# WITTGENSTEIN, LANGUAGE AND INFORMATION

# Information Science and Knowledge Management

## Volume 10

A C.I.P. Catalogue record for this book is available from the Library of Congress.

ISBN-13 978-90-481-7045-6
ISBN-10 1-4020-4583-2 (e-book)
ISBN-13 978-1-4020-4583-7 (e-book)

Published by Springer,
P.O. Box 17,3300 AA Dordrecht, The Netherlands.

*www.springer.com*

*Printed on acid-free paper*

# WITTGENSTEIN, LANGUAGE AND INFORMATION

## 'Back to the Rough Ground!'

*by*

### DAVID BLAIR
*University of Michigan, Ann Arbor, Michigan, USA*

This book is dedicated to my sons, Alain and Christopher.

# Table of Contents

# Acknowledgements

My first book, Language and Representation in Information Retrieval, was so well received that to write a book that was an extension of its theories was a difficult and time-consuming process. I spent 10 years writing this book which extends the analysis of my first book. During that time I greatly appreciated individuals who read my manuscripts and gave me their impression of what I had written. The most dedicated reader of my manuscripts was John Klinkert from Seattle, Washington, who read each of several versions of this manuscript, and sent me written collections of his comments. I'm currently a professor at the University of Michigan. The Michigan faculty member who read early versions of my book was Kevin Kerber. His comments were very supportive and helpful. In Chicago, former University of Chicago professor, Donald Swanson read several versions of my manuscript, and was supportive enough to invite me to his house to discuss what I had written. I also found some of his own publications relevant to my analysis, so they are cited and discussed in the final manuscript.

One of the most supportive acts concerning my early manuscripts of this book was performed by Hubert Dreyfus, professor of philosophy at the University of California at Berkeley. He read an early version of my manuscript and then quoted several paragraphs of it in his new book, On the Internet (Routledge, 2001). This is especially complementary because Hubert Dreyfus is one of the premier philosophers who uses philosophy to analyze practical problems. His 1972 book What Computers Can't Do was an analysis of the potential of Artificial Intelligence, and has proven to be an extremely accurate predictor of the limitations of it. (It's in its 3rd edition now, and has been renamed What Computers (Still) Can't Do, MIT Press) Overall, Dreyfus is the most inspiring modern philosopher for my work in applying philosophy to the practical problems of information systems as I did in this book.

Other individuals who read and responded to early manuscripts of this book were Richard Boland, professor at Case Western University, M.E. Maron, professor emeritus of the University of California, Berkeley, Brian O'Connor, professor at North Texas University, Ron Day, professor at Wayne State University, and Eric Edderer, a professional librarian.

## Major Cited Works by Ludwig Wittgenstein and The Abbreviations Used in This Discussion:

| Works by Wittgenstein: | Abbreviations: |
| --- | --- |
| Blue and Brown Books | BB |
| Culture and Value | CV |
| Last Writings on the Philosophy of Psychology, v. 1 | LWPP I |
| Last Writings on the Philosophy of Psychology, v. 2 | LWPP II |
| Lectures and Conversations on Aesthetics, Psychology and Religious Belief | LC |
| Notebooks 1914–1916 | NB |
| On Certainty | OC |
| Philosophical Grammar | PG |
| Philosophical Investigations | PI |
| Philosophical Remarks | PR |
| Remarks on the Foundations of Mathematics | RFM |
| Remarks on the Philosophy of Psychology, v. 1 | RPP I |
| Remarks on the Philosophy of Psychology, v. 2 | RPP II |
| Tractatus Logico-Philosophicus | TLP |
| Zettel | Z |

# Part I: Introduction

"The more narrowly we examine language, the sharper becomes the conflict between it and our requirement. (For the crystalline purity of logic was, of course, not a result of investigation; it was a requirement.) The conflict becomes intolerable; the requirement is now in danger of becoming empty.—We have got onto slippery ice where there is no friction and so in a certain sense the conditions are ideal, but also, just because of that, we are unable to walk. We want to walk; so we need friction. Back to the rough ground!"[1]

—Ludwig Wittgenstein

This manuscript consists of four related parts: a brief overview of Wittgenstein's philosophy of language and its relevance to information systems; a detailed explanation of Wittgenstein's late philosophy of language and mind; an extended discussion of the relevance of his philosophy to understanding some of the problems inherent in information systems, especially those systems which rely on retrieval based on some representation of the intellectual content of that information. And, fourthly, a series of detailed footnotes which cite the sources of the numerous quotations and provide some discussion of the related issues that the text inspires. The first three of these parts can each be read by itself with some profit, although they *are* related and do form a conceptual whole. Still, the reader who wants an overview of many of the arguments advanced herein, can get them comparatively quickly from Part I, while the reader who wants to see, in some detail, the exegesis of Wittgenstein's late philosophy of language and mind would do well to read Part II with some care. Of course, the central message of the manuscript is presented in Part III, where the implications of Wittgenstein's later philosophy for information systems, especially information retrieval systems, are worked out in some detail, providing a deeper discussion of the issues described in Part I. The only part which cannot be read by itself is, of course, the footnotes, what I would call Part IV. Footnotes have an ambivalent status in writing. Manuals of style insist that if the material is important enough to be included in a manuscript it should be placed in the text and not in the footnotes; if it's not important enough to include in the text, it's not important enough, with few exceptions, to be in the footnotes either. Some individuals are even more pointed in their dislike of footnotes. John Barrymore once said "A footnote in a book is like a knock on the door downstairs while you are on your honeymoon." Certainly footnotes *can* interrupt the flow of the manuscript, and long footnotes can take the reader far enough away from the discussion of the main text that it may be difficult to return to it. Yet, some texts demand the links and extended discussion that footnotes provide, and this present text is one of them. In the first place, any detailed exegesis of Wittgenstein's, admittedly difficult, philosophy, requires citations to identify the wide variety of sources of the frequent quotations and the related or alternative versions of cited passages. Wittgenstein's philosophy, in particular, has generated an enormous amount of critical analysis since his death half a century ago, and to ignore the major points of this analysis would be unwise, so references have been made to discussions

---

[1] **Philosophical Investigations**, §107, 3rd ed. Blackwell Publishers, Oxford, UK, 2001. Translated by G.E.M. Anscombe. 1st ed. published 1953. [Hereafter referred to as **PI**]

or critiques of his work, especially those made by the premier Wittgenstein scholars, G.P. Baker and P.M.S. Hacker, and Wittgenstein's former student and professor of philosophy, Norman Malcolm, who spent his career as professor of philosophy at Cornell University.[2] Wittgenstein himself was not a systematic writer, developing many of the main themes of his work in a sporadic fashion throughout his writings. This unsystematic development of his work demands that the selections from his writings which are used here be carefully cited so that the reader can see where, in the 15 volumes of his currently published writings, the exact quotations come from. Because Wittgenstein's later philosophy is spread out across so many individual works, it would be unreasonable to expect the reader to have copies of all of Wittgenstein's writings for reference. Consequently, I have made every attempt to quote relevant passages as completely as possible, and, in some cases, to give examples of the variations of the same statement in different parts of his writings. To this end, the reader will not be required to have a library of all of Wittgenstein's works cited herein in order to follow the thread of this discussion.

Another reason for the large number of detailed footnotes is the nature of the subject of this discussion—language. The subject of language is as broad and deep a topic as there is. Language permeates almost every aspect of our lives, and the nature of meaning resists concise or comprehensive explanation. Language, it can be argued, is part of the very definition of what it means to be human, and any discussion of the nature of language inevitably brings up myriad links to the cognitive, social and cultural dimensions of mankind. One cannot write succinctly about the nature of language and meaning and still hope to capture its depth and complexity. As Wittgenstein himself put it, "...words have meaning only in the **stream of life**."[3] This is not the first text on language to deal with its complexity in this way, Noam Chomsky's first two, enormously influential, books on language, **Aspects of the Theory of Syntax** (1969) and **Cartesian Linguistics** (1966) had similar styles.[4] Both of these works brought out the complexity and depth of the subject of language by providing detailed footnotes that greatly increased the length of the texts themselves. Any serious discussion of language use and its related issues is, fundamentally, an intellectual adventure. The footnotes in this text are meant to describe the many directions and dimensions of this adventure. Certainly, if the pleasures of the text are enough to make the reader regret the distraction of a footnote, then the best advice is to keep reading and, in John Barrymore's metaphor, simply refuse to answer the knock at the door. As I pointed out above, the text in large part does stand by itself.

## Why Language?—Why Philosophy?—Why Wittgenstein?

Making our way through Wittgenstein's late philosophy of language and mind is a demanding journey, so it will be helpful to first survey Wittgenstein's intellectual landscape

---

[2] The most extensive bibliography of Wittgenstein criticism is **Wittgenstein: A Bibliographical Guide**, by G. Frongia and B. McGuinness [Basil Blackwell, Oxford, UK, 1990]. This work lists references to 1,942 articles and texts published between 1914 and 1987 which discuss Wittgenstein's work. Many of the references have brief annotations.

[3] **Remarks on the Philosophy of Psychology**, v. II, §687. The University of Chicago Press, Chicago, 1980. Edited by G.H. von Wright and H. Nyman, translated by C.G. Luckhardt and M.A. Aue. [Hereafter referred to as **RPP II**]

[4] **Aspects of the Theory of Syntax**. MIT Press, Cambridge, MA, 1969. **Cartesian Linguistics: A Chapter in the History of Rationalist Thought**. Harper Collins, NY, 1966.

to identify its major features and how they relate to the issues of information retrieval. This will give our later analysis a clearer foundation. Wittgenstein wrote frequently of the importance of the "Übersicht," or "Overview" of examples necessary to see how a word is used (see the section in Part II "Five Red Apples" for a more detailed discussion of the German word "Übersicht"). This brief survey of some of his ideas and how they relate to information systems provides a kind of "Übersicht" of his philosophy of language and will set the principal features of the intellectual landscape on which we will make our explorations in Parts II and III.

First of all, why are the issues of language and meaning important to the study of information systems? Information systems are, of course, tools that are used to search for information of various kinds: data, text, images, etc. Information searches themselves inevitably require the searcher to ask for or describe the information he or she wants and to match those descriptions with the descriptions of the information that is available: in short, when we ask for or describe information we must *mean* something by these statements. This places the requests for information as properly within the study of language and meaning.[5] Surely, requests for information, or descriptions of available information, can be clear or ambiguous, precise or imprecise, just as statements in natural language can. In short, understanding how requests for, and descriptions of, information work, and, more importantly, how they can go wrong, is an issue of language, meaning and understanding.

Why, then, is the focus of this discussion on philosophy? Certainly, the fields of linguistics and literature, especially literary criticism, have much to tell us about language and meaning. I would agree, and should I write another book I might be tempted to look to those fields for enlightenment about meaning and language. But I'm turning to philosophy of language first for the principal reason that its *main* concern is with how we *mean* what we say—how does language actually work? These are important issues in linguistics and literary study, but they are not the *central* concerns of these fields. Since the problem of meaning in language is the central concern of this discussion, its aims and focus most closely parallel the aims and focus of the philosophy of language. Another reason why the philosophy of language is particularly pertinent for the present discussion is that for philosophy in general, and Wittgenstein in particular, there is no sharp boundary between understanding language and cognition—how we understand language is closely coupled with how we understand things in general. Not only language, but understanding is important for information systems, too, since information systems are often used to help us understand things better. As we will see in Part III, information systems are part of what I, following Clark,[6] would call the "scaffolding" of our thought. I take the approach of philosophy of language to be the fundamental examination of the issues of meaning, so if there are any clear insights into our understanding of meaning, they will likely be found here first. This is why the philosophy of language is so important to our investigation. Nevertheless, we must be selective about what we use from the philosophy of language. Like any other intellectual discipline, the philosophy of language has its own specific

---

[5] A brief introduction to the relation between information retrieval and the philosophy of language can be found in "Information Retrieval and the Philosophy of Language," by D. Blair [**Annual Review of Information Science and Technology**, vol. 37, pp. 3–50, 2003.]

[6] A. Clark. **Being There: Putting Brain, Body, and World Together Again**. MIT Press, Cambridge, MA, 1997.

puzzles—what Thomas Kuhn called "exemplars"[7]—that preoccupy its practitioners. Some of these are helpful in our investigation, and some are not. Looking at the conduct of the philosophy of language in general, one can discern a number of courses its study has taken: early work, primarily that of Bertrand Russell and Gottlob Frege, was concerned with the relationship between language and the world. For them, language was primarily used to make factual assertions about the world. The central question of this era was "What are the truth conditions of a statement?" that is, "What is the relationship between meaning and truth?" While these are important questions for the philosophy of language, and are still prominent concerns of some present day work, the truth conditions of a statement do not tell us much that would be important to the study of language and information. In recognition of this, our discussion must be selective about what we use from the philosophy of language, and very thorough about extracting the maximum benefit from those aspects of philosophy that are relevant to our present study. "Ockham's Razor" is no less relevant to our present study than it was to the 14th century philosopher William of Ockham in his defense of Nominalism. Another obvious question must be, why is the philosophy of Wittgenstein particularly important for this study; that is, why not just survey the pertinent sections of the Philosophy of Language in general? There are many philosophers of language, and many philosophical theories which have contributed to our understanding of meaning in language. Why should we concentrate our efforts on Wittgenstein's, admittedly difficult, philosophy of language? Surely there are other, easier, routes to furthering our understanding of language and meaning. But Wittgenstein is unique among philosophers in the following respect: early in his career he was the consummate logician, the intellectual heir apparent to the pioneering logical work of Gottlob Frege and Bertrand Russell. Frege and Russell believed that ordinary language was not precise enough to represent the complexity and subtleties of meaning that were becoming increasingly important for analytic philosophy. Russell believed that the goal of analytic philosophy was to clarify what we say about the world. Analytic philosophy should take its inspiration from what Russell believed was the rigor of the scientific method. Since different branches of science often needed their own representational systems to express factual scientific relationships clearly, philosophy would need a similar rigorous representational system to make what it could assert perfectly clear, or so Russell and Frege thought. What we needed, they believed, was a logical language that could faithfully model these complexities and subtleties of expression, and could be used to clarify whether statements of fact were true or false—a language that could be used to bring out and make explicit the underlying logic of language. Early in his career, Wittgenstein was sympathetic with this view of language, believing, like Russell and Frege, that language could be made more precise through the use of formal logic. In his introduction to Wittgenstein's first published work, **Tractatus Logico-Philosophicus**, Russell describes Wittgenstein as being "concerned with the conditions which would have to be fulfilled by a logically perfect language."[8] Russell goes on to describe a logically perfect language as one which "has rules of syntax which prevent

---

[7] T. Kuhn. **The Structure of Scientific Revolutions,** 2nd ed. University of Chicago Press, Chicago, 1970. See the "Postscript" in which he discusses the "disciplinary matrix" of which exemplars are a part.

[8] Bertrand Russell: Introduction to the **Tractatus Logico-Philosophicus**, page ix. Routledge and Kegan Paul, London, 1961. English translated by D.F. Pears and B.F. McGuinness. First German edition published in 1921. [Hereafter referred to as **TLP**]

nonsense, and has single symbols which always have a definite and unique meaning."[9] But as Wittgenstein's thought matured, he began to have serious misgivings about the ability of logic to model or represent the complex and subtle statements of language. Not only was logic inadequate to this task, he thought, ordinary language itself was, if used properly, the best possible medium for linguistic expression, philosophical or otherwise. In short, Wittgenstein's thought evolved from a belief that problems of meaning in language could be clarified by logically analytical methods to a realization that many of the unclarities of language were a result of removing statements from the context, practices and circumstances in which they were commonly used—what Wittgenstein called our "Forms of Life." What determined the truth or meaning of a statement was not some underlying logic, but how the statement was used and what circumstances it was used in. Ambiguities in language are clarified, not by logical analysis, but by looking at how the words or phrases in question are used in our daily activities and practices. Wittgenstein's transition in his view of language is important for the study of information systems for the following reason: our current most widespread model of information systems is the computer model, in particular, the "data model" of information. This has been a very successful and robust model that has had a remarkably long history of implementation. Computers are, in a fundamental sense, logical machines, so we might say that the current most popular model for information systems is the *logical model*. This logical model, as we will show, has worked well for providing access to the precise, highly determinate content of our data bases—things like names, addresses, phone numbers, account balances, etc. But as more and more of our information is becoming managed by computerized systems we find that we must provide access to less determinate information, like the "intellectual content" of written text, images, and audio recordings—for example, searching for information that analyzes the economic prospects of Central European countries, or information that evaluates the impact of government regulation on small businesses. These kinds of access are not as well served by the logical data model of information, as one can easily see when trying to find some specific subject matter (intellectual content) on the World Wide Web using an Internet search engine.[10] Current information systems are in some way, the victims of the success of the more determinate data model of information. The logical/data

---

[9] *Op.cit.*, p. x.

[10] I first made this distinction between the more precise logical model of Data Retrieval and the less precise, more problematic model of Document Retrieval in "The Data-Document Distinction in Information Retrieval." [**Communications of the ACM**, vol. 27:4, pp. 369–374, April 1984.]

Some readers will no doubt rejoin that they have no trouble finding the intellectual content they are seeking on the WWW, and, in a certain sense, this is true—one can always find something relevant to one's search on the web. The key issue here is not finding "something relevant," but finding the best information for some purpose available on the web. Swanson described some time ago what he called the "Fallacy of Abundance":

> A scientist who nowadays imagines either that he is keeping up with his field or that he can later find in the library whatever may have escaped his notice when it was first written is a victim of what might be called the "fallacy of abundance." The fact that so much can be found on any subject creates an illusion that little remains hidden. Although library searches probably seem more often than not to be successful simply because a relatively satisfying amount of material is exhumed, such success may be illusory, since the requester cannot assess the quantity and value of relevant information which he fails to discover. [D.R. Swanson. "Searching Natural Language Text by Computer," **Science**, vol. 132, pp. 1960–1104, 21 October 1960. Quotation p. 1099.]

model of information has become the Procrustean Bed to which many information systems are forced to fit.[11] The effort to fit language and information to the logical model was justified because it was assumed that, as Russell and the early Wittgenstein believed, there is an underlying logic of language that governed its correct usage—an underlying logic which must be uncovered if we wanted to insure the clarity of expression. On this view, information systems used to provide access to "intellectual content" are just sloppy or imprecise versions of data retrieval systems. But it was one of Wittgenstein's clearest reassessments of his early philosophy when he said that "...the crystalline purity of logic was, of course, not a result of investigation; it was a requirement"—that is, the logic that Russell and Frege sought to uncover in their analysis of language, did *not* exist latently in language waiting to be uncovered. The logic of language was something that was a requirement for the analysis *to begin with*—it was something that was imposed on language. Just as Wittgenstein began to have misgivings about the applicability of the logical model, with its requirement for the strict determinacy of sense, to all aspects of language and meaning, some, this author included, are now having misgivings about how applicable the logical/data model of information is to the more complex and subtle problems of access to less determinate information such as the "intellectual content" of written text, images and audio recordings, a kind of access becoming increasingly widespread as more and more of our information starts out in machine readable form. As Douglas van Kirk put it:

> Corporations everywhere are beginning to recognize that information is almost always document-oriented. Because so many companies are in the information business, it stands to reason that the most productive companies will be those that manage documents effectively.

The reason why documents are so important to organizations is that they provide the context that makes information more meaningful. Wittgenstein, the consummate logician, came to see the limitations of logic when used to analyze language, and tried during the remainder of his career to indicate what was rigorous and right about ordinary language. Given that language *does* make sense, how does it do this without the armamentarium of logic? Wittgenstein's answer to this is both relevant to, and important for, access to intellectual content. Ordinary language is good enough for our purposes:

> It is wrong to say that in philosophy we consider an ideal language as opposed to our ordinary one. For this makes it appear as though we thought we could improve on ordinary language. But ordinary language is all right. Whenever we make up "ideal languages" it is not in order to replace our ordinary language by them; but

This was a remarkably prescient insight for 40 years ago, at the very beginning of the explosive growth in available information, and the electronic revolution in information storage and retrieval. Swanson could see this affect of abundance even in the research libraries of that time. Those systems, of course, are dwarfed by the size of today's World Wide Web, with its billions of separately searchable and retrievable pages.

[11] One needs only to look at the advertisements of the largest data base management system manufacturer, Oracle, to see this.

They advocate storing *every* kind of information, data, text, audio, images, video, on their systems, with no indication that each of these information types might require vastly different access methods.

just to remove some trouble caused in someone's mind by thinking that he has got hold of the exact use of a common word.[12] [**BB** p. 28]

On the one hand it is clear that every sentence in our language "is in order as it is." That is to say, we are not striving after an ideal, as if our ordinary vague sentences had not yet got a quite unexceptionable sense, and a perfect language awaited construction by us.—On the other hand it seems clear that where there is sense there must be perfect order.—So there must be perfect order even in the vaguest sentence. [**PI** § 98]

Wittgenstein is not saying that we are never misunderstood when we use ordinary language; of course we are. Wittgenstein is just clarifying how we should identify and resolve these misunderstandings. Instead of building a "logically perfect language" that would be more precise than our day-to-day language, or using logical methods to analyze linguistic mistakes, we must reorient our investigation: Instead of looking for an *underlying logic* of language, we need to look at how language is *actually used*, for it's not an underlying logic that clarifies what we mean, it's the context, activities and practices in which we use language that provide the fundamental clarification of meaning we are looking for. This is why Wittgenstein's work is so relevant to the study of information systems. Formal logic is useful for clarifying or solving a narrow range of problems and puzzles in language. Russell's, and the early Wittgenstein's, mistake was to think logic was applicable for solving a wide variety of linguistic problems that went beyond this narrow range. Like formal logic, the data model of information systems is an enormously successful model for the design of a narrow range of information retrieval tasks—those systems which provide access to highly determinate information (names, addresses, phone numbers, account balances, etc.). The data/logical model of information is a less successful model for providing access to the less determinate "intellectual content" of things like documents and images. The data/logical model cannot always capture the subtleties of language necessary for the retrieval of precise intellectual content on large information systems (again, searching for specific intellectual content on the World Wide Web is a good example). And, like language, there is no underlying logical model of information that we need to uncover— the "crystalline purity of logic" for information systems, like language, is "not a result of investigation; it [is] a requirement." That is, for the data/logical model to be applicable to all information systems, it is *required* that the information on the system be represented in extremely precise or determinate ways. But this process will have the effect, not of making better, "more precise" information systems, but, in the case of the search for "intellectual content," of making dysfunctional information systems—systems which are insensitive to the subtleties of language that are required for highly specific access to intellectual content, especially on large systems. As long as we believe that the precision of representation for data retrieval is possible *for all information systems*, we will run the risk of building such dysfunctional systems.

But recognizing the problems with the logical/data model of information is only part of the problem. What is needed to replace the inadequacies of the logical/data model?

---

[12] **The Blue and Brown Books,** p. 28. **The Blue and Brown Books** were published as a single work by Basil Blackwell, Oxford, UK, 1958. Cited edition is Harper Torchbook, New York, 1965. [Hereafter referred to as **BB**]

Wittgenstein's reassessment of the logical model of language, and his assessment of how language *really works*, is, it is the thesis of this discussion, a good guide for how the logical/data model of information systems must be changed or evolve if it is to provide satisfactory access to less determinate information such as intellectual content. Most philosophers of language have not been logicians, and those who had expertise in logic were not logicians of the first rank, as Wittgenstein was. This is why his reassessment of the usefulness of the logical model of language carries so much weight, and is particularly relevant to the present study. One of the central issues of language, for Wittgenstein, was what he called the "determinacy of sense"—the precision by which meaning can be defined. As we will see, it reappears as a fundamental issue in information retrieval too.

## Surveying Wittgenstein's Landscape

To begin our discussion, it will be useful to provide a brief overview of some of the major themes of Wittgenstein's philosophy of language and mind, and their relation to information retrieval systems. These major themes can be represented by carefully selected quotations from his works.

> 1. ...we don't start from certain words, but from certain occasions or activities.
> [**LC** p. 3][13]

Language does not exist by itself in a static system of definitions and syntax, but is intimately caught up in our activities and practices, what Wittgenstein called our "forms of life."[14] These forms of life comprise what Wittgenstein referred to as the "common behavior of mankind."[15] Language is not so much a collection of "meanings" but something that can be used to *do* things—it is an essential part of our everyday activities and practices. This makes meaning a largely collective notion: meaning *emerges* from the *use* of language in the conduct of day-to-day activities and practices. Emergent phenomena occur when a broad, higher level pattern emerges from the personal interactions of individual entities in the absence of any central controller. In language, "meaning" emerges from the interactions of native speakers using language in their day-to-day activities.[16] A dictionary definition

---

[13] **Lectures & Conversations on Aesthetics, Psychology and Religious Belief**, p. 3. University of California Press, Berkeley, 1972. Edited by C. Barrett. [Hereafter referred to as **LC**]

[14] "...the *speaking* of language is part of an activity, or of a form of life." [**PI** §23]

[15] "The common behavior of mankind is the system of reference by means of which we interpret an unknown language" [**PI** §206]. This is the reason that, as Wittgenstein comments:

> "If a lion could talk, we could not understand him." [**PI** p. 223]

Even if the lion were to use the same vocabulary as we do, because his day-to-day activities are so different from ours, he would use our words in strikingly different ways. He would also have no conception of the specific uses of words which we consider commonplace (e.g., a lion would have no idea what a "pet" is because pets have no role in its day-to-day activities, and what he would consider "food" would be strikingly different from our own conception). If our speaking lion were to say he was "stepping out for lunch" we could be assured that he was not going to a restaurant.

[16] Zipf asserted that the fundamental linguistic interaction which governs language use is the "competition" between speakers and hearers, where the speaker is trying to express himself as economically as possible,

does not *precede* the use of an expression, but *emerges* from the day-to-day use of the expression as a component in a particular activity or practice. As Wittgenstein put it, "...words have meaning only in the stream of life" [**RPPII** §687]. There are no private linguistic meanings or private languages—my sensations are, of course, personal and cannot be felt by others, but while my pain may be personal, I can only talk about it using the expressions commonly used to talk about pain.[17]

The idea of "emergence" is a relatively recent idea, but Wittgenstein seems to have anticipated some of the basic characteristics of this phenomenon. John Holland[18] discusses how the process of emergence can give the impression of something orderly and meaningful arising out of "chaos" or "disorder." Wittgenstein hinted at this possibility of order arising from disorder:

> No supposition seems to me more natural than that there is no process in the brain correlated with associating or with thinking; so that it would be impossible to read off thought-processes from brain-processes. I mean this: if I talk or write there is, I assume, a system of impulses going out from my brain and correlated with

and the hearer is, himself, trying to exert as little effort as possible to understand him. The "competition" occurs because the speaker tries to use as few words as possible, thus minimizing his effort, while the hearer is simultaneously trying to get the speaker to use more words in order to simplify his efforts at understanding the speaker. Zipf calls this the competition between speaker and hearer, or the competition between the forces of "unification" and "diversification." Optimal linguistic understanding occurs when the efforts of the speaker and hearer reach a balance where the sum of their respective efforts is a minimum. It is from these local interactions between speakers and hearers that meaning in language emerges. (for a more detailed presentation of Zipf's theory of language see the section "Implications of the 'Language as City' Metaphor" in Part II).

[17] Wittgenstein's argument against private languages or meanings rests on two assertions: first, private languages can only be discussed or described using the ordinary public language which is available to us all. But if the meaning of private language is expressible only through public language then it is not a private language at all, but merely a somewhat different form of ordinary, public language. As Wittgenstein put it:

> "What goes on within... has meaning only in the stream of life" [**Last Writings on the Philosophy of Psychology**, vol. II, p. 30. Blackwell Publishers, Oxford, UK, 1992.]. [Hereafter referred to as **LWPP II**]

Secondly, language requires exemplary uses of words as guides to meaningful usage. We do the same kind of thing when we suggest that certain paintings are exemplars of a particular style. In art we can say that if you want to look at an exemplar, or, good example, of impressionist painting look at Monet's work. In language, similarly, we can say that if you want to know when to use the word "charisma" think of John F. Kennedy at a presidential press conference, or if you want to know how to use the word "compassion" think of Mother Teresa's work with the desperately poor—these are exemplary cases. But since the meanings of words in a private language would be entirely personal, you would not be able to establish such exemplars—that is, since, in a private language, a word can mean anything you want it to, there could be no examples which are better than others—in other words, there could be no role for exemplars to play. Even if you could establish exemplars in a private language, how would you know whether you were applying the exemplars correctly or not? The essential interplay between speakers and hearers, by which we gauge the correctness of our usage, and from which correct usage emerges, would be missing. There are no criteria for the establishment of exemplars in a private language, in fact there are no coherent criteria for the correct usage of any words of a private language. Since the speaker and the hearer are the same individual in a private language, there is no chance of there ever being a misunderstanding. Again, for Zipf, meaningful language arises from the "balance" achieved by the competition of Speakers and Hearers, yet in a private language there is no such interplay and no "balance" of usage, hence, there can be no private linguistic meaning in the ordinary sense.

[18] J. Holland. **Emergence: From Chaos to Order**. Helix Books, Addison-Wesley, Reading, MA, 1998.

my spoken or written thoughts. But why should the system continue further in the direction of the centre? Why should this order not proceed, so to speak, out of chaos?[19]

**Relevance to Information Systems:** The underlying order of information systems, in so far as they are linguistic systems, is not so much words and categories, but "occasions and activities." Yet often it is the relation to "occasions and activities" that is lost when information is organized for retrieval, especially when it is placed on a computerized retrieval system. Consider a simple example. Paper-based information has some obvious disadvantages regarding storage and copying when compared to the same information in electronic form. But paper-based information has one distinct advantage over electronic information: since a paper document does not need delicate electronic equipment to present it, it can be carried and used almost anywhere, from the office, to the home, to a bus, to a rainy construction site, etc. It is also easy to mark up, annotate or highlight paper, and parts of it can be clipped out or xeroxed and distributed. Further, small accidents such as dropping the paper or spilling coffee on it do not render it unreadable, though information on a laptop computer could not stand such abuse. Consequently, paper-based information can remain close to the activities that produce or use it, and these activities can provide an interpretive context for that information. But when that information is computerized, the very act of computerization may have the effect of removing the information from the activity context that provides much of its meaning and interpretation.[20]

> 2. The best example of an expression with a very specific meaning is a passage in a play.[21]

We learn our native language not so much by memorizing the definitions of words and phrases, but by watching it being used, trying to use it ourselves, and having new expressions or subtleties of meaning demonstrated to us by others. The best definition of a new word or expression is not a dictionary definition, but a scene in a play. For Wittgenstein, descriptions or demonstrations (e.g., plays) are better ways of conveying or clarifying meaning than explanations (dictionary definitions). In fact, "stage setting" can be an essential component of meaning even for a linguistic act as simple as giving something a name:

> When one says "He gave a name to his sensation" one forgets that a great deal of stage setting in the language is presupposed if the mere act on naming is to make sense. [**PI** §257]

A dictionary definition is a kind of shorthand explanation, what Wittgenstein was later to call a kind of "Language Game," and typically can only help us if we already understand the general role of the word in language. When we understand a new expression, what we have is not the ability to recall its definition, but the ability to *use* the expression in

---

[19] **Zettel,** §608. University of California Press, Berkeley, 1967. Edited by G.E.M. Anscombe and G.H. von Wright, translated by G.E.M. Anscombe. [Hereafter referred to as **Z**]

[20] The importance of the proximity of information systems to the activities and practices they serve was a major theme of Blair's **Language and Representation in Information Retrieval**. [Elsevier, 1990]

[21] **Last Writings on the Philosophy of Psychology, v. I**, §424. University of Chicago Press, Chicago. Edited by G.H. von Wright and Heikki Nyman, translated by C.G. Luckhardt and Maximilian A.E. Aue. [Hereafter referred to as **LWPP I**]

the appropriate circumstances and context. We may be able to use many words correctly without being able to define them—Modern English, the language since Shakespeare, existed until the18th century without dictionaries, and it was many more years before dictionaries were widely available. Prior to the wide use of dictionaries, all language learning had to be done through the personal interactions of native speakers in, or with reference to, the relevant daily activities or circumstances. Yet these daily interactions, unaided by dictionaries, produced the rich and nuanced language of Shakespeare's plays and a wealth of literature, essays, history and philosophy. If dictionaries were not widely available until fairly recently, then, it seems that before that we had no central or "essential" criteria for correct meaning or usage.[22] But there is no evidence that the lack of dictionaries caused any great confusion in communication: There are other criteria for correct usage, criteria that are available to every native speaker, literate or not.

> Suppose you came as an explorer into an unknown country with a language quite strange to you. In what circumstances would you say that the people there gave orders, understood them, obeyed them, rebelled against them, and so on?

> The common behavior of mankind is the system of reference by means of which we interpret an unknown language. [**PI** §206]

The criteria for correct usage come from our understanding of the "common behavior of mankind."[23] (NB: It is important to note that Wittgenstein is *not* equating behavior and meaning, only that behavior is the "system of reference" with which we can "interpret an unknown language." See Part II, sections "The Foundation of Language in Instinctive Behavior" and "Why Wittgenstein is not a Behaviorist.")

**Relevance to Information Systems:** Plays are fundamentally stories. So if the best example of a word's use is a scene in a play, then the fundamental structure of linguistic meaning is the narrative.[24] Insofar as language is used in information systems to represent or describe what is stored on the system, its meaning, too, may be more faithfully

---

[22] This lack of a set of "central criteria" for correct meaning comes out in Hilary Putnam's notion of the "Division of Linguistic Labor." Putnam insists that the meaning of a word is not one thing that can be in any single person's possession, but is distributed among a variety of speakers who use the word in question for a variety of activities and purposes. [**Representation and Reality**, p. 22ff. MIT Press, Cambridge, MA, 1996.]

[23] The philosopher W.O. Quine wrote in his famous essay on "the indeterminacy of translation," that if someone speaking a language we did not understand, consistently uttered the word "gavagai" in the presence of a rabbit we still could not be assured that "gavagai" actually meant "rabbit"—it could mean, he claimed, "undetached parts of rabbits" or "rabbithood" [**Word and Object**, §12, p. 52. MIT Press, 1960]. Wittgenstein admitted that language is extremely variable and we may have trouble understanding a language we don't know. But there is more of a common basis for mutual understanding than Quine would admit to. In so far as the activities and practices are the same between two linguistic groups, there will be mutual understanding of their respective languages (Quine makes no claim that the activities of the speakers are at all dissimilar). Differences of meaning are proportional to the differences in respective activities and practices. Since the practice of pointing out and naming things like rabbits is common to virtually all linguistic groups, it is doubtful that "gavagai," when uttered in the presence of a rabbit scurrying by, would ever mean "undetached rabbit parts" in any major languages. In short, the word "rabbit" and the practice of pointing things out, have roles in our activities, but the description "undetached rabbit parts" does not (at least for activities other than philosophical ones).

[24] Mark Turner takes the narrative to be even more basic. For him, the narrative is the fundamental structure of not just language, but cognition itself. He distinguishes between the narrative and the parable. The parable is

interpreted in terms of a narrative. This fits more closely with the idea that information is most productively seen as part of an activity or practice—an activity or practice, like a story or a play, can be described as a sequence of events over time.[25]

> 3. When I think in language, there aren't "meanings" going through my mind in addition to the verbal expressions: the language is itself the vehicle of thought. [**PI** §329]

Language, that is, speech or writing, is not a *product* of thought, but a *means* by which we think. This reversal of the usual way of looking at the relation between what we say or write and what we think, is one of Wittgenstein's most important insights. Language gives us words, phrases and ways of expressing ourselves that serve as a set of implements with which we carry out the activities of speaking, understanding others, and thinking. In his primary later work, **Philosophical Investigations**, Wittgenstein's discussion of the nature of language is replete with metaphors of tools and implements (see Part II of this manuscript: "Words are Like Tools and Language Use is Like Tool Use").

If language is a vehicle of thought, then a number of important consequences follow. In the first place, the words and expressions that we have available in our language represent a kind of limit not only for what we say, but, more importantly, for what we can think, verbally. As the painter is limited by the kinds of paint she has, and the size and style of her brushes, so too are we limited in our verbal thought by the kinds of words and expressions we have available to us—the words and expressions we understand and know how to use. Language is not a straitjacket, though, we can use common words and expressions in new and creative ways, of course. But our verbal thoughts are quite clearly *anchored* in our language, and though we may find ways to express new ideas, what we say must be grounded in the bedrock of our common tongue.

One of the ways in which we use familiar expressions to express new ideas is through metaphors. When Wittgenstein tells us that much of our language use is like a "game" he gives us a clearer sense of the intimacy, dynamics and complexity of language use than he could by describing the detailed processes of expression without the analogy to games [see the section "Language Games" in Part II]. Wittgenstein's frequent use of metaphors in his writings enabled him to stretch the boundaries of philosophical expression into the new areas he wanted to discuss [see the section "Philosophy of Language and Metaphor" in Part II].

Of course, we can also think with images and sound, and Wittgenstein was not denying that this kind of thought occurs, too, but he was primarily concerned with the conduct of philosophy, and philosophy must be written or spoken.

**Relevance to Information Systems:** If the words of language represent a toolset for expression, and, as such, define the limits of our ability to think and express ourselves

---

a narrative that the listener has interpreted in a way that makes it meaningful for him. [**The Literary Mind**. Oxford University Press, Oxford, 1996.]

[25] The idea that information is best seen as part of an activity or practice, was one of the central themes of Blair's **Language and Representation in Information Retrieval**. Elsevier Science, New York, 1990.

verbally, then the words used to represent information must define the limits of our ability to think about and to express our information needs.

> 4. Our craving for generality has another main source: our preoccupation with the method of science. I mean the method of reducing the explanation of natural phenomena to the smallest possible number of primitive natural laws .... Philosophers constantly see the method of science before their eyes, and are irresistibly tempted to ask and answer questions in the way science does. This tendency is the real source of metaphysics, and leads the philosopher into complete darkness. I want to say that it can never be our job to reduce anything to anything, or to explain anything. Philosophy really is "purely descriptive!" [**BB** p. 18]

Although Wittgenstein made this statement against reduction in the **Blue and Brown Books**, one of his earlier writings, his distrust of reduction was an attitude that he carried with him through the remainder of his work.[26] For Wittgenstein, we cannot reduce linguistic meaning to anything more primitive than what we say and do. It is true that we ask for and give definitions of individual words, but asking for and giving definitions is a particular kind of language game, and we can only understand the definition of an individual word if we already understand its general role in our language. Further, these individual definitions of words are not the complete meanings of words, nor can they usually be put together to arrive at the meaning of sentences or longer text—that is, the meaning of a sentence is not always *reducible* to some aggregate of the meanings of the individual words it contains. If we want to understand the meaning of a sentence we must look at how it is used—this is the most basic level of analysis that we can do in language[27] [This point will be presented in more detail in a subsequent section discussing the Augustinean model of language.].

**Relevance to Information Systems:** Since we cannot generally reduce ordinary language to more primitive components of meaning without losing some of the meaning that emerges from its use, we should not expect that a statement that requests information of some kind could be analyzed into more primitive components without some semantic deficit, either. Like language, if we want to understand the meaning of an information request we need to look at how the expression is used, that is, to look at the background of the person making the request, the purpose or rationale for his/her request, the activity that the request serves, and the particular circumstances in which the request was made. Each of these can have a bearing on determining what the request "means," that is, what information would prove useful to the inquirer. Wittgenstein was quite clear in his insistence that

---

[26] Strictly speaking, the **Blue and Brown Books** is not one of Wittgenstein's "writings" in the sense that **TLP** and **PI** are. It is actually a collection of class notes put together by some of his students in the late 1930's as material to accompany his seminars. Although they were not written entirely by Wittgenstein, they do reflect the issues he was grappling with in his seminars, and the notes themselves were thoroughly vetted by Wittgenstein before being distributed. Further, the ideas expressed in **BB** are entirely consistent with the issues that he worked on during the remainder of his life. **BB** is often referred to as "Preliminary Studies for the **Philosophical Investigations**"

[27] Wittgenstein would have a particular disagreement with the kinds of reductive analysis of language that Chomsky engaged in with his "Transformational Grammar." Chomsky's linking of the "surface structures" of language with "deep structures" in the mind, commits two major mistakes on Wittgenstein's analysis: first, in designating "deep structures" as the foundation of language it makes internal, unconscious mental phenomena the determinant of meaning; and, second, it assumes that the expressions we use can be transformed, or reduced, into more primitive units which form the "building blocks" of expression.

we can best express ourselves in ordinary language. This means that our best means of articulating what we want from an information system is with our ordinary, everyday language. When we "reduce" a searcher's information request, stated in ordinary language, to a set of search terms, some loss or distortion of the searcher's meaning must inevitably result.

> 5. Our language can be seen as an ancient city: a maze of little streets and squares, of old and new houses, and of houses with additions from various periods; and this surrounded by a multitude of new boroughs with straight, regular streets and uniform houses. [**PI** §18]

One of Wittgenstein's most compelling metaphors is of language being like a *city*. We live in our language in the same way that we live in our cities. We find our way about our cities by *doing* things, that is, by engaging in our day-to-day activities. It is through the conduct of such day-to-day activities that we learn our way about a city, and it is through the conduct of day-to-day activities that we learn our way about our language. It is also the case that a large city offers many alternative routes for going from one place to another. Similarly, language offers us many alternative ways to say the same thing. The city, no matter how large, can also exist quite efficiently without any kind of central planner or controller. The day-to-day local interactions within cities even as large as New York are sufficient to keep the whole functioning, and, although the city, at any time, contains only a limited supply of essentials such as food, it never runs out, even during major disruptive events—snow storms, labor strikes, power outages, etc. Likewise, language needs no central authority to control usage, it needs only the day-to-day interactions of its native speakers to establish and retain its meaning [See the section "Language as a City" in Part II for a more detailed discussion of this metaphor.].

**Relevance to Information Systems:** The language of information systems is like a city, too, in the following ways: like a city, it is constantly evolving and changing in response to the activities that it serves; like a city, there is no need for central planning if the day-to-day interactions of searchers can provide feedback about how language is used, that is, if searchers can learn the correct usages of search terms from day-to-day searches on the system. The meaning of search terms or descriptions of information *emerges* from the day-to-day interactions of users.

> 6. But how many kinds of sentences are there? Say assertion, question, and command?—There are countless kinds; countless different kinds of use of what we call "symbols" "words," "sentences." And this multiplicity is not something fixed, given once for all; but new types of language, new language-games, as we may say, come into existence, and others become obsolete and get forgotten.[28] [**PI** §23]

---

[28] Wittgenstein's quotation continues:

"Here the term 'language-game' is meant to bring into prominence the fact that the speaking of language is part of an activity, or of a form of life.

Review the multiplicity of language-games in the following examples, and in others:

Giving orders, and obeying them—
Describing the appearance of an object, or giving its measurements—

Language does not work in just one way. Wittgenstein begins **PI** with a quotation from the medieval philosopher Augustine who believed that language worked in just one way: words stood for "objects," and language was taught by pointing to the objects that words "stood for." Subsequent theorists have assumed a more subtle version of Augustine's view holding that words stand for "ideas" (Locke) and that the meaning of a word must be somehow "pointed out" or explained to the person who wants to understand it. But for Wittgenstein, language is so diverse that there are uncountable different ways in which it can be used—language works in different ways in different activities or practices. Expressions can be used to "point things out," but they can also be used ironically, sarcastically, or metaphorically. Language is not used primarily to assert facts, as Frege, Russell and the early Wittgenstein, in **TLP**, believed, but can be used to make a promise, tell a joke, order someone to do something, to lie, to exaggerate, to collude, to elaborate, to tell a story, declare war, or to do any of an uncountable number of things.[29] Each of these uses involves using words or expressions in different ways, and fits in to the needs of many kinds of activities or practices [Wittgenstein's critique of the Augusintean view of language will be presented in more detail in Part III].

**Relevance to Information Systems:** The words used in information systems to represent information are not just a collection of "labels" that are somehow linked to information content, like Augustine's notion that words were names for objects. In information systems, like language in general, language is not used in just one way. An index term can describe the intellectual content of information, like a subject description, but it can also link the information to activities or practices. It can be used to assert the quality of the information, to link information to other related information, to describe how the information has been used (as a contract, a directive, a declaration, etc.), or it can name various contextual information such as the author(s) of the text, the date it was published, the source of the

Constructing an object from a description (a drawing)—
Reporting an event—
Speculating about an event—
Forming and testing a hypothesis—
Presenting the results of an experiment in tables and diagrams—
Making up a story; and reading it—
Play-acting—
Singing catches—
Guessing riddles—
Making a joke; telling it—
Solving a problem in practical arithmetic—
Translating from one language into another—
Asking, thanking, cursing, greeting, praying. [**PI** §23]

---

[29] This assertion that language works in a multitude of ways runs counter to Searle's theory of "speech acts." He takes issue specifically with Wittgenstein's claim, in paragraph 23 of **PI** (see previous footnote) that there are "countless different kinds" of "symbols, words, sentences" [J.R. Searle. **Speech Acts, An Essay in the Philosophy of Language**. Cambridge University Press, NY, 1969]. But Searle's speech acts are based on John Austin's "illocutionary acts," and Austin is quite clear that there are many more kinds of illocutionary acts than the few he names. Austin, like Wittgenstein, insisted on the great multiplicity of usage types—that is, illocutionary verbs—in natural language, though he limited their number to between 1,000 and 10,000 [Austin. **How to Do Things With Words**, p. 150, n. 1. Oxford, 1962.]. Searle, in contrast, limits the number of different kinds of Speech Acts to fewer than ten.

text (a magazine, journal, book, etc.) or the type of document it is (published article, report, minutes of a meeting, evaluation, white paper, regulation, etc.). The number of ways that index terms can be used is similar to the number of ways that the information represented by the terms can be used.

> 7. Many words . . . then don't have a strict meaning. But this is not a defect. To think
> it is would be like saying that the light of my reading lamp is no real light at all
> because it has no sharp boundary. [**BB** p. 27]

One of the clearest breaks that Wittgenstein had with his "old way of thinking" in the **Tractatus Logico-Philosophicus** (**TLP**) was over the "determinacy of sense." The early Wittgenstein, along with his mentors Frege and Russell, believed that for language to be useful in philosophical analysis it must have a "strict determinacy of sense," that is, each word must have a precise, unambiguous "sense," or meaning, that was independent of context, and would hold for all its possible uses. In the **Tractatus** Wittgenstein was even more insistent on the importance of the "determinacy of sense" in language—he felt that "sense" in language had to be determinate for language to be possible at all:

> The requirement that simple signs be possible is the requirement that sense be
> determinate. [**TLP** §3.23]

This is a natural consequence of the belief that language was used primarily to assert facts or make propositions. Facts are generally precise and unambiguous and stay this way regardless of the context in which they appear. So, if language asserts facts, then it should be as precise and unambiguous as the facts it represents. Ordinary language, of course, is not like this, as Frege and Russell saw.[30] Consequently, they believed, ordinary language could not be used for the precise kinds of philosophical analysis—the clarification of propositions, or statements of fact—that Frege and Russell wanted to systematize. This was the reason for their insistence on constructing a language of philosophical analysis that did not have the indeterminacy of ordinary language. The exemplar of the kind of language they wanted was formal logic. In logic, as in other formal systems such as arithmetic, the symbols *do* have a strict determinacy of sense—a logical or mathematical symbol, once defined, means the same thing regardless of what equation or "phrase" it is used in. This is why logic was the model for the philosophical language Frege and Russell deemed necessary for analysis. In his early work, Wittgenstein believed, too, that ordinary language lacked the necessary strict determinacy of sense for philosophical analysis, but he differed from Frege and Russell about how to mitigate this indeterminacy of language. In the **TLP**, Wittgenstein argued that we didn't need another language to do philosophy, we just needed to be more careful about our use of ordinary language. In short, ordinary language clearly makes sense most of the time, so it must have an underlying logical order. The ambiguity of language is an illusion, Wittgenstein asserted, we just need to bring out this underlying logical order, the strict determinacy of sense, of language. What Wittgenstein saw later was that language did *not* get its determinacy from some underlying logical order. Like logic, its "crystalline purity" was "not a result of investigation, it was a requirement." Wittgenstein grew to see that "Many words. . . then don't have a strict meaning. But this is not a defect."

---

[30] As Russell wrote in the his introduction to Wittgenstein's **TLP**: "In practice, language is always more or less vague, so that what we assert is never quite precise." [**TLP**, p. x]

(*supra*) Language can be as determinate as necessary. To see the indeterminacy as a defect is to look at ordinary language as if it were a kind of formal calculus, which it is not. We can make language very precise if we want, not by bringing out some kind of hidden logical underpinning, but by looking at the context, circumstances and practices in which language is used. In **Philosophical Investigations**, Wittgenstein takes a final jab at Frege's insistence on a strict determinacy of sense in language:

> Frege compares a concept to an area and says that an area with vague boundaries cannot be called an area at all. This presumably means that we cannot do anything with it.—But is it senseless to say: "Stand roughly there?" Suppose that I were standing with someone in a city square and said that. As I say it I do not draw any kind of boundary, but perhaps point with my hand—as if I were indicating a particular spot. [**PI** §71]

Wittgenstein's analogy between the meaning of words and the boundary of the light from his reading lamp (*supra*) is particularly *apropos*. The determinacy of sense, or precision of meaning, needs only to be as strict as is necessary for the task at hand—there is no absolute level of determinacy to which all language aspires. In the same way, a light doesn't have a single standard of brightness, it only needs to be bright enough for the task at hand. To decry the ambiguity of individual word meaning is to apply the requirements of a particular Language Game, scientific discourse, for example, to all language. This, of course, is exactly what Russell did, since he claimed that the purpose of philosophy was to clarify scientific assertions about facts.

**Relevance to Information Systems**. As we will see in Part III, the "determinacy of sense" is one of the central issues of Information Systems. In fact, we can line up different kinds of information systems along a spectrum of their respective determinacies of representation. At one extreme we have data base management systems which provide access to highly determinate information such as names, addresses, phone numbers, and account balances. Such data items are unambiguous and stay pretty much the same regardless of the context in which they appear. At the other end of the determinacy spectrum would be a document retrieval system which provides access to the "intellectual content" of a large collection of documents many of which deal with similar topics. Here, a retrieval request for a document detailing the "reasons for the failure of the Marxist economic model" might be very hard to make without retrieving too many or too few documents (imagine devising a search query to do this for use with an Internet Search Engine). This issue of the determinacy of sense in Information Systems will be central to the discussion of Part III.

> 8. We want to establish an order in our knowledge of the use of language: an order with a particular end in view; one of many possible orders; not *the* order. [**PI** §132]

Although Wittgenstein was concerned with identifying errors in our use of language, his goal was to correct philosophical mistakes that arose because of errors in language, not to correct errors in ordinary usage or to create a separate, more precise, ideal language. Although Wittgenstein felt that philosophers needed to be reminded of their "diseases of thinking" which arise from the misuse of language, he believed that ordinary native speakers of a language needed no such reminders.

**Relevance to Information Systems:** Similarly to ordinary language, the language of representation in information systems does not aspire, in theory or in practice, to some ideal language. As with ordinary language, the principal criterion of quality for a search language is whether or not its users, that is, searchers, can *use it* to find what they want. It is also the case that, like ordinary language, the language of information representation and searching is not a fixed entity, but changes insofar as the uses for the information that it provides access to change. Further, just as Wittgenstein insisted that ordinary language usage is the final arbiter in questions of meaning, even philosophical meaning, ordinary language usage will likewise be the final arbiter in questions of meaning about search requests and information representations. Specifically, ordinary language is the best medium for us to express our information needs, and any subset of ordinary language that may be used as an access language to an information system will be correspondingly *less effective* than ordinary language for searching. This poses a particular problem in information systems, namely, that if ordinary language is the best medium in which to express our information requirements, then *computerized* information systems, with which we *cannot* interact using our ordinary means of expression, will constrain our ability to express our information requirements.[31] It may mean also that the best content-retrieval systems, in general, are those which can understand the subtle meanings and nuances of information requests stated in ordinary language. At this point, only experienced search intermediaries can do this.

> 9. My method is not to sunder the hard from the soft, but to see the hardness of the soft. [**NB** p. 44]

Ordinary language, and the practices and activities of which they are a part are our primary references for meaning, even philosophical meaning. The "softness" of meaning in ordinary language cannot be improved by the "hardness" of logic. We don't need a separate more determinate language to eliminate the indeterminacies in meaning, we just need to be more careful about how we *use* language. Further, no such more determinate language is possible since there can be no single comprehensive notion of the determinacy of sense applicable to all uses of language in all contexts and circumstances.[32] The determinacy of sense is not a *property* of individual words, but a function of how those words are used, and can be influenced by the context and circumstances in which they are used or the backgrounds and experience of the participants. The same word can have different levels of determinacy in different usages. More importantly, Wittgenstein saw that when issues of meaning in language come up, as they did frequently in philosophy, the final arbiter of linguistic meaning is not philosophical analysis, but *ordinary usage*.[33] In fact, many of the problems of analytic philosophy arose, Wittgenstein believed, because

---

[31] While there has been work in the fields of Computer Science and Artificial Intelligence to build natural-language front ends to information systems (most commonly, to data base systems where the language, as we have said, is more precise), none of these operates in a fully conversational mode that would be comparable to the kind of semantically rich and complex conversation that an inquirer might have with a reference librarian in a research library.

[32] The notion of the determinacy of sense and its problems is the focus of a major portion of **PI** beginning with §65.

[33] "When I talk about language (words, sentences, etc.) I must speak the language of every day. Is this language somehow too coarse and material for what we want to say? Then how is another one to be constructed?—And how strange that we should be able to do anything at all with the one we have!" [**PI** §120]. Wittgenstein's question is, of course, rhetorical.

philosophers forgot these quotidian constituents of linguistic meaning. Language that has lost its connection to ordinary usage can indeed "bewitch" us.[34] Language leads us into some of these difficulties so frequently and predictably, that Wittgenstein called these systematic errors "diseases of thinking."[35]

In particular, Wittgenstein disagreed with Frege and Russell's belief that, in general, logic would form a better, more precise, foundation for linguistic expression—that language somehow aspired to the "crytaline purity of logic." Wittgenstein came to see that the "rough ground"[36] of ordinary language, as it is caught up in the "hurly-burly"[37] of day-to-day usage, gives us more precision in meaning than philosophers had previously thought possible. This is not a despairing observation, in fact, Wittgenstein reminded his readers that it is surprising how *well* ordinary language works:

> We are under the illusion that what is peculiar, profound, essential, in our investigation, resides in its trying to grasp the incomparable essence of language. That is, the order existing between the concepts of proposition, word, proof, truth experience, and so on. This order is a super-order between—so to speak—super-concepts. Whereas, of course, if the words "language," "experience," "world," have a use, it must be as humble a one as that of the words "table," "lamp," "door."

> On the one hand it is clear that every sentence in our language "is in order as it is." That is to say, we are not striving after an ideal, as if our ordinary vague sentences had not yet got a quite unexceptionable sense, and a perfect language awaited construction by us.—On the other hand it seems clear that where there is sense there must be perfect order.—So there must be perfect order even in the vaguest sentence. [**PI** §§97–98]

**Relevance to Information Systems:** The language of an information system is often created by system designers as they build the system, in much the same way that logicians such as Frege and Russell proposed constructing logical languages to be used in philosophical analysis. Like them, system designers often despair that ordinary language is not precise enough to be useful as a language for content searching, especially on large text or image retrieval systems. But while the language of an information system may be a subset of ordinary language, and its uses may differ, the system designer should not overlook the fact that there may be more precision in ordinary language than he may at first think. In particular, there are often contextual aspects of language that can be used to provide better access to available information. One of the great dangers of building *computerized* information systems is that the computer seems to give us a precision in

---

[34] "Philosophy is a battle against the bewitchment of our intelligence by means of language." [**PI** §109]

[35] "There is a kind of general disease of thinking which always looks for (and finds) what would be called a mental state from which all our acts spring as from a reservoir." [**BB** p. 143]

[36] "The more narrowly we examine language, the sharper becomes the conflict between it and our requirement. (For the crystaline purity of logic was, of course, not a result of investigation; it was a requirement.) The conflict becomes intolerable; the requirement is now in danger of becoming empty.—We have got onto slippery ice where there is no friction and so in a certain sense the conditions are ideal, but also, just because of that, we are unable to walk. We want to walk; so we need friction. Back to the rough ground!" [**PI** §107]

[37] "How could human behavior be described? Surely only by showing the action of a variety of humans, as they are all mixed up together. Not what one person is doing now, but the whole hurly-burly, is the background against which we see an action, and it determines our judgement, our concepts, and our reactions." [**RPP II** §629]

access that is not possible in non-computerized systems. As Wittgenstein remarked about logic, "the crystalline purity of logic was, of course, not a result of investigation; it was a requirement." Some of this belief that the precision of a computer confers an advantage in searching is due to a confusion between *physical access* and *intellectual access*. *Physical access* consists of the means by which a computer locates and retrieves information whose precise address is known, while *intellectual access* consists of the means by which certain information is determined to be what a particular inquirer will be satisfied with, having submitted a specific query to the information system. Computers *can* give us rapid, precise *physical access*, no matter how complex the search requirements are, as long as they are decidable. But rapid, precise *physical access* does not always guarantee rapid, precise *intellectual access,* because in some situations, such as with text or image retrieval, the specific item(s) of information that will satisfy an inquirer often remain(s) an open question during the search. Of course, in data retrieval, where the descriptions of available information—addresses, phone numbers, account balances, etc.—are quite precise, then improvements in *physical access* can improve *intellectual access*. Where does this misconception about precision in language come from? For Frege and Russell, formal logic was the model for all language, leading them to believe that the precision of logical propositions could be attained for any semantic meaning. In the same way, information systems designers have often assumed that the precision of representation and retrieval of a data retrieval system—one that provides access to, for example, names, addresses and phone numbers—is attainable in text or image retrieval systems where the searchers are looking for items with specific intellectual content. But it is clear that, as Wittgenstein states, ". . . every sentence in our language 'is in order as it is' " (*supra*). If there is no better way to express ourselves than in ordinary language, then it is also evident that the farther away from ordinary usage that we get, the less likely we are to express ourselves well. Insofar as information systems employ means of expression different than our ordinary means of expression, our ability to express our information needs will be impoverished. Currently, the only "information system" that uses the full range of expression of our ordinary language is another human being.

> 10. One of the most dangerous of ideas for a philosopher is, oddly enough, that we think with our heads or in our heads.

> The idea of thinking as a process in the head, in a completely enclosed space, gives him something occult. [**Z** §§605–606]

Thinking and meaning are not entities that have simple "locations" in the way that the anatomical parts of the brain have physical places. Our thinking is frequently assisted by implements that exist outside of our skulls: Much information that we use does not exist "in our heads" but in books, audio tapes, computer data bases, the notes we make to ourselves and the people with whom we interact. In some instances, our ability to think may require a calculator, a computer spread-sheet, or just pencil and paper. This sort of augmentation of the human intellect has been called "scaffolding," and will be discussed in Part III.

If our thought processes must sometimes be assisted by implements and information storage media that are *external* to our heads, then there can be no comprehensive psychophysical parallelism. In other words, brain processes cannot always be complete explanations of mental processes. As Wittgenstein put it:

> No supposition seems to me more natural than that there is no process in the brain correlated with associating or with thinking; so that it would be impossible to read off thought-processes from brain-processes. [**Z** §608]

Hilary Putnam came to a similar conclusion in his "Twin Earth" thought-experiment. There he claimed that "meaning" in language was not something that was entirely mental. As he put it so succinctly, "Cut the pie any way you like, 'meanings' just ain't in the head!"[38] (The "Twin Earth" thought experiment is described in the text surrounding footnote 247, *infra*)

**Relevance to Information Systems:** The idea that we think "in our heads" is misleading in the following sense: it implies that everything we need in order to think is either in our heads or potentially so. This can make us disregard how important the context that surrounds us is, and how our circumstances and the implements we use to assist our thinking may be essential to our thought processes—in short, the boundaries of "the mind" are broader than the boundaries of the skull. The purely cognitive, context-free notion of the mind where all thought takes place entirely within our heads may lead us to believe that, like our own minds, everything that we need for retrieval, that is, for understanding the meaning of information and its representations, can be put into the information system.[39] We will discuss this in more detail in Part II ("Psychophysical Parallelism"), in particular, the claim of some epistemologists that we are a "brain in a vat" and "everything we need to represent the world" can be in our heads. The "brain in a vat" metaphor leads us to think of the mind as separate from its milieu, taking from it what it needs for understanding in the form empirical data and abstractions. This can lead us to believe that everything we need to search for or make sense of the information we search through can be contained within the information system itself—that the context or circumstances in which the information system exists or the background and intentions of the searchers and system designers impart no additional meaning to, or interpretation of, the information which exists on the system. This is a "disease of thinking" that Wittgenstein specifically argued against:

> There is a kind of general disease of thinking which always looks for (and finds) what would be called a mental state from which all our acts spring as from a reservoir. [**BB** p. 143]

---

[38] H. Putnam. "The Meaning of 'Meaning'." **Language, Mind and Knowledge**, v. VII, pp. 131–193. Minnesota Studies in the Philosophy of Science, 1975.

[39] This analogy is implicit in the model first proposed by Hilary Putnam where the mind is related to the brain in the way that a computer program is related to the hardware of a computer. This view came to be known as "Functionalism." As he described it, "The proper way to think of the brain is as a digital computer. Our psychology is to be described as the software of this computer—its 'functional organization.' " Putnam has come to reject this view, as he discusses in his more recent work, **Representation and Reality**, in the chapter "Why Functionalism Didn't Work," MIT Press, Cambridge, MA, 1991. Interestingly, one of the reasons he now rejects functionalism is the same conclusion he reached in his "Twin Earth" thought experiment, namely, that "meanings ain't 'in the head'." In other words, if our thoughts and their "meaning" cannot be understood without reference to context and circumstances, then in general, thoughts cannot exist as independent, context-free entities. But the very nature of a computer program is that it *is context-free* and, like an expression of formal logic, its "meaning" is wholly self-contained. The mind lacks this kind of context-free closure.

The view that the mind, or an information system, can hold everything which it needs to represent, and thereby understand, the world is a view with which this manuscript will explicitly take issue, starting with our discussion of "scaffolding," in Part III.

> 11. Let's not imagine the meaning as an occult connection the mind makes between a word and a thing, and that this connection *contains* the whole usage of a word as the seed might be said to contain the tree. [**BB** pp. 73–74]

Words don't stand for objects, nor do they "have meanings" when "meaning" refers to something separate and definite that a word is somehow linked to, and to which we must refer when we want to understand the word in question. We *do* talk of the "meanings" of words, but this is a kind of language game that should not be taken to grant the ontological status of meanings as independent entities to which words and expressions are linked. Wittgenstein is breaking away from two powerful traditions in the study of language: First, by saying that words don't have meanings to which they are somehow linked, he breaks with the "referential" view of language, a tradition in the study of language that reaches back at least to Aristotle.[40] Secondly, and perhaps more importantly, Wittgenstein also broke with the tradition of language study that insists that meaning is something that is either definite, or aspires to a definiteness that is a *sine qua non* of understanding. Wittgenstein writes:

> If a pattern of life is the basis for the use of a word then the word must contain some amount of indefiniteness. The pattern of life, after all, is not one of exact regularity.[41] [**LWPP I** §211]

---

[40] Hilary Putnam spells out the intellectual antecedents of meaning and reference, and its persistence:

> . . . Aristotle was the first thinker to theorize in a systematic way about meaning and reference. In De Interpretatione he laid out a scheme which has proved remarkably robust. According to this scheme, when we understand a word or any other "sign," we associate that word with a "concept." This concept determines what the word refers to. Two millenia later, one can find the same theory in John Stuart Mill's Logic, and in the present century one finds variants of this picture in the writings of Bertrand Russell, Gottlob Frege, Rudolph Carnap, and many other important philosophers. [**Representation and Reality**, p. 19. MIT Press, 1991.]

Wittgenstein found a clear statement of this referential view of meaning in the writings of Augustine, and spends much of the early part of his Philosophical Investigations presenting and criticizing it. We will cover Wittgenstein's explicit rejection of the Augustinian model of language in Part III.

[41] The idea that words must have precisely defined meanings is a view that was central to Frege's philosophy. As we have discussed, this was a view that Wittgenstein was sympathetic to early in his work, and was apparent in **TLP**. In **PI** he made quite clear that he no longer held this view:

"But is a blurred concept a concept at all?"—Is an indistinct photograph a picture of a person at all? Is it even always an advantage to replace an indistinct picture by a sharp one? Isn't the indistinct one often exactly what we need?

Frege compares a concept to an area and says that an area with vague boundaries cannot be called an area at all. This presumably means that we cannot do anything with it.—But is it senseless to say: "Stand roughly there?" Suppose that I were standing with someone in a city square and said that. As I say it I do not draw any kind of boundary, but perhaps point with my hand—as if I were indicating a particular spot. [**PI** §71]

One of the cornerstones of the analytic philosophy of Frege, Russell and the early Wittgenstein was what they referred to as the "strict determinacy of sense." The "sense" or meaning of a word, they insisted, must be completely "determinate," or unambiguous, in order to be used in philosophical analysis. If the meanings of words were not completely determinate, then statements using those words would be indeterminate, since they believed that the meaning of a sentence was composed of the meanings of its words. Thus, any philosophical analysis that used those statements would be intolerably uncertain. This need for a strict determinacy of sense was what made logic and the scientific method so appealing to Frege, Russell and the early Wittgenstein, and why they, in particular, Russell, believed that the clarity and certainty of philosophical analysis could only be assured if its language had the strict determinacy of sense that logic and science seemed to have. Since they believed that ordinary language could never have the determinacy of sense necessary for philosophical analysis, ordinary language could never be the language of philosophy. The clarity of meaning necessary in language could only be brought out by logical analysis. But the reassessment and ultimate rejection of this position is one of the clearest breaks which Wittgenstein made with his early work—what he was to call his "old way of thinking" [**PI** preface, p. ix]. The "strict determinacy of sense" that Frege, Russell and early Wittgenstein believed necessary for philosophy was a false ideal. In the first place, precision in meaning is not a property of words but may vary in different circumstances. Some language uses don't require an ideal precision of meaning: when I make the statement that "The birds are eating all the raspberries that I planted." the meaning that I intend to convey by this statement is perfectly understandable even though the word "birds" is not strictly determinate, in Frege's sense, because it is not clear which, of the thousands of species of birds, it refers to. There is no absolute standard of precision in meaning. Furthermore, when clarity of expression is required, ordinary language can be just as precise as formal logic can, it just gets its clarity in a different manner—not from truth tables and rules like the "excluded middle," as logic does, but from the context and circumstances, what Wittgenstein would call "Language Games" and "Forms of Life," in which the statement was uttered. If meanings don't have some separate, independent existence, and the meanings of the words we use are, in many ways, indefinite, how do we manage to understand each other as well as we do? In many cases, the ambiguity of a statement or a word is resolved by the context or circumstances in which it was uttered or written—in fact, when we are in particular circumstances the ambiguity of a word simply doesn't come up: If I am with a friend at a baseball game and he remarks that "The pitcher looks great!" I know he is *not* commenting on the aesthetic quality of a water container—the ambiguity of the word "pitcher" simply doesn't arise.[42] Here, the word still conveys what its speaker intended, in spite of its seeming ambiguity.

**Relevance to Information Systems:** If the indefiniteness of words or expressions is resolved by a consideration of their context or circumstances of occurrence, then it is no great intellectual leap to see that the indefiniteness of the language of representation and

---

[42] Part of the purpose of Wittgenstein's admonition to not ask for the meaning of a word, but to ask for its use, is to get us away from the ambiguity that often comes up when we ask for the meaning of a word. That is, words can often seem ambiguous when we try to define them, but, and this is Wittgenstein's key point, the same words don't seem ambiguous when we use them in our daily activities and practices. It is perfectly consistent for someone to use a word correctly without being able to give a precise definition of it.

searching used by information systems might be resolved in a similar manner. This means that information systems are *not* context free but are *situated* in an important and essential way. They are influenced by the context and circumstances of their use, in particular, they must be considered part of the common activities and practices in which they are used, and an understanding of these activities and practices may be necessary for the full potential of an information system to be exploited. We will pursue this in greater detail in Part III. The determinacy of sense is one of the central issues of Information Systems. In fact, we can line up different kinds of information systems along a spectrum of their respective determinacy of representation. At one extreme we have data base management systems which provide access to highly determinate information such as names, addresses, phone numbers, credit limits and account balances. Such data items are unambiguous and stay pretty much the same regardless of the context they appear in. At the other end of the determinacy spectrum would be a document retrieval system which provides access to the "intellectual content" of a large collection of documents many of which deal with similar topics.[43] Here, it might be very hard to come up with a formal retrieval request for a document that retrieves neither too many nor too few documents (imagine formulating a search query for use by an Internet Search Engine to retrieve documents discussing the "impact of computer technology on modern management"). This issue of the determinacy of sense in Information Systems will be central to the discussion of Part III.

> 12. For remember that in general we don't use language according to strict rules—it hasn't been taught us by means of strict rules either. We, in our discussions on the other hand, constantly compare language with a calculus proceeding according to exact rules.
>
> This is a very one-sided way of looking at language. In practice we very rarely use language as such a calculus. For not only do we not think of the rules of usage—of definitions, etc.—while using language, but when we are asked to give such rules, in most cases we aren't able to do so. We are unable clearly to circumscribe the concepts we use; not because we don't know their real definition, but because there is no real "definition" to them. To suppose that there must be would be like supposing that whenever children play with a ball they play a game according to strict rules. [**BB** p. 25]

In a calculus the meanings of the words/symbols do not vary from context to context, and their use is governed by the application of a strict, finite set of rules. Language is not like this. The idea of language being like a calculus fails in at least two ways: (1) Meaning in language is dependent on more than just the words and the placement of those words in a sentence. The meaning of an expression can vary according to context, circumstances, tone of voice, etc.[44] Yet, clearly, this is not the case with the symbols of a calculus; these must

---

[43] Don Swanson has pointed out [personal communication] that searching for intellectual content on a document collection of texts dealing with similar topics (what he called a "homogeneous" collection) is much more demanding than searching for intellectual content on a document collection of texts dealing with many disparate topics. An example of a topically homogeneous collection would be the articles on medical research included in the Medline retrieval system. A topically heterogeneous collection might be a collection of newspaper articles published in a major newspaper during a particular span of time.

[44] Consider how the meaning of the sentence "John stole the money." changes as it is spoken with a different word being emphasized (emphasized word is capitalized):

mean the same thing in all contexts. (2) No set of rules can determine how an expression could be used in all contexts and all circumstances since there are an indefinitely large number of possible circumstances and contexts, and the rules must not only specify how the expression should be used, there must also be *meta*-rules which specify when the rules of usage are applicable and when they are not. The rules would have to provide for new or metaphorical uses of the expression, as well.

**Relevance to Information Systems:** Index and search terms do not have fixed meanings that are invariant from system to system. Most obviously, the *extension* of a particular index term—the information, for example, documents or images, which it actually represents—will vary from system to system since different systems will often contain different information. Even within one system the extension of index terms can vary over time, as the coverage of the collection changes—when, for example, new information is added, and previously stored information is removed. And, even when the same document is assigned index terms by different experienced indexers, they often disagree in the terms they select to represent the intellectual content.[45]

Computerized information systems are largely composed of complex assemblages of computer programs. But if we consider the kinds of computer programs that are most successful, they often have the properties of a calculus: they contain relatively context-free variables that are governed by strict rules that can be precisely specified in a program. Computers, in general, do not handle context well so any rules or meaning that are dependent on context or circumstances outside of the computer will not be represented well on a computerized system. So if information systems are dependent on language, and language is context-dependent and not governed by strict rules, then there will often be something Procrustean about computerizing the search processes of certain information systems—those that provide access to content. It means that when using the system to find relatively context-free information, such as news releases that mention certain proper names or dates, then a computerized system may confer some advantages over a non-computerized one. But when looking for information that has a particular "intellectual content" or *meaning*—for example, "advice for investing in Central European service industries"—computerized systems, by themselves, may lack the necessary ability to provide precise intellectual access, especially if the amount of information searched through is large and comparatively homogeneous, and the amount of relevant information is comparatively small.

Computers are, fundamentally, "logical machines" and the attempt to get them to handle language in "meaningful" ways is similar to philosophers' attempts to represent meaning in language using formal logic. As we pointed out earlier, this was an effort that Wittgenstein participated in early in his career, when he supported the work of Frege and Russell. But he soon became disillusioned with this work, saying, in the **Philosophical Investigations**:

> "John *STOLE* the money?" (i.e., I thought he earned the money but it turned out he stole it.)
> "John stole the *MONEY*?" (i.e., he was supposed to steal the jewelry, but he stole the money instead.)
> "*JOHN* stole the money?" (i.e., I thought Matt stole the money, but it turned out that John was the one who stole it.)

[45] See, for example, P. Zunde and M. Dexter. "Indexing Consistency and Quality," **American Documentation**, vol. 20:3, pp. 259–267. July 1969.

> The more narrowly we examine actual language, the sharper becomes the conflict
> between it and our requirement. (For the crystalline purity of logic was, of course,
> not a *result of investigation*: it was a requirement.) [**PI** §107]

Here, Wittgenstein makes clear that the formal rigor—the "crystalline purity"—of logic
and, by inference, computers, is not the "result" of an "investigation" that *uncovers* some
underlying formal structure of language. The formal rigor is a "requirement" for doing
logic in the first place. Similarly, computers don't give us access to an underlying formal
semantic model of language, they *require* that language be transformed into a formal
model as a prerequisite for automation. Only the formal, context-free aspects of language,
such as the location and tabulation of word occurrences, will fit this model. The more
complex semantic and pragmatic aspects of language will be difficult to express in the
"crystalline purity" of logic and computers. Wittgenstein continues:

> We see that what we call "sentence" and "language" has not the formal unity that
> I imagined, but is the family of structures more or less related to one another.—
> But what becomes of logic now? Its rigour seems to be giving way here.—But
> in that case doesn't logic altogether disappear?—For how can it lose its rigor? Of
> course not by our bargaining any of its rigor out of it.—The *preconceived idea* of
> crystalline purity can only be removed by turning our whole examination round.
> (One might say: the axis of reference of our examination must be rotated, but about
> the fixed point of our real need.) [**PI** §108]

How should we turn "our whole examination round?" Wittgenstein expresses it best when
he says:

> ...we don't start from certain words, but from certain occasions or activities.
> [**LC** p. 3]

This could be interpreted to mean that reasonably large computerized information systems for accessing intellectual content are doomed to failure. This is not the case. When
computers work with relatively determinate, context-free information—names, addresses,
phone or social security numbers—like most data base management systems do, they can
be very precise and efficient tools of retrieval. And when text retrieval systems are used
to retrieve documents that mention specific context-free words like proper names or dates
(e.g., when retrieving news articles about a specific person), they too can be extremely
precise and useful. Or, when the document collection to which they provide access is
comparatively small and the documents are all about different subjects, or the searchers
are not very demanding, retrieval can be frequently successful. But when someone wants
to retrieve text containing certain specific intellectual content from a large, homogeneous
document collection, and that content is not associated with a precise context-free representation, such as a proper name or a specific date, then retrieval will be more problematic.
This is why the retrieval of information with a specific intellectual content has been called
an inherently "trial-and-error process."[46]

---

[46] D.R. Swanson. "Information Retrieval as a Trial-and-Error Process." **Library Quarterly**, vol. 47:2, pp. 128–
148. April 1977.

# Part II: Wittgenstein's Philosophy of Language and Mind

> "I am convinced, Yorick," continued my father, half reading and half discoursing, "that there is a northwest passage to the intellectual world; and that the soul of man has shorter ways of going to work, in furnishing itself with knowledge and instruction, than we generally take with it."
>
> —Lawrence Sterne, **Tristram Shandy**

Describing Wittgenstein's philosophy is a daunting endeavor. His currently published works span 15 volumes, only one of which, the **Tractatus Logico-Philosophicus**[47] was published in his lifetime. Of the rest, only **Philosophical Investigations** and **The Blue and Brown Books**[48] benefited from any comprehensive editorial efforts by Wittgenstein himself. The rest, from **Zettel**[49] to, most recently, **Last Writings on the Philosophy of Psychology, v. II**[50] have been put together from Wittgenstein's *Nachlass*, his literary estate, by a number of individuals.[51] These may not be the last publications coming from

---

[47] **Tractatus Logico-Philophicus**. Routledge and Kegan Paul, London, 1961. Translated by D.F. Pears and B. McGuinness. [Hereafter referred to as **TLP**]

[48] **Philosophical Investigations**. Macmillan, NY, 1953. Translated by G.E.M. Anscombe. [Hereafter referred to as **PI**]. NB **The Blue and Brown Books** profited from Wittgenstein's editing, but they were notes for the use of his students and were not meant for publication. There is some indication that Wittgenstein considered the **Brown Book** as the preliminary notes for a possible book, but it was never carried further than that. Much of the **Blue and Brown Books** was revised and incorporated into **PI**. [**The Blue and Brown Books**. Harper, New York, 1976]. Hereafter referred to as **BB.**

[49] **Zettel**. Oxford, Basil Blackwell, 1967. Edited by G.E.M. Anscombe and G.H. von Wright, translated by G.E.M. Anscombe. [Hereafter referred to as **Z**]

[50] **Last Writings on the Philosophy of Psychology, Vol. II: The Inner and the Outer, 1949–1951**. Oxford, Basil Blackwell, 1992. Edited by G.H. von Wright and H. Nyman, translated by C.G. Luckhardt and M.A.E. Aue. [Hereafter referred to as **LWPP II**]

[51] "Wittgenstein bequeathed in his literary estate an unusually complex body of work, with no adequate indications as to which manuscripts should be published and how, nor indeed, with the exception of the **Tractatus Logico Philosophicus**, any model for doing so. His instructions were limited to the following terms in his will:

> 2. I Appoint my friend Mr. R. Rhees of 96 Bryn Road Swansea to be the Executor of this my Will and I hope that he will accept fifty pounds for his personal expenses in discharging this trust. 3. I Give to Mr. R. Rhees, Miss G.E.M. Anscombe and Professor G.H. von Wright of Trinity College Cambridge all the copyright in all my unpublished writings and also the manuscripts and typescripts thereof to dispose of as they think best but subject to any claim by anybody else to the custody of the manuscripts and typescripts. I intend and desire that Mr. Rhees Miss Anscombe and Professor von Wright shall publish as many of my unpublished writings as they think fit but I do not wish them to incur expenses in publication which they do not expect to recoup out of royalties or other profits"

[**Ludwig Wittgenstein**, Vienna Edition, p. 52, Introduction. Springer-Verlag, Wien, New York, 1993. Edited by Michael Nedo.]

Although the books published after Wittgenstein's death were put together from his Nachlass by his former students, these selections have not been made without disagreement. A description of the major points of

his unpublished writings, either. But while most of the editors who have put together these works were personal friends and students of Wittgenstein himself, future publications will be unlikely to profit from that advantage. Although Wittgenstein focused his philosophical work on many specific themes, the published works themselves do not separate his writings into categories—**Remarks on the Foundations of Mathematics**[52] contains many remarks on language as well as mathematics, **Philosophical Investigations** contains remarks on philosophy in addition to mathematics, logic and psychology, and **Remarks on the Philosophy of Psychology, v. II** contains remarks on language as well as psychology. Wittgenstein's discussion of any given topic is spread throughout his writings, but not collected or summarized in any one place. Successive paragraphs may deal with a specific topic, but the topic is dropped in favor of another and picked up again, seemingly at random, later in the work, or in another work. Certainly one of the reasons for this scattershot approach to philosophy is that Wittgenstein was continually grappling with very deep and elusive problems, problems that had defied systematic solution by the best analytical minds of the 20th century. So, many of his recorded comments were not *solutions* to these problems, but the remnants of intellectual battles which he fought all his life (his published writings go right up to a few days before he died, when he succumbed to a long illness).[53] The careful reader may be reminded of Borges' short story "The Garden of the Forking Paths"[54]:

> Ts'ui Pên . . . was Governor of Yunnan and gave up temporal power to write a novel with more characters than there are in the Hung Lou Mêng, and to create a maze in which all men would lose themselves. He spent thirteen years on these oddly assorted tasks before he was assassinated by a stranger. His novel had no sense to it and nobody ever found his labyrinth.

The answer comes later in the story:

> At one time, Ts'ui Pên must have said; "I am going into seclusion to write a book," and at another, "I am retiring to construct a maze." Everyone assumed these were separate activities. No one realized that the book and the labyrinth were one and the same.

It is ironic that Wittgenstein himself uses the metaphor of the "labyrinth" to describe how language often works:

contention appears in "The Wittgenstein Controversy" [**The Atlantic Monthly,** pp. 28–41, June 1997]. Michael Nedo and the publisher Springer-Verlag have undertaken to publish the entire **Nachlass** of Wittgenstein—over 30,000 pages. This is the first attempt to publish Wittgenstein's entire work in the original order in which he left it, thereby addressing one of the major points of contention: that the selections of Wittgenstein's work that were published after **Philosophical Investigations** were taken out of the original chronological order.

[52] **Remarks on the Foundations of Mathematics,** 2nd ed. Oxford/Cambridge, MA, Basil Blakwell/MIT Press, 1978. Edited by G.H. von Wright, R. Rhees, and G.E.M. Anscombe, translated by G.E.M. Anscombe. [Hereafter referred to as **RFM**]

[53] Many of these remarks were published in his **On Certainty** [Oxford, Basil Blackwell, 1969]. Hereafter referred to as **OC**.

[54] J.L. Borges. "The Garden of the Forking Paths," **Ficciones**. Grove Press, New York, 1956. Translated by E. Editores. Quotations from p. 93 and 96, respectively.

> Language is a labyrinth of paths. You approach from *one* side and know your way about; you approach the same place from another side and no longer know your way about. [**PI** §203]

To many of Wittgenstein's readers, his books and the labyrinth of language are, like Ts'ui Pên's novel, "one and the same." **Philosophical Investigations** contains not only remarks on the labyrinth of language but it is itself an embodiment of language's complexity. Metaphors aside, the careful reading, not to mention the understanding, of Wittgenstein's thought requires unusual effort by the reader. Wittgenstein, it is clear, was aware of this problem (from the preface of **Philosophical Investigations**):

> The thoughts which I publish in what follows are the precipitate of philosophical investigations which have occupied me for the last sixteen years. They concern many subjects . . . I have written down all these thoughts as *remarks*, short paragraphs, of which there is sometimes a fairly long chain about the same subject, while I sometimes make a sudden change, jumping from one topic to another.—It was my intention at first to bring all this together in a book whose form I pictured differently at different times. But the essential thing was that the thoughts should proceed from one subject to another in a natural order and without breaks.

> After several unsuccessful attempts to weld my results together into such a whole, I realized that I should never succeed. The best that I could write would never be more than philosophical remarks; my thoughts were soon crippled if I tried to force them on in any single direction against their natural inclination.—And this was, of course, connected with the very nature of the investigation. For this compels us to travel over a wide field of thought criss-cross in every direction. The philosophical remarks in this book are, as it were, a number of sketches of landscapes which were made in the course of these long and involved journeyings. [**PI** pp. ix–x]

The philosopher John Searle provides a convincing explanation of this aspect of Wittgenstein's writings:

> . . . you have the feeling when you take up one of [Wittgenstein's] later works and read it that it's a bit like getting a kit for a model aeroplane [*sic*] with no instructions as to how you are supposed to put all the pieces together. That also can be extremely frustrating. Each of his later works is something of a do-it-yourself book.

> Now why did he write like that? . . . I think he honestly and sincerely was struggling to say something new and different, and he always had the feeling that he hadn't quite said what he really meant, that he was still struggling to find a mode of expression. And in his own mind, he never really succeeded. Finally, I think we need to say for English-speaking readers that this style, though it looks strange to Anglo-American eyes, is not so unusual in German. There is a tradition in German philosophy of writing aphoristically. You find it in Nietzsche, Schopenhauer and Lichtenberg, to mention just a few.[55]

---

[55] Taken from an interview with Searle on Wittgenstein, reported in Bryan Magee's **The Great Philosophers**, p. 341. Oxford University Press, 1988.

Various keys to the **Tractatus Logico-Philosophicus** and **Philosophical Investigations** have appeared in recent years,[56] but the serious reader must, in the final analysis, find his own way through Wittgenstein's philosophical landscape. Like other difficult and, at first flush, seemingly jumbled intellectual works, such as Joyce's **Ulysses** and Sterne's **Tristram Shandy**,[57] there is an implicit methodology that guides Wittgenstein's work, and with understanding, can guide the reader too.[58] It may be the case that Wittgenstein's foremost contribution to philosophy is not his critiques of philosophical views, or his epistemology, but the *method* by which he achieves them—a method that is frequently overlooked by his readers. While the subjects of his philosophical remarks in his later writings seem to be, as we have said, random, the method by which he produces these remarks remains consistent—though unstated—throughout his later writings. This, I think, is the key to his statement (from the preface to **PI**):

> I should not like my writing to spare other people the trouble of thinking. But, if possible, to stimulate someone to thoughts of his own. [**PI** p. x]

Rather than *explaining* his methodology the way Western philosophers have done, traditionally, Wittgenstein, in these later works, *shows* us how to approach the various epistemological problems that confront us.[59] The reader is like an apprentice looking over the

---

[56] Inter alia. Max Black: **A Companion to Wittgenstein's "Tractatus."** Cornell University Press, Ithaca, NY, 1964. G.P. Baker and P.M.S. Hacker. **Essays on the Philosophical Investigations: Wittgenstein: Meaning and Understanding**. University of Chicago Press, 1980; **An Analytical Commentary on Wittgenstein's Philosophical Investigations**, v. I. University of Chicago Press, 1980; Volume 2 of an **Analytical Commentary on the Philosophical Investigations: Wittgenstein: Rules, Grammar and Necessity** [Basil Blackwell, Oxford, Basil Blackwell, 1985]; P.M.S. Hacker: Volume 3 of an **Analytical Commentary on the Philosophical Investigations: Wittgenstein: Meaning and Mind: Part I: Essays** [Basil Blackwell, Oxford, 1990]; Volume 3 of an **Analytical Commentary on the Philosophical Investigations: Wittgenstein: Meaning and Mind: Part II: Exegesis** §§**243–427**. G. Hallett. **A Companion to Wittgenstein's "Philosophical Investigations."** Cornell University Press, Ithaca, NY, 1977.

[57] A further irony is that one of Wittgenstein's favorite books was Lawrence Sterne's **Tristram Shandy**, a book that has a similar seemingly fragmented structure as his own works. A contemporary of Wittgenstein recalled his making the following statement: "Now a book I like greatly is Sterne's **Tristram Shandy**. That is one of my favorite books. You remember the incident where they are discussing infant prodigies, and after several have mentioned examples, one of the company caps the lot by saying that he knew an infant who produced a work on the day he was born. Whereupon Dr Slop replies that it should have been wiped up and nothing more said about it. Now that you could say about a lot that is written today." M.O'C. Drury. "Conversations with Wittgenstein," **Recollections of Wittgenstein**. Oxford University Press, Oxford, 1984. Edited by R. Rhees.

[58] P.M.S. Hacker, one of the principal commentators on Wittgenstein's work, made a similar observation:

> . . . although the **Investigations** is written in brief and often apparently disconnected remarks, although it frequently jumps from topic to topic without indicating the reasons for such sudden transitions, and although it has seemed to many readers to be a philosophy that revels in lack of systematicity, it is in fact . . . a highly systematic, integrated work, and anything but a haphazard collection or *aperçus*. [**Wittgenstein's Place in Twentieth-Century Analytic Philosophy**, p. 97. Blackwell, Oxford, 1996.]

[59] There is some indication that Wittgenstein meant for his approach to philosophical problems to be a general methodology to be used for the more common problems that trouble us:

> Our concepts, judgements, reactions never appear in connection with just a single action, but rather with the whole swirl of human actions. [**LWPP II**, p. 56]

shoulder of a master craftsman—a craftsman who refuses to explain his methods in any detail but continually gives demonstrations of them.[60] Wittgenstein's writings are incomplete from a systematic point of view, they do not cover all the questions that might occur to the average reader or philosopher and some of the questions he does raise he does not answer at all. But if the reader "gets" the method that Wittgenstein demonstrates, then he can apply it to the conceptual problems—philosophical or otherwise—that trouble him. This was one of Wittgenstein's goals. To rid the reader of the "diseases of thinking" that prevent him from getting out of the intellectual dead ends in which he may find himself.[61] Since my goal in this work is to apply Wittgenstein's later thought on language to the problems of building and using computerized information systems—a topic Wittgenstein obviously had nothing to say about—we must try to be clear about how this methodology works. Because of this, I will spend some time discussing his methodology, but first I would like to lay the foundation for this by discussing the relation between language and thought.[62]

## Language and Thought

What must first strike the reader of Wittgengstein's later works is the apparent conflict between one of his goals, to cure us of our "diseases of thinking," and his concentration on the way we use and understand language. Traditional epistemology assumes that language is a product of thought. As Locke wrote, "Words in their primary or immediate signification, stand for nothing but the ideas in the mind of him that uses them."[63] That is, we think, then translate these thoughts into words or expressions. This, in fact, is the view Wittgenstein held during his early work as presented in the **Tractatus Logico Philosophicus**. Since

We can take this to mean that even though Wittgenstein wrote about philosophical problems, he did not divorce these problems from the broader context of human activities in which they are embedded. So a philosophical remark has the potential to be a remark connected to the broader context of human life.

[60] H. Putnam comments on Wittgenstein's method:

> Mary Warnock once said that Sartre gave us not arguments or proofs but "a description so clear and vivid that when I think of his description and fit it to my own case, I cannot fail to see its application." It seems to me that this is a very good description of what Wittgenstein was doing . . . over and over again in his work. [H. Putnam, p. 74.**Renewing Philosophy**. Harvard University Press, Cambridge, MA, 1992.]

[61] For example:

> There is a kind of general disease of thinking which always looks for (and finds) what would be called a mental state from which all our acts spring as from a reservoir. [**BB** p. 143]

[62] I am well aware that by "explaining" how Wittgenstein's methodology works I am guilty of taking a non-Wittgesteinean approach. In my defense I would point out that Wittgenstein's methodology is difficult to grasp if you must get it by just observing his work. Explaining it deprives the reader of this experience of discovery, but provides him with a quicker grasp of its essentials. A "deep" understanding of Wittgenstein still requires one to read his work in the original, and, to this end, in the following discussion I have tried to quote as many of the relevant passages in his works as possible.

[63] J. Locke. "An Essay Concerning Human Understanding." See Book III "Of Words." Quotation from section 3.2.2 in **British Empirical Philosophers**. Routledge and Kegan Paul, London, 1985. Edited by A.J. Ayer and R. Winch.

language is a *product* of thought by this view, it seems a difficult task to examine language and then infer how our thoughts produced these words. But, as Wittgenstein returned to his philosophical work after World War I, he began to reassess and revise many of his early views. Wittgenstein no longer believed that language—that is, what we say or write—was a product of thought. He argued for a virtual Copernican reversal of this epistemological relationship. Instead of language being a *product* of thought, he insisted that language is "the *vehicle* of thought"—loosely, thought is a *product* of language:

> When I think in language, there aren't "meanings" going through my mind in addition to the verbal expressions: the language is itself the vehicle of thought.[64] [**PI** §329]

Or, stated somewhat differently:

> Knowledge is not *translated* into words when it is expressed. The words are not a translation of something else that was there before they were. [**Z** §191]

Obviously, not all our thought involves language, for we can surely "think about" music or visual images without reference to language at all. The point Wittgenstein is making is not that *all* thought uses language as a foundation, but that *when we use language* we usually use it as a means for thinking, not as medium to translate thoughts that are already completely formulated.[65]

Wittgenstein's assertion is based, at least in part, on the observation that we frequently speak without thinking beforehand—that is, we just *speak*. Since conscious thought does not always precede speech (or writing) it follows that it is not a *necessary* precursor to language use. But how is Wittgenstein to answer the objection that the reason we don't have to consciously think before we speak is that the prerequisite thought is unconscious or tacit?

For Wittgenstein, we formulate our thoughts using the tools of language, in the same way that we might say that an artist (e.g., a painter) formulates her images through the tools of her trade—paints, brushes, canvases. The artist need not develop a mental image of what

---

[64] Max Black reports a comment by Wittgenstein:

> ...the anecdote of the girl who, on being told to "think before she spoke," replied, "How do I know what I think until I hear what I say?" Her situation is not unusual: one important function of verbal expression is to reveal to the author what he thinks. He thinks in speaking or writing: as Wittgenstein liked to say, one can think with pen as well as in one's head. [**The Labyrinth of Language**. Encyclopaedia Britannica, Frederick A. Praeger, New York, 1968. Footnote, p. 86]

[65] This is not to say, either, that we never express our thoughts by means of language, for we do—think of answering the question "What are you thinking?"
Wittgnstein makes a similar case for music:

> Speech with and without thought is to be compared with the playing of a piece of music with and without thought. [**PI** §341]

In other words, we don't have to hum a tune to ourselves before we play it.

she wants to paint in any detail *before* she paints—or even while she paints. She creates the artistic image *through* the use of her artistic tools. It is even the case that painting or drawing can help us to see things better—Wittgenstein comments:

> How can one learn the truth by thinking? As one learns to see a face better if one draws it. [**Z** §255]

The detailed artistic image is not necessarily prior to the artistic creation. Neither is it necessarily an internal/mental event. Certainly, there may be artists who *do* begin with a final image of what they want to portray, but it is not necessary that they do so. Some artists, I would imagine, are quite unaware of what the precise end product of a particular project will be, and if they do start with a mental image, it is one that is subject to constant revision in the course of the creative process. Further, what the artist can portray is limited by the kinds of paints, brushes, etc. that are available to her, and the skill she has in utilizing them. While the exceptional artist can transcend the art that has preceded her, she will not be able to achieve certain effects that are beyond the capability of her artistic tools—for example, she will not be able to paint in three dimensions since her canvas is limited to two dimensions.

Like the painter, we must rely on the "tools" of our language for our ability to express ourselves.[66] While it is sometimes the case that we have a thought and express it in words, it is not necessary that we first have such an explicit thought. Our thinking takes place *through* our use of language, and is constrained by language in the same way that the artist's tools and her ability to use them constrain what images she can create.[67] If language contains the tools and elements of thought, then the limits of our verbal thinking are prescribed by the limitations of language—and these limitations can vary from speaker to speaker (consider the language of an educated adult *versus* the language of an adult trying to speak a foreign language that he does not know well). But Wittgenstein goes even further than this. He claims that language—both the words and the formal structures that determine how they are used—is not only the vehicle of thought, but often the source of our "diseases of thinking." So the causes and the evidence for our misunderstandings are in language:

> Philosophy is a battle against the bewitchment of our intelligence by means of language. [**PI** §109]

---

[66] Wittgenstein was not the only person to draw the analogy between words or language and tools, for example: G.K. Zipf also saw words as tools of expression [**Human Behavior and the Principle of Least Effort**. Hafner, NY, 1965 (Facsimile of the 1949 edition)]. The implementational views of language advocated by Zipf and Wittgenstein are presented together in D.C. Blair's **Language and Representation in Information Retrieval**, pp. 139ff. Elsevier Science, Amsterdam, 1990.

[67] While most of us take for granted our ability to think and express ourselves, one remarkable survivor of a severe brain injury, was left without memories of the past, anticipation of the future or the ability to think in an organized and sustained manner. He was able to recover his ability to think only by slowly and painfully learning to write again. In fact, the writing itself was, for a time, the only way he could think:

> This writing is my only way of thinking. If I shut these notebooks, give it up, I'll be right back in the desert, in that "Know-nothing" world of emptiness and amnesia. [A.R. Luria. **The Man with the Shattered World: The History of a Brain Wound**, p. 86. Harvard University Press, 1972.]

It is no great leap of the imagination to see that if we want to understand how we think, and, especially, how we make mistakes in our thinking, we must examine language and how we use it. By focusing his analysis on language, Wittgenstein keeps his efforts oriented towards external phenomena available for us all to see and avoids the problems inherent in examining inner mental phenomena.

## Benjamin Lee Whorf

Wittgenstein's insistence on the dependence of thought on language was a novel idea in philosophical circles, but two linguists, Edward Sapir and Benjamin Lee Whorf, were making similar claims in the 1930's and early '40's.[68] There is no evidence that Wittgenstein was aware of their work, nor were they aware of Wittgenstein's, yet there are parallels between their respective works. Sapir writes:

> Human beings do not live in the objective world alone, nor alone in the world of social activity as ordinarily understood, but are very much at the mercy of the particular language which has become the medium of expression for their society. It is quite an illusion to imagine that one adjusts to reality essentially without the use of language and that language is merely an incidental means of solving specific problems of communications or reflection. The fact of the matter is that the "real world" is to a large extent unconsciously built up on the language habits of the group ... We see and hear and otherwise experience very largely as we do because the language habits of our community predispose certain choices of interpretation.[69]

For Whorf, his discoveries about thought and language came in stages. He first saw that the meaning of various words could lead speakers into false views of reality:

> [Whorf] I came in touch with an aspect of this problem before I had studied under Dr. Sapir, and in a field usually considered remote from linguistics. It was in the course of my professional work for a fire insurance company, in which I undertook the task of analyzing many hundreds of reports of circumstances surrounding the start of fires, and in some cases, of explosions. My analysis was directed toward purely physical conditions, such as defective wiring, presence or lack of air spaces between metal flues and woodwork, etc., and the results were presented in these terms. Indeed it was undertaken with no thought that any other significances would or could be revealed. But in due course it became evident that not only a physical situation qua physics, but the meaning of that situation to people, was sometimes a factor, through the behavior of the people, in the start of the fire. And this factor of meaning was clearest when it was a LINGUISTIC MEANING, residing in the name or the linguistic description commonly applied to the situation. Thus, around a storage of what are called "gasoline drums," behavior will tend to a certain type, that is, great care will be exercised; while around a storage of what are called "empty gasoline drums," it will tend to be different—careless, with little repression of smoking or of tossing cigarette stubs about. Yet the "empty" drums are perhaps

---

[68] The claims made by Sapir and Whorf are usually referred to as the "Sapir-Whorf Hypothesis." But it is clear that their statements do not amount to a hypothesis in the traditional sense, that is, their views are not stated in the form of a testable claim. For simplicity's sake, I will refer to Sapir and Whorf's claim as "Whorf's Conjecture."

[69] Quoted by B.J. Whorf. "The Relation of Habitual Thought and Behavior to Language," **Language, Thought, and Reality: Selected Writings of Benjamin Lee Whorf**, p. 134. MIT Press, Cambridge, 1956. Edited by J.B. Carroll. Original article published in 1939.

the more dangerous, since they contain explosive vapor. Physically the situation is hazardous, but the linguistic analysis according to regular analogy must employ the "empty," which inevitably suggests lack of hazard. The word "empty" is used in two linguistic patterns: (1) as virtual synonym for "null and void, negative, inert," (2) applied in analysis of physical situations without regard to, e.g., vapor, liquid vestiges, or stray rubbish, in the container. The situation is named in one pattern (2) and the name is then "acted out" or "lived up to" in another (1), this being a general formula for the linguistic conditioning of behavior into hazardous forms.

In a wood distillation plant the metal stills were insulated with a composition prepared from limestone and called at the plant "spun limestone." No attempt was made to protect this covering from excessive heat or the contact of flame. After a period of use, the fire below one of the stills spread to the "limestone," which to everyone's great surprise burned vigorously. Exposure to acetic acid fumes from the still had converted part of the limestone (calcium carbonate) to calcium acetate. This when heated in a fire decomposes, forming inflammable acetone. Behavior that tolerated fire close to the covering was induced by use of the name "limestone," which because it ends in "-stone" implies noncombustability.[70] [Whorf continues with several more examples]

These incidents prefigured Whorf's more remarkable claims about grammatical structure and thought. An important role for language is the way it influences how reality is divided up:

GRAMMATICAL PATTERNS AS INTERPRETATIONS OF EXPERIENCE
:
:
A category such as number (singular vs. plural) is an attempted interpretation of a whole large order of experience, virtually of the world or of nature; it attempts to say how experience is to be segmented, what experience is to be called "one" and what "several."[71]

Whorf shows that language does not necessarily mirror reality, in fact it can create impressions of reality that do not exist:

In our language, that is SAE [Standard Average European[72]], plurality and cardinal numbers are applied in two ways: to real plurals and imaginary plurals. Or more exactly if less tersely: perceptible spatial aggregates and metaphorical aggregates. We say "ten men" and also "ten days." Ten men either are or could be objectively perceived as ten, ten in one group perception—ten men on a street corner, for instance. But "ten days" cannot be objectively experienced. We experience only one day, today; the other nine (or even all ten) are something conjured up from memory or imagination. If "ten days" be regarded as a group it must be as an

---

[70] *Op.cit.*, pp. 135–136.

[71] *Op.cit.*, p. 137.

[72] Whorf: "Since, with respect to the traits compared, there is little difference between English, French, German, or other European languages with the POSSIBLE (but doubtful) exception of Balto-Slavic and non-Indo-European, I have lumped these languages into one group called SAE, or 'Standard Average European'." [*Op.cit.*, p. 138]

"imaginary," mentally constructed group. Whence comes this mental pattern? Just as in the case of the fire-causing errors, from the fact that our language confuses the two different situations, has but one pattern for both. When we speak of "ten steps forward, ten strokes on a bell," or any similarly described cyclic sequence, "times" of any sort, we are doing the same thing as with "days." CYCLICITY brings the response of imaginary plurals. But a likeness of cyclicity to aggregates is not unmistakably given by experience prior to language, or it would be found in all languages, and it is not.[73]

As Whorf began to study non-Indo-European languages (primarily, the Native American language of the Hopi), he was able to see the relation between thought and language. This relation was not limited to the connotations of words, like in his fire insurance examples, but was extended to the grammatical structure of language. Like Wittgenstein, Whorf believed that the grammar of language influenced the structure of our thought (though, as we will see, Wittgenstein's notion of grammar, especially what he called "depth grammar," was different than Whorf's). The reason why linguists had not seen this before according to Whorf was that they had studied Indo-European languages primarily. The lexical and grammatical structures of these languages are so similar that we are lead to the conclusion that all languages work this way. As Whorf learned the languages of American Indians, he saw that they were not just semantically and phonetically different from European languages, but grammatically different, and that this grammatical difference influenced how native Americans "saw," or thought about, reality:

> [Whorf]When linguists became able to examine critically and scientifically a large number of languages of widely different patterns ... It was found that the background linguistic system (in other words, the grammar) of each language is not merely a reproducing instrument for voicing ideas but rather is itself the shaper of ideas, the program and guide for the individual's mental activity, for his analysis of impressions, for his synthesis of his mental stock in trade. Formulation of ideas is not an independent process, strictly rational in the old sense, but is part of a particular grammar, and differs, from slightly to greatly, between different grammars. We dissect nature along lines laid down by our native languages. The categories and types that we isolate from the world of phenomena we do not find there because they stare every observer in the face; on the contrary, the world is presented in a kaleidoscopic flux of impressions which has to be organized by our minds—and this means largely by the linguistic systems in our minds. We cut nature up, organize it into concepts, and ascribe significances as we do, largely because we are parties to an agreement to organize it in this way—an agreement that holds throughout our speech community and is codified in the patterns of our language. The agreement is, of course, an implicit and unstated one, BUT ITS TERMS ARE ABSOLUTELY OBLIGATORY; we cannot talk at all except by subscribing to the organization and classification of data which the agreement decrees.
>
> This fact is very significant for modern science, for it means that no individual is free to describe nature with absolute impartiality but is constrained to certain modes of interpretation even while he thinks himself most free.[74]

---

[73] *Op.cit.*, p. 139.
[74] *Op.cit.*, "Science and Linguistics," pp. 212–214. Original article published in 1940.

Whorf continues:

> As I said in the April 1940 *Review*,[75] segmentation of nature is an aspect of grammar—one as yet little studied by grammarians. We cut up and organize the spread and flow of events as we do, largely because, through our mother tongue, we are parties to an agreement to do so, not because nature itself is segmented in exactly that way for all to see. Languages differ not only in how they build their sentences but also in how they break down nature to secure the elements to put in those sentences. This breakdown gives units of the lexicon. "Word" is not a very good "word" for them; "lexeme" has been suggested, and "term" will do for the present. By these more or less distinct terms we ascribe a semifictitious isolation to parts of experience. English terms, like "sky, hill, swamp," persuade us to regard some elusive aspect of nature's endless variety as a distinct THING, almost like a table or chair. Thus English and similar tongues lead us to think of the universe as a collection of rather distinct objects and events corresponding to words. Indeed this is the implicit picture of classical physics and astronomy—that the universe is essentially a collection of detached objects of different sizes.

> The examples used by older logicians in dealing with this point are usually unfortunately chosen. They tend to pick out tables and chairs and apples on tables as test objects to demonstrate the object-like nature of reality and its one-to-one correspondence with logic. Man's artifacts and the agricultural products he severs from living plants have a unique degree of isolation; we may expect that languages will have fairly isolated terms for them. The real question is: What do different languages do, not with these artificially isolated objects but with the flowing face of nature in its motion, color, and changing form; with clouds, beaches, and yonder flight of birds? For, as goes our segmentation of the face of nature, so goes our physics of the Cosmos.

> ⋮

> The Indo-European languages and many others give great prominence to a type of sentence having two parts, each part built around a class of word—substantives and verbs—which those languages treat differently in grammar. As I showed in the April 1940 Review, this distinction is not drawn from nature; it is just a result of the fact that every tongue must have some kind of structure, and those tongues have made a go of exploiting this kind.[76]

Whorf even attributes some advances in science to the way scientists talk about their work:

> The revolutionary changes that have occurred since 1890 in the world of science—especially in physics but also in chemistry, biology, and the sciences of man—have been due not so much to new facts as to new ways of thinking about facts. . . . I say new ways of THINKING about facts, but a more nearly accurate statement would say new ways of TALKING about facts . . . we must face the fact that science begins and ends in talk.[77]

---

[75] *Op.cit.*, "Science and Linguistics," pp. 207–219
[76] "Languages and Logic," *op.cit.*, pp. 240–241. Original article published in 1941.
[77] "Linguistics as an Exact Science," *op.cit.*, p. 220. Original article published in 1940.

*Problems With Whorf's Conjecture*

The philosopher Max Black, although sympathetic with Whorf's claims about the relation between thought and language, observes, correctly, that Whorf had not proved his case. After quoting Whorf, he makes the following comment:

> Even in so crude a summary as the more detailed and more suggestive accounts supplied by Whorf and other anthropologists, a sympathetic reader may darkly discern unfamiliar ways of patterning the universe, remote from our own familiar distinctions between past, present, and future, between "mental" and "physical"— and the like. . . . And when we come to the supposed linguistic "reflections" of the delineated "world-view," the course of the argument becomes dubious indeed. . . . So long as communication between members of radically different cultures remains as crude as it is apt to be at best, the perception of patterns of thought embodied in the formal structure of a language will remain a controversial and speculative exercise. And even if some reliable procedures for conducting this kind of investigation were to be evolved, it would be a further and a very difficult step to argue from such formal features to the existence of causal influence upon the thought habits of the language users. (The existence of diverse philosophical systems, all expressed with equal facility in such a language as English or German, must cast doubt upon the possibility of a *simple* causal relation between grammar and thought.)[78]

Black does not completely reject Sapir and Whorf's conjecture on the influence of language on thought, but he does conclude that " . . . the results remain inconclusive, if suggestive for future scientific research." But his comment, above, that "diverse philosophical systems [can be] expressed with equal facility in such a language as English or German" does not provide evidence against Whorf's position. In the first place, Whorf stated quite clearly that one of the main reasons that we do not see the influence of grammar on thought is that our basis for comparison is what he called the SAE (Standard Average European) languages, which have very similar structures. Whorf would not be surprised that Black sees little difference between expressions in English and German. Black's second point, that "diverse philosophical systems [can be] expressed with equal facility in such a language as English or German" is not as clear cut as Black implies that it is. If it were, there would be no debate about the translation of these works into various languages, yet there is. Texts in formal logic may be translated from one SAE language to another without undue argument, but there are significant debates over the translations of many other European philosophers, Heidegger or Merleau-Ponty, for example. One needs only read the discussions concerning the translation of what Wittgenstein calls "Übersicht" to see that there are points where even English and German do not match up well.[79] But is this difficulty in translation because English speakers don't have the *concept* that the Germans express by "Übersicht?" That is not as clear.

But Black's point that Whorf and Sapir do not provide enough evidence to support their conjecture is well taken. What we see in Whorf is a provocative insight and the beginnings

---

[78] M. Black. **The Labyrinth of Language**. Mentor Book, New York, 1968. Black goes even further than this in observing that neither Whorf nor Sapir had even proposed a testable hypothesis. (see p. 94, in the above work)

[79] Baker, G.P. and P.M.S. Hacker. "Übersicht," **Essays on the Philosophical Investigations, Vol. 1: Wittgenstein: Meaning and Understanding**, chapter 14. Basil Blackwell, Oxford, 1980.

of his attempt to marshal data in its support. Unfortunately, Whorf died in 1941 at the age of 44 while Sapir died in 1939 and their cause was taken up by only a few other linguists or anthropologists. But these followers lacked Whorf's and Sapir's enthusiasm and focus on the relation of language and thought.[80]

Although Whorf's conjecture of linguistic relativity has been out of fashion for decades, there has been a recent renewed interest in what he wrote. Ellis, extending Whorf's conjecture, has claimed that language's primary purpose is not to act as a medium of communication, but to provide the structure or segmentation of reality that enables communication to take place:

> The essential and distinctive feature of language is not its ability to transmit information ... but a logically prior attribute, the process of analysis, evaluation, and organization of experience which must have taken place before communication can occur.[81]

> Language must first have had something to do with what there is to communicate and with what will be counted as communication. It is not just a means of transferring information, it is also, and far more importantly, the locus of the process of deciding what information is to be, and of instituting the kinds of information that will be available for communication.[82]

Ellis' statement recalls a similar statement from Wittgenstein:

> [Philosophical problems] are, of course, not empirical problems; they are solved, rather, by looking into the workings of our language, and that in such a way as to make us recognize those workings: *in despite of* an urge to misunderstand them. The problems are solved, not by giving new information, but by arranging what we have always known. [**PI** §109]

Whorf followed his conception of the dependency of thought on language to its inevitable conclusion. Namely, that we can study how we think, not by introspection or the reporting of mental events, as psychologists and philosophers often do, but, like Wittgenstein, by examining the structure and use of our language:

> [Whorf]Actually, thinking is most mysterious, and by far the greatest light upon it that we have is thrown by the study of language. This study shows that the forms of a person's thoughts are controlled by inexorable laws of pattern of which he is unconscious. These patterns are the unperceived intricate systematizations of his own language—shown readily enough by a candid comparison and contrast with other languages, especially those of a different linguistic family. His thinking itself is in a language—in English, in Sanskrit, in Chinese. [footnote: To anticipate the text, "thinking in a language" does not necessarily have to use WORDS. An uncultivated Choctow can as easily as the most skilled litterateur contrast the tenses or the genders of two experiences, though he has never heard of any WORDS like "tense" or "gender" for such contrasts. Much thinking never brings in words at

---

[80] For example, the work of C. Kluckhohn (see footnote 87).
[81] J. Ellis. **Language, Thought and Logic**, p. 18. Northwestern University Press, Evanston, IL, 1993.
[82] *Op.cit.*, p. 17.

all, but manipulates whole paradigms, word-classes, and such grammatical orders "behind" or "above" the focus of personal consciousness.] And every language is a vast pattern-system, different from others, in which are culturally ordained the forms and categories by which the personality not only communicates, but also analyzes nature, notices or neglects types of relationship and phenomena, channels his reasoning, and builds the house of his consciousness.[83]

Whorf brought out another important, but subtle, point that bears reiterating. That is, the influence of language on our thought not only shapes our thought in language, but it also shapes our non-linguistic thought—thought that deals with images or sound. In other words, we formulate images of objects such as tables, chairs, the sky, marshes, musical passages and other similar entities, at least in part, because our language breaks up our reality this way. This is not to say, of course, that the structures of reality and language are totally independent. Philosopher of Language John Searle describes this relationship between language and reality:

> I am not saying that language creates reality. Far from it. Rather, I am saying that *what counts* as reality—what counts as a glass of water or a book or a table, what counts as the same glass or a different book or two tables—is a matter of the categories that we impose on the world; and those categories are for the most part linguistic. And furthermore; when we experience the world we experience it *through* linguistic categories that help to shape the experiences themselves. The world doesn't come to us already sliced up into objects and experiences: what counts as an object is already a function of our system of representation, and how we perceive the world in our experiences is influenced by that system of representation. The mistake is to suppose that the application of language to the world consists of attaching labels to objects that are, so to speak, self-identifying. On my view, the world divides the way we divide it, and our main way of dividing things up is in language. Our concept of reality is a matter of our linguistic categories.[84]

Wittgenstein demonstrates how language can shape the way we see reality in the following example. He shows us a drawing of a triangle with the angles labeled A, B, and C, and the sides labeled a, b, and c. Then he says:

> See the triangle in such a way that c is the base and C the apex; and now, so that b is the base and B the apex. [**RPP I** §23]

If we look at the triangle in each of these two ways, we have two distinct visual experiences. Yet the visual data we perceive is the same in both instances. Here is a clear example of how language can make us see the same thing two different ways. Note also, that only someone with a basic understanding of the language of plane geometry can have this experience. A monkey could see the same visual data that we do, but he would not be able to see it in the two different ways that Wittgenstein wants us to—*not* because he doesn't see it as well as we do, but because he does not understand the language of geometry. Understanding the *language* of geometry is the *sine qua non* of this perception. It is interesting to note

---

[83]"Language, Mind and Reality," *op.cit.*, p. 252. Original article published in 1942.
[84]J. Searle."The Philosophy of Language" in Bryan Magee's **Talking Philosophy**, p. 156, 2001 edition. Oxford University Press, Oxford, UK, 1978.

that Whorf did not have any formal schooling in linguistics or anthropology before he gained his first insights into the relation between language and thought (as a young man, he attended MIT and majored in chemical engineering). His first insights came as a claims adjuster for the Hartford insurance company,[85] and even as his stature grew with his publications on language, he steadfastly refused academic appointments that were offered to him, "... saying that his business situation afforded him a more comfortable living and a freer opportunity to develop his intellectual interests in his own way."[86] This would not have been a surprise to Wittgenstein. Wittgenstein believed that professional philosophers were so thoroughly locked into the grammatical forms of their language, that is, the way that they formulated their philosophical puzzles, that it was extraordinarily difficult for them to gain the objectivity necessary to see how language was affecting the way they thought about, and eventually answered, these puzzles. By working as a claims adjuster, Whorf was not encumbered by the points of view of professional linguists, and was free to gain his own insights about language. What Whorf discovered by intuition, Wittgenstein came to after a long and intense reexamination of his own early work; and the fragmentary evidence that Whorf gathered to support his conjecture about linguistic relativity paled in comparison to the myriad examples that Wittgenstein marshalled in his attempt to show the relationship between language and thought. Part of the problem with Whorf's conjecture was that he required comparisons between European languages (SAE) and obscure and difficult languages such as Hopi or Navaho. Most readers did not command the necessary familiarity of two such different languages, so the few examples that Whorf gave to support his thesis had to be taken on faith by his readers. But there is a further problem with Whorf's work, although no one, to my knowledge, has articulated this difficulty. That is, Whorf cannot reject the hypothesis that the reason why Hopi Indians and their English speaking contemporaries think differently may *not* be only because their respective grammars are different, but because the *activities* on which their languages are based are so different. Those Native Americans who lived during Whorf's lifetime who maintained fluency in their ancestral language, probably lived day-to-day lives that were strikingly different than that lived by an English-speaker of European descent. This, alone, might account for the differences in their respective languages, and their respective thought patterns. The major objection to Whorf's conjecture about the dependency of thought on grammar and language is that no matter how differently Native American and English speakers talked about everyday affairs, it was always possible for these differences to be somehow articulated in English. For example, Clyde Kluckhohn, a contemporary of Whorf's who sympathized with his belief about the dependency of thought on language, offered a number of examples of differences between English and Navaho:

---

[85] The Hartford Insurance Company must have been an interesting place to work; the Pulitzer prize-winning poet, Wallace Stevens worked in their legal division during the same time, and eventually became a vice president. One might venture that Hartford had, in Stevens and Whorf, a greater number of nationally influential scholars than many colleges did.

[86] J. Carroll. **Introduction to Language, Thought, and Reality: Selected Writings of Benjamin Lee Whorf**, p. 5. MIT Press, Cambridge, 1956. Whorf often took classes at nearby universities, but never considered pursuing a higher degree. His most noticeable association was with the linguist Edward Sapir. He knew Sapir casually at first but began taking his classes and working more closely with him after Sapir accepted a faculty position at Yale in 1931. Sapir encouraged Whorf's work on Uto-Aztecan languages and introduced him to a native Hopi speaker who lived nearby in New York City.

When a Navaho says that he went somewhere he never fails to specify whether it was afoot, astride a horse, by wagon, auto, train, or airplane. This is done partly by using different verb stems which indicate whether the traveler moved under his own steam or was transported, partly by naming the actual means. Thus, "he went to town" would become:

| | |
|---|---|
| *kintahgóó 'ííyá* | He went to town afoot or in a nonspecific way. |
| *kintahgóó bil 'i 'ííbááz* | He went to town by wagon. |
| *kintahgóó bil 'o 'oot 'a '* | He went to town by airplane. |
| *kintahgóó bil 'i 'íí 'éél* | He went to town by boat. |
| *kintahgóó bil 'o 'ooldloozh* | He went to town by horseback at a trot. |
| *kintahgóó bil 'o 'ooldghod* | He went to town by horseback at a run (or perhaps by car or train). |
| *kintahgóó bil 'i 'nooltáá'* | He went to town by horseback at a gallup.[87] |

The problem with such examples, is that even though the expressions in Navaho seem unusually detailed to English speakers, it is still possible to have English expressions that convey the same meanings as the Navaho ones do. In fact, it is easy to imagine circumstances where you would make these distinctions naturally. Consider:

"Bill went to town yesterday."
"That's a long way. How did he get there?"
"He went on horseback."
"I didn't know he could ride a horse."
"He's not good at it, he just rode at a trot."

What is different between Navaho and English is not so much the grammar or the "thoughts" that depend on them, but the *circumstances* in which such fine distinctions are made. Navahos make these distinctions routinely, while English speakers require a more complex set of circumstances, but they can make them nevertheless. These are the kinds of examples that Whorf, *et alia*, used to support their conjecture about the dependence of thought on language, but it seems clear that, collectively, they are *not* really convincing evidence.

What would be required to lend plausibility to Whorf's conjecture? Well, at the very least, there would have to be a situation where, given the same circumstances or stimuli, an English-speaking person would consistently interpret the situation differently than a Navaho would, and these differences would have to be attributable to their respective languages. The difference in interpretation would be most noticeable if it resulted in actions that showed a clear difference between the two. But the strongest support for Whorf's conjecture would be if a Navaho and an English speaker both saw the same situation and stimuli, heard each other's description of the situation, *and* disagreed in their interpretations. That is, both speakers would be lead, by the grammar of their respective

---

[87]C. Kluckhohn and D. Leighton. **The Navaho**, p. 274. The Natural History Library, Anchor Books, Doubleday, Garden City, NY, 1962. Originally published by Harvard University Press, 1946. Kluckhohn and Leighton give numerous similar examples in their chapter "The Tongue of The People."

languages, to not only disagree with each other, but to insist that the other is wrong. Whorf's examples do not give us these kinds of distinctions, but Wittgenstein's do.[88]

## Wittgenstein on Language and Thought

Wittgenstein's philosophy of language had insights that were similar to Whorf's but did not have the failings that Whorf's work had. Wittgenstein did not have to compare two distinctly different languages to prove his point, he found ample evidence for his claims about the dependence of thought on language entirely within his own language.[89] And these examples were so striking that they have been translated convincingly from German into English. Whorf believed that the effect of linguistic relativity could occur only between two languages of sufficiently different origins; Wittgenstein's great insight was to show that these formal differences could occur *within* the boundaries of a single language as well. Where Whorf focused his analysis on different languages, Wittgenstein focused his analysis on the processes *within* a single language—processes which he termed *language games*. The effect that Whorf believed he saw between sufficiently different languages, Wittgenstein saw between language games, in a single language; and while Whorf's attempts to find support for his claims were largely *ad hoc*, Wittgenstein had a rigorous method for uncovering these discrepancies of language use—what he came to call "diseases of thinking."

Whorf had an original and notable observation, but, as Black justifiably pointed out, the facts that he marshalled in support of it were not sufficient to confirm his hypothesis. In fact, the way that Whorf presented his supposition, as we have noted, is not a testable hypothesis at all. Often this sort of conjecture appears in science with inadequate support and the originator is pushed into a debate over the validity of the conjecture. Through this debate, the conjecture is turned into testable hypotheses and various ways are devised to support or reject it. It is then either supported or not. Unfortunately, Whorf died, comparatively young, before this debate could be engaged, so his conjecture about the dependence of thought on grammar and language was left with little for his supporters to pin their allegiance on.

The dependence of thought on language is central to Wittgenstein's later philosophy. The structure and grammar of language determine, or influence, the structure and course of our thinking. Wittgenstein's most famous example is:

---

[88] There has been at least one experiment that lends support to Whorf's view of language and thought. In this experiment, half the subjects were English speakers and half were native Tarahumara speakers (Tarahumara is an Uto-Aztecan language found in Mexico). The point of difference under investigation concerned the fact that Tarahumara speakers use the same word (siyóname) for the colors blue and green. In the first test, subjects were given three color chips: one green, one blue and one, alternately, somewhat green or somewhat blue. The task was to select the one color chip of the three that was the most different from the other two. English speakers selected the correct color chip 29 out of 30 times, while the Tarahumara, with no linguistic means to distinguish blue and green, selected the correct color chip only half the time: that is, no better than random. While this experiment offers support for Whorf's conjecture, it is difficult to come up with such decisive demonstrations. In other words, if Whorf's view of language is taken to be valid, it is clear that it is probably a very small effect and not as pervasive as he suggested. [P. Kay and W. Kempton. "What is the Sapir-Whorf Hypothesis?," **American Anthropologist**, 86:1, pp. 65–79.]

[89] Although Wittgenstein's native language was German, he lived most of his life in England and usually lectured in English. His major philosophical works, other than **The Blue and Brown Books** were written in German and translated into English by his former students and colleagues.

What is the meaning of a word? [**BB** p. 1]

This sort of statement, according to Wittgenstein, gets us into serious conceptual trouble.[90] Most obviously, the structure of the question leads us to expect a certain kind of answer. The difficulty here is that the grammatical form of this question is similar to the form of a set of more common questions. For example:

> What is the length of a marathon?
> What is the color of Alain's car?
> What is the height of Niagara Falls?

Each of these questions has a reasonably precise answer—a marathon is 26 miles and 385 yards long; Alain's car is blue; Niagara Falls (on the Canadian side) is 167 feet high. The question, "What is the meaning of a word?" *looks* like the three questions above. This similarity is a similarity of what Wittgenstein called the "surface grammar" of the questions. But this similarity disguises a very deep semantic difference between the first question and the following three. What is the consequence of this misperceived similarity? The consequence is that when we ask the question "What is the meaning of a word?" we expect the same kind of precise answer that we would get when we ask "What is the length of a marathon?" This leads us to look for a precise entity or statement that would count as a "meaning." The *grammar* of the question about the meaning of a word compels us to think that there is a precise answer to this question. When we don't find it easily, we continue our search, believing that the precise answer we seek is somehow just out of our reach, or that the answer is some sort of complex componential analysis of the meaning such as that done in Eco's work.[91] Wittgenstein's answer to this question is to rephrase it:

> For a large class of cases—though not for all—in which we employ the word "meaning" it can be explained thus: the meaning of a word is its use in language.[92]

---

[90] As Wittgenstein continues:

> The questions "What is length?," "What is meaning?," "What is the number one?" etc., produce in us a mental cramp. We feel that we can't point to anything in reply to them and yet ought to point to something. (We are up against one of the great sources of philosophical bewilderment: a substantive makes us look for a thing that corresponds to it.) **BB** p. 1.

[91] U. Eco. **A Theory of Semiotics**. Indiana University Press, Bloomington, IN, 1976. See also, J. Lyons' **Semantics**, vol. 1. Cambridge University Press, Cambridge, 1977.

[92] **PI** §43. My translation of this passage differs from the published translation. The original translation is:

> For a large class of cases—though not for all—in which we employ the word "meaning" it can be defined thus: the meaning of a word is its use in the language.

What Anscombe, the translator of **Philosophical Investigations**, renders as "defined" is the German word "erklären." But "erklären" is translated, more commonly, as "explained" rather than "defined." "Explain" is the first meaning given for "erklären" and "define" is the ninth meaning in **The New Cassell's German Dictionary** [Funk and Wagnells, New York, 1958]. Given Wittgenstein's distrust of definitions, the Anscombe translation seems somewhat misleading. It appears that Wittgenstein is "defining" what "meaning" is, something that is inconsistent with his philosophy of language. It fails on two counts: In the first place, Wittgenstein specifically argues that language does not work in only one way. "Defining" meaning as "use" is basically saying that meaning arises in only one way, through "use." Further, Wittgenstein distrusts "definitions" in general. They give a false

Reading this formulation of the statement we do not expect a precise answer as we did when we asked the first question. In fact, it is no longer clear what would "count" as the meaning of a word—and this is exactly what Wittgenstein wants. For Wittgenstein, "meaning" is not a clearly describable entity, in fact, it is not an entity at all, as the form of the original question leads us to believe. If we want to understand the meaning of a word, there is no substitute for looking at its *use*; and to come to understand a word's *use* we must look, as John Wisdom, one of Wittgenstein's students, stated, at "cases and cases."[93] And how do we know if we understand what the word "means?" We understand it if we can use it and we get the appropriate response from those to whom we are speaking.

It is also the case that these three questions (*supra*) have a further implication: not only do they all have clearly specifiable answers but they also have clear ways of determining what the correct answers are. If we want to know the length of a marathon or the height of Niagara Falls, we can look it up in an encyclopedia. If we want to know the color of Alain's car we simply look at it. There are clear criteria for correctness here. This is not the case with the "meaning" of a word since the same word can have different meanings in different contexts.

Another important problem with "asking for the meaning of a word" is that this formulation of the question also implies that there is a clear stopping point in our search for the answer. Again, this is the same conclusion that we arrive at with questions like, "What is the length of a marathon?" When we answer this question (by finding out the precise length) we know that our search for an answer has ended.[94] Once you know that a marathon is 26 miles 385 yards, or that Alain's car is blue, or that the height of Niagara Falls is 167

---

sense of precision that has no place in understanding how language works. I believe that translating "erklären" as "explained" gives a rendering of this passage which is more faithful to Wittgenstein's philosophy.

A further reason for translating "erklären" as "explain" is actually given by Anscombe herself. In the paragraph following the one above, Anscombe translates the German:

> Und die Bedeutung eines Namens erklärt man manchmal dadurch, daß man auf seinen Träger zeigt.

as,

> And the meaning of a name is sometimes explained by pointing to its bearer.

Here, "erklären" is translated, more appropriately, I think, as "explained."

[93] See quotation at footnote 177.

[94] One might argue that quantities such as length or height can never be accurately measured. We can measure them with increasing precision, but there must be a point—perhaps at the molecular level, where our notion of accuracy of measurement breaks down completely. But this is a red herring. When we talk about the length of a marathon, the height of a waterfall or the color of a car, we are using these particular measurements in specific language games that require no more accuracy than the use of these values in ordinary life requires. To say that the measurement of the length of a marathon or the height of Niagara Falls must be calculated to the millionth of a centimeter is to confuse language games. We do have language games which require as much accuracy as possible—some scientific measurements may require all the accuracy we can muster. But our notion of the "accuracy of measurement" varies from language game to language game and situation to situation. A tourist looking at Niagara Falls and asking a guide how high it is would not need a measurement accurate to the millionth of an inch. This is not because the tourist is sloppy or fuzzy-minded, but because there is nothing he can do with such an accurate measurement—he does not participate in the activities for which such accurate measurements are used . Wittgenstein talks about how "certainty" can vary from language game to language game:

feet, there is no more for you to do. One cannot then ask "But what else is the length of a marathon?" etc. This is not the case with "What is the meaning of a word?" After someone has answered the question "What is the meaning of this word?," we can legitimately ask, "But what else is the meaning of this word?," or, perhaps more typically, "What other meanings does this word have?" And we could get reasonable answers to such a question. By being able to ask the follow-up question in the case of the meaning of a word, but not have it appropriate in the other three cases shows what Wittgenstein would call a clear *grammatical difference* between the first question and the other three; and by showing such a *grammatical difference*, by inference we have shown a difference in the way that we think about such things. We can see that we think of marathons as having a precisely measurable length, of cars having clearly specifiable colors, and of Niagara Falls having a precisely measurable height. We can also see another difference between the "meaning of a word" and the "length of a marathon": the question about the "meaning" of a word is not only imprecise, it is open-ended. When one proposes what the "meaning" of a word is, it is usually the case that this meaning can be added to or modified because the complete description of such a meaning can almost never be given. In fact, it is not clear at all what a "complete description of meaning" would be.[95] It is also the case that the "meaning" of a word can change, often radically, over time (think of the word "watergate" before Nixon's time as president, and after he resigned). But the length of a marathon or the height of a

> I can be as certain of someone else's sensations as of any fact. But this does not make the propositions "He is much depressed," "25 × 25 = 625" and "I am sixty years old" into similar instruments. The explanation suggests itself that the certainty is of a different *kind*.—This seems to point to a psychological difference. But the difference is logical.
>
> :
>
> The kind of certainty is the kind of language-game. [**PI** p. 224]

In the same way, the degree of precision in measurement can vary from language game to language game; and, as Wittgenstein emphasizes, this is not a psychological difference, although it seems that it is, but a logical or grammatical difference.

> Am I inexact when I do not give our distance from the sun to the nearest foot, or tell a joiner the width of a table to the nearest thousandth of an inch?
>
> No *single* ideal of exactness has been laid down; we do not know what we should be supposed to imagine under this head—unless you yourself lay down what is to be so called. But you will find it difficult to hit upon such a convention; at least any that satisfies you. [**PI** §88]

[95] The incompleteness of linguistic meaning was proposed before the turn of the century by C.S. Peirce. He talks of the meaning of a "representation" which is somewhat broader than, but includes, language. Representations can be any sign, linguistic or otherwise. A sign or representation, according to Peirce, is "something which stands to somebody for something in some respect or capacity" [**Philosophical Writings of Peirce**. Dover, NY, 1955. Edited by J. Buchler]. Peirce describes the unlimited nature of meaning and representation:

> The meaning of a representation can be nothing but a representation. In fact it is nothing but the representation itself conceived as stripped of irrelevant clothing. But this clothing never can be completely stripped off: it is only changed for something more diaphanous. So there is an infinite regression here. Finally, the interpretant is nothing but another representation to which the torch of truth is handed along; and as representation, it has its interpretation again. Lo, another infinite series. [C.S. Peirce, quoted by Eco. **A Theory of Semiotics**, p. 69. Indiana University Press, Bloomington, IN, 1976.]

water fall does not change in any appreciable way over time. Wittgenstein shows this, not by conceptual analysis, but by a *grammatical* analysis. This can be done by juxtaposing statements such as:

> If you give me the meaning of a word, your answer will never be complete, and it will change over time.
> If you give me the height of Niagara Falls, your answer will never be complete, and it will change over time.

Clearly, the first statement is OK but the second one strikes us as decidedly odd, perhaps even incorrect. This sort of grammatical analysis is central to Wittgenstein's methodology and consists of what he called the analysis of "depth grammar."

## Wittgenstein's Methodology

> I am not interested in constructing a building, so much as in having a perspicuous view of the foundations of possible buildings.—Wittgenstein **Culture and Value**

### The Analysis of Depth Grammar

There is an old joke that goes like this:

> Two individuals are talking:
> "The only people who live in Green Bay, Wisconsin are football players and prostitutes."
> "My mother comes from Green Bay!!!!"
> "Really? What position did she play?"

This, of course, is an example of what logicians call the "excluded middle." A question subject to the excluded middle affords only two options for its answer. There are, of course, instances where such a binary choice is perfectly all right:

> Do you want the light on or off?

But in the joke above it shows how the logical, that is, grammatical, form of a statement can lead us ineluctably to only two alternatives, and, in cases like that of the joke, neither alternative is correct. Here, in a very obvious way, we see that the grammatical structure of a statement can lead to the humorous inference that the respondent's mother plays professional football. There are other similar quirks of language structure, many of them emphasized through jokes.[96] But what Wittgenstein found was that there were equally decisive problems with the structure of language that lead us astray in far more subtle and important ways. Unlike the excluded middle, these misleading expressions are harder to

---

[96] For example, the question, "When did you stop stealing?" (first asked of Zeno by the Megarian philosopher Alexius). Malcolm quotes Wittgenstein as saying, " ...a serious and good philosophical work could be written that would consist entirely of jokes (without being facetious). Another time he said that a philosophical treatise might contain nothing but questions (without answers). In his own writing he made wide use of both. To give an example: 'Why can't a dog simulate pain? Is he too honest?' " N. Malcolm. **Ludwig Wittgenstein: A Memoir**, p. 29. Oxford University Press, London, 1958 (reprint 1972).

detect. Consider the time-worn philosophical problem of "Theseus' ship" as described by Plutarch:

> The ship wherein Theseus and the youth of Athens returned [from the labyrinth in Crete] had thirty oars, and was preserved by the Athenians down even to the time of Demetrius Phalereus, for they took away the old planks as they decayed, putting in new and stronger timber in their place, inasmuch that this ship became a standing example among the philosophers, for the logical question of things that grow; one side holding that the ship remained the same, and the other contending that it was not the same.[97]

Even philosophers of the stature of David Hume have contributed their own analysis of this problem:

> A ship, of which a considerable part has been changed by frequent reparations, is still considered as the same, nor does the difference of the materials hinder us from ascribing an identity to it. The common end in which the parts conspire is the same under all their variations, and affords an easy transition of the imagination from one situation of the body to another.[98]

If a few planks of the ship are replaced, most individuals are willing to accept that the ship is still Theseus', but as you continue to replace the planks one by one, eventually, in the limiting case, *all* of the planks will be replaced and the philosopher (even Hume, I think) cannot convincingly assert that the identity of the ship is unchanged. If you agree with Hume that it is still Theseus' ship when "a considerable part has been changed," consider this variation of the problem: What if, instead of *replacing* each rotting plank in the original ship, you began to build an entirely new *separate* ship, plank by plank as the planks in the old ship rotted. It's the same plank by plank replacement process as before, but doing it separately from Theseus' ship now, I think, makes one less willing to say that we still have Theseus' ship after "a considerable part has been changed."[99] The question is not whether Hume, *inter alia,* are right or wrong here—cases can be made for both sides. What is at issue for Wittgenstein is why anyone sees a puzzle here at all.

---

[97] **Plutarch: The Lives of the Noble Grecians and Romans**, p. 14. Modern Library, NY (reprint of the edition published in 1864). Translated by J. Dryden and revised by A.H. Clough.

[98] D. Hume. **A Treatise of Human Nature, in the Philosophy of David Hume**, p. 178. The Modern Library, NY, 1963. Edited by V.C. Chappell.

[99] This problem of incremental change that eventually produces a state change is similar to an even older puzzle, the "paradox of the heap" (originally called "sorites," the adjective form of the word soros, the Greek word for "heap"): you begin with no sand to which you add a single grain of sand. When you have no sand you clearly do not have a "heap" of sand, and if you add a single grain of sand, you still don't have a heap. When one accepts that the addition of a single grain of sand to anything that is not a heap does not produce a heap, then it becomes impossible to create a heap no matter how many single grains of sand are added. A heap is created by a process that, it is agreed, could not produce a heap. It's reasoning is like:

If x is not a heap, then x+1 grains of sand is not a heap;
If x+1 is not a heap then (x+1)+1 is not a heap;
If x+2 is not a heap then (x+2)+1 is not a heap:

Eventually, you are confronted with the paradox, or contradiction, that:
If x+1,000,000 is not a heap then (x+1,000,000)+1 is not a heap.

The philosopher sees a paradox of profound nature, but, to follow Wittgenstein's analysis of similar problems, what we have is not a profound puzzle, but merely a grammatical confusion which results from taking the word "same" out of its ordinary usage. The error is a grammatical error, in part, because no amount of empirical investigation can resolve the issue—no amount of investigation of Theseus' ship will tell you definitively whether it is still his ship or not. The word "same" has no grammatical role in the language game of comparing Theseus' ship (with the replaced parts) to itself. "Same" *does* have a role in the language game of comparing one ship with itself when there is some question of its physical identity (e.g., "Is that the same ship that we sailed to Juneau in last year?"), but it does not have a role in the game of comparing a ship with itself when its physical identity is not an issue, such as our example of Theseus' ship (i.e., we all know that the rotting ship was originally Theseus' ship). Here "same" does not have a legitimate role in comparing Theseus' ship with itself, that is, there are no criteria for usage here as there are in everyday usage of the word "same." Consider what the criteria would be for determining, in the case of legitimate comparison, whether the ship you are considering is the same one that you sailed to Juneau in last year. You might refer to the name of the ship and its home port as printed on the bow or stern (knowing that ships are not permitted duplicate names under international registry). Or, you might show a receipt you have showing that you had purchased passage on the ship in question; or, you might show someone a picture of yourself standing next to the ship in Juneau's harbor; or, you might say, "Just ask my wife and sons, they were with me on the trip"; or, if the name of the ship you are looking at is different, you might ask the captain or the harbor master whether it had a different name last year; etc., etc. None of these justifications would work with the puzzle of Theseus'

This paradox is attributed to Eubulides, a contemporary critic of Aristotle and member of the Megarian school of philosophy. Megarian philosophy was most influenced by Socrates and the Eleatics. Eubulides' most memorable contribution to philosophy was a series of paradoxes: "Sorites" (*supra*), the paradox of the "Hooded Man" the paradox of the "Bald Man," and, most famously, the "Liar's Paradox." (A detailed presentation of the history of sorites and its influence on modern philosophy is given by T. Williamson in his **Vagueness**, Routledge, London, 1994.)

These paradoxes have some similarities with Zeno's earlier, but better known paradox of Achilles and the Tortoise, where the fleet Achilles must catch up to the slower tortoise who has started ahead of him in a race. According to Zeno, Achilles can only catch the tortoise if he traverses half the distance between himself and the tortoise. No traversal of half the distance between Achilles and the tortoise will result in Achilles catching the tortoise. But the distance between Achilles and the tortoise no matter how short can always be halved. Thus there are an infinite number of distances Achilles must go before he can catch the tortoise. Hence, Achilles can never catch the tortoise.

Wittgenstein would say that each of these paradoxes arises, as the paradox of Theseus' ship, because of a confusion of language usage. Interestingly, a recent activity has given rise to an activity/language game in which a similar decision of identity must be made. This occurs in litigation dealing with software "piracy." When a computer program is "stolen," what is usually taken is not the entire program, but critical parts of it. To confuse the identity of the program further, the thief can change the names of variables and files used in the program and may even change the order in which program modules appear physically in the source code. All of this makes it increasingly difficult for the plaintiff to argue convincingly that the defendant's program was, in large part, stolen from the plaintiff. What makes it even more difficult is that for any two programs designed to do the same thing, there will be parts that are the same or similar even when one is not copying the other. This does not mean, however, that the issue of Theseus' ship could be settled in court. The software piracy case is sufficiently different in key ways from the question of Theseus' ship. But it does show how a legitimate language game can come into existence enabling us—here, forcing us—to make distinctions that we did not make before.

ship, that is, it's not an empirical problem.[100] In another example, the convicted murderers Leopold and Loeb carried this kind of reasoning to an extreme when, after serving some time in prison they said that they should be released from jail since they were no longer the same two individuals who had been tried and convicted before. Their reasoning was that since their body's cells were constantly replacing themselves, all of their cells had been replaced since their conviction, hence they were no longer the same individuals who were convicted. Wittgenstein would not have called their reasoning a biological mistake, but a grammatical one. That is, it is not scientifically wrong, as far as I know, to say that an individual's cells can be replaced entirely in a given period of time. But it is incorrect to say that, in ordinary circumstances, an individual's identity is solely determined by the precise set of cells that exist in his body at a specific point in time. Why is this the case? Well, it's easy to make up reasonable sentences that concern identity that have no reference to (and no dependence on) cellular biology (e.g., "Was that Fred wearing the lampshade at the party"). We don't have a language game or *form of life* which relates personal identity and human cellular structure (*that is, cells are not criteria for personal identity*), though it is possible we may someday have such a usage—the FBI's use of "DNA identification" (the identification of criminals based on just a few of their body cells) comes close to dealing with this notion, and is evidence of how such language games can evolve. The problem of personal identity in everyday usage can be seen as a grammatical problem because the form and structure of our language determine how we usually talk about personal identity; and the way we talk about identity gives us a format for raising issues of identity (i.e., what questions or statements are legitimate) and how to resolve these issues (i.e., which *further* questions are legitimate and which are not). How do issues of personal identity come up? They come up in the conversations—that is, the *language games*—we have. For example, we can say, "John is the person who deposited the money," or, "Mary was the winner of the award"; but we cannot say, in normal circumstances, "Although I saw John go to the bank, and everyone agreed that it was John, it was not he."[101] This is not an empirical

---

[100] Wittgenstein saw the relationship between humor and philosophy (*vid.* footnote 50). Perhaps the humorist, like the philosopher, is similarly sensitive to these grammatical irregularities. Comedian George Carlin offers his own variation on the puzzle of Theseus' ship:

> If a radio station changes its call letters, moves its studio across town, hires all new disk jockeys, and changes the style of music it plays, but keeps the same frequency, is it still the same radio station? Suppose they change only the music? On a given day, Flight 23 goes from New York to Los Angeles. The following month, Flight 23 goes from New York to Los Angeles again, but the crew is different, the passengers are different and it's a completely different airplane. How can both flights be Flight 23? [**Brain Droppings**, pp. 43–44. Hyperion, NY, 1997.]

[101] Some might object that when I make a reference to John, I am implicitly also referring to a specific, biological being; and when I refer to someone else, say, Tom, I am referring to someone who does not, indeed, cannot, have the same cellular makeup as John does. But such an objection does not support the assertion that identity is definitively cellularly based. In the case of Leopold and Loeb, their contention was that similarity at the cellular level was the sole criterion for personal identity. To say that the person I knew as John this morning has most of the same biological cells as the person whom I saw in the evening, is to say something that is, at best, only trivially true. If I were to be asked whether the person whom I saw in the morning was John or not, saying that that person and John had the same cells would be a decidedly odd answer. Further, it would not be the first thing that you would look for if you wanted to establish John's identity. The Language Game of talking about someone's identity would not generally make references to identity at the cellular level, except, as was mentioned, in the

problem because no observation of John in these circumstances will resolve the issue. By saying "I saw John go into the bank, but it was not he" the speaker has committed a grammatical, or logical, error, not an empirical one. To be an empirical problem empirical evidence must be decisive; empirical evidence is not necessary here because we do not have to see John to know that the statement "I saw John go into the bank, but it was not he" is false, or senseless. Likewise, there is no grammar or language game for talking about the identity of something like Theseus' ship when it changes incrementally. This, in fact, was one of Wittgenstein's complaints against philosophy, that it focused on puzzles that were puzzles merely because they were based on an unusual or unconventional uses of language. In short, Wittgenstein believed that many philosophical puzzles are really grammatical puzzles disguised as conceptual or empirical puzzles. It is the unorthodox use of language that gives the puzzle its mystery, not the conceptual problem it supposedly represents. As he put it so succinctly,

> philosophical problems arise when language goes on holiday. [**PI** §38]

Until Wittgenstein's work, there was no method for uncovering these kinds of problems, although Ryle comes close to a systematic study of the pathology of expressions in his 1932

---

case of criminal DNA comparisons. But here the notion of a "person" is somewhat different than our normal usage, *viz.*, for the FBI the DNA analysis can establish whether someone was physically at a particular place at a specific time. But it says nothing about whether the individual in question was awake, asleep, comatose or even dead. But DNA type is a very narrow interpretation of individuality—only one form of life among many that are concerned with identity. It cannot be an unequivocal criterion for identity since there are situations where two "different" individuals can have the same cellular identity. For example, "confidence men" who pretend to be someone they are not in order to fool an unsuspecting "mark." Or, cases where individuals have literally lead more than one life, maintaining two complete identities and, in the case of clever male bigamists, spies or double-agents, sometimes even two separate families. We can even say, on meeting an old friend, that he is "not the person he once was." The famous 19th century case of Phineas Gage comes immediately to mind. Gage was the first person known to have suffered severe damage to the frontal lobes of his brain and survive. But, although he was the same biological person he was before and suffered no deterioration in his physical abilities, he did not have the same personality:

> So radical was the change in him that friends and acquaintances could hardly recognize the man. They noted sadly that "Gage was no longer Gage." So different a man was he that his employers would not take him back when he returned to work, for they "considered the change in his mind so marked that they could not give him his place again." The problem was not lack of physical ability or skill; it was his new character. [A. Damasio. **Descartes' Error: Emotion, Reason and the Human Brain**, p. 8. Avon Books, NY, 1994.]

Finally, there are rare, but documented cases of individuals suffering from a multiple personality disorder (dissociation of the personality), where the subject appears to switch between two or more sometimes dramatically different personalities, some of "whom" don't even know of the existence of the others. [C. Thigpen and H. Cleckley. **The Three Faces of Eve**. 1957] All this is to say that our concept of personal identity in ordinary circumstances is not resolved solely by some reference to cellular identity. The notion of personal identity is much more dependent on the regularities in the way we talk and interact than any reference to cellular identity. These issues are, of course, the subject of much good fiction, M. Twain's **Puddinhead Wilson**, the French films "Mr. Klein," and "The Return of Martin Guerre" (which was based on fact), and Edward Wooll's play (later, movie) "Libel" being examples of how complex our notion of identity can be, and how resistant it can be to the testimony of physical evidence.

paper, "Systematically Misleading Expressions."[102] Ryle, though, did not use the mis-statements of language as a foundation for further philosophical analysis, as Wittgenstein

[102]G. Ryle. "Systematically Misleading Expressions," **Proceedings of the Aristotelian Society**, v. XXXII (1931–1932), pp. 139–170. Collected in **The Linguistic Turn: Recent Essays in Philosophical Method**. The University of Chicago Press, Chicago, 1967. Edited by R. Rorty. Ryle identifies a number of types of misleading expressions (Like Wittgenstein, Ryle insists that these expressions are misleading for the philosopher, not the day-to-day speaker of English):

> 1. **"Quasi-Ontological Statements"**: Assertions such as "Satan does not exist" cause confusion be-cause they deny existence to an entity, Satan, while at the same time referring to "him" and thereby seeming to also assert his existence. Similar cases can be made for "Carnivorous cows" and "Unicorns." Even newspapers make such implicit assertions with headlines like "Crowds Fail to Appear." Figures in literature pose the same problem when we assert, for example, that Dickens' Mr. Pickwick " . . . is not a real person."
>
> 2. **"Quasi-Platonic Statements"**: Statements such as "Virtue is its own reward," or "Unpunctuality is reprehensible" implicitly assert the existence of universals such as "virtue" and "unpunctuality." This is the source of the insistence that universals have an existence in the same way the individual objects, or particulars, do. What the phrase "Unpunctuality is reprehensible" really means, according to Ryle, is that "Whoever is unpunctual deserves that other people should reprove him for being unpunctual."
>
> 3. **"Quasi-Descriptions"**: Descriptions such as "The Vice-Chancellor of Oxford University" seem to refer to some person who is "The Vice-Chancellor of Oxford University." Yet it is clear that although we can give such descriptions, the entity so described may not exist. That is, although there is a position for Vice-Chancellor of Oxford, there might not be anyone currently holding that position. Such phrases seem to describe something, but in actuality do not.
>
> 4. **"Quasi-Referential Phrases"**: Phrases such as, "the top of the tree" or "the center of the bush" or "the idea of having a holiday" suggest the existence of entities such as "tops of trees," "centers of bushes" and "ideas." Yet it is not clear at all that such entities do, in fact, exist, and there are less philosophically misleading ways to say the same thing (e.g., instead of saying "I had an idea for a holiday" I could say, "I thought of a nice place to go for a holiday.").

The common pathology that runs through all of Ryle's examples is that they each suggest the existence of "new sorts of objects." Interestingly, Ryle claims that one of the most fertile areas for these misleading statements to do damage is not in philosophy but in physics:

> "I suspect that a lot of Cartesian and perhaps Newtonian blunders about Space and Time originate from the systematically misleading character of the 'the'—phrases which we use to date and locate things, such as 'the region occupied by x,' 'the path followed by y,' 'the moment or date at which z happened.' It was not seen that these are but hamstrung predicative expressions . . . " [*op.cit.*, p. 96]

Were Ryle to be writing today he might see the same kind of conceptual errors being made by Artificial Intelligence when it talks of "concepts," "ideas," "intelligence," or "meanings" as if they were "things" that could be studied by themselves and modeled in computer programs.

> Wittgenstein made a similar observation:
>
> Imagine a language in which, instead of "I found nobody in the room," one said "I found Mr. Nobody in the room."
>
> Imagine the philosophical problems which would arise out of such a convention. [**BB**, p. 69]

did.[103] Wittgenstein showed how language can mislead us, especially when we are doing philosophy. But these problems in language are not obvious. When we ask for the "meaning" of a word, or assert that "I know what I am thinking" it seems like we are saying something quite simple and straightforward. But we are not. The uncomplicated syntax of surface grammar sometimes gives us a deceptive sense of meaningfulness that masks the turmoil of "deeper" misunderstanding. Wittgenstein was particularly interested in showing how the structure, or grammar, of language can lead us astray. This is not something that can be easily described or explained, but it can be *shown,* so this is what he does. Wittgenstein sums up his method succinctly:

> My aim is: to teach you to pass from a piece of disguised nonsense to something that is patent nonsense.[104] [**PI** §464]

While Wittgenstein's method was central to his later work, he spends precious little time describing how he does it. Of course, the reader of **Philosophical Investigations** can watch him do this grammatical analysis, but there is no explicit attempt on Wittgestein's part to describe his methodology except in the briefest detail. Wittgenstein felt, no doubt, that this kind of analysis was better shown rather than explained. But because of Wittgenstein's reluctance to explain his method, even the careful reader may miss how he does it, seeing only the philosophically interesting linguistic puzzles that he uncovers, and not the method by which he does it. Wittgenstein's first mention of the method of his grammatical analysis comes in §150 of **Philosophical Investigations**:

> (a) "Understanding a word": a state. But a *mental* state?—Depression, excitement, pain, are called mental states. Carry out a grammatical investigation as follows: we say
>
> "He was depressed the whole day."
> "He was in great excitement the whole day."
> "He has been in continuous pain since yesterday,"—
>
> We also say "Since yesterday I have understood this word." "Continuously," though?—To be sure, one can speak of an interruption of understanding. But in what cases? Compare: "When did your pains get less?" and "When did you stop understanding that word?"
> (b) Suppose it were asked: "*When* do you stop understanding that word?" All the

---

[103] Although Wittgenstein was the first major philosopher to focus so much of his analysis on grammar, he is not the first to recognize the importance of this point of view. His mentor, Bertrand Russell once wrote before he met Wittgenstein:

> The study of grammar, in my opinion, is capable of throwing far more light on philosophical questions than is commonly supposed by philosophers. Although a grammatical distinction cannot be uncritically assumed to correspond to a genuine philosophical difference, yet the one is prima facie evidence of the other, and may often be most usefully employed as a source of discovery. [**The Principles of Mathematics**, p. 42. Cambridge, 1903.]

[104] Or, as Wittgenstein puts it, more metaphorically, "What is your aim in philosophy?—To shew [*sic*] the fly the way out of the fly-bottle." [**PI** §309]

time? or just while you are making a move? And the *whole* of chess during each move?—How queer that knowing how to play chess should take such a short time, and a game so much longer! [**PI** §150]

We can see how important Wittgenstein's grammatical analysis is for the investigation of, here, mental states. But this method is clearly at odds with the traditional ways philosophers or psychologists often went about such an investigation. Philosophers often use some form of introspection to analyze "mental states," or some kind of reduction in which "mental states" are broken down into constituent properties, while psychologists generally get subjects to report on their mental states looking for what is common in these various reports.[105] Wittgenstein, though, takes the proper study of even something as complex and elusive as a "mental state" to be best approached by grammatical analysis. He starts out with some things that most would agree are mental states: depression, excitement or pain. We can say things like, "He was depressed the whole day," or, "He was excited the whole day," or, "He was depressed until she came back," or, "He was excited, at first, but then he heard something that calmed him down." The question Wittgenstein raises here is whether "understanding" is a mental state or not. If it is, then we should be able to use the word "understanding" in the same grammatical ways that we can use the words for mental states like "depression" and "excitement." So the following sentences should be OK:

"He understood the whole day." (versus, "He was excited the whole day.")
"He understood until she came back." (versus, "He was depressed until she came back.")

These sentences with "understood" make us somewhat uncomfortable. But perhaps the problem is that "understand" is a transitive verb while "was depressed" or "was excited" is not: Let's try the following:

"He understood geometry for the whole day."
"He understood Spanish until she returned."

It is clear that an object of "understanding" does not improve things. To make the distinction sharper, let's try making the time more precise:

"He was depressed from 4:00 to 6:00 today."

This seems OK, but if we substitute "understood" here we get:

"He understood geometry from 4:00 to 6:00 today."

---

[105] The total reliance of philosophical inquiry on introspection is called "psychologism," a position first articulated in the early 19th century by German philosophers Jakob Fries and Friedrich Beneke as a reaction to the dominant philosophy of Hegel. Wittgenstein does not argue against psychologism, per se, and no prominent philosopher contemporary with him held allegiance to its most strict version (i.e., that introspection is the only foundation of philosophical inquiry). Frege, an early influence on Wittgenstein, was a critic of German psychologism, while Carnap, a member of the Vienna Circle, argued against psychologism in his **Der Logische Aufbau der Welt** (Berlin, 1928). Wittgenstein was just reacting to the tendency among his contemporary philosophers and psychologists to look predominantly at mental events (either introspected or reported by others) when investigating cognition.

The last sentence doesn't sound right at all. This casts doubt on the idea that "understanding" is a mental state like "depression" or "excitement." This is the crux of Wittgenstein's "depth grammatical analysis." Notice that in doing this we didn't rely on introspection or reduction, as some philosophers might do, nor did we ask a number of subjects to report their own mental events, as a psychologist might. Yet we have uncovered some of the characteristics of a comparatively "deep" notion of how our mind works.

One of the more interesting confusions we can have is when we think we have made an empirical statement when, in fact, we have not. Consider Wittgenstein's observation:

> "I know . . . only from my own case."—what kind of proposition is this meant to be
> at all? An experiential one? No—a grammatical one? [**PI** §295]

The grammar of the verb "to know" can mislead us in the following sense: we all understand the assertion, "I know that this tree is an oak." But when we say, "I know that I am in pain" are we making the same kind of statement? The surface grammar of the two statements is identical, but Wittgenstein says "no," they are not the same kind of statement. The reason for this is evident from the following grammatical analysis where we change the above statements slightly:

> "I know that this tree is an oak, but I could be mistaken."
> "I know that I am in pain, but I could be mistaken."

The first statement is fine, but the second one is clearly strange—how can we be mistaken about the physical sensations we feel? We simply feel pain or we don't—there is no mistake about it. Yet being mistaken is certainly part of our understanding of what it means to *know* something—part of the language game of "knowing." But in the second sentence it is clear that being mistaken simply doesn't enter into the situation at all. Looking at the surface grammar of the two statements, it appeared that we had two ordinary assertions about what we know. But when we performed a *depth* grammatical analysis like we did above, we saw that they were quite different. In fact, the two statements come from two entirely different, but similar, language games. The statement, "I know that this tree is an oak" is an assertion about observable facts. The statement, "I know that I am in pain" is not a statement about observable facts. "I know that I am in pain" merely declares that "I am in pain." Personal *doubt* and *being mistaken* do not enter at all into the language game of reporting one's feelings—they have no *grammatical* place in them (of course, the listener can have *his own* doubts and *his own* criteria for judging the truthfulness of such reports by others, but that is a different issue). No amount of self-observation can confirm or deny the statement, "I know that I am in pain." Hence, the statement "I know that I am in pain" is a "grammatical" proposition, not an "experiential" one. By this Wittgenstein means that the statement attains its validity or usefulness by virtue of its grammatical structure and placement, not by virtue of any experience of self-observation.

The most important aspect of Wittgenstein's *depth grammatical analysis* is that we have learned something about how our mind works without investigating any mental events at all. We have moved the inquiry away from the difficult and unreliable investigation of mental events, that are by definition private and therefore hard to generalize from, to the examination of events that we all have easy access to. It would be difficult for anyone to answer the question, "Is 'understanding' a mental state?," but it would probably take only an average grasp of the English language to see the distinctions that Wittgenstein wants us to see with his examples. Nothing is hidden in this kind of analysis, but the comparative ease with which we can see these distinctions makes us think that we have somehow missed the solution—it's too easy. We expect that because these problems—such as the analysis of mental states—are so "deep" their solution must be "deep" and difficult, too. But Wittgenstein warns us that we must resist the temptation to look for something deeper or more essential in our analysis, here, of the mental status of "understanding":

> We feel as if we had to penetrate phenomena: our investigation, however, is directed not towards phenomena, but as one might say, towards the "possibilities" of phenomena. We remind ourselves, that is to say, of the kind of statement that we make about phenomena.
>
> ⋮
>
> Our investigation is therefore a grammatical one. Such an investigation sheds light on our problem by clearing misunderstandings away. Misunderstandings concerning the use of words, caused, among other things by certain analogies between the forms of expression in different regions of language—some of them can be removed by substituting one form of expression for another; this may be called an "analysis" of our forms of expression, for the process is sometimes like one of taking a thing apart.[106] [**PI** §60]

Although Wittgenstein continually refers to "grammar" in **Philosophical Investigations**, and other of his later writings, it is important to point out that the object of his analysis is "depth grammar" rather than "surface grammar." "Surface grammar" can be taken as what we normally refer to as syntax—the relations between parts of speech such as nouns, verbs, participles or adverbs. Rules of *surface grammar* tell us that sentences like, "The boys is coming" are incorrect. These relationships are of little concern for Wittgenstein. His "depth grammar" concerns how words go together in specific situations and circumstances, in other words, how they fit in their respective *language games*.

> In the use of words one might distinguish "surface grammar" from "depth grammar." What immediately impresses itself upon us about the use of a word is the way it is used in the construction of the sentence, the part of its use—one might say—that can be taken in by the ear.—And now compare the depth grammar, say

---

[106] Malcolm recounts one of Wittgenstein's lectures in which he (Wittgenstein) described his philosophical method somewhat differently:

> What I give is the morphology of the use of an expression. I show that it has kinds of uses of which you had not dreamed. In philosophy one feels forced to look at a concept in a certain way. What I do is to suggest, or even invent, other ways of looking at it. I suggest possibilities of which you had not previously thought. You thought that there was one possibility, or only two at most. But I made you think of others. Furthermore, I made you see that it was absurd to expect the concept to conform to those narrow possibilities. Thus your mental cramp is relieved, and you are free to look around the field of use of the expression and to describe the different kinds of uses of it. [N. Malcolm. **Ludwig Wittgenstein: A Memoir**, p. 50. Oxford University Press, London, 1972 (reprint of 1958 edition).]

of the word "to mean," with what its surface grammar would lead us to suspect. No wonder we find it difficult to know our way about. [**PI** §664]

Hacker spells out the difference between "surface" and "depth" grammar in more detail:

> There are no "surface rules" and "deep rules," such that the deep rules have the status of hypotheses which explain the surface rules. Wittgenstein's contrast between surface and depth grammar (**PI** §664) is the contrast between the immediate appearance of a word, its mode of occurrence in a given sentence, and the "multitudinous paths leading off from it in every direction"—that is, the different transformations of which the sentence admits, the kinds of consequences it implies, the manner of its context dependence, its role in the language-game, the various combinatorial possibilities of the word and so forth. These are not "hidden" from view, but visible to any speaker of the language who is willing to look around—at the common use of the expression in question. They are not hypotheses, but familiar truisms of which we need to be reminded. Hence the methods of philosophy are descriptive, and argumentative . . . [107]

To see "what is the meaning of a word" and "what is the length of a marathon" as grammatically similar is to only look at the *surface grammar* of these expressions. It is the *surface grammar* of expressions that confuses us, because from this point of view sentences look like they have the same structure when they, at a deeper level, do not.[108] One aspect of Wittgenstein's method that will strike the reader with a background in philosophy is the almost total lack of introspection it contains. Much Western philosophy is the result of the reflections of very bright individuals on their own thought processes. Wittgenstein is mistrustful of these reflections. In fact, he believes that they cannot form the basis of any significant epistemology. While the philosopher has some insight into how he arrives at certain thoughtful outcomes, he has no reliable basis for showing that others do this the same way that he does. In fact, as Wittgenstein demonstrates, for almost any intellectual activity that we can engage in, the supposed thoughtful prerequisites can be entirely missing, just as they were for the artist in our earlier example. We can speak, argue, promise, direct, joke or any number of other intelligent activities without preceding or accompanying them with any conscious thought whatsoever.[109] If conscious thought

---

[107] P.M.S. Hacker. **Wittgenstein's Place in Twentieth-Century Analytic Philosophy**, p. 241. Blackwell, Oxford, 1996.

[108] Although Wittgenstein's early philosophy of language had significant differences from his later views, his metaphorical sense of language as having a visible, or "surface" aspect, which lay above a "deeper" less obvious aspect had very early roots in his work. This can be seen from the following description of language found in his **Notebooks 1914–1916** predating even his **TLP** which was first published in 1921:

Words are like the film on deep water. [p. 52]

[109] Although I will discuss Wittgenstein's argument for such non-conscious, intelligent activity in a later section, it is useful to note here two of the best discussions of this issue apart from Wittgenstein's writings: Norman Malcolm's "Wittgenstein: The Relation of Language to Instinctive Behavior," **Wittgensteinean Themes: Essays 1978–1989**. Cornell University Press, Ithaca, 1995. Edited by G.H. von Wright. And John Canfield's "Wittgenstein and Zen." **Philosophy**, vol. 50, 1975, pp. 383–408. Also of related interest is Polanyi's notion of "tacit knowledge." Polanyi realizes that conscious thought does not necessarily precede intelligent activity. But instead of saying that such thought does not have to be there at all, as Wittgenstein does, he claims that this intelligent

need not precede or accompany such intelligent activity, then it is clear that examining such thought when it does exist will not give us any deeper insight into these cognitive processes. For Wittgenstein, since conscious thought is not necessary for intelligent action, then to understand intelligence we must look elsewhere. If we look at what people who perform the same intelligent activity have in common we find, not common intellectual processes, but common language, abilities, practices, and customs. These common abilities and practices Wittgenstein called the "forms of life," or the "natural history" of mankind. They are "...simply what [we] do." [**PI** §217]

> What we are supplying are really remarks on the natural history of human beings; we are not contributing curiosities, however, but observations which no one has doubted, but which have escaped remark only because they are always before our eyes. [**PI** §415]

Having established Wittgenstein's method of investigation—analysis of *depth grammar*— we can now look more closely at the results of his investigations.


### *Wittgenstein at Work: Philosophical Investigations*

In order to see how Wittgenstein analyzes language it is perhaps best to look at the first few paragraphs of **Philosophical Investigations** in some detail. The basic framework of his methodology and a description of the major issues of language and thought exist in these opening statements.

Wittgenstein begins with a quotation from Augustine[110]:

> [Augustine]When they (my elders) named some object, and accordingly moved towards something, I saw this and I grasped that the thing was called by the sound they uttered when they meant to point it out. Their intention was shewn by their bodily movements, as it were the natural language of all peoples: the expression of the face, the play of the eyes, the movement of other parts of the body, and the tone of voice which expresses our state of mind in seeking, having, rejecting, or avoiding something. Thus, as I heard words repeatedly used in their proper places in various sentences, I gradually learnt to understand what objects they signified; and after I had trained my mouth to form these signs, I used them to express my own desires. [**PI** §1]

Wittgenstein then comments:

> These words, it seems to me, give us a particular picture of the essence of human language. It is this: the individual words in language name objects—sentences are combinations of such names.—In this picture of language we find the roots of the following idea: Every word has a meaning. This meaning is correlated with the word. It is the object for which the word stands.

---

mental activity must be there, only "tacitly." This is why we are not aware of it. Wittgenstein finds no evidence that this is the case.

[110] PI §1, from Augustine. **Confessions, I. 8**.Translation from the original Latin by G.E.M. Anscombe.

> Augustine does not speak of there being any difference between kinds of word. If you describe the learning of language in this way you are, I believe, thinking primarily of nouns like "table," "chair," "bread," and of people's names, and only secondarily of the names of certain actions and properties; and of the remaining kinds of word as something that will take care of itself.[111] [**PI** §1]

Wittgenstein's comments don't directly dispute the Augustinean view of language, they merely point out some of the major implications of it. This is the way that Wittgenstein often presents views that he differs with, and on a first reading it can sometimes appear that Wittgenstein is presenting a view that he agrees with (some of the quotations that he makes and responds to in **Philosophical Investigations** are actually views that *he* held at one time). He does not agree with the Augustinean view of language meaning and language acquisition. But the reader can only see this in retrospect since most of the arguments against these positions are not offered until later.

Several things stand out in these first few comments. Of particular importance are the words "picture" and "essence." Augustine, Wittgenstein states, gives us a "picture of the essence of human language." Augustine has encapsulated a theory of meaning in just a few short remarks, but this description is misleading in several important ways. In the first place, the notion of a "picture" being an explanation strikes at the root of one of the major differences between Wittgenstein's early and later thought (as represented by the **Tractatus Logico Philosophicus** and **Philosophical Investigations**, respectively). In Wittgenstein's early work he insisted that meaning in language, in particular, propositions, could be represented by a picture. It was only later that he saw that pictures were not unambiguous representations, that they also required interpretation. But Wittgenstein did not explicitly say this until later in the **Philosophical Investigations**. In a footnote at the bottom of page 11, Wittgenstein states:

> Imagine a picture representing a boxer in a particular stance. Now this picture can be used to tell someone how he should stand, should hold himself; or how he should not hold himself; or how a particular man did stand in such-and-such a place; and so on. [PI §22]

This is not Wittgenstein's last word on the subject. Forty-three pages later, in another footnote, he comments:

> I see a picture; it represents an old man walking up a steep path leaning on a stick.— How? Might it not have looked just the same if he had been sliding downhill in that position? Perhaps a Martian would describe the picture so. I do not need to explain why *we* do not describe it so. [**PI** §139]

But it isn't until §663, fully 157 pages later that Wittgenstein finally takes an explicit stand against the picture theory of meaning:

> If I say "I meant *him*" very likely a picture comes to my mind, perhaps of how I looked at him, etc.; but the picture is only like an illustration to a story. From it

---

[111] **PI** §1. The idea that words are "names" goes much further back in history, at least to Plato ["The Republic," **Book X. The Dialogues of Plato**, vol. 1. Random House, New York, 1920. Translated by B. Jowett.

alone it would mostly be impossible to conclude anything at all; only when one knows the story does one know the significance of the picture. [**PI** §663]

Not only does one need to know the story before one can understand the significance of the picture, one needs to know the story *before one formulates the picture*. Like medieval monks illuminating manuscripts, we create the images in our consciousness to *accompany* our understanding, not represent it. Imagine looking at an old text with illustrations to accompany the text of a story. Now look at another illustrated text, but look only at the pictures without reading the text. In most cases, it would be impossible to grasp the entire story by just looking at the pictures. We can usually understand the story without the accompanying pictures, but we cannot understand the full significance of the pictures without the story. Even comic books, which tell their stories almost entirely with pictures, usually need some text to accompany the illustrations. It is extremely difficult to tell an explicit story of reasonable length and modest complexity solely with illustrations. (By "reasonable length" I mean a story requiring more than a few pictures.) Wittgenstein illustrates the "danger" of pictures in the following description:

> Of course, if water boils in a pot, steam comes out of the pot and also pictured steam comes out of the pictured pot. But what if one insisted on saying that there must also be something boiling in the pictured pot? [PI §297]

The final comment about the picture theory of meaning comes in part II of **PI** on page 184:

> What this language primarily describes is a picture. What is to be done with the picture, how it is to be used, is still obscure. Quite clearly, however, it must be explored if we want to understand the sense of what we are saying. But the picture seems to spare us this work: it already points to a particular use. This is how it takes us in.

For a more amusing debunking of the view that pictures are unambiguous representations, consider Mark Twain:

> In this building we saw . . . a fine oil painting representing Stonewall Jackson's last interview with General Lee. Both men are on horseback. Jackson has just ridden up, and is accosting Lee. The picture is very valuable, on account of the portraits, which are authentic. But, like many other historical picture, it means nothing without its label. And one label will fit it as well as another:
>
>> First Interview Between Lee and Jackson.
>> Last Interview Between Lee and Jackson.
>> Jackson Introducing Himself to Lee.
>> Jackson Accepting Lee's Invitation to Dinner.
>> Jackson Declining Lee's Invitation to Dinner—with Thanks.
>> Jackson Apologizing for a Heavy Defeat.
>> Jackson Reporting a Great Victory.
>> Jackson Asking Lee for a Match.
>
> . . . a good legible label is usually worth, for information, a ton of significant attitude and expression in a historical picture. In Rome, people with firm sympathetic natures stand up and weep in front of the celebrated "Beatrice Cenci the Day Before

Her Execution." It shows what a label can do. If they did not know the picture, they would inspect it unmoved, and say, "Young Girl with Hay Fever; Young Girl with Her Head in a Bag." [M. Twain. **Life on the Mississippi**, p. 216. Airmont Publishing, NY, 1965.]

The second word that stands out in the quotation from **PI** §1 (*supra*) is the word "essence"— Augustine's stated view of language has said something that applies to *all* language. Again, it is only on further reading that we see that Wittgenstein differs markedly with any attempt to stipulate an "essential" view of meaning in language. The desire to find and describe the "essence" of language, leads to a very deep and fundamental mistake in philosophical analysis. Wittgenstein's strongest statement against trying to find an "essence" of language comes in **PI** §65, in his discussion of *language games*:

> Here we come up against the great question that lies behind all these considerations.—For someone might object against me: "You take the easy way out! You talk about all sorts of language-games, but have nowhere said what the essence of a language-game, and hence of language, is: what is common to all these activities, and what makes them into language or parts of language. So you let yourself off the very part of the investigation that once gave you yourself most headache, the part about the *general form of propositions* and of language."

> And this is true.—Instead of producing something common to all that we call language, I am saying that these phenomena have no one thing in common which makes us use the same word for all—but that they are *related* to one another in many different ways. And it is because of this relationship, or these relationships, that we call them all "language."[112] [**PI** §65]

But if Wittgenstein says that looking for the *essence* of language is a mistake, then what should we do in its place? Wittgenstein gives us a hint 16 pages later:

> When philosophers use a word—"knowledge," "being," "object," "I," "proposition," "name"—and try to grasp the *essence* of the thing, one must always ask oneself: is the word ever actually used in this way in the language-game which is its original home?—

> What *we* do is to bring words back from their metaphysical to their everyday use. [**PI** §116]

Wittgenstein brings up one of the major mistakes of philosophical, analysis: he argues that what the philosopher should be concerned with is not the *essence* of language, but with how these words are used in ordinary contexts. The meanings of words such as "knowledge," "being," etc., appear to refer to very deep concepts, and philosophers have focused much of their analysis on finding general, essential, definitions of these words that would be applicable in all cases. To Wittgenstein, this is a mistake. If we want to find out what these words *really* mean, we shouldn't take them out of their ordinary context, but look at the multitude of their everyday uses:

---

[112]Note in particular, Wittgenstein's equivalence of the "essence" of language games and the "essence" of language.

Only in the stream of thought and life do words have meaning.[113] [**Z** §173]

Where does this desire to reduce meaning in language to *essential* general definitions come from? Wittgenstein tells us in an earlier work:

> Our craving for generality has another main source: our preoccupation with the method of science. I mean the method of reducing the explanation of natural phenomena to the smallest possible number of primitive natural laws; and in mathematics, of unifying the treatment of different topics by using a generalization ... it can never be our job to reduce anything to anything, or to explain anything. Philosophy really *is* "purely descriptive" ...
>
> Instead of "craving for generality" I could also have said "the contemptuous attitude towards the particular case."[114] [**BB** pp. 17–18]

---

[113] Also: "For words have meaning only in the stream of life." [**RPP II** §686]. Even if we want to relate word meaning to something mental, that is, something internal, Wittgenstein reminds us that "What goes on within also has meaning only in the stream of life." [**LWPP II**, p. 30]

[114] Our "craving for generality" may have an even more fundamental source than "our preoccupation with the method of science." Some investigators have asserted that our ability to break things down into their constituent parts and put them back together again in new ways is the characteristic that distinguishes us from other mammals. All mammals have the ability to perform "holistic pattern recognition" since they can recognize things like different animals, situations or geographical settings by picking out the salient features of these entities from the welter of accompanying sense data. But only humans can break these perceived things down into constituent parts and then reassemble them in new or different ways [Warren, as reported in Donald, infra] This ability to break something down into its constituent parts and then reassemble them in various ways is called "generativity." [Corballis] It originated in primitive man's ability to make tools from a number of constituent parts. Having done this with objects in his environment, man, over many eons, was able to internalize this ability until he could break less tangible things—like concepts or mental images—into their constituent parts. Having broken something down into its constituent parts, man was then able to assemble these parts in new and different ways; that is, he was able to "generate" new objects by varying how the parts went together. This "generative" ability is an essential component of what we now call reduction. The distinction between generativity and holistic perception is instantiated in our brains: generativity exists largely in the left hemisphere of our brain while holistic perception, or pattern recognition exists in the right hemisphere. Donald comments:

> In his evolutionary scenario, Corballis argued that generativity first emerged in the left hemisphere for praxic skill and was essential to the development of tool making, where categorical analysis of the fashioned object was essential to the ability to reproduce it, that is, generate new ones. This generative ability expanded its range and eventually enabled the development of, among other things, language. The evolution of language was secondary, somehow dependent upon the pre-existence of the underlying generative capacity. Since generativity is the distinguishing feature of left-hemisphere cognition, laterality of function must have been a key neuropsychological aspect of human cognitive evolution, perhaps because it allowed humans to retain their traditional cognitive skills in the right hemisphere, while developing new ones in the left. [M. Donald. **Origins of the Modern Mind: Three Stages in the Evolution of Culture and Cognition**, p. 72. Harvard University Press, Cambridge, 1991. Donald discusses Warren and Corballis: M.C. Corballis. "Laterality and Human Evolution," **Psychological Review**, vol. 96, pp. 492–505, 1989. R.M. Warren. "Auditory Perception and Speech Evolution," **Annals of the New York Academy of Sciences**, vol. 280, pp. 708–731, 1976.]

If it is true that this reductive capability is not just cognitively based, but physiologically based, then it must take remarkable self-control *not* to look for the constituent parts of things—real or imagined. Our "craving for generality" may be as strong as any other physiological craving we can have. This desire to break things down

Wittgenstein continues:

> The idea that in order to get clear about the meaning of a general term one had to find the common element in all its applications has shackled philosophical investigation; for it has not only led to no result, but also made the philosopher dismiss as irrelevant the concrete cases, which alone could have helped him to understand the usage of the general term. [**BB** p. 19]

The focus of philosophical analysis on essential definitions of words is not a new concern. Socrates spent many of Plato's dialogues trying to find essential definitions of important words like "truth," "beauty," "good," etc. Socrates was smart enough to see that these essential definitions were impossible to formulate. But since Socrates believed that "true knowledge," required these essential definitions, then, *a fortiori*, man cannot have "true knowledge." Like Socrates, Wittgenstein would have agreed that such essential definitions are impossible to formulate, but unlike Socrates, Wittgenstein would not have seen that as important.

> We are unable clearly to circumscribe the concepts we use; not because we don't know their real definition, but because there is no real "definition" to them. To suppose that there *must* be would be like supposing that whenever children play with a ball they play a game according to strict rules.[115] [**BB** p. 25]

Our knowledge is not grounded in essential definitions, but in ordinary language and the "bustle of life":

> We judge an action according to its background within human life, and this background is not monochrome, but we might picture it as a very complicated filigree pattern, which, to be sure, we can't copy, but which we can recognize from the general impression it makes.

into constituent parts and reassemble them in new ways permeates even our mythology and has given us many fanciful creatures: unicorns, centaurs, Pegasus, Medusa & Pan. Here we conceive of creatures composed of "parts" which can be combined in unique and curious ways to produce mythical beings which conjoin "parts" from two unrelated animals. Wittgenstein had some sense of how powerful this compulsion is to look for the simple constituent parts of things very early on in his philosophy. In his **Notebooks 1914–1916** he states:

> *And it keeps on* forcing itself upon us that there is some simple indivisible, an element of being, in brief a thing.

> It does not go against our feeling, that *we* cannot analyze PROPOSITIONS so far as to mention the elements by name; no, we feel that the WORLD must consist of elements. [**Notebooks 1914–1916**, p. 62. Harper and Brothers, NY, 1961.]

The importance of Wittgenstein's rejection of reduction cannot be overemphasized. So central to his later philosophy was this rejection that he at one time considered using the following quotation from Butler as the epigraph for his **Philosophical Investigations:**

... everything is what it is and not another thing. [G. Kreise. "The Motto of **Philosophical Investigations** and the Philosophy of Proofs and Rules," **Grazer Philosophische Studien**, vol. 6, p. 15, 1978.]

[115]"When Socrates asks the question, 'what is knowledge?' he does not even regard it as a preliminary answer to enumerate cases of knowledge." **BB** p. 20. Wittgenstein was referring to Plato's "Theaetetus," 146D–147C.

The background is the bustle of life. And our concepts point to something within this bustle. [**RPP II** §§624–625]

If we return to our original quotation in which Wittgenstein continues his comments on the Augustinean view of language, we can see several other implications that he draws:

... the individual words in language name objects—sentences are combinations of such names—In this picture of language we find the roots of the following idea: Every word has a meaning. This meaning is correlated with the word. It is the object for which the word stands. [**PI** §1]

This is a simple referential theory of meaning: that words stand for "objects" or things. Wittgenstein makes no comment about the validity of such a claim, here, though he certainly disagrees with it. He waits until **PI** §27 to raise an objection:

"We name things and then we can talk about them: can refer to them in talk."—As if what we did next were given with the mere act of naming. As if there were only one thing called "talking about a thing." Whereas in fact we do the most various things with our sentences. Think of exclamations alone, with their completely different functions.

> Water!
> Away!
> Ow!
> Help!
> Fine!
> No!

Are you inclined still to call these words "names of objects?"[116] [**PI** §27]

A simple referential theory that applies to all words is easy to dismiss, as Wittgenstein does here. But if we go back to the original quotation we see that Wittgenstein is less interested in showing the poverty of the simple referential theory of language than he is to show what it implies.

In this picture of language we find the roots of the following idea: Every word has a meaning. This meaning is correlated with the word. It is the object for which the words stands. [**PI** §1]

The notion that each word has a "meaning" associated with it is a much more difficult claim to refute than "words name objects." These remarks demonstrate one of Wittgenstein's techniques of analysis: he begins with a plausible statement about some phenomenon, then shows that it can be easily changed—by substitution of different words—into something that is incorrect and misleading. In describing Augustine's theory of language he does not initially criticize it, as we have shown. This, I think, is on purpose. Wittgenstein's

---

[116]Note in this citation that Wittgenstein's statement begins with a quotation. In general, Wittgenstein's remarks made within quotation marks are not statements that he necessarily agrees with, but are ones that he wants to react to in some way. Sometimes he even quotes a statement that he himself once made.

uncritical portrayal of the simple referential theory of language—words stand for objects—gives it an initial plausibility, and it is an easy view to hold if we think of words like "chair," "shoes" or "tree." But if we hold this simple view, and then think of things that are not physical objects, such as the exclamations—"Help! ... No!"—we have only two alternatives: give up the simple referential theory of meaning, or alter it in some way so that it can accommodate anomalies such as the ones above. If one begins with the assumption that language has an *essence* and the observation that many words appear to be definable ostensively, then it will be hard to give up the simple referential theory of meaning. Wittgenstein's claim that this view of language has some similarities to the scientific method, which is highly esteemed, makes it even more attractive. So, before giving up the theory, the observer will try to find another kind of "object" for which words stand.[117] Of course it is easy to find such an object: a "meaning" or "concept." But although this gives us a plausible way of accommodating the anomalies of reference that Wittgenstein describes, it really just gets us in deeper trouble. The reason why this view is more misleading than Augustine's original formulation is that it directs the analysis of language away from specific, observable activities to "concepts" or "meanings"—mental events—which are much more difficult to examine objectively. When Augustine wants to show us what the word "chair" means, he points to a chair and utters the word. We can immediately see what he means by this (we teach children the meanings of many words this way). But if we say that the word "Help" is defined by a "concept" or "meaning," what do we "point to?" For Wittgenstein, the analysis of internal, or mental, events can be the source of much confusion.[118]

There is one more problem implicit in the view that "Every word has a meaning. This meaning is correlated with the word. It is the object for which the word stands." [**PI** §1] Simply stated, this view can lead one to think that *all* meaning—regardless of what the "meaning" is—is tied to individual words, and that the meanings of sentences or expressions are merely the combination of the meanings of the words they contain. What this view misses is that the context in which the words or sentences are uttered can have a role in determining the meaning of a statement. Wittgenstein does not bring up or deal with this difficulty here, but this issue will become one of the main concerns of his later philosophy and its origin can be traced to the idea that "... the individual words in language name objects—sentences are combinations of such names."

---

[117] Karl Popper called this tendency for investigators to alter a theory to fit new incompatible observations the "conventionalist stratagem":

> Some genuinely testable theories, when found to be false, are still upheld by their admirers—for example, by introducing ad hoc some auxiliary assumption, or by reinterpreting the theory ad hoc in such a way that it escapes refutation. Such a procedure is always possible, but it rescues the theory from refutation only at the price of destroying, or at least lowering, its scientific status. (I later described such a rescuing operation as a "conventionalist twist" or a "conventionalist stratiegem.") [**Conjectures and Refutations**, p. 33. Harper and Row, NY, 1968.]

[118] The reader should not construe that Wittgenstein holds that ostensive definition is a simple matter and works well with clear objects, such as trees, chairs, etc. He actually believes that there must be a lot of "stage setting" before such ostention works. Here he only means to show that such a theory is plausible in certain cases, and how that plausibility, plus a belief that language works in only one way, leads to a major misunderstanding.

Continuing our discussion, we find that Wittgenstein hints at another cause for believing that all words have meanings:

> Augustine does not speak of there being any difference between kinds of word. If you describe the learning of language in this way you are, I believe, thinking primarily of nouns like "table," "chair," "bread," and of people's names, and only secondarily of the names of certain actions and properties; and of the remaining kinds of word as something that will take care of itself. [**PI** §1]

He says that this results from our considering an example of just one kind of word, and then assuming, without examination, that all other kinds of words must have similar meanings. Wittgenstein was to state this problem more forcefully later on:

> A main cause of philosophical disease—one-sided diet: one nourishes one's thinking with only one kind of example. [**PI** §593]

In summary, then, the Augustinian view of language claims that:

- i. Words name objects.

- ii. The meaning of a word is the object for which it stands.

- iii. Every word has a meaning.

- iv. The meaning of a word is independent of context.

- v. The meaning of a sentence is composed of the meanings of its words.

- vi. Teaching consists of pointing to objects and saying their names.[119]


*"Five Red Apples"*

Wittgenstein continues his analysis of language by presenting the following example:

> Now think of the following use of language: I send someone shopping. I give him a slip marked ["five red apples"]. He takes the slip to the shopkeeper, who opens the drawer marked "apples"; then he looks up the word "red" in a table and finds a color sample opposite it: then he says the series of cardinal numbers—I assume that he knows them by heart—up to the word "five" and for each number he takes an apple

---

[119] G.P. Baker and P.M.S. Hacker. **An Analytical Commentary on Wittgenstein's Philosophical Investigations**, vol. 1, p. 22. The University of Chicago Press, Chicago, 1985. Baker and Hacker rightly point out that Wittgenstein would agree with at least two of the implications of Augustine's view of language:

> [Augustine] stresses bodily behavior as "the natural language of all peoples" and as a precondition of language and language-acquisition, a point Wittgenstein himself emphasizes §§185, 202–207, etc. Secondly, he insists that the child's learning required hearing "words repeatedly used in their proper places in various sentences" and hence that meaning and understanding presuppose mastery of combinatorial possibilities of expressions. (*op.cit.*, p. 22) ["§§" refer to paragraphs in **PI** ]

> of the same color as the sample out of the drawer.—It is in this and similar ways
> that one operates with words.—"But how does he know where and how he is to
> look up the word 'red' and what he is to do with the word 'five'?"—Well, I assume
> that he *acts* as I have described. Explanations come to an end somewhere.—But
> what is the meaning of the word "five?"—No such thing was in question here, only
> how the word "five" is used. [**PI** §1]

Although Wittgenstein does not explicitly state it, he formulated the above example, at least in part, as a response to the claim that, "Augustine does not speak of there being any difference between kinds of word" *(supra)*. For Augustine, all words are names for objects. The phrase "five red apples" has three words, each of which is plausibly a "name": "five" is a name for a number; "red" is the name for a color; and, "apple" is the name for a fruit. "Names" are things we often "look up": we look up the *name* of a restaurant in the Yellow Pages; we look up the *name* of a particular bird in a bird identification book; we bring a sample of paint to a hardware store and the clerk compares it with paints they carry to find the *name* of the paint which matches it most closely. So the actions of the shopkeeper in Wittgenstein's example constitute an entirely plausible way to act.

This example raises several important points. In spite of the fact that we can describe the three words as "names," it is clear that they are being *used* differently. It is also the case that the act of "naming" is not as simple and straightforward as it may seem:

> When one says "He gave a name to his sensation" one forgets that a great deal of
> stage-setting in the language is presupposed if the mere act of naming is to make
> sense. And when we speak of someone's having given a name to pain, what is
> presupposed is the existence of the grammar of the word "pain"; it shews [*sic*] the
> post where the new word is stationed. [**PI** §257]

Understanding the word "five" requires a background in basic arithmetic and an ability to count and see similar objects as different individuals (so they can be counted). Understanding the word "red" requires not only an understanding of the names correlated with colors, but—and this is important—an understanding of how close the "color sample" of red must be to the color of the apples. The major substantive distinction here between "five" and "red" is that "five" refers to a discrete number whose application is either correct or incorrect and does not allow degrees of compliance. If the customer wants "five red apples," only "five" apples, and neither "four" apples nor "six" apples nor "5.3" apples will do. There is little ambiguity in counting a simple number (providing one knows how to count). The color "red," though, is much more problematic. The color is not a discrete entity like the number "five" is. "Red" can vary continuously across a wide spectrum of shades and hues. Here the shopkeeper must know how to apply the sample color of "red" to the colors of the apples. Unlike the word "five" there may be a significant difference between the "red" in the sample and the "red" of the apples. Many of the individual apples will also be different shades of "red," so the shopkeeper must have in mind how much variation in the color of the apples there can be for apples to still be considered "red." There is a degree of latitude in applying colors that does not exist in the application of numbers, and this latitude can only be understood through experience. One can easily construct examples where colors or numbers might be used according to different criteria. For example, if I want to match the color of paint for my car in order to paint a place where the original paint has been scratched, I need a much more precise matching of colors than I need in the "five red apples" example. Further, if I am installing a new floor in my hallway and I measure it to be 5.25 feet wide, then only planks of wood of precisely 5.25 feet in length will fit there. A plank that is 5 feet or 6 feet long will not do—this job requires measurements more precise than the integers 1, 2, 3, 4, 5, 6, ... used in the "five red apples" example.

The word "apples" has a different kind of latitude in its application, too. First of all, the shopkeeper must be able to distinguish "red apples" from "red peaches," and among the apples he must not give the customer red apples that have spoiled or been bruised. The application of the word "apples" requires a knowledge of what condition the apples must be in for a customer to want them. This is tied up in a very complex way with how customers will use the apples, and what the customer's expectations are for this kind of transaction. So while the application of the names "five" and "red" are reasonably straightforward in this example, the application of "apples" is much more caught up in the behavior and expectations of people who buy apples (we can imagine a dog or a monkey being trained to pick up five apples, and to be able to distinguish between red apples and, say, green or yellow ones. But it would be hard, I think, to train a dog or monkey to distinguish apples that are in good enough condition to sell and those that are not. This requires an involvement and understanding of human affairs that dogs and monkeys do not—and cannot—have).

After giving the "five red apples" example, Wittgenstein asks, "But what is the meaning of the word 'five'?" He then replies, "No such thing was in question here, only how the word 'five' is used."*(supra)* Although he does not state it explicitly, Wittgenstein's point in raising this issue is to show how irrelevant the question "... what is the meaning of the word 'five'?" is. If someone wanted to know what "five red apples" *meant*, it would be perfectly reasonable to describe the circumstances in which the phrase is used and what consequences arose from its use. As Wittgenstein shows later, this is all one needs to do to make the phrase "five red apples" understandable. This issue—the "meanings" of individual words *versus* the "use" of words—becomes the cornerstone on which Wittgenstein builds his theory of language and philosophical analysis. It also moves the object of philosophical analysis from a quest for the "meanings" of words to an analysis of their "uses"—that is, from an analysis of "mental events" to an analysis of, primarily, "external events." This idea is the source of one of Wittgenstein's most quoted remarks:

> For a large class of cases—though not for all—in which we employ the word "meaning" it can be explained thus: the meaning of a word is its use in language.[120]
> [**PI** §43]

Perhaps a better statement of Wittgenstein's views on "meaning" and "use" is:

> Let the use of words teach you their meaning. (Similarly one can often say in mathematics: let the proof teach you what was being proved.) [**PI** p. 220]

Here, we can see that "use" and "meaning" are separate things—"use" *teaches* us the "meaning" of words. "Use" and "meaning" are not the same thing as they seem to be in

---

[120] See footnote 92 for a discussion of this translation.

the first quotation, above: "the meaning of a word is its use in language." "Use" is not one thing, and neither is "meaning." More importantly, "meaning" is often taken as an internal, mental event, while "use" is more commonly taken as an external event. By emphasizing the importance of "use" over "meaning" Wittgenstein continues to focus his analysis on external rather than internal phenomena. One might wonder about the seeming inconsistency of the two quotations, but the two statements are an accommodation, of sorts, to ordinary usage. That is, given that we use the word "meaning" and such uses are not entirely senseless, Wittgenstein is offering us a way to use the word "meaning" without its being as misleading as before. One can almost imagine Wittgenstein shrugging his shoulders and saying "Alright, if you must use the word 'meaning' here's the way you should do it . . . "

If the proper subject of philosophical analysis is "language usage" and not the examination of "concepts" or other abstractions, then there is one subtle, but important consequence: *nothing that is relevant to analysis is hidden.* Wittgenstein was fighting a tendency in philosophy to base philosophical analysis on the examination of mental events that were elusive or hidden in some way. This is the most important consequence of moving philosophical analysis away from inner mental events to external observable phenomena. It means that the answers we seek are, in some sense, right before our eyes.[121] If there is anything "hidden" about these it is that they are "hidden" by their familiarity:

> The aspects of things that are most important for us are hidden because of their simplicity and familiarity. (One is unable to notice something—because it is always before one's eyes.) The real foundations of his enquiry do not strike a man at all. Unless that fact has at some time struck him.—And this means: we fail to be struck by what, once seen, is most striking and most powerful. [**PI** §129]

Wittgenstein leaves the "five red apples" discussion with a final metaphor that summarizes the difficulties with analyzing language:

> If we look at the example in §1 [the "five red apples" example], we may perhaps get an inkling how much this general notion of the meaning of a word surrounds the working of language with a haze which makes clear vision impossible. It disperses the fog to study the phenomena of language in primitive kinds of application in which one can command a clear view of the aim and functioning of the words. [**PI** §5]

---

[121] The idea that mental processes can be hidden, or have hidden components pervaded much of the intellectual life of *fin de siècle* Vienna, where Wittgenstein grew up. Most prominent at this time was, of course, the dichotomy of the conscious mind and the unconscious mind proposed by Freud. No doubt, this tendency to assume that our thought processes contain significant unconscious, or hidden, components was a kind of reasoning quite familiar to Wittgenstein even before he began studying philosophy. Wittgenstein only mentioned Freud a few times, mostly in conversations with friends (*vid.* M.O'C. Drury's "Conversations with Wittgenstein," **Recollections of Wittgenstein**, pp. 97–171. Oxford University Press, Oxford, 1984. Edited by R. Rhees. There is also a chapter in **LC** that records some of his views on Freud.). Jacques Bouveresse offers a more extended discussion of what Wittgenstein actually said, or implied, about Freud in his **Wittgenstein Reads Freud: The Myth of the Unconscious**. Princeton University Press, Princeton, NJ, 1995. Translation from the French by C. Cosman. For a more critical view, see F. Cioffi's "Wittgenstein on Freud's 'abominable mess,' " **Wittgenstein Centenary Essays**, pp. 169–192. Cambridge University Press, Cambridge, 1991. Edited by A.P. Griffiths. The one Freudian concept that Wittgenstein did seem to respect was Freud's idea that many of our mental problems are really "illnesses" brought on by faulty thinking. This is similar to Wittgenstein's notion that many of our philosophical problems are brought on by what he called "diseases of thinking."

In this statement, Wittgenstein brings up two major aspects of his method of analysis: First, he says that in order to deal with the "hazy" notions of meaning in language, one needs to "disperse the fog" with actual examples of language use. Instead of trying to define the meanings of words, we should try to see how we come to understand words through actual examples of their use. But we don't formulate *any* examples of usage, we need to formulate examples that give us a "clear view of the aim and functioning of the words." Wittgenstein introduces a very important concept in his statement, the notion of a "view" of language. The German word that Wittgenstein uses is the noun "Übersicht" (or the verb form, "übersehen"). There is no single, good English equivalent to this word. Various translations of the word that have been used are, "view," or "survey" or the neologism "surview" suggested by Baker and Hacker.[122] Its most common appearance in **Philosophical Investigations** is in the adjectival form, "übersichtliche Darstellung," translated by Anscombe as "perspicuous representation"[123] **[PI §122]**. What Wittgenstein is getting at is that the examples of word usage one should look at when trying to discern the meaning/usage of a word are examples that are "perspicuous" or "salient," ones that reveal more about the proper usage of a word than a random example might. Perhaps another translation of "übersichtliche" that might be more faithful to what Wittgenstein meant would be "exemplary." This translation of the German would recall Kuhn's use of "exemplars" as a component in his disciplinary matrix of scientific fields.[124] Kuhns' "exemplars" are really "exemplary puzzles." By working through these puzzles the students in a scientific discipline come to understand, that is, get a "clear view" of their field. It is only after working through these exemplars that the student really comes to understand what the basic concepts of the field are, and what the language of the field really means. Kuhns' emphasis on the educational value of his exemplars resonates with Wittgenstein's claim that the usage of language, especially the "übersichtliche Darstellung," can "teach us the meaning" of words. Like Kuhns, Wittgenstein's examples must be perspicuous/exemplary and educational.[125] The word "Darstellung" also has other translations besides "representation." It

---

[122] See the essay "Übersicht" in their **Wittgenstein, Meaning and Understanding**, pp. 295–309. University of Chicago Press, Chicago, 1985.

[123] Even Anscombe, Wittgenstein's principal translator, is not consistent about her translations of "Übersicht." Later, in **Zettel** (§464), Ascombe renders "Übersichtlichkeit" as "synoptic view." Whether this represents a reconsideration of her earlier translation, or is just an unconsidered variation is not clear. (**Zettel** was published in 1967 while **Philosophical Investigations** appeared 14 years earlier in 1953.)

[124] The components of the "disciplinary matrix" are: Symbolic generalizations; Shared commitment to beliefs; Shared values; and Exemplars. Kuhn, Thomas. **The Structure of Scientific Revolutions**. University of Chicago Press, Chicago, 2nd ed., 1970. pages 183ff.

[125] It is important to note that Kuhn's claim that exemplary puzzles are central to the conduct of science is not without its critics. Feyerabend writes:

> According to [Kuhn's] interpretation it is the existence of a puzzle-solving tradition that de facto sets the sciences apart from other activities. It sets them apart in a "far surer and more direct" way, in a manner that is "at once ... less equivocal and ... more fundamental," than do other and more recondite properties which they may also possess. But if the existence of a puzzle-solving tradition is so essential, if it is the occurrence of this property that unifies and characterizes a specific and well recognizable discipline; then I do not see how we shall be able to exclude say, Oxford philosophy, or, to take an even more extreme example, organized crime from our considerations.

can also mean, *inter alia*, a "performance," "presentation" or, in the context of the theatre, a dramatic "production."[126] While "representation" is a perfectly reasonable translation, "Darstellung's" translation as a "presentation," or "performance," etc., gives the word the connotation of a *process* or *activity*. This connotation is, I think, a very important aspect of Wittgenstein's "Darstellung" because he emphasizes that words are intimately caught up in the *activity* of language usage. Examples of this usage must be both *exemplary* and *dynamic*—they must reflect the meaning of the words as they occur within the context of ongoing activities.[127] So while "perspicuous representation" has been the most widely used translation of Wittgenstein's "übersichtliche Darstellung," "exemplary presentation" brings out some of the other connotations of this complex description.

## *The "Builder's Language"*

Wittgenstein next tries to show what a language that fits the Augustinean model, where words are names for things, might look like:

> Let us imagine a language for which the description given by Augustine is right. The language is meant to serve for communications between a builder A and an assistant B. A is building with building-stones: there are bricks, pillars, slabs and beams. B has to pass the stones, and that in the order in which A needs them. For this purpose they use a language consisting of the words "block," "pillar," "slab," "beam." A calls them out;—B brings the stone which he has learnt to bring at such-and-such a call.—Conceive this as a complete primitive language. [**PI** §2]

> For organized crime, so it would seem, is certainly puzzle-solving par excellence. Every statement which Kuhn makes about normal science remains true when we replace "normal science" by organized crime; and every statement he has written about the individual scientist' applies with equal force to, say, the individual safebreaker. [P. Feyerabend. "Consolations for the Specialist," in **Criticism and the Growth of Knowledge**, pp. 197–230. Cambridge University Press, 1970. Edited by I. Lakatos and A. Musgrave.

In his comparison of the puzzle solving capability of normal science and organized crime, Feyerabend leaves out an important element. When normal science solves a puzzle, it immediately moves on to another puzzle, leaving the solved puzzle out of consideration for further analysis (the solved puzzle can be used for training, though). In this way, normal science is "progressive" in its puzzle solving. Organized crime, though, is not overtly progressive. Once criminals learn how to break open a particular kind of safe, they then concentrate their efforts on seeking situations where they only have to break open that kind of safe. The typical scientist actively seeks new puzzles and is not very concerned with puzzles that have been solved.

[126] **The New Cassell's German Dictionary**. Harold T. Betteridge, Funk and Wagnalls, NY, 1958.

[127] The fact that "Darstellung" can be associated with the theater or drama (as a "production") may also have been in Wittgenstein's mind when he used it. Part of his theory of meaning was that words have a context in which they are used, and this context helps to give them their "sense," it contributes to their meaning. When Wittgenstein referred to this context he often referred to it as the "stage setting" necessary to provide the words with their appropriate sense:

> The contexts in which a word appears are portrayed best in a play; therefore, the best example for a sentence with a certain meaning is a quote from a play. And who asks the character in a play what he experiences when he speaks?

> The best example of an expression with a very specific meaning is a passage in a play. [**LWPP II** p. 7]

In this example we can see another aspect of Wittgenstein's method: he constructs hypothetical examples to demonstrate the plausibility of some assertion about language usage or philosophy. There are two ways that Wittgenstein can make his points about language and philosophical analysis: he could *explain* why he believes that his assertions are the case and offer justifications to support his beliefs, or he could give examples which demonstrate perspicuously whether the point in question is valid or not without any explanation. Wittgenstein's preference for constructing examples rather than explaining or justifying his assertions is entirely consistent with his claim that philosophical analysis should consist primarily of *descriptions* or *demonstrations* rather than *explanations*. Carefully constructed examples, he believed, demonstrate philosophical points more clearly than detailed explanations. The reason for this emphasis on examples or demonstrations is that this is the way that we teach and learn language: a child does not ask for definitions and explanations when he is trying to master new words. He needs examples or demonstrations of how these words are used. Explanations and definitions are not necessarily absent from this process, they are just relegated to a minor role and can be often dispensed with entirely. One of the greatest writers in the English language, Shakespeare, did all of his writing *before* there was a published dictionary of the English Language. Clearly Shakespeare's audiences didn't need definitions to understand the subtle verbal nuances of his dialogues and soliloquies.[128]

Wittgenstein maintains the importance of description, or examples, over explanations throughout much of his writings. In his **Blue and Brown Books** (written before **Philosophical Investigations**) he makes the point strongly:

> I want to say that it can never be our job to reduce anything to anything, or to explain anything. Philosophy really is "purely descriptive!" [**BB** p. 18]

In **Philosophical Investigations** we find Wittgenstein's strongest statement about the importance of description rather than explanation:

---

[128] It is interesting to note that for most of its history, the English Language was spoken by individuals without the aid of a dictionary. Dictionaries are a relatively recent phenomenon, with Nathan Bailey's **Universal Etymological English Dictionary**, published in 1721, being the first English dictionary of modern form. Shakespeare wrote his plays and poems over a century before, so it can be assumed that his masterful use of the English Language was gained without the use of any dictionary, as we know it. In addition, his plays were popular with a broad cross section of Elizabethan society who, except for a small educated aristocracy, were largely illiterate and could not use a dictionary even if they had one. All of this is not to say that dictionaries and definitions are useless for language acquisition. They are useful. They are just not necessary, and much learning of linguistic meaning can be, and is, done without them.

One can argue, as we will later in this discussion, that the reason that Shakespeare was able to convey his clever puns and nuanced uses of language to his audiences was that he not only controlled the dialogue of his plays, but also the context (scenery, music, situations, actors, props, etc.) in which the words were uttered. This context helped the audience to understand the dialogue even when it consisted of new or creative uses of the language. Wittgenstein often drew the analogy between drama and understanding by saying that "The best example of an expression with a very specific meaning is a passage in a play" [**LWPP I** §424].

The analogy between the portrayal of meaning in language and dramatic representation is a very important metaphor in Wittgenstein's philosophy of language. We will discuss this in more detail in a subsequent section: "Wittgenstein and Drama: A Dramatic Theory of Meaning."

We must do away with all explanation, and description alone must take its place... The problems are solved, not by giving new information, but by arranging what we have always known.[129] [**PI** § 109]

Wittgenstein appears to exclude explanation entirely from philosophical analysis. But, viewed from our position some 50 years after these words were written, we might find this statement somewhat extreme. Western philosophy has a long tradition of using explanation in philosophical analysis, and this analysis has produced significant insights. Wittgenstein surely does not want to throw all of this out or call all of its results into question. His concern about explanation is not so much that it never works, since it *can be* useful, even in philosophy. Wittgenstein was concerned that philosophers, particularly the analytic philosophers of the first half of the 20th Century, were not wary enough about how explanations, by their very structure, *can* lead us astray. There are Language Games in which explanation is perfectly suited, particularly in scientific fields, but there are Language Games, some of which are common in philosophy, where Wittgenstein believed it is not suited. Bertrand Russell, Wittgenstein's philosophical mentor, believed that philosophical analysis could be improved by making it more like scientific analysis, which he took as the ideal method of inquiry. Since explanation is a major method of scientific inquiry, Russell believed that explanation should be used more in philosophy. In his later philosophy, Wittgenstein was to take the opposite view—that the explanatory model was not only not as useful to philosophy as Russell believed, but that it could be misleading, too. The quotation from **BB** p. 18, above, is preceded by the sentence:

Philosophers constantly see the method of science before their eyes, and are irresistibly tempted to ask and answer questions in the way science does. This tendency is the real source of metaphysics, and leads the philosopher into complete darkness. [**BB** p. 18]

The primary difficulty with explanation is that it is difficult to know when to stop. No matter how "complete" an explanation may be one can always imagine further explanation is possible. Young children are particularly adept at playing this *language game*:

Parent: "I have to fix the roof."
7 year old child: "Why?"
Parent: "Because there is a hole in it."
7 year old child: "Why is there a hole in it?"
"Because the tree branch fell on the roof."
"Why did the branch fall on the roof?"
"Because we had a big storm yesterday."
"Why did we have such a big storm?"
"Because we get storms from time to time."

---

[129] In 2001 a revised edition of **Philosophical Investigations** was published as the 50th anniversary commemorative edition. In the above quotation [**PI** §109] the last sentence was rendered somewhat differently:

The problems are solved, not by reporting new experience, but by arranging what we have always known.

"Why isn't the weather always good?"
"Because the weather can't always stay the same."
"Why can't it stay the same?"
"Because ... "

    ⋮

Wittgenstein saw the same kind of problem with explanation in philosophy, namely, that there is no obvious stopping point for this kind of analysis. The open-ended nature of explanation often causes its users to miss the point where analysis has gone far enough.

> The expression "that is all that *happens*" sets limits to what we call "happening."

> Here the temptation is overwhelming to say something further, when everything has already been described.—Whence this pressure? What analogy, what wrong interpretation produces it?

> Here we come up against a remarkable and characteristic phenomenon in philosophical investigation: the difficulty—I might say—is not that of finding the solution but rather that of recognizing as the solution something that looks as if it were only a preliminary to it. "We have already said everything.—Not anything that follows from this, no, *this* itself is the solution!"

> This is connected, I believe, with our wrongly expecting an explanation, whereas the solution of the difficulty is a description, if we give it the right place in our considerations. If we dwell upon it, and do not try to get beyond it.

> The difficulty here is: to stop.[130] [**Z** §§312–314]

[130] Wittgenstein, no doubt, would have liked Wallace Stevens' poem "The Snow Man" which artfully presents the requirements for pure description:

> One must have a mind of winter
> To regard the frost and the boughs
> Of the pine-tree crusted with snow;

> And have been cold a long time
> To behold the junipers shagged with ice,
> The spruces rough in the distant glitter

> Of the January sun; and not to think
> Of any misery in the sound of the wind,
> In the sound of a few leaves,

> Which is the sound of the land
> Full of the same wind
> That is blowing in the same bare place

> For the listener, who listens in the snow,
> And, nothing himself, beholds
> Nothing that is not there and the nothing that is.

[**The Collected Poems of Wallace Stevens**, p. 9. Alfred A. Knopf, NY, 1978.]

Why do we demand explanations? In the first place, explanation is obviously widely used in ordinary discourse. If Wittgenstein wants to ground philosophical analysis in ordinary language then explanation must be a valid subject for that analysis. Here there are places for some kind of explanation—our dictionaries, for example. But dictionaries are a convenience rather than a necessity. It would take a dictionary of great size and scope to present meanings to the reader entirely by way of examples (the large, multi-volume **Oxford English Dictionary** provides both definitions and examples of usage. We might expect a dictionary devoted only to examples of usage to be even larger, because you would need lots more examples to convey all the nuances that might characterize a word's meaning. In addition, you would also have to have fairly detailed descriptions of the context in which the word might be used.). The explanations of a dictionary are a kind of shorthand presentation of meaning that constitutes a particular language game. They assume that the reader already has a basic familiarity with the concepts that surround the word's use. The reader is still left to find out how the words he looks up are used in everyday life.

To understand the reasons for Wittgenstein's categorical exclusion of explanation from his philosophy, we need to remember that the philosophical analysis of his day aspired to the seeming objectivity and certitude of scientific explanation. Troublesome philosophical statements, it was believed, could be broken down and analyzed in the way that a botanist identifies a particular flower by breaking it down into its constituent parts. For Wittgenstein, *scientific explanations* are not the *complete* explanations that they are claimed to be, and, by inference, philosophical analysis that is based on the scientific model of explanation is not complete either. Nevertheless, in the writings he completed just before his death (published in the volume **On Certainty**)Wittgenstein appeared to see that there was *some* role for explanation in philosophical analysis:

> At some point one has to pass from explanation to mere description. [**OC** §189]

Explanations work up to a point, but the foundation on which explanations gain their validity consists of observations that we can't analyze or break down further. Getting back to the "Builder's Language," Wittgenstein presents us with a situation that seems to be a realistic example of Augustine's notion of language (correlating words with objects). There are no verbs, prepositions, participles, adjectives or adverbs—words that would be difficult to find "objects" for. The "Builder's Language" appears to be complete, but consists only of nouns which are seemingly correlated with objects: "blocks," "pillars," "slabs," and "beams." Wittgenstein also gives us a scenario showing how these words are used. It is a convincing description, and it is a simple matter to imagine that people could talk to each other this way.[131] But having given us such a reassuring example he quickly

---

[131] In **PI** §6 Wittgenstein states:

> We could imagine that the language of [the Builders] was the whole language of A and B; even the whole language of a tribe.

This is a sweeping statement, and Wittgenstein does not offer an extensive justification for it. Whether the Builder's Language is complete or not is not relevant here. If we can imagine that two individuals talk like this in some kind of realistic situation, and I think we can, then that is all that is required. (One can imagine a scene

begins to undermine our confidence in it. Seemingly talking about a third kind of language, he gives us the following example:

> Imagine a script in which the letters were used to stand for sounds, and also as signs of emphasis and punctuation. (A script can be conceived as a language for describing sound-patterns.) Now imagine someone interpreting that script as if there were simply a correspondence of letters to sounds and as if the letters had not also completely different functions. Augustine's conception of language is like such an over-simple conception of the script. [**PI** §4]

The "over-simple conception" of Augustine's view of language is that words (or sounds or letters) can function in only one way. If they do function in one way, then teaching individuals what words mean is a fairly simple process. But if words can have more than one function, or mean different things in different contexts, then there are a lot of ways for people to get the wrong meaning. One can look at a word in one sentence and it means one thing; but in another sentence the same word could mean something entirely different—or, in one sentence a word is an adjective and in another it is a noun (e.g., "An American" vs. "An American car"). Since Wittgenstein is criticizing Augustine's view of language, he is, by transitivity, criticizing the "Builder's Language." But the "Builder's Language" seems to be fairly well grounded in the real world of objects—how could it be ambiguous? Wittgenstein begins his analysis by examining how a child might learn the "Builder's Language":

> A child uses such primitive forms of language [i.e., the "Builder's Language"] when it learns to talk. Here the teaching of language is not explanation, but training. [**PI** § 5]

Wittgenstein makes the point that the teaching of meaning in language involves primarily *training* rather than *explanation*. This is really the same distinction that he makes between *descriptions* and *explanations*. *Training* involves either putting the child in situations where the words in question might be used, or *describing* the situations for him (if the child is old enough to understand such descriptions). Wittgenstein uses a child as an example because the learning of the child is the foundation of understanding for the adult. Adults are familiar enough with the process of using dictionary definitions that they might think, erroneously, that such definitions are the primary way we learn language. They are not.

in an operating room with a surgeon talking to her assistant: "Scalpel!"; "Retractor!"; "Suction!"; etc.) Rush Rhees, a former student of Wittgenstein's, disagrees with the notion that the Builder's Language could be the complete language of a tribe:

> The trouble is not to imagine a people with a language of such limited vocabulary. The trouble is to imagine that they spoke the language only to give these special orders on this job and otherwise never spoke at all. I do not think it would be speaking a language. ["Wittgenstein's Builders," **Discussions of Wittgenstein**, p. 76. Routledge and Kegan Paul, London, 1970.]

One might not limit his native language to such a simple language as the Builder's Language, but we can imagine someone speaking English who speaks only enough of another language, say German, that his entire mastery of German consists of something like the Builder's Language. Norman Malcolm responds to Rhees and defends Wittgenstein's position in his "Language Games" [in Malcolm's **Wittgensteinean Themes: Essays, 1978–1989**. Cornell University Press, Ithaca, 1995. Edited by G.H. von Wright.]

The use of dictionary definitions presupposes that the adult can imagine the context in which the words in question can be used appropriately. Wittgenstein continues:

> We could imagine that the language of §2 [the "Builder's Language"] was the *whole* language of A and B; even the whole language of a tribe. The children are brought up to perform *these* actions, to use *these* actions, to use *these* words as they do, and to react in *this* way to the words of others.

> An important part of the training will consist in the teacher's pointing to the objects, directing the child's attention to them, and at the same time uttering a word; for instance, the word "slab" as he points to that shape. (I do not want to call this "ostensive definition," because the child cannot as yet *ask* what the name is. I will call it "ostensive teaching of words."—I say that it will form an important part of the training, because it is so with human beings; not because it could not be imagined otherwise.) This ostensive teaching of words can be said to establish an association between the word and the thing. But what does this mean? Well, it can mean various things; but one very likely thinks first of all that a picture of the object comes before the child's mind when it hears the word. But now, if this does happen—is it the purpose of the word?—Yes, it *can* be the purpose.—I can imagine such a use of words (of series of sounds). (Uttering a word is like striking a note on the keyboard of the imagination.) But in the language of §2 it is *not* the purpose of the words to evoke images. (It may, of course, be discovered that that helps to attain the actual purpose.)

> But if the ostensive teaching has this effect,—am I to say that it effects an under-standing of the word? Don't you understand the call "Slab!" if you act upon it in such-and-such a way?—Doubtless the ostensive teaching helped to bring this about; but only together with a particular training. With different training the same osten-sive teaching of these words would have effected a quite different understanding. [**PI** §6]

For Wittgenstein, Augustine's "ostensive teaching of words" is not the unambiguous pro-cess that it seems: ". . . an ostensive definition can be variously interpreted in *every* case" [**PI** §28]. Ostensive teaching must be accompanied by *training*. It is not enough for the child to understand the object that is correlated with the word "slab," he must also be able to react or do something in the appropriate way. What other ways could B act when A calls out "Slab!?" First, he must know that "slab" is a real word and not just gibberish or a curse; then, he must understand that the word is directed at him, and not someone else; he must then recognize the word as a command (this may mean that B must recognize in A's gestures and tone of voice that the word is a command, and that a command would be an appropriate thing for A to say to him in this situation). But even if B understands all of this, are there still other ways that he could react to the command "Slab!?" Certainly. "Slab!" could mean "Bring me a slab!," "Take away the slab!," "Turn over the slab!" "Put the slab in the trash!" "Break the slab up into pieces!," "Jump up and down on the slab!," "Put the proper postage on the slab and mail it!" etc., etc. The only limit to the number of interpretations of "Slab!" is the number of different things that you can do to or with the slab (here, it is also limited by the number of things B can do with the slab within the ac-tivity of building, and, although this is fewer things to do, there still might be a significant number of different procedures that the builder can carry out with a slab). How would the teacher get B to understand that "Slab!" means "Bring me a slab!?" The teacher must show how "Slab!" is used, perhaps by showing A giving the order "Slab!" to someone else. But, of course, all of this presupposes that B understands the concept of a command, and the concept of following orders, and that if you work for someone, that person can give you commands and expect them to be carried out, and that when you build something you must bring the appropriate pieces of construction together at the right time, etc., etc. Even this simple command presupposes a fairly high level of understanding of common human activities before the command "Slab!" can be understood—as Wittgenstein put it: "a great deal of stage-setting in the language is presupposed if the mere act of naming is to make sense" [**PI** §257] Wittgenstein waits until **PI** §19 to take up a major objection to his description of what role understanding and training play in understanding the word "Slab!." Since Wittgenstein does not answer this objection here, it is important to spend some time to illustrate his unstated opinion. He proposes that "Slab!" is an elliptical, sentence . . . the command "Slab!" is merely a shortened version of "Bring me a slab!." This is a tempting explanation, since we can imagine A saying "Bring me a slab!" a number of times until B understands what it means, then A can shorten the command by stages to "Bring a slab!," "Slab, here!" and finally, "Slab!." Most adults have experienced such elliptical sentences, and it is well known that words or phrases that are used frequently will gradually become shortened in ordinary usage (e.g., how the word "automobile" became shortened over time to "auto" and then "car"). But Wittgenstein resists this explanation, even though it is possible that it could have happened this way (not for the builder and his assistant in Wittgenstein's example, though, since they only have four words in their vocabulary). Why is it so important to resist the disambiguation of "Slab!" by "lengthening" it into the less ambiguous sentence, "Bring me a slab!?" In the first place, the semantic preciseness of "Bring me a slab!" is not as unambiguous as it may seem at first. "Bring me a slab!" could be construed to be a "shortening" of "Bring me a slab and put it near me. Then wait for my next order."; or, "Bring me a slab and help me put it in the right place, which I'll point to."; or, "Bring me a slab, but be careful not to hurt yourself. Ask for help if you need it."; or, "Bring me a slab now/quickly/soon/when you get around to it/tomorrow/etc."; or, "Bring me a slab and place it so the better side is face up."; or, "Bring me a slab, but be careful not to drop it since it may break. If it breaks, we can't use it, we will lose money and you will be fired."; etc. But even with all of these longer, more detailed variations of "Bring me a slab!" one might still insist that we could formulate a single longer, unambiguous sentence, or set of sentences, that explains all that is implicit in the command "Slab!" in these circumstances. It might be a very long sentence or set of sentences, but it is certainly possible to do it. But Wittgenstein's objection is not that we cannot come up with such an unambiguous sentence. We probably could (though just like explanation in general, it may be difficult to know when to stop). He takes issue with the assumption that it would be a proper explanation of what "Slab!" *really* means. This assumption is not only wrong, it gives us a false sense of understanding. Again, the *real* meaning of "Slab!" is *not* more words and sentences. The solution is, as Wittgenstein often says, right before our eyes. We understand the *real* meaning of "Slab!" because we are *trained* to do so and we can use it successfully in some established practice, not because there is some "more detailed" verbal description that is implicit in "Slab!." B understands A's command because B has worked with him or other builders, or on similar projects, and understands what sort of things he is expected to do. This training does not take the form of explaining what B is to do, it takes the form of *showing* or *demonstrating* what he is to do, and this process may be largely non-verbal, even with individuals who have a more complex language than the builder does. Wittgenstein continues the above quotation [**PI** §6] with the following metaphor:

> "I set the brake up by connecting up rod and lever."—Yes, given the whole of the rest of the mechanism. Only in conjunction with that is it a brake-lever, and separated from its support it is not even a lever; it may be anything, or nothing. [**PI** §6]

When Wittgenstein puts a comment in quotation marks, he is usually identifying a statement that he wants to react to. Generally it is a statement that one would consider reasonable, sometimes it is even a statement that Wittgenstein himself has made. Wittgenstein's comments are aimed at the quoted statement. This statement epitomizes a particular type of problem that can afflict analysis, the tendency to look at superficial aspects of a problem and ignore, or just not see the complexity of the "rest of the mechanism." For Wittgenstein, words are the part of language that is most visible to us. At first it seems that these words are the only part of language that really matters. When we say that each word in our language has its own meaning, and sentences are combinations of these meanings, then it is easy to make the further inference that a word somehow carries its entire meaning—nothing need be added to the analysis of meaning than the analysis of words. But for Wittgenstein, if we do this we are like the person who believes that to "set the brake" all he needs to do is connect "up rod and lever." Connecting the rod and lever is seen as a complete explanation of how to set the brake. But this explanation ignores the "whole of the rest of the mechanism" that is necessary for the rods and levers to work. What is the "rest of the mechanism" for language—what underlying mechanism exists that is necessary for language to work? Wittgenstein doesn't say a lot here, but the careful illumination of this "mechanism" is the subject of much of the rest of **Philosophical Investigations**. Briefly, the "rest of the mechanism of language" consists of the surrounding context of human activities—the "forms of life,"—and a number of dynamic formal linguistic practices that are embedded in these activities—what he called "language games." These are what enable the "mechanism" of language to work.

## Language Games

In the next paragraph Wittgenstein introduces the "language game":

> We can also think of the use of language (2) [the "Builder's Language"] as one of these games by means of which children learn their native language. I will call these games "language games" and will sometimes speak of a primitive language as a language-game.
>
> And the processes of naming the stones and of repeating words after someone might also be called language-games. Think of much of the use of words in games like ring-a-ring-a-roses.
>
> I shall also call the whole, consisting of language and the actions into which it is woven, the "language-game." [**PI** §7]

The *language-game* is one of the most important components of Wittgenstein's philosophy of language. Wittgenstein resists, as we might expect, giving a rigorous definition of it, but that does not mean that it is not a rigorous notion. As usual, we must see its rigor in the examples Wittgenstein gives us. The problem that Wittgenstein faced was how to reconcile the need in language for a predictable structure that determines how the words in language go together, with the simultaneous need for flexibility in usage. Further, the structure must be dynamic: it must be able to account for regularities in language that extend over time (such as holding a discussion). Structure in language is necessary so that we can speak in predictable ways and be understood, but flexibility is necessary, too, in order to permit new or creative uses of language—something important when we face new or different situations, or have to describe something we don't understand well. These situations do not have to be *entirely* new, but merely new to the speaker. The notion of a *language-game* provides both the predictable structure in language as well as the flexibility that allows us to talk about new or unusual situations. Consider the game of baseball, for example: there are rules, that can be codified and written down, but within these rules there is enormous latitude for innovative play. Importantly, the rules of baseball do not prescribe every possible action within the game. They specify what may be called a "fair ball," but do not prescribe how the runner should run to first base, except to say that he must stay within the base path—he may run, hop, skip or do somersaults down the base path if he wants to. On the defensive side, it provides general rules for what counts as an "out," but it says nothing about how a fielder may catch a "fly-ball"—he can catch the ball in front of him, behind his back or he can do a back-flip before his catch. He doesn't even have to catch the ball in his glove, either. He can catch the ball in his bare hand, as infielders often have to, or he could catch the ball in his cap or his shirt.

The aspects of games that are important for *language-games* may consist of the following characteristics:

1. *A predictable structure*: Usually codified as a set of rules and may be written down in some sports, like basketball or football, or may be proposed informally by casual players of a game, such as two children playing catch.[132] For games in which the

---

[132] It may be useful to distinguish different kinds of rules here. Searle makes the distinction between "constitutive rules" and "regulative rules":

> ... regulative rules regulate antecedently or independently existing forms of behavior: for example, many rules of etiquette regulate inter-personal relationships which exist independently of the rules. But constitutive rules do not merely regulate, they create or define new forms of behavior. The rules of football or chess, for example, do not merely regulate playing football or chess, but as it were they create the very possibility of playing such games... Regulative rules regulate a pre-existing activity, an activity whose existence is logically independent of the rules. Constitutive rules constitute (and also regulate) an activity the existence of which is logically dependent on the rules. [J. Searle. **Speech Acts**, pp. 33–34. Cambridge University Press, 1969.]

Constitutive rules are of three general kinds: implicit, explicit and ad hoc (Searle does not draw these distinctions). Implicit constitutive rules are like the U.S. Constitution or the Bill of Rights. They already existed before we were born, and we accept them implicitly by virtue of our growing up in the United States. We may choose to disobey them, as criminals do, or we may argue about their validity or consistency, which lawyers sometimes do. But in general, such implicit constitutive rules are accepted, eo ipso, by U.S. citizens. In information systems,

rules are written down, a continual violation of the rules might mean that the players are not really playing the game. That is, they are disobeying the *explicit constitutive rules* of the game. By violating the *constitutive rules* they, in effect, deny the existence of the game as it is formally set up. For example, if we allowed two goalies for each side in a hockey game, we would be playing a game that is *like* hockey, but the actions of the players and the character of the game would be subtly changed by the addition of the extra goalies. Thus, we would not be playing hockey as it is normally known. These codified rules specify what counts as a fair game, but they do not specify certain basic regularities that the game assumes by being embedded within the broader context of human activities. Games in particular are embedded in our understanding of games in general. For example, we need not have rules that state that the losing player should not beat up the winning player, or that basketball players cannot eat the ball. These actions would be considered bizarre *in any game* as we presently know it. In ancient Rome, though, wrestling matches were sometimes conducted until one player was killed. One might conclude that the Roman notion of "game" was different in this regard than ours is. Some of the rules of games are left open to interpretation, such as a rule against cheating. Such a rule rarely specifies what counts as cheating, they merely specify the penalties for getting caught. How do we know what cheating is? This requires training and experience. We must play or observe the game we are interested in repeatedly, until we get a grasp of what kind of actions constitute cheating and which do not. Some games, especially at the higher more skillful levels have referees that make immediate rulings on the legitimacy of certain actions (think of the umpire in baseball, or the referee in a boxing match). Sometimes rules that may appear the same actually are quite different when they are applied to different games. For example, both football and hockey have rules against fighting, but, at least at the professional level in the United States, fighting is tolerated much more in hockey than in football. But hockey does not permit as much fighting as boxing—fighting is the point of boxing. But even in boxing there are some things that opponents can't do that are permitted in football, such as throwing a block at an opponent's knees, and in hockey you are sometimes permitted to hit players from behind, which you

established federal regulations governing how long certain information, such as personnel records, must be kept by an employer is an example of implicit constitutive rules.

Explicit constitutive rules are those constitutive rules which we formally accept, and do not bind us unless we do accept them (and often the acceptance follows a precise procedure). For example, the institution of marriage or membership in the Moose Lodge requires that we formally accept the constitutive rules of these institutions. Often, too, institutions based on explicit constitutive rules have specific procedures for getting out of the institution (e.g., married couples get divorced, Moose Lodge members have second thoughts, etc.).

Finally, there are ad hoc constitutive rules which we not only formally accept, but also formulate ourselves, often with the agreement of others. For example, we can start our own version of the Moose Lodge.

All constitutive rules are based on agreement between individuals, and naturally they are all subject to change, modification or interpretation. Agreements can change over time, and such rules may vary greatly in their difficulty or requirements necessary to change. We could also classify the institutions based on these rules as implicit, explicit and ad hoc. (see Searle's **The Construction of Social Reality** [The Free Press, 1995] for more discussion of constitutive and regulative rules.)

cannot do in football or boxing. There may also be changes in the rules over time. For example, in professional American football two decades ago, the defensive linemen, as they tried to stop the offense, could slap the side of an offensive lineman's helmet in their rush. Sometime later, this move was outlawed and there is now a penalty against any defensive player who does it. In professional basketball, up until a number of years ago all shots (excluding free throws) counted two points. Now, shots from farther away than the top of the key count three points. These are just a few examples of how dynamic the notion of a "game" is. Wittgenstein believed that this sort of dynamic structure was necessary for language, too. This is why the metaphor of a "game" fits so well with language usage.

2. *A point or goal*: This provides a focus for the intentions of the "players," although not all games, as Wittgenstein rightly points out, have a goal or an explicit point. We can imagine children kicking a ball back and forth without any explicit goal other than to return the ball in the general direction of the other person. [See quotation 12 in the section in Part I "Surveying Wittgenstein's Landscape"]

3. *Flexibility of performance*: There is a wide latitude in terms of what kind of performance is permitted within the boundaries of the game's structure. One needs only to think of the thousands of plays that a professional football quarterback must commit to memory to understand how much diversity there can be, even in something as regulated as American football.

4. *The need for training and practice*: In order to "play" the game, one needs to be taught how to play. Some of this teaching may take the form of explanation, but most of it takes the form of being coached—trying to play the game and have a coach offer suggestions as the play goes on. The learning may also take the form of watching skilled players. Playing a game is like mastering a technique with demonstrations being more useful to the novice than explanations. But one must attain a certain minimum level of expertise before coaching can be effective.

5. *Performance is not necessarily accompanied by conscious mental processes*: Many highly skilled athletes claim that they have little conscious thought during their performance. They perform at an intuitive or instinctive level. In fact, there is evidence that consciously thinking about your performance may actually makes your performance worse—as professional baseball star Yogi Berra put it, "You can't think and hit at the same time." This is the main point of the popular book **The Inner Game of Tennis**.[133] The author asserts that in order to learn a sport or improve your performance, it is better for you to watch better players or visualize your successful performance. Trying to, for example, break down your swing in tennis into its "components" will lead to mediocre performance, at best. Likewise, conscious thoughts are not usually necessary for Language Games either, which is why Wittgenstein

---

[133] W. T. Gallwey. **The Inner Game of Tennis**. Random House, NY, May 1974. In fact, Gallwey suggests that when your opponent is beating you, the best way to get him to start playing badly is to ask him what he is doing to play so well. This will get him to begin consciously thinking about his game which will, in turn, lead to poorer play on his part.

sees little point in examining our thoughts if we want to understand how we use language. It is also better to watch others use language if we want to learn how to use it ourselves. The importance of instinctive behavior in language will be discussed in the subsequent section "The Foundation of Language in Instinctive Behavior."

6. *The ability to formulate families of games—to derive new games out of old ones.* Many games grow out of existing games and derive their rules and intent from previous games. One needs only to think of the relation of American baseball and its antecedent game of English cricket. American football, Canadian football, rugby, and Australian football form a "family of similar games." For language, there are families of similar activities that provide the basis for similar Language Games—for example, promising to pay borrowed money back to a friend, promising to mow a neighbor's lawn, and signing a business contract to provide specific products or services, are all variations in the family of Language Games called "promising." Interestingly, many athletic games build themselves on certain individual skills that are developed in childhood, often independently of any formal game: skills like jumping, running, holding one's balance, throwing an object, catching an object, etc. Language Games are also often built on individual skills that are learned apart from language games: skills like acting honestly and forthrightly, being kind and respectful to others, doing what you're supposed to do, etc.

7. *Games can rely on other games for some of their codification.* For example, some of the constitutive rules for American baseball grew out of the British game of cricket. Similarly, much of the structure of American football grew out of the game of rugby. These games were probably more civilized versions of ancient games that served to improve and maintain the warrior skills of their participants.

8. *Games are embedded in, and influenced by, the larger context of human activities.* This provides a way of instilling extraordinary complexity into a game without having to codify all of the complexity. It also means that from a superficial point of view games look rather uncomplicated. Consider the notions of "fairness," "cheating" or "unsportsmanlike conduct." These concepts are set within a broader context than the individual games of which they are a part. We might say that it would be unfair for college basketball teams to play high school teams, or, for a professional boxer to fight an amateur. We might say it is *cheating* for a card player to surreptitiously look at this opponent's cards, or, for a golfer to make a sudden loud noise when his opponent takes a swing at his ball. We might say that it is *unsportsmanlike* for a defeated player to refuse to shake hands with the winner, or, for a tennis player to throw a tantrum when a line-call goes against him. In none of these cases is the use of these concepts prescribed solely by the rules or conduct of the game in which it occurs. And these concepts are learned, not by learning definitions and rules for their application, but by seeing demonstrations or having instances of their occurrence in actual games pointed out to us.

9. *Games help individuals build and refine their social and interpersonal skills*, such as, the ability to follow rules reliably, the ability to make and interpret rules, the ability to coordinate one's actions with others, etc.

10. *Games take place over time*, consisting of certain broadly-prescribed "moves" and "counter moves" or "responses." Language too, is not just a collection of words and meanings, but consists of a number of predictable transactions extending over time such as those known as "Speech (or, Illocutionary) Acts." Traditional grammar specifies the structure of individual sentences or clauses, but there are many linguistic transactions that extend beyond the single sentence. Speech acts (or, Illocutionary acts) have been more successful at categorizing some of these transactions over time. There are 6 major kinds of Speech Acts:

Directives (orders)

Commissives (promises)

Expressives (expressions of opinion, such as an evaluation or an apology)

Assertives (claims for existence)

Declarations (formal pronouncements, such as a declaration of marriage, where the statement, by virtue of its expression in the appropriate circumstances, creates something; here, a marriage. In short, "Saying makes it so.")

Assertive Declarations (where a declaration is based on an observed occurrence; for example, an umpire calling a base runner "out." Here, the declaration is also an assertion that the runner failed to perform in a way that would have made him "safe.")

What is also important for speech acts, which echoes Wittgenstein's view of *language games,* is that there is a surrounding context and circumstances that are prerequisites for the linguistic transactions to work. For example, only a minister, justice of the peace or a ship captain can declare a couple married, and the couple must themselves be willing and eligible to marry. Any one else making such a declaration would not be able to officially marry a couple. Austin called these "felicity conditions." Without them the speech act cannot work.[134]

---

[134] Austin's [**How to do Things with Words,** Oxford University Press, 1962] description of illocutionary acts as having a grammatical structure and a set of felicity conditions prescribed by social context and conventions has a rough parallel with Wittgenstein's description of language usage as being based on language games, which consist of "... language and the actions into which it is woven..." [**PI** §7]. There is no evidence that Austin's work was in any way influenced by Wittgenstein's, even though they were both prominent in British philosophy in the 1940's (Austin at Oxford, and Wittgenstein at Cambridge). In fact, Austin considered himself more aligned with G.E. Moore's work than Wittgenstein's. Hacker recounts:

> If Ryle, among the leading Oxford figures, had learnt the most from Wittgenstein, Austin was the least influenced. "Some people like Witters," he remarked, "but Moore is my man." [Hacker attributes Austin's remark to the recollections of P. Strawson and P. Grice. **Wittgenstein's Place in Twentieth-Century Analytic Philosophy**, p. 172. Blackwell, 1996. Hacker goes on to identify the principal similarities and differences between Austin and Wittgenstein, pp. 172–173.]

Although there are similarities in some of their work, their main point of difference lies in their entirely different purposes in studying language. Wittgenstein hoped to uncover mistakes in reasoning that were due to linguistic

This list is not meant to be complete or unchangeable. Further, it is not necessary that every kind of game have all these characteristics. Although Wittgenstein introduces the

confusions. These confusions, he thought, underlay many prominent philosophical problems. Austin was less interested in fighting the brushfires of traditional philosophical debate than in analyzing the ordinary use of language for its own sake (he did not claim, as Wittgenstein did, that his analysis would clear up any long-standing philosophical disputes). Hacker gives an example:

> [Austin] found linguistic investigations of interest in their own right, and delighted in uncovering subtle, unnoticed differences in linguistic idiom. (Why "very" allows the substitution of "highly" in some cases ("very unusual") but not in others ("very depressed" or "very wicked") is not a question which is likely to have interested Wittgenstein.) [*ibid.*]

Austin's work was extended by J. Searle [**Speech Acts: An Essay in the Philosophy of Language**. Cambridge University Press, 1969]. While Searle describes a number of differences between his own and Austin's work (primarily, that Austin was describing illocutionary verbs, not illocutionary acts, as Searle wanted to do), their work has many striking similarities. Searle's classification of speech acts into Representatives, Directives, Commissives, Expressives and Declarations, has unmistakable antecedents in Austin's work. Austin has the same basic number of categories of illocutionary acts, but calls them Verdictives, Exercitives, Commissives, Behabitives and Expositives. (Searle also described two further categories, Assertive Declarations, and (later) Indirect Speech Acts). Searle's contribution to speech act theory was to focus on the acts themselves and to try to describe the conditions necessary for the successful performance of those acts. Austin and Searle also showed that the proper study of language was not just the formal features of words and sentences (syntax, statistical properties of language, etc.) but of the broader context of speech acts:

> A great deal can be said in the study of language without studying speech acts, but any such purely formal theory is necessarily incomplete. It would be as if baseball were studied only as a formal system of rules and not as a game. [*op.cit.* p. 17]

What is implicit in this quotation is that the body of rules of a game are not complete explanations or representations of the game. The notion of "a game" is much broader than an explicit set of constitutive or regulative rules can convey. It is an intensely human activity much of which cannot be codified entirely in a set of rules. Wittgenstein would be sympathetic with such a portrayal. If there is a difference between Searle's work and that of Austin and Wittgenstein, it is that Searle claimed that his categories of speech acts covered all such transactions that were possible in language. Austin saw these categories as only rough approximations of the kinds of speech acts, of which he believed were between 1,000 and 10,000 [Austin, *op.cit.*, p. 150, n.1]. Wittgenstein believed that there were simply too many different kinds of language games to count or classify. For example, consider the following two instances:

> One corporation agrees to provide some service or product to another corporation. This agreement takes the form of a contract, which is drawn up and handled by the corporate counsel in each company.

> Neighbor A promises to pick up neighbor B's mail and to mow his lawn while neighbor B is away on vacation.

For Searle, both of these instances are promises (what he calls "commissives") and, from a categorical point of view, they are the same. Wittgenstein, and probably Austin too, would see these as very different activities. It is true that both involve a promise, of sorts. But clearly the "felicity conditions" (Austin) or the "stage-setting" (Wittgenstein) that make these two promises work are vastly different. Certainly Neighbor B would not hold Neighbor A legally liable if he did not mow his lawn for him, but a business would certainly hold another business legally liable if they did not meet the terms of their contract. To say these commissives are both the same would be like saying a mosquito and a Stealth Bomber are the same because they both have wings and fly.

Paragraph §23 in **PI**, in which Wittgenstein talks of the enormous number of language games, is the statement that Searle takes issue with. But Wittgenstein anticipates Searle's more narrow point of view in the next paragraph:

concept of a *language game* in **PI** §7 of **Philosophical Investigations**, he does not discuss it at any length until **PI** §§65–67:

Here we come up against the great question that lies behind all these considerations.—For someone might object against me: "You take the easy way out! You talk about all sorts of language-games, but have nowhere said what the essence of a language-game, and hence of language, is: what is common to all these activities, and what makes them into language or parts of language. So you let yourself off the very part of the investigation that once gave you yourself most headache, the part about the general form of propositions and of language."

And this is true.—Instead of producing something common to all that we call language, I am saying that these phenomena have no one thing in common which makes us use the same word for all,—but that they are related to one another in many different ways. And it is because of this relationship, or these relationships, that we call them all "language." I will try to explain this.

Consider for example the proceedings that we call "games." I mean board-games, card-games, ball-games, Olympic games, and so on. What is common to them all?—Don't say: "There must be something common or they would not be called 'games'"—but look and see whether there is anything common to all. For if you look at them you will not see something that is common to all, but similarities, relationships, and a whole series of them at that. To repeat: don't think, but look!— Look for example at board-games, with their multifarious relationships. Now pass to card-games; here you find many correspondences with the first group, but many common features drop out, and others appear. When we pass next to ball games, much that is common is retained, but much is lost.—Are they all "amusing?" Compare chess with noughts and crosses. Or is there always winning and los-ing, or competition between players? Think of patience. In ball games there is winning and losing; but when a child throws his ball at the wall and catches it again, this feature has disappeared. Look at the parts played by skill and luck; and at the difference between skill in chess and skill in tennis. Think now of games like ring-a-ring-a-roses; here is the element of amusement, but how many other characteristic features have disappeared! And we can go through the many, many other groups of games in the same way; can see how similarities crop up and disappear.

And the result of this examination is: we see a complicated network of similarities overlapping and criss-crossing: sometimes overall similarities, sometimes similar-ities of detail.

If you do not keep the multiplicity of language-games in view you will perhaps be inclined to ask questions like: "What is a question?"

That is, if you do not keep this multiplicity of language games in mind then you are likely to clump them together in general categories that span large numbers of examples but which will mask important differences that exist between specific examples. Asking "What is a question?" implicitly assumes that a "question" is one kind of thing, and misses the enormous diversity that different questions can take (direct questions vs. rhetorical questions vs. leading questions, etc.). In our example, grouping all promises together into one category obscures important differences they may have.

I can think of no better expression to characterize these similarities than "family resemblances"; for the various resemblances between members of a family: build, features, color of eyes, gait, temperment, etc. etc. overlap and criss-cross in the same way.—And I shall say: "games" form a family.

And, for instance the kinds of number form a family in the same way. Why do we call something a "number?" Well, perhaps because it has a—direct—relationship with several things that have hitherto been called number; and this can be said to give it an indirect relationship to other things we call the same name. And we extend our concept of number as in spinning a thread we twist fibre on fibre. And the strength of the thread does not reside in the overlapping of many fibres.

But if someone wished to say: "There is something common to all these constructions—namely the disjunction of all their common properties"—I should reply: Now you are only playing with words. One might as well say: "Something runs through the whole thread—namely the continuous overlapping of those fibres." [**PI** §§65–67]

Baker and Hacker describe some of the characteristics of what they call "invented language games." These are the games that Wittgenstein makes up to demonstrate a particular grammatical point. But these characteristics must be similar to those that comprise *language games* that Wittgenstein does not invent—ones that already exist in our language. Again, these characteristics do not define what *language games* are, but give us some properties that might help us to understand them. Wittgenstein's invented language-games display many features which are given varying prominence for philosophical purposes at hand. A language-game contains the following:

(i) Words, and sentences formed from them according to combinatorial rules: the vocabulary is given and its use in speech acts (moves in the language-game) specified.

(ii) Instruments: ... Wittgenstein calls (a) gestures, as used in teaching the use of "there," (b) patterns, whether samples, words, or figure drawings, and (c) pictures in a table which correlates words and pictures ... This accords with his favored tool analogy for words. Most importantly, it extends the concepts of language and grammar to include elements hitherto regarded (by linguists and philosophers) as extraneous. This is a remarkable innovation ...

(iii) Context (*Zusammenhang*): it is important to distinguish the generality of the notion of context that is being used and the purpose for which it is brought into view. Like any other game, a language-game is "played" in a setting. Wittgenstein's stress on the context of the game appears to be motivated by the wish to bring to the fore elements of linguistic activities which, while not obviously involved in the explanation of the meaning of constituent expressions (hence unlike instruments), are nevertheless pertinent to their meaning. At its most general the notion of context encompasses the presuppositions of meaning ... These may be very general features of the natural world, for example, agreement in responses (to injury, color, pointing. etc.) ...

(iv)   Activity of the game: this feature is related to the former. It is in the activities constitutive of a language-game that the point and purpose of linguistic expressions is evident . . .

(v)   The use, purpose, role, and function of instruments, words, sentences (and occasionally even language-game themselves): these are crucially important features . . . in [Wittgenstein's] view the cardinal error of 20th-century philosophy has been the focus upon form and structure of expression rather than upon these features.

(vi)   Learning games: we do learn games, and the foundation of this learning is training. In many of his invented language games Wittgenstein sketches the different kinds of training necessary for a participant to be able to play . . . This highlights the nature of rule-following, and the way in which the "gap" between rules and their application is bridged. It emphasizes the presuppositions of explanation and the prerequisites of doubt and question. It is the crucial component of the claim that all explanation comes to an end . . .

(vii)   Completeness: Wittgenstein commonly emphasizes that his invented games are not fragments of a language, but should be considered as complete.[135]

A number of questions arise in response to Wittgenstein's concept of *language games*. In the first place, Wittgenstein brings up *language games* within the context of a child's learning language:

> Language games are the forms of language with which a child begins to make use of words. The study of language games is the study of primitive forms of language or primitive languages. [**BB** p. 17]

This seems to imply that the *only* use of *language games* is for children learning to master "primitive forms of language." If this is the case, then the large areas in language of adult discourse appear to lack *language games*; in other words, *language games* only cover a small, primitive part of language. This is not a correct inference. If it is the case that children use *language games* to learn language, then why shouldn't *language games* be a means for *all* learning in language? It stands to reason that the method that the child uses to learn language should be useful for adult language learning, too—that the method the child uses to learn language would not suddenly change to some other method when the child becomes an adult. Wittgenstein never states that adults learn language differently than children do, nor does he even hint that it might be the case. From a methodological point of view, there is no good reason for adults to learn new words and phrases any differently than children do.

Wittgenstein often refers to *language games* as "primitive," leaving one to question whether all *language games* are primitive. But this notion is dispelled on further reading:

[135] Backer and Hacker, **Essays on the Philosophical Investigations: Wittgenstein: Meaning and Understanding** [University of Chicago Press, 1985, pp. 54–55].

> If we want to study the problems of truth and falsehood, of the agreement and disagreement of propositions with reality, of the nature of assertion, assumption, and question, we shall with great advantage look at primitive forms of language in which these forms of thinking appear without the confusing background of highly complicated processes of thought. When we look at such simple forms of language the mental mist which seems to enshroud our ordinary use of language disappears. We see activities, reactions, which are clear-cut and transparent. On the other hand we recognize in these simple processes forms of language not separated by a break from our more complicated ones. We see that we can build up the complicated forms from the primitive ones by gradually adding new forms. [**BB** p. 17]

If it is the case that the employment of *language games* pervades both our simple and complex uses of language then it is a reasonable inference that *language games* are, in aggregate, a kind of *grammar* of our language—more precisely, they embody, at least in part, what Wittgenstein was to call the "*depth grammar*" of our language. Finally, there is a more fundamental question that arises naturally in response to Wittgenstein's model of language use comprising games. Some readers may object that Wittgenstein's reliance on games as a framework for his philosophy of language and mind is naive or, at best, trivial. How could something as serious as a philosophy of language and mind be based on something as trivial as "games?" Wittgenstein never addresses this issue, but some comment may be in order. In the first place, when we think of games we usually think of children's games, or casual adult games such as bridge or charades. But many of these games grew out of more serious social activity. Certainly throwing a ball or wrestling have their counterpart activities in primitive warfare, and the engagement in such activities was, in part, a source of training for such endeavors. Some activities like archery, hunting or boxing have direct links to traits that were necessary for our survival in not too distant times. At times, less-serious games have even displaced the practice of more serious games related to warfare, and such a shift in the appeal of games may signal a shift in social or cultural attitudes as well. The conflict between casual sports and the practice of the skills of warfare was evident in 15th century Scotland. Golf originated in The Netherlands, but reached its greatest appeal in Scotland:

> It is uncertain at what date golf was introduced into Scotland, but in 1457 the popularity of the game had already become so great as seriously to interfere with the more important pursuit of archery. The Scotish king James IV announced that it was forbidden to play golf.

> Futeball and Golfe forbidden. Item, it is statut and ordainit that in na place of the realme there be usit fute-ball, golfe, or uther sik unprofitabill sportis.[136]

In Scotland, the urge to play "golfe" was so strong that it displaced even the need to practice the skills of warfare. Certainly, a practice that is motivated this strongly must be closely tied to the fundamental desires and practices of the human community. There are authors who have argued that, contrary to initial impressions, games are not only an important component of society, but are a *sine qua non* of human society as we know it. One author, Johan Huizinga, sees the "play" aspect of culture as so essential that he claims we should

---

[136]**The Encyclopædia Britannica**, 11th ed., vol. 12, p. 219. The Encyclopædia Britannica Company, NY, 1910.

not be named *homo sapiens* ("rational man") but *homo ludens* ("playing man"). Huizinga's notion of "play" is broader than Wittgenstein's concept of "games," but his conception of "play" includes "games." One of the most important aspects of play for Huizinga is the order that it brings to a situation:

> Inside the play-ground an absolute and peculiar order reigns. Here we come across another, very positive feature of play: it creates order, *is* order. Into an imperfect world and into the confusion of life it brings a temporary, a limited perfection.[137]

The notion of "the confusion of life" that Huizinga describes has a certain resonance with Wittgenstein when he writes of the "hurly burly of human actions":

> How could human behavior be described? Surely only by sketching the actions of a variety of humans, as they are all mixed up together. What determines our judgment, our concepts and reactions, is not what *one* man is doing *now*, an individual action, but the whole hurly-burly of human actions, the background against which we see any action. [**Z** §567]

If Wittgenstein, like Huizinga, sees life as a "confusion" or "hurly-burly" then it must surely be one of the functions of Wittgenstein's games, like Huizinga's, to provide order. Games are not just for amusement, but are, like Huizinga claims, part of who we are. For Wittgenstein, language games are, similarly, part of "what [we] do."[138]

## Language and Categorization

Categorization is one of the most important aspects of language and, by inference, thought. The central issue of categorization is how we can see individual things as being the same in some regard even though there may be many ways in which they are different. Most utterances contain explicit references to categories: tables, chairs, cars, people, trees, feelings, colors, etc. In fact, it is difficult to imagine an utterance that does not contain a reference to at least one category. Yet this description of how pervasive categories are doesn't get at the central position of importance they hold for language. Ellis has argued persuasively that categories are the very foundation of language, that without them we simply could not have language at all.[139]

> Categorization, not syntax, is the most basic aspect of language, and it is a process that must be understood correctly if anything else (incuding syntax) is to be understood, and categorization, not communication, is the most important function of language, one that is prior to all others. . . . Every language is a *particular* system of categorization . . .[140]

---

[137] J. Huizinga. **Homo Ludens: A Study of the Play Element in Culture**, p. 10. Beacon Press, Boston, 1950.

[138] If I have exhausted the justifications I have reached bedrock, and my spade is turned. Then I am inclined to say: "This is simply what I do." [**PI** §217]

[139] J. Ellis. **Language, Thought and Logic**. Northwestern University Press, Evanston, IL, 1993. See especially, chapter 3: "The Heart of Language: Categorization."

[140] *Op.cit.*, p. 27.

Like the nominalist, Ellis holds that the individual things that make up our everyday life are, fundamentally, unique. Two Shetland Sheepdogs have much more that is different about them than alike—they might weigh different amounts, stand at different heights, have slightly different coloring, have barks that sound different, prefer to eat different kinds of food, are different ages, have different temperaments, can run at different speeds, know different kinds of tricks, be loyal to different people, etc.[141] Similar lists of differences can be drawn between two members of any category. The world is composed of unique objects: *this* person, *this* tree, *this* situation, *this* Shetland Sheepdog, etc. Yet if we only had unique objects in our world—objects that do not belong to categories—it is clear that we would not be able to talk of them at all. All linguistic references would be as unique as the objects that they referred to and would thereby be significantly less informative.

---

[141] While it may seem that this kind of variety in perception is more of an intellectual exercise than a practical reality, there actually are individuals who are so overcome with the variety of visual perception that they find it extremely difficult to recognize and form categories of objects. Oliver Sacks reports that individuals who become blind early in life but then have their sight restored as adults inevitably have such problems with visual recognition. He writes of one such individual, a fifty-year-old man who had his sight recently restored:

> Unfamiliar objects were much more difficult [for him]. When I took a blood-pressure cuff from my medical bag, he was completely flummoxed and could make nothing of it, but he recognized it immediately when I allowed him to touch it. Moving objects presented a special problem, for their appearance changed constantly. Even his dog, he told me, looked so different at different times that he wondered if it was the same dog. He was utterly lost when it came to the rapid changes in others' physiognomies. Such difficulties are almost universal among the early blinded restored to sight. [Another patient] could not recognize individual faces, or their expressions, a year after his eyes had been operated on, despite perfectly normal elementary vision. What about pictures? ... when we tried him first on still pictures, pictures in magazines, he had no success at all. He could not see people, could not see objects—did not comprehend the idea of representation. [**An Anthropologist on Mars**, p. 129. Vintage Books, NY.]

The existence of individuals with such deficits indicates that our perceptions are not as unequivocal as we might assume. It also argues against the realist's view that the categories of perceived objects are in any way obvious, and for the nominalist's view that all things are unique until we, consciously or unconsciously, group them into classes. This sort of visual confusion is difficult for the non-visually impaired person to understand. Perhaps a good analogy would be to imagine what it would be like to look at newspaper pictures through a magnifying glass where the visual impression is of clusters of dots rather than images. One would find it very difficult to identify even familiar images when looking at the pictures in such detail, because it would be difficult to, in gestalt terms, separate the figure from the ground. All visual impressions would be equally salient making it difficult to separate them into meaningful groups.

The poet T.S. Eliot describes this imperfect match between knowledge and perception more elegantly:

> ... There is, it seems to us,
> At best, only a limited value
> In the knowledge derived from experience.
> The knowledge imposes a pattern, and falsifies,
> For the pattern is new in every moment
> And every moment is a new and shocking
> Valuation of all we have been.
> ["The Four Quartets: East Coker: II")

Language would not add any information other than a different noise sounding for every different situation or thing. In fact, language as we know it would not be possible.Since all references would be to unique items, then new utterances would have to be made up with every new object or event, and this would tell us nothing we could use in subsequent instances. It is a reasonable inference that we could not even function in our day-to-day activities if we saw every object, situation or event as unique—we would have no categories for things like "food," "danger," "friend," "water," etc. As a consequence, we would not only be unable to deal with these concepts in any kind of general way, we would not have any knowledge about them to use in the future or pass on to others.[142] Categorization, then, is a means of simplification. It provides a basic reference system in which things that are fundamentally different, are treated *as if* they were alike. And what does it mean for things to be "alike?" It means, at least in part, that they have the same role for us in what we do, that their differences are of no consequence for their use. Any two Shetland Sheepdogs, though each is unique, can be treated as being members of the same category. This is done by setting the criteria for class membership to treat some aspects as important (such as the color and markings on the fur and the size and shape of the ears) and others (such as precise weight, sound of voice or birthplace) as irrelevant. It is also true that members of one category can be members of other categories: two Shetland Sheepdogs could also be in the category of "my dogs," or one might be in the category "show dog" while the other is not, or they both might be in the category of "guard dog," etc.: [Ellis]

> If situations themselves present a limitless variety, a language can only have a finite set of categories. It follows that language functions as the instrument of human knowledge and communication only because it simplifies the complexity of experience by reducing an infinite variety to a finite set of categories—the categories of a particular language ... This *simplification* is the central fact and process of categorization, and thus the central fact of language and the knowledge it affords us of our world. For communication to be possible, then, there must first have been a considerable degree of processing of experience—of analyzing it, abstracting from it, focusing and shaping it. It is in this complex process that the essence of language is to be found, not in communication per se. Indeed, communication is only of value

---

[142] Zipf discussed this issue in his statistical theory of language [**Human Behavior and the Principle of Least Effort**. Hafner, NY, 1965 (facsimile of the 1949 edition)]. He said that language is the result of the struggle between two competing economies: the Force of Unification and the Force of Diversification. The Force of Unification is the tendency for language to have just one word that would be used to express all linguistic meaning. The Force of Diversification is the tendency for language to have a unique word for every linguistic meaning. Zipf also called these forces the Speaker's Economy and the Hearer's Economy, respectively: If a language consisted of one word it would pose the least effort for the speaker, but would demand the most effort from the hearer (i.e., he would have to figure out what the single word meant for each of its different uses). This is the Speaker's Economy. If, at the other extreme, a language had a different word for every meaning, this would minimize the effort for the hearer while maximizing the effort for the speaker for he would have to find the precise, unique word for every meaningful expression. This is the Hearer's Economy. Language cannot function at either of these extremes so the forces compete to form a balance where some words can be used to express a lot of meanings (general words like "people") and some can be used to express only a few meanings (specific words like "the current President of the U.S."). Word usage in all natural languages fall somewhere along a continuum stretching from very general words to very specific words. This "vocabulary balance," as Zipf called it, represents the minimum total effort for the speaker and hearer combined, and can be represented by a predictable statistical pattern of word frequencies (for a more detailed discussion of Zipf's Law see Colin Cherry's **On Communication** [Basic Books, 1972], or Blair's **Language and Representation in Information Retrieval** [Elsevier Science, New York, 1990]).

to us because this prior process creates something that can be communicated and is worth communicating. Words do not label situations, they must relate one situation to others in order to be able to talk about them at all. Only a prior typology of situations and their aspects allows communication about any one of them to take place, because what is communicated is *not the facts of the situation merely in itself* (again, that is an impossible notion) but the place of that situation within the set of categories of the language.[143]

But language is not just a means of simplification, its importance is even more fundamental. The categories that are explicit in language determine how we experience reality—in fact, they determine what we consider reality *to be*. This relation between language and reality was expressed most clearly by philosopher John Searle: "Our concept of reality is a matter of our linguistic categories." (see entire quotation at footnote **84**).

Getting back to Ellis' point about how language simplifies the complexity of experience, consider the following sentence:

Bill got into his car and drove to the store.

"Got into" tells us that Bill entered his car, but it does not tell us specifically how he did it. If we had to draw a picture of exactly how he got in the car we could not do so (he may have opened the door and stepped in, or crawled in through an open window, or entered a number of other ways). "His car" refers to a particular car, but it tells us no more. It could be a Ford, a Cadillac or a SAAB, it could be old or new, rusty or recently repainted, it could have a cracked windshield and bald tires, it could have in-state or out-of-state license plates, etc. "Drove" tells us that Bill used the car when he went to the store, but it does not say which route he used to go to the store, nor does it say whether he drove fast or slowly, or whether he stopped along the way. "The store" doesn't tell us what kind of store he went to, it doesn't say how big it is, or what Bill was looking for, nor does it even say whether it was open or not. All of this possible complexity—and it could be even more complex than this—is left out of this sentence, even the name "Bill" is not as precise as it could be, we could have several friends who have the name "Bill." In fact, if we were to talk always at a very detailed level of complexity it might be difficult for us to communicate at all. An important point is what criteria determine the level of complexity required for the utterance. Different levels could be appropriate for different circumstances. If a friend asked you casually where Bill was, the above sentence might

---

[143] Ellis, *op.cit.*, p. 29. The idea that what we perceive are not facts, but sensory data that has already been processed in some fundamental way, is difficult to grasp. But this is not a new notion. Even Goethe could see this:

The most important thing is to understand that everything that is factual is already theory. [Werke. **Hamburger Ausgabe**, 10th ed. Munich, 1982. 12:432. Cited in chapter 2 of Ellis, *op.cit.*, p. 127]

or,

...and so it can be said that every time we look attentively at the world we are already theorizing. [Farbenlehre (Werke 13:317) **Hamburger Ausgabe**, 10th ed. Munich, 1982, cited by Ellis, *op.cit.*, p. 134.

be fine, but if a policeman is asking you about Bill's trip to the store because he is filling out an accident report for a mishap Bill got into, you might be required to give a lot more detail than the above sentence does. The level of detail required for an utterance is based on the particular use and circumstances in which it is made. So our use of categories not only allows us to simplify our utterances and focus them on what is important, but they also allow us a wide latitude in how detailed we want to be. Further, the use of certain categories can be a signal for the level of complexity desired. We could say, for example:

> Bill vaulted over the door of his classic, red 1955 Thunderbird convertible, landing squarely behind the wheel. He jabbed the key into the ignition, started the engine and roared off in a cloud of dust. Taking the Shore Highway, he turned East on Noriega, stopped at the small Safeway store near 25th street and bought some cigarettes.

Such an utterance would be bizarre in response to a simple query about where Bill is, but would certainly be imaginable as a description in a short story. It might be asked how we know what level of detail is required for our utterances. Certainly some of this level of detail can be negotiated in a conversation:

> 1st person: "Bill got into his car and drove to the store."
> 2nd person: "What did he go to the store for?"
> 1st person: "To get a pack of cigarettes."
> 2nd person: "How long ago did he leave?"
> 1st person: "Just a few minutes ago."
> 2nd person: "What kind of car was he driving?"
>
> $\vdots$
>
> etc.

But what is surprising is that we often begin our conversation or answer a question with just the right level of detail, so no negotiation is required. Although this does not always happen, the fact that it does at all, given the unlimited number of things we could say, is remarkable. What give us a sense of the correct level of detail required are the context and circumstances—the Forms of Life—in which the statement is uttered.[144] Paul Grice has stated that our ordinary conversations are governed by what he calls "conversational implicatures." These implicatures are considered to be in force during our conversations unless there is some clear indication that they are not. [This will be discussed in more detail in the section "Conversational Implicatures," *infra*] It is clear that categorization

---

[144] It is remarkable how quickly and intuitively we can assess the level of detail needed in conversation. Some time ago, a study was done in New York City which observed the way that people gave directions to strangers they met on the street. The study had individuals go up to random people on the street and ask directions to a well-known place in the city, say, Times Square or Central Park. When the person who asked directions spoke with a New York City accent, the person asked would give the directions, but make their description relatively simple and often reference other New York city landmarks. But when the person asking directions spoke with a heavy Southern accent, the person who was asked would immediately give the directions in much more detail than they would to a New Yorker. Clearly, the responder was able to make the immediate inference that someone with a New York accent would have some familiarity with the city and could be given very brief directions, but someone with a Southern accent would likely be entirely new to the city requiring much more detailed directions.

is an essential aspect of language. But there are a number of competing theories about how categorization takes place. In philosophy, the subject of categorization is traditionally referred to as the relation between "universals and particulars."

## Universals and Particulars: An Old Debate

One of the major problems in philosophy has been understanding how we can have general, unchanging ideas or concepts of things when all we can observe are things that are subject to constant change—or, putting it more traditionally, how can we arrive at a universal concept when we can observe only unique particulars? Traditionally, this debate has been organized around three points of view: realism, conceptualism and nominalism. Realism's first major proponent was Plato (427–347 B.C.). For Plato, true knowledge must be permanent and unchanging. But the things we observe in our day-to-day experience are always subject to change and decay. Therefore, according to Plato, our everyday experience, no matter how careful, cannot be the source of true knowledge. But there *are* some things that are permanent and unchanging, namely our ideas of categories. That is, although actual tables and chairs are infinitely variable in construction and are subject to constant change—nicks, scratches, and other wear and tear—our conception of a "table" or "chair" remains constant. As Socrates explains to Glaucon:

> Let us take any common instance; there are beds and tables in the world—plenty of them, are there not?
>
> Yes.
>
> But there are only two ideas or forms of them—one the idea of a bed, the other of a table.
>
> True.
>
> And the maker of either of them makes a bed or he makes a table for our use, in accordance with the idea—that is our way of speaking in this and similar instances—but no artificer makes the ideas themselves: how could he?
>
> Impossible.[145]

The general, unchanging ideas of such entities had to come from some place. Since Plato believed that they couldn't come from our observations of everyday things, he proposed that they actually existed independently in a "realm of forms (or ideas)." This realm of forms exists separately from our everyday world. Our general ideas of things like "tables" and "beds" are recollections that we have of these ideas or forms that we have seen before we were born (the realm of forms was where people existed before birth). With this foundation, it was easy to attribute all general prototypical ideas to the realm of

---

[145] Plato. "The Republic," **Book X**, pp. 852–853. **The Dialogues of Plato**, vol. 1, Random House, NY, 1920. Translated by B. Jowett. Plato's doctrine of forms did not just attempt to resolve the problem of categories but also tried to resolve the problems of contradiction and perfection. Plato felt that everyday objects were inherently contradictory because any one could be, for example, beautiful from one point of view and ugly from another. Further, geometric entities, such as circles and lines, lacked a perfection in their everyday appearances that our ideas of them did not.

forms—ideas of not just material objects but also attributes like "beautiful" and "good" and relations such as "greater than" or "equal to."

Aristotle (394–322 B.C.) found some problems with Plato's theory of "universals." Specifically, Plato could not explain satisfactorily how the forms of his ideal realm could be related to the particulars or individuals of everyday life. This is the fundamental problem with all dualistic systems—how do you explain the influence of one component on the other given that they are, by definition, separate? In order to be related to particular instances there must be some feature in common between the form and the instance. But if that were true, then this feature in common must have its own form. This objection was rendered more figuratively as the "third man" argument, Aristotle's most famous objection to Plato: The "first man" is the individual or particular man, and this is related to the "second man" which is the type, or ideal man. But for the "first man" and the "second man" to be related, as they must, we need a "third man" which is the general form for this relationship. It is not possible for the form of the relationship to be part of the first man or second man, so it must be separate from both of them. But if this is the case, then we will need a "fourth man" to be the form of the relationship between the first man and the third man. This "fourth man" then necessitates a "fifth man," and the "fifth man" requires a "sixth man," and so on leading to an infinite regress. But this infinite regress does not mean that we cannot get to the end, but that there is, more importantly, no "end" to get to. Wittgenstein made this important observation about infinite regresses:

> The reasoning that leads to an infinite regress is to be given up not 'because in this way we can never reach the goal', but because here there is no goal; so it makes no sense to say "we can never reach it." [**Z** §693]

For Aristotle, Plato's realm of forms introduced a separate "reality" that caused more problems than it solved. Bertrand Russell comments:

> . . . a universal cannot exist by itself, but only *in* particular things.

> Suppose I say "there is such a thing as the game of football," most people would regard the remark as a truism. But if I were to infer that football could exist without football-players, I should be rightly held to be talking nonsense. Similarly, it would be held there is such a thing as parenthood, but only because there are parents; there is such a thing as sweetness, but only because there are sweet things; and there is redness, but only because there are red things.[146]

Aristotle then proposed that instead of universals being a separate reality, they were better seen as common elements in real objects of the same category—form could not be separate from existing individuals. The universal "table" consists of whatever is in common with all tables. Plato's theory came to be known as *universalia ante rem* (universals *before (prior to)* things) while Aristotle's was known as *universalia in rebus* (universals *in* things).[147]

---

[146] B. Russell. **A History of Western Philosophy**, p. 163. Simon and Schuster, NY, 1945. Russell does not hold Aristotle's view, but continues on and criticizes it, though his criticisms are different than the ones I present here.
[147] Aristotle's criticism of Plato did not stop here. He had a total of at least 7 objections to Plato's notion of universals:

Platonic and Aristotelian realism both enjoyed long periods of support, with medieval philosophers Augustine favoring Plato's version of realism and Aquinas supporting Aristotle's view. Variations of Aristotle's realism have found even more recent support.[148] But in spite of the long support these theories of knowledge have enjoyed, there are some problems with strict versions of realism. Most prominently there is the observation that, as we pointed out above in our discussion of Ellis, there are often more aspects of members of the same category that are different than are the same. Further, individual members of one category can be seen to be members of other categories, too, and some of this variation is not due just to the entity in question, but may be contingent on context and circumstances—for example, a can of soup on the shelf of a supermarket is merely a can of soup; but that same can of soup on display in the Chicago Art Institute is a legitimate art object (and worth substantially more $). In short, the number of ways that particular entities can be the same, or can be different, is uncountable, especially when you include context and circumstances. Clearly, then, empirical similarities or differences between things are not *decisive* in establishing their membership, or non-membership, in different categories. This was one of nominalism's major criticisms of realism.

Nominalism's first major proponent was William of Ockham (1280–1347).[149] Ockham was a 14th century figure who, in addition to his scholarly work, was pronounced a heretic, excommunicated and eventually became one of the many victims of the Black Plague. The Plague wiped out much of the 14th century intelligentsia of Northern Europe, plunging

In criticizing the Platonic theory of ideas, [Aristotle] offers seven arguments, which group themselves in such a way that there are virtually only two main criticisms of Plato. The first criticism is that the ideas, although they are intended to explain the nature of things, are not adequate to do so. This thesis is developed in four special arguments: (1) the ideas are mere abstractions and as such cannot account for the existence of concrete things; (2) they are static and eternal, and are thus unable to explain the motion and change of concrete things; (3) ideas are posterior rather than prior to particular things, and cannot therefore be used to explain them; in short, ideas are copies of things, not their causes; (4) the ideas are unnecessary reduplications of things and not explanations of them. The second broad criticism of the ideal theory is that the relation between things and ideas is inexplicable. This criticism is expanded into the following three arguments: (1) nothing is explained by saying that things are the "copies of" or "participate in" ideas; to say that the individual man participates in the ideal man adds nothing to our understanding of the individual; (2) the alleged relation between the ideas and the corresponding things leads to an infinite regress—the "third man" argument as discussed above. (3) the theory of ideas completely separates the essence of form of a thing from the thing itself, but such a separation is at variance with the unity of the particular as observed by the mind. [F. Thilly. **A History of Philosophy**, p. 104. Holt, Rinehart, and Winston, NY, 1965. Revised by L. Wood.]

[148] Most notably, Frege, Russell, and Moore, all contemporary influences on Wittgenstein's early work. Hacker points out the debt Wittgenstein's early philosophy had to the early Platonic/metaphysical realism of these individuals:

> [Wittgenstein] accepted a version of metaphysical realism. The simple objects of the Tractatus [**TLP**] are heir to the realist ontologies of Frege, Moore and Russell. They resemble Fregean concepts in being "unsaturated," Fregean and Moorean concepts and terms in being unanalysable and indecomposable, and all three in being conceived to be constituents of reality. [**Wittgenstein's Place in Twentieth-Century Analytic Philosophy**, Blackwell, Oxford, 1996.]

This was one of the tenets of his early philosophy that Wittgenstein was later to reject.

[149] Earlier figures who held nominalist-like views, but who were not as prominent as William of Ockham, were Roscelin de Compiègne and Peter Abelard. ("Ockham" is sometimes spelled "Occam.")

it into a century of intellectual darkness. Ockham remains a last glimmer of rationality before a long period in which intellectual issues were not prominent. Ockham could see the principal flaw with realism: that positing the separate existence of "universals," as Plato, Aristotle and their followers insisted on, does not explain how we see only individual, unique things, yet can somehow group them by general characteristics. Further, making universals separate from particulars introduces the principal attendant problem with any dualism: *viz.* how do the separate entities interact? Ockham's legacy to philosophy, the notion of "Ockham's razor," was a defense of nominalism, because it "shaved off" the unnecessary universals of realism.[150] For Ockham, all knowledge begins with the particulars or individual entities of our experience. We abstract from the objects of our experience the characteristics common to them, and form universal concepts. But these universals only exist in our mind and are only expressed as words or some other signs. They do not exist outside our minds, as Plato believed, nor do they exist in things, as Aristotle thought. To make separate entities of universals is to create something that doesn't help to explain how we acquire general concepts.[151]

Nominalism found an early articulation in the works of Thomas Hobbes (1588–1679):

> The manner how speech serves to the remembrance of the consequence of causes and effects consists in the imposing of *names* and the *connection* of them.

> Of names, some are *proper* and singular to one only thing, as *Peter, John, this man, this tree*; and some are *common* to many things, *man , horse, tree*, every of which, though but one name, is nevertheless the name of diverse particular things, in respect of all which together it is called a *universal,* there being nothing in the world universal but names, for the things named are every one of them individual and singular.

> One universal name is imposed on many things for their similitude in some quality or other accident; and whereas a proper name brings to mind one thing only, universals recall any one of those many.[152]

---

[150] Entia non multiplicanda praeter necessitatem ("Entities or principles should not be unnecessarily multiplied"). F. Thilly. **A History of Philosophy**, p. 248. Holt, Rinehart, and Winston, NY, 1965. Revised by L. Wood. Russell (*op.cit.*) claims that Ockham never wrote this, nor is there any mention of a "razor" in Ockham's work. Russell attributes the following similar statement to him: "It is vain to do with more what can be done with fewer." [p. 472]. Russell, himself, came closest to the view of realism: "I think a logical argument could be produced to show that universals are part of the structure of the world" [**The Analysis of Mind**. London, 1921]. Some years later he wrote: "I conclude, therefore, though with hesitation, that there are universals, and not merely general words." [**An Inquiry Into Meaning and Truth**. London, 1940.]

[151] While this discussion deals with traditional versions of realism and nominalism, this does not mean that there are not tenable later formulations. For example, see Goodman and Quine's "Steps Towards a Constructive Nominalism," **Journal of Symbolic Logic**, vol. 12, pp. 105–122, 1947. Goodman answers some of the major objections to his version of nominalism in his "A World of Individuals." Originally published in 1956, reprinted in **The Problem of Universals**, pp. 292–305. Basic Books, NY, 1971. Edited by C. Landesman. Also, of interest is Max Black's critique of recent versions of nominalism in the field of linguistics: "A crude nominalism . . . is often to be found, nowadays, expressed by overenthusiastic devotees of the popular movement known as General Semantics" [**The Labyrinth of Language**, p. 149. Mentor Books, NY, 1961]. Black cites S.I. Hayakawa's **Language, Meaning and Maturity** [Harper and Row, NY, 1954] as an introduction to General Semantics.

[152] T. Hobbes. **Leviathan: Parts I and II**. Introduction by Herbert W. Schneider. [The Library of the Liberal Arts, Bobbs-Merrill, NY, 1958.]

Hobbes admits that there must be something about things in the same category that is similar for them to be referred to by universals. This avoids the problems of the more rigid realisms of Plato and Aristotle by not specifying exactly how entities in the same category are similar. But Hobbes never ventures further in his description of how things in the same category are similar, leaving his reader to wonder what precisely constitutes this "similitude." Later critics claimed that Hobbes had not, in fact, excluded universals— things that are similar, they pointed out, must be similar in some general respect. This made similarity contingent on implicit universals.

A somewhat different theory of universals was proposed by John Locke (1632–1704).[153] This view is often referred to as "conceptualism," and is close enough to nominalism that some writers, such as Russell and Windelband, insist that Locke was really a nominalist.[154] While the nominalist claims that the only general things we have are words, Locke pushed the analysis of universals back another step by claiming that a word is general or meaningful only insofar as there is a general concept associated with it. This view adds a complication to the nominalist theory by including another element, the "general idea," with it. While nominalism rejects the dualism of realism, Locke's conceptualism brings another form of dualism back. It is difficult to understand why Locke made his theory of universals *more* complicated than traditional nominalism, in effect, reversing the parsimony of Ockham's "razor." But a good guess might be that Locke saw that general ideas can change over time, and that it is difficult to reconcile this change with the nominalist view. For example, one could form a general idea of horses having seen a number of dark Arabian thoroughbreds. The word for this particular category of animals, of course, is "horse." But suppose that at a later time, the same individual sees other kinds of horses too: Clydesdales, Pintos, Mustangs, Piebalds, Lipizzaner stallions, etc. We would still call these examples "horses," but something has changed. We have a different "idea" of "horse" now than we had before. Yet, for the nominalist, since words are "names" and the word "horse" remains the same in both situations, it is difficult to see how the observer's view of horses has changed. For Locke, what has changed is not the word "horse" but the general idea that it stands for. Locke's formulation, then, can help us to understand general ideas when they change—something that strict nominalism has a harder time with.[155]

Locke's theory of universals works like this:

---

[153] Locke's theory was criticized by two subsequent Empiricists, Berkeley (1685–1753) and Hume (1711–1776).

[154] See Russell, *op.cit.,* p. 610: "Chapter III [of Locke's **Essay On Human Understanding**] ... takes up an extreme nominalist position on the subject of universals." And W. Windelband [**A History of Philosophy**, v. II. Harper Torchbooks, Harper and Row, NY, 1958 (original copyright, 1901).]: "Like the greater part of English philosophers, Locke was an adherent of Nominalsim, which professed to see in general concepts nothing but internal, intellectual structures." [p. 451].

[155] Wittgenstein's solution to this problem, of course, would be to say that what changes is neither the word "horse" nor some idea associated with it. What changes are the uses to which the word "horse" can be put and the situations in which it is appropriate. One can use "horse" to refer to these other kinds of horses within a wider range of contexts than it could be used before. In other words, the role that the word "horse" plays in our life changes as we see more kinds of horses. Certainly we can still describe a horse as having certain characteristics, or we can talk about our "idea" or image of a horse, but these exercises are merely two of the language games that can be used when we are talking about horses, and are not the basis for understanding what a "horse" is. Only the use of the word can teach us that.

> The mind makes the particular ideas, received from particular objects, to be-
> come general; which is done by considering them as they are in the mind such
> appearances—separate from all other existences, and the circumstances of real ex-
> istence. ... This is called *abstraction*, whereby ideas taken from particular things
> become general representatives of all of the same kind ... Thus, the same colour
> being observed today in chalk or snow, which the mind yesterday received from
> milk, it considers that appearance alone, makes it a representative of all of that
> kind; and having given it the name "whiteness," it by that sound signifies the same
> quality wheresoever to be imagined or met with; and thus universals, whether ideas
> or terms are made.

The traditional problem with universals or general ideas is that they are clearly different
from our ideas of individual things. This apparent dichotomy between universals and
particulars has proved the undoing of many theories of categorization (recall Aristotle's
"third man" argument against Plato's realism). Locke attempted to resolve this issue by
claiming that we did not have separate universal and particular ideas, but only particular
ideas. The universal idea is merely a particular idea regarded in a different way. Since
universals were particular ideas taken in a different way, it means that we have the ability
to turn any particular ideas we might have into universal ideas. We can *choose* to regard
a particular idea in a general way. This means that we are not bound to a particular
interpretation of universals, nor are we prevented from changing our mind about the
membership of categories, or even the existence of the categories themselves. Woozley
summarizes Locke's position:

> We do not find objects and their features divided by nature of God into real and
> objectively delimited classes; we observe objects and their features, but the dis-
> tinction between one class and another is something we ourselves make by criteria
> of convenience and utility. Similarities and differences are there for us to *observe*;
> whether the similarities are sufficiently close so that we can place the objects in the
> same or in different classes is for us to *decide* ...
>
> A consequence of this kind of conceptualism will be that concepts are not per-
> manently fixed, as on a simple realist theory they would be; a concept is liable to
> development and change, as fresh experience or changes of view show the need or
> utility of it.[156]

Locke's most significant contribution to the debate over universals and particulars was to
recognize that any theory must be able to account for possible changes in the categories
themselves. In this regard he sounds very modern. The problem with Locke's conceptualism is that it falls prey to the difficulties of any mentalistic theory of language—
where the "meaning" of a word is taken to be the idea that it stands for, or, as Locke put
it: ."... words in their primary or immediate signification stand for nothing but the ideas
in the mind of him that uses them ... "[157] The main problem with mentalistic theories of
meaning is that if the meaning of a word is a concept, and this concept is, by definition,

---

[156] A.D. Woozley. "Universals," **The Encyclopedia of Philosophy**, vol. 8, p. 201. Macmillan, NY, 1967. Paul
Edwards, editor in chief.

[157] J. Locke. **An Essay Concerning Human Understanding**, 5th ed., chapter 3.2.2. New York and London,
1961. Edited by J.W. Yolton.

private, then how can one be sure that he has the "correct" concept when he learns the meaning of a word? In truth, we cannot observe what is in others' minds, so any appeal of the question of meaning to concepts or other mental states cannot be verified.[158] In short, Locke made the important observation that categories are subject to change, and category membership is subject to a decision by the observer based on the "criteria of convenience and utility."

## Wittgenstein's Approach: The Rejection of Strict Nominalism and Realism[159]

The *nominalist* claims that all perceivable entities are unique, and that entities that we put in the same categories, such as Shetland Sheepdogs, have many more things that are different about them than alike. Consequently, the similarity of entities in the same category cannot be based on just observable characteristics. The strict *nominalist* would claim that the only thing that Wittgenstein's games have in common is that they are *called* games.

The *realist's* view of categorization claims that universals have a separate existence outside of the mind, that is, they are not dependent on any perception or mental abstraction for their existence. This view has taken a number of forms including the existence of universals separate from particular entities (Plato) and the existence of universals as common features in particular entities (Aristotle). The *realist* would say that what Wittgenstein's games have in common is that they possess some feature, or features, in common *in addition to* the fact that they are games. Having discussed some of the history of the debate over universals and particulars, and having collected some of Wittgenstein's views on the issue, it is important now to reconcile these points of view. First, it would be important to discuss any actual references that Wittgenstein makes to the *nominalist:realist* debate. Unfortunately, he makes only one direct reference to these points of view.[160] In **Philosophical Investigations** he remarks:

> We are not analysing a phenomenon (e.g., thought) but a concept (e.g., that of thinking), and therefore the use of a word. So it may look as if what we were doing were Nominalism. Nominalists make the mistake of interpreting all words as *names*, and so of not really describing their use, but only, so to speak, giving a paper draft on such a description.[161] [**PI** §383]

---

[158] As Max Black put it: "It is part of the 'mentalistic' conception [of meaning] to assume that the 'idea' is something 'private' to its possessor, something of which only he can be directly aware. But if so, how am I to convey my 'idea' to you—or to be sure that the idea you have corresponds sufficiently closely to my own?," **The Labyrinth of Language**, p. 194. Frederick A. Praeger, NY, 1968. Conceptualism (or mentalism) did not die with Locke, but exists in various forms today. Most prominently, the field of semiotics is strongly conceptualistic (see, especially, Umberto Eco's **A Theory of Semiotics**, Indiana University Press, Bloomington, Indiana, 1976). This conceptualistic, or mentalistic, view is criticized in detail in Blair's **Language and Representation in Information Retrieval** [Elsevier Science, Amsterdam, 1990].

[159] The discussion in this section is taken largely from R. Bambrough's "Universals and Family Resemblances," **The Problem of Universals**, pp. 266–279. Humanities Press, NJ, 1992. Edited by A.B. Schoedinger [reprinted from the "Proceedings of the Aristotelian Society," vol. 61, 1960–1961].

[160] Wittgenstein does mention "realism" in some of his later work [see, §§338–339 in his **RPPII**], but he is not referring to the view of realism we have been discussing.

[161] This is one of the clear breaks which Wittgenstein had with his past philosophy. In the **Tractatus** he claimed that the basic purpose of words is to name objects. That is, words stand for objects in reality, and these objects are the meaning of the words.

Wittgenstein's rejection of this aspect of nominalism is brief, but clear. Since he has already established that meaning in language is "explained"[162] by how words are used, any philosophy that does not recognize the relationship between meaning and use is going to be rejected by Wittgenstein. On Wittgenstein's view, the nominalists make three mistakes: (1) By saying that all words are names, they are saying that language only works in one way. In his criticism of the Augustine theory of language (see section "Wittgenstein at Work: **Philosophical Investigations**," *supra*), Wittgenstein specifically rejected the notion that language could work in only one way, regardless of what that way might be. (2) The claim that words are merely names is not supportable for much language use. (see section "Five Red Apples," *supra*). (3) Nominalists don't consider the importance that context, circumstances and activities play in the meaning of language—in effect, a word that is a name in one context might be something entirely different in another (e.g., if I say "Bring the chair over here" I am using the word "chair" as the name for a particular object. But if I say that "Bill is the chair of the Executive Committee" I do not mean that Bill is an object that people can sit on. I am using the word "chair" in a metaphorical or idiomatic sense.). These three objections are not rejections of all of nominalism's claims, though; there are some aspects of nominalism that Wittgenstein agrees with, at least implicitly, as we shall see.

The most extensive discussion that Wittgenstein has about universals—what he calls "generality"— is to be found in **The Blue and Brown Books**. Although this is an earlier work than **Philosophical Investigations** it contains the seeds of some of the discussions that he devoted the **Philosophical Investigations** to.[163] Wittgenstein begins the discussion by saying that what we need to look at if we are examining language, is specific examples of how particular words, phrases or sentences are used. But in saying that this is what we *should do*, Wittgenstein implies that this is precisely what we *don't do*. In fact, we have an inherent distrust of this kind of analysis. This prejudice has lead us away from fruitful investigations and towards a kind of analysis that is not likely to show us what is going on.

> If we say thinking is essentially operating with signs, the first question you might ask is: "What are signs?"—Instead of giving any kind of general answer to this question, I shall propose to you to look closely at particular cases which we should call "operating with signs."
>
> ⋮
>
> Now what makes it difficult for us to take this line of investigation is our craving for generality.
>
> This craving for generality is the result of a number of tendencies connected with particular philosophical confusions.

---

[162] The reader is reminded that "explain" is my translation of the German word "erklären." This word is usually rendered as "define" in the Anscombe translation of **Philosophical Investigations** (see quotation 92 and the following text).

[163] The generally accepted subtitle for **BB** is **Preliminary Studies for the "Philosophical Investigations."** It comprises two sets of class notes that Wittgenstein dictated for his students' use in 1934–1936. While the "Blue Book" was never intended for anything more than class notes, Wittgenstein had hoped that the "Brown Book" might be a draft of a longer written work, but this never came to pass [R. Rhees. The preface to **BB**].

[One tendency is] to look for something in common to all the entities which we commonly subsume under a general term ... It is comparable to the idea that properties are ingredients of the things which have the properties; e.g. that beauty is an ingredient of all beautiful things as alcohol is of beer and wine, and that we therefore could have a pure beauty, unadulterated by anything that is beautiful.[164]
[**BB** pp. 16–17]

Wittgenstein is objecting to a view of universals that has its roots in Aristotle's realism. His most articulate rejection of this is his attempt to show that if we were to look at what we all agree are "games" there is no single characteristic that they all have. Further, we can see that some games, for example, chess and hopscotch, have so little in common that it is remarkable that we classify both as "games," at all. The basis for this judgment, according to Wittgenstein, is to resist the attempt to find a general definition of "games" and to look at as many different kinds of games as possible. If we do this, we will see that no such general definition of games is at all possible:

Here we come up against the great question that lies behind all these considerations.—For someone might object against me: "You take the easy way out! You talk about all sorts of language-games, but have nowhere said what the essence of a language-game, and hence of language, is: what is common to all these activities, and what makes them into language or parts of language. So you let yourself off the very part of the investigation that once gave you yourself most headache, the part about the general form of propositions and of language."

And this is true.—Instead of producing something common to all that we call language, I am saying that these phenomena have no one thing in common which makes us use the same word for all,—but that they are related to one another in many different ways. And it is because of this relationship, or these relationships, that we call them all "language." I will try to explain this.

Consider for example the proceedings that we call "games." I mean board-games, card-games, ball-games, Olympic games, and so on. What is common to them all?—Don't say: "There must be something common or they would not be called 'games' "—but look and see whether there is anything common to all. For if you look at them you will not see something that is common to all, but similarities, relationships, and a whole series of them at that. To repeat: don't think, but look!— Look for example at board-games, with their multifarious relationships. Now pass to card-games; here you find many correspondences with the first group, but many common features drop out, and others appear. When we pass next to ball games, much that is common is retained, but much is lost.—Are they all 'amusing'? Compare chess with noughts and crosses. Or is there always winning and losing, or competition between players? Think of patience [a form of solitaire]. In ball games there is winning and losing; but when a child throws his ball at the wall and catches it again, this feature has disappeared. Look at the parts played by skill and luck; and at the difference between skill in chess and skill in tennis. Think now of games like ring-a-ring-a-roses; here is the element of amusement, but how many other characteristic features have disappeared! And we can go through the many, many other

---

[164]Ryle called such references to "beauty" "quasi-Platonic statements" since they implied a kind of Platonic realism [*vid.* footnote 102].

groups of games in the same way; can see how similarities crop up and disappear.
[**PI** §§65–66]

This tendency of ours to look for essential definitions of words rather than looking at lots of cases of their use, is not only misleading when we consider games, it is a prejudice that underlies much philosophical analysis:

> The idea that in order to get clear about the meaning of a general term one had to find the common element in all its applications has shackled philosophical inves- tigation; for it has not only led to no result, but also made the philosopher dismiss as irrelevant the concrete cases, which alone could have helped him to understand the usage of the general term. When Socrates asks the question, "what is knowl- edge?" he does not even regard it as a preliminary answer to enumerate cases of knowledge.[165] [**BB** pp. 19–20]

Wittgenstein only rarely made such sweeping statements, so its impact is doubly impor- tant. It underscores the breadth and seriousness with which he considered this problem. Wittgenstein continues with a second reason for this "craving for generality":

> ... There is a tendency rooted in our usual forms of expression, to think that the man who has learnt to understand a general term, say, the term "leaf," has thereby come to possess a kind of general picture of a leaf, as opposed to pictures of particular leaves ... This again is connected with the idea that the meaning of a word is an image, or a thing correlated to the word. (This roughly means, we are looking at words as though they all were proper names, and we then confuse the bearer of a name with the meaning of the name.) [**BB** pp. 17–18]

In this view, a universal is like a "general picture." It is most like Locke's theory of ideas, namely, that general ideas are formed by considering particular ideas in a general way. One might arrive at this general picture by looking at lots of individual leaves until we somehow form a general picture of what the leaves have in common. This is similar to an early view that Wittgenstein held: the picture theory of meaning.[166] This view of meaning is flawed in one major way, specifically, a picture cannot be the "meaning" of a word because

---

[165] **BB** pp. 19–20. Wittgenstein is referring to Plato's dialogue "Theaetetus," 146D–147C.

[166] Malcolm has stated that Wittgenstein's early philosophy, as presented in the **Tractatus Logico-Philosophicus**, has some striking resemblances to Locke's:

> If I am giving a correct interpretation of the **Tractatus**, it reveals that the conceptions of the **Tractatus** belong to a traditional framework of philosophical ideas about the relation of thinking to language. John Locke, for example, declared that a man's thoughts "are all within his own breast, invisible and hidden from others, nor can of themselves be made to appear." In order for there to be a communication of thoughts "it was necessary that man should find out some external sensible signs, whereof those invisible ideas, which his thoughts are made up, might be made known to others." This is substantially the same as Wittgestein's idea that thoughts, composed of "psychical constituents," have an existence apart from physical signs, but can be given an expression in physical signs, by which the thoughts are made perceptible to the senses. The notion is that thoughts are independent of spoken or written language. [N. Malcolm. **Nothing is Hidden: Wittgenstein's Criticism of his Early Thought**, p. 71. Basil Blackwell, 1986. Malcolm quotes Locke's **An Essay Concerning Human Understanding**, vol. 2, book III, chapter 2, section 1. Clarendon Press, Oxford, 1894. Edited by A.C. Fraser.]

a picture or image can have more than one interpretation. We have already presented Wittgenstein's rejection of the picture-theory of meaning so we will not reiterate it here (see the section "Wittgenstein at Work: **Philosophical Investigations**," *supra,* especially quotation **PI** §22).

Wittgenstein continues his attack on "generality":

> ...Again, the idea we have of what happens when we get hold of the general idea "leaf," "plant," etc. etc., is connected with the confusion between a mental state, meaning a state of a hypothetical mental mechanism, and a mental state meaning a state of consciousness (toothache, etc.)

> ...Our craving for generality has another main source: our preoccupation with the method of science. I mean the method of reducing the explanation of natural phenomena to the smallest possible of primitive natural laws; and, in mathematics, of unifying the treatment of different topics by using a generalization ...This tendency is the real source of metaphysics, and lead the philosopher into complete darkness. I want to say here that it can never be our job to reduce anything to anything, or to explain anything. Philosophy really is "purely descriptive." (Think of such questions as "Are there sense data?" and ask: What method is there of determining this? Introspection?)

> Instead of "craving for generality" I could also have said "the contemptuous attitude toward the particular case." [**BB** p. 18]

## Wittgenstein's Categories: Family Resemblances

In his discussion of *games,* Wittgenstein introduces another important concept: "family resemblances."

> ...the result of this examination [to find what games have in common] is: we see a complicated network of similarities overlapping and criss-crossing: sometimes overall similarities, sometimes similarities of detail.

> I can think of no better expression to characterize these similarities than "family resemblances"; for the various resemblances between members of a family: build, features, color of eyes, gait, temperment, etc. etc. overlap and criss-cross in the same way.—And I shall say: "games" form a family. [**PI** §§66–67]

The need to classify or categorize things is essential for language, but finding a basis for categorization that accommodates the subtleties of Wittgenstein's philosophy of language is difficult. The dominant view of categorization, especially in the biological sciences, during Wittgenstein's time was fundamentally Aristotelian—that items in the same categories had specifiable properties in common. Dogs were dogs because they had properties that all dogs had, and these properties, for the most part, were different than those of other mammals. This method of analysis has a long tradition, as we have shown. Nevertheless, there must be good modern reasons to hold this view. Baker and Hacker, in their writings on Wittgenstein, show that this model of analysis gains its currency by mimicking successful methods of scientific analysis, here, chemical analysis:

(i) Chemical analysis comes to an end in atoms or elements that cannot be further decomposed (at least chemically). It is natural to think that the analysis of concepts must similarly terminate in simple ideas, in what is unanalysable and hence indefinable, that is, the atoms or elements of thought and language ...

(ii) Given a familiar object, we know that it must be compounded out of the familiar chemical elements; or at least this is an accepted working assumption. The parallel idea is familiar, for example, in British empiricism. We are thought typically to have the full range of simple ideas, and we know in advance of carrying out an analysis of any given idea that it must be compounded somehow out of these basic building blocks. Any failure to analyze our idea into its simple constituents must be ascribed to limitations of our abilities.

(iii) Chemical analysis yields the elements out of which any substance or stuff (e.g., water) is compounded, but equally those out of which any particular object (e.g., a metal bar) is compounded. It seems to be simultaneously an analysis of individual things and of kinds of stuff (conflated with kinds of things). The analysis of concepts is often conceived to be parallel. It reveals both the constituents of concepts or ideas and the ingredients of particulars or individuals; the property of rigidity is both a logical part of the concept of a beam and the ingredient of any object that is a beam.[167]

In his earlier work, **The Tractatus Logico Philosophicus**, Wittgenstein held that such a reductive method was the proper means of philosophical analysis. But by the time that he was writing **Philosophical Investigations**, he was skeptical of this method. He begins his criticism by attacking the reduction itself:

> When I say: "My broom is in the corner,"—is this really a statement about the broomstick and the brush? Well, it could at any rate be replaced by a statement giving the position of the stick and the position of the brush. And this statement is surely a further analyzed form of the first one.—But why do I call it "further analyzed?"—Well, if the broom is there, that surely means that the stick and brush must be there, and in a particular relation to one another; and this was as it were hidden in the sense of the first sentence, and is expressed in the analyzed sentence. Then does someone who says that the broom is in the corner really mean: the broomstick is there, and so is the brush?—If we were to ask anyone if he meant this he would probably say that he had not thought specially of the broomstick or specially of the brush at all. And that would be the right answer, for he meant to speak neither of the stick nor of the brush in particular. Suppose that, instead of saying "Bring me the broom," you said "Bring me the broomstick and the brush which is fitted on to it.!"—Isn't the answer: "Do you want the broom? Why do you ask so oddly?"—is he going to understand the further analyzed sentence better?" [**PI** §60]

Wittgenstein's first argument is to appeal to our own experience—the activities in which we might *use* a broom. Here, no further breakdown of a "broom" can be made if we still want to keep our day-to-day understanding of what a "broom" is. The reason that we don't

---

[167]Baker and Hacker. **Wittgenstein: Meaning and Understanding. Essays on the Philosophical Investigations**, v. I, p. 186. University of Chicago Press, Chicago, 1980.

break a broom down into the components "broomstick" and "the brush which is fitted on to it" is that it just doesn't make sense to do this; that is, we can't use the distinction in every day life, and even if we were to use it, it would cause more confusion than it resolved. We can see this if you look at how a broom is used (and, of course, this parallels the use of the word "broom." It would be used in the same circumstances.). We talk about "brooms" when we are talking about *sweeping* or *cleaning*. Within *this context* it makes no sense to speak of a "broomstick and the brush which is fitted on to it." If you said, "Bring me the broom" and I replied, "Do you want the broomstick with the brush fitted onto it?" you would not think of my question as being *wrong*, but as being *odd*, or *inappropriate*. If a statement can be construed as correct or incorrect, then we can assume that it is relevant to the discussion at hand. The problem here in the broom analogy is that my reference to the "broomstick with the brush fitted onto it" is neither correct nor incorrect, it is simply inappropriate, or, more to the point, without a clear *use*. Our desire to break down the broom into its constituent parts has caused us to take the broom out of context:

> When philosophers use a word—"knowledge," "being," "object," "I," "proposition," "name"—and try to grasp the *essence* of the thing, one must always ask oneself: is the word ever actually used in this way in the language-game which is its original home?—
>
> What *we* do is to bring words back from their metaphysical to their everyday use.
> [**PI** §116]

If we are talking about the *language game* in which we can refer to "brooms," *there is no grammatical place* for speaking about a "broomstick and the brush which is fitted on to it." Following Wittgenstein's methods, we might redirect our analysis by asking how we might use the words "broomstick and the brush which is fitted on to it." Clearly, we cannot use it in an ordinary context, such as we have described above. Could we use this phrase at all? Probably. We can imagine someone working in a broom-making factory saying, "Did you fit the right brush on the stick?" This might make sense in this context, but there is no ordinary usage of the word "broom" that can be replaced with the "broomstick and the brush which is fitted on to it," hence, the word "broom" cannot be "further analyzed" as in Wittgenstein's example, above.

Philosophy has frequently worked under the assumption that ordinary language is not robust enough to discuss the deep conceptual problems that are the object of philosophical analysis. What is needed, it is claimed, is to make language more rigorous by defining the words used in the analysis more carefully. Wittgenstein disagrees. In fact, he makes the point that our reluctance to use ordinary language in philosophical analysis is the source of many of our philosophical puzzles.

> When I talk about language (words, sentences, etc.) I must speak the language of every day. Is this language somehow too coarse and material for what we want to say? *Then how is another one to be constructed?*—And how strange that we should be able to do anything at all with the one we have![168] [**PI** §120]

---

[168] In Wittgenstein's time, the major proponents of the view that ordinary language was not sufficiently precise for philosophical analysis were Russell and Whitehead (among other deficiencies ordinary language lacked

Wittgenstein's questions, of course, are rhetorical. Everyday language *is not* too coarse to discuss philosophical problems, nor can we construct another, presumably better, language for this kind of use. One suspects that Wittgenstein would be skeptical of any such artificially constructed language, even if the ones creating it are philosophers:

> It is wrong to say that in philosophy we consider an ideal language as opposed to our ordinary one. For this makes it appear as though we thought we could improve on ordinary language. But ordinary language is all right. Whenever we make up "ideal languages" it is not in order to replace our ordinary language by them; but just to remove some trouble caused in someone's mind by thinking that he has got hold of the exact use of a common word. That is also why our method is not merely to enumerate actual usages of words, but rather deliberately to invent new ones, some of them because of their absurd appearance. [**BB** p. 28]

Making up an "ideal language" should not be a prerequisite for philosophical analysis. Formal logic, or any other ideal language, has only a minor role in clearing up problems one may have in thinking. It is certainly *not* to be used to replace ordinary language. Ordinary language is robust enough to be used in philosophical analysis. There is no "ideal language" to which it aspires:

> On the one hand it is clear that every sentence in our language "is in order as it is." That is to say, we are not *striving after* an ideal, as if our ordinary vague sentences had not yet got a quite unexceptionable sense, and a perfect language awaited construction by us.—On the other hand it seems clear that where there is sense there must be perfect order.—So there must be perfect order even in the vaguest sentence. [**PI** § 98]

Wittgenstein broadens his argument against reduction, now applying it to everyday objects:

> But what are the simple constituent parts of which reality is composed?—What are the simple constituent parts of a chair?—The bits of wood of which it is made? Or the molecules, or the atoms?—"Simple" means: not composite. And here the point is: in what sense "composite?" It makes no sense at all to speak absolutely of the "simple parts of a chair."

> Again: Does my visual image of this tree, of this chair, consist of parts? And what are its simple component parts? Multi-colouredness is one kind of complexity; another is, for example, that of a broken outline composed of straight bits. And a curve can be said to be composed of an ascending and a descending segment.

> If I tell someone without any further explanation: "What I see before me now is composite," he will have the right to ask: "What do you mean by 'composite'? For there are all sorts of things that that can mean!"—The question "Is what you see

the necessary "definite sense"—its propositions were not always definitely true or false) . In their **Principia Mathematica** they state that "Ordinary language yields no such help [in philosophical analysis]." Wittgenstein did not wait until the **Philosophical Investigations** to disagree with this:

> ...all the propositions of our everyday language, just as they stand, are in perfect logical order. [**TLP** §5.5563]

composite?" makes good sense if it is already established what kind of complexity—
that is, which particular use of the word—is in question. [**PI** §47]

If language use is largely concerned with discussing everyday affairs, and these everyday
affairs often deal with common observable objects, these objects are not "composite" or
"simple" in any absolute sense. They can be seen variously as "simple" or "composite,"—
and not "simple" or "composite" in one or two ways, but in many ways. Their "simpleness"
or "compositeness" is dependent on what we are using them for, or in what circumstances
we talk about them. If we are talking about things that we sit on, then clearly a "chair" cannot
be logically broken down into smaller parts. You wouldn't say, "Get me the seat with the legs
and back attached to it" when you wanted a chair. When you are looking for something to
sit on, you don't look for parts of a chair, except in very unusual circumstances (one might
imagine needing a chair of some sort in an urgent situation and making do with a couple
of boxes stacked together if that was all you have. But this is a rare situation.). Playing the
devil's advocate, Wittgenstein tries to resurrect the dying sense of absolute compositeness:

> But isn't a chessboard, for instance, obviously, and absolutely, composite?—You
> are probably thinking of the composition out of thirty-two white and thirty-two
> black squares. But could we not also say, for instance, that it was composed of the
> colours black and white and the schema of squares? And if there are quite different
> ways of looking at it, so you still want to say that the chessboard is absolutely
> "composite?"—Asking "Is this object composite?" outside a particular language-
> game is like what a boy once did, who had to say whether the verbs in certain
> sentences were in the active or passive voice, and who racked his brains over the
> question whether the verb "to sleep" meant something active or passive. [**PI** §47]

Here Wittgenstein shows us where the distinction between the "simpleness" or "compositeness" of a chessboard shows up. It shows up in the *language games* that refer to
chessboards. Here we might take, for example, the request, "Get your chessboard out, I
want to play a game." In this instance, the chessboard is simple, no further breakdown of
the "parts" of a chessboard would make any sense in this *language game* (remember that
Wittgenstein's definition of *language game* included not just the words one might use, but
the circumstances in which they are uttered). But we also can imagine two people talking
about making a chess board. Here it would be quite reasonable for one to ask, "What
kind of wood did you use for the white squares?," or, "How did you cut the squares so
well, they fit perfectly?" Clearly, this example treats the chessboard as composed of small
squares of different colored wood. And we can make up other examples to show variations
on these uses. This points to an important aspect of Wittgenstein's method of analysis.
That is, the way that we decide whether an object is "simple" or "composite" is *not* an
empirical investigation of the object—*but a grammatical investigation of the language
that discusses it* (taking "grammar" in Wittgenstein's sense of "depth grammar" which
includes the activities in which the words or phrases are typically used). An empirical
investigation may lead us astray because we will be trying to determine whether the object
in question is "simple" or "complex" in some kind of absolute way—that is, in some way
that can be verified empirically and is independent of its description in language. This is an
important point, and bears further elaboration. For Wittgenstein, if we want to determine
whether something is "simple" or "composite" we don't conduct an empirical investigation, we try to formulate different sentences that emphasize the object's "simpleness" or

"compositeness" and see if they sound all right. The grammar of a *language game* mirrors the one way, out of many possible ways, that we structure our view of the world for the situations in which that *language game* is appropriate. For example, is a "tree" simple or composite? Well, if trees are "composite" then sentences like, "Did you see the parts of the tree?" would make sense. Since this sentence would strike most people as odd, we might find it hard to accept that trees are composite. But there could be circumstances where such a statement might be understandable. For example, I might say, "John told me that he cut down the tree already. Did you see any parts of the tree lying around?" This is probably a marginally acceptable statement, the question might be better phrased, "Did you see any logs or cut wood lying around?" But it is clear that, on average, trees are not composite—and this is *not* an empirical statement, but a *grammatical* one. That is, we can look at any number of trees and not be able to tell, in any kind of final way, whether they are "simple" or "composite"—they could be either. But if we construct some hypothetical sentences that treat trees as, on the one hand, "simple," and on the other, "composite," we can often immediately see which sentences look all right, and which do not. For example, we might consider the appropriateness of the following sentences:

> "Did you plant the tree?"
> "What kind of tree is that?"
> "How many kinds of oak tree are there?"
> "Cut the tree up and put the logs in the firewood bin."
> "The gardener trimmed the tree by cutting off the lower branches."
> "The leaves of the walnut tree are a brilliant yellow in the Fall."
> "The roots of the tree were breaking the sidewalk."

Here we can see that when we refer to trees we usually talk about them with the word "tree" or "trees," and do not refer to "parts" of the tree. When we want to refer to a part of the tree rather than the whole, we do not call them "parts," but "logs," "branches," "leaves" or "roots" (although the statement "What part of the tree was damaged in the storm?" would be acceptable). But if "logs," "branches," "leaves," and "roots" are composite parts of the tree, in the same way that "transmissions," "fuel injectors," and "differentials" are composite parts of a car's engine, then we should be able to say:

> "All trees are composed of logs, branches, leaves and roots."

This sentence is marginally acceptable (and may be made more acceptable by replacing "logs" with "a trunk") even though bamboo trees have no branches, deciduous trees have no leaves in winter, and dead trees, which are still trees, have no leaves at any time. But the above sentence is not the usual way that we refer to trees, and is certainly not the kind of "compositeness" that we have with automobiles. Such a sentence, as Wittgenstein remarked, gives us a "mental cramp." We can see the difference by comparing other statements about cars and trees:

> "I took the engine apart and put it back together"
> "I took the tree apart and put it back together"

The first statement is OK, but not the second, so the compositeness of cars is very different from the compositeness of trees, if we can even say that trees are composite in any way.

When we refer to parts of a tree certain parts are appropriate to specific situations—that is, specific *language games*—and not to others. For example, if we are talking about cutting a tree up into firewood we might refer to "cut logs" or "kindling," but not to "branches" or "roots." If we refer to "branches" or "roots" we refer to them in the context of gardening, not making firewood. So our answer, if we were to construct more examples is that, in general, trees are not treated *grammatically* as being "composite" in the same way that a car can be seen as composite, but there are special circumstances where it makes sense to talk about the parts of a tree using such specific terms as "branches," "logs," "leaves," and "roots." Wittgenstein comments:

> We use the word "composite" (and therefore the word "simple") in an enormous number of different and differently related ways. (Is the color of a square on a chessboard simple, or does it consist of pure white and pure yellow? And is white simple, or does it consist of the colours of the rainbow?—Is this length of 2 cm. simple, or does it consist of two parts, each 1 cm. long? But why not of one bit 3 cm. long, and one bit 1 cm. long measured in the opposite direction?) To the philosophical question: "Is the visual image of this tree composite, and what are its component parts?" the correct answer is: "That depends on what you understand by 'composite'." (And that is of course not an answer but a rejection of the question.)[169]
> [**PI** §47]

Getting back to the discussion of "games," we can see that a definition of "games" that tries to establish a set of necessary and sufficient properties that all games have is doomed to failure. No game has all the properties of other games, nor is there a necessary and sufficient set of properties that could determine whether something is a game or not. Further, there is no single property that exists in all games. In fact, the only thing that games have in common is that *they are all games.*[170] This sounds facetious, but it is not. It resists any reductive analysis of the category "games." Games are simply games, they are non-reducible concepts in the *language games* that refer to them. This does not mean we cannot identify some features of games, but such features are heuristic not definitional. The difference between heuristic and definitional is that the heuristic use of features utilizes them primarily in training those who don't understand the concept of "games" or those who must distinguish games from other things for some purpose. Once they understand what games are (i.e., they can use the word "games" correctly) they often dispense with the identification of games by features and see games simply *as games*. Many individuals who know what games are, would not be able to give a definition of "games." The definition of "games" is simply not a necessary prerequisite to understanding what "games" are.[171]

---

[169] This is a common technique of Wittgenstein's method of analysis, to show how something that we think is simple is really complex.

[170] This point will be elaborated below.

[171] One alternative to reductive definitions that was not known in Wittgenstein's time is the idea of "emergence." Instead of saying that games are defined by certain characteristics, we can say that our concept of games *emerges* from certain kinds of activities and circumstances. Philosopher Paul Humphries states that emergent phenomena must satisfy two criteria: (1) The emergent phenomenon must be qualitatively different from what it emerged from, and must exhibit novel features. (2) The emergent phenomenon must be autonomous from lower level phenomena (emergent phenomena are subject to different rules than the lower level phenomena from which they emerge). "Two Models of Emergence." Presentation given at the University of Michigan, 7 March 2003. A case could probably be made that "games" do satisfy these two criteria.

If "games" were a composite notion then we should be able to have clear answers to the following questions:

> "Of what parts is baseball composed?"
> "Of what parts is hockey composed?"
> "Of what parts is canasta composed?"
>         etc.

One can come up with valid sentences such as:

> "Baseball consists of 9 innings"
> "Hockey consists of 3 periods."

These *look* like statements that satisfy the notion that at least some games are composite. But these examples are misleading. Certainly games that occur over time can be said to be "composed of" a number of discreet time intervals, but this does not mean that games are essentially composite in the same way that, from a manufacturing point of view, cars are composed of discrete parts. If games were composed of time intervals in the same way that cars are composed of machined parts, then the parts of the game could exist independently of the games. For example, it makes sense to say that differentials exist independently of any car, but it does not make sense to say that "innings" exist independently of any baseball game: such a statement sounds like a Zen Koan. Of the two sentences below, the first is grammatically correct, but the second is not:

> "John took the transmission out of the car and put it over there."
> "John took the third inning out of the ball game and. . . "

So, one *grammatical* criterion of the way we talk about parts that truly compose a more complex object is that in normal circumstances we can speak of them as existing independently of the complex object. Further, if we could say that some games are truly composed of time intervals, then we could also say that people are composed of time intervals since they exist over a succession of years. In fact, it would be hard to find anything that did not exist over specific periods of time. So, being composed of time intervals is a property of virtually everything we know. As a result, the composition of entities existing over time offers no information that distinguishes games from anything else. Existence over time is a property of everything, hence it is a *defining property* of nothing (by *defining property* I mean a property that distinguishes something from other related entities).

But if there is no set of properties that all games have, how do we identify games? Wittgenstein says that this is really not a major problem if we think about it. We identify games by having someone show us examples of games, or by playing in games ourselves. In fact, if we are a typical individual who lives in modern society, we will have no difficulty identifying games even though no one has explicitly defined them for us. The only problem that occurs is when we try to define all games as having some specific set of properties in common.

> The idea that in order to get clear about the meaning of a general term one had to find
> the common element in all its applications has shackled philosophical investigation;

for it has not only led to no result, but also made the philosopher dismiss as irrelevant the concrete cases, which alone could have helped him to understand the usage of the general term. [**BB** pp. 19–20]

Certainly, there may be grey areas where an activity may or may not be a game. But this does not concern Wittgenstein either:

> Many words ... then don't have a strict meaning. But this is not a defect. To think it is would be like saying that the light of my reading lamp is no real light at all because it has no sharp boundary. [**BB** p. 27]

and,

> Is it always an advantage to replace an indistinct picture by a sharp one? Isn't the indistinct one often exactly what we need? [**PI** §71]

This is not, of course, an argument for sloppy definitions. It is merely the observation that looking for definitions in this case gets us away from the true foundation of our ability to analyze and classify things like "games." By trying to find a common set of properties that we can use to determine set membership, we are guilty of trying to make an "indistinct picture into a sharp one." This is an interesting analogy, not just because it argues against the forcing of precision on to an imprecise process, but for something more subtle. If we take an indistinct picture and turn it into a sharp one there are *any number* of "sharp" images that we can construct from the indistinct one. Further, there are no criteria to tell us which, of the many sharp pictures we can construct, is the one that is most faithful to our original image. Think of a blurry photograph of a person you do not know. If it is digital, we can certainly make it sharper with computer programs like Photoshop, but will it be a better likeness of the actual person who was photographed?—won't the sharper picture introduce a misleading precision into the image? The computerization of intelligent activity, such as the modeling of expert judgement in an expert system, is sometimes guilty of this. They take the vague or "blurry" rules of expert decision-making and make them more precise, that is "sharper," because computers work best with precise commands. For computer programs, just as for formal logic, precision is not a *result* of the process, but a *requirement* for it. As Wittgenstein comments:

> The more narrowly we examine language, the sharper becomes the conflict between it and our requirement. (For the crystalline purity of logic was, of course, not a *result of investigation*; it was a requirement.) The conflict becomes intolerable; the requirement is now in danger of becoming empty.—We have got onto slippery ice where there is no friction and so in a certain sense the conditions are ideal, but also, just because of that, we are unable to walk. We want to walk; so we need *friction*. Back to the rough ground! [**PI** §107]

But what happens when we codify expert behavior in precise rules? What often happens is that we cease to have expert judgments any more. We turn an expert decision process into a novice decision process.[172]

---

[172] H. Dreyfus and S. Dreyfus pointed out that only novices use precise rules, experts do not. [**Mind over Machine: The Power of Human Intuitive Expertise in the Era of the Computer**. Free Press, 1986]

We do not think of a set of properties when we think of games. We think of *examples* of games, examples that form a *family* of similar activities. What helps us the most in understanding which of our activities are games and which are not is our *involvement* in activities that we come to describe as "games." This gets us back to Wittgenstein's insistence that when we want to understand some general term, such as "games," we should not ask for a general definition or essence that holds for all games—this will lead us away from what we want. Definitions may also give us a false sense of analytical rigor. We need to ask how we would *use* such a term like "games," and this entails some description or demonstration of what games are. John Wisdom, a student of Wittgenstein's, and later a philosopher himself, understood this well when he talked about Wittgenstein's technique:

> . . . the substitution of 'Ask for the use' for 'Ask for the meaning' is linked with the procedure of explaining meaning by presenting not a definition but cases, and not with one case but cases and cases.[173]

Wittgenstein applies the same methods to his analysis of *language games* as he does to "games" alone. That is, when we start tabulating what we perceive to be *language games*, we find that there is not a single common set of properties that define them. Instead, there is a prodigious diversity of them:

> But how many kinds of sentences are there? Say assertion, question, and command?—There are countless kinds; countless different kinds of use of what we call "symbols" "words," "sentences." And this multiplicity is not something fixed, given once for all; but new types of language, new language-games, as we may say, come into existence, and others become obsolete and get forgotten. (We can get a *rough picture* of this from the changes in mathematics.)

> Here the term "language-*game*" is meant to bring into prominence the fact that the *speaking* of language is part of an activity, or of a form of life.[174] [**PI** §23]

Does Wittgenstein's resistance to philosophical reduction mean that it can never be used to analyze something? No, it does not. There are lots of *language games* where it is appropriate to talk about entities that are composed of smaller, simpler objects. When we talk about a manufacturing process, such as making a car, it is clearly part of the *grammatical structure* of this *language game* that cars are composed of many precisely identifiable components. But if we are talking about driving a car, such as when we ask a friend to give us a ride, the components that are part of the manufacturing process become irrelevant. Here we engage in a different *language game,* a *language game* where passenger capacity, power steering, air conditioning, and automatic transmissions may be important components of the car. Even within the automobile manufacturing *language game* the parts breakdown is not as obvious as might first appear. Cars have welds, glue, anti-freeze, brake fluid, gasoline, and oil, but from the point of view of manufacturing

---

[173] J. Wisdom. **Paradox and Discovery**, pp. 88–89. University of California Press, Berkeley, 1970.
[174] J. Searle [**Speech Acts: An Essay in the Philosophy of Language.** Cambridge University Press, 1969] attempted to show that this kind of diversity does not exist in language (this was discussed in more detail in footnotes 29, and 134) and that there are only a few distinct types of language games or speech acts (he specifically objected to this quotation from **PI**).

these are not considered components of a car; that is, while the gas tank is a component, the gas in the tank is not.

Since there are language games where some reduction is acceptable when we want to know what a word "means," the natural question becomes, "Where do we stop our reductive analysis?" Wittgenstein's answer to this is to focus our attention back on the activities or situations where the word in question is used. If we are talking about how a car is manufactured, then it makes sense to break the car down into the components of the car— carburetor, differential, transmission, etc. We may even break these components down into individual parts such as nuts, bolts, washers, etc. But this is where we stop. We don't break the individual car parts down into their chemical components. Such a level of analysis would not make sense if we were discussing how cars are put together; it might make sense, though, if we are talking about how foundries prepare the metal for casting the different components of a car, using different alloys for different components. If, on the other hand, we are concerned with renting a car, we would probably not care whether the car has a carburetor or fuel injection. We would be more concerned with how much the rental cost is, what the fuel efficiency is, and whether the car had enough room to seat several passengers comfortably. These different uses of the word "car" form a "family" of related usages. They resemble each other in the same way that members of a family may resemble each other. But even *family resemblance* is not a single notion: think of how two brothers resemble each other, and how this might be different from how a brother and a sister resemble each other, or, how family members from different generations resemble each other. *Family resemblance* is not always just a question of physiognomy, either. Two individuals who look strikingly similar but are not related would not be said to have a *family resemblance*. But, even here, we can extend the usage of *family resemblance* beyond blood relatives by saying something like, "If those two young men were related, I would say that they had a remarkably strong *family resemblance*." This, perhaps, gets more closely to what Wittgenstein meant by *family resemblances, viz.,* the resembling entities don't necessarily *come* from a family—though this is the paradigm case—they *form* a family of resembling entities.

It is important to note that the resemblance between different family members is of a different sort than the resemblance between cars, or between paintings. What enables us to see these various kinds of resemblance is that there is a *grammatical place* for such resemblance in the *language games* where they occur. For example, seeing a resemblance in the physical characteristics of a car may be useful in purchasing a car ("I want a car that looks sporty"); or, seeing the resemblance between paintings may help us to see the relationships between different schools of painting ("Notice how the striking colors and severe brushstrokes of the Fauvist painters seem to be a reaction to the delicacy and subtlety of Impressionism."). The notion of *family resemblance* can be applied variously in sundry *language games* and situations. If this is the case, then the question arises, "Has Wittgenstein substituted an uncontrolled relativity for the rigor of reduction?" Surely he must still explain how we can avoid complete subjectivity in the application of linguistic categories. How can we use words correctly that have such a wide variety of applications? Wittgenstein gives us no direct explanation there. He asks us, simply, to look at our everyday use of words. If the application of words is strongly subjective, in the way, for example, that our personal appreciation of art often is, then we should be in a constant state of linguistic confusion and misunderstanding, but we are not. Further, if estimations of *family resemblance* are as subjective or varied as aesthetic judgments then we should be able to substitute references to *family resemblances* for references to aesthetic judgments in grammatically correct sentences:

> "Only an expert can judge whether art is from the same artist or school (i.e., that two works resemble each other in a way that indicates they are by the same artist or from the same school)"
> "Only an expert can judge whether two individuals look like they come from the same family."

Here, the first sentence sounds all right, but the second does not. Clearly, the judgment of *family resemblance* is not of the same *genre* as aesthetic judgments. It is a skill that is not reserved exclusively for experts, but available to and practiced by us all. Wittgenstein is not concerned with how often we might be mistaken or misunderstood, he asks us to focus on our correct usage of language in these kinds of situations. What is truly remarkable, for Wittgenstein, is not how many times we are misunderstood, but how often we are understood perfectly well. We can somehow take ordinary words, such as "car" or "tree" or "friend" and, although we can use them in a wide variety of contexts and situations and they appear to have many related "meanings," we somehow seem to use them and are understood most of the time. This is what is truly remarkable about our use of language. How can we account for the fact that we can say something very precise with such seemingly ambiguous words? The answer, according to Wittgenstein, is right before our eyes. What accounts for our precise use of language is not some latent or unconscious understanding of the essential definitions of words, or some kind of access to "deep language structures," but our participation in common activities or practices:

> Suppose you came as an explorer into an unknown country with a language quite strange to you. In what circumstances would you say that the people there gave orders, understood them, obeyed them, rebelled against them, and so on?

> The common behavior of mankind is the system of reference by means of which we interpret an unknown language.[175] [**PI** §206]

What we have in common with others is not so much our language, but our common participation and involvement in the intensely human activities of mankind. When we use words in a particular way that conveys our meaning unambiguously we understand this usage, not because the words have some common, essential meaning to them, but because we share the activities or practices in which the word is used. These common activities and practices are what Wittgenstein referred to as the "forms of life":

> ... to imagine a language means to imagine a form of life. [**PI** §19]

or,

---

[175] Wittgenstein gives a more detailed discussion of a similar example on pages 101ff of **BB** (as noted before, much of the writings in the **BB** were preliminary discussions of ideas that were developed in the later **PI**.).

> What has to be accepted, the given, is—so one could say—*forms of life.*[176] [**PI** p. 226]

We can see how Wittgenstein's assessment of meaning in language has moved from a formal logical model (in **The Tractatus ...**) to a pragmatic/anthropological model (in **Philosophical Investigations**). It seems at first glance that Wittgenstein is trading away the rigor of his earlier logical model for a less rigorous, but more realistic model of meaning, but he is not. The more pragmatic, activity-oriented model of language has a deceptive rigor about it—in Wittgenstein's terms:

> My method is not to sunder the hard from the soft, but to see the hardness of the soft. [**NB** p. 44]

### Wittgenstein's Place in the Nominalist-Realist Debate

Looking back on the nominalist:realist debate we can now see Wittgenstein's place in this controversy. Given a category such as "chairs," Wittgenstein would agree with the realist that there are observable differences between chairs and other common objects such as refrigerators. But the realist concludes from this correct observation that there must be properties that all chairs have *in addition to* the fact that they are chairs. Wittgenstein agrees with the realist's observation, but disagrees with his inference: in short, Wittgenstein claims that what chairs have in common is that *they are chairs*. Chairs, like games, may have some features in common, but they do not need to have a single common feature, nor do they need some subset of features with different chairs having different subsets of the features. For us, chairs are simply chairs; they cannot be reduced to a necessary, defining set of properties—what features they have are heuristic rather than definitional.

The nominalist, on the other hand, makes the correct observation that all observable entities are unique, and infers from this that there is no single way for a group of things to be categorized. Wittgenstein makes a similar claim in another way: there is no limit to the number of ways an entity can be categorized. Consequently, he agrees with the nominalist's inference that there can be no single observable way that entities can be classified. But he does not agree with the nominalist's further inference: that because there are so many ways to classify things, no classification based on observed features is possible—in effect, what chairs have in common is that we call them "chairs." Bambrough observes:

> The nominalist says that games have nothing in common except that they are called games.

> The realist says that games must have something in common, and he means by this that they must have something in common other than that they are games.

---

[176] A slight variant of this quotation appears in **Remarks on the Philosophy of Psychology, v. I:**
What has to be accepted, the given—it might be said—are facts of living [§630] [**Remarks on the Philosophy of Psychology**, v. I. University of Chicago Press, Chicago, 1980. Edited by G.E.M. Anscombe and G.H. von Wright, translated by G.E.M. Anscombe.]. Hereafter referred to as **RPP I.**
In the 50th Anniversary commemorative edition of **Philosophical Investigations**, published in 2001, the quotation is the same but it appears on p. 192 instead of p. 226.

Wittgenstein says that games have nothing in common except that they are games.

Wittgenstein thus denies at one and the same time the nominalist's claim that games have nothing in common except that they are called games and the realist's claim that games have something in common other than that they are games. He asserts at one and the same time the realist's claim that there is an objective justification for the application for the word "game" to games and the nominalist's claim that there is no element that is common to all games.[177]

Bambrough continues:

There is no limit to the number of possible classifications of objects. (The nominalist is right about this.)

There is no classification of any set of objects which is not objectively based on genuine similarities and differences. (The realist is right about this.) The nominalist is so impressed by the infinite diversity of possible classifications that he is blinded to their objectivity.

The realist is so impressed by the objectivity of all genuine classifications that he underestimates their diversity.

Of course we may if we like say that there is one complete system of classification which marks all the similarities and all the differences. (This is the realist's summing up of what we can learn by giving critical attention to the realist and the nominalist in turn.)

[177] R. Bambrough's "Universals and Family Resemblances," **The Problem of Universals**, pp. 266–279. Humanities Press, NJ, 1992. Edited by A.B. Schoedinger [reprinted from the **Proceedings of the Aristotelian Society**, vol. 61, pp. 274–275, 1960–1961]. Bambrough makes clear the importance of Wittgenstein's work:

I believe that Wittgenstein solved what is known as "the problem of universals," and I would say of his solution, as Hume said of Berkeley's treatment of the same topic, that it is "one of the greatest and most valuable discoveries that has been made of late years in the republic of letters."

I do not expect these claims to be accepted by many philosophers. [p. 266]

Bambrough was correct in that at least a few philosophers leveled criticisms against his interpretation of, and optimism about, Wittgenstein's views on universals. Most of these criticisms hinge on philosophical points that are not significant for our present discussion, but the interested reader might find the following critical discussions of Bambrough of interest:

R.I. Aaron. "Wittgenstein's Theory of Universals," **Mind**, vol. 74, pp. 249–251.
N.W. Griffin. "Universals and Family Resemblances," **Canadian Journal of Philosophy**, vol. 3, pp. 635–651, 1986.
J.W. Thorp. "Whether the Theory of Family Resemblances Solves the Problem of Universals," **Mind**, vol. 81, pp. 567–570.
J. Nammour. "Resemblances and Universals," **Mind**, vol. 82, pp. 516–524.

Bambrough is not without his supporters, though. For an attempt to extend Bambrough's interpretation of Wittgenstein's notion of properties to that of relationships see D.J. Packard. "A Note on Wittgenstein and cyclical comparatives," **Analysis**, vol. 36, pp. 37–40.

Or we may say that there are only similarities and differences, from which we may choose according to our purposes and interests. (This is the nominalist's summing up.)

In talking of genuine or objective similarities and differences we must not forget that we are concerned with similarities and differences between *possible* cases as well as between actual cases, and indeed that we are concerned with the actual cases only because they are themselves a selection of the possible cases.[178]

## Forms of Life

Wittgenstein introduces the notion of a *form of life* early in **Philosphical Investigations**. But although *forms of life* are essential components of Wittgenstein's philosophy of language, he only explicitly uses the phrase five times in this work: in addition to the two quotations above (the one at footnote 180 and the preceding quotation), the three other references that Wittgenstein makes to *forms of life* in **PI** are:

But how many kinds of sentences are there? Say asseration, question, and command?—There are countless kinds; countless different kinds of use of what we call "symbols" "words," "sentences." And this multiplicity is not something fixed, given once for all; but new types of language, new language-games, as we may say, come into existence, and others become obsolete and get forgotten. (We can get a rough picture of this from the changes in mathematics.)

Here the term "language-game" is meant to bring into prominence the fact that the speaking of language is part of an activity, or of a **form of life**. [**PI** §23]

"So you are saying that human agreement decides what is true and what is false?"— It is what human beings say that is true and false; and they agree in the language they use. That is not agreement in opinions but in **form of life**. [**PI** §241]

One can imagine an animal angry, frightened, unhappy, happy, startled. But hopeful? And why not?

A dog believes his master is at the door. But can he also believe his master will come the day after to-morrow?—And what can he not do here?—How do I do it?—How am I supposed to answer this?

Can only those hope who can talk? Only those who have mastered the use of a language. That is to say, the phenomena of hope are modes of this complicated **form of life**. [**PI** p. 174]

The mere counting of references does not indicate the importance of this notion for Wittgenstein, and these five quotations have enough variety that they are probably not sufficient to get precisely what he is talking about. But although he only uses the words "form(s) of life" five times in **Philosophical Investigations**, the concept that is behind

[178] *Op.cit.*, pp. 277–278.

them runs like an undercurrent through much of his work, and is closely linked, I think, to a "family" of related concepts:

| | |
|---|---|
| "background" | [*Hintergrund*] |
| "background within human life" | [*Hintergrund im menschlichen Leben*] |
| "bustle of life" | [*Getriebe des Lebens*] |
| "human behavior" | [*Menschliche Handlungsweise*] |
| "circumstances" | [*Umständen*] |
| "common behavior of mankind" | [*Gemeinsame menschliche Handlungsweise*] |
| "natural history" | [*Naturgeschichte*] |
| "pattern of life" | [*Lebensmuster*] |
| "weave of life" | [*Lebensteppich*] |
| "stream of life" | [*Fluss des Lebens*] |
| "occasions" | [*Anlässen*] |
| "activities" | [*Tätigkeiten*] |
| "swirl of human actions" | [*Gewimmel der menschlichen Handlungen*] |
| "This is simply what I do" | [*So handle ich eben*] |

In order to understand the concept of *forms of life* (or the family of concepts relating to it), we can look at the specific references for the above related concepts:

"background within human life," "bustle of life," "hurly-burly":

We judge an action according to its **background within human life**, and this background is not monochrome, but we might picture it as a very **complicated filigree pattern**, which, to be sure, we can't copy, but which we can recognize from the general impression it makes. [**RPP II** §624]

The **background** is the **bustle of life**. And our concepts points to something within this bustle. [**RPP II** §625]

And it is the very concept "**bustle**" that brings about this indefiniteness. For a **bustle** only comes about through constant repetition. And there is no definite starting point for "constant repetition." [**RPP II** §626]

How could **human behavior** be described? Surely only by showing the action of a variety of humans, as they are all mixed up together. Not what one person is doing now, but the whole **hurly-burly**, is the **background** against which we see an action, and it determines our judgement, our concepts, and our reactions.[179] [**RPP II** §629]

Wittgenstein often refers to "background" as an "inherited background":

---

[179] Boldface type added. §629 is similar to §567 in Z:

How could human behavior be described? Surely only by sketching the actions of a variety of humans, as they are all mixed up together. What determines our judgment, our concepts and reactions, is not what one man is doing now, an individual action, but the whole hurly-burly of human actions, the background against which we see any action.

> But I did not get my picture of the world by satisfying myself of its correctness; nor do I have it because I am satisfied of its correctness. No; it is the **inherited background** against which I distinguish between true and false. [**OC** §94]

What Wittgenstein is trying to get at here is that we assume without question many of the concepts and background by which we distinguish between what is the case and what is not. This background is not inferred or constructed by us after intense observation, we assume it, for the most part, without question during our formative years because it has been accepted by others. And what we assume is not a set of rules or a precise framework. What we learn is to act *as if* much of this background or context is the case. For example, one does not learn that gravity causes a ball to fall to the earth, one learns to play games where this assumption *is the basis for playing the game*—it is not questioned, nor even raised:

> Language—I want to say—is a refinement; "in the begining was the deed."[180]

It also would be strange to question much of this background, and in some cases, it would be impossible to do so. But there are kinds of background that are less fundamental which we can question and choose to assume or not. An example might be the assumption of the context of the military when one enlists in the service. This would take some time to acquire and much of the military context would be at odds with the civilian one—such as the license to kill people during wartime. But, in general, what we can question about our context or background is probably only a small part of the totality that we assume.[181]

> "circumstances," "common behavior of mankind":

> Suppose you came as an explorer into an unknown country with a language quite strange to you. In what **circumstances** would you say that the people there gave orders, understood them, obeyed them, rebelled against them, and so on?

> The **common behaviour** [*sic*] **of mankind** is the system of reference by means of which we interpret an unknown language. [**PI** §206]

---

[180] Page 31, **Culture and Value** [hereafter referred to as **CV**], Blackwell, Oxford, 1980. Translated by P. Winch. This will be discussed in more detail in the section "The Foundation of Language in Instinctive Behavior."

[181] Much of Wittgenstein's discussion in his **On Certainty** is directed at what you can question and what you cannot question about reality. Statements like "I know that this is a hand," when you are referring to your own hand [**OC** §19], appear to be empirical claims, but, according to Wittgenstein, they are really logical, or grammatical, statements. Such statements are not claims about reality for there is no observation that could confirm or deny the existence of your hand in normal circumstances. These statements reveal the grammatical or logical structure of factual assertions. As Monk writes:

> ... if the contrary of a proposition makes sense, then that proposition can be regarded as an empirical hypothesis, its truth or falsity being dependent on the way things stand in the world. But if the contrary of a proposition does not make sense, then the proposition is not descriptive of the world but of our conceptual framework; it is then a part of logic. Thus: "Physical objects exist" is not an empirical proposition, for its contrary is not false but incomprehensible. [**Ludwig Wittgenstein: The Duty of Genius**, p. 563. Free Press, NY, 1990.]

"Circumstances" are not the same thing as *forms of life*, but they are a necessary background for them. That is, *forms of life* can be specifiable activities such as walking, fixing the house, raking the leaves, driving a car, etc. But each of these actions presupposes a set of circumstances which are needed for the activity to make sense. For example, driving a car is a structured activity that many of us have engaged in at one time or another, but to do this requires a specific set of circumstances for us to carry it out—for example, we must have a working car available, there must be a road or some other drivable surface nearby, we must have a key to the car, we must have a valid license if we are to drive on a public road, etc. Wittgenstein calls these circumstances "normal circumstances" or "stage setting." But what are "normal circumstances?" Wittgenstein continues:

> . . . we recognize **normal circumstances** but cannot precisely describe them. At most, we can describe a range of abnormal ones.[182] [**OC** § 27]

The reason that we can't describe "normal circumstances" is that we just don't notice them—and we don't notice them because we *don't need to notice them*. We frequently act as if we assume that they are constantly around us, which they usually are. But why is it so difficult for us to describe them or even to notice them in any detail? Wittgenstein would probably answer that, except in rare circumstances, we just don't have a *language game* for describing "normal circumstances"—there is no *grammatical* place for this kind of description in our language. If we can assume that we usually find ourselves in "normal circumstances," then why would we need to describe them? If we felt a need to describe these circumstances we would probably frequently utter sentences like:

> "In normal circumstances, I will mail the letter at the post office."
> "In normal circumstances, I will drive to the store and buy some milk."

Such sentences would be considered odd in everyday usage because they state the obvious and don't really add any information to the statement. In fact, the only information that they might add is that the speaker needs to speak oddly for some reason or other. The listener's reply might be:

> "Why are you speaking so oddly—are you afraid that 'normal circumstances' will somehow not occur?"

But we do have *language games* for describing "abnormal circumstances"—the description of abnormal circumstances *does* play a role in our lives. We need to describe them from time to time, if only to describe how some event has differed from our normal expectations, for example we might say, "I would have come at 2:00 but the bridge washed out." But even here, there is never a "complete" description of such circumstances. What we describe is what is important for the situation at hand.[183] "natural history":

---

[182] There are, of course, language games and circumstances where an anthropologist might describe "normal circumstances," viz. when describing the "normal circumstances" of a culture different than his own. Even here, though, "normal circumstances" would not be described in detail, but only insofar as they differ from those of the anthropologist's own culture.

[183] There are anthropologists who have tried to describe some of the "normal circumstances" of different countries or cultures. Edward Hall is a well known writer in this regard (**The Silent Language**. Anchor Books/Doubleday, NY, 1959, **The Hidden Dimension**. Anchor Books/Doubleday, NY, 1966, **Beyond Culture**.

...commanding, questioning, recounting, chatting, are as much a part of our **natural history** as walking, eating, drinking, playing. [**PI** §25]

Anchor Books/Doubleday, NY, 1976 and, **Hidden Differences: Doing Business with the Japanese**. Anchor Books/Doubleday, NY, 1987). But even here Hall does not try to describe all the characteristics of "normal circumstances" for any culture, but limits himself to describing the differences between the normal circumstances of two or more cultures. Hall, though, is characteristically modest about what he can say about cultural differences:

> Culture hides much more than it reveals, and strangely enough what it hides, it hides most effectively from its own participants. Years of study have convinced me that the real job is not to understand foreign culture but to understand our own. I am also convinced that all that one ever gets from studying foreign culture is a token understanding. The ultimate reason for such study is to learn more about how one's own system works... Simply learning one's own culture is an achievement of gargantuan proportions for anyone. [**The Silent Language**, p. 30]

Seventeen years later, Hall was still convinced that inter-cultural interaction is a great source of knowledge:

> ...the great gift that the members of the human race have for each other is not exotic experiences but an opportunity to achieve awareness of the structure of their own system, which can be accomplished only by interacting with others who do not share that system—members of the opposite sex, different age groups, different ethnic groups, and different cultures—all suffice. [**Beyond Culture**, p. 44]

Hall says that most individuals have stopped learning by the time they are young adults. For these individuals, the study of foreign culture has an important positive result:

> ...man's tremendous brain has endowed him with a drive and a capacity for learning which appear to be as strong as the drive for food or sex. This means that when a middle-aged man stops learning he is often left with a great drive and highly developed capacities. If he goes to live in another culture, the learning process is often reactivated. [*ibid.*]

This statement may have an interesting relevance to Wittgenstein's work. Specifically, Wittgenstein was one of the few major philosophers who lived most of his adult life in a culture different from the one in which he grew up. Not only were the countries different (Austria vs. England), but they were on opposite sides of two world wars, which only served to heighten the differences between them (Wittgenstein served in the Austrian army in WWI, but lived in England during WWII, volunteering as a hospital orderly for a period of time). Further, Wittgenstein also lived, as an adult, in a different socio-economic group than the one in which he grew up. He came from an extremely wealthy Viennese family with strong ties to the musical and artistic life of Vienna. His father, Karl, was a wealthy industrialist and an avid patron of the arts—composers Brahms, Walter, Mahler and Labor were frequent guests in the "Palais Wittgenstein." Wittgenstein's sister Margarete was the subject of a famous portrait by Gustav Klimt and Ravel wrote a piano piece for Wittgenstein's brother Paul. (Paul had lost an arm in WWI, but still managed a respectable career playing entirely with his remaining hand. Ravel wrote his 1931 "Concerto for the Left Hand" specifically for him.)

Although Wittgenstein remained in England for nearly all of his adult life, he maintained a critical attitude towards British culture: "[A] fundamental difficulty was Wittgenstein's dislike of English culture in general..."[Monk. **Wittgenstein: The Duty of Genius**, p. 568. Free Press, NY, 1990.]. If Hall is correct in his assertion that cultural differences keep man's "learning process" active, Wittgenstein's living in a culture that was not only different from his native one, but also one which he disliked may have kept his intellect more focused and productive later in his life. It may also help to explain his later concern about how our "forms of life," or shared activities— loosely, our "culture"—affect the way we think. Wittgenstein often felt emotionally estranged from others—he was rarely completely comfortable with his friends or even his family. While this may have been the source of much personal pain, it may also have been the means by which he attained the necessary objectivity to see how others are influenced by "what we do"—even when we are doing philosophy.

What we are supplying are really remarks on the **natural history** of human beings; we are not contributing curiosities however, but observations which no one has doubted, but which have escaped remark only because they are always before our eyes. [**PI** §415]

"pattern of life," "weave of life," "stream of life":

If a **pattern of life** is the basis for the use of a word then the word must contain some amount of indefiniteness. The **pattern of life**, after all, is not one of exact regularity. [**LWPP I** §211]

Seeing life as a **weave**, this **pattern** (pretence, say) is not always complete and is varied in a multiplicity of ways. But we, in our conceptual world, keep on seeing the same, recurring with variations. That is how our concepts take it. For concepts are not for use on a single occasion. [**Z** §568]

"Grief" describes a **pattern** which recurs, with different variations in the **weave of our life**. If a man's bodily expression of sorrow and of joy alternated, say with the ticking of a clock, here we should not have the characteristic formation of the pattern of sorrow or of the pattern of joy. [**PI** p. 174]

For words have meaning only in the **stream of life**. [**RPP II** §687]

What goes on within has meaning only in the **stream of life**. [**LWPP II** p. 30]

"occasions," "activities":

... we don't start from certain words, but from certain **occasions** or **activities**.[184]

"swirl of human actions":

Our concepts, judgements, reactions never appear in connection with just a single action, but rather with the whole **swirl of human actions**. [**LWPP II** p. 56]

"simply what I do":

If I have exhausted the justifications I have reached bedrock, and my spade is turned. Then I am inclined to say: "This is **simply what I do**." [**PI** §217]

All of these variants form a "family" of concepts related to *forms of life*. They do not comprise a *definition* of *forms of life*, but, taken together, they give us a better understanding of the kinds of things that Wittgenstein meant. But this indefiniteness about what *forms of life* are is somewhat disconcerting, especially since we find it difficult to give up our need for definitions and explanations. Wittgenstein understands this:

---

[184]**Lectures and Conversations on Aesthetics, Psychology, and Religious Belief**. Edited by Cyril Barrett [University of California Press, Berkeley, 1972, p. 3]. Hereafter referred to as **LC**.

Remember that we sometimes demand definitions for the sake not of their content but of their form. Our requirement is in architectural one; the definition a kind of ornamental coping that supports nothing. [**PI** §217]

Pitkin comments on the lack of a clear definition for *forms of life*:

That notion [forms of life] is never explicitly defined, and we should not try to force more precision from it than its rich suggestiveness will bear. But its general significance is clear enough: human life as we live and observe it is not just a random, continuous flow, but displays recurrent patterns, regularities, characteristic ways of doing and being, of feeling and acting, of speaking and interacting.

Because they are patterns, regularities, configurations, Wittgenstein calls them *forms*; and because they are patterns in the fabric of human existence and activity on each, he calls them forms *of life*. The idea is clearly related to the idea of a language game, and more generally to Wittgenstein's action-oriented view of language. "The *speaking* of language," he says, "is part of an activity, or form of life." How we talk is just part of it, is embedded in, what we do. "Commanding, questioning, recounting, chatting, are as much a part of our natural history as walking, eating, drinking, playing." We all know our shared forms of life, these basic, general human ways of being and doing, though they have never been taught to us and we could not begin to be able to put into words what we know about them. Wittgenstein says that they are part of our "natural history," regularities "which no one has doubted, but which have escaped remark only because they are always before our eyes." ... The notion of forms of life should help us to understand the sense in which language may be said to be conventional.[185]

Even though Wittgenstein spends little time describing or discussing these *forms of life* in any detail, one should not infer that they are unimportant components of his philosophy. In fact, just the opposite is true. As Malcolm points out:

Wittgenstein says that his philosophical observations are "remarks on the natural history of human beings." It would be difficult to exaggerate the significance of that comment. It is often said that Wittgenstein's work belongs to "linguistic philosophy"—that he "talks about words." True enough. But he is trying to get readers to think of how the words are tied up with human life, with patterns of response, in thought and action. His conceptual studies are a kind of anthropology. His descriptions of the human forms of life on which our concepts are based make us aware of the kind of creature we are.[186]

Readers of Wittgenstein's early work such as that in the **Tractatus Logico-Philosophicus** would be struck by the absence of any detailed reference to the *forms of life* and related concepts. Nowhere is this more significant than his remarks on language. In his early work, Wittgenstein believed that expressions in language—primarily propositions or, as

[185] H. Pitkin. **Wittgenstein and Justice**, pp. 132–133. University of California Press, Berkeley, 1972, pp. 132–133]. Pitkin quotes Wittgenstein's **Philosophical Investigations**, §23, §25, and §415, respectively.
[186] N. Malcolm. "Wittgenstein on the Nature of Mind," **Studies in the Theory of Knowledge**, pp. 9–29. Oxford Press, 1970. Edited by N. Rescher. Quotation from p. 22.

he called them, "pictures of facts"—had a "definite sense." This definite sense, or meaning, stayed the same no matter where or when a statement was uttered or occurred. It is significant that Wittgenstein aims some of his earliest criticism in **Philosophical Investigations** at this kind of "essentialism" in language. For early Wittgenstein, language consists largely of propositions, and propositions are like pictures. But we have already discussed how pictures can be interpreted, or seen, variously, so pictures—and by inference propositions—cannot have a "definite sense." Later, Wittgenstein saw that even with words which are simple references to objects the "meaning" of these words is not always clear. Consider the "slab language" again (*supra*). Wittgenstein showed that although the single expression, "Slab!" has the same appearance wherever it occurs, and its reference to a specific object can be clear, its meaning can still vary radically from context to context, or activity to activity. It can also vary according to the *training* of those who understand it. As we pointed out, the single word "Slab!" can mean "Bring the slab here!," "Put the slab over there!," "Break the slab up!," etc. It is easy to imagine additional situations where "Slab!" might mean something entirely different. Malcolm comments:

> A shrug of the shoulders is a familiar gesture that means something different in different situations. It does not have a *fixed* meaning. Neither does a familiar sentence.

> Wittgenstein's repudiation of the assumption that the *sense* of language is independent of the circumstances of life in which the language is used, is perhaps the single most important aspect of his break with what he calls in the preface of the Investigations "my old way of thinking."[187]

The relation between the sense of a statement and the *context* in which it occurs is clearly articulated in Wittgenstein's last work, **On Certainty**:

> The words "I am here" have sense only in certain contexts, and not when I say them to someone who is sitting in front of me and sees me clearly—and not because they are superfluous, but because their meaning is not *determined* by the situation, yet stands in need of such determination. [**OC** §348]

One might assume that the lack of a definition for *forms of life* leaves us unclear about what they are. Not so, according to Wittgenstein. In fact, there really is no "definition" to them. But how do we know what they are? The answer is relatively straightforward: We know them by participating in them; we are actively involved in them on a daily basis. If I say that walking, eating, driving, explaining, questioning, etc. are all *forms of life*, will you have any difficulty understanding what I mean? Not likely. But we don't begin our lives with an understanding of many of these *forms of life* (an infant can certainly eat, but it cannot walk, drive or talk). So how do we learn these activities? We don't learn them by memorizing a set of rules or definitions. We learn them by having them demonstrated to us. We then try to perform them ourselves and have our attempts refined through the coaching of others who are more knowledgeable about them than we are. Here Wittgenstein's concept of a game is important for nonlinguistic activity too. The easiest way to see this is to imagine how you might come to learn some card or athletic game. Some of the teaching might be

[187] N. Malcolm. **Nothing is Hidden**, p. 271. Basil Blackwell, Oxford, 1986.

verbal, and some might not be. There may also be rules that govern our behavior in some of these activities, but the rules do not completely cover all the actions of the activity, in the way that the rules of basketball do not cover every aspect of the game (e.g., there is no description of how a player can shoot the ball other than he cannot kick it). It is important to understand that although there may be a great deal of variability in the conduct of these activities, they are not totally arbitrary. We know that they are not arbitrary because we do have a sense of how they can be done badly or incorrectly—basketball games can be played incorrectly, the rules of etiquette can be violated, our statements to others may inadvertently offend them, etc.

From these examples we can make the following general observations about *forms of life*:

1. They are *dynamic*. The *forms of life* are not static, but can change over time. The rate of change varies according to the rate of change of the activities that they represent. For example, the activity of "riding a horse" as a common mode of transportation gave way to "driving a horse-drawn cart," and this, in turn, gave way to "driving an automobile." These activities were similar in many respects and different in others. Even within the category of driving modern cars there is a significant amount of variation (some cars have four gear stick shifts, some have five gears, some have automatic transmissions, some have different size engines, etc.).

2. *Forms of life* are *not definable* in any complete way; there is no essential definition to them. In fact, were we to find a "complete definition" such a definition would not be able to account for our ability to act in accordance with the loose structure of these *forms of life*. Such a definition would not contain any instructions on how to apply it to the activity in which it is used. Since these activities can vary a lot within the rough boundaries of a *form of life*, there must be something that shows how the concept of an activity can be applied. In general, this is not done by rules, but by training.

3. *Forms of life* have an inherent *"indefiniteness"* to them:

   > If a pattern of life is the basis for the use of a word then the word must contain some amount of indefiniteness. The pattern of life, after all, is not one of exact regularity. [**LWPP I** §211]

   Consider the *form of life* or activity "pitching a baseball." It is clear that in American baseball all the pitchers do roughly the same thing: they throw the ball towards the catcher and the batter who are positioned near "home plate." The pitcher's intent is to strike out the batter, or have him hit the ball badly. In addition, he must throw the ball close enough to the batter that he will not "walk" him. The batter, on the other hand, wants to hit the ball well or force the pitcher to walk him. This duel between the batter and pitcher is the essential tension of the game. Now from this general description, pitching a baseball appears to be the same thing for all pitchers. But if we look at, say, professional baseball pitchers we find a great deal of variety in the way this is done. In the first place, there are many ways to throw the ball: overhand, three quarters, sidearm, and underhand. There is also a wide range of speeds that a pitcher can throw the ball at, and a wide variety of pitches: fast ball, slider, screwball, overhand curve, knuckleball, forkball, split-fingered fastball, etc. Each pitcher will often throw these pitches differently than others ("Nobody could throw a curve like Koufax!"). Additionally, pitchers may have different "windups": some pitch from the "stretch" and some do not, and some have truly unique deliveries, such as Luis Tiant or Hideo Nomo. But in spite of all these differences, we can still see that the activity all these pitchers have in common is *pitching the ball.*

4. *Forms of life* (and the activities that are "woven" into *language games*) have meaning for us in relation to the role or importance they play in our lives. If we are not professional baseball players, then the distinctions between "sliders," "forkballs," and "curves" will have little meaning to us. We can understand a baseball player's assessment that the reason Greg Maddux is such a great pitcher is that he has remarkable control of his pitches, but we would not be able to make that assessment by ourselves. Our concept of baseball pitching is not at the same level of complexity as a professional player's is. We would have to accept such a statement on faith (and accepting something "on faith" is another *form of life* that plays a role in our lives—we all accept some things "on faith").

5. *Forms of life do not exist by themselves,* but are caught up with others in the "pattern" of life:

> Seeing life as a weave, this pattern (pretence, say) is not always complete and is varied in a multiplicity of ways. But we, in our conceptual world, keep on seeing the same, recurring with variations. That is how our concepts take it. For concepts are not for use on a single occasion.
>
> And one pattern in the weave is interwoven with many others. [**Z** §§568–569]

6. *Forms of life* are best taught by *demonstration and coaching,* not by explanation, explicit rule-following or by using definitions.

7. *Forms of life* arise in our lives through *repetition*:

> We judge an action according to its background within human life... The background is the bustle of life. And our concept points to something within this bustle.
>
> ... it is the very concept "bustle" that brings about this indefiniteness. For a bustle only comes about through constant repetition. And there is no definite starting point for "constant repetition." [**RPP II** §§624, 625, and 626]

8. We *cannot isolate* a single *form of life* from others. They are often dependent on other *forms of life* for their structure and significance. The game of baseball is similar to and dependent upon the earlier game of cricket. Baseball is also dependent on abilities learned in other activities, such as hand–eye coordination, or the ability to run fast. The notion of "fairness" in a game is a broad concept

that goes beyond any single game, and takes on a character set by society at large. Our riding a bicycle is dependent on a number of prior abilities: the ability to find one's way about; the ability to understand and follow traffic regulations; the ability to balance oneself and master a physical skill; the ability to make minor repairs of the bike; the ability to drive the bike so as not to endanger others; etc. Most children do not learn to ride a two-wheel bicycle until they are 7 or 8 years old, at least. It usually takes this long for children to master the related physical and mental abilities that are needed as a foundation for riding a bicycle.

## Language Games and Forms of Life

Having roughly sketched the notions of *language game* and *form of life*, we should now look at how they are related. Wittgenstein briefly states what this relation is:

> ... we don't start from certain words, but from certain occasions or activities. [**LC** p. 3]

*Language Games* are embedded in, and dependent on, the recurring "occasions or activities" which make up our "natural history."

> ... the term "language-game" is meant to bring into prominence the fact that the speaking of language is part of an activity, or of a form of life. [**PI** §23]

Zabeeh writes:

> The introduction of *actions* into the fabric of language links the idea of "language game" with the idea of "form of life."[188]

But if we go back to Wittgenstein's discussion of *language games* we find that the activity that surrounds a *language game* is part of the *language game* itself:

> I shall also call the whole, consisting of language and the actions into which it is woven, the "language-game" [**PI** §7]

If Wittgenstein included the "actions into which it is woven" as part of the *language game*, then why does he introduce the notion of *forms of life*? It seems that the *forms of life* are already part of the definition of *language games*. It is true that these two notions are related and, in a sense, overlapping, but there are *forms of life* that do not have any direct relation to language use. I am speaking of the nonlinguistic, or prelinguistic activities that do not require language for their execution. Activities such as the physical act of eating, throwing an object, walking, jumping, sleeping, driving a car, hammering a nail, tightening a bolt, whistling, etc. These activities can be named and referred to, and the use of language can take place during their execution, but they do not *require* language to execute and can be performed entirely without recourse to language at all. These *forms of life* can be contrasted with the activities that are part of *language games* and require language for their execution. Activities such as giving orders, describing the appearance of an object,

---

[188] F. Zabeeh. "On Language Games and Forms of Life," **Essays on Wittgenstein**, p. 341. University of Illinois Press, Chicago, 1971. Edited by E.D. Klemke.

singing, making a joke, requesting, thanking, cursing, greeting, etc.[189] These actions are generally not possible without language.

Baker and Hacker bring out this relation between forms of life and language games:

> The notion of a form of life is connected with that of a language-game, but is more general and elemental. A form of life is a given unjustified and unjustifiable pattern of human activity (part of human natural history [**PI** §25]). It rests upon, but is not identical with, very general pervasive facts of nature. It consists of shared natural and linguistic responses, of broad agreement in definitions and in judgements, and of corresponding behavior.
>
> A language perforce contains moves which are not justified by reference to anything, but are simply accepted as appropriate, as a common pattern of linguistic behavior by reference to which other moves are justified. Equally, any cognitive claims, as well as any doubts, occur within a framework of propositions that are not doubted, that belong to the frame of reference of the system of knowledge (propositions of the *Weltbild*). Training in what counts as justification, acceptance of undoubted truths of the world-picture, is acculturation in the form of life of the community.[190]

Language can only be understood within the context of related activities—both with those which require language and those that do not. As Zabeeh points out:

> The idea that a language game is something that "plays a particular role in our human life" (though vaguely) is important. Since even at this early stage it connects language games with specifiable activities and in an oblique way shows that a mere use of words (or even use of a grammatically well-formed expression in the absence of certain actions, such as informing or warning or referring) is not to be considered as playing a language game.[191]

It is easy to see the relation between *language games* and activities that require language to execute, such as "telling a story." One must not only have something to say, one must tell it at an appropriate time, to an appropriate audience, and formulate the story using one's knowledge of certain real or fictitious events that may be relevant, among many other things. All of these are largely linguistic activities that are relevant to the task at hand. But how does language relate to something that is nonlinguistic, such as "eating?" It's clear, of course, that one can eat without any recourse to language, but there are times when one might say something that would not be understandable outside the activity of eating. For example, we might ask "How do you like the salad?," or we might say, "Please pass the salmon," or , "I am full," or instruct someone, "Use the small fork for salad and the large one next to it for your entrée." These linguistic events are not required for us to perform the act of eating, but they don't make much sense unless we are eating (or are referring to the act of eating) when we hear or utter them. Were these statements to be uttered outside the context of eating, they would be seen as odd, perhaps even incomprehensible.

---

[189] These examples are from **PI** §23.
[190] G.P. Baker and P.M.S. Hacker. **An Analytical Commentary on Wittgenstein's Philosophical Investigations**, vol. 1, p. 48. University of Chicago Press, 1985.
[191] Zabeeh, *op.cit.*, p. 331.

A grammatically correct sentence just won't make sense in the wrong context (imagine getting on a bus and telling the driver, "I am full."). Zabeeh makes a further point: the *language games* and the activities in which they are embedded are not just *any* ones, but are the *language games* and activities which play a role or have importance, in our life. For people who have never seen or played Mah Jong, any *language game* that is linked to the playing of Mah Jong would be incomprehensible. One could not understand a statement that such-and-such "is similar to Mah Jong." Having a role in one's life can also determine the degree to which a language game is understood. For example, if one were asked, "Isn't that a good chess move?," the meaning of this statement might depend on the listener's chess playing ability. A casual, amateur's concept of a "good move in chess" would be much different than a grand master's concept of a "good move in chess." It is useful to distinguish between those *forms of life* that play a role in everyone's life, like eating, and those that play a role in our lives by our choice, such as pitching baseballs or driving a car—the latter activities being characterized by varying levels of ability and commitment.

*Language* and *forms of life* work together to put a structure on our use of language and our participation in regular human activities, respectively. But they do it without providing a list of rules which we must refer to, consciously or unconsciously, in order to speak or act appropriately. Instead, they provide a kind of natural structure that encourages us to act or speak in certain ways, but not in others. A list of rules would not be enough to describe or define *language games* and *forms of life* because in most cases rules cannot completely describe how an activity is to be performed. To be adequate a formal system of rules must be embedded in a broader context which limits the coverage or applicability of those rules. Otherwise, one doesn't know when to stop applying the rules, and new rules are needed for every possible exception which comes up. There will be no end to such rules if they are not bounded by human activities, conventions and training. One might object that the rule system for a game such as chess is complete and sufficient to regulate every possible legal move. But these rules are embedded in a context that excludes many possible moves and chess-like activities without our even thinking about them (in the way that we would think of a chess move). We don't need a chess rule that says that a player must not knowingly cheat, or eat the chess pieces, or turn off the lights during his opponent's moves, or threaten him if he declares "checkmate," etc. These actions are considered bizarre or inappropriate because they are excluded by the *forms of life* or activities in which the playing of chess games is embedded. The rules of chess don't have to address these situations at all. It is true that a "complete" set of rules for chess, such as those used to regulate international competition, might include a rule stipulating that a player may not interfere with his opponent. But the rules assume that a typical player would know what "interference" means, and he *does*, not by virtue of the rules of chess, but because he is a normal social individual familiar by experience with the natural conventions of playing competitive board games. Wittgenstein comments:

> How should we have to imagine a complete list of rules for the employment of a word?—What do we mean by a complete list of rules for the employment of a piece in chess? Couldn't we always construct doubtful cases, in which the normal list of rules does not decide? Think e.g. of such a question as: how to determine who moved last, if a doubt is raised about the reliability of the players' memories?

The regulation of traffic in the streets permits and forbids certain actions on the part of drivers and pedestrians; but it does not attempt to guide the totality of their movements by prescription. And it would be senseless to talk of an "ideal" ordering of traffic which should do that; in the first place we should have no idea what to imagine as this ideal. If someone wants to make traffic regulations stricter on some point or other, that does not mean that he wants to approximate to such an ideal. [**Z** §440]

Because *language games* and *forms of life* are not constituted or regulated by explicit rules they cannot be defined or explained in the same way that more rule-governed systems such as chess or mathematics can be. *Language games* and *forms of life* are primarily demonstrated or shown; they cannot be described or defined in any complete way. Explanations and definitions may help, but only if the student already understands a similar *language game* or *form of life* and can himself fill in what is left out by the explanations. Wittgenstein comments:

> For remember that in general we don't use language according to strict rules—it hasn't been taught us by means of strict rules either. *We*, in our discussions on the other hand, constantly compare language with a calculus proceeding according to exact rules.
>
> This is a very one-sided way of looking at language. In practice we rarely use language as such a calculus. For not only do we not think of the rules of usage—of definitions, etc.—while using language, but when we are asked to give such rules, in most cases we aren't able to do so. We are unable clearly to circumscribe the concepts we use; not because we don't know their real definition, but because there is no real "definition" to them. To suppose that there must be would be like supposing that whenever children play with a ball they play a game according to strict rules. [**BB** p. 25]

Wittgenstein continues:

> But what does a game look like that is everywhere bounded by rules? Whose rules never let a doubt creep in, but stop up all the cracks where it might?—Can't we imagine a rule determining the application of a rule, and a doubt which it removes—and so on? [**PI** §84]

Wittgenstein's question is, of course, rhetorical. A game, in the normal sense of the word, cannot be "everywhere bounded by rules," and neither can *language games* (this kind of analogy is what Wittgenstein hoped to convey by calling these linguistic activities "games"). What, in addition to rules, do you need to learn or master a practice? Wittgenstein is quite clear about this:

> Not only rules, but also examples are needed for establishing a practice. Our rules leave loopholes open, and the practice has to speak for itself.[192] [**OC** §139]

---

[192] P. Ziff pointed out that people frequently confuse rules with "regularities":

> I am concerned with regularities: I am not concerned with rules. Rules have virtually nothing to do with speaking or understanding a natural language ...

## The Big Picture: Philosophy of Language and Metaphor

In the course of his discussions of language in **Philosophical Investigations**, Wittgenstein draws a number of analogies between language and other activities:

> The grammar of language use is like the dynamic structure of a game.
> Words are like tools, and language use is similar to tool use.
> Words have a uniform appearance in different contexts, but their uses may be as different as the uses of the handles in a locomotive.
> Language as a city.
> Language as a labyrinth.
> The background in which we accept propositions is like a mythology, or a river-bed.

Each of the above metaphors is useful for understanding Wittgenstein's philosophy of language, and each illuminates different aspects of language. But what strikes us is how divergent the use of these analogies is from the usual way of doing analytic philosophy. It may appear at first that Wittgenstein is merely being eloquent in using these metaphors—as Mark Twain once remarked, they are included "for general literary gorgeousness."[193] Perhaps Wittgenstein could make his points in more analytic ways without recourse to

> ...those who speak of "the rules of language" ... are I believe misusing the word "rule."..it is possible to misuse a screwdriver, to use it correctly or incorrectly: are there rules for using screwdrivers? This too would be of use of the word...

> ...A rule is easily confused with a regularity. This may be one reason why rules have been thought to be of some importance in the use of language. By first confusing "George regularly walks to school." with "As a rule, George walks to school." and then confusing that with "The rule is that George walks to school.," one can easily arrive at the view that rules have a significant part to play in language.

A general model relating rules to proficiency in any human task (of which language use is one) has been proposed by Bert and Stuart Dreyfus in their **Mind Over Machine: The Power of Human Intuition and Expertise in the Era of the Computer** [The Free Press, Macmillan, NY, 1986]. They identify five stages in the acquisition of proficiency: Novice, Advanced Beginner, Competence, Proficiency and Expert. Only Novices and Advanced Beginners follow rules to any significant extent. Those who are proficient or expert at some skill—either cognitive or physical—do not follow rules, nor can they articulate rules to explain their expertise in any kind of complete way. Their expertise consists of "know-how" or intuition rather than skills which could be precisely described. Wittgenstein would say that the expert has an ability to perform a particular task well rather than an ability to follow a set of rules. In fact, attempts to model expert behavior usually produce only novice or beginner's performance. As Pascal wrote in 1670:

> Mathematical formalizers wish to treat matters of intuition mathematically, and make themselves ridiculous... The Mind... does it tacitly, naturally, and without technical rules. [Pensées (1670). Quoted in Dreyfus and Dreyfus, p. 16]

The intuitively applied know-how of the expert would appear in what Csikszentmihaly calls a "flow-state" (*vid.* footnote 237). Csikszentmihaly describes the flow-state as being "rule-bound" (*q.v.*), But he must use the phrase loosely because his definition of a flow-state would exclude the conscious following of rules.

[193] From **A Tramp Abroad**, Abridged and Edited with an introduction by Charles Neider. [Perennial Library, Harper and Row, NY, 1977].

analogies. But Wittgenstein introduced these metaphors for a number of reasons. In the first place, metaphors are a form of *showing* or demonstrating a concept, rather than explaining or defining it. This dovetails nicely with Wittgenstein's assertion that explanations do not teach as well as having a concept demonstrated to us. The second reason for his use of metaphor is that by focusing on metaphors Wittgenstein has shifted our attention away from internal or mental events and towards entities and processes that are external to us and available for us all to observe and consider. When we try to understand what language *is*, our natural tendency is to see it as springing from some mental event. But if we say that language is like a city, or like a game, then we have shifted our focus to entities that are available for us all to examine and discuss. When we argue over the precise nature of mental events, we are on slippery ground since there is no common basis for comparing the mental event of one person with the mental event of another, except in the most general or adumbrative way. This redirection of our attention from internal events to external ones is a major component in Wittgenstein's analysis, and marks a significant difference with the traditional methods of analytic philosophy. Malcolm comments:

> When we are philosophically perplexed about the nature of belief, or remembering, or meaning something, our natural tendency is to search inwardly into our minds or brains. That is a dead-end. Wittgenstein teaches us to look outwardly—to take note of how a difference in circumstances changes the meaning of what we say and do. Giving an account of this role of circumstances is not easy. In everyday life we learn to use the psychological terms in various circumstances. But the needs of everyday life do not require us to learn to describe those circumstances.[194]

Even though these metaphors can stand on their own, it will be useful to point out some of the implications these analogies have for language. We begin with a common metaphor for language that is more misleading than helpful, a metaphor that Wittgenstein, in his early work, believed reflected the way that language worked.

### Language as a Kind of Calculus

In one of his early works, **Philosophical Grammar,** Wittgenstein writes:

> The understanding of language, as of a game, seems like a background against which a particular sentence acquires meaning.—But this understanding, the knowledge of the language, isn't a conscious state that accompanies the sentences of the language. Not even if one of its consequences is such a state. It's much more like the understanding or mastery of a calculus, something like the ability to multiply.[195]

---

[194] Malcolm. **Nothing is Hidden: Wittgenstein's Criticism of his Early Thought**, p. 191. Blackwell, Oxford, 1986. Wittgenstein comments:

> One learns the word "think", that is, its use, under certain circumstances, which, however, one does not learn to describe.
> But I can teach a person the use of the word! For a description of those circumstances is not needed for that.
> I just teach him the word under particular circumstances. [**Z** §§114–116]

[195] **Philosophical Grammar**, §11. University of California Press, Berkeley, 1974. Edited by R. Rhees and A. Kenny. **Philosophical Grammar** hereafter referred to as **PG**.

We can see that Wittgenstein's early view of language was that it operates in much the same way that calculus does—language use consists of the mastery of a set of symbols, their operational definitions, and rules that govern their uses and transformations. But we can see the change in Wittgenstein's view later in the **Blue and Brown Books**:

> For remember that in general we don't use language according to strict rules—it hasn't been taught us by means of strict rules either. We, in our discussions on the other hand, constantly compare language with a calculus proceeding according to exact rules.
>
> This is a very one-sided way of looking at language. In practice we very rarely use language as such a calculus. For not only do we not think of the rules of usage—of definitions, etc.—while using language, but when we are asked to give such rules, in most cases we aren't able to do so. We are unable clearly to circumscribe the concepts we use; not because we don't know their real definition, but because there is no real "definition" to them. To suppose that there must be would be like supposing that whenever children play with a ball they play a game according to strict rules. [**BB** p. 25]

Here Wittgenstein shows that since calculus consists entirely of strict, general rules and precise definitions, that it cannot be a model for language. Language has neither strict rules that govern every usage nor precise definitions of its terms (symbols). It is true that we do sometimes use language with precise rules and fairly clear definitions, such as when we say:

> John rides the horse.
> and not,
> John ride the horse.

The second sentence is a clear violation of the simple and precise rule that subject and verb must agree in number. This rule is context free in the sense that it holds for any subject and any verb. Further, the nouns, "John" and "horse," are semantically unproblematic. This simple example may lead us to believe that all language operates in more or less the same way, that complex sentences are merely variations on these simple ones in the same way that complex formulae are variations or combinations of simple ones. But if we recollect Wittgenstein's criticism of Augustine's view of language, we are reminded that language is not used in just one way.

What Wittgenstein argued against is the notion that language, like calculus, is composed of a precise set of rules that prescribe all possible transformations within the system, and operate on terms or symbols that are clearly defined. Further, these transformations would be context free. But this view of language has some problems. In the first place, while we have rules of grammar that govern the agreement between sentence parts, these rules do not tell us why some apparently grammatically correct sentences don't make sense:

> Colorless green ideas sleep furiously

This example was used by the linguist Noam Chomsky to demonstrate the independence of meaning and grammar—that grammatically correct sentences can still be meaningless.

The independence of grammar, or syntax, and meaning is an essential characteristic of calculus, and insures that (1) Changes in the meaning of the symbols do not change the valid rules that operate on them, and (2) The context in which the symbols are used does not change the meaning of those symbols once they have been defined. In his early thought, Wittgenstein himself believed this to be the case. In the **Tractatus Logico-Philosophicus** he states:

> In logical syntax the meaning of a sign should never play a rôle. It must be possible to establish logical syntax without mentioning the *meaning* of a sign. . . [**TLP** 3.33]

But this was one view which he was later to revise in his distinction between *surface grammar* and *depth grammar*. The independence of grammar and meaning in language only holds if we look at *surface grammar*—the syntax of statements—not if we look at *depth grammar*—the context and circumstances in which they are used. But Wittgenstein felt that *surface grammar* does not tell us enough about what makes a sentence meaningful or not. What was important in this regard is the *depth grammar* of a sentence, how the sentence relates to the circumstances and context—the *language game*—in which it is appropriate. In Wittgenstein's *depth grammar*, grammar and meaning are not separate, and Chomsky's sentence is both meaningless *and* ungrammatical.[196] We can see this if we do a Wittgensteinean analysis of the *depth grammar* of Chomsky's sentence:

If "colorless green" is really a color, then it should be all right to use it in other sentences, for example:

> The artist went to the art-supply store and bought some colorless green paint.
> My new car is colorless green.

These, clearly, are odd sentences. In fact, they are so deviant that one cannot even guess what the speaker might mean by them, so they can't even be interpreted as metaphorical. "Colorless green" has a logical structure like $(\neg A \bullet A)$—where we can approximate the phrase in question by making A = "color." This leaves us with a contradiction. A description such as "colorless green" is not an empirical mistake, but a logical or grammatical one. No amount of empirical investigation could result in a confirmation or disconfirmation of "colorless green."

There are other problems with the *depth grammar* of Chomsky's statement. It makes an implicit claim that "ideas" can have colors. If this is the case, then the following sentences should be alright:

> My ideas are mostly red or blue. . .
> I had a green idea this morning, but later had a purple one.

Again, these sentences are very odd, so odd that it would be difficult to even guess what the speaker might mean. One might make a case that ideas, like moods, can be "blue" or

---

[196] J. Ellis makes the same point by insisting that grammar and lexicon (meaning) are not separate. [**Language, Thought, and Logic**. Northwestern University Press, Evanston, IL, 1993. See chapter 4 "Grammar".]

"black," but this is stretching the point, and is clearly not what Chomsky meant. Continuing, if "ideas sleep," then we should be able to say some other things about them like:

> His idea slept soundly all night.
> His idea woke up.
> My best ideas require little sleep.

Again, we are forced into accepting an intolerable bizarreness if we want to hold on to the claim that Chomsky's sentence is grammatical. A similar analysis can be made of "sleep furiously."

A Wittgensteinean analysis of the *depth grammar* of Chomsky's sentence demonstrates that meaning and grammar are not independent in natural language, and that language, therefore, does not operate like a kind of calculus.[197]

A further argument against the independence of meaning and grammar came with George Lakoff's examples of how the grammatical soundness of a sentence can depend on the context in which it is uttered:

> John is a Republican, and Bill is a crook, too.

A Democrat might not see anything wrong with the above statement, while a Republican might consider it not just wrong, but, according to Lakoff, ungrammatical.[198] Another aspect of calculus that Wittgenstein, at one time, believed it shared with language is the notion of the "definite sense" of words or terms. The logic of calculus requires that once the meaning of a term is established, no change in the context in which it is used will cause a change in the meaning of that term. This means that the terms in calculus have a "definite sense." Wittgenstein believed, early in his career, that the words used in propositional statements had a definite sense too—that they had a meaning that was independent of context. In the **Tractatus Logico-Philosophicus,** language consisted of definite propositions which represented or, more accurately, pictured, reality and could be seen as either true or false. These propositions, as long as they were grammatically well formed, had the same sense regardless of the context in which they were uttered or written. Wittgenstein was later not only to reject the idea of a definite sense of a sentence or proposition, saying that they did not have fixed meanings, but he was also to insist that context is an important determinant of the sense of language:

> The words "I am here" have sense only in certain contexts, and not when I say them
> to someone who is sitting in front of me and sees me clearly—and not because they

---

[197] The phrase structure grammars which were a natural outgrowth of Chomsky's emphasis on the autonomy of grammar represent the extreme to which these syntactic structures can be taken. Eco's semiotics was an attempt to shore up the failing syntactic model of language by introducing semantic and pragmatic components to the grammatical representation of language. Eco, *et al.*, spent a lot of effort trying to keep Chomsky's view of language afloat, but it's hard to build a sound edifice on such weak foundations.

[198] The example was given in personal communication at the University of California, Berkeley. Lakoff gives a more detailed argument against the autonomy of grammar in his **Irregularity in Syntax**. [Holt, Rinehart and Winston, 1970]

are superfluous, but because their meaning is not determined by the situation, yet stands in need of such determination.[199] [**PI** §348]

As Malcolm comments:

> A shrug of the shoulders is a familiar gesture that means something different in different situations. It does not have a fixed meaning. Neither does a familiar sentence.

> Wittgenstein's repudiation of the assumption that the sense of language is independent of the circumstances of life in which the language is used, is perhaps the single most important aspect of his break with what he calls in the preface of the Investigations "my old way of thinking."[200]

Another problem with the calculus-model of language is that calculus has no clear connection with behavior and common human activities the way that language does. Calculus does not spring from the things that we do, except in a very restrictive sense.[201] As we will argue soon, Wittgenstein believed that language was grounded in instinctive behavior, it was not, at its most basic level, built on conscious, or what we might call "rational," thought. Calculus, in contrast, is nothing if it is not conscious. A further difference between the calculus model of language and the later model of language that Wittgenstein developed is that, according to Baker and Hacker, "It is false that a complete understanding of language is derivable from knowledge of definitions and forms alone."[202] Again, the problem is that language requires context to complete its sense, while calculus is relatively context-free in this regard. The clearest example of this is to consider the meaning of sentences, or utterances that are exactly the same in construction but are presented in different circumstances. Take Wittgenstein's example (from above):

> I am here.

---

[199] O.K. Bouwsma recalled the following incident which occurred in August of 1949 when he visited Wittgenstein who was the guest of Norman Malcolm at Cornell University:

> When does a sentence make sense? There was talk about Moore's sentence: "I am here." Moore thought one could decide that "I am here" made sense, by some introspective questioning. Does it make sense? Now, of course, all these sentences have a use. The question is whether, if one shouted such a sentence under any circumstances whatever, it has a use. I can see what moves [philosopher Max] Black. Black says that the sentence obviously has no particular point, nobody gets any information by it. But if it were a question in a True-False questionnaire, you would clearly answer "True" or "Yes" if asked: Yes or No. [Wittgenstein] said: "No! No! Of course not, etc. Context determines use." [Bouwsma. **Wittgenstein: Conversations 1949— 1951**, pp. 14–15. Hackett, Indianapolis, IN, 1986. Edited by J.L. Craft and R.E. Hustwit.]

[200] N. Malcolm. **Nothing is Hidden**, p. 271. Basil Blackwell, Oxford, 1986.

[201] This and the following differences between language and calculus were taken from Baker and Hacker's **Wittgenstein: Meaning and Understanding: Essays on the Philosophical Investigations**, vol. 1, pp. 49–50. The University of Chicago Press, Chicago, 1985. Baker and Hacker simply list these differences. The explanations and inferences drawn from these differences are entirely my own.

[202] *Ibid.*

We can imagine it uttered by someone to his blind friend whom he is meeting in a crowded place (and who would recognize his voice and know who the "I" is without a name accompanying it). Or we could imagine it as a response over the telephone:

> When will you get here?
> I *am* here.

In the first case, the sentence could mean that the speaker is physically near his blind friend and might be stated in order to give him reassurance. But in the second case, it could mean that the speaker has arrived in the city of his friend, is probably early, and has called his friend to get directions to his house. The knowledge of the surface grammar and the possible meanings of the individual words in this sentence could not provide us with these two disparate meanings of the sentence. For Wittgenstein, thinking of language as a kind of calculus puts us on "the very brink of a misunderstanding." This misunderstanding not only misleads us about how language actually works, but it does something far more insidious: it leads us to believe that an ideal logical language—a language that is "better. . . than our everyday language"—is somehow possible. As Wittgenstein writes:

> . . . in philosophy we often *compare* the use of words with games and calculi which have fixed rules, but cannot say that someone who is using language *must* be playing such a game.—But if you say that our languages only *approximate* to such a calculi you are standing on the very brink of a misunderstanding. For then it may look as if what we were talking about were an *ideal* language. As if our logic were, so to speak, a logic for a vacuum.—Whereas logic does not treat of language—or of thought—in the sense in which natural science treats of a natural phenomenon, and the most that can be said is that we *construct* ideal languages. But here the word "ideal" is liable to mislead, for it sounds as if these languages were better, more perfect, than our everyday language; and as if it took the logical to shew [*sic*] people at last what a correct sentence looked like.
>
> All this, however, can only appear in the right light when one has attained greater clarity about the concepts of understanding, meaning, and thinking. For it will then also become clear what can lead us (and did lead me) to think that if anyone utters a sentence and *means* or *understands* it he is operating a calculus according to definite rules.[203] [**PI** §81]

### The Structure of Language is Like the Dynamic Structure of a Game

Since we have already discussed the metaphorical connection between language and games, we will not repeat that analysis here. But there is a variant of the language:game analogy that bears some scrutiny—the idea that language is like a chess game.

### Language and Chess

> The question "What is a word really?" is analogous to "What is a piece in chess?"
> [**PI** §108]

---

[203] Note, in the last sentence, Wittgenstein's admission that he, too, once saw language in this misleading way (in his early work **TLP**).

Here Wittgenstein begins by drawing an analogy between a word and a chess piece. It is clear that it would be odd to ask what a chess piece *means*—it doesn't really mean anything. But it does make sense to ask how the chess piece is *used*. The same is true of words. But there is something rather subtle about this analogy, namely, it makes no sense to talk about a chess piece *outside* the context of a chess game.

Wittgenstein makes the analogy between chess and language in other places in his writing:

> How should we counter someone who told us that with him understanding was an inner process?—How should we counter him if he said that with him knowing how to play chess was an inner process?—We should say that when we want to know if he can play chess we aren't interested in anything that goes on inside him.—And if he replies that this is in fact just what we are interested in, that is, we are interested in whether he can play chess—then we shall have to draw his attention to the criteria which would demonstrate his capacity, and on the other hand to the criteria for the "inner states." [**PI** p. 181]

> How should we have to imagine a complete list of rules for the employment of a word?—What do we mean by a complete list of rules for the employment of a piece in chess? Couldn't we always construct doubtful cases, in which the normal list of rules does not decide? Think, e.g., of such a question as: how to determine who moved last, if a doubt is raised about the reliability of the player's memories? [**Z** §440]

The chess analogy brings out two important similarities with language: first, chess pieces have no use/meaning outside of a chess game. The dependence of chess pieces on the context of a chess game is the same as the dependence of words on specific language games and circumstances. Words taken out of their respective language games may be misleading or nonsensical. Secondly, like chess, the use of language is not governed by a "complete list of rules." For chess and language, what resolves the ambiguities of usage left by what rules there may be, are *training* and *relevant circumstances* (Forms of Life).

*Words are Like Tools and Language Use is Like Tool Use*
> Think of the tools in a tool-box: there is a hammer, pliers, a saw, a screw-driver, a rule, a glue-pot, glue, nails and screws.—The functions of words are as diverse as the functions of these objects. (And in both cases there are similarities.)[204] [**PI** §11]

[204] **PI** §11. Compare with **BB** pp. 67–68:

> Think of words as instruments characterized by their use, and then think of the use of a hammer, the use of a chisel, the use of a square, of a glue pot, and of glue. (Also, all that we say here can be understood only if one understands that a great variety of games is played with the sentences of our language: giving and obeying orders; asking questions and answering them; describing an event; telling a fictitious story; telling a joke; describing an immediate experience; making conjectures about events in the physical world; making scientific hypotheses and theories; greeting someone, etc. etc.).

Baker and Hacker make the point that Germans consider "glue," "nails," and "screws" tools, though we usually do not. [**An Analytical Commentary on Wittgestein's Philosophical Investigations**, vol. 1, p. 37. University of Chicago Press, 1985.]

Wittgenstein's analogy between words and tools is one of the central insights of his philosophy of language. In the quotation above, the tool analogy reiterates his criticism of Augustine's view of language—that words function in only one way. But if words are like tools, and language use is like tool use, then we only need look at the diversity of tool usage to see that a similar diversity exists in language. Think of a hammer. It can be used to drive nails, to break or crack something solid (like chipping flakes off a stone so it will fit in a particular place), to weight something down on a windy day (like holding down a schematic while a carpenter works outside on a project), to tap a water pipe to free it of an obstruction, to hammer something together or apart, to tap a chisel when cutting wood, or even to fend off an attacker. Or, think of a screwdriver which can be used to turn screws, to try open the lid of a can of paint, to hold a door open when wedged underneath it, to apply small dabs of glue to specific places, to make a crude hole in something or to use as a spindle to wind string or wire on.

Another point of the tool analogy is to show how misleading questions about the meaning of a word can be. Tools have *uses* but they do not really have *meanings*. This is evident in a sentence such as:

> What is the *meaning* of a hammer?

While this might be good poetry, it is not good semantic analysis, and the oddity of this statement, when taken literally in everyday discourse, should be obvious to us all—in fact, it isn't at all clear what would even count as an answer to it. Wittgenstein's reply to such a question might be:

> Why do you put it so oddly?[205] [**PI** §60]

Further, if we insist that tools do have "a" meaning, then we are forced into trying to find some single, essential "meaning" that applies to all hammers, or all screwdrivers, etc. The same holds for words: like tools, they do not have *meanings*, in any strict sense, but they certainly do have *uses*.

Earlier, Wittgenstein makes a related point:

> "I set the brake up by connecting up rod and lever."—Yes, given the whole of the rest of the mechanism. Only in conjunction with that is it a brake-lever, and separated from its support it is not even a lever; it may be anything, or nothing. [**PI** §6]

The brake is a kind of tool, and the example here is meant to show how superficial some kinds of analysis can be. We look at the brake and think that it works by "connecting up rod and lever." But this is not how the brake really works. For it to work, it requires the "whole of the rest of the mechanism." The analogy to language is clear: we often think that language works because of some superficial relationships—relationships like syntax, transformational grammar, or the proximity of other words. But such analysis misses the

---

[205] This was his reply to the question of asking for the "broomstick and the brush which is fitted onto it" instead of asking for the "broom" [**PI** §60]. This was discussed in the previous section **Wittgenstein's Categories: Family Resemblances**.

"whole of the rest of the mechanism." What is the "rest of the mechanism" for language? The "rest of the mechanism" is the *context* in which language works: the activities, circumstances, and practices in which language is used, and the background and training of the speakers or hearers. We can see this relationship even in Wittgenstein's simple "slab" language (see the discussion in the previous section **The "Builder's Language"**). The context which enables the slab language to work consists of the activities of construction and the experience of the workers. Without that context, the "rest of the mechanism" for language is missing and nothing in the syntax of the language can tell us what "Slab!" means. That is, there are too many possibilities for what it might mean, and no criteria for choosing the right one. Wittgenstein continues with his tool analogy:

> Of course, what confuses us is the uniform appearance of words when we hear them spoken or meet them in script and print. For their application is not presented to us so clearly. . .

> It is like looking into the cabin of a locomotive. We see handles all looking more or less alike (Naturally, since they are all supposed to be handled.). But one is the handle of a crank which can be moved continuously (it regulates the opening of a valve); another is a the handle of a switch, which has only two effective positions, it is either off or on; a third is the handle of a brake-lever, the harder one pulls on it, the harder it brakes; a fourth, the handle of a pump; it has an effect only so long as it is moved to and fro.[206] [**PI** §§ 11–12]

The fact that the same word appears in different contexts and has different uses gives us the impression that there must be something that is the same that follows the word from context to context—some general, essential meaning. Words are like the handles in a locomotive. But if we grab the handles and manipulate them we find that although they all look the same, their functions are quite diverse. Wittgenstein considered one of the problems with the analysis of language is that we consider only one or a few examples. It would be like reaching into the locomotive, manipulating one or two handles, then assuming that all other handles work the same way because they look similar. To understand how handles that look alike really work we have to try a number of them. It is the same way with language: we have a tendency to look at one or two examples of a word's usage and infer that all instances of that word work the same way. Consider the following examples of the word "pitch":

> "Randy Johnson is the best **pitcher** in professional baseball."
> "The brewer **pitched** the yeast."
> "The sales **pitch** was very convincing."

Seeing these examples, one might be tempted to say that the word "pitch" in the different sentences has some semantic similarities: they all involve "throwing something" (albeit in the sales example, the "sales pitch" is metaphorical). It may be tempting to think that

---

[206] In the complete quotation, Wittgenstein included a pointed observation about philosophy:

> Of course, what confuses us is the uniform appearance of words when we hear them spoken or meet them in script and print. For their application is not presented to us so clearly. ***Especially when we are doing philosophy!***.

it might be possible, in theory, to come up with a definition of "pitch" that would be the same in each of the above three cases. But if we take John Wisdom's suggestion that when we use Wittgenstein's analysis of "depth grammar" we need to come up," . . . not with one case but cases and cases" (*vid.* See quotation at footnote 177), we can see immediately that a uniform, essential meaning for "pitch" that applies to all usages is impossible:

"They **pitched** their tent."
"They all **pitched** in."
"He covered his roof with **pitch**."
"The armies fought a **pitched** battle."
"He sang at a much higher **pitch** than before."
"Faldo **pitched** the ball within two feet of the cup."
"The falcon soared to a very high **pitch**."
"The roof was sharply **pitched**."
"He drank all the water in the **pitcher**."
"They worked at a feverish **pitch**."

Even a cursory examination of these additional examples leads us to the ineluctable conclusion that no uniform definition could possibly exist that would tell you what the meanings of these instances of "pitch" would be in each case. At best, there are "families" of meanings for "pitch": some are similar to each other, and some are quite divergent. This brings up an important point, namely, that if there are many meanings or uses for the word "pitch," how can you sort through them to find the right one that is presented to you? The answer is simple: you don't have to go through all the possible meanings every time you want to use the word "pitch," the particular meaning or usage of "pitch" comes with the circumstances in which it is used. For example, if you are watching a baseball game with someone and he makes a remark about the "pitcher" you know immediately what he means. There is no need to ask yourself, "Does he mean a 'baseball pitcher', or a 'pitcher of water'?" The context gives us the particular meaning of the word that is relevant to the situation at hand. The need to sift through various meanings of the words we use would simply be too time-consuming to do, because if we do it for one word, like "pitch," we would have to do it for *all* the words in all our sentences, not just words like "pitch," the nouns and verbs, but all the adjectives, adverbs and words like "the," "and," "is," which can be used variously too.[207] The only thing similar in the uses of "pitch" in different contexts is the spelling of the word. You could have made up a word different than "pitch" for any of these contexts and the difference would be of no consequence whatsoever.[208] That is,

[207] It is hard to see how "the," "and," etc. can be used differently, but they can: consider, "the car" versus "the pain in my leg." In both, "the" identifies something specific, but the specificity of a "car" is quite different than the specificity of a "pain." One way to see this is to ask how you would verify statements like "I saw the car you were talking about," as opposed to "I see you still have the pain in your leg." The definite article ("the") works differently in each case. ("The" can also create an illusion of existence, and, as such, is one of Ryle's "systematically misleading expressions" (*vid.* discussion of Ryle in footnote 102). Similar cases can be made for the different uses of "and" and "is" ("he bought an apple and an orange" versus "he is a scholar and a gentleman." Or, speaking about the various uses of "is": consider, "the car is black" versus "his mood is black." Again, the differences in use here can be seen if we look at how we might verify each statement.)

[208] In fact, it is not uncommon for ordinary words to be exchanged for other words in certain contexts. The individual who enlists in the Navy and arrives at his new ship will at first find it confusing that "stairs" are called "ladders," "floors" called "decks", "ceilings" called "overheads," "doors" called "hatches," "ropes" called

it is of no consequence whether it happened that we say, "He covered his roof with *pitch*," or we say, "He covered his roof with *veeblefletzer.*" The meaning of the word "pitch" in this context is in no way dependent on any of the other uses of the word "pitch" in other contexts. As a result, the word that comes to be used in this context is largely accidental. Before the first utterance of a sentence with this usage, it was probably no more likely for it to contain "pitch" than it was to contain any other word.

Context is often strong enough to make the right reference without the word even mentioned. For example, we are watching a baseball game as the pitcher strikes out three batters in a row. My friend turns to me and says, "Boy, he's got good stuff!" Is this an ambiguous phrase? Not in normal circumstances. "He" is obviously the pitcher who is now pitching, and his "good stuff" refers loosely to the high quality of his pitches, as evidenced by his three consecutive strikeouts. Yet if my friend utters the same sentence as we stand in line at the concession stand between innings, I might not know what he's talking about.[209]

"lines," "rooms" called "spaces," "left" called "port," "right" called "starboard," etc. There are also many Naval descriptions, such as "abaft the beam," or "on the port quarter," that have no simple equivalent in "civilian" English. Perfectly ordinary sentences can sound like a foreign language. Herman Wouk brings this out in his WW II novel **The Caine Mutiny**: The central figure in the story is Willie Keith who reports aboard the ship the USS Caine with no prior shipboard experience. Willie listens to a sailor explaining why a mine-sweeping maneuver had been done badly:

> "Sir, it was my fault," spoke up the boatswain's mate. He began an alibi that sounded to Willie [Keith] like this: "The port bandersnatch got fouled in the starboard rath when we tried to galumph the cutting cable so as not to trip the snozzle again. I had to unshackle the doppelganger and bend on two snarks instead so we could launch in a hurry." "Well," said De Vriess, "couldn't you have vorpaled the sillabub or taken a turn on the chortlewort? That way the jaxo would be clear of the varse and you could forget about dudelsak. It would have done the same thing."

> "Yes, sir," said Bellison. "That might work okay. I'll try it tomorrow."

> Willie's heart sank. He was certain that if he sailed a hundred years on the Caine he would understand such abracadabra no better than he did at the moment.[H. Wouk. **The Caine Mutiny**, p. 102. Doubleday, Garden City, NY, 1951.]

[209] As another example of the variability of use/meaning, consider the word "line":

"Make him toe the **line**."
"He put his reputation on the **line**."
"Give me the bottom **line** on the investment."
"The batter **lined** out to third."
"I can't follow his **line** of thought."
"He took a pencil and drew a **line**."
"The soldiers stood in **line**."
"The coat was **lined** with down."
"Don't give me that old **line**!"
"The actor forgot his **lines**."
"The ocean **liner** weighed anchor and put out to sea."
"The fishing **line** was hopelessly tangled."
"The store carried a **line** of small tools."

But suppose that we *can* get a uniform, essential meaning or definition of a word that is similar in all contexts. Would this work for us? Wittgenstein is clear in his answer:

> When we say: "Every word in language signifies something" we have so far said *nothing whatever*; unless we have explained exactly *what* distinction we wish to make. [**PI** §13]

Wittgenstein quickly follows this example with a similar one that purports to give a single essential meaning of the word "tools":

> Imagine someone's saying: "All tools serve to modify something. Thus the hammer modifies the position of the nail, the saw the shape of the board, and so on."—And what is modified by the rule, the glue-pot, the nails?—"Our knowledge of a thing's length. The temperature of the glue, and the solidity of the box."—Would anything be gained by this assimilation of expressions? [**PI** §14]

Again, Wittgenstein's question is rhetorical, nothing would be gained by such a general definition.[210] This is easy to see if we look at the *use* of the word "tools" and not the definition. If we try to *use* the general definition of the word "tool" we find that it is really not good for anything. What we can use, though, is a family of examples of how the word "tools" is actually employed.

> The desire to find essential definitions of words that work in a variety of contexts is part of our "craving for generality" and our "contemptuous attitude towards the particular case." [**BB** p. 18]

Wittgenstein continues to elaborate on the tool-like nature of language usage:

> It will be possible to say : In language (8) [the "expansion" of the "Builder's language"] we have different kinds of word. For the functions of the word "slab" and the word "block" are more alike than those of "slab" and "d." But how we group words into kinds will depend on the aim of the classification,—and on our own inclination.
>
> Think of the different points of view from which one can classify tools or chess-men. [**PI** §17]

Once again, Wittgenstein lets us draw the conclusion he wants; and if we think of the different points of view or uses for tools, it is not too hard to come up with other classifications:

> "His actions were completely out of **line**."
> "Drop me a **line** when you get there."

---

[210] Pitkin comments: "First, [Wittgenstein] seeks to show... that the grasping of definitions or essences or universals cannot explain what needs to be explained. And, second, he tries to show that even the mastery of definitions, principles, generalities, depends ultimately on our natural human capacities and inclinations, which do not themselves have any further explanation... The kind of training that is necessary to the acquisition of a natural language, Wittgenstein says, requires 'inducing the child to go on' in the same way, in new and different cases. This is different from training for repetition, which 'is not meant to apply to anything but the examples given'; this teaching 'points beyond' the examples given." [**Wittgenstein and Justice**, p. 45. University of California Press, Berkeley, 1972. Pitkin quotes from **PI** §208.]

Carpenter's tools
Painter's tools
Antique tools
German tools
My tools
Sturdy tools
Poorly made tools
Farm tools
Small tools
Unusual tools
"Tools You Never Knew Existed" (the title of a mail-order catalog)
⋮
etc.

What Wittgenstein wants us to see is that there is no *obvious* way that we can break up reality into categories (this is the main point of Nominalism). The possible categories we might use to group familiar things (here, tools) are simply too numerous for one category to be obviously more prominent than others. Categories imply a "point of view," and the number of "points of view" are too many for there to be a single obvious one. Even botanical classifications, which are often seen as providing the only possible categories for plants, presuppose a scientific framework or point of view. For example, we could classify trees by their scientific categories: oaks, maples, hawthornes, mulberries, pines, etc. as we normally do. But if we get away from our scientific categories, we can see a number of other ways of categorizing trees: we could imagine that the trees could be arranged by their utility, as an aborigine population might see them. They might break them up into groups by whether they are good for making bows, building houses, making arrows, building boats or making firewood. Trees could also be categorized by their size, with all large trees being in one category and smaller ones in other categories. We could even imagine trees being classified by their aesthetic appearance, with trees that we consider in the same category, for example, oaks, grouped differently by aesthetic taste. Perhaps there could be a medicinal classification of trees, or a geographical one (pines North of the Great Lakes being called one thing, and pines South of the Great Lakes called something else). Again, as we start looking at lots of cases, we see that the scientific categories of our own world are not the only possible ones. Some classifications that are used by other cultures may be inconceivable from our point of view: As Whorf pointed out:

> The Hopi actually call insect, airplane, and aviator all by the same word, and feel no difficulty about it.[211]

Further, it is not just that we can group things in various ways, but even what we call a "thing" may differ from situation to situation. If it is the case that things can be categorized in a number of different ways, and that these ways of categorizing them are not obvious when they are investigated empirically, then the natural question is: how do we know what category a thing belongs to?

---

[211] B.L. Whorf. "Science and Linguistics," **Language, Thought, and Reality: Selected Writings of Benjamin Lee Whorf**, p. 216. MIT Press, Cambridge, MA.

*Language as a City*

Wittgenstein draws another analogy with language: He describes language as a "city" or "town"[212]:

> Do not be troubled by the fact that languages (2) [the "Builder's Language"] and (8) [the extended "Builder's Language"] consist only of orders. If you want to say that this shews them to be incomplete, ask yourself whether our language is complete:—whether it was so before the symbolism of chemistry and the notation of the infinitesimal calculus were incorporated in it; for these are, so to speak, suburbs of our language (And how many houses or streets does it take before a town begins to be a town?). Our language can be seen as an ancient city: a maze of little streets and squares, of old and new houses, and of houses with additions from various periods; and this surrounded by a multitude of new boroughs with straight, regular streets and uniform houses. **[PI §18]**

The first comparison between language and a city is brought up to show that the artificial languages that Wittgenstein discusses earlier—(2) The "builder's language," and (8), the "extended builder's language"—are complete languages. There is no question about these simple languages being complete or incomplete in the same way that there is no question about "how many houses or streets does it take before a town begins to be a town" [*supra*]? Why is this important? If we thought of these simple languages as being incomplete, then we would miss what really makes them work, and we could write them off as simplistic or elliptical. Some would say that the way these simple languages work is somehow "hidden" from us—that these languages are simple versions of more complex utterances which we can refer to unconsciously in order to disambiguate the simple languages Wittgenstein described. But Wittgenstein says that incompleteness is not the problem here for the simple reason that these languages are not incomplete. They are complete because they are used perfectly well by the builder to accomplish his tasks. The reason for our misapprehension is our faulty notion of how language works. If we believe that words "stand for meaning" in some way, then we tend to think that when the words, by themselves, seem insufficient or ambiguous then "meaning" can only be completed or clarified by *additional* words. For Wittgenstein, this is wrong. What compensates for the perceived ambiguities or incompleteness in language is not more words, but *context,circumstances* and the *training* or *experience* of the speakers. While the single word "Slab!" may be ambiguous to the philosopher, it is not ambiguous to the builder. The ambiguity that the philosopher sees is not a function of the sentence, but a function of his point of view. He has taken the "Builder's Language" out of context, out of the "stream of life":

> For words have meaning only in the stream of life. **[RPP II §687]**

If the philosopher had worked with the builder, he would no doubt come to see the "Builder's Language" as working perfectly well—nothing about the meaning of the sentence "Slab!" is hidden or elliptical. The criterion for the "completeness" of a sentence is

---

[212] Robert J. Ackermann makes ample use of Wittgenstein's metaphor of language being like a city. He argues that Wittgenstein's two philosophies of language exemplified in the early **TLP** and the much later **PI**, are not two distinct philosophies but are like two neighborhoods in the same city. [**Wittgenstein's City**. The University of Massachusetts Press, Amherst, 1988]

whether you can accomplish what you want with it. If a sentence, no matter how abbreviated, *works*, then, *a fortiori*, it is complete—if a number of houses, no matter how few, functions as a town, it is a town.

Wittgenstein continues in a similar vein:

> But why should I not... have called the sentence "Bring me a slab" a *lengthening* of the sentence "Slab!?"—Because if you shout "Slab!'" you really mean: "Bring me a slab."—But how do you do this: how do you *mean that* while you *say* "Slab!?" Do you say the unshortened sentence to yourself? And why should I translate the call "Slab!" into a different expression in order to say what someone means by it? And if they mean the same thing—why should I not say: "When he says 'Slab!' he means 'Slab!'?" Again, if you can mean "Bring me the slab," why should you not be able to mean "Slab!?"—But when I call "Slab!," then what I want is, *that he should bring me a slab!*—Certainly, but does "wanting this" consist in thinking in some form or other a different sentence from the one you utter? [**PI** §19]

To argue that "Slab!" is merely a shortened version of "Bring me a slab!" is to fall again into the trap that when the meaning of a sentence appears to be incomplete, what it needs is *more words*, or more explanation. But the surface dissimilarity of "Slab!" and "Bring me a slab!" dissolves if we focus on the *use* of the sentences rather than their meaning. The mistaken inference about these two sentences is just the opposite of a previous mistaken inference that we have already discussed. Before, Wittgenstein noted that the similar appearance of words or sentences in different contexts leads us to the incorrect conclusion that there is some underlying essential "meaning" that runs through all the occurrences of words that appear in disparate contexts. Here, Wittgenstein is looking at the other side of that question, namely, that words or sentences that look different are really the same—that "Slab!" and "Bring me a slab!" have the same function or meaning, with the longer statement being a more "complete" and less ambiguous version of the shorter one. Wittgenstein asks, rhetorically:

> But doesn't the fact that sentences have the same sense consist in their having the same *use*? [**PI** §20]

What makes "Slab!" a "complete" sentence for the builder is not that it refers in some unconscious way to a longer "more complete" sentence, but that it is used in an *appropriate context* and *circumstances* that enable it to be understood. One could even imagine that in the terse, direct vernacular of the builder, the "complete" sentence "Bring me a slab!" might be thought odd or even an insult, implying that the hearer does not understand the simple command "Slab!." What Wittgenstein doesn't say, but which, I believe, agrees with his view of the "completeness" of statements, is that even if we wanted to accept "Bring me a slab!" as a more "complete" version of "Slab!," what grounds would we have for ending our analysis with "Bring me a slab!" as the final "complete" version of the command "Slab!?" Couldn't we also say that "Bring me a slab!" is merely a shortened version of:

> "Bring me a slab, right now!"

And this, in turn, could be a shortened version of:

"Bring me a slab, right now, and be careful not to drop it!"

And, again, we can "lengthen" the sentence to:

"Bring me a slab, right now. Be careful not to drop it, and put it next to my feet."

This list could be extended indefinitely by, for example, providing detailed instructions about how to pick a slab up and set it down, among other things. Of course there could be circumstances where you might want to use such sentences, but they would not be "longer" versions of "Slab!" within the context of the "Builder's Language." The reason why they are not longer versions of "Slab!" is that the command "Slab!" works perfectly well for the builder. No more clarification is necessary. This leads Wittgenstein to the important conclusion:

> On the one hand it is clear that every sentence in our language "is in order as it is." That is to say, we are not *striving after* an ideal, as if our ordinary vague sentences had not yet got a quite unexceptionable sense, and a perfect language awaited construction by us.—On the other hand it seems clear that where there is sense there must be perfect order.—So there must be perfect order even in the vaguest sentence.[213] [**PI** §98]

Wittgenstein might have found some sympathy with Walt Whitman's poetry:

> There was never any more inception than there is now,

---

[213] Wittgenstein's rejection of the need for an "ideal language" for doing philosophy, is one of his later positions that has its roots in the **Tractatus (TLP)**. In his early work, this was a rejection of Frege's and Russell's claim that ordinary language is not adequate for doing analytic philosophy, as they saw it. Hacker writes:

> Frege and Russell had held that natural languages are. . . only partial guides to the objective logical structures of reality (of a third realm, or of the world), whereas the **Tractatus** had argued that every possible language must, as a condition of sense, mirror (on analysis) the logical forms of what is represented. [P.M.S. Hacker. **Wittgenstein's Place in Twentieth-Century Analytic Philosophy**, p. 80. Blackwell, Oxford, 1996.]

What natural language lacked, according to Russell and Frege, is a strict determinacy of sense. Since, language, they believed, was primarily used to assert facts, and facts either are, or are not the case, then language, too, should only make statements that are clearly true or false. They felt that the vagueness or indeterminacy of natural language was an inherent flaw that made it an inadequate tool for philosophical inquiry. This could only be remedied by the construction of an ideal logical language—a goal of both Frege and Russell. Wittgenstein rejected the need for an ideal language because he felt that the indeterminacy of ordinary language was just a superficial phenomenon that could be corrected by philosophical analysis. Later, in **PI**, he rejected this, preferring to see determinacy of sense not as a function of language itself, but as a function of particular language games and/or forms of life. That is, there is no absolute standard of determinacy in language, as Russell and Frege thought, but determinacy of language varied according to the activities and circumstances of its use. The goal of language use is not to adhere to some exalted standard of determinacy, but to have just enough determinacy of sense that it can be used appropriately, the circumstances of its use will clear up any remaining indeterminacy. Meaning in language is not determined by uncovering the essential unchanging meanings of words, but by looking at how those words are actually used.

Nor any more youth or age than there is now,

And will never be any more perfection than there is now,

    :
    :

To elaborate is no avail, learn'd and unlearn'd feel that it is so.[214]

Wittgenstein is not saying that there are no ambiguous sentences in ordinary language, or that some explanation might not be necessary for some statements. He is saying that if a sentence makes sense, it must be complete, no matter how ambiguous it may seem when considered apart from the context and circumstances in which it usually occurs. And if we want to know how a brief, seemingly ambiguous sentence can convey a precise idea, we should not look for some other more "complete" sentence, we should look at how the circumstances and context of the sentence give it sense. To use one of Chomsky's examples, the single sentence "Flying planes can be dangerous" can be interpreted in two different ways and seems in need of further clarification. But this ambiguity occurs when we take the statement out of its context, out of the "stream of life" in which it makes sense. If we see a friend climbing out of the cockpit of a small plane that he has just landed, and his face appears ashen and his hands trembling as he says, "Flying planes can be dangerous!" we know exactly what he means.[215]

---

[214] W. Whitman. "Song of Myself," **The Oxford Book of American Verse**, part 3, p. 281. Oxford University Press, NY, 1950. Edited by F.O. Matthiessen.

[215] Chomsky used examples like this to make a much more profound claim, *viz.*, that sentences that are structurally ambiguous such as "Flying planes can be dangerous" or "I saw a grizzly bear driving to Los Angeles" must have a "deep structure" that we can access to resolve the ambiguity. Yet, as Wittgenstein showed us, if we look to some "inner" or "deep" mental mechanism to resolve ambiguity in language, we are looking for the answer in the wrong place. The resolution of this kind of ambiguity comes from the context and circumstances of the utterance not its purported "deep structure." As Baker and Hacker comment on this form of "ambiguity":

> The "ability to detect ambiguity" allegedly forces us to attribute knowledge of a grammatical theory to children or adults. Two examples are notorious: (i) "Visiting aunts can be boring." Of this two modern linguists claim "in order to assign an unambiguous semantic interpretation to the sentence, we need access to information contained in its deep structure."**
> (ii) "They are flying planes." ... If I ask "Where are Tom and Dick?" and am told "They are flying planes," I do not need any system of internal formulae or mental representation to know that the answer means that Tom and Dick (the well-known aces of the 25th Squadron) are flying their Harriers (or, in a different context, that Tom and Dick those well-known model-plane builders are currently flying their latest models in the park). Similarly, if I am walking through the aeronautics museum and the guide points at some full-scale model planes, saying "These are only reconstructed planes, but those over there, they are flying planes," I do not need any deep structures to enable me to understand. Pari passu, if "Visiting aunts can be boring" is a response to "That old bag, Aunt Doris, is visiting us tomorrow," or a response to "What a bore, I have to visit my Aunt Doris tomorrow," it wears its meaning on its face, not in its "depth grammar," let alone in any "mental representations" thereof.
> Not only does an ordinary speaker not need to have recourse ("deep in his unconscious mind") to hidden rules of transformational-generative grammar, but he could not do so if he needed to [G.P. Baker and P.M.S. Hacker. **Language, Sense and Nonsense: A Critical Investigation of Modern Theories of Language**, pp. 292–293. Basil Blackwell, 1984.] . The authors cite the following reference in the above quotation: [J.P.B. Allen and P. van Buren. **Chomsky: Selected Readings**, p. 103. Oxford University Press, Oxford, 1971.]

**The Implications of the "Language as City" Metaphor**

The analogy between language and a city is a very powerful and suggestive metaphor, and it may be useful to bring out some of the implications this has for the study of language. Let's first take another look at the quotation in which Wittgenstein makes this analogy:

> (And how many houses or streets does it take before a town begins to be a town?) Our language can be seen as an ancient city: a maze of little streets and squares, of old and new houses, and of houses with additions from various periods; and this surrounded by a multitude of new boroughs with straight, regular streets and uniform houses. [**PI** §18]

One of the first characteristics of a city to come to mind is that it is constantly changing: new parts of the city are being constructed and older parts are falling into disuse. Some parts of the city are no longer used at all. This metaphor brings out the same dynamic quality in language. Our language changes on a continual basis in a number of ways. We often borrow words and phrases from other languages, such as the expressions "savior faire" or "gung ho." We also create entirely new sets of words and phrases to deal with new activities, such as manned space missions ("Apollo," "power up," "space shuttle," "lunar module," and "launch pad"). These newer words and phrases occur in concert with the growth of a new activity, and are most frequently seen in scientific disciplines since these are the activities that are currently changing the most. Before World War II we had no words to express such things as "DNA," "hovercraft," "fusion reaction," "gene splicing," "data base management," "telecommunications," "throughput," "mini-, micro-, or mainframe computer," etc. Sixty years ago we had no words to express these concepts because we had yet to begin the activities that they emerged from. We have also completely abandoned some words and phrases, like we abandon old neighborhoods, primarily because they refer to activities in disuse. The practices of phrenology and bloodletting being cases here, and, more recently, the references to "cold fusion." Another dynamic that encourages change in our language is the use of slang. Each generation seems to develop its own vernacular: what was "cool!" "far out!" or "groovy!" for the "beat generation," of the 1950's, is now "rad!" or "fresh!" to today's youth. It is also the case that there may be parts of Wittgenstein's city that are temporary, and some parts that are more enduring (slang being a case of the former and religious texts being a case of the latter).

One of the most interesting, but subtle, characteristics of the city is that it creates right-of-ways through certain parts of the city and obstacles to other passageways. One cannot go *anywhere* one might want to, buildings or other edifices may be in our way. Language

---

In some sense, Wittgenstein (and his advocates such as Baker and Hacker) offers a reversal of the old joke about the man looking for his lost keys at night under a street lamp—"Where did you lose your keys?" a passerby asks. "Down the street," he replies. "Why aren't you looking for the keys where you lost them?" asks the passerby. "Because the light is much better here," he replies. This has been offered as an example of how misleading it may be to use quantitative modelling methods to investigate mental processes—using the "brighter clarity" of quantitative modelling to represent "darker" less well-understood mental phenomena. Yet, with Chomsky's insistence that we should be looking at "deep structures" if we want to understand meaning, and not at the actual usage of language, as Wittgenstein insists, he moves our investigation of language away from the "bright light" of usage (what Chomsky calls "performance") and towards the "darkness" of the "deep mental structures" (what Chomsky terms "competence"). Chomsky is looking for the proverbial black cat in a dark room, never asking the more fundamental question of whether the cat is there at all.

operates in the same manner. We are not free to talk in any way that we might want to. There are "roads" and "passageways" that influence how we speak. This does not mean that we can *never* speak in certain ways, but that we are encouraged to speak in other specific ways. Language is a not a *product* of thought, as we noted earlier (see the previous section "**Language and Thought**"), but the *vehicle* of thought:

> When I think in language, there aren't "meanings" going through my mind in addition to the verbal expressions: the language is itself the vehicle of thought. [**PI** §329]

Another parallel between language and a city is that the city functions with few, if any, explicit rules that govern how it works. It has been noted that New York City contains, at any given time, only enough food to feed its inhabitants for a few days. Yet it never runs out of food, even during trucking or railroad strikes or after severe snow storms. But there is no set of rules that governs the supply of food for New York City, and it is doubtful that such a set of rules could be set up to control all eventualities. In the same way, language is a large, enormously complex system that defies complete regulation by explicit rules. It is true that language has rules of syntax, and New York has a variety of civil regulations. But neither the rules of syntax nor the city regulations completely determine the functioning of language or the city, respectively. The activities of supply and demand in New York attain a kind of equilibrium in which the demand for goods and services balances with the available supply. This balance can shift in favor of supply or demand in certain situations, but it always seems to come back into balance when things return to normal:

> The regulation of traffic in the streets permits and forbids certain actions on the part of drivers and pedestrians; but it does not attempt to guide the totality of their movements by prescription. And it would be senseless to talk of an "ideal" ordering of traffic which should do that; in the first place we should have no idea what to imagine as this ideal. If someone wants to make traffic regulations stricter on some point or other, that does not mean that he wants to approximate to such an ideal.[216] [**Z** §440]

Language, too, has no ideal ordering that it aspires to, but like the supply of food in New York, language achieves a kind of balance as a result of competing forces. The individual who originally described the balancing of competing forces in language was George Kingsley Zipf.[217] Like Wittgenstein, Zipf believed that the words and phrases in our language are like tools, and these tools are used to perform linguistic acts:

---

[216]The idea that rules cannot govern all the actions in a process is a recurrent theme in Wittgenstein's work. See also **PI** §84 at the end of the previous section **Language Games and Forms of Life**.

[217]**Human Behavior and the Principle of Least Effort**. Hafner, NY, 1965 (facsimile of the 1949 edition). Zipf found that if you tabulate the occurrences of all words in a sufficiently large text and rank them according to their frequencies, with the most frequent word holding rank number one, then the product of the rank of any given word and its frequency will approximate a constant. If you plot this distribution on logarithmic scales by decreasing frequency, the plot will be linear with a slope of −1. Further, because of the slope of -1 the x and y intercepts will be the same (x = rank, y = frequency), meaning that the total number of different words in the vocabulary being studied will be equal to the frequency of the most frequently occurring word (the word of rank one). Zipf's Law was observed in such diverse linguistic samples as, James Joyce's novel **Ulysses**, newspapers, Homer's **Iliad**, Chinese, German, Plains Cree, Dakota, Aelfric's Old English, etc., so there is little doubt that it describes a fairly well-established statistical regularity of natural language.

... words are tools that are used to convey meanings in order to achieve objectives.[218]

The balance in language is a product of the "competition" between tools (i.e., words) and jobs (i.e., the linguistic tasks that we use words to complete).

> The problem of *tools-and-jobs* is the same as the problem of *means* and *ends*, or of *instruments* (or agents) and *objectives*. We shall adopt the homelier term, *tools-and-jobs*, to emphasize the common-place nature of the problem under discussion.[219]

But this tools-and-jobs nature of language is fundamentally reciprocal. It means that tools require certain kinds of jobs in order to be used, and jobs require certain kinds of tools in order for the job to be accomplished. This reciprocity has the function of fitting available tools to required jobs, and, at the same time, altering the jobs to be performed to fit the functions of available tools.

> ... there are two aspects of the economy of the *tools-and-jobs* in question. In the first place, there is the economy of *tools*. In the second place, there is the economy of *jobs*... To clarify the significance of these two economies, let us illustrate them briefly in terms of carpentry *tools* and carpentry *jobs*... We *all* know from experience that when a person has a carpentry *job* to be performed, he directly or indirectly seeks a set of carpentry *tools* to perform the job. And, in general, we may say that *jobs seek tools*... But what is often overlooked is the equally obvious fact that when a person owns a set of carpentry *tools*, then, roughly speaking, he directly or indirectly seeks a carpentry *job* for his tools to perform. Thus, we may say that *tools seek jobs*.[220]

Zipf calls this the "reciprocal economy of matching tools to jobs and jobs to tools." In linguistic behavior, this reciprocal economy manifests itself in the following way: The words and phrases in language are, of course, the tools, and the expression of meaning is the job for which these words/tools can be used. For example, if I want to ask someone what time it is, I have certain words and phrases that are more-or-less suitable for this task (consider how the use of conventional English as opposed to the use of slang can be used to accomplish this job differently). We are so fluent in our native language that this reciprocal economy of tools and jobs is not readily apparent. But we can see this reciprocity more clearly if we imagine ourselves in Germany with only a modest ability to speak German. Here, the job is the same—to find out what time it is. But suppose we don't know the standard phrase, "Wieviel Uhr ist es?" Here, we must fit our limited tools (the few German words and phrases we know) to the task of finding out what time it is. We may be able to get by with the contrived phrase "Was ist die Uhr?"—"What is the hour?" (accompanied, perhaps, by appropriate gestures), but if we look closely at this situation, we can see another change taking place. Because our command of German is minimal, we would not comprehend a detailed or precise explanation of the time such as, "Es ist zehn nach halb acht." We can only comprehend such phrases as "Sieben Uhr"—"Seven o'clock" or, "Ungefär Sieben Uhr"—"About seven o'clock." Thus, the limited tools available to

---

[218] *Op.cit.*, p. 20.
[219] *Op.cit.*, p. 10.
[220] *Op.cit.*, p. 8.

use have *changed* our task at hand from finding out *exactly* what time it is to finding out *roughly* what time it is—this is how tools and jobs can influence each other.

The important thing to remember is that, like our example of supplying food to New York City, we don't need codified rules to bring about the vocabulary balance in language. In fact there is no set of rules that could do this. All we need to do is to use language to accomplish our day-to-day tasks. A natural equilibrium will result. Another aspect that cities share with language concerns how we find our way about. In a city, we learn to find our way about through our active involvement in our daily affairs. Sometimes we might need a map to find our way, but often we just ask or travel with others in the course of our activities and come to know our way about in a casual rather than formal way. By "casual" I do not mean "imprecise" or "haphazard." I merely mean that when we learn our way about there is no systematic attempt to learn our way *apart from the activities we engage in*. We simply participate in the activities we want to engage in and, in so doing, we learn how to get around the city. These activities could be for business or pleasure. It is also the case that we often can find our way about without being able to explain to someone how to do it in any kind of precise way. While we can *show* another person how to get from A to B by driving him and pointing out landmarks along the way, we are often at a loss to give detailed instructions about exactly what route to take without actually taking them along that route. Wittgenstein comments:

> It could very well be imagined that someone knows his way around a city perfectly, i.e., would confidently find the shortest way from any place in it to any other,—and yet would be quite incompetent to draw a map of the city. That, as soon as he tries, he produces nothing that is not completely wrong. [**Z** §121]

Language is quite similar. We learn much of our native language by using it in day-to-day activities rather than learning it in a formal way apart from the activities that we might use it in. Of course, we do have formal classes in English grammar and composition, but we usually do not take such classes until we have been in school for a number of years and already have a good ability to use our language—that is, we can get things done with it. The formal classes merely refine an ability that already exists, and there are many individuals who achieve a remarkable ability with language with little or no formal training. Our understanding of cities and language comes about primarily through interaction and participation. We can read a tourist guide to New York, but we won't really know our way about until we stay there for some time. Wittgenstein comments:

> People who always keep asking "why?" resemble tourists who read Baedeker while they stand before a building and through reading about the building's history, origins, and so on are kept from seeing it.[221]

A final similarity between a city and language is that we can know a lot about getting around a city without knowing *every single place* in the city. There may be large areas

---

[221] Wittgenstein. **Unpublished Manuscript number 163** (1941). Cornell University Library. Wittgenstein's low estimation for "tourists" is reflected in his reply to a student who wanted to attend some of Wittgenstein's lectures, but not all of them: "My lectures are not for tourists." [Malcolm. **Ludwig Wittgenstein: A Memoir**, p. 28. Oxford University Press, London, 1958.]

that we will never see. We won't see them because our activities don't take us there. In language, there will always be expressions that we don't understand. There will even be entire "neighborhoods" of language we will never know (a "neighborhood" of language would be like a dialect of language or the jargon of a scientific field, e.g., the language of chemistry or electron microscopy, or other "suburbs" of our language (see **PI** §18 at the beginning of the section **Language as a City** (*supra*)). Like cities these "neighborhoods" of language do not have distinct borders; words and phrases can be used in common with a variety of activities.

### *Language as a Labyrinth*

Closely related to Wittgenstein's notion of language as a city is his metaphor of language as a "labyrinth."

> Language is a labyrinth of paths. You approach from one side and know your way about; you approach the same place from another side and no longer know your way about. [**PI** 203]

An unknown city can seems like a labyrinth or maze so Wittgenstein's metaphor seems to be just a variation on the "city" metaphor. But there is one aspect of a labyrinth that is important to language but does not fit with the city metaphor. This would be the concept of a labyrinth that was constructed *as a* labyrinth, and is not part of a city. In this kind of labyrinth, all the passageways look the same so it is difficult to know just where you are (whereas, in a city most of the "passageways," i.e., streets, looks different). This is like the case in language where the words look the same in different contexts so we assume that they are all used in the same way:

> Of course, what confuses us is the uniform appearance of words when we hear them spoken or meet them in script and print. For their *application* is not presented to us so clearly. [**PI** §11]

This is a minor point, but much of Wittgenstein's philosophy comes as a succession of such minor points, things, as he said, that are important but which slip by our observation because they are so familiar.

### *Reality and Myth: The Background of Reality on Which Language is Based is Like a Mythology, and its Structure is Like a Riverbed*

Propositions, that is, assertions of fact, hold an important place in 20th century philosophy's analytic tradition and its philosophy of language. It is through factual assertions that we can describe what we know to be the case. Some would even claim that the *only* role of philosophy is to examine the truth or falsity of factual propositions. Wittgenstein, in his early work, **TLP**, took as one of his primary tasks to define the boundaries of factual discourse.

Once we know that something is the case, it does not change readily—this is the inherited background of facts that we accept, much of it on faith. Wittgenstein comments:

> But I did not get my picture of the world by satisfying myself of its correctness; nor do I have it because I am satisfied of its correctness. No; it is the inherited background against which I distinguish between true and false.
>
> The propositions describing this world-picture might be part of a kind of mythology. And their role is like that of rules of a game; and the game can be learned purely practically, without learning any explicit rules.
>
> It might be imagined that some propositions, of the form of empirical propositions, were hardened and functioned as channels for such empirical propositions as were not hardened by fluid; and that this relation altered with time, in that fluid propositions hardened, and hard ones became fluid.
>
> The mythology may change back into a state of flux, the river-bed of thoughts may shift. But I distinguish between the movement of the waters on the river-bed and the shift of the bed itself; though there is not a sharp division of the one from the other.
>
> But if someone were to say "So logic too is an empirical science" he would be wrong. Yet this is right: the same proposition may get treated at one time as something to test by experience, at another as a rule of testing.
>
> And the bank of that river consists partly of hard rock, subject to no alteration or only to an imperceptible one, partly of sand, which now in one place now in another gets washed away, or deposited.[222] [**OC** §§94–99]

Wittgenstein is not talking about *all* language here, but only that part of our language which deals with propositions—statements of fact. These propositions express the "inherited background" of facts that make up our view of the world. It is important to point out that the propositions we are able to articulate cannot completely describe our "picture of the world." It is also the case that much of what we take as our "inherited background" by which we can judge the truth and falsity of factual statements was not given to us in the form of propositions. This factual background came to us, in part, through training—as a parent shows the child the names of things—and, in part, through our involved experience and interaction with our surroundings (e.g., our discovery of how painful bee stings are). Nevertheless, Wittgenstein's point is well-taken. If our descriptions of facts are constrained, not just by the "facts" of our world, but in some cases by the formal structure of those propositions, then we can see that the influence of the formal structure of language (here, propositions), like a riverbed, influences what we can assert and not assert, and that, in turn, can influence how we think. Wittgenstein speaks of this as a kind of "mythology." He is not saying that our empirical world is a myth, but that, like a myth, parts of it are presented to us as the truth, even though we cannot verify them. We must remember that what we take as a mythology, such as the myths of the ancient Greeks and Romans, was taken by them to be a picture of their factual world. The pantheon of gods that the Greeks

---

[222] This statement stands in marked contrast to statements that Wittgenstein made in his earlier philosophy: "It isn't possible to believe something for which you cannot imagine some kind of verification" [**Philosophical Remarks**, §59. University of Chicago Press, Chicago, 1975]. Since Wittgenstein does not explicitly address his earlier views in his later writings it is sometimes difficult for the reader to see exactly where he has revised his earlier thought.

believed in were not seen to be products of their imagination, they were considered to be just as valid a part of their reality as their everyday affairs were.

In the above quotation, Wittgenstein is saying that the propositions that we can formulate in language have a kind of structure like the riverbed of a river. In many cases, this propositional structure or grammar has a fixed nature to it, like the "hard rock" bank of a river, but in others it consists of "sand" and may shift easily. Propositions that have a "hard rock" structure are like:

Alain is 6 feet tall.
Chris weighs 190 pounds.
Bill planted a copper-beech tree in his yard.
The Lufthansa flight from Vienna is scheduled to arrive at 5:00 pm.

These kinds of propositions have a comfortable familiarity about them. Most importantly, they have clear criteria for testing their truthfulness—we can measure Alain's height and Chris' weight, we can look at the trees Bill has planted, we can call the airport and ask when the Lufthansa flight is due. One can be as certain about the truth of these propositions as one can for just about anything, and there are not too many ways for an adult of reasonable intelligence to go wrong here. These are all propositions that we can confirm personally. Another kind of proposition that we generally accept but which is beyond our personal ability to establish is:

Pluto is the farthest planet from the sun in our solar system.

Most of us would accept this proposition as being true, but it is certainly beyond the ability of the average person to confirm directly. This is a proposition that we accept on authority and is part our background knowledge, even though it does not affect us personally.

But sometimes we think that the "hard rock" of propositions like those above exists for other propositions when it doesn't. We have already given an example of this phenomenon, but it bears repeating. When we ask:

What is the height of Mt. Hood?

we have a clear sense of what would count as an answer, and we would go about finding it in much the way that we would answer questions of similar form or grammar. But what about the question:

What is the meaning of a word?

On the surface, this looks like the previous question. Consequently, it's easy to assume that it has the same "hard rock" structure as that question. If this were so, then like "the height of Mt. Hood," the "meaning of a word" should not only be easily answerable, but there should be just one clear answer to the question. But this is not the case. Not only is there not a clear answer for our "meaning" question, but even answers that are deemed true at one point in time, are subject to continual debate and revision. The "meaning of a word" lies on a bed of shifting sand rather than a firmament of hard rock. To carry Wittgenstein's river metaphor to its conclusion, we might say that looking at the "surface grammar" of the above two questions is like looking at the surface of a river and not questioning the nature of the riverbed on which it flows. In the "river" metaphor we are again led back to Wittgenstein's distinction between "surface grammar" and "depth grammar," with "depth grammar" being concerned with the "riverbed." The most common way for the "hard rock" riverbed of propositions to change is after the introduction of new technology. The way that we see the facts of our world can change dramatically. The electron microscope lets us see detail that simply was not possible before; telephones let us talk to friends and relatives who were unreachable, conversationally, except by physical journey; the Hubble telescope enables us to see farther in the universe than we have ever seen before, etc. Wittgenstein unwittingly gives us another example:

> Suppose some adult had told a child that he had been on the moon. The child tells me the story, and I say it was only a joke, the man hadn't been on the moon; no one has ever been on the moon; the moon is a long way off and it is impossible to climb up there or fly there. [**OC** §106]

Now, of course, the child could have talked to Neil Armstrong—the hard rock riverbed has shifted here creating a possibility that never existed before. In another case we could compare the following statements:

> Jack is over 6 feet tall.
> Jack is a paranoid schizophrenic.

Sometimes, the "riverbed" for the same proposition can vary significantly. The first assertion (above) is fairly clear, but the second may or may not make a clear distinction, depending on the backgrounds of those who might utter it. Some psychiatrists insist that paranoid schizophrenia, or at least extreme cases of it, is a real "sickness" and can be diagnosed with relative confidence. So to them the second statement and the first both have clear grounds for asserting. But for other psychiatrists the diagnosis of paranoid schizophrenia is not nearly as clear-cut. Psychiatrist Thomas Szasz sees the distinction between the mentally fit and the mentally ill as a false dichotomy. They are of no more consequence than other human characteristics that distinguish us (such as the differences between shy individuals and extroverts). For Szasz, we feel a need to define and treat those we label as psychotics, not because they are "sick" but because we find their behavior upsetting. Interestingly, like Wittgenstein, Szasz sees the failure to distinguish physical from mental illness as a consequence of language:

> The upshot of this psychiatric-psychoanalytic "revolution" is that, today, it is considered shamefully uncivilized and naïvely unscientific to treat a person who acts or appears sick as if he were not sick. We now "know" and "realize" that such a person is sick; that he is obviously sick; that he is mentally sick.

> But this view rests on a serious, albeit simple, error: it rests on mistaking or confusing what is real with what is imitation; literal meaning with metaphorical meaning; medicine with morals. In other words, I maintain that mental illness is a metaphorical disease: that bodily illness stands in the same relation to mental illness as a defective television set stands to a bad television program. Of course, the word

"sick" is often used metaphorically. We call jokes "sick," economies "sick," sometimes even the whole world "sick"; but only when we call minds "sick" do we systematically mistake and strategically misinterpret metaphor for fact—and send for the doctor to "cure" the "illness." It is as if a television viewer were to send for a television repairman because he dislikes the program he sees on the screen.[223]

According to Malcolm, this metaphorical mistake is echoed in the philosophy of mind:

What is happening in today's philosophy of mind is truly extraordinary. The idea that thoughts and feelings are "inner," in a metaphorical sense, has been transformed into what is believed to be a precise, hard-headed, scientific theory, namely, that thoughts and feelings are actually *in* the head. This seems to be building a philosophical position on a pun: what was first regarded as *metaphorically* "inner" is now taken to be *literally* "inner."[224]

There are other kinds of propositions that are upheld in a different kind of way than the more readily testable ones we described above. Wittgenstein writes:

However, we can ask: May someone have telling grounds for believing that the earth has only existed for a short time, say since his own birth?—Suppose he had always been told that,—would he have any good reason to doubt it? Men have believed that they could make rain; why should not a king be brought up in the belief that the world began with him? And if Moore and this king were to meet and discuss, could Moore really prove his belief to be the right one? I do not say that Moore could not convert the king to his view, but it would be a conversion of a special kind; the king would be brought to look at the world in a different way.

Remember that one is sometimes convinced of the correctness of a view by its simplicity or symmetry, i.e., these are what induce one to go over to this point of view. One then simply says something like: "That's how it must be."[225] [**OC** §92]

---

[223] T. Szasz. **The Myth of Mental Illness**. Perennial Library, Harper and Row, NY, 1973 (revised edition). This failure of psychiatry, according to Szasz, occurs because of a problem of language, specifically, it occurs because psychiatry has taken the metaphor "mental illness" too literally. No doubt, Wittgenstein would see this as a "disease of thinking," of confusing two language games—"sickness" as defined by physiological medical practice, versus, "sickness" defined in psychiatric practice.

It may sound trivial to distinguish between those psychiatrists who accept the clear diagnosability of paranoid schizophrenia and those who do not. But the acceptance of one view over the other is not just the acceptance of a single diagnosis. Those who hold one view really hold an entire system of views. As Wittgenstein remarked:

When we first begin to believe anything, what we believe is not a single proposition, it is a whole system of propositions. (Light dawns gradually over the whole) [**OC** §141]

Interestingly, Wittgenstein has even had an impact on the field of psychiatry. A book that takes a Wittgensteinean view of schizophrenia is Louis Sass' **The Paradoxes of Delusion: Wittgenstein, Schreber, and the Schizophrenic Mind**. Cornell University Press, Ithaca, NY, 1994.

[224] Malcolm. **Nothing is Hidden: Wittgenstein's Criticism of his Early Thought**, p. 191. Blackwell, Oxford, 1986.

[225] The "Moore" whom Wittgenstein referred to was his fellow Cambridge philosopher G.E. Moore. Wittgenstein spent much of OC describing his objections to Moore's philosophy as described in Moore's 1939 paper "Proof of an External World."

Here, Wittgenstein gives us examples of "facts" that do not lend themselves to proof the way that more common ones do. He shows that there are other, more complex criteria for our acceptance of them. These are the kinds of facts that comprise religious beliefs, such as the assertion that the world was created in 6 days, or that all people are descended from Adam and Eve, or that heaven and hell actually exist. These are facts that an astronomer, who would not accept the existence of a tenth planet without substantial evidence, might accept without scientific proof. These facts are more like the "mythology" that Wittgenstein describes in the quotation at footnote 227 (*supra*). The rationale for these kinds of beliefs, according to Wittgenstein, might be something like "simplicity" or "symmetry." These beliefs tend to fill out the unknown parts or processes of our universe, such as, how the universe could have come about, or, what happens to us when we die. Belief in them gives us a kind of closure in our personal cosmology, it fills in the gaps and thereby creates a kind of symmetry in our sense of the universe and our place in it. It is also simple, and therefore easy to grasp and to pass on to others, unlike many scientific explanations.[226]

In the quotation at footnote 227 (*supra*) we see another metaphor. Wittgenstein draws an analogy between the "inherited background" of facts and mythology:

> The propositions describing this world-picture might be part of a kind of mythology.

This seems to be a decidedly odd statement coming from a philosopher with such a strong analytical bent. How is our description of the factual world to be compared to a mythology? On the one hand, we seem to have strong empirical justification for our reality, while mythology exists without such justification. But if we look more closely, we find that there *are* similarities between what we take to be empirical reality and mythology. For both, explanations have to stop somewhere, and when this point is reached we must simply say that that is the way things are. When we try to explain how our universe began, we can explain things back to the "Big Bang," but we cannot go any further. Wittgenstein's analysis of meaning in language, which he considers the fundamental problem in philosophy, runs up against a similar endpoint. We can talk about how we use language, we can give examples of language use, and we can explain this usage *up to a point*. But we cannot go further. For Wittgenstein, of course, the terminal point for our explanations of language use and meaning comes in the activities in which we use the language in question. We can

---

[226] The rigor with which Wittgenstein approached philosophical problems might lend one to believe that he might be disdainful of religion. But he was not. Normam Macolm brings out Wittgenstein's religious point of view:

> As a child Ludwig Wittgenstein received formal instruction in Roman Catholicism. Later on, conversations with his sister Gretl destroyed his childish faith. He became indifferent to, perhaps even contemptuous of, religious belief. When he was about 21 years of age, however, something occurred that had a lasting impact on him. He saw a play in Vienna which was mediocre drama: but there was a scene in which a person whose life had been desperately miserable, and who thought himself about to die, suddenly felt himself to be spoken to in the words, "Nothing can happen to you!" No matter what occurred in the world, no harm could come to him! Wittgenstein was greatly struck by this thought (as he told me approximately forty years later): for the first time he perceived the possibility of religious belief . . . [**Wittgenstein: A Religious Point of View?**, p. 7. Cornell University Press, Ithaca, NY, 1994]. Later in life, Wittgenstein told his friend Drury, "I am not a religious man but I cannot help seeing every problem from a religious point of view." [**Ludwig Wittgenstein, Personal Recollections**, p. 94. Oxford University Press, Oxford, 1984. Edited by R. Rhees.]

explain how language is used in, say, singing a song, but we can't explain why we sing songs. Singing is just something we do, which has no further justification. Of course we can continue the explanation of, here, singing, as a means of bonding people of the same culture together, or for promoting social contact, or for inducing an infant to sleep, etc. But we still have to ask why we do *these* things, and eventually we will reach the endpoint that Wittgenstein reminds us of, where we will have to say, "This is simply what I do." Like mythology, the foundation of language is not rational:

> It is so difficult to find the *beginning*. Or, better: it is difficult to begin at the beginning. And not try to go further back.
>
> When a child learns language it learns at the same time what is to be investigated and what not. When it learns that there is a cupboard in the room, it isn't taught to doubt whether what it sees later on is still a cupboard or only a kind of stage set.
>
> ⋮
>
> Language did not emerge from some kind of ratiocination. [**OC** §§471–472, 475]

What is true of language is also true of language games:

> ... for why should the language-game rest on some kind of knowledge? [**OC** §477]

In fact, we don't have "reasons" until we have language-games:

> Instinct comes first, reasoning second. Not until there is a language-game are there reasons. [**RPP II** §689]

The child is not taught to *believe* that the cupboard exists, but is taught to open cupboards, put things in cupboards, close cupboards, get things from cupboards, etc. The issue of the cupboard's existence never comes up.

## The Foundation of Language in Instinctive Behavior

In spite of our discussion so far, it still must seem odd to some that language does "... not emerge from some kind of ratiocination." But Wittgenstein is certain that it does not.[227]

---

[227] This objection to a rational basis for language may seem like a minor point, but it is not. One of the most influential modern linguists, Noam Chomsky, insists that the process of language acquisition is distinctly rational:

> To learn a language... the child must have a method for devising an appropriate grammar, given primary linguistic data. As a precondition for language learning, he must possess, first, a linguistic theory that specifies the form of the grammar of a possible human language, and, second, a strategy for selecting a grammar of the appropriate form that is compatible with the primary linguistic data. [N. Chomsky. **Aspects of the Theory of Syntax**, p. 25. MIT Press, Cambridge, 1965.]

This "linguistic theory" that the child possesses, Chomsky was later to call a "universal grammar":

> [Chomsky] Suppose we assign to the mind, as an innate property, the general theory of language that we have called "universal grammar"... The theory of universal grammar, then, provides a schema to which any particular grammar must conform. Suppose, furthermore, that we can make this schema sufficiently restrictive so that very few possible grammars

As Wittgenstein pointed out, language is not the product of thought, it is "the vehicle of

> conforming to the schema will be consistent with the meagre and degenerate data actually available to the language learner. His task, then, is to search among the possible grammars and select one that is not definitely rejected by the data available to him. [Chomsky. **Language and Mind**, p. 88. Harcourt Brace Jovanovich, NY, 1972.]

Why do we need the "universal grammar?" To Chomsky, there just isn't enough linguistic information to enable the child to learn language without some additional innate knowledge or ability:

> We cannot avoid being struck by the enormous disparity between knowledge and experience— in the case of language, between the generative grammar that expresses the linguistic competence of the native speaker and the meager and degenerate data on the basis of which he has constructed this grammar for himself. [*op.cit.*, p. 78.]

If we just look at the linguistic information that the child has access to, then Chomsky is right, there is not enough linguistic data for the child to build up his linguistic competence. But Chomsky's missing the most important component of language—a mistake that Wittgenstein doesn't make:

> . . . we don't start from certain words, but from certain occasions or activities. [Wittgenstein. **LC**, p. 3]

What lies at the foundation of a child's learning language is not just linguistic data, but the child's understanding of the situations, activities and context that give that "meager and degenerate" linguistic data meaning. The foundation of language lies not in some innate, mental, "deep structures" but surrounds us all in the "common behavior of mankind." Chomsky's recourse to innate mental mechanisms is just the sort of "disease of thinking" that Wittgenstein abhorred, since it encourages us to look for the foundation of language in the wrong place. Not only does it ignore what is truly essential to linguistic meaning—situations, context, activities and practices—but it is presented in such a way that it would be impossible to prove, or disprove. What would count as evidence that the child has a "universal grammar" and uses it in the way Chomsky insists he must? Chomsky feels he doesn't have to prove his hypothesis because he believes it is the only one that can explain the child's ability to acquire language. But surely Wittgenstein's theory of language use is a reasonable alternative to Chomsky's, and, if so, means that Chomsky must provide evidence for his version of language acquisition. This he cannot do. Constructing a theory that embodies the only possible explanation of a phenomenon is a common method of science, and Chomsky is to be commended for his rigor in analyzing language. But the rigor that characterized his language theory was not a rigor that he discovered but a rigor he imposed on his work. Wittgenstein saw this distinction quite clearly:

> The more narrowly we examine language, the sharper becomes the conflict between it and our requirement. (For the crystalline purity of logic was, of course, not a result of investigation; it was a requirement.) The conflict becomes intolerable; the requirement is now in danger of becoming empty.—We have got onto slippery ice where there is no friction and so in a certain sense the conditions are ideal, but also, just because of that, we are unable to walk. We want to walk; so we need friction. Back to the rough ground! [**PI** §107]

Chomsky ignored the "rough ground" of language use (what he called "performance"). Ironically, Malcolm points out that Chomsky's view of language is remarkably similar to Wittgenstein's early view—a view that he, Wittgenstein, later rejected, in large part:

> One striking feature of Chomsky's views about language is that they have a strong resemblance to the conceptions of the **Tractatus** (published with English translation in 1922); and a second striking feature is that they seem to totally ignore the devastating criticism of those conceptions in the **Philosophical Investigations** (published with English translation in 1951). [Malcolm. **Wittgenstein: A Religious Point of View?**, p. 48. Cornell University Press, Ithaca, NY, 1994.]

thought" (see quote at footnote 64). But if language does not have its origin in thought or "some kind of ratiocination," from what does it come? Wittgenstein is quite clear in his answer:

> The origin and the primitive form of the language-game is a reaction; only from this can the more complicated forms grow.

> Language—I want to say—is a refinement; "in the begining was the deed." [**CV** p. 31]

The origin of language is in the things that we do. We can imagine people existing who do not have a language—perhaps someone suffering from aphasia. They would not be able to say anything nor understand things that are said to them. But can we imagine the opposite: a person who has linguistic ability but no routine activities, even of the most primitive sort? Someone who is not active, who has never played, never run or jumped, never thrown an object or even walked? The closest that we can imagine to someone fitting this image might be some unfortunate individual who has been brain-damaged from birth, someone who hasn't the ability or understanding to perform the simplest human acts. Such an unfortunate individual would not have the characteristics, other than appearance, of a person at all. What defines us as humans is not so much a common linguistic ability, but a common ability to engage in many simple and complex human activities. In short, we can imagine people without language but not people without shared activities.[228]

---

[228] As pointed out, aphasics are the best examples of people who do not have the ability to use or understand language. The very existence of aphasia indicates that our ability to use language is modular and can be selectively removed without affecting most of our other cognitive abilities. The sufferers from aphasia are usually stroke or tumor victims and aphasia itself can be either expressive—the inability to use language—or receptive—the inability to understand language—or both. Unfortunately, once aphasics are afflicted with this disability, they can no longer report, or report reliably, to observers what they are going through, since the very medium by which they would report what they experience—language—has been removed or corrupted. But Merlin Donald describes a remarkable case of a paroxysmal aphasic, referred to as "Brother John," who suffered periodic bouts of aphasia which lasted anywhere from a few minutes to a few hours [**Origins of the Modern Mind**. Harvard University Press, Cambridge, MA, 1991]. After these periods of aphasia, Brother John was able to remember what it was like to be aphasic, explaining, in detail, how his perceptions and abilities had changed. Further, during his aphasic episodes, he was able to remember and carry out requests that were suggested by medical observers. In this way, Brother John's abilities during aphasia could be tested, as no aphasics had been tested before.

The important fact about Brother John's spells was that they selectively shut down language processing, while he remained conscious and able to remember what he was experiencing. During his long spells, his cognitive abilities returned gradually, progressing through several stages of recovery. The authors recorded his responses and comments in detail and thus had an unusual opportunity to observe what a person can do in the absence of speech (including internal speech) and written language [*op.cit.*, p. 83].

Up until the appearance of subjects like Brother John it was not clear just what the dividing line was between linguistic ability and other forms of intelligence that we consider uniquely human. But the following remarkable story helps us to understand better where this boundary is:

> The extent to which [Brother John] retained the ability to cope with practical challenges was quite remarkable. One episode, while he was traveling in Switzerland, was particularly striking. He found himself at the peak of one of his seizures as he arrived at his destination, a

town he had never seen before. He took his baggage and managed to disembark. Although he could not read or speak, he managed to find a hotel and show his medic-alert bracelet to the concierge, only to be sent away. He then found another hotel, received a more sympathetic reception, communicated by mime, and was given a room. He was able to execute various procedures which formed a framework for linguistic operations; for example, he was able to point out to the desk clerk where in his passport to find the information required to fill out his registration slip, while not being able to read it himself. Finding himself too hungry and miserable to sleep, he went to the hotel restaurant. He could not read the menu, but he pointed to a line which he thought might be the hors d'oeuvres and randomly chose an item, hoping he would like it. In fact, it was a dish he detested, but he ate it, returned to his room, and slept for the remainder of his paroxysmal attack. When he awoke, he went to the hotel desk and explained the episode in detail. [Donald, *op.cit.*, pp. 84–85]

What Brother John's aphasia showed is that the aphasic can understand and interact with his surroundings appropriately in spite of his lack of expressive or receptive abilities in language. He could find a hotel he had never seen before even though he could not read or recognize a sign designating a hotel. As Donald concludes:

A number of important conclusions can be drawn from this case. First, despite the complete absence of language, internal or external, Brother John was able to cope in ways that are uniquely human. He was capable of coherent thought, able to recognize music, voices, and faces, and the uses of objects and places. His spatial orientation and basic mechanical intelligence were intact. His episodic memory for the events of his seizures was accurate (this was objectively verified by the authors) and organized. During a seizure, he was able to remember and execute a request given to him weeks earlier by the authors—for example, taping his spontaneous speech as it recovered during the spell.

     :

Finally, both gestural ability and practical knowledge were intact. He could imitate or reproduce on demand a wide variety of gestures. He could tune a radio, operate an elevator, and, as the Switzerland episode shows, assess and respond appropriately to a social situation of some complexity. All of this was achieved in the absence of visual or oral language, and in the absence of internal speech as well. In his own introspective account, he claimed that he could not "find the words" for things and events. Nevertheless, he could think about them coherently, deal with them appropriately, and remember them later.

This case suggests strongly that human intellectual skill is uniquely powerful, even in the absence of language. Most of the behaviors demonstrated by this man during his seizures were well beyond the abilities of any other primate or mammal. Language was obviously not the vehicle by which he assessed events, formulated plans, and evaluated his own responses. Nor was it important in his vivid and perceptive episodic registration of events or in the execution of gestures and mime. Moreover, his semantic representations of the world were accessible and useful to him, quite independently of language... the boundaries between the linguistic and nonlinguistic worlds have seldom been so clearly seen... [*op.cit.*, pp. 85–86].

What was lost, then, from knowledge and memory, by excising all forms of language and internal speech? In particular, what happened to his semantic memory, and what of propositional knowledge? The verbal forms of this material were not available to him, and any cognitive operations that were dependent upon symbolic representations could not be executed. But he evidently knew many of the things that he normally would have expressed, and probably learned, via the language system. Therefore, a great deal of his knowledge must have been nonverbal, or at least stored outside of the language system in nonsymbolic form... Deaf people who learn some form of language typically recall episodes from their youth, despite the absence of normal language development. Thus, the human brain, without language, can still record the episodes of life, assess events, assign meanings and thematic roles to agents

Wittgenstein's point is that people build their linguistic ability on a set of common human activities and abilities—activities and abilities that we all share as well as activities and abilities that are shared by only those of a particular culture, class or background. It is easiest to see this grounding of language in common activities when we think of learning a new language:

> Suppose you came as an explorer into an unknown country with a language quite strange to you. In what circumstances would you say that the people there gave orders, understood them, obeyed them, rebelled against them, and so on?
>
> The common behavior of mankind; is the system of reference by means of which we interpret an unknown language. [**PI** §206]

If we do not share or understand the customs and activities of a strange people then the result is quite different:

> We. . . say of some people that they are transparent to us. It is, however, important as regards this observation that one human being can be a complete enigma to another. We learn this when we come into a strange country with entirely strange traditions; and, what is more, even given a mastery of the country's language. We do not understand the people. (And not because of not knowing what they are saying themselves.) We cannot find our feet with them.
>
> ⋮
>
> If a lion could talk, we could not understand him.[229] [**PI** p. 223]

> in various situations, acquire and execute complex skills, learn and remember how to behave in a variety of settings. [*op.cit.*, p. 87 and p. 89]

> Among the uniquely human capacities found in the complete absence of language are a capacity for spontaneous gesture and mime, which can be retained after language loss; toolmaking and praxis in general; emotional expression and social intelligence, including an ability to comprehend complex events and remember roles, customs, and appropriate behavior. These fundamental abilities, robust and so important to human survival, might have emerged early in the human line, before language evolved. Their neuropsychological dissociability from language suggests a distinctly human, but prelinguistic, level of cognitive development and a possible basis for an early hominid adaptation that set the scene for the later arrival of language. [*op.cit.*, pp. 93–94]

The relevance of this to our present discussion is clear: although language is intimately tied up with our activities, language itself can operate largely independently of our activities, giving support to Wittgenstein's assertion that "Language—I want to say—is a refinement; 'in the beginning was the deed'." Further, the statement that "semantic representations of the world were accessible and useful to him, quite independently of language. . . " lends support to Ellis' assertion that language helps to set up categories of perception that can then exist independently of language use.

(NB: There are actually a number of different forms of aphasia, *viz.*, anomia, conduction aphasia, paraphasia, jargonaphasia, fluent aphasia, *et al.* For the purpose of this discussion their differences are not important. An early advocate of the singularity of these afflictions was P. Marie. ["Révision de la question sur l'aphasie: La troisième convolution frontale gauche ne joue aucun rôle spécial dans le fonction du language." **Semaine Medicale** (Paris), vol. 21, pp. 241–247, 1906.])

[229] **PI** p. 223. Cf. **Z** §187:

For Wittgenstein, the foundation of language is in shared activities—but not just any activities. The foundation of language rests on the shared activities that we perform *instinctively*. There are two related characteristics of instinctive behavior: it is performed without conscious thought, and is unaccompanied by doubt. Such behaviors are commonplace in our everyday affairs. We eat without thinking, drive our cars without thinking, play handball without thinking, mow the lawn without thinking, shower without thinking—we can even talk without thinking (see section **Language and Thought**, *supra*). That does not mean that we have never thought during such activities, or will not in the future, it only means that it is possible to perform them without thinking. Malcolm links instinctive behavior with lack of doubt:

> Absence of doubt manifests itself throughout the normal life of a human being. It appears, first, in advance of any learning: for example, in the spontaneous behavior of reacting to a cause. This behavior is "instinctive" in the primary sense of the word. Second, it appears in the young child when it is taught to respond to orders such as "Sit in the chair," "Hold out your hands," and so on, before the child can itself employ words. Third, it appears in the behavior, due to teaching, of employing the names of objects. At these second and third levels, the confident way of acting and speaking could be called "instinctive" in a secondary sense.

> The absence of doubt, at all three levels, can be called "instinctive" because it isn't learned, and because it isn't the product of thinking... The knowledge is not something that underlies and explains the behavior.

> ⋮

> One of the most striking illustrations of what I am calling the "instinctive element" in the employment of language and in language-like activities, is the way in which people who have been given some instruction in a procedure (such as continuing a mathematical series, or drawing a design, or building a brick wall) will, when told to carry on from there, spontaneously and on their own continue in the same way. It would seem that from the original instruction those people could branch out in an indefinitely large number of directions, each one going a different way. It is true that they could. But they don't! Almost all of them will go on in a way that the others will agree is the same way. This "agreement in reactions" is impressive. And it cannot be explained by saying that they have "intuitively grasped the rule," or something of the sort. This confident going on in the same way, without any doubt, cannot be given any rational foundation. This is a reason for calling it "instinctive."

Why can't a cat be taught to retrieve? Doesn't it understand what one wants? And what constitutes understanding or failure to understand here?

Retrieving is not one of the activities that cats do normally. As a consequence, we cannot train them to do this. More importantly, since language is built on activities, we cannot link a command to a cat's retrieving the way we can with dogs when we tell them to "Fetch!" Paul Ziff gives a similar example:

> I throw a cat a piece of meat. It does not see where the meat fell. I point to the meat; the cat smells my finger. [Paul Ziff. **Semantic Analysis**. Cornell University Press, Ithaca, 1960, pp. 92–93.]

Without this kind of natural agreement, this instinctive going on in the same way, there could not be language.[230]

[230] N. Malcolm. **Wittgensteinean Themes: Essays 1978–1989**, pp. 79–80. Cornell University Press, Ithaca, NY, 1995. Edited by G.H. von Wright. Wittgenstein does not consider doubting and thinking to be the same process, rather, doubting is a special kind of thinking:

> A child that is learning to use the word "tree." One stands with it in front of a tree and says "Lovely tree!" Clearly no doubt as to the tree's existence comes into the language-game. But can the child be said to know: "that a tree exists?" Admittedly it's true that "knowing something" doesn't involve thinking about it—but mustn't anyone who knows something be capable of doubt? And doubting means thinking. [**OC** §480]

And doubting, like verbal thinking, operates within language games. There is a place for doubting in our daily language use—that is, our language games—and a place for it in the activities that are part of our language games. But while we can doubt things within the scope of a language game, we cannot doubt the empirical foundations of these games:

> ...the absence of doubt belongs to the essence of the language-game. [**OC** §370]

> You must bear in mind that the language-game is so to say something unpredictable. I mean: it is not based on grounds. It is there—like our life. [**OC** §559]

The doubt that exists within a language game can only rest on empirical foundations that are beyond doubt:

> Admittedly, if you are obeying the order "Bring me a book," you may have to check whether the thing you see over there really is a book, but then you do at least know what people mean by "book"; and if you don't you can look it up,—but then you must know what some other word means. And the fact that a word means such-and-such, is used in such-and-such a way, is in turn an empirical fact, like the fact that what you see over there is a book.

> Therefore, in order for you to be able to carry out an order there must be some empirical fact about which you are not in doubt. Doubt itself rests only on what is beyond doubt. [**OC** §519]

One can see how the ordinary doubt that can be part of a language game differs from the more fundamental doubt of the empirical foundations themselves:

> Imagine that the schoolboy really did ask "and is there a table there even when I turn round, and even when no one is there to see it?" Is the teacher to reassure him—and say "of course there is!?"

> Perhaps the teacher will get a bit impatient, but think that the boy will grow out of asking such questions.

> That is to say, the teacher will feel that this is not really a legitimate question at all...this pupil has not learned how to ask questions. He has not learned the game that we are trying to teach him.

> This doubt isn't one of the doubts in our game. [**OC** §§314–315, 317]

The relation of doubt and activity are close enough that were doubt to permeate all of our language games, it would have a devastating effect on our lives. Malcolm comments:

Instinctive behavior can be just a reaction—our jumping when hearing a loud noise. But it can also be learned. Consider learning an athletic game like handball. We start by being told how to hold our hands, then how to hit the ball, then we can be told the rules of the game so we can see where we are allowed to hit the ball fairly, how to keep score, etc. As we get better, we are coached on how to respond to specific game situations ("serve conservatively when you're behind and go for winners when you are ahead," "every once in a while reverse the spin on the ball when you hit it to throw your opponent's timing off"). All of this sort of coaching starts as a kind of background for our learning to improve our game, and we may consciously repeat the coach's instructions as we play. But if we practice and play enough, there comes a time when these pointers will in large part recede from consciousness and we will play primarily without thinking.[231] If language is grounded in learned and unlearned instinctive behavior, what can it be used for? In the first

> Now it is true that if a previously normal adult began to be in constant doubt about the meanings of ordinary words, not only could he not continue to carry on the everyday employment of language, but also his behavior would fall into disarray. [Malcolm, *op.cit.*, p. 82]

I'm reminded of the comedian Gallagher talking about dictionaries: "Have you ever noticed that in a dictionary they list words like 'door', 'table' and 'chair'? Who would need to look those up?! If you didn't know what a 'chair' or 'table' is, you wouldn't know what a dictionary is either" (approximate quotation). As Wittgenstein said, "Doubt itself rests only on what is beyond doubt." (*supra*)

[231] This kind of non-thinking performance is related to what the psychologist Csikszentmihaly calls a "flow state." Although he is talking about a kind of optimal experience, it is clear that even when one is performing at a very high level in a complex task, one can engage in learned activities such that there is no accompanying conscious thought. In fact, conscious thought will interfere with attaining such a state:

> We have seen how people describe the common characteristics of [a flow-state]: a sense that one's skills are adequate to cope with the challenges at hand, in a goal-directed, rule-bound action system that provides clear clues as to how well one is performing. Concentration is so intense that there is no attention left over to think about anything irrelevant, or to worry about problems. Self-consciousness disappears, and the sense of time becomes distorted. [M. Csikszentmihaly. **Flow: the Psychology of Optimal Experience**, p. 71. Harper and Row, NY, 1990.]

That this was not just a theoretical notion and had practical relevance is confirmed by the fact that Csikszentmihaly was hired by a professional football team to help its players achieve flow states and perform instinctively. Another analogy for Wittgenstein's unthinking behavior is, as philosopher John Canfield points out, the practice of Zen Buddhism:

> Wittgenstein's later philosophy and the doctrines of Mahayana Buddhism integral to Zen coincide in a fundamental aspect: for Wittgenstein language has, one might say, a mystical base; and this base is exactly the Buddhist ideal of acting with a mind empty of thought. [J. Canfield. "Wittgenstein and Zen," **Philosophy**, vol. 50, pp. 59–84, 1975. Quotation p. 59.]

Canfield continues:

> This "just doing" of something is an example of what Wittgenstein means by a "practice" when he says that practice (and not some idea or other) is bedrock for the understanding of language... Thus in this case it is doing, or practice, that stands as the foundation of the understanding of language, and not the formation of ideas. Given these observations, the view that it is necessary that understanding, at some point, proceed via thoughts, is no longer attractive. For simply: if understanding can function at the ground level without benefit of thoughts (as it must) then why think that thoughts are necessary at any level?

place, it can replace some forms of instinctive behavior, such as that which is related to sensations:

> A child has hurt himself and he cries; and then adults talk to him and teach him exclamations and, later, sentences. They teach the child new pain-behavior. "So you are saying that the word 'pain' really means crying?"—On the contrary: the verbal expression of pain replaces crying and does not describe it. [**PI** §244]

Language can also extend, refine and elaborate on instinctive behavior. Malcolm comments:

> Wittgenstein says that not only does language replace prelinguistic behavior, but also that it serves as an extension, refinement, or elaboration of that behavior... But the language of sensation provides finer descriptions of sensation than would be possible with purely non-linguistic behavior. One says, "It still hurts but not as much as it did yesterday"; or "There is a slight pain in my hip but not enough to bother me." These reports could not be conveyed in prelinguistic behavior.[232]

Language can also describe circumstances that can give an utterance sense when those circumstances are not in effect. For example, if someone asks us what the word "charisma" means, we might say, "Do you remember seeing a film of a press conference with President Kennedy? Do you recall his self confidence, his good humor and the control he had over the situation? Do you remember how reporters were so deferential towards him when they asked questions? That's what we mean when we say that Kennedy had 'charisma'." Or, a tennis coach might counsel an athlete, "When your opponent is charging the net hit your return right at his feet—if he is already at the net when you hit the ball, lob it over his head."

It is not just the basic or primitive examples of language that are grounded in instinctive behavior, but also all of our more complex uses of language. Malcolm comments:

> Not merely is much of the first language of a child grafted onto instinctive behavior—but the whole of the developed, complex, employment of language by adult speakers embodies something resembling instinct.[233]

Wittgenstein's grounding of language use in instinctive behavior has a further consequence: we can justify or explain our language use by referring to how it originates from instinctive

> ...we can view language as nowhere needing thought forms in order to function. [*op.cit.*, p. 65]

[232] Malcolm, *op.cit.*, p. 68. Wittgenstein writes:

> Being sure that someone is in pain, doubting whether he is, and so on, are so many natural, instinctive, kinds of behavior towards other human beings, and our language is merely an auxiliary to, and further extension of, this relation. Our language-game is an extension of primitive behavior. [**Z** §545]

[233] Malcolm, *op.cit.*, p. 75.

behavior, but we can offer no *further* justification; that is, we cannot justify or explain the instinctive behavior itself. For example, if someone asked us, "Why did you cry out?," we could answer, "I dropped the hammer on my foot and it hurt." But if we were asked, further, "Why did dropping the hammer on your foot hurt you?" we would not know what to say—it simply happens that way. This is easy to see when we are dealing with sensations, but the same holds true for more complex linguistic acts. For example, if we were asked, "Why did you laugh when you talked to Bill?" we might reply, "He told me a very funny joke." But if we were then asked, "But why do you laugh when you hear something funny?," again, we would not know what to say. When we hear something funny we usually laugh—that's simply what we do.

> If I have exhausted the justifications I have reached bedrock, and my spade is turned. Then I am inclined to say: "This is simply what I do."[234] [**PI** §217]

By setting limits to what we can explain, Wittgenstein is cautioning us not to look further than our shared, instinctive behavior if we want to understand how language use is grounded:

> It is so difficult to find the beginning. Or, better: it is difficult to begin at the beginning. And not try to go further back.

> When a child learns language it learns at the same time what is to be investigated and what not. When it learns that there is a cupboard in the room, it isn't taught to doubt whether what it sees later on is still a cupboard or only a kind of stage set.

> Just as in writing we learn a particular basic form of letters and then vary it later, so we learn first the stability of things as the norm, which is then subject to alterations.

> This game proves its worth. That may be the cause of its being played, but it is not the ground.

> I want to regard man here as an animal; as a primitive being to which one grants instinct but not ratiocination. As a creature in a primitive state. Any logic good enough for a primitive means of communication needs no apology from us. Language did not emerge from some kind of ratiocination.

> Children do not learn that books exist, that armchairs exist, etc. etc.,—they learn to fetch books, sit in armchairs, etc.[235] [**OC** §§471–476]

[234] Compare with William James' statement:

> ... it takes a mind debauched by learning to carry the process of making the natural seem strange so far as to ask for the "why" of any instinctive act. [Quoted in O. Morton's "Doing What Comes Naturally: A New School of Psychology Finds Reasons for your Foolish Heart," *The New Yorker*, p. 102, 3 November 1997.]

[235] The child has no doubt whether books, armchairs, etc. exist. The issue of doubt is not part of the activities that use books, armchairs, etc. Wittgenstein also states:

> The squirrel does not infer by induction that it is going to need stores next winter as well. And no more do we need a law of induction to justify our actions and predictions. [**OC** §287]

Wittgenstein's views on the foundation of language use are important in themselves, but they also fit with Wittgenstein's more general method for examining language and the forms of our thought. Previously, Wittgenstein urged us to examine the "depth grammar" of language if we wanted to understand the structure of thought. Traditional epistemological inquiry has been primarily concerned with examining mental events—our thoughts—through either introspection (the method of choice for philosophers) or the questioning of reliable subjects (the method of choice for psychologists). But these methods can go wrong in a number of ways: Introspection is unreliable because I cannot know precisely whether the mental event that I experience is like someone else's mental event. For example, I say that hearing a children's song reminds me of third grade. But what does this consist of?—a recollection of my classroom (only the vaguest image here, I can remember no one exactly)? A recollection of the school building? A recollection of my teacher, a middle-aged woman named Mrs. Espinshade? A recollection of the joy or disappointment of that time in my life? How could I possibly communicate this image accurately? I probably could not communicate it at all to anyone who had not seen my third grade school and teacher, and knew me at the time. Even if someone were to respond to me saying that he *too* thinks of his third grade class when he hears the same song, certainly his image, though seeming to be similar, would be very different from mine since, obviously, he went to a different school than I did, perhaps at a different time, too. Even if two subjects were to agree that they both had the same "thought" pop into their minds the similarity may be an illusion. For example, someone mentions the "Cuban Missile Crisis" and both of us immediately have an image of John F. Kennedy float before our minds. This appears to be the same "thought," but it may not be so. My image of Kennedy may be of him making his inaugural speech. The image may be animated and I may even "hear" a sentence or two of that speech in his distinctive Boston accent. My friend, though, has an image of a black and white photo of Kennedy on vacation at Hyannis Port playing with his daughter Caroline. Are these two mental associations the same? Only in the most general, and uninformative, sense. And even if the images *were* the same, their interpretations, like the interpretation of any picture, could be decidedly different. Wittgenstein comments:

> Images tell us nothing either right or wrong, about the external world. . . Images are subject to the will. . .

> It is just because forming images is a voluntary activity that it does not instruct us about the external world. [**Z** §621, 627]

Wittgenstein also refers to the "animal" nature of certainty:

> One might say: " 'I know' expresses comfortable certainty, not the certainty that is still struggling."

> Now I would like to regard this certainty, not as something akin to hastiness or superficiality, but as a form of life. (That is very badly expressed and probably badly thought as well.)

> But that means I want to conceive it as something that lies beyond being justified or unjustified; as it were, as something animal. [**OC** §§357–359]

The other method of examining mental events is to record the recollections of reliable subjects as they describe their own thoughts or mental images. Again, there is a problem. Whatever similarity we may find in the descriptions that the subjects give is just that—a similarity of the descriptions, not a similarity of the mental images they purport to describe. The irony of this is that the similarity of descriptions appears to reflect a similarity of mental images—that is, a similarity of internal/mental events. Yet what is really similar are two *external* events—the two descriptions—not two internal events. The impression that such reports give us any precise information about mental events that could be compared is illusory. Again, the example about John F. Kennedy is apropos: two subjects are asked about the mental image that they formed in response to some suggestion, and they report that they each had an image of JFK appear in their minds. What is the same here is not the mental images that the two subjects conjure up; what is the same are the descriptions they give to those mental events. In this light, it is not surprising that Wittgenstein moves his analysis of inner mental events to outer linguistic/grammatical events.[236]

Through his use of *depth grammatical analysis*, Wittgenstein showed that we could examine the way we think by looking at external events—examples of language use—that

---

[236] This reliance on reports of mental processes is probably one of the reasons that Wittgenstein disliked the experimental methods of psychology:

> The confusion and barrenness of psychology is not to be explained by calling it a "young science"; its state is not comparable with that of physics, for instance, in its beginnings. (Rather with that of certain branches of mathematics. Set theory.) For in psychology there are experimental methods and conceptual confusion. (As in the other case conceptual confusion and methods of proof.)

> The existence of experimental methods makes us think we have the means of solving the problems which trouble us; though problem and methods pass one another by. [**PI** p. 232]

An almost identical series of statements exist in **RPP I** §1039. It differs only in that it includes the following penultimate sentence (*supra*):

> While, however, in mathematics one may be pretty sure that a proof will be important, even if it is not yet rightly understood, in psychology one is completely uncertain of the fruitfulness of the experiments.

Gestalt psychologist Köhler offered an explanation for psychology's unscientific nature:

> Why does this difficulty beset behavioristic psychology, and not occur in physics? The answer is simple enough: Physics is an old science and psychology is in its infancy. [From "Psychology as a Young Science" in his **Gestalt Psychology**, NY, 1929.]

Wittgenstein has a response, though:

> Misleading parallel: psychology treats of processes in the psychical sphere, as does physics in the physical.

> Seeing, hearing, thinking, feeling, willing, are not the subject of psychology in the same sense as that in which the movements of bodies, the phenomena of electricity etc., are the subject of physics. You can see this from the fact that the physicist sees, hears, thinks over, and informs us of these phenomena, and the psychologist observes the external reactions (the behavior) of the subject. [PI §571]

Wittgenstein never said explicitly what he disliked about psychology, but there are a number of characteristics of the field that he would likely be uncomfortable with:

1. As we mentioned above, psychology relies too much on subjects' reporting of mental events. This reliance arises from two beliefs: the first is a belief that if we want to understand human cognition we should look primarily at our conscious thought processes. This belief is questioned in one of Wittgenstein's most quoted statements:

> There is a kind of general disease of thinking which always looks for (and finds) what would be called a mental state from which all our acts spring as from a reservoir. [**BB** p. 143]

The second belief is in a parallelism between descriptions of thoughts and the thoughts themselves. It assumes that the same verbal descriptions of mental events by different individuals indicate that the mental events they are describing are the same too. Yet when two individuals give the same description of their respective thoughts, does this mean that they have the same thoughts? How could we possibly know?

Implicit in psychology's reliance on personal reports of mental events is the belief that we can't "really know" what others are thinking, without their telling us, drawing a sharp boundary between public knowledge and private knowledge. Wittgenstein attempts to show that this boundary is not as sharp as is traditionally thought, that we can, in fact, know a great deal about what goes on "in others' minds," without their having to report what they are thinking; in fact, much of our behavior is based on our being able to correctly surmise what others are thinking or believe. But we have to look at the right things. If we only look at the descriptions of mental events as criteria for what someone is thinking, then, rightly, we can't know what is going on in someone else's head, unless he tells us (but even here, we cannot accept what he says except under certain circumstances, so statements by themselves are not sufficient). But if we look instead at circumstances, criteria, etc. that surround us all in our day-to-day activities, then we can figure out quite a bit about what someone else is thinking. (I will discuss this dichotomy between inner and outer processes in more detail in the section "Wittgenstein and Crime.")

2. Wittgenstein would also be concerned about the way that psychology talks about the subjects that concern it. The obvious example is when we ask for the meaning of a word we are led to look for some "entity" that is "the meaning." In the same manner, we often treat "concepts," "subconscious," "ego," "phobias," etc. like they are definite psychological entities. This gives us a sense that they must exist in the same way that "meanings" are thought to exist for words. We then reserve a place for these entities in our theory of mind and begin the process of looking for something that will fit. Of course, we will always find something that will provide some kind of "fit" (and if we don't, we won't adjust our theory to account for why they are missing, we will adjust our theory to account for why we can't find them—e.g., they are unconscious, or, they go by our consciousness so quickly we can't see them).

This is the same misleading process that Ryle talked about in his "Systematically Misleading Expressions" in which he demonstrates how the use of the word "the"—as in the idea—gives a misleading ontological status to whatever follows it. [*vid.* footnote 102, *supra*]

3. Wittgenstein would also be suspicious of the experimental method's need for statistically significant numbers of cases to prove its hypotheses. That is, we may be tempted to treat things as the same which are not really the same. For example, when the psychologist looks at "fear" or "suspicion" or "anger" is he always looking at the same thing? Is my fear of lions the same as my fear of spiders? Is my fear of nuclear war the same as a general's fear of nuclear war? Is our love of humanity the same as our love of ice cream? Can an American love the taste of a uniquely Hungarian desert like Dobos Torta the way a Hungarian does? Wittgenstein is not saying that such comparisons are impossible, nor is he saying that all is diversity and there are no entities that can be classified in the same category. Wittgenstein is merely saying that our "craving for generality"…"our contempt for the particular case" is so strong that we must be constantly on guard that we are not reducing dissimilar things into a misleading similarity. For Wittgenstein, the tabulation of significant numbers of cases is not as compelling evidence as a single, well-chosen example—in his words, an "übersichtliche Darstellung" ("perspicuous representation," or "exemplary presentation").

4. There is a final possible explanation for Wittgenstein's dislike of psychology: viz. he may have criticized set

theory along with psychology in the quotation above because he dislikes both fields for the same reason. While Wittgenstein didn't state explicitly why he disliked psychology, he does elaborate on his dislike for set theory:

> The error in the set-theoretical approach continually consists in treating laws and reports (lists) as basically one and the same. [**Manuscript 108**. 1929–1930, p. 180. Quoted in Hallett's **A Companion to Wittgenstein's "Philosophical Investigations,"** p. 756. Cornell University Press, Ithaca, NY, 1977.]

Wittgenstein is complaining that set theory confuses, in more formal terminology, extensionality and intentionality. The intension of a set is the law or definition that can be used to determine set membership: for example that the set of dogs consists of quadraped mammals with certain physical characteristics. The extension of a set consists of the actual members that have been included in the set at this time: for example, the set of dogs consists of this cockerspaniel, this doberman, this shelty, etc. Intentionality and extensionality are not the same for the obvious reason that we can define sets intentionally that have no members, that is, have no extension: for example, the set of people who are ten feet tall, or the set of left-handed major-league third basemen.

Psychology, as an empirical science, deals continually with sets, both intentional (e.g., people with claustrophobia) and extensional (e.g., the people who have read this sentence). Much psychological research consists of determining what the characteristics are of certain groups of individuals: for example, what characteristics do excellent chess players have in common? The most common mistake that psychology can make in this process is a form of reductionism: to take a group of individuals that are defined extensionally by some activity (e.g., like playing chess well) and trying to reduce them to a set of intentional psychological characteristics (e.g., having an IQ above 130, having a good aptitude for mathematics as a youth, etc). The confusion comes up in two ways. In the first place, it is not always clear that references to psychological states, such as an "aptitude for mathematics" refers to well-determined empirical phenomena. (*vid.* Ryle, footnote 102)

The second way in which this confusion occurs is in the assumption that an extensionally-defined group of people can be meaningfully described by a set of intentionally-defined characteristics. For example, even if it is the case that we can define mathematical aptitude empirically, can measure it reliably, and can show that good chess players have it and poor ones don't, it is entirely possible that such an observation really tells us little about what it means to be a good chess player. In short, just because we can measure it doesn't mean that it's significant or important. This is why Wittgenstein says "... in psychology one is completely uncertain of the fruitfulness of the experiments" (*supra*). Further, because of the empirical need for measurement in psychology, intentional definitions may be subtly altered to make them more measurable, thus confounding intension and extension. This is why Wittgenstein asserts:

> The existence of experimental methods makes us think we have the means of solving the problems which trouble us; though problems and methods pass one another by. [*supra*]

For Wittgenstein, it may be the case that the only important thing that good chess players have in common is that they are good chess players (*vid.* section **Wittgenstein's Approach—The Rejection of Nominalism and Realism,** *supra*), a claim which has a less problematic connection between its extension and intension than the more reductionistic psychological statements. The "disease of thinking" that psychologists commit here Wittgenstein referred to in a slightly different context:

> The desire to find essential definitions of words that work in a variety of contexts is part of our "craving for generality" and our "contemptuous attitude towards the particular case." [**BB** p. 18]

Here, we might take the specific usages of words as their extension and their "essential definition" as their intension. Even though Wittgenstein is here objecting to the attempt to provide essential definitions of words, it is not, I think, an incorrect intellectual reach to apply this to the attempt to find the "essential definitions" of psychological phenomena. In short, Wittgenstein's statement can, I think, be taken to express his caution about trying to define or characterize an intensely human activity, such as playing chess well, as a set of psychological characteristics or states.

are accessible to us all; we need neither introspection nor truthful reports of our thoughts to do this. Similarly, Wittgenstein is saying here that if we want to find the foundations of language use we should be looking at external processes, not some elusive or idiosyncratic descriptions of internal mental processes. As Malcolm comments:

> We have the inclination to suppose that all mastery of language, as well as all meaningful behavior, is based on and emerges from mental states or attitudes that should be expressible in psychological terms. But what we find is that all of the psychological terms either redescribe, or else presuppose, ways of acting. It is these ways of acting that provide the foundation for the psychological concepts. They are "the main thing" (die Hauptsache), which shows itself when one reflects on the practice of language, but which itself is not supported by any mental process or structure.[237]

By shifting our analysis from internal events and processes to external ones, Wittgenstein can also prescribe a limit or end point for such analysis:

> Giving grounds, however, justifying the evidence, comes to an end;—but the end is not certain propositions' striking us immediately as true, i.e. it is not a kind of seeing on our part; it is our acting, which lies at the bottom of the language-game.[238]
> [**OC** §204]

### Instinctive Behavior and Forms of Life

*Instinctive behavior* and *forms of life* appear to have some similarities. They are both comprised in large part of conventional, repeated activities that, in aggregate, make up many of the "things that we do." In this sense they are the same. But while *instinctive behavior* is comprised of human activities which we perform without thinking, *forms of life* are not so narrowly defined. As we have pointed out, when someone is learning certain kinds of *instinctive behavior* (what Malcolm called the "second" and "third" levels of *instinctive behavior*—see quotation at footnote [236]) he will probably go about it quite consciously. Consider a handball coach: "Swing your hand with your palm perpendicular to the floor, stride into the ball as you make contact, hit the ball near the top of your hand

---

[237] Malcolm. **Wittgensteinean Themes: Essays 1978–1989**, pp. 85–86. Cornell University Press, Ithaca, NY, 1995. Edited by G.H. von Wright.

[238] It is easy to get caught in the downward spiral of reductive explanation and hard to know when to stop. One of the least considered failures of psychoanalysis is that its explanation of unconscious motivation suffers from the same infinite regress that Aristotle saw in Plato's realism (see the description of the "third man" argument in the section **Universals and Particulars—An Old Debate**, *supra*). Psychoanalysis explains inconsistencies that occur between the way people act and the way that they profess to want to act. For example, an individual may profess to have the utmost respect for business associates, but is continually flagrantly late for meetings. The psychoanalyst might say that while the individual consciously expresses his respect for others, unconsciously he really feels hostile towards them, and acts out this hostility by keeping them waiting repeatedly. The failure with this kind of explanation is that if we need an unconscious mind to interpret what the conscious mind presents, then why do we assume that the unconscious mind is the final arbiter of psychological conflicts? In short, if the conscious mind can be false or misleading, how can we not suspect the unconscious mind of being false too? We would then need a deeper unconscious mind to explain the unconscious mind. Of course, if this is the case, then we need an even deeper unconscious mind to explain the deeper unconscious mind. Hence, the infinite regress. Just as Occam applied his "razor" to pare off the unnecessary universals of realism, Wittgenstein would have us remove the unconscious mind, and even much of the conscious mind from any epistemological investigation.

if you want a natural spin on the ball and with the bottom part of your hand if you want a reverse spin, snap your wrist on contact and follow through. . . " If our subject practices this enough, he will eventually be able to do this "instinctively"—without conscious thought. During the learning period, our novice handball player could not be said to be engaging in *instinctive behavior*, but he could be seen to engage in an activity that might be characterized as a *form of life*. In this sense, *instinctive behavior* is a restricted subset of *forms of life*, while *forms of life* comprise activities that may or may not be instinctive.[239]

Since language use is grounded in activities, both instinctive and conscious, and language is "the vehicle of thought," it is not hard to see that the nature and form of our thinking is largely grounded in our activities. While this is an important inference, its import for cognition is even more profound than may at first appear. Merlin Donald suggests that there is enough evidence from research in neurophysiology to establish the claim that our participation in shared activities—what we would call, our "culture"— actually affects the physical structure of our brains:

> In has been known for some time that the immature brain is highly plastic; that is, it can grow connections, and lose connections, in many different ways, depending on early experience. Changeux has proposed an epigenetic theory of brain develop-ment, in which the young brain proliferates new connections fairly indiscriminately, that is, invents many possible routes of development, of which only a few will sur-vive, due to the selective effects of experience. . . Changeux was aware of the cultural corollary of this notion: namely, that culturally specific, highly redundant patterns of brain use would imply the existence of cultural traditions that have an indirect *neurological* instantiation—that is, the brains of many individuals in one culture are broadly programmed in a specific way, while in another culture they may develop differently, because use patterns are fundamentally different. . . Cultures restructure the mind, not only in terms of its specific contents, which are obviously culture-bound, but also in terms of its fundamental neurological organization. . . Culture can literally reconfigure the use patterns of the brain; and it is probably a safe in-ference from our current knowledge of cerebral plasticity that those patterns of use determine much about how the exceptionally plastic human central nervous system is ultimately organized, in terms of cognitive structure.[240]

---

[239] Even when we think about what we need to do while we are doing it—that is, when we are following the coach's instructions—there are many movements that we engage in that are not conscious. For example, when the coach tells us that we must follow through with our swing, we don't tell ourselves to "dip my shoulder 4 inches, bend my elbow 107 degrees at the beginning of the swing, keep my elbow 2 inches below the plane of my hand, accelerate my hand at 32 ft/sec/sec, tense my hand at 15 pounds/sq.inch, make contact with the ball one half inch below the base of the ring finger, etc. etc." Such explanations could go down to an almost unlimited level of granularity. So when we say that such descriptions are conscious, we are not saying that every minute aspect of the directions must be described. It is only necessary for some of the action to be conscious. It is also true that even when we are conscious of what we are doing, it is likely that there is much that we do that is not conscious—that is, that conscious activity rests on a broad stratum of non-conscious activity.

[240] Donald. **Origins of the Modern Mind: Three Stages in the Evolution of Culture and Cognition**, pp. 13–14. Harvard University Press, Cambridge, MA, 1991 [Donald cites J. Changeux. **Neuronal Man**. Pantheon Books, NY, 1985]. Donald equates "culture" with the "shared patterns of acquired behavior characteristic of a species" [p. 9]. Although he does not state explicitly that culture consists of shared activities, his notion of "shared patterns of acquired behavior" is reasonably similar to our notion of the shared activities or "forms of life" that underlie our use of language. It is not, then, unreasonable to conclude that participation in the shared activities that underly language use can affect the very physiological structure of the brain. This means, in turn,

### Language and Cognition: What Do We Have in Our Heads, and What is it Good for?

Wittgenstein's desire to move epistemological analysis from the examination of internal, mental events to the examination of external events—language use, activities, and their surrounding context and circumstances—continues in his analysis of cognition. It is clear that we often have something "in our heads" at times, so it is important to consider these mental events to determine what they are and what their role is in what we do. Let's look first at a familiar activity: Consider teaching someone to throw a baseball. We would demonstrate the proper grip on the ball, the proper motion of the arm, the release, where

that changing some of the language and thought patterns that depend on the physiological structure of the brain may be extremely difficult to do, and explains why we sometimes cannot see another's point of view no matter how hard we try. Anthropologist Edward Hall has observed that cultural differences are extremely difficult for us to overcome. If these differences are largely instantiated in neurological structure, as Donald argues, then it gives support to Hall's claim [E. Hall.**Beyond Culture**. Anchor Books, New York, 1976]. Wittgenstein's assertion that "The common behavior of mankind is the system of reference by means of which we interpret an unknown language" (*supra*) takes on an even more profound import.

Donald even sees the influence of culture on cognitive structure as the essential component of human evolution:

> ...what humans evolved was primarily a generalized capacity for cultural innovation. Part of that capacity was linguistic communication; part of it was the ability to think and represent the environment...

> Dunbar has recently proposed that encephalization was driven not by the cognitive demands of tool making or spatial mapping of the environment but by growth in the size of social groups. In other words, it was not instrumental intelligence that drove brain expansion but rather social intelligence. Complex societies make great demands on memory...

> ...the actual cognitive structure of an individual mind is heavily influenced by culture. [*op.cit.*, pp. 10–11. Donald cites Dunbar, "Ecological Modeling in an Evolutionary Context," **Folia Primatologica** (Basel), vol. 53, pp. 235–246.]

From this we might surmise that the greatest achievement of ancient cultures such as the Egyptians was not so much the building of the pyramids at Giza and the spectacular temple of Karnak, but the organizing of large numbers of people into a complex society dedicated to the common effort of large projects. Since, as Donald says, "specific types of human culture have direct effects upon individual cognition," we can see that the large projects engaged in by the Egyptians, and, later, other cultures, may have had a direct developmental effect on the cognitive structures and abilities of the people involved and their descendents. [*op.cit.* pp. 9–10] So many ancient cultures engaged, independently, in large building projects (Pueblo Bonito, Ankor Wat, Stonehenge, Teotihuacán, The Great Wall of China, etc.) that one is tempted to hypothesize that such large projects were part of a natural social and cognitive evolution. Certainly, some of these projects can be justified on practical grounds: they not only served some purpose of habitation or defense, but they also kept their inhabitants busy and, presumably, unable to foment rebellion—unity being a major concern as societies grew larger. But if Donald is correct, these building projects may have encouraged commensurate changes in the brain's physiological structure that enabled increasingly large groups of individuals to live together successfully (the projects, of course, did not cause the change in physiological brain structure, but provided a means by which increasingly adaptive changes in brain physiology could be selected—those individuals who were "better" at participating in or leading these large projects, would be rewarded economically, and this reward would better enable them to produce and provide for a family, thus passing on their adaptive genes).

In terms of our later discussion, we must ask how the structure and processes of large computerized information systems may affect the way we think, and, perhaps, are compelled to think, about accessing information.

to throw it, etc. Wouldn't it be odd if after our demonstration our pupil were to turn to us and ask, "But what went on in your mind when you were throwing the ball? I need to know that too." We see this question as odd when we are teaching someone a physical technique, but we do not see this as odd when we talk about meaning and language. When we begin to see language usage as a technique, like pitching in baseball, we will also see questions about an inner process that precedes or accompanies all language use as somehow misplaced. This is not to deny that something might have gone on in my mind when I was pitching, it is only to deny that what did go on in my mind is a necessary accompaniment of the pitching and that I need to know it before I can pitch successfully. We can also see a bit better why Wittgenstein insisted that forms, not facts, are what guide our meaningful activities (and language use is an activity). There is no "fact" about my arm that influences my pitching, but its general form influences how I will throw the ball (how far it is possible to throw it, what kind of spin I can put on it, how accurately I can throw, etc.). The general form of the anatomy of my arm does not cause me to throw in a particular way, but it does influence it. But, again, the anatomy of my arm is not the only influence on how I throw. The form or requirements of the game of baseball influence how I will throw, too. It also depends on how much I practiced, who taught me, how much time my coach spent with me, etc. And of course, there are outside factors that may influence my pitching on a daily, or even pitch by pitch basis, such as the temperature, the wind and its direction, and the skill of the batters I face. Can we pitch in our minds? Of course. In fact, such imagining of athletic performance is often recommended to athletes by coaches as a way of sharpening or refining their skills (One is reminded of the serene portrait of Olympic skiers waiting at the top of a downhill run, dreamily swaying their heads, eyes closed, as they imagine themselves skiing down the course.). But it's important to get the cart and the horse the right way round. In general, one must be able to perform, or at least observe, the activity or skill *externally* before one can perform it internally, that is, mentally—one must be able to pitch in reality before one can pitch in his imagination.

Let's look at a more cerebral practice, such as addition. Most parents have had experience teaching a small child to add. How is it done? Well, one puts two similar things—say, oranges—together and says, "Two," or "Two oranges" (Of course the child must know what oranges are, be able to count, and be of otherwise normal intelligence.). The parent then puts three more oranges next to the original two, and says, "...plus three oranges, is how many oranges?" The parent may then show how to count all the oranges, "...one, two, three, four, five oranges..." If done repeatedly, then the child will be able to "add" small numbers of objects together in the same way. A variety of more complicated skills can be built on this simple one. For example, the parent could then show the child how to add more things together by making series of small marks with a pencil on a piece of paper, and eventually, could teach addition using base-ten arithmetic. The important thing is that one can perform any of these procedures without having any accompanying conscious thoughts whatsoever. One could do practically all the "thinking," so to speak, with pencil and paper. Like learning to pitch, the technique of addition is taught without any recourse to conscious thought. Teaching someone to add consists entirely of demonstrating processes that are external to the mind—nothing about teaching elementary addition needs to refer to mental abilities or techniques (one certainly must have an ability to recognize things as separate entities, but this is not an ability that is *referred to*. It is the instinctive background which is the basis for counting). Malcolm comments:

> People often do arithmetical calculations in their minds or, as we say, "in their heads." Are all calculations done in the head? Certainly not. Someone who laboriously worked out a complicated multiplication on paper, did not do it "in his head." This is not how this expression is used. One may be inclined to say: "He must have done the calculation in his head as well as on paper. Surely he would not have been able to do it on paper unless he had done it in his head!" What a peculiar idea! In writing out the calculation, was he copying the calculation that he did in his head? Was the outward calculation guided by an inward calculation? Then what guided the inward calculation? To avoid an infinite regress one has to say that nothing guided it. But if one has to stop, why not stop with the calculation on paper? And the explanation of his being able to calculate would simply be that he learned it in school.
>
> There are people who are unable to calculate in their heads. Most of us cannot do complex arithmetical calculations in that way. There is a philosophical temptation to think that calculating in one's head comes first, and that calculating on paper or aloud is derivative from it. But... the exact reverse is the case. We do not say of someone that he does calculations in his head, unless he has learned to calculate in writing or aloud. This is where the logical priority is.
>
> "Calculating in one's head" is one of those expressions that seem to have been deliberately invented to mislead philosophers. It looks as if "in one's head" must mean, in one's brain. So at least some calculations literally occur in the brain. But if we don't just look at the words but consider the circumstances in which they are used, we see that nothing is implied about an occurrence in the brain.[241]

Wittgenstein makes a similar point more succinctly:

> Only if you have learnt to calculate—on paper or out loud—can you be made to grasp, by means of this concept, what calculating in the head is.[242] [**PI** p. 216]

Some observers may counter that we still, in fact, do such things "in our heads," but that these conscious accompaniments are so subtle or brief that we just don't see them. When one considers this explanation, though, it is hard to find evidence to support it, and Wittgenstein is quite outspoken in his objection to it:

> If it is asked: "How do sentences manage to represent?"—the answer might be: "Don't you know? You certainly see it, when you use them." For nothing is concealed.

[241] N. Malcolm. **Nothing is Hidden: Wittgenstein's Criticism of his Early Thought**, pp. 187–188. Basil Blackwell, Oxford, UK, 1986.

[242] Compare to **PI** §366:

> Is a sum in the head less real than a sum on paper?—Perhaps one is inclined to say some such thing; but one can get oneself to think the opposite as well by telling oneself: paper, ink, etc. are only logical constructions out of our sense-data.

⋮

But given this answer: "But you know how sentences do it, for nothing is concealed" one would like to retort "Yes, but it all goes by so quick, and I should like to see it as it were laid open to view."

Here it is easy to get into that dead-end in philosophy where one believes that the difficulty of the task consists in this: our having to describe phenomena that are hard to get hold of, the present experience that slips quickly by or something of the kind. Where we find ordinary language too crude, and it looks as if we were having to do, not with the phenomena of every-day, but with ones that "easily elude us, and, in their coming to be and passing away, produce those others as an average effect." (Augustine: Manifestissima et usitatissima sunt, et eadem rusus nimis latent, et nova est inventio eorum.)[243] **[PI** §§435–436]

And nothing is more wrong-headed than calling meaning a mental activity! Unless, that is, one is setting out to produce confusion. **[PI** §693]

It is important to note that Wittgenstein says not only that the foundation of meaning in language *is not* a mental process, but that it *cannot* be a mental process. This is relatively simple to demonstrate, since it is clear that our intentions or thoughts are never sufficient to give our utterances or gestures meaning—otherwise we would never be misunderstood. If I make a particularly vulgar gesture that is known to Italians, it will not be understood, no matter how much I mean it to, unless I am in the company of Italians who might comprehend it. That is, the gesture must have the right context. But even this is not enough, for the circumstances must be appropriate too. That is, the Italians to whom I make the gesture, may understand that I am trying to insult them, but see my gesture as only funny—an amusing attempt at insult by a silly American. We might say that the gesture did not fit the language game we were engaged in—there was no role for the gesture to play there. Not only is it not the case that intentions and thoughts are insufficient to give meaning to language or, here, gestures, but these intentions and thoughts can be entirely absent and yet the words or gestures can still be meaningful in conventional ways. For example, I am engaged in a heated debate with Italian friends and, during a lull, I unknowingly make an obscene gesture to the people I am talking to. Here I have neither the intention nor the thought of insulting anyone, but the gesture, unintended though it is, still works in a conventional way. The accidental insult works because there is a place for the expression of insults—even by silly Americans—in the language game of arguing. In fact, even if I plead that I did not intend the insult, my friends—soon to be ex-friends—may insist that, unconsciously, I really *did* intend to insult them. Similar examples can be constructed using words and phrases instead of gestures. Such inadvertent signification is the substance of much good fiction. It is the circumstances and context that surround language use that give it meaning, not our intentions or the meanings that might be "running through our minds." This does not mean to say that intention has *nothing* to do with meaning, only that intention is not the determiner of meaning. Intention certainly plays a role in meaning: when we *intend* to express some meaningful communication we then look for the appropriate context

---

[243] English translation of Latin: "Augustine: They are perfectly obvious and ordinary, and yet the same things are too well hidden, and their discovery comes as something new." From **A Companion to Wittgenstein's "Philosophical Investigations,"** p. 472 [G. Hallett. Cornell University Press, Ithaca, NY, 1977.]

and circumstances that will support that communication. But it is the circumstances, not the intention that play the bigger role in determining meaning. These circumstances are sometimes so dominant that they may even prevent an intended meaning no matter how much the speaker/gesturer wishes it to be the case. Can the Pope or the Dalai Lama make an obscene gesture? Can Saddam Hussein apologize to the Kurds? Probably not, no matter what they say or do, or in what circumstances they do it.[244]

So the foundation of meaning in language cannot be exclusively grounded in conscious thoughts or intentions. This is not to say that language does not, or cannot, have any conscious accompaniment, nor is it meant to say that *some* language games may refer exclusively to conscious thought (e.g., children might play a game in which they try to guess what each other is thinking). This can happen. It's just that, in general, these conscious accompaniments are not necessary for meaningful communication.[245] We are not saying that *nothing* mental happens when we, say, engage in some nonmental activity. We are saying that *nothing important to the understanding of that activity* occurs in our conscious mental processes. In fact, like our learning to pitch baseballs "in our imagination," the conscious accompaniments of the meaningful use of language *follow* our correct use of language rather than *precede* it. Since language is grounded in instinctive behavior, and such behavior is nonconscious, then whatever conscious accompaniment it may have is, in Malcolm's words, "a refinement" of the behavior, and thereby follows it.

Still, one may be tempted to hypothesize that if language is not grounded in conscious thought it must thereby be grounded in unconscious thought. But such a supposition is no more tenable than the belief that language can be grounded in conscious thought. Unconscious thought must, by definition, be similar in structure and dynamics to conscious thought. If this is the case, then, why would we assume that unconscious thought can impart any more meaning to language than conscious thought can? To do so it would have to have properties very different than conscious thought, and it is not at all clear what those properties would be. To my knowledge, no one has proposed that unconscious thought is substantively different than conscious thought, other than, in Freudian terms, it is seen to be more "objective" or "uncensored" than the conscious mind. The hypothesis that the unconscious mind can somehow supply the meaning to language that the conscious mind cannot, is to merely shift the quest for meaning to a mechanism—the unconscious—that is even harder to investigate than conscious mental phenomena. In fact, the very difficulty

---

[244] It is interesting how circumstances can legitimate an expression. Lee Atwater, President Bush's 1988 presidential campaign director was the instigator of the vicious and misleading "Willie Horton" campaign ad that contributed significantly to Bush's come-from-behind defeat of Michael Dukakis. A few years later, Atwater, on his death-bed, asked Dukakis' forgiveness for the ads. One wonders whether such a poignant request would have been considered sincere had Atwater not been terminally ill.

[245] As we quoted before:

> When I think in language, there aren't "meanings" going through my mind in addition to the verbal expressions: the language is itself the vehicle of thought. [**PI** §329]

An interesting position on the necessity of consciousness is presented by Julian Janes. He describes many human activities which do not require consciousness, and asserts that for much of man's early history, until about 3000 years ago, individuals were not conscious at all. [**The Origin of Consciousness in the Breakdown of the Bicameral Mind**. Houghton Miflin, 1990 (Reprint)]

that we have investigating the unconscious serves those who hold its primacy in thought. Since its character is so elusive to investigate, the unconscious can, hypothetically, fulfill whatever requirements we might want that we don't find in the conscious mind. The belief in the primacy of the unconscious mind is merely a disease of thinking grounded in the assumption that all our intelligent acts must have their origin in some mental activity:

> There is a kind of general disease of thinking which always looks for (and finds) what would be called a mental state from which all our acts spring as from a reservoir. [**BB** p. 143]

The belief in the unconscious as a foundation for thought and language shifts epistemology in the wrong direction: deeper into our minds rather than out into the context and circumstances where Wittgenstein feels it belongs.

*Externalism*

Wittgenstein's distrust of meaning being a mental activity prefigures a more recent movement in the philosophy of language and mind called "Externalism." The beginnings of Externalism, as a distinct movement in the philosophy of mind, finds its roots in Putnam's "Twin Earth" thought experiment.[246] Putnam asked us to imagine that there was a "Twin Earth" that was exactly like our own earth, even to the point of having a "twin" of every person on this earth. But there was one aspect of Twin Earth that was different: on Twin Earth they had a substance they called "water" which was exactly like our own water except that instead of having a chemical structure $H_2O$ it had a different structure which Putnam called "XYZ." Except for the different chemical structure, Twin Earth water had exactly the same function there as it does here: Twin Earthers drank it, washed in it, poured it on their plants, and used it in squirt guns for amusement. Twin Earth "water" came out of the sky in the form of rain, and large amounts of it formed rivers, lakes and oceans, just like ours does. Since the Twin Earthers' use of their "water" was exactly like our own use of water, their conception of water, that is their idea of what it was and how it was used, was exactly the same as our own idea of what we called "water." In other words, what the average Twin Earther had "in his head" about water was exactly the same as what we have in our heads about our version of water. Yet, Putnam wrote, Twin Earth water was different from our water because it had a different chemical structure (XYZ vs. $H_2O$). For Putnam the ineluctable conclusion of this thought experiment is that semantic meaning is not entirely internal; at least part of the definition of what water is, is external to our skulls because what we and the Twin Earthers have in our heads cannot distinguish our water from Twin Earth water. As Putnam put it, "Cut the pie any way you like, 'meanings' just ain't in the head!" (Putnam (1975), p.144). Tyler Burge[247] published an article a few years after Putnam's extending Putnam's externalist interpretation of semantics to

[246] H. Putnam. "The Meaning of 'Meaning'." **Language, Mind and Knowledge, Minnesota Studies in the Philosophy of Science**, v. VII, pp. 131–193, 1975. Collected in Pessin and Goldberg (eds). **The Twin Earth Chronicles: Twenty Years of Reflections on Hilary Putnam's "The Meaning of 'Meaning'."** M.E. Sharpe, Armonk, NY, 1996.

[247] T. Burge. "Individualism and the Mental," **Midwest Studies in Philosophy, 4, Studies in Metaphysics**, pp. 73–122. University of Minnesota Press, Minneapolis, 1979. Edited by P. French, *et al.*

include intentional mental states such as beliefs, desires, hopes and fears. Burge called the internalist interpretation that he and Putnam criticized, "individualism."

Although the Twin Earth thought experiment is entirely fanciful, similar phenomena occur every day. In most categories there is a level of generality where different people will call different things by the same name—for example, what I call a "sparrow" and another person calls a "sparrow" might actually be different species of birds, even though they have the same behavior, general appearance and habitat. Two women can have identical appearing necklaces and thereby have the same mental conception of each's jewelry. But while one necklace is made of precious stones, the other is made of fake stones. Again, what each woman has in her head is identical since both believe their jewelry is genuine, but their respective necklaces are not actually the same. The Twin Earth thought experiment has had a profound effect on philosophy over the last 3 decades. As Pessin and Goldberg observed, "Twin Earth and 'The Meaning of Meaning,' the article in which it became famous, comprise perhaps the most influential single philosophical episode in the past half century." (This quotation was taken from the preface of a valuable 20 year retrospective collection of prominent articles written about Putnam's Twin Earth thought experiment [Pessin and Goldberg (eds), 1996, p. xi] See footnote 246).

*Psychophysical Parallelism*

Some of those who wish to ground meaning in our mind will not give up even when our conscious and unconscious minds are shown to be untenable foundations for meaningful activity. For these individuals, if meaning is not grounded in the conscious mind or the unconscious mind, then it must be grounded even "deeper" in the biological strata of the brain. This is a kind of mind–brain, or psychophysical, parallelism where whatever is in the conscious or unconscious mind must have a corresponding process or structure in the neurology of the brain. Malcolm; describes the beliefs of psychophysical parallelism:

> According to the viewpoint of [psycho-physical] parallelism, for each thought, sensation, or feeling there is a corresponding event, process, or state in or of the brain (or central nervous system). For each difference in a thought or sensation, there is a matching difference in the corresponding brain-occurrence. It should be mentioned that even if a philosopher does not regard the word "mind" as a term that designates a thing that thinks, he may still adopt the doctrine of parallelism. A thought, decision, or intention is conceived of a non-material event or state, to which there corresponds a brain-event or brain-state.[248]

Even when the cognitive foundations for language are not found in the conscious or unconscious mind, it is easy to insist that they none-the-less exist tacitly in the neurological structure or processes of our brains. To some, this *must* be the case, since meaning has to be a mental event of some kind, and any mental event *must* have its origin and foundation in neurological processes and structures. This belief in psychophysical parallelism is held by both prominent philosophers and psychologists. Philosopher John Searle presents his support of this theory quite clearly:

---

[248] N. Malcolm. **Nothing is Hidden: Wittgenstein's Criticism of his Early Thought**, p. 183. Basil Blackwell, Oxford, 1986.

The brain is all we have for the purpose of representing the world to ourselves and everything we can use must be inside the brain. Each of our beliefs must be possible for a being who is a brain in a vat because each of us is precisely a brain in a vat; the vat is a skull and the "messages" coming in are coming in by way of impacts on the nervous system.[249]

The views of many psychologists resonate with Searle's statement:

There are two theories of mind, speaking very generally. One is animistic, a theory that the body is inhabited by an entity—the mind or soul—that is quite different from it, having nothing in common with bodily processes. The second theory is physiological or mechanistic; it assumes that mind is bodily process, an activity of the brain. Modern psychology works with this latter theory only.[250]

Wittgenstein's disagreement with this psychophysical parallelism comes in some of his most striking statements:

One of the most dangerous of ideas for a philosopher is, oddly enough, that we think with our heads or in our heads.

The idea of thinking as a process in the head, in a completely enclosed space, gives him something occult.

Is thinking a specific *organic* process of the mind, so to speak—as it were chewing and digesting in the mind? Can we replace it by an inorganic process that fulfills the same end, as it were use a prosthetic apparatus for thinking? How should we have to imagine a prosthetic organ of thought?

No supposition seems to me more natural than that there is no process in the brain correlated with associating or with thinking; so that it would be impossible to read off thought-processes from brain-processes. I mean this: if I talk or write there is, I assume, a system of impulses going out from my brain and correlated with my spoken or written thoughts. But why should the system continue further in the direction of the centre? Why should this order not proceed, so to speak, out of chaos?

It is thus perfectly possible that certain psychological phenomena cannot be investigated physiologically, because physiologically nothing corresponds to them.

I saw this man years ago: now I have seen him again, I recognize him, I remember his name. And why does there have to be a cause of this remembering in my nervous system? Why must something or other, whatever it may be, be stored up there in any form? Why must a trace have been left behind? Why should there not be a psychological regularity to which no physiological regularity corresponds? If this upsets our concept of causality then it is high time it was upset.

[249] J. Searle. **Intentionality,** p. 230. Cambridge University Press, Cambridge, 1983. Quoted in Malcolm's **Nothing is Hidden: Wittgenstein's Criticism of his Early Thought,** p. 185. Basil Blackwell, Oxford, 1986.
[250] D.O. Hebb. **Textbook of Psychology**. Saunders, 1958, p. 3. Quoted in Malcolm, *op.cit.,* p. 186.

The prejudice in favour of psychophysical parallelism is a fruit of primitive interpretations of our concepts. For if one allows a causality between psychological phenomena which is not mediated physiologically, one thinks one is professing belief in a gaseous mental entity.[251] [**Z** §§610–611]

It is a travesty of the truth to say 'Thinking is an activity of our mind, as writing is of the hand'. (Love in the heart. The head and heart as loci of the soul.) [**PG** §64]

Meaning it is not a process which accompanies a word. For no process could have the consequences of meaning. [**PI** p. 218]

If God had looked into our minds he would not have been able to see there whom we were speaking of.[252] [**PI** p. 217]

Malcolm; makes a number of more strident comments on Searle's assertion:

... It makes as little sense to ascribe experiences, wishes, thoughts, beliefs, to a brain as to a mushroom.

Searle says that each of us *is* a brain in a vat, the vat being one's skull. Now if you *are* your brain then you are inside your own skull. You cannot walk or talk or see your friends. Searle says that you can receive "messages." But in that predicament, who wants messages?

Searle's idea is amusing—but at the same time one feels dismayed by the fact that an intelligent philosopher could assert such a view in all seriousness. It is a symptom of a grave disarray in the philosophy of mind.[253]

---

[251] These paragraphs exist in Wittgenstein's **RPP I** as §§903–906. They are identical except for the last sentence of the penultimate paragraph and the last paragraph:

If this upsets our concepts of causality then it is high time they were upset.

The prejudice in favour of psycho-physical parallelism is also a fruit of the primitive conception of grammar. For when one admits a causality between psychological phenomena, which is not mediated physiologically, one fancies that in doing so one is making an admission of the existence of a soul alongside the body, a ghostly mental nature. [**RPP I** §§905–906]

The change from "primitive interpretations of our concepts" to "primitive conception of grammar" is of some note.

It is ironic that Wittgenstein writes about "a prosthetic apparatus for thinking." One senses that he mentions it because of its very impossibility. Yet today, there are many who believe a computer is just such a device.

[252] Putnam comes to a similar conclusion:

... reference is socially fixed and not determined by conditions or objects in individual brains/minds. Looking inside the brain for the reference of our words is, at least in cases of the kind we have been discussing, just looking in the wrong place. [H. Putnam. **Representation and Reality**, p. 25. MIT Press, Cambridge, MA, 1996.]

[253] **Nothing is Hidden: Wittgenstein's Criticism of His Early Thought**, p. 186. Basil Blackwell, Oxford, 1986.

Wittgenstein comments on the related ability of understanding how to continue a mathematical series when it is shown to us. Even here it is not necessary that there be a perceivable mental process that accompanies or grounds such an ability:

> If there has to be anything "behind the utterance of the formula" it is particular circumstances, which justify me in saying I can go on—when the formula occurs to me.

> Try not to think of understanding as a "mental process" at all.—For that is the expression which confuses you. But ask yourself: in what sort of case, in what kind of circumstances, do we say, "Now I know how to go on," when, that is, the formula has occurred to me?—

> In the sense in which there are processes (including mental processes) which are characteristic of understanding, understanding is not a mental process.

> (A pain's growing more or less; the hearing of a tune or a sentence: these are mental processes.) [**PI** §154]

For Wittgenstein, it is no more likely that we "think" with our "brains" than we "love" with our "hearts." If we hold some sort of psychophysical parallelism then our belief is in some sense due to a failure of language. We are taking a metaphor—like "calculating in our heads"—too literally.[254] If we take as a "given" that we literally "calculate in our heads" and do not find *conscious* processes that always, necessarily accompany this ability, then we will look for or postulate some tacit or *unconscious* processes that satisfy these conditions; if these *unconscious* processes become untenable as a basis for calculating, then one is tempted to "go deeper" and look for these processes in the physiology of the brain itself. The fact that CAT scans and MRI's of the brain show that "something" is going on in specific regions of the brain when we calculate, seems to offer support that we are looking in the right place for what we want. There is no denying that "something" must go on in the brain while we are calculating (Wittgenstein would not deny this either), but that is a long ways from believing that such brain activity is a *complete explanation* of what we mean by "calculating." This is an example of how a simple metaphor—"calculating/thinking in our heads"—can not only mislead us about the location of such an ability, but also misleads us about where to look when we don't find the ability where we expect it (i.e., it keeps us looking "in the head" when we don't find what we expect at first). There is no reason to believe that the neurological processes offer some kind of endpoint for this sort of examination either. Neurons are made up of molecules, so if we do not find the foundation of intelligent activity in the neurology of the brain, we may be tempted to suppose that the foundation of meaning that we seek is located at the molecular level. Further, brain chemistry plays such an important role in neurological activity with neural synapses facilitated or inhibited by the presence or absence of neurotransmitters such as norepinephrine, dopamine or serotonin that if we do not find the foundation of thought in

---

[254] This is the same problem with metaphor that Szasz described as the basis for the "myth of mental illness." That is, psychiatrists are confusing the metaphorical use of "illness" in "mental illness," for the literal use of "illness" in "physical illness." See footnote 228.

neurological structures, we may then be tempted to look for a chemical basis for cognition. For Wittgenstein, we would be, both literally and figuratively, *deepening* our error.

There are also intelligent activities that are not entirely thought-based. Driving a car, for example. We may consciously think about how to drive when we are learning, but at a certain point, we drive and make decisions with our body, and not just with our mind. Certain reactions that we have while we drive, such a jamming on the brakes in an emergency, can happen almost entirely at the body level—that is, feeling an unexpected bump in the road in certain situations can cause us to perform a rapid action that happens so fast that it is our body reacting to the stimulus rather than the body feeling the stimulus, transmitting it to the brain which evaluates it and sends an emergency message back to the relevant body parts for response. This happens when the doctor tests our "knee jerk" reactions with a rubber hammer, so why can't it plausibly happen at least some of the time or, in part, for higher level bodily responses including those which are learned?

It is also the case that by linking thought processes to brain processes we are being arbitrarily selective. Surely, there are other physical processes, besides brain processes, that are necessary for thought. We need to eat nutritiously, get enough sleep and breathe before we can do any thinking "in our heads." Why, then, aren't eating, sleeping, and breathing, along with brain processes, part of the physiological basis for thought? And why stop with just these bodily processes—there are myriad others that keep us alive. Further, it is surely the case that such physical processes can influence how we think, too, making their relation to thought even more compelling. If I have a stomachache or a headache my thinking is likely to be less intense, perhaps even confused, especially if my physical ailments are disturbing enough. Late in life, the great Swiss mathematician Euler did some of his best mathematical work while relaxing in the evening after dinner. Do we owe as much to Euler's agreeable digestive system as we do to his brain for the brilliant advances in mathematics he conceived? Let's return to Wittgenstein's striking example (from the quotation above):

> I saw this man years ago: now I have seen him again, I recognize him, I remember his name. And why does there have to be a cause of this remembering in my nervous system? Why must something or other, whatever it may be, be stored up there in any form? Why must a trace have been left behind? Why should there not be a psychological regularity to which no physiological regularity corresponds? If this upsets our concept of causality then it is high time it was upset. [**Z** §610]

We have all had experiences of recognizing an old friend after a period of absence. How do we do this? It is easiest to suppose that we have some kind of mental image of what our friend looked like. We recognize our friend when we match our recollection of him with those people we are currently looking at. It seems like we are just matching pictures, though even this is not as straightforward as it first appears. But is this all there is to it? Wittgenstein doesn't think so:

> It is easy to have a false picture of the processes called "recognizing"; as if recognizing always consisted in comparing two impressions with one another. It is as if I carried a picture of an object with me and used it to perform an identification of an object as the one represented by the picture. [**PI** §604]

If recognition is simply a matter of matching a mental image with a visual one we should be able to recognize our friend in any circumstances, given the time to make the comparison. After all, comparing pictures should work anywhere and anytime, like extracting a picture from your wallet or purse whenever you wanted to compare it to someone you meet. But our memory doesn't always work so predictably. That is, although we may recognize our old friend at a high school reunion, we may not recognize him if he were to pass us on the street. There is nothing inconsistent about this, we would say that while we would expect to see our friend at the reunion, we would not expect to see him on the street (perhaps we were under the impression that he lived in another city). In this situation, we might say that we recognize our friend because of the circumstances in which he appears. So our recollection then, is not simply the matching of a mental image with an individual we see, but the matching of such an image in certain specific circumstances. There might be some circumstances in which our friend appears where we would actually refuse to believe it is our friend even though it looks just like him. For example, we might see a picture of him being knighted by Queen Elizabeth, but surmise that she must be knighting someone who looks like our friend, since we believe it to be impossible that he would ever be knighted by the ruling British Monarch. Or, we may see him in a major Hollywood movie, but believe that such an event to be impossible since he had never demonstrated a desire to act when we knew him before. If our recollection of our friend were purely a matter of matching what is in our heads with people we meet, then circumstances would have no influence on the process. But circumstances clearly do have some influence, sometimes a dominant influence. Further, even if we look just at the physical appearance of our friend, we find that our recollection of him can be strikingly different from his present appearance. Those of us who have gone to school reunions decades after our graduation know that some of our best friends can change not only in physical appearance—balder or fatter—but also in the clothes they wear and even their mannerisms, opinions and tone of voice. And, more importantly, they can change in ways that we do not anticipate at all. Yet in spite of these clear changes in their appearance or mannerisms we often still recognize them. Some of our recollections, then, are modified by our expectations of how our friend might have changed. For example, if we haven't seen our friend since high school, 25 years ago, we might *expect* him to be heavier, balder and more conservatively dressed, but we would not expect him to be shorter, or have blue eyes rather than brown. Our recognition of our friend is not simply the matching of a mental image with someone we see because there are circumstances and expectations that would alter how we might expect him to look. The role of the mental image we have of our friend can have even a curious *negative* quality about it. That is, if it has been sufficiently long since we last saw our friend we might be reasonably sure that our friend *does not* look like our recollection of him. Confronted with someone who looks exactly like our friend did 25 years ago, we might surmise that we are looking at someone else, his son perhaps, but not him. And seeing our friend after 10 years would give rise to different expectations than if we saw him after 40 years. As Wittgenstein observed:

> Images tell us nothing, either right or wrong, about the external world (Images are not hallucinations, nor yet fancies).

> While I am looking at an object I cannot imagine it.

Difference between the language-games: "Look at this figure!" and "Imagine this figure!"

Images are subject to the will.

Images are not pictures. I do not tell what object I am imagining by the resemblance between it and the image.

    ⋮

I might also have said earlier: The tie-up between imaging and seeing is close; but there is no similarity.

The language-games employing these concepts are radically different—but hang together.

A difference: "trying to see something" and "trying to form an image of something." In the first case one says: "Look, just over there!," in the second "Shut your eyes!"

It is just because forming images is a voluntary activity that it does not instruct us about the external world.

What is imaged is not in the same *space* as what is seen. [**Z** §§621, 625–627]

So, while it is tempting to say that the way we recognize things is by comparing them to a mental image, this explanation fails on a number of significant points:

1. The mental image does not match reality in exact ways. At best, it is a rough copy.

2. If the image is a rough copy of reality, then there must be something—perhaps rules—that governs the application of the image to what it purports to represent. But, as the Nominalist will remind us, reality is infinitely variable, so there must be separate rules for the application of the image to each different reality. Since there is an uncountable number of different realities that the image in question could apply to, there must be a correspondingly uncountable number of rules governing its application to reality. This, of course, is impossible.

3. An important part of the recognition process includes the particular circumstances and context where the recognition takes place. Thus, the mental image *by itself* could not be sufficient for recognition. That is, the image alone does not explain what is recognized.

4. Implicit in the activity of seeing something familiar is the assumption that it involves the process of recognition. That is, we see something unfamiliar, and then by exercising whatever mental abilities are appropriate we then come to recognize the unfamiliar as familiar. This does happen sometimes, but most of the time we just see things as familiar—I don't see a strange car, then recognize it as *my* car, I simply see *my* car.

5. Finally, and perhaps most decisively, if we look at the recognition process we see that often, and for some a majority of the time, we have no conscious impression of a mental image *at all*. When we see a friend we simply *recognize* him; as Wittgenstein said:

> If I have exhausted the justifications I have reached bedrock, and my spade is turned. Then I am inclined to say: "This is simply what I do."[255] [**PI** §217]

Searle, *et al.*, claim that:

> The brain is all we have for the purpose of representing the world to ourselves and everything we can use must be inside the brain. (*supra*)

If the claim "everything we can use [to represent the world] must be inside the brain" is not taken to be trivially circular, then to refute it we need to identify something that "we can use [to represent the world]" which is not "inside the brain." Consider the following example: many of us cannot make mathematical calculations without the aid of a pencil and paper. Yet no matter how many times we write out our calculations we may never be able to perform these calculations without a pencil and paper. In this case the brain cannot

---

[255] Some have claimed that the dearth of conscious images is merely because the necessary images are unconscious rather than conscious. But this begs the question, substituting a supposition for a missing observation. The weakness of such an assumption is apparent when we try to distinguish between knowledge with unconscious images, knowledge without unconscious images and ignorance. Clearly there is no observable distinction between knowledge with unconscious images and knowledge without them, so this distinction is untenable. Wittgenstein makes a similar point.

Psychologist J. Shotter argues that there is a further reason to distrust strict psycho-physical parallelism. ["Wittgenstein and Psychology: on our 'Hook Up' to Reality," **Wittgenstein Centenary Essays**. Cambridge University Press, Cambridge, 1991. Edited by A. Phillips Griffiths.]. Specifically, it has been asserted for some time now that the recollection of a memory is not the retrieval of some memory trace that exists in detail in some part of the brain. Rather, it is an unconscious process of retrieving the gist of a memory and then actively filling out its details, thereby including information that the subject did not actually observe, but which may still be correct.

> In all ordinary instances [the person] has an overmastering tendency simply to get a general impression of the whole; and, on the basis, of this, he constructs the probable detail. Very little of his construction is literally observed and often, as was easily demonstrated experimentally, a lot is distorted or wrong so far as the actual facts are concerned. But it is the sort of construction which serves to justify his general impression. [F. Bartlett. **Remembering: A Study in Experimental Psychology**, p. 206. Cambridge University Press, London, 1932. Quoted in Shotter, *op.cit*, p. 204]

Further, CAT scans and MRI's have shown that the recollection of a simple memory often consists of utilizing two or more different parts of the brain, indicating that the memory must be somehow constructed, or reconstructed, from more than one physical element. This reconstructive recollection may be part of the reason that false memories can be rather easily induced for some subjects, even when the memory conflicts with their initial recollection ["Creating False Memories." **Scientific American**, pp. 70–75. September 1997. See also, **Memory Distortion: How Minds, Brains and Societies Reconstruct the Past**. Harvard University Press, Cambridge, 1995. Edited by D.L. Schacter, et al.; and, E. Loftus and K. Ketcham's **The Myth of Repressed Memory**, 1994, St. Martin's Press, New York]. That is, since recollection is, in part, reconstruction, slight alterations in relatively insignificant cues may cause a subject to recall, that is reconstruct, something that did not actually take place, or did not take place in the way remembered.

get along without the pencil and paper for the obvious reason that if you take the pencil and paper away, we cannot calculate, no matter what is in our brain or how many times we performed the calculation before. Here we have a case where the claim "everything we can use must be in the brain" is not true—here we cannot represent the process of addition by means of the brain itself. The brain is no substitute for pencil and paper.

Getting back to our example of recognizing an old friend, is there anything outside of the brain that might be necessary for this recognition to take place? Surely the context and circumstances in which the recognition takes place are important. Context and circumstances are outside the brain, and we cannot recognize our friend without being in the right circumstances. Like our math example, we cannot remove the appropriate context and circumstances and still expect to recognize our friend. Thus, some or all of the context and circumstances *must* be there for the recognition to take place—the brain is simply not able to take in *everything it needs* to perform the recognition correctly. I am not denying that the brain may abstract something from the circumstances that might help in the recognition process. But what it abstracts will often not be enough for it to perform the recognition without physically being in the appropriate context and circumstances. Now we can see what Wittgenstein was getting at when he said, "... why does there have to be a cause of this remembering in my nervous system?" (*supra*). There can't be a "cause of this remembering in my nervous system" because much of what enables us to remember our friend is in the circumstances we find ourselves. Whatever we have "in our heads" that enables us to recognize our friend is, in itself, incomplete, adumbrative. Not only that, the circumstances where we might see our friend may vary considerably, and our expectations of what he might look like, and even our desire to see him may vary from time to time (based on how long it has been since we saw him, what mutual friends might have told us or how preoccupied I might be with something else at the time). It may be the case that what we have "in our heads" that enables us to recognize our friend is in constant flux. What is constant about our ability to recognize an old friend is not something "in our head"; what is constant is *our ability to recognize our friend*—as Malcolm and Wittgenstein put it so well: "*nothing is hidden*."

Wittgenstein is not saying that there are no mental processes at all accompanying conscious intellectual activities. He is saying that the conscious accompaniments that may occur are not necessary, and, if they do not occur in the conscious mind they cannot be replaced by unconscious mental activity. But surely something goes on in the brain when we perform meaningful activities like speech. Wittgenstein does not deny this, he merely says that any analysis of these processes would not give us an explanation of how we use language:

> But you surely cannot deny that, for example, in remembering, an inner process takes place.—What gives the impression that we want to deny anything? When one says "Still, an inner process does take place here"—one wants to go on: "After all, you see it." And it is this inner process that one means by the word "remembering."— The impression that we wanted to deny something arises from our setting our faces against the picture of the "inner process." What we deny is that the picture of the inner process gives us the correct idea of the use of the word "to remember." We say that this picture with its ramifications stands in the way of our seeing the use of the word as it is.

> Why should I deny that there is a mental process? But "There has just taken place in me the mental process of remembering..." means nothing more than: "I have just remembered..." To deny the mental process would mean to deny the remembering: to deny that anyone ever remembers anything.

> "Are you not really a behaviorist in disguise? Aren't you at bottom really saying that everything except human behavior is fiction?"—If I do speak of fiction, then it is a grammatical fiction.[256] **[PI §§305–307]**

This is similar to the act of pitching, which we discussed previously, where there are obvious "inner processes" that are a necessary part of the pitching activity (e.g., the contracting and relaxing of muscles in a specific sequence during the pitching movements). Many of these "inner processes" are also controlled by the nonconscious brain, but none is relevant to any conscious mental part of pitching.

### *The Mind and Reality: Mental Models or Scribbled Jottings?*

Some individuals hold that we don't have just images of reality, but a more complex "mental model" of the world which allows us to deal with reality. This view is, according to one psychologist, the view that dominates the mainstream of modern psychology [Shotter]:

> The mainstream [of psychology] is following through all the implications of what it calls "the cognitive revolution"; the idea that everything intelligent we do involves a "cognitive process" working in terms of "inner" *mental representations* of the "external" world, and that the way to study such processes is by modeling them in computational terms.
>
> ⋮
>
> Wittgenstein's philosophical investigations... offer good reasons for thinking that the current "cognitive" orientation in psychology is radically misconceived, and the idea, that computer models are relevant to the understanding of human activities, will eventually lose its credibility...[257]

In their simplest form *mental models* are merely *pictures* of the external world, an explanation of understanding that Wittgenstein rejected relatively quickly in his later philosophy:[258] First of all, we don't seem to have a *mental model* when we try to analyze

---

[256] The issue of whether Wittgenstein is a behaviorist or not will be taken up in the subsequent section **Wittgenstein and Behaviorism**, at the end of Part II.

[257] J. Shotter. "Wittgenstein and Psychology: on our 'Hook Up' to Reality." **Wittgenstein Centenary Essays**. Cambridge University Press, Cambridge, 1991. Edited by A.P. Griffiths. Quotation from p. 193. Shotter cites Boden ["Formalism and Fancy," **New Universities Quarterly**, vol. 36, 1982] and Johnson-Laird [**Mental Models**. Cambridge University Press, Cambridge, 1983] as two of the better known proponents of this view. Shotter does identify several nonmainstream psychologists who do not subscribe to a theory of mental models: J. Gibson. **The Ecological Approach to Visual Perception**. Houghton Mifflin, London, 1979; M. Billig, **Arguing and Thinking: A Rhetorical Approach to Social Psychology**, Cambridge University Press, Cambridge, 1987; K. Gergen, "The social constructionist movement in modern psychology," **American Psychologist**, vol. 40, 1985; J. Shotter. **Social Accountability and Selfhood**. Blackwell, Oxford, 1984; Shotter and Gergen. **Texts of Identity**. Sage, London, 1989.

[258] In rejecting the picture theory of meaning, Wittgenstein is rejecting a view that he himself held and was the cornerstone of his early philosophy which he developed in the **Tractatus Logico-Philosophicus**. Here,

Wittgenstein's view of language was that it's main purpose was to represent "facts." This was a common belief in early 20th century analytic philosophy, so Wittgenstein was not alone. Bertrand Russell wrote in his preface to the **Tractatus Logico-Philosophicus** that the "business of language is to assert or deny facts" [**TLP** p. x]. In the **Tractatus**... Wittgenstein writes:

> The world is all that is the case. [**TLP** 1]
> The world is the totality of facts, not things. [**TLP** 1.1]
> We make ourselves pictures of facts. [**TLP** 2.1]
> A picture is a model of reality. [**TLP** 2.12]
> In a picture the elements of the picture are the representation of objects. [**TLP** 2.131]
> The fact that the elements of a picture are related to one another in a determinate way represents that things are related to one another in the same way. [**TLP** 2.15]
> Pictorial form is the possibility that things are related to one another in the same way as the elements of the picture. [**TLP** 2.151]
> That is how a picture is attached to reality; it reaches right out to it. [**TLP** 2.1511]
> [The picture] is laid against reality like a measure. [**TLP** 2.1512]

Such a perspective is mirrored in more recent work in psychology by Johnson-Laird:

> ... the psychological core of understanding... consists in your having a "working model" of the phenomenon [you are concerned with] in your mind. [**Mental Models**, p. 2. Cambridge University Press, Cambridge, 1983.]

Wittgenstein came to reject this view, referring to it as part of his "old way of thinking" [**PI**, preface]. He rejected it for two principal reasons: First, the link between the picture and reality is not a simple correlation since pictures are always open to interpretation. Secondly, the role of language is not just to represent "facts"—it has myriad other uses. As Wittgenstein comments:

> But how many kinds of sentences are there? Say assertion, question, and command?—There are countless kinds; countless different kinds of use of what we call "symbols" "words," "sentences." And this multiplicity is not something fixed, given once for all; but new types of language, new language-games, as we may say, come into existence, and others become obsolete and get forgotten (We can get a rough picture of this from the changes in mathematics.). Here the term "language-game" is meant to bring into prominence the fact that the speaking of language is part of an activity, or of a form of life.
>
> Review the multiplicity of language-games in the following examples, and in others:
>
> Giving orders, and obeying them—
> Describing the appearance of an object, or giving its measurements—
> Constructing an object from a description (a drawing)—
> Reporting an event—
> Speculating about an event—
> Forming and testing a hypothesis—
> Presenting the results of an experiment in tables and diagrams—
> Making up a story; and reading it—
> Play-acting—
> Singing catches—
> Guessing riddles—
> Making a joke; telling it—
> Solving a problem in practical arithmetic—
> Translating from one language into another—
> Asking, thanking, cursing, greeting, praying.
> —It is interesting to compare the multiplicity of the tools in language and of the ways they are used, the multiplicity of kinds of word and sentence, with what logicians have said about the structure of language. (Including the author of the **Tractatus Logico-Philosophicus**.) [**PI** §23]

our own thoughts, and even if we assume that we have it, but in some kind of tacit or otherwise inaccessible form, we still must explain how we can apply it to reality.[259] A model of reality would, like a picture, stand in need of interpretation so it could be linked to reality, consequently, we would need a set of rules, or some similar device, to perform this interpretation. For example, we might have a general mental model of a tree that, it is said, might be used to help us identify real trees. But each tree that we see is unique, as the nominalist says. So we would not just need a set of rules to apply the model of a tree to a tree in reality, but we would have to have a slightly different set of rules to apply the tree mental model to every different individual tree we might possibly encounter. Without this ability, we would not be able to classify many unique objects, as even a child can. But for computational reasons, we probably could not work out all the possible rules that might enable us to apply a general mental model of a tree in every case, for we would not have mental models for just trees, but for all the myriad categories that we need to distinguish in reality—trees, bushes, dogs, birds, cars, bicycles, furniture, wine, mushrooms, rugs, etc. If our minds were busy working out all the rules for applying the mental models or images we have to all the possible unique cases of classification in reality, our minds would no doubt be totally preoccupied in this task, leaving little capacity to do anything else.

If propositions are not pictures of facts, what are they? Wittgenstein sidesteps this question by considering, not what a proposition is, but how would you explain what sense it has.

> When I ask "What sense does it make?"—I want someone to answer me not with a picture or a series of pictures, but with the description of situations. [**RPP I** §132]

It is not the photographer who captures reality, but the playwright.

[259] I will not address the issue here of "tacit knowledge," though we might reject any theory of mental models on the basis of the untenability of such knowledge. As Baker and Hacker put it:

> The questions of what distinguishes tacit knowledge from explicit knowledge on the one hand, and of what distinguishes tacit knowledge from ignorance on the other, must be answered coherently. For it is far from obvious that theorists' use of the term "tacit knowledge'" is intelligible. Like Locke's notion of tacit consent, tacit knowledge may be no more than a device for tacitly burying problems raised by the theory itself. If we are to ascribe tacit knowledge of a theory of meaning to a person there must be something that will reveal the difference between tacitly knowing the theory and total ignorance of it, something other than the mere fact of the speaker's correct discourse. If his correct discourse is all that shows his tacit knowledge and incorrect discourse is all that shows ignorance, then the hypothesis that he can produce and understand sentences because of such tacit knowledge is both untestable and vacuous. [G.P. Baker and P.M.S. Hacker. **Language, Sense and Nonsense: A Critical Investigation into Modern Theories of Language**, p. 341. Basil Blackwell, New York, 1984.]

Baker and Hacker are specifically addressing the assertion—popularized by Chomsky—that ". . . the speaker of a language has tacit knowledge of the theory of meaning." However, their comments apply to all notions of "tacit knowledge." [*Op.cit.* p. 340] [*vid.* N. Chomsky. **Rules and Respresentations**. Blackwell, London, 1980.] As Wittgenstein put it:

> Philosophy simply puts everything before us, and neither explains nor deduces anything.— Since everything lies open to view there is nothing to explain. For what is hidden, for example, is of no interest to us. [**PI** §126]

Further, it is not clear at all where all these rules would come from, or how they might be applied.

But suppose, it is countered, that we do not have precise mental models or images that are in constant need of rules to apply them in exceptional cases. Suppose we have "rough" mental models or images that can "fit" a lot of applications without requiring them to fit exactly (and hence not requiring special rules to adapt to every case). This is similar to Rosch's "basic level" of abstraction, around which we supposedly organize many of the categories we use in everyday life.[260] But this doesn't help us either because even though our "rough" mental model can be applied more efficiently to large numbers of unique objects, there would still need to be rules, or some method, that would enable us to determine whether the "rough" fit is adequate *in each case.* And some of the properties of a tree can be very loose (like the number of leaves it might have or its height) and others might be very precise (like whether is needs sap or bark). To distinguish which properties can fit loosely and which must be precise, and, further, in what way they must be precise or can be loose, throws us back into the situation where we need increasingly more information to match the model with an ever-expanding reality of individual cases. In short, there are likely to be just as many ways that a "rough" model of a tree can be applied to actual cases as there are ways for a more precise model to be applied. Both situations— the precise model and the "rough" model—must be adapted to an uncountable number of possible cases. The "rough" model does not really save us any effort when we consider all the possible situations in which the model might be matched with reality. Trying to say that "rough" mental models require fewer adaptive cases and rules than "more precise" mental models might is like saying that there are fewer even integers than there are odd *and* even integers—yet, as is well known to mathematicians, the set of even integers can be mapped one-to-one onto the set of all integers, meaning that from the point of view of denumerability, neither set is greater than the other. Paradoxically, there are just as many even integers as there are odd *and* even integers. Similarly, when dealing with unlimited sets of unique objects in reality we are faced with the paradox that there are likely to be, at least from a practical point of view, just as many exceptions to the application of a general mental model as there are variations of more precise mental models. Nothing is saved by the "rough" model over the precise one. There are other inconsistencies with "rough" mental models. For example, there are multiple criteria for "rough" fitting, and these criteria are not based on how, in our example, the tree fits a formal model or image in the mind, but on how the tree identification might be used in particular circumstances and for different purposes. For example, the precision of fit for tree identification for a botanist might be very different than that of a casual hiker. And this may vary with different situations too: the botanist who needs to fell a small tree to help him cross a stream in a hurry is not going to care this time what type of tree it is, but whether it satisfies some general "tree across the stream" properties; and these properties might have little to do with what the botanist might normally look at in a tree. But just like our problem with applying rough and precise mental models to reality, it is clear that any set of rules that might permit a botanist to select a good candidate tree for bridging a stream could not be unambiguously interpreted themselves in every type of circumstance; consequently, these

---

[260] E. Rosch. (Cited in **The Literary Mind**, by M. Turner).

rules would require further rules to insure *their* correct application in other cases—in one case, the botanist must fell a tree to make a bridge across a small stream, in another, he must fell a tree to cross a large raging torrent, in another the best possible trees grow too far away from the stream, so a compromise must be reached; in another case his axe breaks limiting his cutting ability, in another he sprains his wrist while chopping, etc., etc. This leads us again into the potentially infinite regress of rules for the application of rules to each new case, etc.[261] Wittgenstein states the issue more succinctly:

> ...the idea of "agreement with reality" does not have any clear application. [**OC** §215]

Wittgenstein is quite clear about his disagreement with the use of mental images to provide an understanding of reality. He says that if we look at what we remember when we recall something we find that we don't have a very precise picture of the desired object.

> If I say "I saw a chair in this room," I can mostly recall the particular visual impression only very roughly, nor does it have any importance in most cases. The use that is made of the sentence bypasses this particular feature. [**Z** §25]

But, it could be countered, a mental model is likely to be a more complex entity than a mental picture or image. Consider a structured, intelligent activity—finding one's way around a city. We have all probably done something like this at one time or another. We can do it, do it well, do it in some circumstances and not in others, or, perhaps, not be able to do it all. But if we look at our ability to find our way around a city, even when we are particularly good at it, we notice a curious inconsistency. Wittgenstein comments:

> It could very well be imagined that someone knows his way around a city perfectly, i.e. would confidently find the shortest way from any place in it to any other,—and yet would be quite incompetent to draw a map of the city. That, as soon as he tries, he produces nothing that is not *completely wrong*. [**Z** § 121]

If our subject truly had a working model of reality, the city, in his head—a "mental map," as the metaphor might suggest—then he should be able to reproduce it, at least in its essential features.[262] The fact that he often cannot means that he does not need to have

---

[261] For a more detailed discussion of the problem of rules, see, "The Structure of Language" in my book **Language and Representation in Information Retrieval**, pp. 149ff. Elsevier Science, 1990.

[262] The persistence of the "mental map" metaphor is remarkable even though we have no real evidence that it truly models what is in our minds. Some cognitive psychologists take the existence of a mental map as the assumed foundation for research rather than an object for verification itself. Consider UCLA's Dr. Bruce Gallistel, "a leading authority on animal navigation" who is reported to claim that "Most animals have a rudimentary mental map of the world encoded in nerve tissue that helps them figure out how and where to move..." [from "Navigating Life's Maze: Styles Split The Sexes," The New York Times, May 26, 1992, p. B1]. In such a situation, psychologists are making the same mistake that Szasz claims psychiatrist's make when they take the metaphor "mental illness" literally, or that Malcolm claims philosophers make when they take the metaphor of thoughts and feelings being "in the head" too literally (see quotation at footnote 229). It's not hard to see how a psychologist can make this mistake. When we want to find our way we generally use a map. This works very well. So when animals can somehow find their way across difficult geography, or when people do it intuitively, it is easy to infer that the external process is a model for the internal process. What else could it be? By claiming that the "mental map" is in the "nerve tissue" of the animal, and, by inference, in the people who can orient themselves without maps or conscious thought, Dr. Gallistel has removed the model of a "mental map" from empirical investigation. It also

such an exact mental model or even a mental model at all. Some might counter that the subject has the representation but may not be a good enough illustrator to reproduce it. But surely he could reproduce it with simple drawings that are within his capability (i.e., while the drawing might not be exact, it would clearly have the necessary detail and be correct in what it does represent). But in most cases, he cannot even do this. If our subject has no mental model of reality that stands behind such simple skills as finding his way around a city, where does he get his ability to do this? Where is the information that enables him to drive around the city? The information about the city is certainly available to the subject, but it is not the kind of literal or predictive mental model that many want. In short, our subject does not need a mental model of the city to find his way around because *he already has the city "out there."* In other words, why do you need to make a model of something that you already have? It would be like insisting that in order to read the map before our eyes we must have a copy of the map in our heads, in the same way that, as Malcolm pointed out, some assume erroneously that we must calculate in our heads before we can calculate on paper. Surely, Ockham's Razor is needed here. This is what Wittgenstein was getting at when he stated:

> Images tell us nothing, either right or wrong, about the external world. (Images are not hallucinations, nor yet fancies).
>
> While I am looking at an object I cannot imagine it. [**Z** §621]

The mental image is not only unnecessary as a correlative to something real, it, according to Wittgenstein, cannot even be brought up at all when the object it might represent is present. Reality, it seems, precludes the imagination.[263]

Getting back to our subject finding his way around the city, all he needs in addition to the city itself, is such things like an ability to see parts of the city as familiar as he drives around, an ability to tell which direction he is going, some general understanding of how streets are usually laid out in cities (i.e., that numbered streets lie parallel to each other in numerical order, or that street names do not usually change with each passing cross street—and this additional information can vary greatly in kind and amount, as can the driver's skill in using it). Our subject cannot recall a detailed map of the city, but he can recognize the right ways to turn *as he drives around in the city.* In fact, the presence of the city is a prerequisite for his recollection of how to find his way—without the city he cannot "remember" how to get around. Those of us who have lived in a large metropolitan area realize that it is not unusual for us to be able reliably to drive a complex route of many turns

---

conveniently explains why we can't find it when we look for it in the conscious mental processes of well-oriented individuals. While the idea of a "mental model" appears to be an empirical claim, it is in actuality a somewhat dogmatic assumption. We don't have to have "mental maps" to orient ourselves in the same way that we don't have to fly the same way that birds do if we want to build machines that fly. The belief that we must fly like birds, if we are to fly at all, hindered the early development of powered, heavier-than-air flight craft. Perhaps the use of metaphors such as "mental models" to explain how we understand things is a "disease of thinking" that holds back cognitive psychology in the same way that Szasz and Wittgenstein claim that psychiatry and epistemology are held back by the literal interpretation of metaphors such as "mental illness" and "thinking in our heads," respectively.

[263] It is not too farfetched to suppose that when the imagination can substitute for, replace or alter real perceptions we would have a pathological mental state of some kind: psychosis or drug-induced hallucination.

across the city, but to not be able to tell, in sufficient detail, someone else how to drive the same way. Some of us, through practice may learn to be able to give detailed directions of this kind (a tour guide might develop this ability). But such a detailed descriptive ability is *not* a necessary condition of the ability to find one's way about in a reliable manner, nor is it a latent ability that we can learn to make explicit. Since the presence of the city is often a prerequisite for remembering how to get around, Searle's claim that "the brain is all we have for the purpose of representing the world to ourselves and everything we can use must be inside the brain" (*supra*) cannot be right. If "everything we can use must be inside the brain" then our recollection of how to get around the city would be just as reliable whether the city is there or not. But it isn't. Therefore "everything we can use" is *not* in the brain.

It is also the case that two individuals who can find their way around a large city may do it in quite different ways. That is, they may differ greatly in the details that they keep in mind, and differ also in the landmarks which they use as guides to following the same route. What is the same between two individuals is not some mental phenomena that enable them to get across town, but their *ability to get across town*. Again, Wittgenstein pushes our focus away from "inner mental processes" and towards the "outer" abilities that we have: "The uncertainty about the inner is an uncertainty about something outer" [**LWPP II** p. 88]. Our mistake is that we try to explain our "outer" abilities by resorting to some "inner/mental processes"—this is our "disease of thinking": "There is a kind of general disease of thinking which always looks for (and finds) what would be called a mental state from which all our acts spring as from a reservoir" [**BB** p. 143]. Our "outer" abilities don't need explaining, Wittgenstein insists, they are ". . . simply what [we] do" [**PI** §217]. "What has to be accepted, the given, is—so one could say—*forms of life*" [**PI** p. 226].

One of the central questions in epistemology concerns the relationship between mental phenomena or processes and the ability to do things. Cognitive Science concentrates primarily on "mental processes/mental models," assuming that people who can do the same things must have identical mental processes from which these actions "spring as from a reservoir." Wittgenstein rejects this and asserts that the only thing people who can do the same thing have in common is the *ability to do the same thing*. They do not have the same mental processes lying behind these abilities or somehow instigating them. To disprove this assumption, Wittgenstein only has to show that there are cases where people who can do the same things have different things going on in their minds, or that they don't have *anything* going on in their minds. For Wittgenstein, positing a "mental model" as a basis for being able to perform intelligent activities does not add anything to our understanding of these processes. Such a theory can be misleading, too.[264] This false

---

[264] It may be the case that even from a physiological point of view there may be important differences in the ways that the same ability or function may be instantiated at the neuronal level. Merlin Donald writes:

> Classical neuropsychology has tended to assume that localization of [cognitive] function follows a roughly similar course in each individual, provided gender and handedness are taken into account. But this principle is almost certainly wrong, given the competitive maturational environment of neurons at the microbiological level and the tremendous culturally programmed changes in environmental patterning of the brain on the psychological level.

assumption that common mental processes underly our common intelligent abilities, is what Wittgenstein was getting at with the following statement:

> It is sometimes said that animals do not talk because they lack the mental capacity. And this means: "they do not think, and that is why they do not talk." But—they simply do not talk. Or to put it better: they do not use language...[265] [**PI** §25]

> ...the degree of consistency across individuals that has been assumed in neuropsychology may not exist in tertiary cortical regions at all. This might be expressed as the *principle of singularity*: the individual human brain develops a unique functional organization at the representational level. This has serious implications for optimal research strategies in neuropsychology; at the very least, it is a very strong argument in favor of the single-case approach. The regions of the brain that are most characteristically human—especially the great expanses of the frontal and anterior temporal lobes—are likely to be the most malleable neurological structures in nature, taking on many forms. They are configurable and reconfigurable to a remarkable degree, because their resources are allocated on a *competitive* basis to the many input paths impinging on them. In effect, *the physical structure of mind has become less and less fixed as neocortical evolution has progressed.* This leaves room not only for the kinds of radical reconfiguration introduced by literacy but also (presumably) for larger differences between the brains of individual human beings than are possible in primates. It also leaves room for further cognitive restructuring, possibly in fundamental ways. [M. Donald. **Origins of the Modern Mind: Three Stages in the Evolution of Culture and Cognition**, p. 380. Harvard University Press, Cambridge, MA, 1991. Italics are in the original text.]

In his discussion of "neurological indeterminacy," Donald makes use of the work of Edelman [**Neural Darwinism**. Basic Books, NY, 1987]:

> Most of the greatly expanded cortical regions in the human brain... receive great quantities of highly digested inputs from all over the brain. They lack a single genetically entrenched dominant input path; therefore, in theory, maturational competition could produce a wide variety of different "wiring" schemes in tertiary regions, depending on the patterns of early experience. In principle, this would create an opportunity for considerable individual variability in the functional organization of the adult neocortex.

> ...Edelman [*op.cit.*] has considered this issue in detail and has proposed a theory of competitive neuronal group selection, which he calls "neural Darwinism." In his conception of neuronal genesis, there is room for a great deal of individual variability in neuronal organization; in fact, it is an essential feature of his system. No two animals will evolve the same nervous system, not even during the earliest stages of development. [Donald, *op.cit.*, p. 379]

We can now see that we have an ineluctable cognitive variability on at least two levels: on the conscious level, when we actively use different cues and heuristics to perform the same task as others do, and at the neuronal level where the ability to perform conscious and nonconscious tasks is instantiated. Clearly there is ample evidence for the cognitive variability that Wittgenstein describes in the brain and the mind.

[265] The idea that speech is a criterion for thought goes back a long ways in western epistemology. Thomas Hobbes wrote:

> When a man, upon the hearing of any speech, has those thoughts which the words of that speech and their connection were ordained and constituted to signify, then he is said to understand it, understanding being nothing else but conception caused by speech. And therefore if speech be peculiar to man, as for aught I know it is, then is understanding peculiar to him also. [**Leviathan**, p. 44. Bobbs-Merrill, NY, 1958 (Chapter 4: "Of Speech")]

The fact that an animal cannot talk is not evidence that it cannot think, it is simply evidence that it cannot talk—nothing is hidden. The fact that two individuals can drive a complex route across a large city is not evidence that they have the same "mental model," or set of mental processes, as some might insist, it is merely evidence that they both have the *same ability to drive across town*. What each of these individuals has "in mind" to enable him to drive across town is probably quite different from what the other has "in mind," even when they drive the same route. Each individual would have a complex combination of highly subjective "mental jottings," or notes, combined with an ability to recognize certain features of the landscape as familiar (e.g., although they all turn left at the same place, one individual turns left at the "third stoplight after the exit from the highway," the other turns left "across from the dry cleaners on Cedar street," a third individual turns left where it "just feels like he should"). The "mental jottings" that we might have that enable us to follow the route across town, might be like the written jottings of a student listening to a lecture. Wittgenstein comments:

> Imagine the following phenomenon. If I want someone to take note of a text that I recite to him, so that he can repeat it to me later, I have to give him paper and pencil; and while I am speaking he makes lines, marks, on the paper; if he has to reproduce the text later he follows those marks with his eyes and recites the text. But I am assuming that what he has jotted down is not writing, it is not connected by rules with the words of the text; yet without these jottings he is unable to reproduce the text; and if anything in it is altered, if part of it is destroyed, he gets stuck in his "reading" or recites the text uncertainly or carelessly, or cannot find the words at all.—This can be imagined!—What I called jottings would not be a rendering of the text, not so to speak a translation with another symbolism. The text would not be stored up in the jottings. And why should it be stored up in our nervous system?
> [**Z** §612]

We can imagine a student taking actual notes in the way that students normally do during a lecture—that is, the notes may include actual words as well as any other marks or symbols the student finds useful. The notes are not an exact reproduction of the lecture, yet by means of them plus some background knowledge and understanding the student may be able reproduce the lecture in detail; and another student, with a different set of jottings, may be able to reproduce the lecture just as accurately as the first student. Clearly, two students don't need the same "jottings" (mental or actual) in order to reproduce the lecture. In fact, it is unlikely that any two students would, independently, have the same jottings for the same lecture even if they tried. The rejoinder to this example might be that the combination of the written lecture jottings *plus* what is in the student's head would be a literal copy of the lecture. But it can be shown that this is not the case either, for recapitulating the lecture does not have to be like reading a literal copy. Much of what we do when we recall something is inferential or reconstructive in nature. That is, I begin by stating, from literal memory, the speaker's opening few sentences, but then, because I know the "gist" of his lecture, I can infer what he says next because "it follows" from his opening statements. I may jot down a word or phrase in my notes, not because it is a complete rendition of what was said, but because it recalls for me an "old joke" or hackneyed story that I know already and can reconstruct in the style and emphasis that the speaker would have told the story (i.e., I not only know the story, but I can fit it into the speaker's talk because I know the speaker's aim or point in using it). It follows that much of what we call memory is not literal recall, but a complex and often idiosyncratic process of reconstruction. If we had a literal copy of a talk in our heads, would we really have remembered the talk? I think that Wittgenstein would say no. The exact copy of the talk (a kind of mental image of text that we could read like a book) would fail to do what we want in the same way that a picture or any other literal representation fails to have an unambiguous interpretation. A literal text is like a "picture" of the talk and, like any picture, can be taken in more than one way. See how different the meanings of three copies of the same literal sentence, "John stole the money," are when the emphasis is on "John" in the first case, "stole" in the second, and "money" in the third:

> "*John* stole the money." (i.e., I thought it was *Bill*, but found out to my surprise that it was *John*)
>
> "John *stole* the money." (i.e., I thought John *borrowed* the money, but it turned out that he *stole* it)
>
> "John stole the *money*." (i.e., John was supposed to steal the *jewelry*, not the *money*)

Missing also from the literal text are the tone and pacing of the talk, the speaker's gestures and facial expressions, not to mention his beliefs or point of view as evidenced by his previous talks or writings. The student may use these too, in order to "read between the lines" of the talk (what the naive listener takes as literal, the informed listener may see as facetious or allegorical). In fact, the less we "understand" a lecture, the more literal we must be in our recollection, and we can memorize by rote what we do not understand at all (even such a literal rendering of the lecture, as we noted before, may not be a "complete" or accurate rendering of what the speaker wanted to convey—imagine what would be "missing" from Martin Luther King's invigorating "I have a dream" speech if we were to hear it recited in a quiet monotone).[266]

If much of our knowledge is "out there" rather than in our heads, why don't we see it? Wittgenstein says that we often cannot see what is right before our eyes.

> The aspects of things that are most important for us are hidden because of their simplicity and familiarity (One is unable to notice something—because it is always before one's eyes.). The real foundations of his enquiry do not strike a man at all. Unless <u>that</u> fact has at some time struck him.—And this means: we fail to be struck by what, once seen, is most striking and most powerful. [**PI** §129]

> If it is asked: "How do sentences manage to represent?"—the answer might be: "Don't you know? You certainly see it, when you use them." For nothing is concealed. [**PI** §435]
>
> ⋮
>
> Here it is easy to get into that dead-end philosophy, where one believes that the difficulty of the task consists in this: our having to describe phenomena that are

---

[266] Autistic or similarly afflicted individuals who have what is called "savant syndrome," can memorize, seemingly without effort, incredible amounts of text, sometimes without the ability to understand it at all. [O. Sacks. "Prodigies," **An Anthropologist on Mars**, pp. 188–243. Vintage Books, NY, 1995.]

hard to get hold of, the present experience that slips quickly by, or something of the kind. [**PI** §436]

We don't have a need to internalize our knowledge any more than we have a need to memorize the contents of our libraries. We don't need to memorize the books in libraries, except in special circumstances, because whenever we need the information in the library we simply go there and look it up. As Samuel Johnson once observed, "Knowledge is of two kinds. We know a subject ourselves, or we know where we can find information on it."[267] Our surrounding context and circumstances, like the library, can be the repository for much of the everyday information and knowledge we need to use, so we don't have to remember it literally. If we can go to the library for written information, why can't we "go to" our surroundings for some of our everyday information? As Malcolm comments:

> The world is represented to us in history books and maps, drawings and diagrams, newspapers, novels, paintings, plays and music.[268]

Some of our problem in seeing that much of what we "know" exists outside our heads is that it is difficult for us to see how this knowledge or information is often subtly embedded in the circumstances that surround what we do. In large part, we have a blind spot about this essential source of our knowledge because we have no way of describing it—and if we can't describe it, it is hard to be aware of it (*vid.* earlier section **Language and Thought**). Why don't we have the general ability to describe this knowledge that is embedded in our surroundings, circumstances and practices? That's simple, we don't need to. A language game for describing these surroundings, circumstances and practices, and the knowledge embedded in them, is not generally available to us (although there may be activities that would require such linguistic ability—say the work of anthropology or sociology, for example. The necessary language games may grow out of those activities). Our difficulty seeing the importance circumstances, surroundings and practices for language is a direct consequence of a faulty view of how language works. If we believe that language is learned by explanation and definition, we will look for the definitions and explanations which *must* be used in this process. Not finding them, we refuse to give them up, and so we hypothesize that they must be part of some hidden mental processes.[269] We believe that the definitions and explanations are there, but merely latent or hidden. But all we need to understand

---

[267] J. Boswell. **The Life of Samuel Johnson**. 18 April 1775. [Oxford University Press, Oxford, 1980, p. 627]

[268] N. Malcolm. **Nothing is Hidden: Wittgenstein's Criticism of his Early Thought**, p. 185. Basil Blackwell, Oxford, 1986.

[269] The belief in "false consciousness" and the hiddenness of some of our thoughts is particularly strong in 20th century, as evidenced by the continuing popularity of its principal proponents Freud and Marx. Freud's work was very prominent in the intellectual circles of *fin de seicle* Vienna, where Wittgenstein grew up, so Wittgenstein was well aware of it (his sister Margarete was a personal friend of Freud). False consciousness is the supposed solution to the inconsistency between what we profess to believe is the case, and what we "actually" believe (as based on, e.g., how we act). For example,. we profess to like so-and-so but we continually mistreat him. Freud would say that we unconsciously dislike him and that our positive conscious attitude towards him is false. This false consciousness serves to hide our dislike for him even from ourselves. Wittgenstein, though he did not write about Freud much, would probably consider the doctrine of false consciousness to be a "disease of thinking." Where Freud looked "deeper" in our psyche—the unconscious—for the resolution of inconsistencies in consciousness, Wittgenstein, on the other hand, would shift his attention outwardly to the context and circumstances where such inconsistencies really manifest themselves. Wittgenstein would probably say that the only thing that is important is how we act. The contradictory positive conscious statements do not "hide" anything, they just point

language use is right before our eyes. It is not hidden in some kind of Chomskean "Deep Structures," nor does it consist of explanations and definitions. It consists of, among other things, the circumstances, context, activities and practices that surround and permeate our use of language. We have no need to describe these circumstances in any detail because these descriptions have no real use for us. But how do we teach others about this subtle embedded knowledge if we cannot describe it? Well, we can still convey the necessary information by *showing* the student the proper usage in the relevant circumstances (In some cases, if the student already has a personal familiarity with the circumstances or situation in question, I may not have to wait for them to occur, but can merely refer to them. Here we are teaching a new usage, or a refinement of definition to someone who is already familiar with the relevant circumstances, so no detailed description is needed.). Wittgenstein comments on this problem:

> One learns the word "think", i.e. its use, under certain circumstances, which, how-ever, one does not learn to describe.

> But I *can teach* a person the use of the word! For a description of those circumstances is not needed for that.

> I just teach him the word *under particular circumstances*.

> :

> I cannot enumerate the conditions under which the word "to think" is to be used—but if a circumstance makes the use doubtful, I can say so, and also say *how* the situation is deviant from the usual ones. [**Z** §§114–116, 118]

If our student understands the circumstances or situations relevant to the linguistic usage that we want to teach, I can merely refer to those situations without describing them in detail. But if he is not familiar with these relevant circumstances, I must show him the actual circumstances for that language use. If he has not experienced the situation I refer

to an inconsistency between our actions and our statements. Wittgenstein remained ambivalent about Freud, as evidenced by a letter he wrote to Norman Malcolm in 1945:

> I, too, was greatly impressed when I first read Freud. He's extraordinary.—Of course he is full of fishy thinking and his charm and the charm of the subject is so great that you may easily be fooled... Unless you think very clearly psycho-analysis is a dangerous and a foul practice, and it's done no end of harm and, comparatively, very little good...—All this, of course, doesn't detract from Freud's extraordinary scientific achievement. Only, extraordinary scientific achievements have a way these days, of being used for the destruction of human beings." [Malcolm. **Ludwig Wittgenstein: A Memoir**, pp. 44–45. Oxford University Press, London, 1972 (Reprint of 1958 edition).]

Some years earlier (1930) he had made the following comment to Drury:

> I was walking about in Cambridge and passed a bookshop, and in the window were portraits of Russell, Freud and Einstein. A little further on, in a music shop, I saw portraits of Beethoven, Schubert and Chopin. Comparing these portraits I felt intensely the terrible degeneration that had come over the human spirit in the course of only a hundred years. [M.O'C. Drury. "Some notes on conversations with Wittgenstein." **Recollections of Wittgenstein**, p. 112. Oxford University Press, 1984. Edited by R. Rhees.]

to, or some similar situation, then the teaching becomes more complex and subject to misunderstanding. As Wittgenstein summed it up:

> One of the most dangerous of ideas for a philosopher is, oddly enough, that we think with our heads or in our heads.

> The idea of thinking as a process in the head, in a completely enclosed space, gives him something occult. [**Z** §§605–606]

Since everything we need to perform a complex, intelligent task, such as finding one's way around town, is *not* in our heads, as Searle insists it is, but is, at least in part, in the "lived world" of our experience, and since such information is a necessary foundation for thinking, it is no great intellectual leap to see that our thinking does not always take place entirely "in the head, in a completely enclosed space" but, at least partially, in our "lived world." And this should be no surprise since much of our thinking takes place using tools, information and knowledge that are outside our heads: most of us cannot perform complex arithmetic without paper and pencil; we cannot figure out the strengths and weaknesses of a country's economy without the use of almanacs, encyclopedias and newspapers; we cannot make sound financial decisions without reliable stock market information and the advice of a broker; etc.[270]

---

[270] It is interesting to note that the idea of thinking taking place entirely in one's head is a view of cognition that seems to lie at the foundation of Artificial Intelligence. If, as Searle insists, everything necessary to thought resides in the "enclosed space" of the brain—the "brain in a vat"—then isn't a computer rather like a "brain in a vat?" And if the human brain—the "brain in a vat"—can, according to Searle, have within it all it needs to represent the world, then it is not surprising that those working in or supporting Artificial Intelligence would take as a given that the computer can, at least in theory, have the capacity for holding everything needed "to represent the world," that is, everything necessary for intelligent activity. If, on the other hand, Wittgenstein is right, then much of what is necessary to thought is outside our heads. For Artificial Intelligence to be successful in performing intelligent activities, then, computers would need to interact and "live" in our milieu in the same way that we do. Such a requirement on Artificial Intelligence might severely limit not only what it might do, but also what it could possibly do. Research in Artificial Intelligence could no longer follow the course it has.

One rejoinder Artificial Intelligence might make to Wittgenstein's argument is that even though much information that we need may reside outside our heads, there is no theoretical reason to suspect that the complete representation of the world within the brain and, by analogy, the computer, is not possible. This, of course, would make efforts to do this on computers a difficult, but not pointless, endeavor. There is no real direct evidence that might refute this, and the known abilities of individuals with eidetic memories may indicate that we have the potential for the literal storage of information in our heads at a great capacity [For a compelling description of eidetic memory, see O. Sack's "The Landscape of His Dreams" in his **An Anthropologist on Mars**, Vintage Books, NY, 1995]. This may be true, but the literal memorization of our entire milieu is not likely to be a solution to the problem. In the first place, not all memory is literal representation, so other kinds of prodigious memory capacities—such as the knowledge of how to do things or the ability to formulate and use abstract concepts and relationships) are necessary too. We have less evidence for these kinds of remarkable memory than we do for literal or eidetic memory (e.g., while we know of individuals, like the conductor Toscaninni, who was documented to have recall of virtually every note of every instrumental part of every major orchestral work he conducted , we have no evidence that someone could remember how to play every instrument in the orchestra [ G. Marek. "Toscanini's Memory," **Memory Observed: Remembering in Natural Contexts**. W.H. Freeman, NY, 1982. Edited by U. Neisser]. Even the musically gifted can master only a small number of instruments at a time, and not because they do not have the time to learn them, but because we just don't have the capacity to possess a great number of abilities like that). (Dreyfus argues persuasively that the knowledge which would provide the foundation for intelligence is not just a collection of "facts" as early workers in Artificial Intelligence proposed. He points out that intelligent discernment and decision-making require know-how, something that is very difficult to represent computationally. As Dreyfus put it:

> "... the research program based on the assumption that human beings produce intelligence using facts and rules has reached a dead end, and there is no reason to think it could ever succeed." [from p. ix of the introduction to **What Computers Still Can't Do: A Critique of Artificial Reason**, MIT Press, Cambridge, MA, 1992.]

It is also the case that the vast capacity for literal recall of extraordinary amounts of information may, at a certain point, be disfunctional. Luria's famous mnemonist, S., remembered practically everything that happened to him or anything he could memorize by rote [A.R. Luria. **The Mind of a Mnemonist**. Henry Regnery, Chicago, 1976. Translated from the Russian by L. Solotaroff.]. S. recalled things, at least in part, because he made so many associations with the items he wanted to remember; numbers weren't just indications of amount, they also conjured up images of taste, smell and vision. Such combinations of images employing different senses is termed "synesthesia." While synesthesia serves to give memorized items more cues, it also increases the number of associations to a remembered item and that often complicated S.'s understanding of some text. Luria observed:

> Thus, trying to understand a passage, to grasp the information it contains (which other people accomplish by singling out what is most important), became a tortuous procedure for S., a struggle against images that kept rising to the surface in his mind. Images, then, proved an obstacle as well as an aid to learning in that they prevented S. from concentrating on what was essential. Moreover, since these images tended to jam together, producing still more images, he was carried so far adrift that he was forced to go back and rethink the entire passage. Consequently a simple passage—a phrase for that matter—would turn out to be a Sisyphean task. These vivid, palpable images were not always helpful to S. in understanding a passage; they could just as easily lead him astray. [Luria, *op.cit.*, p. 113]

Dan Shacter, a specialist in the psychology of memory, comments on Luria's mnemonist:

> ... [S.] was overwhelmed by detailed but useless recollections of trivial information and events. He could recount without error long lists of names, numbers, and just about anything else that Luria presented to him. This served him well in his job as a newspaper reporter, because he didn't have to write things down. Yet when he read a story or listened to other people, he recalled endless details without understanding much of what he read or heard... he had great difficulty grasping abstract concepts. [D. Schacter. **Searching for Memory: The Brain, the Mind, and the Past**, p. 81. Basic Books, New York, 1996.]

One wonders if the same fate is destined for Doug Lenat's computer program to internalize commonsense knowledge. Years in the making, the program may eventually store so much information that it becomes impossible for it to find and use the information effectively. This is not a problem of selecting the "best" storage techniques or access procedures. That is, it is not a problem of searching memory faster. The size of the memory to effect such a large storage will be so great that faster access methods will only get us faster to the wrong place—and there are too many wrong places to go to for even extraordinarily fast search techniques to be effective. What slows such systems down is not the physical speed of searching, it's the large number of decisions of relevance or non-relevance that it must make in the course of its searching. As the size of the search space goes up, the number of decision points goes up rapidly, too (This is the essence of the Information Retrieval problem, an issue we will deal with in some detail in Part III.). Perhaps not being able to recollect everything that happens is necessary for adequate mental functioning. Our ability to act intelligently is not so much based on our ability to understand and memorize by rote, but on our ability to understand, remember the gist of what we know or see, and forget what we don't need. People, unlike computers or Luria's mnemonist, can remember the gist of things, and forget the "obvious." Schacter comments:

> Forgetting, though often frustrating, is an adaptive feature of our memories. We don't need to remember everything that has ever happened to us; engrams that we never use are probably best forgotten. The cognitive psychologist John Anderson has argued convincingly that forgetting

Wittgenstein rejects the dualism of the *mind* and the*brain* believing that those who hold it to be the case are confusing a grammatical distinction with an empirical one. Talk about the "mind" and the "brain" involves engaging in two different Language Games which are embedded in two different sets of activities and practices ("Forms of Life"). He also rejects the reduction of the mind *to* the brain. But if we can't build our epistemological foundation on *minds* and *brains*, or the reduction of minds *to* brains, what *do* we build it on? What lies at the foundation of Wittgenstein's epistemology is *not* just physical brain processes, but human activity and interaction:

> Only of a living human being and what resembles (behaves like) a living human being, can one say: it has sensations; it sees; is blind; hears; is deaf; is conscious or unconscious.

> memories over time is an economical response to the demands placed on memory by the environment in which we live. We are better off forgetting trivial experiences than clogging our minds with each and every ongoing event, just in case we might want to remember one of those incidents someday. But we do need to form an accurate picture of the general features of our world, and it turns out that we are reasonably adept at doing so. Our recollections of the general contours of our pasts are often reasonably accurate. Perhaps paradoxically, if we, like [S.], were constantly overwhelmed by detailed memories of every page from our pasts, we would be left without a coherent story to tell. [Schacter, ibid.]

But there is a further argument against the practical possibility of being able to internalize all the information that we require for intelligent activity. Namely, we don't ever need to do this, neither now nor at any time in our historical past. Evolutionary development is remarkably efficient. Abilities that a species does not need rarely get developed, and those that do come up from time to time in the course of random genetic change are not sustained for long if they are not useful. Memory of the extraordinary capacity needed to represent the world to the "brain in a vat" is most closely approximated by S.'s ability, yet it is clear that there are major drawbacks to such a large literal memory. Our present range of mental capacity, then, may represent an "optimum" of sorts—a useful blending of literal memorization, recognition and reconstruction that allows us to remember the things and abilities that we need to be functioning social beings, but to forget the welter of non-relevant detail that surrounds these things. Any greater literal mental capacity would be, like that of Luria's mnemonist, disfunctional. From such an evolutionary point of view, the practical possibility of complete internal representation is not convincing because such a complete internal representation probably could not be the foundation of intelligent activity, and intelligent activity is a *sine qua non* for human life as we know it. The existence of nonliteral memory has some support in neurological research. Neurologist Antonio Damasio comments:

> Images are not stored as facsimile pictures of things, or events, or words, or sentences. The brain does not file Polaroid pictures of people, objects, landscapes; nor does it store audiotapes of music and speech; it does not store films of scenes in our lives; nor does it hold the type of cue cards and TelePrompTer transparencies that help politicians earn their daily bread. In brief, there seem to be no permanently held pictures of anything, even miniaturized, no microfiches or microfilms, no hard copies. Given the huge amount of knowledge we acquire in a lifetime, any kind of facsimile storage also poses difficult problems of retrieval efficiency. We all have direct evidence that whenever we recall a given object, or face, or scene, we do not get an exact reproduction but rather an interpretation, a newly reconstructed version of the original. In addition, as our age and experience change, versions of the same thing evolve. None of this is compatible with rigid, facsimile representation, as the British psychologist Frederic Bartlett noted several decades ago, when he first proposed that memory is essentially reconstructive. [A. Damasio. **Descartes' Error: Emotion, Reason, and the Human Brain**, p. 100. Avon Books, NY, 1994. Damasio cites F.C. Bartlett: **Remembering: A Study in Experimental and Social Psychology**. Cambridge University Press, Cambridge, UK, 1964.]

⋮

We do indeed say of an inanimate thing that it is in pain: when playing with dolls for example. But this use of of the concept of pain is a secondary one. Imagine a case in which people ascribed pain *only* to inanimate things; pitied *only* dolls.

⋮

Only of what behaves like a human being can one say that it *has* pains.

⋮

Look at a stone and imagine it having sensations.—One says to oneself: How could one so much as get the idea of ascribing a *sensation* to a *thing*? One might as well ascribe it to a number!—And now look at a wriggling fly and at once these difficulties vanish and pain seems to get a foothold here, where before everything was, so to speak, too smooth for it.[271] **[PI §§281–284]**

Or, as Malcolm, discussing Wittgenstein, wrote:

> ... the thing which perceives, thinks, imagines is neither a non-corporeal entity that "inhabits" the body, nor a brain—but a living human being.[272]

For Wittgenstein, the foundation of epistemology is *not* some kind of *mind:brain* dualism. Nor is it the reduction of mental processes to neurological events or the reduction of mental processes to behavior. The foundation of epistemology is, instead, the intensely human activities—forms of life—of mankind. This helps to explain one of Wittgenstein's more curious predilections—his love of mystery stories.

### *Wittgenstein and Crime: The Breakdown of the Distinction Between Inner and Outer Processes*

Malcolm writes:

> ... in February 1940 I returned to the United States after one and a half years in Cambridge. Wittgenstein and I kept up a correspondence. I knew that he was fond of detective magazines. They could not be obtained in England during wartime, and periodically I sent some to him from America. He had a preference for a magazine published by Street and Smith, each number of which contained several short detective stories. Wittgenstein acknowledged the arrival of a package of magazines, in a letter from Cambridge.

⋮

In subsequent letters during and after the war Wittgenstein referred to detective magazines more than once:

---

[271] Malcolm asserts that the first part of this quotation "Only of a living human being..." is "One of Wittgenstein's most profound insights, largely ignored in present-day philosophy..." **Nothing is Hidden: Wittgenstein's Criticism of His Early Thought**, p. 184. Basil Blackwell, Oxford, 1986.

[272] Malcolm, *op.cit.*, p. 186.

It'll be fine to get detective mags from you. There is a terrible scarcity of them now. My mind feels all underfed.

They are *rich* in mental vitamins and calories.

The one way in which the ending of Lend-Lease really hits me is by producing a shortage of detective mags in this country. I can only hope Lord Keynes will make this quite clear in Washington. For I say: if the USA won't give us detective mags we can't give them philosophy, and so America will be the loser in the end. See?

He compared "Street and Smith mags" with **Mind**, the prominent international philosophy journal:

If I read your mags I often wonder how anyone can read **Mind** with all its impotence and bankruptcy when they could read Street and Smith mags.

Well, everyone to his taste.

Two and a half years later he repeated the comparison:

Your mags are wonderful. How people can read **Mind** if they could read Street and Smith beats me. If philosophy has anything to do with wisdom there's certainly not a grain of that in **Mind**, and quite often a grain in the detective stories.

Once Wittgenstein was so pleased with a detective story that he lent it to both Moore and Smythies and wished me to try to find out what else the author had written:

It may sound crazy, but when I recently re-read the story I liked it again so much that I thought I'd really like to write to the author and thank him. If this is nuts, don't be surprised, for so am I.[273]

Wittgenstein's former student Drury recalled the following conversation with him:

Today at lunch the conversation turned to discussing "detective stories." Wittgenstein said how much he enjoyed the stories of Agatha Christie. Not only were the plots ingenious but the characters were so well drawn that they were real people. He thought it was a particularly English talent to be able to write books like this. One of the company advised him to read Chesterton's "Father Brown" stories. He made a grimace. "Oh no, I couldn't stand the idea of a Roman Catholic priest playing the part of a detective. I don't want that."[274]

---

[273] N. Malcolm. **Ludwig Wittgenstein: A Memoir**, pp. 35–36. The detective novel which Wittgenstein liked so much that he wanted to write to the author was, according to Monk, Norbert Davis' **Rendezvous with Fear** [R. Monk. **Ludwig Wittgenstein: The Duty of Genius**, p. 528. The Free Press, NY, 1990]. **Rendezvous with Fear** was the British title of the novel that was originally published in the US as **The Mouse in the Mountain**. (While **Rendezvous with Fear** has been out of print for some time, **The Mouse in the Mountain** is still in print, as of 2003).

[274] M.O'C. Drury. "Conversations with Wittgenstein," **Recollections of Wittgenstein**, p. 133. Oxford University Press, Oxford, UK, 1984. Edited by R. Rhees.

What was it that Wittgenstein liked about detective stories? For most of us, mysteries are light diversionary reading. Is it possible that Wittgenstein turned to them as a diversion from the exhausting rigors of philosophical analysis? Not likely. In the first place, Wittgenstein was not given to diversionary activities. His life, thoughts and work were in almost every way dedicated to serious pursuits. Bertrand Russell related the following incident after attending a boat race which they watched when Wittgenstein was first at Cambridge University in 1912 (he had gone there on Frege's recommendation to study with Russell;)

> "[After the race, Wittgenstein] suddenly stood still and explained that the way we had spent the afternoon was so vile that we ought not to live, or at least he ought not, that nothing is tolerable except producing great works or enjoying those of others, that he has accomplished nothing and never will, etc.—all this with a force that nearly knocks one down. He makes me feel like a bleating lambkin."[275]

This extreme pessimism was neither temporary, nor a reaction to specific events. It was part of his character. Malcolm writes:

> It was Wittgenstein's character to be deeply pessimistic, both about his own prospects and those of humanity in general. Anyone who was on an intimate footing with Wittgenstein must have been aware of the feeling in him that our lives are ugly and our minds in the dark—a feeling that was often close to despair.[276]

Some of this intense pessimism may have originated in Wittgenstein's youth, a time when his sister Hermine reported that he ". . . found it particularly difficult to fit in, for right from earliest childhood he suffered almost pathological distress in any surroundings which were uncongenial to him."[277] Whether the source of his distress was to be found in his nature or his nurturing, there can be no doubt that his family presented a very difficult milieu in which to grow up—his older brothers Hans and Rudi had already committed suicide by the time Wittgenstein first went to Cambridge, and a third older brother, Kurt, was to commit suicide soon at the close of World War I.[278] Wittgenstein himself was suicidal much of his youth. Although he managed to make it through life without intentionally harming himself, there can be no doubt that pessimism and despair dominated his thinking, maintaining his thoughts at an intense level of seriousness that he was rarely able to rise above.[279]

---

[275] Russell in a letter to Lady O. Morrel, 11 September 1912, quoted on p. 76 in M. Nedo and M. Ranchetti's **Ludwig Wittgenstein: Sein Leben in Bildern und Texten**. Suhrkamp Verlag, Frankfurt am Main, 1983.

[276] N. Malcolm. **Ludwig Wittgenstein: A Memoir**, p. 72. Oxford University Press, London, 1972 (reprint of 1958 edition).

[277] H. Wittgenstein. "My Brother Ludwig," **Recollections of Wittgenstein**, p. 11. Oxford University Press, Oxford, UK, 1984. Edited by R. Rhees.

[278] There is some question whether Hans actually committed suicide, though there is no doubt about Rudi or Kurt. Hans had simply "vanished" from a boat in the Cheasapeake Bay, but the two major biographers of Wittgenstein, McGuinness and Monk, both agree that the circumstances and Hans' state of mind were such that suicide was the most likely explanation of his death. McGuinness comments: "[Hans] vanished from a boat in Cheasapeake Bay at the age of 26 in circumstances suggesting suicide: as such, certainly, from whatever indications, his death was always regarded in the family." [**Wittgenstein: A Life. Young Ludwig 1889–1921**, p. 26. Brian McGuinness, The University of California Press, Berkeley, 1988. See also R. Monk's **Ludwig Wittgenstein: The Duty of Genius**. The Free Press, a division of Macmillan, NY, 1990.]

[279] Wittgenstein's good friend D. Pinsent wrote in his diary in 1912:

The one exception to this obsession with serious pursuits might have been his attending the cinema after delivering one of his intense lectures. His favorite films were westerns and musicals, clearly not "serious" film *genres*. If Wittgenstein can be accused of diversionary activities this, alone, is the best candidate. Wittgenstein said that he attended the movies, often sitting in the front row, as a way of recovering from the mental intensity that he needed to conduct his lectures. His students attested to the tortured manner in which he lectured. One of Wittgenstein's students, Theodore Redpath gives the following description of his lecture style:

> [During his lectures, Wittgenstein's] train of thought would frequently come to a halt. On such occasions he would sometimes sit astride a small upright chair, resting his arms on the back or holding the tops of the uprights, and curse himself roundly in such terms as "Damn my bloody soul!" Sometimes, on the other hand, he would shout out "Help me, someone!"[280]

He stated that his attendance of films after his lectures was like a "shower bath," washing away the disgust with which his difficult lectures often left him. In this sense, films were more of a purgative than a diversion.[281] But these experiences were very different than what he got from his detective stories. In the first place, he never referred to these films as providing anything intellectually deep at all. Detective stories, on the other hand, were something that interested Wittgenstein. His statement (*supra*) that there was more wisdom in detective stories than in the prominent philosophy journal **Mind** indicates that these detective stories were probably of interest to him from an intellectual, if not philosophical, point of view. This does not mean that he did not enjoy reading them, nor does it mean that they contributed directly to his philosophy, it merely means that his enjoyment was coincident with his interest in them. He never mentions that there was any wisdom in the westerns and musicals he saw.

> [Wittgenstein] was very communicative and told me lots about himself: that for nine years, till last Xmas, he suffered from terrific loneliness (mental—not physical): that he continually thought of suicide then, and felt ashamed of never daring to kill himself [D. Pinsent. **A Portrait of Wittgenstein As a Young Man**, p. 6. Basil Blackwell, Cambridge, MA, 1990. Edited by G.H. von Wright.]

[280] T. Redpath. **Ludwig Wittgenstein: A Student's Memoir**, p. 20. Gerald Duckworth, London. 1990.
[281] N. Malcolm remarks in his memoir of Wittgenstein:

> Wittgenstein was always exhausted by his lectures. He was also revolted by them. He felt disgusted with what he had said and with himself. Often he would rush off to a cinema immediately after the class ended. As the members of the class began to move their chairs out of the room he might look imploringly at a friend and say in a low tone, "Could you go to a flick?" On the way to the cinema Wittgenstein would buy a bun or cold pork pie and munch it while he watched the film. He insisted on sitting in the very first row of seats, so that the screen would occupy his entire field of vision, and his mind would be turned away from the thoughts of the lecture and his feelings of revulsion. Once he whispered to me "This is like a shower bath!" [**Ludwig Wittgenstein: A Memoir**, pp. 27–28. Oxford University Press, Oxford, 1972.]

Again, we're brought back to the question of what was the "wisdom" that Wittgenstein found in detective stories? He only mentions detective stories once in his published writings, in a section of **LWPP I** in which he discusses "dissimulation" at length:

> But isn't the concept such that for any behavior, etc., one can imagine (construct) a larger context in which even this behaviour would be dissimulating behavior? Isn't this, for example, the basis for the problem of any detective story? [**LWPP I** §254]

He doesn't say specifically that the constant theme of "dissimulation" is what attracted him to detective stories, but a consideration of the philosophical issues that occupied him late in his life does yield a related issue that he returned to repeatedly—the distinction between "inner and outer processes." It is in this context that the "wisdom" of the detective stories can be seen.

Traditionally, there has been a more or less sharp dividing line between what we say or do—those things that are available for all to see—and what we think or feel—those things that we consider private. In Wittgenstein's later writings, especially that included in his **Last Writings on the Philosophy of Psychology, v. II**, we see that he does not believe that there is such a sharp distinction between what we consider public and what we consider private. Traditionally, our "private" thoughts and feelings are thought to be understandable to others only if we choose to reveal them. But for Wittgenstein, much of what we consider private, and revealed to others only through confession, is not hidden at all—even if we try to keep it private. These private thoughts and feelings are as "open" to others as any public display can be—they are merely open to us in a "different way":

> My thoughts are not hidden from him, but are just as open to him in a different *way* than they are to me. [**LWPP II** pp. 34–35]

> And one cannot answer : "I draw certain conclusions from my knowledge, even if no one else can"—for *conclusions* must be valid for all.
>
> ⋮
>
> One could even say: The uncertainty about the inner is an uncertainty about something outer.[282] [**LWPP II** p. 88]

Wittgenstein is not saying that we are all infallible mind-readers. He is merely saying that what we think or feel can be surmised sometimes by others even when we don't specifically

---

[282] Understanding someone's unstated thoughts was not an unfamiliar event for Wittgenstein. In his memoir of Wittgenstein, Malcolm writes:

> Wittgenstein had an extraordinary gift for divining the thoughts of the person with whom he was engaged in discussion. While the other struggled to put his thought into words Wittgenstein would perceive what it was and state it for him. This power of his, which sometimes seemed uncanny, was made possible, I am sure, by his own prolonged and continuous researches. He knew what someone else was thinking because he had himself travelled innumerable times through those twists and turns of reasoning. He once remarked to me that it was very unlikely that anyone in his classes should think of something of which he had not already thought. This was not braggadocio. [N. Malcolm. **Ludwig Wittgestein: A Memior**, p. 55. Oxford University Press, London, 1972 (reprint of 1958 edition).]

admit to what we think or feel. When we say that we are uncertain about what someone thinks or feels we are really stating an uncertainty about some outer, external event or process that is open to us all, and the conclusions we draw "must be valid for all" (*supra*). We are not expressing an uncertainty about something "inner." Likewise, if I am *certain* about some internal event or process in someone else I am really expressing certainty about something external—something that can be experienced by all.

> Ask not: "What goes on in us when we are certain that. . . ?—but: How is 'the certainty that this is the case' manifested in human action?" [**PI** p. 225]

The reason why these conclusions must be "valid for all" is that they are based on the "common behavior of mankind"—the *forms of life*. These *forms of life* are the foundation for language, and, as we have shown, language is the foundation for thought—it is the "vehicle of thought." Wittgenstein goes on to make a subtle point:

> Here the connection of evidence with what it is evidence for is not ineluctable. And I *don't* mean: "the connection of the outer with the inner." [**LWPP II** p. 88]

Wittgenstein makes clear that he is not *connecting* the inner with the outer. To do so would make the inner into a "something"—an ontological status he is unwilling to concede. Since we have no direct access to the inner events or processes of others we cannot connect anything to them—there is no "them" to connect to. At most, an inner event is a "something about which nothing could be said."[283] When we make a statement about what someone thinks or feels we are merely making a statement about what may happen in a form that is available for us all to see—actions, social events, statements, personal observations, etc.:

> I say "This man is hiding what is in him." How does one know that he is hiding it? Thus there are signs for it and signs against it.
>
> There is an *unmistakable* expression of joy and its opposite.
>
> Under these circumstances one *knows* that he is in pain, or that he isn't; under those, one is uncertain.
>
> But ask yourself: what allows one to recognize a sign for something within as infallible? All we are left with to measure it against is the outer. Therefore the constrast between the inner and the outer is not an issue. [**LWPP II** p. 32]

Traditionally, we have a sense of "outer" phenomena being exposed to view, and "inner" phenomena being, by definition, hidden. Wittgenstein continues:

---

[283]"But you will surely admit that there is a difference between pain-behaviour accompanied by pain and pain-behaviour without any pain?"—Admit it? What greater difference could there be?—"And yet you again and again reach the conclusion that the sensation itself is a nothing."—Not at all. It is not a something, but not a nothing either! The conclusion was only that a nothing would serve just as well as a *something* about which nothing could be said. We have only rejected the grammar which tries to force itself on us here. [**PI** §304]

> It is only in particular cases that the inner is hidden from me, and in those cases it
> is not hidden because it is inner. [**LWPP II** p. 33]

Wittgenstein makes the subtle, but important point that being "hidden" is *not* an inherent
property of "inner" phenomena. Being hidden is a particular aspect of some of our *forms
of life* and *language games.*

> ...what goes on in him is... a game, and pretence is not *present* in him like a
> feeling, but like a game.
>
> For also, if he speaks to himself his words only have meaning as elements of a
> language-game. [**LWPP II** pp. 31–32]

If we lie to someone and wish to keep him from the truth, then it is generally *not* sufficient
for us merely not to tell him the truth. We must also guard ourselves from revealing the truth
through our actions, dealings with others, and the things we say that might *imply* the truth
without our saying it explicitly. *Hiding our thoughts* is, in many cases, something attained
through conscious effort; that is, it is something that we *add* to "inner" phenomena.

Thus, for a phenomenon to be seen as "inner" or "outer" and subsequently as "hidden"
or not, is a function of the *language game* or *form of life* it occurs in and not of some
inherent property it possesses independently of its role in these *language games* or *forms
of life.* The references to "inner phenomena" are thus not so much references to actual
things as they are simply a way of talking—a Language Game. But is Wittgenstein merely
saying that *all we have* are "outer" phenomena—that the "inner" phenomena are somehow
irrelevant? If he were, he might justifiably be called a behaviorist. But Wittgenstein *does*
believe in both the existence and importance of "inner" phenomena, even those that are
never revealed—voluntarily or not (this will be discussed in more detail in the section
"Wittgenstein and Behaviorism" (*infra*)). Such "inner phenomena" are legitimized by
their existence in accepted *language games* and *forms of life.*

It is also not the case that the discovery of "inner phenomena" is contingent solely on the
consequences that may follow them. Certainly the consequences of "inner phenomena"
help us to learn how to detect something that is hidden, but they are not *decisive.* For
example, we believe what someone tells us but later find out that he was lying. If we
experience this enough times we may be able to tell when that person lies in the future.
But, although consequences are often important in the learning process, we can often
attain a certainty about whether someone is lying that exists independently of the possible
consequences. For example, someone we trust tells us that we should never believe Frank's
fishing stories because he always "lies about what he caught"—we never see any of the
fish, we just, "on good authority," don't believe him. Wittgenstein comments:

> It could be that someone uttered signs of gladness and then behaved in a completely
> unexpected way, and that we still could not say that the first expression was not
> genuine. [**LWPP II** p. 90]

Certainty or genuineness, then, is a function of a particular *language game* or *form of
life*, and is not necessarily determined empirically. Even though our justifications for our

beliefs must be valid for all, there may be circumstances when, for example, we can tell when someone is lying, but we cannot describe or give precise criteria about how we do it—that is, we are convinced we are right, but can give no criteria to support our assertion:

> But does there have to be *a reason*? Couldn't I simply know whether he is pretending without knowing how I know it?
>
> I simply would have "an *eye*" for it. [**LWPP II** p. 31]

What Wittgenstein is saying is that just because one's "conclusions must be valid for all" (*supra*) does not mean that we can always articulate the criteria that convinced us we were correct. Two people can agree that a third person is lying or "hiding something" without being able to articulate the reasons for such a conclusion—this is like the detective's "hunch."

It is also important to note that our assessment of some inner phenomenon—that so-and-so is lying—does not necessarily express a *probability* of our being correct:

> I do not say that the evidence makes the inner merely probable. [**LWPP II** p. 40]

There are cases where we can say we are *certain*. Does this mean that we are implicitly asserting a *probability* that we are correct? Not necessarily. What is the difference between *certainty* and a *probability* of being correct? Well, things look different in the two cases: if we are *certain* that someone is thinking such-and-such, we may act differently, we may take different things as criteria, or there may be different consequences than if we take it to be only *probable* that the person is thinking such-and-such. Believing something is *certain* rather than just *probable*, may just "feel" different. Being *certain* does not mean you are correct, though. It just commits you to a particular attitude or point of view. *Probability* is part of some *language games*, but not all. Some decision theorists would like to substitute assessments of subjective *probability* for all our assertions, but this is a Procrustean bed and not all assertions will "fit" it.[284] Even a confession, which purports to link the inner with the outer, is a very complex process.

> Let us assume that there was a man who always guessed right what I was saying to myself in my thoughts (It does not matter how he manages it.). But what is the criterion for his guessing *right*? Well, I am a truthful person and I confess that he has guessed right.—But might I not be mistaken, can my memory not deceive me? And might it not always do so when—without lying—I express what I have thought within myself?—But now it does appear that "what went on within me" is not the point at all (Here I am drawing a construction-line).

---

[284] A good example of giving a probability, or probability-like assessment, for assertions that are not initially quantitative such as linguistic "hedges" (like "very," "almost," "somewhat," etc.) occurs in Fuzzy Sets Theory (the originator of Fuzzy Sets theory was Lotfi Zadeh, who is the author of many works on the subject). Here, if we assert that John—who stands at 6 feet 5 inches—is "very tall" we are, in terms of fuzzy-sets, saying that John's probable membership in the group of "very tall people" is 90%, or so. While such a quantitative rendering of uncertainty is useful in computer modeling, for which it was originally intended, it does not capture the subtle differences between quantitative and nonquantitative assessments in our day-to-day discourse. That is, when we say "John is very tall" we are not, even unconsciously, assigning a probability to his being very tall—we simply see him as being "very tall."

> The criteria for the truth of the *confession* that I thought such-and-such are not the criteria for a true *description* of a process. And the importance of the true confession does not reside in its being a correct and certain report of a process. It resides rather in the special consequences which can be drawn from a confession whose truth is guaranteed by the special criteria of *truthfulness*. [**PI** p. 222]

We might distinguish between two kinds of "private" entities: feelings and thoughts. It is relatively easy to see how our personal feelings may be discernable by others:

> If I see someone writhing in pain, with evident cause I do not think: all the same, his feelings are hidden from me. [**PI** p. 223]

Correctly discerning what someone is thinking is somewhat more complex, but also accessible:

> There is a game of "guessing thoughts." A variant of it would be this: I tell A something in a language that B does not understand. B is supposed to guess the meaning of what I say.—Another variant: I write down a sentence which the other person cannot see. He has to guess the words or their sense.—Yet another: I am putting a jig-saw puzzle together; the other person cannot see me but from time to time guesses my thoughts and utters them. He says, for instance, "Now where is this bit?"—"*Now* I know how it fits!"—"I have no idea what goes in here,"—"The sky is always the hardest part" and so on—but I need not be talking to myself either out loud or silently at the time.

> All this would be guessing at thoughts; and the fact that it does not actually happen does not make thought any more hidden than the unperceived physical proceedings.

> "What is *internal* is hidden from us."—The future is hidden from us. But does the astronomer think like this when he calculates an eclipse of the sun? [**PI** p. 223]

Language use comprises a set of activities, and like other common activities—or *forms of life*—they usually follow more or less predictable patterns. It is like, in Wittgenstein's example, the assembling of a jigsaw puzzle: there are things that you generally do first—like putting together all the pieces with a straight side to form the outer border of the puzzle, then building the puzzle in from there, or concentrating on assembling those pieces with a distinct color or design and leaving other parts until the end ("the sky is always the hardest part"(*supra*)). In another example, if I see a friend coming towards me first thing in the morning, I am sure he will greet me and ask how I'm doing. If he knows that my son has been ill he will likely ask after his health. If I answer his greeting saying I feel especially good this morning, he will likely ask what the reason is for my unusually good mood, etc., etc. We often make such assumptions and draw such inferences about others so readily that we aren't even aware of how much we anticipate in our normal dealings with others.[285]

---

[285] There was a television commercial for Excedrin, a headache tablet, in which a wife offers her husband some Excedrin. Since he had not complained, he wonders how she knew he had a headache. She says that his headache is so bad "it shows." This leads into the product endorsement: "For a headache so bad that it shows, take Excedrin." (quotation is approximate).

But we don't make inferences about everything that happens around us. In fact, we often don't make inferences at all—we act as if routine events and things will remain the same: I act as if the people who were my friends yesterday will be my friends today; I act as if people who know me will recognize me, and people whom I have not seen before will not; I act as if shopkeepers will be friendly and acquiesce to my requests for service; I act as if family members will still share personal family knowledge with me; I act as if the streets and buildings in my town will remain in their places; etc.:

> But I did not get my picture of the world by satisfying myself of its correctness; nor do I have it because I am satisfied of its correctness. No; it is the inherited background against which I distinguish between true and false.

> The propositions describing this world-picture might be part of a kind of mythology. And their role is like that of rules of a game; and the game can be learned purely practically, without learning any explicit rules.

> It might be imagined that some propositions, of the form of empirical propositions, were hardened and functioned as channels for such empirical propositions as were not hardened by fluid; and that this relation altered with time, in that fluid propositions hardened, and hard ones became fluid. [**OC** §§94–96]

There is much that we do not question in our day-to-day activities. Some of this is assumed merely by our being ordinary, social people: for example, we assume that everyone we know has biological parents. Some things, on the other hand, are contingent on certain circumstances: for example, we might fear for our personal safety if we walk in certain parts of some major cities late at night, but would not have the same fears walking in a crowded shopping mall at any time; and some of what we assume is dependent on our personal experience: for example, that my good friend Milt will be sure to pay back any small loan I make to him, because he has always done so in the past. So some of the things we assume are things that we do not, and in some cases, *cannot* test for ourselves, such as the one about biological parents, above, and some things may not come from our personal experience, but from the experience of others, such as the assumption about our personal safety. The third assumption is one that is based on our own experience, but even that experience is only assumed to hold in "normal circumstances." Wittgenstein brings out this inherited background in his apt example:

> Does my telephone call to New York strengthen my conviction that the earth exists?

> Much seems to be fixed, and it is removed from the traffic. It is so to speak shunted onto an unused siding.

> Now it gives our way of looking at things, and our researches, their form. Perhaps it was once disputed. But perhaps for unthinkable ages, it has belonged to the scaffolding of our thoughts. (Every human being has parents.) [**OC** §§210–211]

As Malcolm comments:

Absence of doubt manifests itself throughout the normal life of a human being.[286]

But, given the inherited background of our world, what allows us to anticipate what others are thinking or feeling? What enables us to do this is our understanding of how we deal with the routine activities which every normal person engages in: asking questions, joking, complaining, arguing, censuring, praising, restraining, lying, speaking sarcastically, misleading, etc. It means that if we see a particular person in certain specific circumstances, engaged in a familiar activity, we can often surmise what he is thinking or feeling. As a character in David Mamet's film "House of Games" says:

> The things we think, the things we want—we can do them or not do them, but we can't hide them.[287]

Returning to Wittgenstein's "detective mags" we can see how they frequently turn on the clever detection of something that appears "hidden"—some knowledge that one or more of the protagonists is keeping secret. It is this, I think, that Wittgenstein found fascinating about detective stories, for it showed that the traditional distinction between what is public and what is private, while held to be largely unbreachable, except by reliable confession, by some philosophers and psychologists, is certainly not the case in everyday life. We not only can often figure out what people are thinking or feeling without their telling us, but, if we are clever, we can find out about the thoughts and feelings of others who go to elaborate lengths to keep those thoughts and feelings secret. The clever detective not only finds out these secrets but he does it himself by piecing together a varying collection of circumstances, evidence and statements by the suspect and/or others that lead to informal inferences about what the suspect *really* thinks or feels.[288] What detective stories do is to describe attractively a kind of folk wisdom that has been available to us for some time, at least in this form.

Perhaps the first modern detective stories were written over 100 years ago by Edgar Allan Poe. Consider the passage from his "Murders in the Rue Morgue":

> We were strolling one night down the long dirty street, in the vicinity of the Palais Royal. Being both, apparently, occupied with thought, neither of us had spoken a syllable for fifteen minutes at least. All at once Dupin [the detective] broke forth with these words:

> "He is a very little fellow, that's true, and would do better for the *Théâtre des Variétés*."

---

[286] Malcolm. **Wittgensteinean Themes: Essays 1978–1989**, p. 79.

[287] The statement is made by a swindler/confidence man to a psychiatrist who has been drawn into the demi-monde of cons and scams where such criminals exist. Both the psychiatrist and the conman earn their living by anticipating what others think, even when others are trying to keep those thoughts secret. The movie offers an interesting contrast between the human understanding of the psychiatrist and the conman: the psychiatrist who asks her patients what they think and infers what may be hidden, and the conman who must know what people think without asking, and can even manipulate what they think to his own ends.

[288] Since the time of Doyle's Sherlock Holmes stories these inferences unfortunately have often been called "deductive." It is clear that they are usually not this rigorous, but involve more informal kinds of inference. One book which tries to systematize some detective story logic is W. Neblett's **Sherlock's Logic**. [Dorset Press, NY, 1985]

"There can be no doubt of that," I replied, unwittingly, and not at first observing (so much had I been absorbed in reflection) the extraordinary manner in which the speaker had chimed in with my meditations. In an instant afterward I recollected myself, and my astonishment was profound.

"Dupin," said I, gravely, "this is beyond my comprehension. I do not hesitate to say that I am amazed, and can scarely credit my senses. How was it possible you should know I was thinking of —-?" Here I paused to ascertain beyond a doubt whether he really knew of whom I thought.

"—of Chantilly," said he, "why do you pause? You were remarking to yourself that his diminutive figure unfitted him for tragedy."

This was precisely what had formed the subject of my reflections. Chantilly was a *quondam* cobbler of the Rue St. Denis, who, becoming stage-mad, had attempted the *rôle* of Xerxes, in Crébillon's tragedy so called, and been notoriously Pasquinaded for his pains.

"Tell me, for Heaven's sake," I exclaimed, "the method—if method there is—by which you have been enabled to fathom my soul in this matter." In fact, I was even more startled than I would have been willing to express.

"It was the fruiterer," replied my friend, "who brought you to the conclusion that the mender of soles was not of sufficient height for Xerxes *et id genus omne.*"

"The fruiterer!—you astonish me—I know no fruiterer whomsoever."

"The man who ran up against you as we entered the street—it may have been fifteen minutes ago."

I now remembered that, in fact, a fruiterer, carrying upon his head a large basket of apples, had nearly thrown me down, by accident, as we passed from the Rue C— into the thoroughfare where we stood; but what this had to do with Chantilly I could not possibly understand.

There was not a particle of *charlatânerie* about Dupin. "I will explain," he said, "and that you may comprehend all clearly, we will first retrace the course of your meditations, from the moment in which I spoke to you until that of the *recontre* with the fruiterer in question. The larger links of the chain run thus—Chantilly, Orion, Dr. Nichols, Epicurus, Stereotomy, the street stones, the fruiterer."

There are few persons who have not, at some period of their lives amused themselves in retracing the steps by which particular conclusions of their own minds have been attained. The occupation is often full of interest; and he who attempts it for the first time is astonished by the apparently illimitable distance and incoherence between the starting-point and the goal. What, then, must have been my amazement, when I heard the Frenchman speak what he had just spoken, and when I could not help acknowledging that he had spoken the truth. He continued:

"We had been talking of horses, if I remember aright, just before leaving the Rue C—." This was the last subject we discussed. As we crossed into this street, a fruiterer, with a large basket upon his head, brushing quickly past us, thrust you upon a pile of paving-stones collected at a spot where the causeway is undergoing repair. You stepped upon one of the loose fragments, slipped, slightly strained your ankle, appeared vexed or sulky, muttered a few words, turned to look at the pile, and then proceeded in silence. I was not particularly attentive to what you did; but observation has become with me, of late, a species of necessity.

"You kept your eyes upon the ground—glancing, with a petulant expression, at the holes and ruts in the pavement (so that I saw you were still thinking of the stones), until we reached the little alley called Lamartine, which has been paved, by way of experiment, with the overlapping and riveted blocks. Here your countenance brightened up, and, perceiving your lips move, I could not doubt that you murmured the word 'stereotomy,' a term very affectedly applied to this species of pavement. I knew that you could not say to yourself 'stereotomy' without being brought to think of atomies, and thus of the theories of Epicurus; and since when singularly, yet with how little notice, the vague guesses of that noble Greek had met with confirmation in the late nebular cosmogony, I felt that you could not avoid casting your eyes upward to the great *nebula* in Orion, and I certainly expected that you would do so. You did look up; and I was now assured that I had correctly followed your steps. But in the bitter *tirade* upon Chantilly, which appeared in yesterday's '*Musée*,' the satirist, making some disgraceful allusions to the cobbler's change of name upon assuming the buskin, quoted a Latin line about which we have often conversed. I mean the line

> Perdidit antiquum litera prima sonum.

I had told you that this was in reference to Orion, formerly written Urion; and, from certain pungencies connected with this explanation, I was aware that you could not have forgotten it. It was clear, therefore, that you would not fail to combine the two ideas of Orion and Chantilly. That you did combine them I saw by the character of the smile which passed over your lips. You thought of the poor cobbler's immolation. So far, you had been stooping in your gait; but now I saw you draw yourself up to your full height. I was then sure that you reflected upon the diminutive figure of Chantilly. At this point I interrupted your meditations to remark that as, in fact, he *was* a very little fellow—that Chantilly—he would be better at the *Théâtre des Variétés*."[289]

Such inferences may seem a bit strained to the modern reader, but they may not have been so for the 19th century reader. There is nothing deductive about inferences such as these,

---

[289] E.A. Poe. "The Murders in the Rue Morgue," **The Complete Poems and Tales of Edgar Allan Poe**. While Poe is usually considered the originator of the modern detective story, the first detective novel written in English was probably W. Collins' **The Moonstone** (1868) which T.S. Eliot called "... the first, the longest, and the best of modern English detective novels" [J.I.M. Stewart's introduction to **The Moonstone**, Penguin Books, London, 1996]. Detective fiction in China predates English works by centuries: "Short stories about mysterious crimes and their solution have existed in China for over a thousand years, and master-detectives have been celebrated in the tales of the public story teller and in theatrical plays for many centuries. The longer Chinese detective novel started later, about 1600, and reached its greatest development in the 18th and 19th centuries" [**Celebrated Cases of Judge Dee (Dee Goong An)**. Translated by Robert van Gulik, Dover Publications, New York, p. 1.]. We can see from these examples that the detection and revelation of what has been hidden is a subject of longstanding interest that cuts across cultural boundaries.

they could be right or wrong, though for the purposes of fiction it is better that they be right. They would certainly be hard to *prove* in any rigorous sense and are certainly defeasible—they can be overturned by further information or inferences. The series of inferences that Dupin makes are also based on different kinds of observations and knowledge: that the subject might be "vexed" when the fruiterer runs into him; that the subject would know about the attempt to replace paving stones with the better stereotomy method of paving, and approve of it; that he, Dupin, could read the subject's lips when he mumbled "stereotomy" to himself; that the subject would know of the philosophy of Epicurus and make the phonetic connection between "stereotomy" and "atomies;" that the subject's glance up to the stars "could only mean" that he was connecting Epicurus to the Orion Nebula—a connection that seems reasonable to Dupin because "...we disussed this subject not very long ago"; that the subject would have been familiar with the recent bad reviews the actor had gotten, and that one prominent reviewer drew a veiled analogy to Orion; that a change in the subject's gait—"I saw you draw yourself up to your full height"—might indicate something about what he was thinking; and that people often follow just such trains of thought where external stimuli, personal knowledge and associations combine to link one thought to another, in a very informal way. But in spite of the tenuous nature of the inferences, there is no doubt that Poe was one of the first authors to explicitly describe a kind of phenomenon that *does* have a realistic basis. We *can*, and *do*, surmise a lot about what others think by observing what they do. Taking Wittgenstein's lead to give examples rather than explanations to demonstrate a point, we might consider some more recent examples of the detective *genre*—examples that would probably appear more plausible to the modern reader. First, take an example from a mystery writer who wrote during Wittgenstein's time and whom he liked, Agatha Christie (see quotation at footnote [274]). One of her detectives, Hercule Poirot, demonstrates his understanding of the subtleties of human behavior in the following passage:

[Poirot] "I was attracted to [your case]... by its striking unimportance."

"Importance?" said Sir Joseph.

"Unimportance was what I said. I have been called in for varying causes—to investigate murders, unexplained deaths, robberies, thefts of jewelry. This is the first time that I have been asked to turn my talents to elucidate the kidnapping of a Pekinese dog."

Sir Joseph grunted. He said: "You surprise me! I should have said you'd have had no end of women pestering you about their pet dogs."

"That, certainly. But it is the first time that I am summoned by the husband in the case."

Sir Joseph's little eyes narrowed appreciatively. He said: "I begin to see why they recommended you to me. You're a shrewd fellow, M. Poirot."[290]

---

[290] A. Christie. "The Nemean Lion," **The Labors of Hercules**, pp. 12–13. G.P. Putnam and Sons, NY, 1993.

In this quotation we can see two major characteristics of this kind of inference. In the first place it begins with a general feeling of uneasiness, a feeling that something is amiss, or inconsistent with one's expectations (Poirot is wondering why the husband of the woman with the lost dog has called him rather than the woman herself). Nothing need be known about *what* exactly is wrong, only the general feeling of unease is noted. Many detective stories begin this way. Often the detective is the only one who has these feelings, a "hunch," so to speak; this, of course, is due to his/her superior insight and experience (the story wouldn't be as interesting if it were composed entirely of observations or inferences that anyone could make). The search for the reason for the detective's uneasiness often occupies the major part of the story. But while the uneasiness may occur in almost any form, the eventual explanation for the uneasiness must be plausible both to those in the story as well as the readers. The author of the detective story must thereby walk a fine line between plausibility and implausibility. That is, the source of the uneasiness must be hidden enough that the reader cannot figure it out when it's presented. But it must also be the case that the eventual explanation of why the situation made the detective or other protagonists uneasy must be plausible. The balancing of hiddenness and revelation is the touchstone of good detective fiction. Sometimes the uneasy feelings come not from what someone says, but from their behavior. Consider Raymond Chandler's detective Phillip Marlowe:

> [Marlowe] "How well did Miss Fromsett know Lavery? Out of office hours?"
>
> His face tightened up like a charleyhorse. His fists went into hard lumps on his thighs. He said nothing.
>
> "She looked kind of queer when I asked her for his address yesterday morning," I said.
>
> He let a breath out slowly.
>
> "Like a bad taste in the mouth," I said. "Like a romance that fouled out. Am I too blunt?"
>
> His nostrills quivered a little and his breath made noise in them for a moment. Then he relaxed and said quietly:
>
> "She—she knew him rather well—at one time. She's a girl who would do about what she pleased in that way. Lavery was, I guess, a fascinating bird—to women."
>
> "I'll have to talk to her," I said.
>
> "Why?" He asked shortly. Red patches showed in this cheeks.
>
> "Never mind why. It's my business to ask all sorts of questions of all sorts of people."
>
> "Talk to her then," he said tightly. "As a matter of fact she knew the Almores. She knew Almore's wife, the one who killed herself. Laverly knew her too. Could that have any possible connection with this business?"

"I don't know. You're in love with her, aren't you?"

"I'd marry her tomorrow, if I could," he said stiffly.[291]

The reader can see that Chandler is trying to convey how upsetting Marlowe's questions are, not by explicitly saying they are upsetting, but by describing the physical appearance of the man he is questioning. A person who is not emotionally involved in the matter would doubtless answer the questions matter-of-factly. Since he does not answer matter-of-factly it indicates that he finds the subject of the questions disturbing. What is interesting in this passage is that this emotional reaction can be conveyed by the simple description of the individual's appearance while he answers the questions. No explanation is given of what the individual actually is thinking or feeling during the questioning. Instead, the appearance of the man being questioned is simply given, but for most intelligent readers this is all that is necessary to get the author's point. In fact, Marlowe not only sees that the fellow he is questioning is upset, he understands *why* he is upset—he is in love with Miss Fromsett and is understandably upset talking about a former affair of hers. If he were not in love with Miss Fromsett, his being upset would not "fit" the situation. For Wittgenstein such descriptions convey what they intend because they are part of a general system of understanding and belief that most intelligent adults know and accept (a kind of "inherited background" that forms the basis for what we take as true). It is also an example of "showing" rather than "telling," of "description" rather than "explanation." Wittgenstein comments:

At some point one has to pass from explanation to mere description.[292] [OC §189]

---

[291] R. Chandler. **The Lady in the Lake**, p. 73. This passage is obviously overdone, from a literary point of view, but it still serves as an example of how a writer can convey, even in popular fiction, the emotions that underlie what is actually said in the dialogue, without explicitly stating what those emotions are. More subtle examples of such techniques, of course, are used extensively in finer fiction: consider James Joyce's short story "The Two Gallants" from his **Dubliners** [The Portable James Joyce, The Viking Press, NY, 1966 (revised edition)]. The story concerns two young men, one of whom is on his way to see an attractive young woman. The second young man waits to see his friend after his friend's evening with the young woman. Afterwards, the second young man is anxious to hear how his friend's time with the young woman went. The story ends as follows:

"Can't you tell us?" he said. "Did you try her?"

Corley halted at the first lamp and stared grimly before him. Then with a grave gesture he extended a hand towards the light and, smiling, opened it slowly to the gaze of his disciple. A small gold coin shone in the palm. [*op.cit.* p. 71]

This ending is understated enough for its meaning to escape the casual reader, yet it shocked Joyce's original printer enough for him to refuse to publish it. [R. Ellmann. **James Joyce**, p. 228. Oxford University Press, NY, 1959.]

[292] Wittgenstein comments on the dangers of explanation:

The expression "that is all that happens" sets limits to what we call "happening."

Here the temptation is overwhelming to say something further, when everything has already been described.—Whence this pressure? What analogy, what wrong interpretation produces it?

Here we come up against a remarkable and characteristic phenomenon in philosophical in-

Sometimes the detective's reasoning approaches more formal logical deductions:

> Degarmo said gratingly: "Who told you she tried to get money from Almore?"
>
> "Nobody. I had to think of something to fit what happened. **If** Lavery or Mrs. Kingsley had known who Murial Chess had been, and had tipped it off, [**then**] you would have known where to find her and what name she was using. You **didn't** know those things. **Therefore** the lead had to come from the only person up there who knew who she was, and that was herself. So I assume she wrote to Almore."[293]

This reasoning follows the valid logical form known as "modus tollens":

> **If** A **then** B.
> **Not** B
> **Therefore**: **Not** A.

The above passage does not explicitly deny the antecedent, A—"Lavery or Mrs. Kingsley had known who Murial Chess had been." It denies A implicitly. The conclusion that "[Murial Chess] wrote to Almore" cannot be deduced from the statements above unless there is also the premiss that *only* Lavery or Mrs. Kingsley knew who Murial Chess was (of course, Murial Chess knew who Murial Chess was). This premiss is implicit in the earlier part of the story. Nevertheless, the inference does conform to propositional logic. Sometimes the detective's observation depends on expected regularities that may differ from culture to culture. Consider the following passage from a Japanese detective novel translated into English:

> As Sekigawa drank his highball, the waiter brought over an appetizer. It was a plate of smoked salmon. Emiko stared at it.
>
> Noticing her gaze, Sekigawa offered the dish to her. "Eat some if you like."
>
> "Thank you. I'll just take this." Emiko pierced the slice of lemon on the plate with a toothpick. Putting it into her mouth, she ate it as if it were delicious.
>
> "Does such a sour thing taste good to you?" Sekigawa asked, watching her.

> vestigation: the difficulty—I might say—is not that of finding the solution but rather that of recognizing as the solution something that looks as if it were only a preliminary to it. "We have already said everything.—Not anything that follows from this, no, this itself is the solution!"
>
> This is connected, I believe, with our wrongly expecting an explanation, whereas the solution of the difficulty is a description, if we give it the right place in our considerations. If we dwell upon it, and do not try to get beyond it.
>
> The difficulty here is to stop.
>
> "Why do you demand explanations? If they are given you, you will once more be facing a terminus. They cannot get you any further than you are at present." [Z §§312–315]

---

[293] Chandler, *Op.cit.*, p. 141. Bold face type has been added.

At this moment, Sekigawa's expression changed. He had realized something. He glared at Emiko. Suddenly shifting his chair around, he moved close to sit next to her.

"You," he said softly in her ear, "can't possibly be..."

Emiko turned bright red. Her hand stopped moving. She sat perfectly still.

"So that's it." Sekigawa was still looking at her intently.

Without uttering a word, Emiko nodded.[294]

Such an inference based on the stated interactions between the characters may be too tenuous for the average Western reader to pick up immediately. Presumably, the Japanese reader would make the desired inference—that Emiko is pregnant—given the circumstances described by the author.

Often the understanding of what is "hidden" in a detective story dawns with the gradual accumulation of evidence—frequently unpredictable—and the stringing together of inferences based on that evidence. This process is brought out nicely by Colin Dexter in his more recent detective novel **The Wench is Dead**.[295] It will be instructive to look at this sequence of inferences in some detail. In the story, Dexter's sleuth, Inspector Morse, is recovering from a painful ulcer in a hospital. He must remain there several days and, being a man of action, he is bored. A friend gives him a book detailing an account of a murder trial that occurred over a century before in which a young woman, Joanna Franks, had booked passage on a canal boat to Oxford, but was murdered by the four boatmen. Two of the boatmen were convicted and hung. But reading this account Morse begins to grow uneasy:

> After reading [the first] few pages, Morse found himself making some mental queries about a few minor items, and harbouring some vague unease about one or two major ones:
>> Far quicker for [Joanna] by rail, of course! And the fare she'd paid, 16s 11d, seemed on the face of it somewhat on the steep side for a trip as a passenger on a working boat. In 1859? Surely so! What would the rail-fare have been then? Morse had no idea. But there were ways of finding out;
> Why on earth [did the boatmen all have] "aliases?" Were the crewmen counted a load of crooks before they ever came to court? Did every one on the Canal have two names—a "bye name", as it were, as well as one written in the christening-book? Surely any jury was bound to feel a fraction of prejudice against such [men].[296]

Morse does not know what these sources of his unease mean, he is just aware that the facts of the case don't seem to fit together as well as they should. The price of the passage on

---

[294] S. Matsumoto. **Inspector Imanishi Investigates**. Soho Press, NY, 1989. Translated by B. Cary. One might even be able to base a study of cultural differences on the differences in the respective detective stories of those cultures.

[295] C. Dexter. **The Wench is Dead**. Bantam Books, NY, 1989.

[296] *Op.cit.* pp. 42, 44, and 45.

the boat is significant because Joanna and her husband were both very poor, so poor in fact that they could not live together. In such a case it would be normal to expect a traveler to seek the cheapest means of transportation. If the traveler does not, one might conclude that there must have been some ulterior motive for purchasing a more expensive ticket. Morse does not know what that motive might be, he has just noticed a seeming deviation from normal expectations. Of course, if it turns out that the boat passage *was* the cheapest transportation available then the purchase of boat passage would fit with the poverty of Joanna.

The "aliases" of the boatmen might prejudice the jury against them, if such aliases were uncommon. Again, it is not entirely clear how this might have been significant in the trial, it is just something that runs counter to what Morse expects. If the boatmen truly were a bad lot and the evidence against them in the trial was overwhelming, then such a prejudice would have little effect on the outcome other than, perhaps, increasing the severity of the punishment. But if the evidence against the boatmen was weak—as it turned out to be—then it might force a conviction where the evidence really didn't justify it. But, if boatmen were commonly held to be a "load of crooks" why would a woman traveling by herself choose to spend several days alone with them? In noting these possibly significant facts, and the questions they raise, Morse has begun a process of detecting and revealing something that might have been hidden in the evidence of the case—something that was kept out of the evidence, willfully. This process is much like Peirce's idea of "abduction":

> The first starting of a hypothesis and the entertaining of it, whether as a simple interrogation or with any degree of confidence, is an inferential step which I propose to call *abduction* (or *retroduction*). This will include a preference for any one hypothesis over others which would equally explain the facts, so long as this preference is not based upon any previous knowledge bearing upon the truth of the hypotheses, nor on any testing of any of the hypotheses, after having admitted them on probation. I call all such inference by the peculiar name, *abduction*, because its legitimacy depends upon altogether different principles from those of other kinds of inference [induction and deduction]... The form of the inference, therefore, is this:
>
>> The suprising fact, C, is observed;
>> But if A were true, C would be a matter of course;
>> Hence, there is reason to suspect that A is true.[297]

---

[297] C.S. Peirce. **Philosophical Writings of Peirce**, p. 151. Dover Publications, NY, 1955. Selected and edited by J. Buchler. W.B. Gallie distinguishes between induction and abduction in the following way:

> ...in the former [induction] we conclude that facts, similar to observed facts, are true in cases not examined, whereas in the latter [abduction] we conclude the existence of a fact quite different from anything observed; the former classifies, and the latter explains...the conclusion [of an abductive inference] is altogether tentative in character: all that is argued or defended is that a certain suggestion as conjecture is worth considering. [**Peirce and Pragmatism**, p. 98. Pelican Books, Edinburgh, 1952.]

The tentative character of abduction is what logicians term "defeasible" reasoning—conclusions whose validity can be "defeated" by further information or inferences.

The uneasiness that Morse feels when he reads the account of the trial stems from expectations he has about how the trial should go. These expectations are based on his
familiarity with purposeful activities that normal individuals participate in. Some of these
expectations—that an impoverished traveler will try to find the cheapest mode of travel
available—come from a general knowledge of how people conduct their affairs. Other
expectations—such as the understanding that a jury might be prejudiced if the defendant has engaged in previous criminal activity—come from Morse' experience as a police
officer. The uneasiness that Morse has prompts him to resolve it in some way, either by dis-
pelling it or by finding a way to accommodate it within the framework of his expectations
(e.g., if Morse were able to figure out what the ulterior motive might be for Joanna to select
a more expensive mode of transportation and willingly travel with "a load of crooks," then
his expectations could be altered to accommodate that seeming inconsistency).

As Morse continues reading his uneasiness grows:

> As with Part One, Morse found himself making a few notes (mentally, this time) as
> he read through the unhappy narrative. For some reason he felt vaguely dissatisfied
> with himself. Something was nagging at his brain about Part One; but for the present
> he was unable to put a finger on it... could anyone, *anyone*, read this story and not
> find himself questioning one or two of the points so confidently reported? Or two
> or three of them? Or three or four?[298]

Although Morse hasn't put his finger on the source of his uneasiness, he begins to look
towards what his experience tells him might be the most fruitful area of inquiry—the
activities and routines of the boatmen:

> What was the normal pattern of entertainment for canal boatmen, like Oldfield,
> on those "protracted stops" of theirs? Changing horses was obviously one of the
> key activities on such occasions, but one scarcely calculated to gladden every soul.
> Dropping in at the local knocking-shop, then? A likely port-of-call for a few of
> the more strongly sexed among them, most surely. And drink? Did they drink their
> wages away, these boatmen, in the low-beamed bars that were built along their way?
> How not? Why not? What else was there to do?
>
> ... So many questions.[299]

But the questions keep coming up for Morse:

> Boots... shoes...
>
> What *was* all that about [Joanna's] shoes? Why were they figuring so repeatedly in
> the story?[300]

And:

---

[298] Dexter, *op.cit.*, p. 56.
[299] *Ibid.*
[300] *Op.cit.*, p. 58.

Forbidding to Joanna as the tall lock-house must have appeared that midnight, standing sentinel-like above the black waters, it presented her with her one last chance of life—had she sought asylum within its walls.

But she made no such request.[301]

And those last complex, confusing paragraphs! [Joanna] had been desperately anxious to get off the boat and away from her tipsy persecutors—so much seemed beyond any reasonable doubt. But, if so, why, according to the self-same evidence, had she always been so anxious to get back *on* again?[302]

But it's the actions of the boatcrew after Joanna's death, and before her body was found, that puzzle Morse the most:

How had it come about—whatever the fortuitous, involuntary, or deliberate circumstances in which Joanna had met her death—that the crew of the *Barbara Bray* had insisted time and time again that the wretched woman had been nothing but one long, sorry trial to them all ever since she'd first jumped on board at Preston Brook? How *was* it that they were still damning and blasting the poor woman's soul to eternity way, way *after* they had pushed her into the Canal and, for all Morse or anyone else knew, held her head under the black waters until she writhed in agony against their murderous hands no longer? Had a satisfactory explanation been forthcoming for such event?. . . the answer was "no."[303]

Did (Morse asked himself) wicked men tend to get more *drunk*—or more *sober*— after committing such callous crimes? Interesting thought . . . [304]

It was not unknown, admittedly, for the odd psychopath to act in a totally irrational and irresponsible manner. But these were *not* a quartet of psychopaths. And, about all, it seemed quite extraordinary to Morse that, even after (as was claimed) the crew had somehow and for some reason managed to murder Joanna Franks, they were—some twenty-four, thirty-six hours later—still knocking back the booze, still damning and blasting the woman's soul to eternity. Morse had known many murderers, but never one who had subsequently acted in such a fashion—let alone *four*. No! It just didn't add up; didn't add up at all. . . One might expect some measure of shame, remorse, fear—yes!—even, in a few cases, triumph and jubilation in the actual performance of the deed. But not—no!—not the fierce anger and loathing perpetrated by the boatmen through the hours and the days after Joanna had met her death.[305]

Morse has drawn on his unusual knowledge of murderers' personalities and habits, a set of *forms of life* he is familiar with, to see that these boatmen do not act like murderers. After all these questions, Morse begins to see what the source of his discomfort is:

[301] *Op.cit.*, p. 55.
[302] *Op.cit.*, p. 59.
[303] *Op.cit.*, pp. 82–83.
[304] *Op.cit.*, p. 84.
[305] *Op.cit.*, pp. 110–111 and 125–126.

> Morse felt he could put his finger on the major cause of his unease. It was all those conversations, heard and duly reported, between the principal characters in the story: conversations between the crew and Joanna; between the crew and other boatmen; between the crew and lock-keepers, wharfingers, and constables—all of it was *wrong* somehow. *Wrong, if they were guilty.* It was as if some inexperienced playwright had been given a murder-plot, and had then proceeded to write page after page of inappropriate, misleading, and occasionally contradictory dialogue. For there were moments when it looked as if it were Joanna Franks who was the avenging Fury, with the crewmen merely the victims of her fatal power.[306]

What is interesting is that when Morse sees what is bothering him—what doesn't "fit" in the narrative of the trial—he sees not one or two things, but a whole *system* of facts or propositions. Again, this parallels Wittgenstein's notion of factual understanding:

> When we first begin to *believe* anything, what we believe is not a single proposition, it is a whole system of propositions. (Light dawns gradually over the whole.)

> It is not single axioms that strike me as obvious, it is a system in which consequences and premises give one another *mutual* support. [**OC** §§141–142]

Again, Morse' narrative follows the general framework of many detective stories. First, the detective or some central character becomes uneasy about the events or circumstances that occur. He often doesn't know *why* he feels uneasy, but the uneasiness persists in spite of his continuing thoughts about the case. The method for resolving this uneasiness is to find an explanation for the events or circumstances in question that somehow shows why these events or circumstances played out in the unexpected way that they did. This (abductive) explanation usually comes after the detective obtains more information about the people, things, motivations or circumstances in the case. The clever thing for the detective is to see that some of these events or circumstances are related in a way that others, including the reader, had not seen. Generally, the detective tries to find more about the specific case with which he is concerned (In our example, Morse supplements the narrative of the murder case with trips to the library to find the actual transcript of the trial along with old newspaper accounts of it.). This additional information can be about a number of things: it could be something previously unknown about the central characters that might give them a motive for committing the crime, or some special skill that gave them a means of carrying out the crime, or some special circumstances that prefigure the crime itself. When it comes down to it, the detective, more often than not, relies on his or her understanding of human nature—both criminal and normal. It is mostly his/her understanding of what Wittgenstein might call the "natural history of mankind" that enables him to find out things that others may willfully try to hide.[307]

---

[306] *Op.cit.*, p. 110.

[307] Out of deference to C. Dexter, the author of **The Wench is Dead**, I have not revealed the conclusion of the story. But I can say that Inspector Morse was correct, there was something "fishy" about the story of Johanna. And when he finds out exactly what it is, all the inconsistencies that bothered him before now "fit," bringing the reported actions of the protagonists back into the "inherited" framework of, in Wittgenstein's words, the "common behavior of mankind." [**PI** §206]

*Wittgenstein and Drama: A Dramatic Theory of Meaning*

Morse' sudden revelation that the recorded testimony of the case reads like a bad play, resonates with Wittgenstein:

> The best example of an expression with a very specific meaning is a passage in a play. [**LWPP I** §424]

> The contexts of a sentence are best portrayed in a play. Therefore, the best example for a sentence with a particular meaning is a quotation from a play. And whoever asks a person in a play what he's experiencing when he's speaking? [**LWPP I** §38]

For Wittgenstein, if we want to demonstrate the meaning of a particular word or phrase we can best do this by describing how those words might be used in a play. So the meaning of the word or phrase is not a dictionary definition, nor is it a description of what we are thinking, but a description of the context and circumstances (and perhaps the background of the characters) that would provide the "stage setting" and motivation for its use in a play; for Morse, a good way to see what the clues or evidence *mean* is to imagine them within the context of a play. Wittgenstein also uses the related metaphor of "stage setting" in the everyday use of language:

> But what does it mean to say that he has "named his pain?"... When one says "He gave a name to his sensation" one forgets that a great deal of stagesetting in the language is presupposed if the mere act on naming is to make sense. And when we speak of someone's having given a name to pain, what is presupposed is the existence of the grammar of the word "pain"; it shews [*sic*] the post where the new word is stationed. [**PI** §257]

By saying that meaning in language is best portrayed as its use in a play, Wittgenstein once again moves us away from the narrow context-free mentalistic semantics of language that he felt did not capture the richness and complexity of language *in use*. One might make the further inference that the best description of a *language game* is a description of that particular language usage in a play. Recall Wittgenstein's description of a *language game*:

> I shall call the whole, consisting of language and the actions into which it is woven, the "language game." [**PI** §7]

Our observation that the criteria on which the detective may base his inferences or hunches may vary between different cultures is also supported by Wittgenstein's "dramatic notion of meaning":

> A play, for example, shows what instances of dissimulation look like.

> Of course, one could imagine variations of the typical manifestations of dissimulation.

> The plays of people who differ from us in this way would then take a different course from ours, and we wouldn't understand them at all.

> What would be completely unmotivated to us would seem natural to them.

> (For example, the way Orestes identifies himself to the king, by pointing to his sword, etc., might seem utterly absurd to some people.)

> A play by these people would be incomprehensible to us. (Indeed, is Greek tragedy comprehensible to us?)[308] **[LWPP I §§263–266]**

Wittgenstein's "dramatic theory of meaning" has given us a way to establish what particular context and circumstances are necessary for the conveying of a specific linguistic meaning (though the context and circumstances used in the play must be familiar to the audience). The use of drama to portray meaning is also an instance of how effective *demonstrating*, or *showing*, what a word or phrase means is, as opposed to *explaining* or *defining* it. Wittgenstein continually insists in his later philosophy that demonstration and description are far better ways of conveying linguistic meaning than explanations and definitions are.[309]

One of the major criticisms of ordinary language philosophy is that when we extend the criteria of meaning in language from a syntactic or semantic foundation to a pragmatic one, we make so much relevant to meaning that it would be impossible to describe in any kind of complete way. As Benson Mates wrote in his criticism of this aspect of "ordinary language philosophy":

> We have all heard the wearying platitude that "you can't separate" the meaning of a word from the entire context in which it occurs, including not only the actual linguistic context but also the aims, feeling, beliefs, and hopes of the speaker, the same for the listener and any bystanders, the social situation, the physical surroundings, the historical background, the rules of the game, and so on ad infinitum. There is no doubt some truth in this, but I fail to see how it helps one get started in an empirical investigation of language. At the very least, provisional divisions of the subject have to be made somewhere.[310]

For Mates, by including all this pragmatic information as essential to linguistic meaning, we have no boundaries to limit what we look at. With no boundaries for what is relevant, then any description or investigation of meaning based on it would be endless and, thus, impossible to complete. But Wittgenstein is not so open-ended in his analysis. His "dramatic theory of meaning" (*q.v.*) puts clear boundaries on what is necessary to convey linguistic meaning. Pragmatic meaning does not include, as Mates implies, *everything*, for, surely, if the dramatist can create the context and circumstances that can convey, faithfully, the

---

[308] If the culture we grow up in influences not only what we think, but also how we think, as Donald claims ("Culture can literally reconfigure the use patterns of the brain" (see footnote [240]), it is not unreasonable to infer that if two individuals came from sufficiently different cultures they may not be able to understand each other in fundamental ways. And the plays of a culture that no longer exists, like Greece Before the Common Era, may be, as Wittgenstein supposes, "...incomprehensible to us" in significant ways.

[309] Wittgenstein's concern with language and meaning was not just philosophical. By living his entire adult life in a culture that did not speak his native language, German, he was constantly confronted with having to find or confirm the meanings of everyday language (English), and, no doubt, was poignantly aware of the differences in meaning that different cultures could impose on language. This gave a constant personal imperative to his work on language.

[310] B. Mates. "On Verification of Statements About Ordinary Language," **Ordinary Language: Essays in Philosophical Method**, p. 71. Dover Publications, NY, 1981 (first published in 1964). Edited by V.C. Chappell.

meaning of ordinary—or even very creative—language use in a play, then *a fortiori*, the description of the context and circumstances necessary to convey linguistic meaning are not endless and impossible to describe completely. The dramatist can do it, so why not the philosopher?[311]


### The Inner and the Outer

> The endless fascination of these people for me lies in what I call their inward power. It is part of the elusive secret that hides in everyone, and it has been my life's work to try to capture it on film. The mask we present to others and, too often, to ourselves, may lift for only a second—to reveal that power in an unconscious gesture, a raised brow, a surprised response, a moment of repose. *This* is the moment to record.[312]
>
> —Yousuf Karsh (portrait photographer)

This discussion of the "hiddenness" and "openness" of our thoughts and feelings brings us to a more general conception of the issue which Wittgenstein termed the "inner" and the "outer," and which occupied much of his thought during the last few years of his life.[313] But the distinction between the inner and the outer is a variation on a much more fundamental set of distinctions, or dualisms, that has occupied philosophers for centuries— the distinction between the physical and the mental, between phenomena of the physical world and the processes or states of the human mind. From a subjective point of view, there is unquestionably a relationship between the inner and the outer: things we observe become subjects of our most private thoughts, and ideas that we have sometimes seem to be the instigation for our actions in the physical world. But what is this relationship between the inner and outer processes? And, just how "private" are our thoughts and feelings? The

---

[311] S. Cavell, who is largely sympathetic with Wittgenstein's view of language, takes issue with this statement by Mates:

> ... I should perhaps justify my very heavy reliance on the idea of context, because on Mates' description of what a statement of context involves, it should be impossible ever to make one [Cavell quotes Mates' statement above]. Isn't this another of those apostrophes to the infinite which prevents philosophers from getting down to cases? Of course if I have to go on about the context... ad infinitum, I would not get very far with it. But I would claim to have characterized the context sufficiently (for the purpose at hand) by the statement that something is, or is supposed to be, fishy about the action. Giving directions for using a word is no more prodigious and unending a task than giving directions for anything else. The context in which I make a martini with vodka is no less complex than the context in which I make a statement with [the word] "voluntary." Say, if you like, that these actions take place in infinitely complex contexts; but then remember that you can be given directions for doing either...

In recommending that we ignore context in order to make "provisional divisions" of a subject and get an investigation started, Mates is recommending the wrong thing for the right reason. It is true that we cannot say everything at once and that for some problems some distinction of the sort Mates has in mind may be of service. My discontent with it is that it has come to deflect investigation—I mean from questions on which Oxford [Ordinary Language] philosophy trains itself.[From "Must We Mean What We Say?," **Ordinary Language: Essays in Philosophical Method**, pp. 89–90. Dover Publications, NY, 1981 (first published in 1964). Edited by V.C. Chappell.

[312] Y. Karsh. **Karsh: A Fifty Year Retrospective**, p. 23. Little Brown, Boston, 1983.

[313] See, especially, his **RPP I**, and **Last Writings on the Philosophy of Psychology: Vol. I and II**.

centrality of the contrast between the inner and the outer to mainstream philosophical thought is emphasized by Glock in his comments on Wittgenstein:

> The inner/outer picture informs not just Cartesian dualism, but the mainstream of modern philosophy, including rationalism, empiricism and Kantianism. Even Frege, who insisted that what we think—"thoughts"—are abstract entities in a "third realm," accepted the traditional contrast between the "second realm" of material objects and the first realm of "ideas" which are the private properties of individuals...Idealism and phenomenalism dispense with the physical world, but cleave to the image of the mind as a private immaterial theatre to which we have immediate access. Behaviorism, by contrast, reduces the mental to human behavior, which it describes in purely physical terms. Finally, materialism rejects the Cartesian conception of the mind as an immaterial substance, but concludes that it must be a material substance, thereby replacing the mind/body dualism with a *brain*/body dualism, in which the brain takes on the role of the inner. These positions question one half of the dichotomy, but not the contrast itself. They ignore that we describe human behavior not as mere bodily movement, but *ab initio* in terms of our mental vocabulary, for example as jumping for joy, chuckling with glee. The mental is neither a fiction, nor hidden behind the outer. It infuses our behavior and is expressed in it.[314]

Wittgenstein insists that our private feelings and thoughts—the "inner"—are really not intrinsically hidden. They are open to others in a "different way" than our more public statements and actions—the "outer"—are. The way that they are open to others is similar to the way that hidden motivations and thoughts are open to the detective. The initial "hunch" that begins the detective's quest for knowledge is like our own feeling that something is, or is not, the case, even though we do not have clear evidence for it. Wittgenstein remarks:

> I go for a walk in the environs of a city with a friend. As we talk it comes out that I am imagining the city to lie on our right. Not only have I no conscious reason for this assumption, but some quite simple consideration was enough to make me realize that the city lay rather to the left ahead of us. I can at first give no answer to the question why I imagine the city in this direction. I have no reason to think it. But though I see no reason still I seem to see certain psychological causes for it. In particular, certain associations and memories. For example, we walked along a canal, and once before in similar circumstances I had followed a canal and that time the city lay on our right.—I might try as it were psychoanalytically to disover the causes of my unfounded conviction.

> "But what is this queer experience?"—Of course it is not queerer than any other; it simply differs in kind from those experiences which we regard as the most fundamental ones, our sense impressions for instance.

> "I feel as if I knew the city lay over there."—"I feel as if the name 'Schubert' fitted Schubert's works and Schubert's face." [**PI** p. 215]

---

[314]H.-J. Glock. **A Wittgenstein Dictionary**, p. 175. Blackwell, Cambridge, MA, 1996. Glock references the following passages in Wittgenstein as being relevant: **PI** §357, pp. 178, 222–223; **LWPP II** pp. 24–28, 81–95.

Of course, such "hunches" can be wrong, but just as surely, and perhaps more strikingly, they can be right. The basis for these feelings may be ineffable. Even on reflection, one might not be able to justify them at all, or only partially. Sometimes, they come from a sense of "symmetry":

> ... one is sometimes convinced of the correctness of a view by its simplicity or symmetry, i.e., these are what induce one to go over to this point of view. One then simply says something like: "That's how it must be." [**OC** §92]

The detective's hunches often come when something doesn't "fit" with everything else. In Morse' case, the description of the boatmen's activities after the crime does not fit with their being guilty—they did not act like men who had just committed a murder. The notion that events, circumstances and statements must somehow "fit" together, is what makes it so difficult for us to hide our thoughts and feelings, that is, to lie. As Sir Walter Scott wrote:

> Oh what a tangled web we weave
>
> When first we practice to deceive![315]

Solving a mystery is somewhat like learning a new language, and Wittgenstein makes it very clear that such education is strongly based on our understanding of the common practices and activities—the life forms—of mankind:

> Suppose you came as an explorer into an unknown country with a language quite strange to you. In what circumstances would you say that the people there gave orders, understood them, obeyed them, rebelled against them, and so on?
>
> The common behavior of mankind is the system of reference by means of which we interpret an unknown language. [**PI** §206]

Inspector Morse is trying to understand what the boatmen meant by their statements damning the murdered woman. The 19th century boatmen are residents in the "unknown country" whose language Morse is trying to understand. Morse does not need to figure out the literal meaning of what the boatmen said—any one who speaks English can understand that. What he needs to figure out is how this literal meaning fits the presumed circumstances—the guilt of the boatmen. And this understanding, like all meaning in language, is grounded in forms of life—here, the forms of life of the boatmen and Joanna in particular, and the forms of life of average working Englishmen of the 19th century, in general ("[Morse] What was the normal pattern of entertainment for canal boatmen, like Oldfield, on those 'protracted stops' of theirs?"). If the detective is to interpret the meaning, connotations and implications of a suspect's language correctly—especially if he is to tell whether the suspect is lying or not—he or she must understand the forms of life of both ordinary people and criminals.

Much of what the detective infers is based on what Wittgenstein called "imponderable evidence" or "fine shades of behavior"—those things that by themselves do not amount

---

[315] Sir W. Scott. "L'envoy," (Verse xvii).

to much but in the right context or circumstances, or with the right assumptions turn out to be key revelations. Inspector Morse comments:

> From the newspaper records, it was soon clear that the [author of the narrative] had omitted no details of any obvious importance. Yet, as in most criminal cases, it was the apparently innocuous, incidental, almost irrelevant, details that could change, in a flash, the interpretation of accepted facts. And there were quite a few details here (to Morse, hitherto unknown) which caused him more than a millimetric rise of the eyebrows.[316]

In a remarkably similar statement, Wittgenstein comments on the importance of the "simple" and "familiar" when doing philosophical analysis:

> The aspects of things that are most important for us are hidden because of their simplicity and familiarity (One is unable to notice something—because it is always before one's eyes.). The real foundations of his enquiry do not strike a man at all. Unless *that* fact has at some time struck him.—And this means: we fail to be struck by what, once seen, is most striking and most powerful. [**PI** §129]

Being a detective and doing analytic philosophy are remarkably similar activities, and philosophy, to Wittgenstein, is an activity, not a doctrine:

> Philosophy aims at the logical clarification of thoughts.

> Philosophy is not a body of doctrine but an activity.

> A philosophical work consists essentially of elucidations.

> Philosophy does not result in "philosophical propositions," but rather in the clarification of propositions.

> Without philosophy thoughts are, as it were, cloudy and indistinct: its task is to make them clear and to give them sharp boundaries.[317] [**TLP** §4.112]

---

[316] Dexter, *op.cit.*, p. 123.

[317] The mathematician Ramsey, who was a friend of Wittgenstein, remarked on this in this review of the **Tractatus Logico-Philosophicus**:

> The conclusion of the greatest modern philosopher, is that there is no such subject as philosophy; that it is an activity, not a doctrine; and that, instead of answering questions, it aims merely at curing headaches. [F.P. Ramsey.**The Foundations of Mathematics and Other Logical Essays**, p. 288. London, 1931. Edited by R. Brathwaite.]

While Wittgenstein rejected or modified many of his views in **TLP**, he maintained this view of philosophy throughout his life, as Baker and Hacker observe:

> ...philosophy is extraordinary in that it adjudicates the bounds of sense. It clarifies which questions are intelligible and which investigations are in principle relevant or irrelevant for answering them. This view Wittgenstein held and argued for throughout his career. It is the sense that he thought of philosophy as the activity of clarifying thoughts. [G.P. Baker and P.M.S. Hacker. **Wittgenstein: Meaning and Understanding. Essays on the Philosophical Investigations,** vol. 1, p. 259. University of Chicago Press, 1985.]

This series of statements about philosophy could be a good description of what the detective's "method" aims at too. Like the philosopher, the detective aims at finding the "simple" and "familiar" things that elucidate his problems (Morse ponders, "Boots... shoes... What *was* all that about [Joanna's] shoes? Why were they figuring so repeatedly in the story?"); like the philosopher, the detective must find out what the right questions are he should be asking ("Did (Morse asked himself) wicked men tend to get more *drunk*—or more *sober*—after committing such callous crimes? Interesting thought..."); like the philosopher, the detective must be wary of how the forms of language and the regularities of our activities compel us to make improper assumptions or draw misleading conclusions (on reading the case of Joanna's murder, one is naturally drawn to believe that Joanna is the victim and the coarse boatmen her tormentors, as the jury did. But, Morse observes, "...there were moments when it looked as if it were Joanna Franks who was the avenging Fury, with the crewmen merely the victims of her fatal power." ); and like the philosopher, the detective is often confronted with resolving paradoxes ("And those last complex, confusing paragraphs! [Joanna] had been desperately anxious to get off the boat and away from her tipsy persecutors—so much seemed beyond any reasonable doubt. But, if so, why, according to the self-same evidence, had she always been so anxious to get back *on* again?").

*Imponderable Evidence* **(Unwägbare Evidenz)**

Wittgenstein talks about the subtleties of evidence that we might gather to support an inference or opinion. Some of this is what he calls "imponderable evidence":

> It is certainly possible to be convinced by evidence that someone is in such-and-such a state of mind, that, for instance, he is not pretending. But "evidence" here includes "imponderable" evidence.

> The question is: what does imponderable evidence *accomplish*?

> Suppose there were imponderable evidence for the chemical (internal) structure of a substance, still it would have to prove itself to be evidence by certain consequences which *can* be weighed.

> (Imponderable evidence might convince someone that a picture was a genuine... But it is *possible* for this to be proved right by documentary evidence as well.)

> Imponderable evidence includes subtleties of glance, of gesture, of tone.

> I may recognize a genuine loving look, distinguish it from a pretended one (and here there can, of course, be a "ponderable" confirmation of my judgement). But I may be quite incapable of describing the difference. And this not because the languages I know have no words for it. For why not introduce new words?—If I were a very talented painter I might conceivably represent the genuine and the simulated glance in pictures.[318] [**PI** p. 228]

---

[318] Wittgenstein had a slightly different version of the last two paragraphs of this in **LWPP I**:

What does "imponderable evidence" mean? (Let's be honest!)

I tell someone that I have reasons for this claim or proofs for it, but that they are "imponderable."

Well, for instance, I have seen the look which one person has given another. I say "If you had seen it you would have said the same thing." [But there is still some unclarity.] Some other time perhaps, I might get him to see this look, and then he will be convinced. That would be one possibility.

To some extent I do predict behavior ("They'll get married, she'll see to that"), and to some extent I don't. [**LWPP I** §§922–923]

"Imponderable evidence" is often the grounds for both the detective's "hunch" as well as the expert's "judgment."[319] Such evidence cannot be marshaled for or against a given hypothesis as "documentary evidence" can, it can only be the unstated basis for one hunch or judgment over another. But such a hunch must lead to certain consequences that are *not* imponderable—"it would have to prove itself" as Wittgenstein states. (One imagines the classic denouement of many British mysteries where the detective gathers all the suspects together in the library of a country estate and begins to recount his discoveries and inferences. Gradually, as one suspect after the other is eliminated from suspicion the tension grows until the guilty one often makes a run for it, thereby confirming his guilt and turning the detective's hunch into the ponderable evidence of a flight, capture and possibly a confession.)

To confirm their "hunches" the detective and the philosopher must turn imponderable evidence into "ponderable" evidence. But there are experts who may never get to the point where they can convincingly justify their judgments to nonexperts. Consider the connoisseur. Wittgenstein observes:

"Imponderable evidence" includes subtleties of tone, of glance, of gesture.

Isn't it really as if here one were looking at the workings of the nervous system? For I would very much like my feigned gesture to be exactly like the real one, but *in spite of everything* it is not the same.

I can recognize a genuine loving look, distinguish it from a pretended one. And yet there is no way in which I can describe it to someone else. If we had a great painter here, he might conceivably represent a genuine and simulated look in pictures, or this kind of a representation could be imagined in a film, and perhaps a verbal description based on it.

Ask yourself: How does a man learn to get a 'nose' for something? And how can this nose be used? [**LWPP I** §§936–938]

[319] Note how, in common parlance, that a detective has a "hunch" while an expert has an "opinion" or "judgment." An expert in art would not normally be said to have a "hunch," while the detective would not be said to have an "opinion" or a "judgment." Following Wittgenstein's deep grammatical analysis, we must conclude that "hunches," "opinions" and "judgments" refer to a family of similar, but subtley different cognitive abilities.

> A *connoisseur* couldn't make himself understood to a jury, for instance. That is, they would understand his statement, but not his reasons. He can give intimations to another connoisseur, and the latter will understand them. [**LWPP I** §927]

It may even be the case that there are no reasons at all for some of our judgments:

> But does there have to be a reason? Couldn't I simply know whether he is pretending without knowing how I know it?
>
> I simply have "an eye" for it. [**LWPP II** p. 31]

But how does the expert acquire such subtle abilities? Wittgenstein comments:

> Is there such a thing as "expert judgment" about the genuineness of expressions of feeling?—Even here, there are those whose judgment is "better" and those whose judgment is "worse."
>
> Correcter [*sic*] prognoses will generally issue from the judgments of those with better knowledge of mankind.
>
> Can one learn this knowledge? Yes; some can. Not, however, by taking a course in it, but through *"experience."*—Can someone else be a man's teacher in this? Certainly. From time to time he gives him the right *tip*.—This is what "learning" and "teaching" are like here.—What one acquires here is not a technique; one learns correct judgments. There are also rules, but they do not form a system, and only experienced people can apply them right. Unlike calculation rules.
>
> What is most difficult here is to put this indefiniteness, correctly and unfalsified, into words.[320] [**PI** p. 227]

What is important here is that learning how to make this kind of expert judgment does not involve following explicit rules or "taking a course in it." It involves having as many relevant experiences as possible in the company of an expert who *coaches* the novice. Experts who can make these judgments well may not be able to describe how they make them in any kind of detail. They can *demonstrate* how these judgments are made in actual cases, but they may not be able to describe any context-free rules that would allow someone without the expertise to systematically make such judgments. Context-free rules are like

---

[320] Compare to a similar statement in **LWPP I** §§925– 926:

An important fact here is that we learn certain things only through long experience and not from a course in school. How, for instance, does one develop the eye of a connoisseur? Someone says, for example: "This picture was not painted by such-and-such a master"—the statement he makes is thus not an aesthetic judgment, but one that can be proved by documentation. He may not be able to give good reasons for his verdict.—How did he learn it? Could someone have taught him? Quite.—Not in the same way as one learns to calculate. A great deal of experience was necessary. That is, the learner probably had to look at and compare a large number of pictures by various masters again and again. In doing this he could have been given hints. Well, that was the process of learning. But then he looked at a picture and made a judgment about it. In most cases he was able to list reasons for his judgment, but generally it wasn't they that were convincing.

Look at learning—and the result of learning.

calculation rules, which can be applied by nonexperts, or even computers. But these aren't like the rules that Wittgenstein refers to. The expert's rules are more like heuristics, and presuppose a minimal level of expertise before they can be applied. Perhaps an example will help. Many of us have used repair manuals to fix our cars, appliances, etc. rather than paying to have an experienced repairman fix them. While these manuals are frequently advertised as enabling complete novices to make complex repairs, they often implicitly presuppose a minimal level of expertise to apply the steps in a repair. For example, in trouble-shooting a car that won't start, one of the steps tells the reader to check to see that all the spark plugs are generating a "good spark." What it doesn't tell you is what a "good spark" looks like. You need some experience to know what a "good spark" really looks like. The ability to blend expertise and rules is what Wittgenstein means when he writes:

> There are also rules, but they do not form a system, and only experienced people can apply them right. [*supra*]

The successful exercise of expert judgments not only doesn't follow the kind of analysis we see in mathematical calculations, the attempt to make expert judgments by analysis can actually prove an impediment to gaining expertise. Consider the following description of learning to play chess at an expert level:

> I was always good at mathematics and took up chess as an outlet for that analytic talent. At college, where I captained the chess team, my players were mostly mathematicians and mostly, like me, at the competent level. At this point, a few of my teammates who were not mathematicians began to play fast chess at the rate of five or ten minutes a game, and also eagerly to play over the great games of the grandmasters. I resisted. Fast chess was no fun for me, because it didn't give me time to *figure out* what to do. I found grandmaster games inscrutable, and since the record of the game seldom if ever gave rules and principles explaining the moves, I felt there was nothing I could learn from the games. Some of my teammates who through fast chess and game studying acquired a great deal of concrete experience have gone on to become masters.
>
> As I look around at my mathematical academic colleagues, most of whom play chess and none of whom have gotten beyond my own competent level, I see how our view of chess as a strictly analytic game has cut us off from absorbing concrete chess experience. While students of mathematics and related topics predominate in the population of young people enthusiastic about chess, you are as likely to find a truck driver as a mathematician among the world's best players. You are more likely to find an amateur psychologist or a journalist. In a way I am glad that my analytic approach to chess stymied my progress, because this helped me to see that there is more to skill than reasoning.[321]

Taking another example, how do we teach someone the difference between Impressionism and Neo-impressionism in French painting? Definitions and explanations alone would likely fail to make the distinctions and similarities that are important. We need to see examples of each of these schools of painting and our expertise will grow as we see more

---

[321] H. Dreyfus and S. Dreyfus. **Mind Over Machine: The Power of Human Intuition and Expertise in the Era of the Computer**, p. 25. Free Press, NY, 1986.

and more examples. The best way to demonstrate these artistic categories is for an expert to take the novice to an art gallery in which both styles of painting are present and point them out to him: "This painting by Cezanne is a good example of Impressionism, while this painting by Seurat is a good example of Neo-impressionism. Both Impressionism and Neo-impressionism reduce the sharp picture of reality that we see to an image that is softer and less sharp, but they do it in different ways—in Neo-impressionism see how the painter constructed the painting with discrete dots of paint; now compare that with the Impressionist who used fuller strokes of the brush," etc. This type of teaching involves the grouping of examples into similar categories, but it also may be accompanied by examples that can be used to distinguish these examples from those outside the categories in question. For example, we might point out Lichtenstein's Pop Art to give an example of an artistic style that uses dots of color to make up larger images but is not an example of Neo-Impressionism; or, we might contrast Impressionism with other painting styles such as Fauvism and Expressionism that create their works with impressionist-like images, but are not considered examples of Impressionism. The simultaneous importance of distinction and similarity in assessing class membership is considered a fundamentally important aspect of how language works.

### The Objective Correlative

The use of literary techniques to reveal the feelings or thoughts of characters without actually stating them is not limited to detective stories, but runs through much established English literature. The poet and dramatist T.S. Eliot discusses this process in his 1919 essay "Hamlet and His Problems." He called this literary device an "objective correlative":

> The only way of expressing emotion in the form of art is by finding an "objective correlative"; in other words, a set of objects, a situation, a chain of events which shall be the formula of that *particular* emotion; such that when the external facts, which must terminate in sensory experience, are given, the emotion is immediately evoked. If you examine any of Shakespeare's more successful tragedies, you will find this exact equivalence; you will find that the state of mind of Lady Macbeth walking in her sleep has been communicated to you by a skillful accumulation of imagined sensory impressions; the words of Macbeth on hearing of his wife's death strike us as if, given the sequence of events, these words were automatically released by the last event in the series. The artistic "inevitability" lies in this complete adequacy of the external to the emotion . . . [322]

We can see the subtleties of such inferences in the commentary which Ezra Pound added to his translation of a Chinese poem by Rihaku:

"The Jewel Stairs' Grievance"

The jewelled steps are already quite white with dew,

It is so late that the dew soaks my gauze stockings,

---

[322] T.S. Eliot. "Hamlet and His Problems," **Selected Essays**. Harcourt, Brace and World, NY, 1932. Quotation is from pp. 124–125.

And I let down the crystal curtain

And watch the moon through the clear autumn.

[Pound's comments] Note: Jewel stairs, therefore a palace. Grievance, therefore there is something to complain of. Gauze stockings, therefore a court lady, not a servant who complains. Clear autumn, therefore [s]he has no excuse on account of weather. Also she has come early, for the dew has not merely whitened the stairs, but has soaked her stockings. The poem is especially prized because she utters no direct reproach.[323]

Pound was a poet and Eliot was a poet as well as a dramatist, but such literary devices are common to prose, too. James Joyce formulated a similar technique which he called an "epiphany." His brother, Stanislaus, discusses this:

Another experimental form which [Joyce's] literary urge took... consisted in the noting of what he called "epiphanies"—manifestations or revelations. Jim always had a contempt for secrecy, and these notes were in the beginning ironical observations of slips, and little errors and gestures—mere straws in the wind—by which people betrayed the very things they were most careful to conceal.[324]

This digression into literary devices is not meant to show that Wittgenstein is unoriginal in his claim that our thoughts and feelings are "open" to others in various ways. It is merely to show that his claim has support in other areas of language use, especially in those areas

---

[323] Rihaku. "The Jewel Stairs' Grievance," **Selected Poems of Ezra Pound**. A New Directions Paperbook, NY, 1957. Translated by E. Pound. "Rihaku" is the Japanese name for the Chinese Poet Li Po.

[324] S. Joyce. **My Brother's Keeper**, p. 124. Viking Press, NY, 1969. The relation between the "clue" in a mystery story and an epiphany has been drawn by Hugh Kenner:

The clue is a bogus epiphany. In itself it has no ontological significance. It doesn't open to contemplative penetration the intelligible depths of some object; rather it suggests to the quick deductive wit discursive attention to the superficies of a dozen other objects. The clue and the chain of reasoning function, like a jigsaw puzzle, in two dimensions. The sleuth's reconstruction of a crime works at the level of efficient causes only; the epiphany implies an intuitive grasp of material, formal, and final causes as well. Though it resembles "Araby" or "The Dead" in that the significance of the whole becomes clear on the last page, the detective story remains a two-dimensional parody of the Joycean short story, as Holmes is a parody of Stephen, as Stephen is a parody of Joyce, and as discursive analysis, once it deserts its job of arranging data in the line of efficient causality, becomes a parody of metaphysical intuition, or of allied aesthetic modes of knowledge. The "meaning" of "The Dead" cannot be reasoned out, as a whole generation of commentators has had opportunity to discover. [**Dublin's Joyce**, pp. 176–177. Beacon Press, Boston, 1962.]

Kenner's criticism of clues as being a lower form of epiphany is, in my opinion, too severe. If Joyce's epiphanies are of a higher order of insight and revelation than clues in mystery stories are then this is not because detective stories are "two-dimensional parod[ies] of the Joycean short story," but because Joyce is simply a greater writer than even the best mystery story writer. Had Joyce turned his hand to writing mystery stories his "clues" would, no doubt, have reached the depth and insight of the epiphanies in his stories. But even apart from the greatness of a writer like Joyce, the clues of a mystery story have a kind of deceptive obviousness about them that encourages us to think of their revelations as clever rather than profound. If we are not familiar with the activities and forms of life of the characters—for example, we come from a different culture—the revelations of the clues may not be so obvious.

where language use has reached a high level of execution, such as poetry and literature. Wittgenstein has merely drawn a reference to a kind of human ability that has existed for a long time, but had not been considered significant by most philosophers.

*Imponderable Evidence and Real Life*

So far, we have drawn supporting evidence for Wittgenstein's claim to the "openness" of inner/mental phenomena from the world of fiction. While such references are intriguing, it is important to look for similar evidence in the details of actual events. Since we initially drew the parallel between Wittgenstein's work on the openness of inner phenomena and detective fiction, it may be instructive to examine whether actual detectives follow their "hunches" as fictional ones do. Although Michael Kurland, author of **How to Solve a Murder: The Forensic Handbook**[325] is initially critical of the accuracy of fiction detectives (and, apparently unaware of mystery writers like Agatha Christie's and P.D. James' use of working police and detectives as advisors), some of his examples of how detective work proceeds are remarkably similar to the progression of unease, hunches, investigation and resolution that we described with Detective Morse. As Kurland described it:

> Many homicide detectives develop a "sixth sense" in recognizing a purposeful murder in what seems on the surface to be a random act of violence, an accidental death, or a suicide. If you ask a detective how he or she knew that a given case was not what it seemed, the response is often, "It just didn't feel right." When, early in the afternoon of Thursday, September 30, 1993, detectives Danny Caudil and Larry Reese of the Columbus, Ohio, homicide squad answered the call to investigate the death of thirty-year-old Greg Williams at Williams' townhouse, the feeling of wrongness was strong.[326]

Greg's wife, Michele, had heard the shot, but did not see the murderer. She told the detectives what she had seen:

> Michele, a sweet young blond who looked like every college man's dream date, told her story between sobs while being physically supported by a family friend to keep from collapsing completely. "You've got to catch that guy!" she told the detectives. Throughout Michele and Greg's storybook romance, they had been the perfect couple, and still adored each other, as far as anyone could tell...
>
> But something about Michele—the way she told her story or perhaps the condition of the house—set off the alarm bells in the detective's minds. It just didn't feel right. Michele and her mother were taken to the police station where Michele was to give her statement, while Caudill and Reese, acting on their hunch, searched the house. In a cardboard box in an upstairs bedroom, they found a laundry bag. And in the laundry bag, a .32 caliber revolver. In her purse, sitting in the kitchen, they found cartridges for the .32, as well as shell casings from the three rounds that had been fired.[327]

---

[325] Macmillan Company, 1633 Broadway, NY, 1995.
[326] *Op.cit.*, p. 35.
[327] *Op.cit.*, p. 36.

Other evidence was found and Michele was eventually convicted of murder.

While the detective is sensitive to how well a suspect's story fits what is known about the case, it is sometimes the case that a suspect's story may be true not because it is *likely* to have happened, but because it is *unlikely* to have happened. In this kind of situation, the abductive inference made is quite different from inductive inferences that are based on finding confirmations of scientific theory. Consider the following example by the same author:

> When the police entered the house of Robert and Barbara Parks on February 18, 1950, they found Robert, a thirty-eight-year-old retired army captain, in the bedroom, dead from a gunshot wound. He was lying on the floor near the door to the dining room, with a bullet hole in his right side. The autopsy established that the bullet had passed from right to left through his chest and stopped just on the far side of his heart.

> Park's wife, Barbara, was twelve years younger than the captain, and the couple had a history of violent quarrels. She was also known to have telephoned someone in San Francisco a couple of weeks before, asking for a one-way ticket so she could leave her husband.

> When the police found Barbara, she was hysterical. Her story was that she had been in the kitchen when she heard a shot. Racing into the bedroom, she found her husband standing by the door. He said, "Honey, the gun backfired," and then fell dead.

> The murder weapon, an automatic pistol, was lying against the far wall of the dining room, with one shot fired. The cartridge case had jammed in the ejection port. Forensic investigation showed that Parks could not have been holding the gun himself when it was fired, regardless of how it could have been thrown across the room.

> Barbara Parks was taken to Luray, the nearest reasonably-sized town, and put in jail.

> The investigators had two questions to answer before winding up the case. One was why Mrs. Parks would tell such an improbable story when so many other more plausible tales were available to her: for example, self-defense, or she thought he was a burglar, or he was teaching her how to shoot it when it went off by accident. The other question was how did the brown-painted hot-air grill in the doorway between the dining room and the bedroom get a brand-new dent on it that chipped the paint away down to the metal?

> The detectives wrapped up the evidence; gun, bullet, cartridge case, and hot-air grill were sent to the FBI Crime Laboratory. The FBI technicians verified that the bullet that killed Captain Parks had been fired from that gun, as had the cartridge, and that the gun had been fired from farther away than Parks could have held it.

> But what of the dent in the hot-air grill? The technicians matched it with two points on the slide and hammer of the automatic, and searched for and found microscopic bits of brown paint from the grill on those spots on the gun. In reconstructing the

scene they found that if the weapon had discharged as it struck the grill, the bullet would have hit Parks just where it actually did. Then how did it get all the way across the room? The only scenario that fit was that Captain Parks, a man with a violent temper, threw the gun away from him in a fit, it hit the grill and fired, the bullet hit Parks, the cartridge jammed when the slide was obstructed in its travel by the heating grill, and then the gun bounced across the dining room.

A firearms expert from the FBI Crime Laboratory came to Virginia to testify to these findings. The judge ruled that Park's death was an accident. Barbara Parks' seemingly unbelievable story was true. She was released from jail and went home.[328]

While detectives are trained to look for such evidence and follow their hunches, it is also the case that ordinary citizens often have their own hunches and make such subtle inferences in support of a criminal investigation. Consider the following case of murder in Ypsilanti, Michigan:

The wife of a 53 year-old real estate salesman, William Curtis, was murdered in an apparent robbery attempt. The suspect, 24 year-old Todd Plamondon, was apprehended a hour later driving Curtis' Cadillac, carrying the gun he used and the wife's jewelry; he also had blood stains on his shirt. The crime seemed to be a simple case of a bungled robbery. But after the pictures of Plamondon and Curtis were shown on local TV, two Ypsilanti bartenders felt that they had seen something odd that might be relevant to the case. They called the police and said that they had seen Curtis and Plamondon meet weekly in their bar a couple of months before the murder. Why was this important? The two bartenders weren't sure but they commented:

It was pretty strange to see those two together sitting at the bar... Plamondon was strictly Ypsi [Ypsilanti] local—torn Levis and a T-shirt—but this guy Curtis was always dressed just like the picture, suit and tie... They could come in within five minutes of each other, talk quietly for two or three hours and, except for one time, leave together... Todd would talk to me about the bands that would be playing at night... Curtis never introduced himself. He was pretty quiet... Curtis always paid for both of them.

Why was this likely to be relevant to the murder? Well, it showed that Curtis and Plamondon knew each other well before the murder, making it unlikely that the robbery was just a random act. It would also be unusual for a conservative businessman to meet regularly with a scruffy young man half his age, unless the young man was related to him or worked for him, neither of which was the case here. Further, since Curtis payed for Plamondon's food and drink each time they met, it implied that Curtis was more generous than he needed to be, or was in debt to Plamondon for some reason. If the latter, how could the wealthier Curtis be in debt to Plamondon—he certainly could not be financially in debt to him (None of these possible interpretations was given by the bartenders at the time, they simply reported what they believed to be an unusual set of events.). Why did the police take what the two bartenders said to be reliable or without an ulterior motive? Well, the bartenders had no obvious connection to Curtis, his wife or Plamondon outside of their duties as bartenders, so an ulterior motive was not likely. Further, the evidence they gave the

---

[328] *Op.cit.*, p. 37.

police was not, from their point of view, likely to influence the case in one way or another, so it had no real "point" to it. It was simply something unusual that they had observed and thought might be relevant to the guilt *or* innocence of the individuals involved. It was also the case that the bartenders were students at nearby Eastern Michigan University who were bartending to help put themselves through college. It seemed clear that they were two earnest, responsible young men whose testimony was likely to be true (the article had a picture of them both looking serious and guileless, one with an EMU sweatshirt on).

On the basis of this hunch, the police investigated further and found that Curtis and Plamondon had a long term homosexual relationship that pre-dated the murder by some time. Curtis had, until then, been considered "cooperative" with the police and was "not a suspect at this point." But Curtis suddenly fled and was arrested on a fugitive warrant in Virginia. He was extradited and eventually tried and convicted along with Plamondon.[329] It is clear that real detectives make subtle inferences based on their intimate knowledge of human behavior in the same way that fictional detectives do, and that ordinary citizens are capable of having their own hunches. Often the use of such subtle clues in criminal detection are described without any explanation or justification:

> MIAMI, Aug. 25—The three wooden cargo crates dropped off by a courier at the international airport in San Juan, P.R., for a Delta Air Lines flight to New York City looked harmless. But when the courier's nervousness raised suspicions about their contents, law-enforcement officials looked inside, and found 1,000 pounds of cocaine.[330]

Why would the nervousness of the courier indicate that the cargo might contain illegal drugs? Further, what actions of the courier would be taken as signs of nervousness? The article doesn't have to answer these questions because virtually every adult reader of the **New York Times** would know the answers. But the reader knows the answers in a special way. For the first question, he may be able to *explain* why the nervousness of the courier might indicate that the cargo contained illegal drugs. But for the second question, he might not be able to *explain* exactly what nervousness looks like. He still could be said to know the answer, though—he knows it insofar as he could *recognize* nervousness were he to see it (knowing how vs. knowing that). Such explanations are taken at face value because they draw on our mutual understanding of what Wittgenstein would call the "common behavior of mankind" or "our natural history":

> The common behavior of mankind is the system of reference by means of which we interpret an unknown language. [**PI** §206]

> ... commanding, questioning, recounting, chatting, are as much a part of our natural history as walking, eating, drinking, playing. [**PI** §25]

---

[329] This description, and the quotation by the bartenders, was drawn from two newspaper articles: "Barkeeps: Victim's husband, accused killer met often," **The Ann Arbor News**, 6 April 1991; "Guilty plea in Curtis slaying," **The Ann Arbor News**, 7 October 1991, p. A1.
[330] "At U.S. Ports, Drug Smuggling is Fast Becoming an Inside Job," **The New York Times**, 26 August 1997, p. A1.

Even if the reporter who wrote the article wanted to describe the actions of the courier that indicated his nervousness he might be at a loss to do so in any kind of complete or convincing manner. He might be able to describe certain physical movements that the courier made that indicated his nervousness, such as fidgeting, or being too much in a hurry, or forgetting to take a receipt for the cargo, or any number of other observable actions. But each of these physical movements could have an entirely innocuous interpretation, too. What is it that he did that made authorities think that he was nervous?—Well, he *acted nervous.*[331] We also make the same kind of subtle inferences based on imponderable evidence in noncriminal situations:

[331] It's interesting that a common tactic for a lawyer who might defend the courier would be to pursue a reductionistic strategy and make the witnesses who noted the courier's "nervousness" explain, in court, precisely what they saw in the actions of the courier that made him appear nervous. Inevitably, when the witnesses try to state exactly what they saw that indicated that the courier was nervous—that the courier's hands were trembling or he couldn't look them in the eye—the defense lawyer can bring up perfectly innocent explanations for this behavior: that the courier had had little sleep the night before, or was in an unusual hurry for personal reasons. If the lawyer can show that the witnesses had no certain, unequivocal reasons to interpret the behavior of the courier as being "nervous," then he might be able to show that the search of the cargo was illegal and any drugs found inadmissible as evidence. Such a reductionistic strategy often works for several reasons. First, one aspect of behavior is that there is no single thing that equates with a characteristic such as "nervousness":

> Our concepts, judgements, reactions never appear in connection with just a single action, but rather with the whole swirl of human actions. [**LWPP II** p. 56]

There may be lots of observable things that, together, might indicate nervous behavior, but such a set might be quite large and would often be both unbounded and varying from situation to situation (e.g., what would a nervous soldier look like compared to a nervous public speaker, or a nervous adult compared to a nervous child, etc. There are individual differences, too, since there is a lot of variety in the ways that individuals show their nervousness. There may be cultural differences, too).

> How could human behavior be described? Surely only by sketching the actions of a variety of humans, as they are all mixed up together. What determines our judgment, our concepts and reactions, is not what *one* man is doing *now*, an individual action, but the whole hurly-burly of human actions, the background against which we see any action. [**Z** §567]

This would make it difficult for the witnesses to give a "complete" explanation of what they saw that indicated the courier was nervous. Further, even if we realize that there may be lots of observable things that, together, constitute "nervousness," we may not be able to describe many of them. Wittgenstein comments:

> . . . we recognize normal circumstances but cannot precisely describe them. [**OC** §27]

It may have been the case that there were no necessary and sufficient physical characteristics that indicated that the courier was nervous; that is, the *complete* explanation of why the cargo was searched was that *the courier looked nervous*:

> If I have exhausted the justifications I have reached bedrock, and my spade is turned. Then I am inclined to say: "This is simply what I do." [**PI** §217]

What Wittgenstein is saying is that describing what "nervousness" looks like may be similar to describing what coffee tastes like. Coffee doesn't taste like anything else—coffee tastes like coffee. In the same way, "looking nervous" may not be the sum of a number of characteristics—"looking nervous" is simply "looking nervous." As Wittgenstein puts it:

> After 27 years of patrolling the Golden Gate Bridge, Ron Garcia says that he can
> spot potential suicides as adeptly as a cabbie does fares.
>
> Overly purposeful walkers catch his watchful eye, as do those with flimsy clothing
> on blustery winter afternoons.
>
> "A lot of the people we pick up are people you'll spot and you'll say, 'That one
> isn't right.' It's like a sixth sense you come up with," said Garcia, bridge captain
> for Golden Gate Bridge, Highway and Transportation District.[332]

While such abductive inferences are dramatic, making good newscopy, we make similar
less spectacular assessments of others on a regular basis: when we meet friends, we can
often assess their mood just by looking at them or listening to their tone of voice; we
judge others we don't know by their mannerisms and the circumstances surrounding our
meeting—a complete stranger who approaches us upon our arrival at a large airport late
at night and offers us a ride wherever we want to go might be looked upon with suspicion,
perhaps even fear, while the same stranger coming up to us on a busy city street at noon
asking for directions to a restaurant may be seen as quite ordinary, even sympathetic.
We often assess the intentions of others—whether they are dissembling or biased in their
statements—by similar asessments of subtle, imponderable evidence. And this ability to
assess intentions is an ability that appears very early in our development. Consider the
following description of a study of infant behavior reported in **Science News**:

> Each of us constantly makes assumptions about what other folks believe, want, and
> feel. Now, a new study shows that these inferences about our compatriots' mental
> states may have developmental roots in the first year of life.
>
> By about age 1, infants tend to attribute positive or negative intentions to self-
> propelled objects that pursue simple goals, assert David Premack and Ann James

> The expression "that is all that *happens*" sets limits to what we call "happening."
>
> Here the temptation is overwhelming to say something further, when everything has already
> been described.—Whence this pressure? What analogy, what wrong interpretation produces
> it?
>
> Here we come up against a remarkable and characteristic phenomenon in philosophical in-
> vestigation: the difficulty—I might say—is not that of finding the solution but rather that of
> recognizing as the solution something that looks as if it were only a preliminary to it. "We have
> already said everything.—Not anything that follows from this, no, *this* itself is the solution!"
>
> This is connected, I believe, with our wrongly expecting an explanation, whereas the solution
> of the difficulty is a description, if we give it the right place in our considerations. If we dwell
> upon it, and do not try to get beyond it.
>
> The difficulty here is: to stop.
>
> "Why do you demand explanations? If they are given you, you will once more be facing a
> terminus. They cannot get you any further than you are at present." [**Z** §§312– 315]

"All that happen[ed]" was that the courier "looked nervous." Here, bad epistemology becomes good legal strategy.
[332]"Suicide patrols eyed for GG Bridge," **San Francisco Examiner**, 2 August 1995.

Premack, psychologists at the National Center for Scientific Research in Paris, France.

$$\vdots$$

This suggests that infants have an inherent capacity for discerning such intentions in the goal-directed actions of their parents or anyone else they observe, argues David Premack.

$$\vdots$$

These responses support the theory that infants possess a basic knowledge about intentional actions, the investigators assert in a report accepted for publication in **Cognition**.

Nonetheless, only older children, beginning between age 3 and 5, understand that others may hold distinct mental states, such as false beliefs. "A major question is how the transition occurs from basic intentional knowledge to an understanding of mental states," David Premack contends.[333]

While assessments of other's thoughts or intentions can be right or wrong, they can often be justified and we can even argue about the validity of such inferences. Consider a critical book review by **New York Times** reviewer Christopher Lehmann-Haupt of a prominent book about the Kennedy's: **The Last Brother**, by Joe McGinniss:

How do you read Joe McGinniss's new biography of Senator Edward M. Kennedy, "The Last Brother," without being overwhelmed by the tempest it has already created? You try to read it objectively, but it all too quickly becomes apparent that its problems are even greater than anticipated. The book isn't bad; it's awful.

$$\vdots$$

Writing classes of the future will be richly rewarded by studying the art of inferred hypotheses as wielded in "The Last Brother." My favorite is Mr. McGinniss's explanation for what he perceives to be Senator Kennedy's rather sudden marriage to Joan Bennett: "It is true that no child was born the following year, but also true that if Joan had miscarried (and she later had at least three miscarriages, as well as three children), it would not have been a development the Ambassador [the Senator's father] would have publicized." From this, one is supposed to conclude that because no announcement of a miscarriage was made, Mr. Kennedy married Ms. Bennett because she was pregnant.

As for imagining thoughts: nothing surpasses the way Mr. McGinniss has it both ways trying to read Joseph P. Kennedy's mind long after the former Ambassador to the Court of St. James's had lost the ability to communicate because of his stroke: "Whatever his agonies, they would be locked inside him until death set him free. And whatever his sins, this punishment seemed sufficiently severe: to be forced, every waking hour, to confront the stark fact that his drive for power, glory and freedom from the laws that governed man had been satisfied only through the spilling of his children's blood."

But the area that raises the greatest difficulties in "The Last Brother" is Mr. McGinniss's uncritical appropriation of sources. Any rumor that suits his purposes is fair

---

[333] "Tots show signs of intentional minds," **Science News**, vol. 149, p. 118, 24 February 1996.

game. For instance, he cites the speculation by John F. Kennedy's biographer Nigel Hamilton that Joseph P. Kennedy may have sexually abused his daughter Rosemary and thereby caused the emotional disturbance that later led him to have her lobotomized, presumably to remove an embarrassing stain from the family's image.

After balancing this speculation with mention of Ms. Goodwin's heated refutation of "any such notion," he hits us ungently with how he imagines Rosemary's sudden disappearance might have affected his subject as a youth: "In the absence of any assurances to the contrary, it might well have begun to seem to the 9-year-old Teddy that this could be the price of failure within the family: to suddenly cease to exist." ["Ms. Goodwin" is Doris Kearns Goodwin who is another Kennedy biographer: **The Fitzgeralds and the Kennedys**, Simon and Schuster, 1987]

Where Mr. McGinniss's indiscriminate use of sources gets him into severe difficulties is in his uncritical embrace of the unproved theory that the Mafia assassinated John F. Kennedy for failing to oust Fidel Castro and revive the mob's criminal stake in Cuba, an obligation that Mr. McGinniss says the Kennedys incurred when Joseph P. accepted illegal election help for his son in West Virginia and Illinois.

Mr. McGinniss's version of this conspiracy is built out of highly speculative books like [3 books are mentioned]

    ⋮

And what is Mr. McGinniss's point in embracing such half-baked history? Not to buttress one conspiracy theory against another, but simply to milk the reader's sympathy for Senator Kennedy.

... one of Mr. McGinniss's most spectacular thought inferences [concerns] when his subject is considering whether to run for the Presidency in 1968, after his brother Robert has been killed: "He knew the time was not right, but he knew also that for him, the time would never be right. Why not just jump in and get it done? Maybe somebody would shoot him and then he, too, could die a hero, like his brothers. Then the family destiny would be complete."[334]

Lehmann-Haupt does a surgical job of exposing the improper use of imponderable evidence in McGinness' book. He gives examples where McGinniss appears to read the literal thoughts of many of the principal characters, something that is tough to do for those with whom we are not intimate. If Teddy Kennedy were to speculate on what John Kennedy may have thought at one time or another, it might be more believable than McGinniss' ruminations. In spite of the subtlety and even *ad hoc* character of such imponderable inferences, there seem to be criteria that can lend or take away support for them. Lehmann-Haupt's attribution of a motive for McGinniss' speculation merely adds another reason why McGinniss seems to have gone beyond the bounds of such legitimate inference.

This is not to say that what we take as evidence for some subtle phenomenon cannot change or be culturally contingent. At the Salem Witch Trials in 1692 the evidence used to substantiate the guilt of the witches were the reports of several young girls that the

[334]"The Minds of the Kennedys as Imagined by McGinniss." Christopher Lehmann-Haupt, **The New York Times**, 29 July 1993.

supposed witches had appeared in their dreams. That is, the witches appeared in the girls' dreams because they, the witches, *chose* to appear in them. At that time it was generally believed that only witches could chose to appear in others' dreams, so the individuals who appeared in the girls' dream *must* have been witches. Such an inference in a court of law in present-day New England would be, of course, absurd.

One of the more common places for challenges to inferences to be made is in a criminal trial. This is often where imponderable evidence is debated and sometimes transformed into ponderable evidence. Consider the murder trial of Eric and Lyle Menendez:

> As jurors showed up for another week of deliberations today in the murder trial of Lyle and Erik Menendez, the two panels appeared to be struggling with the trial's central issue: whether the brothers told the truth when they said they killed their parents out of fear for their lives.
>
> Prosecutors challenged the brothers' account that they killed out of fear arguing that they had planned the killings, concocted an elaborate alibi and then lavishly spent their parents' money after the shootings.
>
> The prosecution says that the brothers killed to inherit $14 million from an over-bearing father and to eliminate their mother as a witness.
>
> The brothers said they had bought shotguns at a San Diego sporting goods store for protection. But the prosecution said the manner of the purchase showed that they had tried to cover their tracks: they went out of town, used false identification and paid in cash, even though they usually used credit cards for purchases.[335]

*Conversational Implicatures*

While we have concentrated here on how we uncover the plausible truth that lies behind our hunches, it is also the case that we often bring unquestioned assumptions to our daily social interactions; that is, in a given situation we do not uncover or infer *everything*. Some of our understanding consists of implicit assumptions about what is the case. This is particularly true in our use of language. Paul Grice has identified a number of assumptions that each speaker brings to ordinary discourse; he calls these "Conversational Implicatures." Conversational Implicatures are based on what Grice terms the "Cooperative Principle":

> Our talk exchanges do not normally consist of a succession of disconnected remarks, and would not be rational if they did. They are characteristically, to some degree at least, cooperative efforts; and each participant recognizes in them, to some extent, a common purpose or set of purposes, or at least a mutually accepted direction.[336]

We engage in conversation to *do* things: we ask questions to gain information; we assert things to convince others that such-and-such is the case; we talk informally to others to establish or maintain relationships; we direct others to do things; we make promises; etc.

---

[335] "Juries Ask: Did Brothers Kill Parents Out of Fear?," **The New York Times**, 28 December 1993.

[336] P. Grice, "Logic and Conversation," **Studies in the Way of Words**, p. 26. Harvard University Press, Cambridge, MA, 1989. (\*\*\*cf. G's criticisms of W in Hacker's **Witt's Place in 20th century Analytic Philosophy** pp. 245ff)

In each of these activities the participants normally have a mutual interest in the success of the communication: if we make a promise, our listener is interested in having the promise be made clearly and properly; if we ask a question, our answerer is interested in our being correctly answered; if we chat casually, both of us are interested in maintaining our relationship; etc. Since it is far too arduous a task to test the other's cooperative sincerity each time one engages in a conversation, we generally begin our conversations with the assumption that our participant is cooperating with us, that is, he wants the conversation we are having to proceed as faithfully as possible. This is not to say that we will always find our conversational partners cooperative: others may exaggerate, dissemble or mislead us, or otherwise violate this principle of cooperation. But it is the case that people do cooperate so frequently that it is generally practical to assume someone is cooperating unless there is evidence to the contrary.

Grice does not discuss why such cooperation would be useful since you could still fulfill the purposes of conversation without being cooperative. It *is* clear, though, that the assumption of cooperation makes conversation much more efficient than it would be without such an assumption. Without this assumption, all cooperation and all the implicatures (which we will discuss below) would have to be tested at the beginning of each conversation. Again, that doesn't prevent the attainment of conversational goals, but it does make such activities extraordinarily inefficient. The nearest analog to the assumption of noncooperation—or the non-assumption of cooperation—is the vetting of testimony in a court of law. Here all testimony must be tested and found truthful to be admitted to the purposes of the court. This is a long, often inconclusive process—certainly not the kind of process that we would want to govern our everyday conversations. The most plausible rationale, then, for the assumption of cooperation is that it makes the conversational process faster and more efficient. But this rationale is not just speculation, it fits with an older view of language proposed by George Zipf. Zipf theorized that language use was governed by the Principle of Least Effort. For Zipf, during any communicative act we have a speaker and a hearer. For the speaker and the hearer to understand each other they must both engage in a certain amount of effort: the speaker must find the right words in language to say what he wants to say; the hearer, on the other hand, must interpret what the speaker says in order to understand it fully. We are all governed, Zipf said, by the Principle of Least Effort, that is, we will try to expend the least effort we can to get a job done at a desired level of effectiveness. Neither the speaker nor the hearer wants to expend any more cognitive effort in conversation than he has to. But there is a problem here. For the speaker, he would expend the least amount of effort if he could be as terse in his speech as possible—in the extreme case he might utter a single word for all his communicative acts. Most of the effort would fall on the hearer who must figure out what the speaker means by this single word uttered in a wide range of situations and circumstances (one can imagine an autocratic ruler who merely grunts when he wants something leaving it up to his frantic subjects to figure out what he might desire). So while the speaker expends a minimal amount of effort, the hearer must expend an exceptionally large amount of effort. On the other hand, the hearer can expend the least amount of effort if he can force the speaker to state everything in great and extensive detail so no possible ambiguity would be left unexplained (consider our autocratic ruler again, forcing his subjects to explain themselves in wearying detail while he lounges on his throne eating grapes). This situation, of course, would cause the speaker to expend a tremendous amount of effort. For Zipf, either of these extreme alternatives requires a non-minimal amount of total effort when considering the speaker and the hearer together, that is, when considering the total act of conversation. According to Zipf, the minimum of effort occurs in conversation when both the speaker and the hearer make reasonable efforts to communicate. Specifically, the speaker gives up his idea of using just one word to express many different things, and expands the number of words he uses so the hearer doesn't constantly need to figure out the different meanings the same words might have. The hearer, on the other hand, relaxes his insistence that the speaker explain himself in great and unambiguous detail in each utterance, and agrees to let the speaker use some general words multiple times and permits him a certain amount of vagueness of expression that can be clarified by the context or circumstances of the utterance or some other knowledge the hearer may have. The hearer, then, must expend a reasonable amount of effort to decipher some tolerated ambiguities of the speaker's expressions. According to Zipf, this tacit agreement between speaker and hearer will cause a "balance" of effort to be reached which causes a minimum amount of *total* effort to be expended during the conversational process. For Zipf, the foundation of language use—in fact, the foundation of all behavior—is the desire to expend the least amount of effort in the process. In his Principle of Cooperation, Grice has articulated one of the mechanisms that Zipf claimed would be necessary for conversationalists to communicate as efficiently as possible; that is, with the least amount of effort.[337]

Grice's Principle of Cooperation is based on the satisfaction of nine maxims which fall into four categories: Quantity, Quality, Relation, and Manner:

There are two maxims of Quantity:

1. Make your contribution as informative as is required (for the current purposes of the exchange).

2. Do not make your contribution more informative than is required.

Two maxims of Quality:

1. Do not say what you believe to be false.

2. Do not say that for which you lack adequate evidence.

One maxim of Relation:

1. Say only what you believe to be relevant.

Four maxims of Manner:

1. Avoid obscurity of expression.

---

[337] Zipf"s theory of language is extensive and detailed, and has some strong correlations with Wittgenstein's philosophy of language, especially with Wittgenstein's notion that words are like tools. For a more detailed description of this relationship, see Blair's **Language and Representation in Information Retrieval** [Elsevier Science, New York/Amsterdam, 1990], especially pages 139ff. Zipf's theory is developed most extensively in his **Human Behavior and the Principle of Least Effort**. [Hafner, NY, 1965 (Facsimile of the 1949 edition).]

2. Avoid ambiguity.

3. Be brief (avoid unnecessary prolixity).

4. Be orderly.

Conversation begins with the participants' assumption that all nine maxims are being followed by the participants. Some maxims are clearly more important than others: an individual who expresses himself obscurely would likely be less criticized than one who has knowingly stated something false. Grice also points out that there is some interdependence among the maxims, notably, that many of the maxims only become relevant if the first maxim of Quality is satisfied. It is also the case that other maxims might be added to this list (Grice comments that other maxims of Manner might be necessary). Be that as it may, we are not looking for a complete theory here, but only some indication of what the structure and dynamics of these implicatures might be. In fact, what Grice has outlined are some of the components of conversational Language Games.

The importance of the assumption of cooperation cannot be overstated. For example, consider the following situation: I come in to work in the morning. As I walk past the secretary I ask if my colleague Bill has arrived yet. The secretary replies, "I saw a yellow Volkswagen in the parking lot." Taken literally, this is a bizarre, even incomprehensible statement. But if I make the assumptions that the secretary has understood my question and has tried to satisfy the maxims of cooperation to the best of his ability, then I may be able to make sense out of the seemingly odd statement. That is, the reference to the "yellow Volkswagen" must be *relevant* to my question, so a reasonable supposition is that it refers to Bill's car. The secretary must also know that I know that if Bill were to be in his office he would have driven and parked his car in the lot this morning. The secretary would also know that, in general, yellow Volkswagens are uncommon enough that the appearance of one in a parking lot is likely to be a unique event, indicating the presence of a particular driver, in this case, Bill. The secretary would also have to assume that I would be aware of such general information too. Contrast the above statement with the statement (in answer to my question), "I saw a white car in the parking lot." What does that tell me about Bill's presence? Not much. Even if Bill owns a white car, so do a lot of other people. The presence or absence of a white car in the parking lot tells me little that I want to know. (Interestingly, it does tell me something about the secretary—either he has entirely misunderstood my question, does not have a good grasp of basic facts, like the comparative rarity of white cars, is making some kind of joke, or has just gone silly.)

But the maxims that Grice has identified are not just members of a static list, they are the foundation for a number of extremely subtle communicative acts. Let's look at some of these. In the first place, the maxims are subject to variation based on other aspects of the circumstances or context in which the conversation takes place. For example, a study showed that if someone with a New York accent asks directions on a New York City street, he will generally be given brief, explicit directions. But if someone with a Texas accent asks for the same directions in exactly the same way as the New Yorker did, the person he asks will often give him much more detailed instructions than he gave the New Yorker. The direction-giver has automatically altered the maxim of Quantity—he has increased the level of informativeness he assumes is needed for the Texan. Why? Because, on the basis of the Texan's accent alone, the direction-giver has surmised that he, the Texan, is not as likely to be as familiar with New York City as an typical New Yorker might be. Consequently, the Texan would need more detailed street directions ("See that street behind you? Go up there two blocks to Broadway, take a left..."), rather than broader references to unconnected landmarks ("Go to Grant's Tomb, then..."). We do the same sort of thing when talking to small children, altering the level of informativeness and perhaps some of the maxims of Manner to talk to them "at their level." The degree by which we alter the levels of satisfaction for the maxims is not something that we calculate. It is something we do based on experience, and the immediate feedback that we might receive from the person we are talking to (e.g., if we are too detailed in our statements our listener might say, "OK, OK, you don't have to be so detailed, I understand the basics."). But there are times when it may be impossible to fulfill all of the maxims, even if the speaker wants to do so. For example, we may not be as informative as we know we should be without violating the second maxim of Quality: to say only that for which we have adequate evidence.

Of particular importance is the subtle information that can be conveyed through the systematic *violation* of one or more of the maxims. That is, it is not just what we *say* that is part of the informativeness of a conversation, our level of compliance with the maxims of cooperation also convey important information. For example, suppose I ask a friend why our car won't start. He replies that it is undoubtedly because I am out of gas. Yet I know that there are innumerable other reasons why my car might not start—wet or grounded electrical system, low battery cranking voltage, poor fuel and oxygen mixture, bad spark plugs, etc. By giving a simplistic answer, my friend has violated the first maxim of Quantity: he has not been as informative as he should have. If I can assume that he has not done this on purpose, his lack of informativeness tells me that he knows little about the workings of an automobile. Yet, he has nowhere explicitly admitted to such, and probably does not even know how naive he really is.

Let's look at some examples of how the intentional violation of the maxims can be used to inform the listener of something implicit in the exchange. Consider a high school student asking a mathematics instructor how to do a particular calculation. The instructor explains how to do it, but the student still doesn't understand. The instructor then explains the calculation again, this time in somewhat more detail. The student claims that he still does not understand how to do the calculation. This is repeated a number of times. Finally, the instructor begins to explain the calculation including trivial detail: "First you find a pencil, then you get a piece of paper, then you add the first two numbers by making marks on the paper with the pencil and counting the marks, 1, 2, 3, 4 ... " It should be obvious to the student that the instructor is purposefully including too much detail for a high school student. If the student believes that the instructor is sincere in wanting to teach him, and that although he made a reasonable effort to explain the calculation, the student must explain why the instructor has switched from being helpful, to being obviously not helpful. The most likely explanation is that the instructor is irritated at the student's inability to understand her, and is telling him, basically, "I've tried to explain this to you, but you don't seem to be making an effort to understand what I am saying (or, you didn't come adequately prepared), therefore I am no longer willing to help you. You must find some other means of learning the calculation."

Another kind of intentional violation of the cooperative principle might be willful equivocation. For example, we ask our friend, "I didn't see you at the meeting last Wednesday, where were you?" Our friend answers, "I couldn't make it." Since he offers no more explanation, we might pursue the issue with, "Why couldn't you make it?" If our friend answers this with, "Some other things came up" he has not only *not* told us what prevented him from attending the meeting, he has also implied that he does not *want* to tell us the reason, either.

Or, another example: I ask a friend, "Is Jennifer seeing Stuart again?" He responds, "I saw his car parked at her house the other evening." I reply, "Are you saying that she *is* seeing him?" Our friend replies, "I didn't say that!" Of course our friend really *is* saying that he believes Jennifer is seeing Stuart, but by implying it then denying that he is implying it he is really saying, in effect, "I think that she is seeing him, but don't tell anyone that *I* said so!" Here our friend is violating the maxim to say only that which he believes to be true. He asserts something—that Jennifer is seeing Stuart again—while at the same time denying that he is asserting it (he is not only violating one of the maxims of Quality, he is also *stating* that he is violating it).

## Wittgenstein and Behaviorism

The mind-body dualism has been both a persistent framework and a longstanding irritant in philosophy. Plato was the first major figure to make this distinction, but it was Descartes who first proposed a system based on the nature and interrelationships between mind and body. This dualism is attractive because it models two kinds of seemingly separate entities, or, at least, two different kinds of statements. But maintaining the dualism poses obvious problems about how, if mind and body are separate entities, they can interact, for clearly they do. Some theories of interaction suffer from the same infinite regression of Aristotle's third-man criticism of Plato (see the previous section "Universals and Particulars-An Old Debate"). It is beyond the scope of this discussion to present the rich history of the mind-body debate, but some discussion of it can illuminate Wittgenstein's position *vis à vis* behaviorism, and help us to understand his later philosophy. One possible solution to the mind-body distinction, which we have already discussed, is to defeat this dualism by reducing the mind to the body—that is, reducing mental processes to brain states (this is commonly called "materialism"). We have already shown how Wittgenstein rejects this "solution." Another monistic "solution" is to go in the opposite direction and reduce the mind to the *externally observable* body—that is, to reduce mental processes to behavior. Because Wittgenstein continually forced our investigation of meaning away from internal, mental phenomena towards outer, observable phenomena his epistemology is often seen to be some form of behaviorism. What's important is not whether Wittgenstein is a behaviorist or not—and there are lots of different versions of behaviorism that could apply—but whether any of these versions of behaviorism when applied to Wittgenstein's work is at all misleading. It is my contention that labeling Wittgenstein's epistemology a form of "behaviorism" misrepresents his work in important ways. Behaviorism traces its antecedents back to Thomas Hobbes who attempted to interpret all mental states as forms of matter in motion. But modern, more attractive forms of behaviorism began in the early 20th century with J.B. Watson. Watson wanted to establish psychology as an objective science by freeing it of the subjectivism of introspection:

The committed behaviorist, Watson declared, will drop "from his scientific vocabulary all subjective terms such as sensation, perception, image, desire, purpose, and even thinking and emotion as they were subjectively defined." This is not merely because these concepts are insufficiently sharply defined for "scientific purposes." Rather, there is no such thing as consciousness as traditionally conceived. "The belief in the existence of consciousness," he wrote contemptuously, "goes back to the ancient days of superstition and magic." The scientific psychologist "can do without the terms 'mind' and 'consciousness,' indeed he can find no objective evidence for their existence." Hence "the behaviorist recognizes no such things as mental traits, dispositions or tendencies."[338]

Since Watson, psychologists, such as Skinner have offered alternative versions of behaviorism, in particular, alternative descriptions of what counts as *behavior* (Watson's notion of behavior was so broad that it included even physiological processes such as the beating of the heart, while Skinner proposed that only the "action of the organism upon the outside world" should count as behavior.).[339] In philosophy, as we pointed out, behaviorism is a direct attack on the duality of the mind and the body. We can identify three major kinds of behaviorism: *metaphysical, methodological* and *logical*. *Metaphysical* behaviorism is the most extreme version, denying that there are mental phenomena at all; *methodological* behaviorism does not deny mental phenomena, but it stipulates that they should not be used to explain behavior since they are not directly accessible by more than one individual; *logical* behaviorism claims that statements about mental phenomena or processes are semantically equivalent to statements about behavior.[340]

Philosopher Gilbert Ryle offered the most sustained attack on mind-body dualism in his **The Concept of Mind**[341] where he termed the Cartesian view "... the dogma of the ghost in the machine." Ryle's work is often called behaviorism, but Wittgenstein's early work is most closely associated with Carnap's logical behaviorism which he, Carnap, called "physicalism." So similar were some of Wittgenstein's early views with Carnap's that Wittgenstein accused him of plagiarism in 1932.[342] The dispute is curious, since, as

---

[338] P.M.S. Hacker. **Wittgenstein, Meaning and Mind. Part I: Essays** [Vol. 3 of an **Analytic Commentary on the Philosophical Investigations**). Blackwell, Oxford, 1990, p. 97]. Hacker cites Watson's **Behaviorism** [Kegan Paul, Trench, Trubner, and Co, London, 1924] pp. 5f (first three quotations), 2, 18, and 98, respectively.

[339] For the antecedents of modern behaviorism, see, principally: Thomas Hobbes. De Corpore; J.B. Watson. *op.cit.* B.F. Skinner. **The Behavior of Organisms**. NY, 1938. Skinner made the most effort to extend his version of behaviorism beyond the traditional boundaries of psychological research. Of particular interest is his behavioral interpretation of linguistic meaning in **Verbal Behavior** (New York, 1957). Noam Chomsky's strident criticism of Skinner's theory of language in his review of **Verbal Behavior** was the opening clarion call of his enormously influential theory of transformational grammar, which dominated linguistics for the next several decades (Chomsky's review appeared in **Language**, vol. 35, pp. 26–58, 1959).

[340] Behaviorism can also be distinguished as either molar or molecular. Molar behaviorism investigates the relations between stimuli and observable responses, while molecular behaviorism attempts to discover the physiological laws that underly and support the relations found by molar behaviorism.

[341] G. Ryle. **The Concept of Mind**. NY, 1949.

[342] P.M.S. Hacker writes:

When Wittgenstein resumed philosophy in 1929, behaviorism was definitely in the air. There is no evidence to suggest that he read Watson's book, but he certainly read Russell's Analysis of Mind, in which Watson's ideas are discussed. It seems likely that at some stage he at least

Hacker points out, Wittgenstein never gave what could be described as a logical behaviorist version of first-person psychological statements.[343] He did give something like a logical behavior analysis of third-person psychological assertions, but that is not sufficient to label him a behaviorist. From that point, Wittgenstein's subsequent philosophy moved much farther away from the model of logical behaviorism, although many readers of his later work still insist that it harbors behaviorist ideas, at least implicitly. Such a belief is unwarranted, as we shall see.

### Wittgenstein *vs.* Behaviorism: What is "Behavior"?

Perhaps the most fundamental difference that Wittgenstein has with behaviorism would be over the definition or concept of "behavior" itself. Most behaviorists insist that behavior consists of observable human actions, either at the social level, for *molar* behaviorism, or at the physiological level, for *molecular* behaviorism. Wittgenstein would accept the relevance of certain physical movements, but considers them only part of what he would call behavior. If behavior were merely physical movements, then we should be able to photograph behavior. As Wittgenstein put it:

> looked at Carnap's **Logische Aufbau**, and he definitely read the first of the **Erkenntnis** articles in 1932, which occasioned a quarrel. Wittgenstein accused Carnap of plagiarism, and held that Carnap's ideas concerning physicalism were derived from the **Tractatus**, conversations Wittgenstein had held with Waismann and Schlick in which Carnap had participated, and reports of Wittgenstein's new ideas circulated to members of the Vienna Circle by Waismann. He abruptly severed relations with Carnap. [Hacker, **Wittgenstein, Meaning and Mind. Part I: Essays**, p. 105 (Vol. 3 of an **Analytic Commentary on the Philosophical Investigations**). Blackwell, Oxford, 1990. The full name of Carnap's book is **Der Logische Aufbau der Welt**. Berlin, 1928 (English translation: **The Logical Structure** of the World, translated by R.A. George. Routledge and Kegan Paul, London, 1967). Carnap's two articles appeared in **Erkenntnis**, pp. 432–465, II, 1932; and **Erkenntnis**, pp. 165–197, III, 1932/ 1933.]

The philosophical connection between analytic philosophy and behaviorism did not originate with Carnap but with Bertrand Russell eleven years earlier. In the preface to his **Analysis of Mind** (1921) he states:

> I think that what has permanent value in the outlook of the behaviorists is the feeling that physics is the most fundamental science at present in existence.

The conflation of psychology and physics—more precisely, behaviorism and empiricism—gave the hope of a "unified science" as at least a theoretical possibility. Such a concept would have had great appeal to the philosophical group called the Vienna Circle, of which Carnap was a part. Wittgenstein's view of such a synthesis could be inferred from his statement about the "barrenness of psychology" in which he insisted that psychology is not like physics, at all (see footnote 241, *supra*).[The above quotation by Russell is not meant to imply that he agreed entirely with Watson's, or behaviorism's views. Quite to the contrary, there is one tenet of Watson's behaviorism that he explicitly rejects:

> [Behaviorism's] denial of images is indefensible: they cannot be interpreted as actual small sensations, or as words. Quoted by R. Monk in his **Bertrand Russell: The Spirit of Solitude: 1872–1921**, p. 545. Free Press, NY, 1996.]

[343] *Ibid.*

> If behaviourism is correct, then it would be intelligible to say that a camera perceives.[344]

Yet it is clear that filming human actions does not necessarily record legitimate behavior. Consider a film which depicts two actors making an agreement and shaking hands. Did they really make an agreement? No, it only looks that way—they just "went through the motions." But the film *by itself* cannot tell us that for it could just as easily be used to record an actual agreement (between heads of state, for example).

Laughing, joking, arguing, persuading, being afraid, being happy, being depressed, etc. All these "behaviors" call up easy images of individuals manifesting them. But because these images are so easy to imagine, we often don't see some important aspects of the behavior they represent. To shake us out of these easy images, Wittgenstein gives us a number of examples of the behavior of animals:

> Can I then speak of one behaviour of anger, for example, and of another of hope? (It is easy to imagine an orang-utan angry—but hopeful? And why is it like this?) [**RPP I** §314]
>
> One can imagine an animal angry, frightened, unhappy, happy, startled. But hopeful? And why not?
>
> A dog believes his master is at the door. But can he also believe his master will come the day after to-morrow?—And *what* can he not do here?—How do I do it?—How am I supposed to answer this? [**PI** p. 174][345]

Wittgenstein answers this question, ironically, in an *earlier* part of **Philosophical Investigations**:

> Why can't a dog simulate pain? Is he too honest? Could one teach a dog to simulate pain? Perhaps it is possible to teach him to howl on particular occasions as if he were in pain, even when he is not. But the surroundings which are necessary for this behaviour to be real simulation are missing. [**PI** §250]

We can imagine a dog frightened or happy, but not hopeful or simulating pain. A dog can be frightened or happy not just because of his actions, but because there are legitimate circumstances in which we might find dogs where these behaviors would be seen as genuine. A dog can't be hopeful or simulate pain because we *cannot* imagine the dog being in circumstances which would legitimate such behavior. What about people? How would we portray a person who is *angry*? Well, we should remember Wittgenstein's "Dramatic Theory of Meaning" ($q.v.$):

---

[344] Wittgenstein's unpublished "Big Typescript" (ca. 1933) p. 462. Cited by Nicholas Gier in his **Wittgenstein and Phenomenology: A Comparative Study of the Later Wittgenstein, Husserl, Heidegger, and Merleau-Ponty**, p. 135. State University of New York Press, Albany, NY, 1981.

[345] In **LWPP II**, §§358–360 are similar to the first two statements, supra, but they include the following statement between them in §359:

> For hoping is quiet, joyful expectation. (Even though there is something repugnant about this kind of analysis.)

> The best example of an expression with a very specific meaning is a passage in a play. [**LWPP I** §424]

The director of a play might have an actor portray anger by scowling, raising his voice (if talking), acting agitated, perhaps shaking his fist, etc. Circumstances seem to play less of a role here; just the mannerisms of the individual in question seem to be sufficient to convey anger, and these mannerisms would probably be convincing in just about any normal context. But what about portraying a person who is *hopeful*? Unlike anger, there are no obvious expressions or other physical mannerisms that are uniquely characteristic of being hopeful. Something more is needed, we need the right "stage settings," as Wittgenstein reminds us. How would we portray being hopeful in a play? Well, it would require more context than portraying anger. Imagine a scene in a play: a man is wheeled into an operating room for a dangerous operation, his wife bids him goodbye with tears in her eyes. Some time later, the surgeon enters the room where the wife is waiting. She looks up as he approaches her. Can't we say here that she looks hopeful? And what about a dog's expecting his master to come the day after tomorrow? Can we devise a scene in a play that would convey that to an audience? Probably not.

We might take Wittgenstein's use of plays to demonstrate meaning and behavior a step further: behavior might be explained as *that which can be portrayed and understood in a play*. This sounds enough like a definition to make anyone who understands Wittgenstein uncomfortable. But, like Wittgenstein's coupling of meaning and use, we can certainly say that *for a large class of cases—though not for all*—we can *explain* behavior as that which can be portrayed and understood in a play.[346] It does not hold for all cases because we can portray some impossible behavior in a play—like someone flying (using a wire), someone disappearing in a puff of smoke, someone reading someone else's mind, etc. But, again, for a large number of cases, what can be portrayed in a play is a touchstone of legitimate human behavior, and while some behaviors portrayed in a play are not legitimate behaviors, there are no legitimate human behaviors that cannot be portrayed in a play. This is as close to a definition of behavior as we can get. The importance of the right circumstances to legitimate behavior can be seen in the following example:

> Why can't my right hand give my left hand money?—My right hand can put it into my left hand. My right hand can write a deed of gift and my left hand a receipt.— But the further practical consequences would not be those of a gift. When the left hand has taken the money from the right, etc., we shall ask: "Well, and what of it?" [**PI** §268]

If circumstances and context are not necessary for legitimating behavior, then my right hand really *could* give my left hand a gift by just making the appropriate bodily movements. But if we try to define behavior as just bodily movements, there is a further problem, namely, that the same bodily movements, without reference to context or circumstances, could mean a wide variety of things. That is, it would be impossible to tell what specific,

---

[346] The quotation I allude to is:

> For a *large* class of cases—though not for all—in which we employ the word "meaning" it can be explained thus: the meaning of a word is its use in language. [**PI** §43]

bodily movements meant outside of the relevant circumstances. For example, imagine two individuals shaking hands: are they actually shaking hands, or is one pulling the other by the hand? Even if they were just shaking hands, are they shaking hands to seal an agreement, shaking hands to say "hello," or, are they shaking hands for the benefit of a photographer. Two hands clasped together tell us very little. This is what Wittgenstein is getting at in the following example:

> Suppose we were observing the movement of a point (for example, a point of light on a screen). It might be possible to draw important consequences of the most various kinds from the behavior of this point. And what a variety of observations can be made here!—This is how it is with the behavior of man; with the different characteristic features which we observe in this behavior. [**PI** p. 179]

Wittgenstein's analogies make us aware of how important circumstances are for legitimating *all* human behaviors. Now we can understand Wittgenstein's description of what he means by "behavior":

> Take the various psychological phenomena: thinking, pain, anger, joy, wish, fear, intention, memory etc.,—and compare the behavior corresponding to each.—But what does behavior include here? Only the play of facial expression and the gestures? Or also the surrounding, so to speak the occasion of this expression? And if one does include the surrounding as well,—how is the behavior to be compared in the case of anger and in that of memory, for example? [**RPP I** §129]

Wittgenstein answers these questions 34 pages later:

> ...the word "behaviour," as I am using it, is altogether misleading, for it includes in its meaning the external circumstances—of the behaviour in a narrower sense. [**RPP I** §314]

So now we see behavior as consisting of specific physical/bodily movements embedded within legitimating context and circumstances. But when we observe behavior, even in specific circumstances, what is it we actually see—just physical movements? Wittgenstein remarks:

> "I see that the child wants to touch the dog, but doesn't dare." How can I see that?—Is this description of what is seen on the same level as a description of moving shapes and colours? Is an interpretation in question? Well, remember that you may also mimic a human being who would like to touch something, but doesn't dare. And what you mimic is after all a piece of behavior. But you will perhaps be able to give a characteristic imitation of this behavior only in a wider context.

> One will also be able to say: What this description says will get its expression somehow in the movement and the rest of the behavior of the child, but also in the spatial and temporal surrounding.

> But now am I to say that I really "see" the fearfulness in this behavior—or that I really "see" the facial expression? Why not? But that is not to deny the difference between two concepts of what is perceived. A picture of the face might reproduce its features very accurately, but not get the expression right; it might, however,

be right as far as the expression goes and not hit the features off well. "Similar expression" takes faces together in a quite different way from "similar anatomy." [**RPP I** §§1066–1068]

Wittgenstein makes a crucial distinction when he asks how he can observe the child's fear of touching the dog. Is what he sees here the same as when he sees "moving shapes and colors," that is, un-interpreted perceptions of physical phenomena? No, it is not. If behavior was just "moving shapes and colors" then, as he commented before, a camera could perceive this kind of behavior. But, clearly, we could not photograph the child's fear of touching the dog. What the observer sees is not the anatomical movements of the child's face and body, he sees *a fearful child.* Fear is not comprised of a fixed set of bodily movements for the simple reason that these bodily movements can be feigned by an individual who is not afraid at all. But even in the case where someone *is* actually afraid, their fear can be manifested behaviorally in a unlimited variety of ways. It is possible that we could see fear manifested in a way that we had never seen before, and *still* know that this new manifestation is *fear.* How would we know this? Well, we see a person caught in circumstances where a reasonable individual with his background *should* be afraid. The behavior of fear is a very complex *form of life* consisting of bodily movements, performed by individuals with certain kinds of experience or training, in particular circumstances, and which often have "further practical consequences." How does our presumption of experience or training in the observed individual help us to understand his behavior? Suppose that we are in a crowded coffee shop and we observe someone moving his hands in quick, distinctive movements. Are his movements just nervous twitches? Is he going through some exercise for physical therapy? Or, is he "talking" with American Sign Language for the Deaf? Clearly, if we know that he is recovering from a severe hand injury, or that he is deaf, or that he is neither of these, then we can make some reasonable assessments of what his hand motions are (or, are *not*) likely to mean. The interpretation of behavior requires not only present, immediate perceptions, but sometimes also a knowledge of the kind of relevant training or experience that the person being observed might have undergone.

For Wittgenstein, a "similar expression" *does not* mean a "similar anatomy." This means that "expression" and "anatomy" are only loosely coupled, and not *causally.* The desire to express a particular feeling might be a *reason* why someone makes certain facial movements, but it is not a *cause.* So here is another difference between behaviorism and Wittgenstein: behaviorism seeks to establish the *causes* for observable behavior, while Wittgenstein believes that there are no *causes* for behavior—there are only *reasons* for acting in particular ways.

It's helpful to see behavior as a kind of language. Traditionally, language had been seen as the representation of thought—that is, we have thoughts and then translate them into written or spoken language. Wittgenstein conflated thought and language by showing that instead of language representing or being a product of thought, language is often the *means by which* we think ("language is itself the vehicle of thought" [**PI** §329]). A similar relation exists between behavior and feeling. Traditionally, behavior was thought to represent feeling—that is, we have feelings and then translate them into certain specific behavior. Wittgenstein conflated this duality, too, by insisting that behavior is part of the feeling itself. We don't have feelings and then translate them into behavior, or have feelings that *cause* behavior, we have *expressive behavior*—behavior that is part of the feeling process. Now we can see why different behaviors can go along with the same feeling: it is analogous to the fact that different words can have the same "meaning." Like language, behavior can be unpredictable and creative, and in the same way that we can understand a sentence we have never seen or heard before, we can often understand behavior we have never seen before.

## Wittgenstein *vs.* Behaviorism: Reductionism

Most versions of behaviorism are characterized by some form of reductionism, for example, mental phenomena being reduced to observable behavior or behavior being reduced to physical movements. But Wittgenstein's later work is strongly anti-reductive:

> Our craving for generality has another main source: our preoccupation with the method of science. I mean the method of reducing the explanation of natural phenomena to the smallest possible of primitive natural laws... This tendency is the real source of metaphysics, and leads the philosopher into complete darkness. I want to say here that it can never be our job to reduce anything to anything... [**BB** p.18]

Any reductive system is implicitly dualistic, so in denying reductive analysis in philosophy, Wittgenstein is also denying the dualisms on which it is based.

## Wittgenstein *vs.* Behaviorism: The Existence of Mental Phenomena

Another difference which Wittgenstein has with behaviorism is with metaphysical behaviorism's belief that mental processes or events are, as Watson put it, "superstition and magic." While Wittgenstein directed our attention away from mental processes and towards those human life forms that we all could observe or experience, he was quite clear that he was not denying the existence of mental phenomena. This is evident from one of his longest and most important discussions about behavior:

> "But you will surely admit that there is a difference between pain-behavior accompanied by pain and pain-behavior without any pain?"—Admit it? What greater difference could there be?—"And yet you again and again reach the conclusion that the sensation itself is a *nothing*."—Not at all. It is not a *something*, but not a *nothing* either! The conclusion was only that a nothing would serve just as well as a something about which nothing could be said. We have only rejected the grammar which tries to force itself on us here.

> The paradox disappears only if we make a radical break with the idea that language always functions in one way, always serves the same purpose: to convey thoughts—which may be about houses, pains, good and evil, or anything else you please.

> "But you surely cannot deny that, for example, in remembering, an inner process takes place."—What gives the impression that we want to deny anything? When one says "Still, an inner process does take place here"—one wants to go on: "After all, you *see* it." And it is this inner process that one means by the word "remembering."— The impression that we wanted to deny something arises from our setting our faces against the picture of the 'inner process'. What we deny is that the picture of the inner process gives us the correct idea of the use of the word "to remember." We

say that this picture with its ramifications stands in the way of our seeing the use of the word as it is.

Why should I deny that there is a mental process? But "There has just taken place in me the mental process of remembering. . . " means nothing more than: "I have just remembered. . . " To deny the mental process would mean to deny the remembering: to deny that anyone ever remembers anything.

"Are you not really a behaviorist in disguise? Aren't you at bottom really saying that everything except human behavior is fiction?"—If I do speak of fiction, then it is a *grammatical* fiction.

How does the philosophical problem about mental processes and states and about behaviorism arise?—The first step is the one that altogether escapes notice. We talk of processes and states and leave their nature undecided. Sometime perhaps we shall know more about them—we think. But that is just what commits us to a particular way of looking at the matter. For we have a definite concept of what it means to learn to know a process better (The decisive movement in the conjuring trick has been made, and it was the very one that we thought quite innocent.).—And now the analogy which was to make us understand our thoughts falls to pieces. So we have to deny the yet uncomprehended process in the yet unexplored medium. And now it looks as if we had denied mental processes. And naturally we don't want to deny them.

What is your aim in philosophy?—To shew[*sic*] the fly the way out of the fly-bottle. [**PI** §§304–309]

These are important, but difficult passages, and deserve some commentary: In paragraph one, Wittgenstein begins with a clear statement about the ". . . difference between pain-behavior accompanied by pain and pain-behavior without any pain." If there is a difference, as Wittgenstein admits there is, then there must be some "inner" mental component of these two identical behaviors that distinguishes them. Having said that, Wittgenstein makes one of his most cryptic remarks about the mental component of pain: "[the sensation] is not a something, but not a nothing either!" Wittgenstein has seemingly placed his conception of sensation in the previously "excluded middle" between "something" and "nothing." Wittgenstein is making a very subtle, but important point: pain sensation is neither an object nor a "thing," in the way that we ordinarily conceive a thing to be. But it cannot be "nothing" either, otherwise there would be no difference between the behaviors of feeling pain and feigning it. What gives us the idea that there is no "middle ground" between "something" and "nothing?" The *grammar* of these two words does it—it forces itself on us. Since we know that we have sensations—that they exist—the sense of the "excluded middle" forces us to think that since a sensation is not "nothing" it *must be* "*some* thing" or "*some* mental phenomenon." What's wrong with this? Well, by treating a sensation as a "thing" we fall into that unproductive disease of thinking whereby we think "sensations" are *objects* that can be found and examined in the same way that a geologist examines rock samples. This leads us to think of "sensations" as *one thing*, or *one kind of thing*. This, in turn, can lead us to look for the "location" of sensations in the brain—if they are "things" then they must be *located* somewhere. If the neurologist sees a difference between the CAT scans of a person who is in pain and someone who is merely feigning pain, this "object-language" of sensations may encourage him to interpret the difference in the CAT scans as an actual physiological representation of the thing we know as "pain." The neurologist's mistake is *not* an empirical mistake, it is, as Wittgenstein insists, a *grammatical* one. Our language has forced us to interpret our milieu in a particular, biased way. What are "sensations," *really*? Wittgenstein gives us no answer, here. He simply resists the grammatical temptation to declare them either "objects" or "nothing"—"It is not a *something*, but not a *nothing* either!" [*supra*]

This simple referential language, as we described above, should sound familiar. It is the language of Augustine (see the section "Wittgenstein at Work: Philosophical Investigations," *supra*). For Augustine, language works in only one way, and words are names for "things"—here, the "things" are "thoughts" or "sensations."[347] The "paradox" that Wittgenstein refers to in the quotation we are considering is, of course, that "pain" is neither a "something" nor a "nothing." The paradox is resolved by the realization of two things: first, language does not work in just one way; and, second, even though there *are* instances where language can best be described as consisting of *names* which refer to *things/objects,* the words "pain" and "sensation" do not fall within the language-game of simple reference. Freed from this grammatical straight-jacket, we can withold our judgment of what sensations *are*, pending further analysis, which, of course, could be either a grammatical or an empirical analysis. To reiterate, the important point is that whether a sensation is a "something" or a "nothing" is *not* an empirical distinction, but a *grammatical* one. If we think that it is an *empirical* distinction then we are forced to choose between two alternatives: if we believe a sensation is a "something" then we are lead down the same fruitless path as the neurologist with his CAT scans; but if we believe that a sensation is a "nothing" then we are forced into the dead end of metaphysical behaviorism which denies the very existence of mental phenomena.

In the third paragraph, *supra*, the Augustinian view of language—that words name objects—rears its head again in a more insidious form. Wittgenstein is asked whether or not he denies that "...in remembering, an inner process takes place." Here, Augustine's simple referential language takes the form of designating a "thing" called an "inner process." Wittgenstein, at one and the same time, admits that there is an "inner process" that occurs when we remember, but denies that what we refer to as an "inner process" is a "thing" of any kind. The danger of giving "something" a precise name, is that, if we are not careful, the naming process can reify what is named as a kind of "object." Having given these mental phenomena names, the empiricist/psychologist will design his experiments to "discover" these "things"—the "inner processes." We should not be surprised when he finds them. But what he finds fits a *grammatical* form, not an *empirical* one.

If the problem we have is *grammatical*, as Wittgenstein insists, then the solution must involve some grammatical change. In the next paragraph, Wittgenstein shows us how: "But 'There has just taken place in me the mental process of remembering...' means nothing more than: 'I have just remembered....'." We need to adopt a non-referential language, here. If we say a "mental process of remembering" took place, we are committed

---

[347] Words need to stand for "thoughts" rather than just "things/objects" in order to allow words to refer to things that do not currently exist; for example, unicorns, Millard Fillmore, water-proof teabags, etc.

to identifying *remembering* with "some-thing." But if we just say, "I remembered..." then we do not fall into this grammatical trap. We can now apply this method to other referential statements: "I *have* a pain" becomes, "I'm hurting"; "I *have* an idea what to do" becomes, "I know what to do." If we recall the discussion in footnote 262 about "mental maps," we can see some of the same kind of grammatical disease of thinking taking place. A "mental map" is, as we pointed out, a metaphor that has been taken too literally; and when we take it literally, we are then committed to the Augustinean language of simple reference again. This leads to such spurious inferences as, "Most animals have a rudimentary mental map of the world encoded in nerve tissue..." If we say that animals "have" a mental map, then it is easy to infer that there must be a "something" that equates with the "mental map." But when we do not find the "mental map" in any obvious "place," it is easy to fall into the trap of locating it in the place where we can't easily look, the "nerve tissue." That is, if we "have" a "mental map," it must be *located* somewhere. Again, this is *not* an *empirical* imperative, but a *grammatical* one.

Is Wittgenstein saying that we should get rid of all such references in our language? No, he is not, for the simple reason that we can "make sense" using these references—people understand me when I say that I "have a pain" or "have an idea." This is a language game that is perfectly legitimate for me to engage in. Wittgenstein's admonishment is for epistemologists and psychologists, or anyone else investigating cognition. These are the people who must avoid the " bewitchment of our intelligence by means of language." [**PI** §109]

Wittgenstein then asks the obvious question (of himself):

> "Are you not really a behaviorist in disguise? Aren't you at bottom really saying that everything except human behavior is fiction?"—If I do speak of fiction, then it is a *grammatical* fiction. (*supra*)

Since Wittgenstein says that sensations are "not a something" it looks like we have no "thing" linked to our behavior. All we have left that is anything is *behavior* itself, hence, Wittgenstein *must* be a behaviorist, though he seems to deny it. But what Wittgenstein denies is not the mental phenomena, but the "particular way of looking at the matter" that is forced on us by our grammar. This particular way of looking at the matter is to see behavior somehow "linked" to mental processes and states, as names are "linked" to objects in Augustine's view of language. How does this happen? Wittgenstein tells us:

> How does the philosophical problem about mental processes and states and about behaviorism arise?—The first step is the one that altogether escapes notice. We talk of processes and states and leave their nature undecided. Sometime perhaps we shall know more about them—we think. But that is just what commits us to a particular way of looking at the matter... (The decisive movement in the conjuring trick has been made, and it was the very one that we thought quite innocent.) (*supra*)

The "decisive movement in the conjuring trick," in Wittgenstein's wonderful metaphor, is the naming of these mental processes and states. Naming them accomplishes two things: first, it separates them and treats them as independent objects, and, second, the name gives the process or state a deceptive familiarity—don't we really *know* what "fear" is, or "enthusiasm?" So we are committed to treating these mental processes as objects which we are basically familiar with. This familiarity keeps us from looking too deeply into what these processes and states are, or, more importantly, whether they exist at all in the independent manner that their names, that is, their grammatical usage, suggest. If we combine this naming and reification of mental phenomena with a penchant for seeing the physical and the mental as separate, then it is easy to see how the grammar of these statements gets us into this particular "disease of thinking." All of this is a "grammatical fiction" because it has no real empirical basis—it is simply a way that we talk about these things that has forced us into a "particular way of looking at the matter"(*supra*).

## Wittgenstein *vs.* Behaviorism: Intersubjective Knowledge

*Methodological* behaviorism rejects the consideration of mental phenomena, not because they don't exist, but because they are not directly accessible to more than one individual. Wittgenstein, as we already discussed, did not believe that our thoughts and feelings were entirely inaccessible to others (this is discussed in the section "Wittgenstein and Crime: The Breakdown of the Distinction Between Inner and Outer Processes."):

> My thoughts are not hidden from him, but are just as open to him in a different way
> than they are to me. [**LWPP II** p. 34]

## Wittgenstein *vs.* Behaviorism: Logical Behaviorism

Wittgenstein's philosophy, albeit his early philosophy, comes closest to the logical behaviorism—termed "physicalism"—of Carnap. In spite of the fact that Wittgenstein accused Carnap of plagiarism in developing physicalism Wittgenstein has clear theoretical differences with him. In particular, Carnap built his theory on a foundation of *methodological solipsism* which holds that the primary source of our knowledge is first-person experience. Our knowledge of other's feelings or thoughts is inferential in character: for example, "He is in pain" is known by inferring that he behaves the same way that I do when I am in pain. There are a number of problems with this self-referential learning. In the first place, not only is it difficult to observe ourselves and make the appropriate inferences, but often we're not even aware that our own behavior can be a reference for determining the behavior of others. Wittgenstein comments:

> If someone imitates grief for himself in his study, he will indeed readily be conscious
> of the tensions on his face. But really grieve, or follow a sorrowful action in a film,
> and ask yourself if you were conscious of your face. [RPP I §925][348]

The answer, of course, is that we are *not* conscious of our own face when we try to interpret another's facial expressions. This is easy to see if we ask ourselves how we determine the meaning of a puzzling expression in another person. If our own face were a reference point, then we might find a mirror, look into it, and try to make the same expression that puzzles us in the other individual. Having made the expression in question in a mirror, though, it is unclear what we would do next. The relation between the expression and a

---

[348] This is very similar to **Z** §503: If someone acts grief in the study, he will indeed readily become aware of the tensions in his face. But be really sad, or follow a sorrowful action in a film, and ask yourself if you were aware of your face.

feeling or thought is not causal, as we have shown, so there is no obvious thought or feeling that would be linked to it and uncovered by this process—one can have a smile on one's face for a lot of different reasons, even when one is in unhappy circumstances. It is clear, though, that we often see puzzling expressions in the faces of others and are somehow able to figure out what they mean. How do we do this? The most direct method is to ask the other person why he made such an expression; but if we can't do that, the next most obvious method is to try to determine what circumstances he is in. Personal knowledge will certainly play a role here, but it is knowledge of shared activites—forms of life—that tell us what the other person is going through, not his physiognomy. This would give us the context and circumstances in which the expression would "make sense." Any expression taken out of the context in which it occurred can be ambiguous. Consequently, facial expressions are usually secondary to circumstances and activities when an interpretation must be made. Wittgenstein continues:

> "Putting the cart before the horse" may be said of an explanation like the following: we tend someone else because by analogy with our own case we believe that he is experiencing pain too.—Instead of saying: Get to know a new aspect from this special chapter of human behavior—from this use of language.
>
> :
>
> Being sure that someone is in pain, doubting whether he is, and so on, are so many natural, instinctive, kinds of behavior towards other human beings, and our language is merely an auxiliary to, and further extension of, this relation. Our language-game is an extension of primitive behavior. (For our language-game is behavior.) (Instinct).[349]

We may need to learn to recognize when people are in pain, and we may make inferences during this learning process. Further, there may be instances where we have to figure out whether someone is in pain or not. But in the ordinary cases, once we have learned to recognize pain in others, what we see is not a set of behaviors from which we infer that so-and-so is in pain—we see *a person in pain*. Wittgenstein comments:

> We do not see facial contortions and make inferences from them (like a doctor framing a diagnosis) to joy, grief, boredom. We describe a face immediately as sad, radiant, bored, even when we are unable to give any other description of the features.—Grief, one would like to say, is personified in the face.
>
> This belongs to the concept of emotion. [Z §225]

There is also a problem with the process of inference. The relation between behavior and a feeling (e.g., pain) is, as we pointed out, not causal—lots of different behaviors can indicate pain. We can see an entirely new manifestation of pain behavior and still know that it is pain we are looking at. More importantly, we can't always make a clear inference to our own behavior because the person we are looking at may exhibit pain behavior that is very different from our own. If the relation between behavior and feeling is not causal, then any inferences necessary to determine what a given behavior means are much

---

[349] **Z** §§542–545, resp. In the section "The Foundation of Language in Instinctive Behavior" we discussed how language can be a form of expressive behavior that can refine and extend nonlinguistic behavior.

more problematic and certainly defeasible. As a consequence, Carnap's attempt to base understanding of behavior on personal, inferential knowledge, is tenuous at best. Carnap went even so far as to claim that our knowledge of ourselves is, like our knowledge of others, inferential in nature. The sentence "I am now excited" is supported by such assertions as "I feel my hands trembling," "I see my hands trembling," "I hear my voice quavering," etc.[350] In effect, we determine how we feel by marshalling evidence for it. Wittgenstein would not agree with this proposal. If we need to gather evidence to determine whether we are "excited," then it implies that there will be cases where we will surmise we are excited, since it is supported by sufficient evidence, and cases where we may think we are excited but do *not* find sufficient evidence to support this. In short, we could be *wrong* about how we feel. Once again, the grammar of our language highlights the problem: We can say, "I know he is excited, but I could be wrong." But we cannot say, "I know I am excited, but I could be wrong." For Wittgenstein, the declaration "I am excited" is not a statement about what we have found out through some sort of investigation. It is not *knowledge* because being mistaken is implicit in the act of knowing. The statement "I am excited" in not a statement of knowledge, it is an *avowal*. In other words, it is not a statement *about* my behavior, it is an expression *of* my behavior. My statement "I am excited" is a substitute for, or extension of, my pain-behavior:[351]

> The truth is: it makes sense to say about other people that they doubt whether I am in pain; but not to say it about myself. [**PI** §246]

## Why Wittgenstein is not a Behaviorist: A Summary

It is fairly clear that Wittgenstein is not a behaviorist in any sense of the term. While his early work in the **Tractatus Logico-Philosophicus** has some *prima facie* similarities with Carnap's logical behaviorism, careful reading indicates that Wittgenstein harbors some decisive differences with even Carnap's work. As Wittgenstein's philosophy moved into its later phase where he looked at language, behavior and psychology more deeply, only a superficial reading would give one the idea that Wittgenstein was a behaviorist of any form. His major differences with behaviorism can be summarized as follows:

1.  Wittgenstein held that "behavior" was not the simple aggregation of bodily move-ments that many behaviorists believed it to be. Wittgenstein's concept of "behavior" included not just physical movements but also the context and circumstances which surround them, and the training and experience of the individuals involved. These are the sorts of things which you would have to put in a play to legitimate an actor's portraying such behavior. Much behavior is embedded in, and derives meaning from, forms of life—the common day-to-day activities that comprise "what we do."

2.  Some forms of behaviorism utilize an explicit reduction of mental phenomena to physiological or behavioral phenomena. Wittgenstein rejects all forms of reduction in this kind of analysis. Reduction purports to apply the scientific method to

---

[350] R. Carnap. "Psychology in Physical Language," **Logical Positivism**, pp. 165–197. Allen and Unwin, London, 1959. Edited by A.J. Ayer.
[351] *Vid.* section "The Foundation of Language in Instinctive Behavior."

psychology. But, according to Wittgenstein, the scientific method is out of place here—it is the wrong language game to be using in psychology or epistemology. One of the aims of philosophy is to clarify our statements. This doesn't require reduction, but is best served by descriptions of "perspicuous representations" of usage.

3. Wittgenstein believed in the existence and importance of mental phenomena, which metaphysical behaviorism does not. Methodological behaviorism, on the other hand, accepts the existence of mental phenomena, but it did not believe that they should be used in analysis since they were not accessible intersubjectively.

4. But Wittgenstein believed that we *can* often know what others are thinking or feeling, even if they do not tell us, and sometimes even when they try to hide their thoughts and feelings from us.

5. For logical behaviorism, our knowledge of others is based on our personal experience and is inferential in nature. Wittgenstein did not agree that this kind of knowledge is inferential, but, in many cases, was directly accessible (e.g., we do not see certain behavior and infer that someone is afraid, we see *someone who is afraid*).

6. Logical behaviorism held that self-knowledge is inferential in nature too—that I observe certain aspects about myself, that my hands are trembling, for example, and infer that I am nervous. Wittgenstein held that statements like "I am nervous" are not expressions of knowledge inferred from observations of ourselves, but are *avowals*—these expressions are not *about* behavior, but are a form of behavior themselves.

# Part III: Wittgenstein, Language and Information

The general features of Wittgenstein's philosophy of language could be summarized as follows:

i. **"Meanings" are not linked to words.**

ii. **"Meanings" are not concepts or any other single thing.**

iii. **To understand the meaning of a word** is not to have some definition in your head, but to be able to use the word correctly in the activities and practices (Wittgenstein's "Forms of Life") in which it is normally used, and to know how to use it (Wittgenstein's "Language Games").

iv. **Meaning emerges from or becomes evident through use.** "... we don't start from certain words, but from certain occasions or activities" [**LC** p.3].—"Let the use of words teach you their meaning." [**PI** p. 220]

v. **While examining the use of language is important for understanding meaning, Wittgenstein is clear that not just *any* usage is relevant. He felt that meaning in language was conveyed most clearly by what he called a "perspicuous representation"** ("übersichtliche Darstellung").
"A main source of our failure to understand is that we do not *command a clear view* of the use of our words.—Our grammar is lacking in this sort of perspicuity. A perspicuous representation produces just that understanding which consists in "seeing connexions" [*sic*]. Hence the importance of finding and inventing *intermediate cases*.
"The concept of a perspicuous representation is of fundamental significance for us. It earmarks the form of account we give, the way we look at things." [**PI** §122]

vi. **Context is important for understanding language.** We often understand the situation in which language is used before we understand the words used. Meaning, in part, is an external notion—what we have in our heads, our ideas, are neither necessary nor sufficient for determining what we mean: context and circumstances are often essential determinants of meaning.

vii. **Indeterminacy in language is not the result of sloppy or irrational usage.** Language meaning reflects the complexity of usage, that is, the wide variety of circumstances and activities in which it can be used, and the same word may have different meanings in different circumstances or activities. "If a pattern of life is the basis for the use of a word then the word must contain some amount of indefiniteness. The pattern of life, after all, is not one of exact regularity" [**LWPP I** §211]. Most of the troublesome indeterminacy in meaning arises, as Wittgenstein put it, "when language *goes on holiday...*" [**PI** §38]. This occurs primarily when language is taken out of its normal circumstances and patterns of usage. The apparent lack of precision in meaning is not something that can be "cured" by better definitions of words or by creating a more "rational" ideal language to replace our present language. Ambiguity in meaning is mitigated by looking at how the words in question are actually used.

viii. We make a variety of assumptions about the **intentions** of those with whom we talk. In particular, unless given evidence to the contrary, we assume that the individuals with whom we talk will cooperate with us and follow Grice's maxims (Although Grice developed his theories of language many years after Wittgenstein's death, since they were based on the interaction between speakers, i.e., on context and circumstances, Wittgenstein would have probably agreed with them.).

## Support for Wittgenstein's Philosophy of Mind: Robotics and "Scaffolding"

### Where is the Mind?

As compelling as Wittgenstein's arguments are for his theories of language and cognition, it is reasonable to ask whether there is any more recent work that support his conclusions. There is. Wittgenstein is quite clear in his related assertions that "meaning" is not a mental entity or activity,[352] that thinking does not take place exclusively in the head,[353] and that the conscious thoughts or other "psychological phenomena" we have do not correspond to parallel brain processes.[354]. Wittgenstein leaves us with these tantalizing assertions without specifically telling us why he believes them to be the case. Although the careful reader can get a sense of why Wittgenstein believed these claims to be true, Wittgenstein nowhere gives us a concise argument for their support (see the section "Language and Cognition" in Part I of this manuscript for a justification of Wittgenstein's position). Fortunately, there is now growing support for these assertions coming out of recent work in robotics and neuroscience. Andy Clark's book **Being There**[355] gives us a clear sense of this movement

---

[352]"And nothing is more wrong-headed than calling meaning a mental activity! Unless, that is, one is setting out to produce confusion." [**PI** §693]

[353]"It makes as little sense to ascribe experiences, wishes, thoughts, beliefs, to a brain as to a mushroom." [N. Malcolm. **Nothing is Hidden: Wittgenstein's Criticism of His Early Thought**, p. 186. Basil Blackwell, Oxford, 1986.]

[354]"No supposition seems to me more natural than that there is no process in the brain correlated with associating or with thinking; so that it would be impossible to read off thought-processes from brain-processes.

⋮

It is thus perfectly possible that certain psychological phenomena cannot be investigated physiologically, because physiologically nothing corresponds to them.

⋮

The prejudice in favour of psychophysical parallelism is a fruit of primitive interpretations of our concepts. For if one allows a causality between psychological phenomena which is not mediated physiologically, one thinks one is making profession that there exists a soul side by side with the body, a ghostly soul-nature." [**Z** selected from §§605–611]

[355]A. Clark. **Being There: Putting Brain, Body, and World Together Again**. MIT Press, Cambridge, MA, 1997.

away from psychophysical parallelism, and offers a more complex view of the "mind" than the simple traditional notion of the mind being "in the head."

To ask the question "Where is the mind?" or even just to use the word "mind" is to commit oneself implicitly to the existence of something called a "mind." In Part I we saw how Wittgenstein warned us that a similar "disease of thinking" occurs when we ask "What is the *meaning* of a word?"—by using the word "meaning" we give meaning an implicit, independent existence, and the form of the question is seductively similar to more straightforward questions like "What is the *height* of Mount Ranier?" This grammatical parallel encourages us to assume that there is the same concise, determinate answer to the question about "meaning" as there is to the question about the height of Mount Ranier. A similar situation occurs with the use of the word "mind." When we ask "where is the mind?" we expect the same kind of answer that we would get with the parallel question "Where is the pineal gland?"

## The Mind: "Who's in Charge Here?"

One aspect of cognition that Clark takes up that Wittgenstein does not explicitly address, is the notion of the mind as being a "central controller" or "central planner." Yet the idea of a central planner is implicit in the idea of cognition being epistemically based and a product of a single entity—the mind. When Wittgenstein insists that we don't "think... in our heads" he is, I suggest, adopting a view that is consistent with Clark's rejection of the "central planner." Wittgenstein's objection to the purely cognitive foundation of behavior is clear when he states:

> There is a kind of general disease of thinking which always looks for (and finds) what would be called a mental state from which all our acts spring as from a reservoir.[356] [**BB** p. 143]

Clark rejects both the need for a central planner and the cognitive foundation of behavior. The principal reason for this, Clark asserts, is that the central planner represents a prohibitively inefficient way for us to manage what we do. Interestingly, the evidence to support this view comes largely from work in robotics:

> The New Robotics revolution rejects a fundamental part of the classical image of mind. It rejects the image of a *central planner* that is privy to all the information available anywhere in the system and dedicated to the discovery of possible behavioral sequences that will satisfy particular goals. The trouble with the central planner is that it is profoundly impractical. It introduces what Rodney Brooks aptly termed a "representational bottleneck" blocking fast, real time response. The reason is that the incoming sensory information must be converted into a single symbolic code so that such a planner can deal with it. And the planners' output will itself have to be converted from its proprietary code into the various formats

---

[356] This does not say, of course, that none of our actions is the result of a mental state, only that our actions are not necessarily the result of a mental state.

needed to control various types of motor response. These steps of translation are time-consuming and expensive.[357]

One of the ways that Clark bolsters his claim that there is no central planner to control our behavior or motor skills is to offer the suggestive analogy of how more observable complex behavior may be carried out in ways that do not require a central planner, either:

> Complex phenomena exhibit a great deal of self-organization. Bird flocks do not, in fact, follow a leader bird. Instead, each bird follows a few simple rules that make its behavior depend on the behavior of its nearest few neighbors. The flocking pattern emerges from the mass of these local interactions—it is not orchestrated by a leader, or by any general plan represented in the heads of individual birds.[358]

Sometimes the overall pattern of behavior of the group emerges from the reactions of individuals to small changes in their local environment. Clark calls this "stigmergy." He gives an example of termites building a nest in which individual termites respond to the placement of mud balls by other termites and place their own mud ball in a position relative to the others. Through the repetition of this process by thousands of termites a complex nest of many arches, cells, chambers, and tunnels is created. The important point is that no single termite has an overall plan for the nest, nor does the overall plan exist in any other form. Yet by means of these basic stigmergic actions a nest can be built that is beyond the planning capability of any individual termite.[359]

## Scaffolding

> Much seems to be fixed, and it is removed from the traffic. It is so to speak shunted onto an unused siding.

> Now it gives our way of looking at things, and our researches, their form. Perhaps it was once disputed. But perhaps, for unthinkable ages, it has belonged to the **scaffolding** of our thoughts. (Every human being has parents.) [**OC** §§210–211]

Some human activities are stigmergic in nature, though Clark makes it clear that true stigmergy is quite inflexible since it mandates a specific response to each triggering condition. People have more flexibility in their responses to triggering events than insects do, but more importantly, they can intentionally alter their environment in ways that will elicit the kinds of responses that they want to get. Clark calls this process "scaffolding." Scaffolding provides external augmentation for intelligent activity that permits us to achieve outcomes that would be difficult or beyond the capability of a single, unassisted individual. This external assistance can be physical (e.g., a hammer, a truck, a boat), cognitive (e.g., reference

---

[357] Clark, *op.cit.*, p. 21. Clark does not give an exact citation for the work of Brooks to which he refers, but he does cite two of his works a couple of paragraphs before: R. Brooks. "Coherent behavior from many adaptive processes," **From Animals to Animals** 3. MIT Press, 1994. Edited by D. Cliff, *et al.* R. Brooks and L. Stein. "Building Brains for Bodies," Memo 1439. Artificial Intelligence Laboratory, Massachusetts Institute of Technology, 1993.

[358] Clark, *op.cit.*, p. 40. Clark claims that this is one of the central messages of his work. He follows this example with several others.

[359] Clark, *op.cit.*, p. 75.

books, methods of estimation, rules of thumb, explicit procedures) or social (e.g., creating guilds of craftsmen to establish professional standards, building professional societies to facilitate the dissemination of professional information, and to monitor professional conduct, or, gathering individuals together to collaborate in the solution of a complex problem).[360] It is this ability to alter our immediate environment to augment our abilities and stimulate specific actions that gives us the capability to perform exceptionally complex tasks: from building a house, to constructing a dam, to designing the equipment that can take astronauts to the moon, and return them safely to the earth. Scaffolding occurs even on a simple level when we make subtle changes in our environment to, for example, help us remember things: we can put an overdue library book on the driver's seat of our car so that when we get into the car next we will see the book and be reminded to return it. Or, we can leave notes to ourselves stuck to prominent places, like the refrigerator, to remind us of things we need to do.

Some of the most interesting scaffolding is that which we do in order to enable several individuals to work together to perform a complex task that would be difficult or impossible for a single person to perform. An exceptionally rich and detailed example of this kind of deliberate scaffolding is described in Hutchins' **Cognition in the Wild**[361] where the author describes a long and detailed study of the complex process of navigation on a Navy ship. This is an interesting example because it involves the collaboration of several individuals, each of whom brings a different kind of expertise to the activity, and it requires a kind of precision and low fault tolerance that puts significant pressure on the individuals involved to work together and get all the procedures right.

## Scaffolding and the Rational Model of Choice

The choices that are available to us are dictated by the scaffolding that surrounds and permeates what we do. We are not, Clark points out, fully rational agents with a comprehensive set of preferences and complete or perfect information about the situations in which we act. Our rationality, as Simon[362] described, is "bounded": we make choices based on the alternatives available to us and the amount of information we are capable of considering in the process of choosing.

But Clark's notion of scaffolding is even more radical than Simon's "bounded rationality." Simon's model is an adjustment, albeit an ingenious one, of the rational model, but, as such, it is still anchored in the model of rational choice. The model of rational choice

---

[360] Clark traces the roots of the idea of scaffolding back to the Soviet psychologist Lev Vygotsky [**Thought and Language**. MIT Press, Cambridge, 1986. Translation of the 1962 edition]. As Clark describes it: "Vygotsky stressed the way in which experience with external structures (including linguistic ones, such a words and sentences...) might alter and inform an individual's intrinsic modes of processing and understanding" [Clark, *op.cit.*, p. 45]. The more general notion of "...mind as inextricably interwoven with body, world and action" [*op.cit.*, p. xvii] has its antecedents in the works of Martin Heidegger [**Being and Time**. Harper and Row, 1961. Translation of 1927 edition. ] and M. Merleau-Ponty [**The Structure of Behavior**. Beacon Press, 1963. Translation of 1942 edition.]

[361] E. Hutchins. **Cognition in the Wild**. MIT Press, Cambridge, MA, 1995. Clark also cites Hutchins' work as an example of scaffolding.

[362] H. Simon. **Models of Bounded Rationality**, vol. 1 and 2. MIT Press, 1982.

dictates that choices can be made entirely by conscious deliberation. That is, we can make the best choices by considering available information and thinking about how it influences the alternatives that we have—rational choice becomes the exercise of rules on data. These data are mostly "facts" about the decision situation, but can also include such values as preferences, utilities, expected monetary values, etc. All of these can be represented in some context-free, objective manner. The rational model claims that all decisions can be represented this way, and in the stronger versions of the rational model, it is held that this is the way that the mind actually makes decisions, even when it is operating unconsciously.

Hubert Dreyfus[363] wrote persuasively decades ago about the inadequacy of the purely rational model of choice or mind. But there is growing evidence that we don't make our choices following anything like the purely rational model, except in a few very limited kinds of decision-making. Nor is it possible to represent all the factors that influence our choices as "facts," "data" or "preferences" of some kind. Even the "transitivity of choice"—one of the central assumptions of the rational model of choice, has proved to be unreliable.[364] One of the most concerted attempts to make the rational model of choice work has been Lenat's "CYC Project," a decades-long, multi-million dollar attempt to enable a computer to have the commonsense understanding of a child. CYC attempts to do this by creating an enormous storage of "facts" and some methods of using these facts to understand ordinary human situations. CYC aims to make use of many of the commonsense things that we all know, but never explicitly mention. Things like, if you go into a restaurant, you are probably hungry, or if something large is between you and the place that you want to go, you will have to go around it to get there. The underlying idea behind CYC is that having commonsense is just a matter of having lots and lots of explicit facts about us, our common circumstances and activities.

Clark considers the CYC project and concludes that the rational model of intelligence that it represents is "absolutely, fundamentally, and fatally flawed."[365] For Clark, much of our knowledge comes not from lists of explicit facts and rules, but from our active involved dealings with the world. Our minds are not objective, independent rational choice calculators, but are pattern completers "embedded" in our daily activities—as Wittgenstein put it, in the "bustle" and "hurly-burly" of "what [we] do."[366] This, of course, is a viewpoint championed by Dreyfus 3 decades ago, and echoed in the pre-Artificial Intelligence philosophies of Wittgenstein, Heidegger and Merleau-Ponty.[367] This kind of

---

[363] H. Dreyfus. **What Computers Can't Do**. The original edition is over 3 decades old and was a sharp critique of Artificial Intelligence's claims that we could model how the mind works with rules and facts. Dreyfus' critique is still relevant today, and his book is now in its 3rd edition (Ironically, this edition was published by MIT Press, the publisher and the institution which adopted the early model of rationality that Artificial Intelligence defended so vigorously and Dreyfus criticized so sharply).

[364] A. Tversky. "Intransitivity of Preferences," **Psychological Review**, vol. 76:1, pp 31–48, 1969.

[365] Clark, *op.cit.*, p. 4.

[366] See Part I, section "Forms of Life."

[367] Clark acknowledges these antecedent criticisms of the rational model of intelligence:

> "Major philosophical critics of AI have long questioned the attempt to induce intelligence by means of disembodied symbol manipulation and have likewise insisted on the importance of situated reasoning (that is, reasoning by embodied beings acting in a real physical environment)." [*Op.cit.*, p. 4]

intuitive, involved knowledge that resists explicit description comes out nicely in Mark Twain's description of his training as a 19th century Mississippi riverboat pilot. Twain describes a critical event in his education as recounted in his semi-autobiographical **Life on the Mississippi.** [In this passage, the pilot has just ordered Twain, the apprentice pilot, to steer the boat over what Twain thinks is a deadly reef which will sink the boat]:

> [Twain] [we] made a straight break for the reef. As it disappeared under our bows I held my breath: but we slid over it like oil.
>
> [Pilot] "Now don't you see the difference? It wasn't anything but a *wind* reef. The wind does that."
>
> [Twain] "So I see. But it is exactly like a [real] reef. How am I ever going to tell them apart?"
>
> [Pilot] "I can't tell you. It is an instinct. By and by you will just naturally *know* one from the other, but you never will be able to explain why or how you know them apart."
>
> [Twain] It turned out to be true. The face of the water, in time, became a wonderful book—a book that was a dead language to the uneducated passenger, but which told its mind to me without reserve, delivering its most cherished secrets as clearly as if it uttered them with a voice. And it was not a book to be read once and thrown aside, for it had a new story to tell every day.[368]

What we have for minds are not rational, objective calculators, but, in Clark's words, "embodied minds"—minds that are not bounded by the skull, but are intimately coupled with bodies which are actively situated in the world and are participating in activities and practices. Much of the information that we garner from our environment cannot be represented formally at all, and can, in some sense, only be *felt* by active participants in the world. This interplay between the rational part of our mind and its inseparable embodied, feeling part is easy to see in Clark's example of solving a jigsaw puzzle. When we work on a jigsaw puzzle, it would probably be impossible to put the right pieces together by just thinking about which pieces might fit, without actually trying to fit them together. By thinking, we can estimate which pieces are good candidates for fitting together, but we can't *really* tell which ones go together without actually trying to fit them together. The decisiveness of the "snap" of two pieces going perfectly together is not possible to have by a purely rational attempt to fit them together.

Another aspect of scaffolding that may be important is the physiological effect it may have on the brains of those who use it, especially the brains of youngsters. In Part I of this manuscript, Merlin Donald pointed out that the young brain is highly plastic and "can grow connections, and lose connections, in many different ways, depending on early experience."[369] The "shared patterns of acquired behavior" that we engage in can literally

---

[368] M. Twain. **Life on the Mississippi.**

[369] See the section in Part I "Instinctive Behavior and Forms of Life," especially the quotation from Donald's work.

"restructure the mind." In this sense, scaffolding can have a self-reinforcing aspect to it, the more it is used, the more necessary it becomes to the behavior it augments, especially for younger individuals. There is already some preliminary evidence of how dependent we have become on the scaffolding of personal computers and PDA's (Personal Digital Assistants). Consider the following news article:

> "Computer-mad generation has a memory crash"
>
> *by* Cherry Norton and Adam Nathan
>
> *The New York Times* [February 4, 2001]:
>
> GROWING numbers of people in their twenties and thirties are suffering from severe memory loss because of increasing reliance on computer technology, according to new research.
>
> Sufferers complain they are unable to recall names, written words or appointments, and in some cases have had to give up their jobs.
>
> Doctors are blaming computer technology, electronic organisers and automatic car navigation systems. They claim these gadgets lead to diminished use of the brain to work out problems and inflict "information overload" that makes it difficult to distinguish between important and unimportant facts.

## Scaffolding and Computerized Information Systems

Scaffolding is clearly one of the important things that computerized information systems can provide. Ideally, computers are designed to augment individual information searching and retention capabilities. They allow us to store increasingly large amounts of information of all kinds—data, text, images, audio, hypertext, and compound documents, etc. They also enable us to search through information at remarkable physical speeds.

## The Boundaries of the Mind

In the section "Language and Cognition: What do We Have in Our Heads, and What is it Good for?" in Part I, we discussed how we not only frequently use implements in our surroundings to help us think, but in some situations these implements may be the *sine qua non* of thought. Wittgenstein mentions passingly about thinking with "pencil and paper" and Malcolm develops this example more carefully.[370] The upshot is that many of

---

[370] Clark also uses the example of mathematical calculation in his discussion of how we can extend the capability of the mind with "pen and paper":

> Most of us... can learn to know at a glance the answers to simple multiplications, such as $7 \times 7 = 49$... But longer multiplications present a different kind of problem. Asked to multiply $7222 \times 9422$, most of us resort to pen and paper (or a calculator). What we achieve, using pen and paper, is a reduction of the complex problem to a sequence of simpler problems beginning with $2 \times 2$. We use the external medium (paper) to store the results of these simple

us simply cannot do basic arithmetic calculations without paper and pencil, and few of us can do complex calculations without being able to write them down. If we take away the paper and pencil, we simply cannot do the calculations—we *cannot think*. And calculations are not the only kinds of mental activity that require some kind of essential augmentation. We cannot compose a scholarly paper of any length, without actually writing it down, reviewing it, revising it, and adding related quotations from books, articles or personal notes. All of these materials are not just supplemental to the process of writing but are essential to it, they are part of the "scaffolding" of scholarly work. Neither I, nor any of my colleagues, can compose a paper, much less a book such as this one, without writing it down, and without reading and looking up a lot of related material in established sources. It is not enough to have the idea or insight, one must be able to look at it and revise it—visions often need revisions. This usually requires us to record it in some way, thereby increasing the accuracy and longevity of our "memory." Thomas Edison's observation that inventions are "1% inspiration and 99% perspiration" is just as applicable to writers as it is to inventors.

This brings us back to the questions what, and where is the *mind*? It is clear that Wittgenstein and Clark do not believe the mind to be exclusively *in the head*, nor do they believe that its capabilities are limited to what we can think. As Clark put it:

> Much of what we commonly identify as our mental capacities may likewise, I suspect, turn out to be properties of the wider, environmentally extended systems of which human brains are just one (important) part.[371]

Wittgenstein said that we can think with pen and paper, accepting the notion of scaffolding, in principle. So, where is the mind? For Wittgenstein, talking about mind and body is to commit one self to a dichotomy that is more of a grammatical distinction than an empirical one. Wittgenstein's solution to the perils of the "mind/body" distinction is simply to not make the distinction. Philosophers are confronted with the problematic nature of the dichotomy between brain and mind forgetting that they made the original distinction to *begin with*. For Wittgenstein the solution is not to find some way of putting mind and body back together again, but of not breaking them apart in the first place. This is easy to do if we avoid the overly abstract view of language and restrict our study of language and its relation to thought to ordinary usage—to examine language in the Language Games and Forms of Life in which it finds its home. The issue of the mind/body dualism simply doesn't come up if we look at ordinary usage. To accept the mind/body dualism is to be caught between Scylla and Charybdis: one is forced to choose between two equally problematic alternatives: either the mind *is* the brain—the materialist's solution—or the mind is the immaterial "inhabitant" of the body, the "ghost in the machine" as Ryle aptly called it—the idealist's solution. But, Wittgenstein's "solution" is that what perceives,

---

problems, and by an interrelated series of simple pattern completions coupled with external storage we finally arrive at a solution. Rummelhart *et al.* comment: "This is real symbol processing and, we are beginning to think, the primary symbol processing that we are able to do. Indeed, on this view, the external environment becomes a key extension to our mind." [*op.cit.*, pp. 60–61]

[371] Clark, *op.cit.*, p. 214.

thinks, or acts is not a "mind" or a "brain" but a living human being who is caught up in the "bustle" and "hurly-burly" of everyday life and interactions with others. This is the foundation for the analysis of intelligent activity, not neurons and synapses. This is Wittgenstein's solution to the mind/body dualism. Clark appears to agree:

> ... we must recognize the brain for what it is. Ours are not the brains of disembodied spirits conveniently glued into ambulant, corporeal shells of flesh and blood. Rather, they are *essentially* the brains of embodied agents capable of creating and exploiting structure in the world.[372]

## Scaffolding and the Role of Language

For Clark, language has a major role in scaffolding. Language gives us a means by which we can dramatically reduce the complexity of intelligent activity. It does this in a number of ways. First, language can give us notational systems such as those used by formal mathematics and logic which permit us to say fairly complex things very concisely and to draw conclusions and make comparisons that would be difficult to do without them. Language also gives us the means by which to construct specialized languages like those for biology and physics. In more mundane tasks we use language to make lists and schedules, and to exchange messages which simplify planning and collaboration. One of the most obvious ways in which we simplify our intellectual tasks is to offload much of our memory into diaries, notebooks, memos, and other recording media, many of which are now in electronic format which adds further capabilities to these recordings (e.g., text which is in electronic format is easier to store, transmit, and copy than paper versions of it would be).

One of the most common uses of language is as a label or sign. These deceptively simple artifacts are of great use for reducing the complexity our immediate environment, and can be made to correlate with other media such as maps or diagrams. Labels and signs are so commonplace that we quite literally could not get along without them—the computational complexity of our tasks would be far too difficult. It is no wonder that one of the first things that resistance fighters often do when their country is invaded is to take down or change all the road signs ahead of the advancing enemy.

The closest affinity that Clark has with Wittgenstein comes when he considers the relation between language and thought:

> ... we use words to focus, clarify, transform, offload, and control our own think-ings. Thus understood, language is not the mere imperfect mirror of our intuitive knowledge. Rather, it is part and parcel of the mechanism of reason itself.[373]

As Wittgenstein put it, "When I think in language, there aren't "meanings" going through my mind in addition to the verbal expressions: the language is itself the vehicle of thought." [**PI** § 329]

---

[372] Clark, *op.cit.*, p. 220.
[373] Clark, *op.cit.*, p. 207.

# Mental Models

One of the more interesting parallels between Clark and Wittgenstein is with the utility of mental models. Wittgenstein, as we showed in Part I, was not an advocate of mental models when the models are taken to be detailed representations of aspects of reality that we are concerned with, and these models are a *requirement* for our understanding of, and interaction with, these aspects of reality [See, "The Mind and Reality: Mental Models or Scribbled Jottings?" in Part I for a more detailed discussion of this.]. As an example, Wittgenstein considers our ability to find our way across a large city. Just because we can find our way across the city does not mean that we have some kind of detailed cognitive representation of the city, a "mental map," that we can look at like a real map. What we have is the *ability to find our way across the city*. This ability, according to Clark is not contingent on our having a detailed mental model of the city but of our ability to use our experience of *being in the city* to complete partially remembered patterns. This is why we often can't remember our way around the city without actually being *in the city*, and why we can only remember a complex route across a city *as we travel it* (see Part I).[374] Like Wittgenstein, Clark is skeptical about the utility of detailed mental models to mediate intelligent activity such as finding our way across the city. Creating and using mental models to mediate complex intelligent activity, according to Clark, would put an intolerable cognitive burden on our ability to do things. In the example of the city, we would not only have the effort of constructing a detailed, three-dimensional mental model of the city, we would also have to continually update it to reflect changes in reality—traffic jams, road construction, detours, or how the lighting at different times of day makes visual landmarks look different. What is the solution? If we can't use complex mental models efficiently, then what do we use? As I stated in Part I, we don't need a mental model of the city because we have the city itself "out there"—it is part of the world we live in, feel comfortable in, and find familiar. We can avoid the creation and maintenance of complex three-dimensional mental models because, "The world is its own best representation."[375] If we refer to the world itself instead of a detailed mental model of the world, then we don't have to keep a model of the world in mind, we don't have to constantly refer to it, and we don't have to continually update the model as we use it.[376] If we don't have detailed mental models of the reality we interact with, then what do we have? Churchland,

---

[374] This criticism of detailed mental models has its origin in Wittgenstein's more general claim that what we "have in mind" are not mental entities that we can examine the way we might examine objects in reality. What we "have in mind" are more or less detailed mental jottings which we can complete with our situated experiences.

[375] Clark, *op.cit.*, p. 46. Clark identifies this phrase as the "moboticists' slogan." This is clearly a rejection of Searle's "Brain in a vat" model of cognition: "The brain is all we have for the purpose of representing the world to ourselves and everything we can use must be inside the brain." If the "world is its own best representation" then "everything" we need to represent the world to ourselves is not in the brain. (See the section "Psycho-physical Parallelism" in Part I)

[376] There is another problem with detailed mental models. Specifically, even if we saw that we had a detailed mental model that appeared when we performed some complex mental activity, such as finding our way across a large city, there is no evidence that such a mental model is what guides us in our actions or understanding. The mental model that we have may only be epiphenomenal, that is it may simply accompany our understanding rather than be the cause of it.

*et al.*, in their cleverly-named paper, "A Critique of Pure Vision"[377] hypothesize that we maintain only sequences of "partial representations" or "visual semi-worlds" which we use in conjunction with our perception of the reality that surrounds us, to provide a complete and detailed model of reality. We update such a model by continually taking glimpses of reality to fill out parts of the model that we don't have or that need to be updated.

In spite of the parallels between Clark's and Wittgenstein's thought on mental models, there are some important differences too. Clark does not completely reject the use of mental models to assist intelligent activity. He believes that the "New Roboticists' rejection of all internal models, maps, and representations"[378] is too extreme. Clark dismisses the use of detailed mental models on purely computational grounds—to "avoid excessive world modeling."[379] If "excessive world modeling" is bad, and the "partial representations" of Churchland, *et al.*, are OK, then simple mental models of simple situations should be OK, too. But for Wittgenstein, the rejection of mental models is a *complete* rejection, whether the models are simple or complex is of no consequence.[380] Clark's willingness to keep some form of mental model as a prerequisite for understanding, even when complex forms of these models seem to be clearly wrong, indicates that he is still sympathetic with the use of mental models to mediate intelligent activity. But if we don't need detailed mental models to mediate complex tasks, then why do we need them to mediate simple ones? Clark's rejection of complex mental models is based on computational grounds, yet by hypothesizing that simple kinds of mental modeling are OK while complex kinds are not, Clark removes one source of complexity but introduces another source of complexity into this process. Specifically, by asserting that there are *two* ways of mediating intelligent activity, one for simple models and one for complex, Clark puts us in a position where we must have some way of determining *which* method, the complete model for simple situations, or the partial model for complex situations, is to be selected for *each* intelligent activity in which we engage. The computational effort needed to determine *when* to apply the complete detailed mental model or the partial mental model, is, obviously, an *increase* in computation, not a reduction. Wittgenstein showed that there is no simple comprehensive way to distinguish the simple from the complex, and that the distinction is usually context dependent; that is, an entity could be simple in one context and composite or complex in another.[381] Furthermore, in the case of the partial model, we would also need to determine

---

[377] P. Churchland, V.S. Ramachandran, and T.J. Sejnowski. "A Critique of Pure Vision," **Large-Scale Neuronal Theories of the Brain**. MIT Press, Cambridge, MA, 1994. Edited by C. Koch and J. Davis. (Cited by Clark, *op.cit.*)

[378] Clark, *op.cit.*, p. 22.

[379] Clark, *op.cit.*, p. 23.

[380] As stated in Part I, Wittgenstein's rejection of mental models is not a claim that we have no mental representations at all during intelligent activity, or that such representations are completely useless. His is merely a rejection of the claim that such mental representations are required for intelligent activity.

[381] Wittgenstein:

> But what are the simple constituent parts of which reality is composed?—What are the simple constituent parts of a chair?—The bits of wood of which it is made? Or the molecules, or the atoms?—"Simple" means: not composite. And here the point is: in what sense "composite?" It makes no sense at all to speak absolutely of the "simple parts of a chair."

> Again: Does my visual image of this tree, of this chair, consist of parts? And what are its simple

exactly *how* the partial model is to be supplemented: in Churchland's terms, which parts of the model need glimpses of reality to supplement or update them, and which do not. Boundary conditions can sometimes be extremely difficult to determine, as the 2,400 year debate over the "sorites" paradox attests.[382] In short, if our aim is to reduce cognitive complexity, as Clark insists, why would we have two ways of mediating intelligent activity instead of just one way?[383] Clark asserts that the mental component of intelligent activity is to complete partially held mental patterns with information from our surroundings. It is likely that instead of having complete or incomplete mental models, we have mental patterns that *all* require some "filling out" with empirical information. Although Wittgenstein did not specifically discuss "mental models," since the phrase is of more recent origin, we must look to his remarks on the use of mental images to mediate intelligent activity to give us a sense of how he conceives of mental models. Wittgenstein states:

> Images tell us nothing either right or wrong, about the external world....
>
> Images are subject to the will....
>
> It is just because forming images is a voluntary activity that it does not instruct us about the external world. [**Z** §§621, 627]

For Wittgenstein, mental images are not entities that can be examined to tell us something about the external world that we did not already know; consequently, they cannot usually be used to store comprehensive objective information about our milieu, nor can we examine them the way that we examine objects in our milieu such as the way we might look up something in a book. Of course we *do* remember things as images, so how is it that they do "not instruct us about the external world?" Wittgenstein is making a subtle point here: the mental image can tell us something about the external world in the sense that we can use our will to create the image in a certain way, and the way that we create it may actually be faithful to the way that our external world is. But, and this is the critical point, mental images are always "subject to the will" so any faithfulness that they have to reality is because we have willed the appropriate image, not because there is any objective, photographic-like recording of the external world. The willed-image, and the way that we interpret it, just happened to represent faithfully the way reality was and it

> component parts? Multi-colouredness is one kind of complexity; another is, for example, that of a broken outline composed of straight bits. And a curve can be said to be composed of an ascending and a descending segment.
>
> If I tell someone without any further explanation: "What I see before me now is composite," he will have the right to ask: What do you mean by "composite?" For there are all sorts of things that that can mean!"—The question "Is what you see composite?" makes good sense if it is already established what kind of complexity—that is, which particular use of the word—is in question. [**PI** §47]

See the extended discussion of the distinction between simple and complex, or composite, in Part I section "Wittgenstein's Categories: Family Resemblances."

[382] See the section "The Analysis of Depth Grammar" in Part I.

[383] Clark actually violates his own "principle of parsimony" in which he asserts that we should know "only as much as you need to know to get the job done." *Op.cit.*, p. 46. The "partial representations" that Clark likes have the same problems that the "rough copies" I talk about in section "Psychophysical Parallelism" have.

can only represent what we *will* it to, so it cannot "instruct us about the external world"—it cannot tell us anything that we did not know in the first place. Even times when we try to remember things in a faithful and objective manner, our memories are notoriously unreliable. There are many examples where the image we remember was supposed to be an objective representation, but turns out not to be—like the bystander who, as a witness to an event that becomes the subject of litigation, tells the court what he thinks he saw, but which turns out not to be the case. Psychologists have found that it is remarkably easy to get people to believe in recollections that are known to be false, even in such a rigorous context as courtroom testimony.[384] Images do not *mediate* intelligent activity, they *accompany* it. Mental images are not like maps which give us objective pictures of reality, they are more like the illuminations of medieval manuscripts which don't convey information so much as represent text that is already understood. Likewise, the "mental model" is not something that can be referred to as a map or a dictionary can be, it is a kind of epiphenomenon that is an illustration of our understanding, not the source of the understanding itself. If there is a role for mental images or models it may not be so much to give us detailed information about our milieu, but to give us the senses of familiarity and relevance which we need to feel when we go about our daily activities.

The reason that we can say that images or mental models are not necessary intermediaries for intelligent activity is that for much of our intelligent activity we simply *don't have them*. We *do* have "something in mind" when we remember a familiar place because we can often describe it or make a rough drawing of it. But just because an image comes to mind when we think of a familiar place does not mean that the image is the source of our understanding, it may only be a *product* of our understanding. Also, we can still have the feeling of familiarity without being able to draw or recall the place, even vaguely. We have all had the experience of coming to a place and seeing it as familiar, but before that occurs having no recollection of the place at all. Quite literally, we may have had to *be in the place* in question *before* we could sense its familiarity. Nothing in our minds alone could give us this sense. *Being there* gives us perceptions which help to complete our recollections of familiar places and circumstances.

Clark's instincts about what is wrong with mental models are good, but he resists the obvious conclusion to the points he raises—namely, if there is something wrong with mental models there is something wrong with *all* mental models, not just some of them (the "complex"ones). In this light, Wittgenstein would be more likely to sympathize with those New Robotcists who reject all forms of "internal models, maps and representations," though, as we said, he does grant the usefulness of "scribbled jottings." (See section "The Mind and Reality: Mental Models or Scribbled Jottings?" in Part I)

## Externalism and the Philosophy of Language

Recent work in the philosophy of language has shown the influence of the trend towards "externalism" in the philosophy of mind.[385] Traditionally, the philosophy of mind has been

---

[384] E. Loftus and K. Ketcham. **Witness for the Defense: The Accused, the Eyewitness, and the Expert Who Puts Memory on Trial**. St. Martin's Press, NY, 1991.
[385] (A good presentation of the various forms of Externalism can be found in McGinn's **Mental Content** [Oxford, Basil Blackwell, 1989]. See also McCulloch's **The Mind and Its World** [Routledge, New York, 1995],

almost exclusively "internalist"—that is, the workings of the mind, our thought processes, have been seen as acting entirely within the physical boundaries of the brain and skull. Internalism has been an implicit, but essential component of the mind:body dualism most strongly associated with Descartes, and is still, in various forms, fundamental to many current models of cognition. Externalism, on the other hand, does not place the boundaries of cognition within the skull, but argues that there are many external facilities or processes that are necessary for cognition. Wittgenstein, who can be said to have had externalist leanings, gave the example of our using a pencil and paper when we perform calculations. Many of us need such external implements for even simple calculations, but all of us need them for complex calculations. If we do not have a paper and pencil handy, we, quite literally, *cannot think through a complex calculation*—the pencil and paper become a *sine qua non* for thought itself. Today, we have many such tools essential for thought: computers, databases, graphical plotters, etc. None of us remembers *everything* he or she needs to conduct his or her daily affairs. Books, databases and personal computers become necessary extensions to our memory. Without these implements, we would not be able to think the way we do.

The beginnings of externalism, as a distinct movement in the philosophy of mind, finds its roots in Putnam's "Twin Earth" thought experiment.[386] Putnam asked us to imagine that there was a "Twin Earth" that was exactly like our own earth, even to the point of having a "twin" of every person on this earth. But there was one aspect of Twin Earth that was different: on Twin Earth they had a substance they called "water" which was exactly like our own water except that instead of having a chemical structure $H_2O$ it had a different structure which Putnam called "XYZ." Except for the different chemical structure, Twin Earth water had exactly the same function there as it does here: Twin Earthers drank it, washed in it, poured it on their plants, and used it in squirt guns for amusement. Twin Earth "water" came out of the sky in the form of rain, and large amounts of it formed rivers, lakes, and oceans, just like ours does. Since the Twin Earthers' use of their "water" was exactly like our own use of water, their conception of water, that is, their idea of what it was and how it was used, was exactly the same as our own idea of what we called "water." In other words, what the average Twin Earther had "in his head" about water was exactly the same as what we have in our heads about our version of water. Yet, Putnam wrote, Twin Earth water was different from our water because it had a different chemical structure (XYZ vs. $H_2O$). The ineluctable conclusion of this thought experiment is that semantic meaning is not entirely internal; at least part of the definition of what water is, is external to our skulls because what we and the Twin Earthers have in our heads cannot distinguish our water from Twin Earth water. As Putnam put it, "Cut the pie any way you like, 'meanings' just ain't in the *head*!" (*op.cit.*, p.144). Tyler Burge[387] published an article

and Rowlands' **The Body in Mind: Understanding Cognitive Processes**. [Cambridge University Press, New York, 1999]

[386] H. Putnam. "The Meaning of 'Meaning'," **Language, Mind and Knowledge**, v. VII, pp. 131–193. Minnesota Studies in the Philosophy of Science, 1975. Collected in Pessin, Andrew and Sanford Goldberg (eds). **The Twin Earth Chronicles: Twenty Years of Reflections on Hilary Putnam's "The Meaning of 'Meaning'."** M.E. Sharpe, Armonk, NY, 1996.

[387] T. Burge. "Individualism and the Mental," **Midwest Studies in Philosophy, 4, Studies in Metaphysics**, pp. 73–122. University of Minnesota Press, Minneapolis, 1979. Edited by P. French, *et al*. Collected in A. Pessin and Sanford Goldberg (eds). **The Twin Earth Chronicles: Twenty Years of Reflections on Hilary Putnam's "The Meaning of 'Meaning'."** M.E. Sharpe, Armonk, New York, 1996.

a few years after Putnam's extending Putnam's externalist interpretation of semantics to include intentional mental states such as beliefs, desires, hopes, and fears. Burge called the internalist interpretation that he and Putnam criticized, "individualism."

Although the Twin Earth thought experiment is entirely fanciful, similar phenomena actually *do* occur every day. In most categories there is a level of generality where different people will call different things by the same name—for example, what I call a "sparrow" and another person calls a "sparrow" might actually be different species of birds, even though they have the same behavior, general appearance and habitat, and they appear the same to us mentally. Two women can have identical appearing necklaces and thereby have the same mental conception of each's jewelry. But while one necklace is made of precious gems, the other is made of fake stones. Since each woman believes that her necklace is made of precious stones, what each woman has "in her head" is identical. But their respective necklaces are, in reality, **not** the same. The Twin Earth thought experiment has had a profound effect on philosophy over the last 3 decades. As Pessin and Goldberg observed, "Twin Earth and 'The Meaning of Meaning,' the article in which it became famous, comprise perhaps the most influential single philosophical episode in the past half century."[388]

## Why is the "Mind" Important for Information Systems?

Information systems are used, of course, to find information of various kinds: data, documents, images, audio recordings, websites, etc. But searchers typically don't find information to just collect it, they find it to *use* it for some purpose. Even the casual Internet "surfer," while seemingly engaged in idle, nonspecific retrieval, still has a purpose in his or her searching, be it simple curiosity, or the escape from boredom. But the typical, purposeful searcher who uses an information system is frequently looking for information that he needs in order to begin or continue some task or activity.[389] All but the smallest information systems contain more information than the searcher could possibly commit to his own memory, so in just the storage sense information systems are an augmentation of the memories of searchers. But information systems augment the searcher's cognitive abilities in many other ways, too. The information that exists on an information system is rarely haphazardly collected; it almost always represents a selection of some subset of the available information by individuals who may be more knowledgeable about that information than the searcher is. In this sense, the selection of information on the system embodies the intelligence and discrimination of the individuals who designed the system, and may reflect abilities and practices that extend more broadly than the information itself (such as, e.g., when practicing physicians have a part in selecting information to be included in a system such as the medical document retrieval system Medline). This too, is an augmentation of the cognitive capabilities of the searcher. Computerized information systems also offer a number of tools that enable the searcher to do things that would be impossibly time-consuming to do on a noncomputerized information system of any

[388] From the preface, edited by A. Pessin and S. Goldberg. **The Twin Earth Chronicles: Twenty Years of Reflections on Hilary Putnam's "The Meaning of 'Meaning'."** M.E. Sharpe, Armonk, New York, 1996.
[389] I first proposed this view of searching in my PhD dissertation, "Pragmatic Aspects of Inquiry." [The University of California, Berkeley, 1981]

typical size (things like sorting large amounts of retrieved information by its date, its author or its title, performing statistical procedures—sum, average, standard deviation—on large collections of data, or searching through the text of information for specific names, dates, words or phrases). These are only a few of the things an information system can do to augment the cognitive abilities of a searcher, and by augmenting these abilities the information system is helping the searcher, quite literally, to *think*. Thus, an information system acts as a kind of *scaffolding* to supplement the searcher's intellect, enabling him to examine information, perform searches, and compare information that he would not be able to do easily or at all by himself. The information system, then, represents a kind of extension of the mind of the searcher, or at least a softening of its boundaries. Since the scaffolding of the information system should assist the intellect of the searcher in ways that are beneficial, it is important that the designers of information systems should know not only what the capabilities of technology are, but also what the capabilities of the human mind are so they can decide how best to supplement or assist them in their information searches. The mind of the searcher can extend, quite literally, into the information system—it can become "embedded" in information technology in the same way that it can become embedded in the implements of any practice. As Clark put it, "I am convinced that it is valuable to (at times) treat cognitive processes as extending beyond the narrow confines of skin and skull."[390] Thus, an understanding of the capabilities and limits of the human mind is essential if we are to design information systems that extend and supplement these capabilities and limits.

## The Structure of Information Systems

At the highest level of abstraction, the level at which the searcher comes into contact with it, an information system is fairly simple. Basically, an information system is an organized process which attempts to provide correct or pertinent information in response to a formal request of some kind. In the broadest sense, people are themselves information systems since they often provide answers or recommendations to others who ask them questions. But our concern here is with information systems which are artifacts designed to provide answers or selected material in response to queries, or to be used by searchers to find relevant information. The following diagram depicts the basic structure and dynamics of an information system:

The Inquirer generally begins the search process with a request of some kind. This can be stated in natural language as a question—"What is Mary Sinico's credit limit?" If we think of the request as a question, we can distinguish between a number of basic kinds: what, who, where, why, how, and when. These can all be reformulated as "What..." questions: what person, what place, what reason, what method, and what time. This request must then be translated into a format that is appropriate for the information system being used. This is the Formal Query. In its simplest form, a Request and a Formal Query might look like this:

Request: "What is the credit limit for the customer Mary Sinico?"

[390] Clark, *op.cit.*, p. 215.

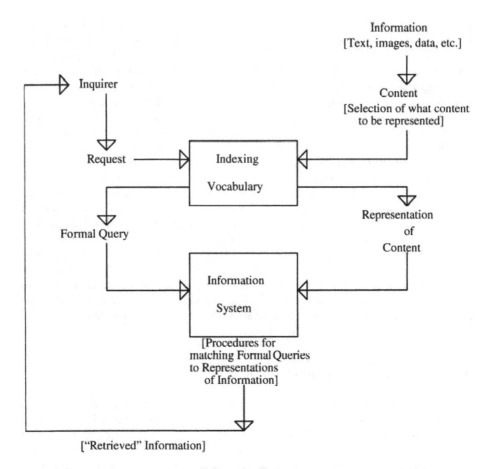

Information System

Formal Query (**SQL**): **SELECT** Credit_Limit
**FROM** Customer
**WHERE** Last_Name = "Sinico"
**AND** First_Name = "Mary";

In order for the Formal Query to select the right information or data there must be some data or information for it to search through and it needs to be structured in a way to facilitate retrieval. For data, like in our example, there are relatively well-understood procedures for structuring it for retrieval: a process called "Normalization."[391] While normalization is not

---

[391] While Database modeling and design is, in most cases, a fairly routine process, this does not mean that it has the precision of a mathematical procedure or that it is without uncertainties or competing viewpoints. Rather than a rigid procedure, normalization is more like a set of heuristics that guides the design of record structures but does not control it. Most data base design theories recommend normalization to third Normal Form, but some recommend that fourth and fifth Normal Forms should be implemented if multi-valued dependencies are present in the data. Even in databases which are normalized, violations of the rules of normalization can be tolerated

without its uncertainties, it is still a fairly straightforward process compared to the design of some more problematic collections of information which we will consider shortly.

In the above example, the database needs to be structured so that customer data is kept in a table, or relation, called "Customer" and that this table has the data fields "Credit_Limit," "Last_Name," and "First_Name." The job of the Information System is to find the appropriate tables or relations in the database and to select the correct rows and fields that match the Formal Query.

What I have described here is what I would call the basic "Data Model" of information systems. Overall, this view of information or data has been enormously successful in managing data over the last few decades, and it has affected our daily lives in significant ways: we can withdraw cash from our personal checking account using an ATM in a distant city or even in another country; we can use a single credit card to handle virtually any purchase of any kind in stores that are thousands of miles away from our home town; we can buy a ticket in Chicago for a play at the Geary Theater in San Francisco so we can attend during a future trip; we can reserve a campsite at any National Park in the US from any telephone with access to 800-level phone numbers; etc. These activities would not be possible without the capacity to find and record precisely defined data like names, account numbers, phone numbers, etc.

## The Fundamental Relationship in Information Systems

The Fundamental Relationship in any information system is the linking of an item or items of information or data with some representation or description of that information. In our example, above, the number representing Mary Sinico's credit limit is given the description "Credit_Limit." In semiotic terms, this is an indexical relation. For data, this indexical relation looks like this:

**Address**

31 Emmett Avenue, Dedham, MA
5822 Jamestown Road, Hyattsville, MD
4413 Chase Avenue, Bethesda, MD
6227 Madawaska Road, Washington, D.C.
400 East Randolph, Chicago, IL.

⋮

and are sometimes even recommended—the most common complaint of normalization being that it breaks data bases up into too many records, making it necessary for the data base users to join them back together again to answer queries. Apart from normalization, there are other issues concerning the treatment of null values in data bases, and, more recently, the handling of object-oriented features like inheritance, encapsulation and class hierarchies. The more recent extension of the data base concept into Data Warehousing and Data Mining have introduced new uncertainties and competing visions into the data design process.

Here the word "Address" is an index of a set of data items. It allows us to refer to the address, or addresses, in a meaningful and parsimonious way. It is parsimonious in the sense that we have a single term "Address" to refer to an entire set of addresses on the information system. The word "Address" also has a "sense" or "meaning" that we are all familiar with, and helps us to understand what kind of data is in this set. Here we can see that indexes do two things: first, they *distinguish* a specific set of data as distinct from the other data in the system, and, second, they *describe* this set of data in a way that makes it meaningful for individuals who use the system.[392]

This basic indexical relation occurs repeatedly in information systems and is the basis for the retrieval of information or data. It allows us to index, that is to *distinguish* and *describe*, a wide variety of familiar data items:

> "Phone Number"
> "Name"
> "Employer"
> "Social Security Number"
> "Date of Birth"
> "Marital Status"
> ' "Job Title"
> "Account Balance"
> ⋮

These index terms have a highly determinate relation between their common meaning or usage and the information or data they can be used to represent. That is, in *ordinary usage*, which Wittgenstein insisted is the touchstone of linguistic meaning, there is usually very little ambiguity about what "phone numbers," "names," "dates of birth," etc., are. This kind of highly determinate relationship between indexes and information or data is one of the major reasons for the success of the data model. We are able to precisely describe a large percentage of the data we need to conduct our daily activities: we can ask directions to a unique address, we can look up our checking account balance which is referred to by our unique Social Security Number, we can order a book or CD with a unique combination of title and author, and we can call a friend whose phone number is, out of the millions of phone numbers in the world, unique. This kind of information system, with highly determinate indexes we can refer to as the "Data Model." As we said, it is an enormously robust and successful model for information or data management. But its very success has led to its widespread application to kinds of information that cannot be indexed with the certainty of the above examples. Even more problematic, it is the source of the belief that all information has, at least potentially, a highly determinate representation that can be used to distinguish a small amount of useful information from large amounts of similar information on an information system. But to insist that there is, potentially, a highly determinate representation of any item of information is like insisting

---

[392] D.C. Blair. "Pragmatic Aspects of Inquiry." PH.D Dissertation, The University of California, Berkeley, CA, 1981. A more recent discussion of "description" and "distinction" (or "discrimination") in information retrieval can be found in D.C. Blair "Information Retrieval and the Philosophy of Language." [**Annual Review of Information Science and Technology**, vol. 37, pp. 3–50. Information Today, Medford, NJ, 2003.]

that there is a clear definition for each of the concepts we use. Wittgenstein considered this a mistake:

> We are unable clearly to circumscribe the concepts we use, not because we don't know their real definition, but because there is no real "definition" to them. [**BB** p.25]

If we believe that every item of information has, potentially, a highly determinate representation that would enable it to be retrieved by those who want it in any situation, then many of the failures of information systems will be attributed to incorrect indexing—not representing the information content correctly, or incorrect search query formulation—not representing what the inquirer wants correctly. But, it is the thesis here, that in many retrieval situations information *does not*, either actually or potentially, have a determinate enough representation to distinguish it from the information a searcher does not want.

## The Fundamental Issue of Information Systems: The "Determinacy of Representation"

There are indexes which are less determinate than the ones above and whose precise meanings are correspondingly less certain. Even some highly determinate indexes may have indeterminate aspects about them. For example, index descriptions such as "debit" or "credit" on a bank statement indicate additions or subtractions from an account but may not indicate what the nature of the credit or debit actually was. Of course, whether such descriptions are considered determinate or indeterminate will depend on *how that information is being used*. Sometimes the specific values for the data and the nature of their use can lower the level of determinacy.[393] For example, while the name "Alex Szabo" appears only once in the Manhattan phonebook, and is thus quite determinate (i.e., it refers to a single individual), the name "Robert Smith" occurs over 90 times in the same phone book, and is correspondingly less determinate. It is less determinate not simply because it repeats a lot, but because the typical *use* of a phone book is to look up unique individuals, not groups of individuals with the same name. No matter how many Robert Smiths there are in Manhattan, there is typically only one Robert Smith to whom we wish to talk. Recalling Wittgenstein, the key to understanding a word, even something as simple as a name, is to look at its *use*.

But there are other kinds of indexes which also have high levels of indeterminacy. The most common of these are the indexes which represent certain aspects of textual information like the "intellectual content" of documents. A given document does have *some* determinate indexes such as the author's name, the title, the date of publication, the title of the journal or edited collection in which it occurred, etc. But it is far more uncertain how to index or precisely describe the "intellectual content" of documents or books—what they are about, or how they can be used—than it is to determine the correct name of the author.

---

[393] I take the phrase "to lower determinacy" and "to raise indeterminacy" to be synonymous. Likewise, "to raise determinacy" and "to lower indeterminacy" are synonymous.

We can see now that there are two basic kinds of information or data which can be managed by an information system—*highly determinate* information which we can refer to with precise indexes, and *less determinate* information which varies in its precision of representation. This distinction we take as fundamental; it differentiates two different kinds of information systems or retrieval situations. Originally,[394] it was taken that data management systems provided access to highly determinate information—phone numbers, account balances, order numbers—while document and image retrieval systems had much less determinate representations of their stored information, particularly when looking for documents with a specific "intellectual content" or images of a particular type or subject. But, on further consideration, we can see that the distinction between highly determinate and less determinate representations of information does not fall precisely on the dividing line between data retrieval and document/image retrieval systems. There can be indeterminate representations of data and highly determinate representations of documents or images. Let's look at our phonebook example in more detail: We would usually consider the names in a phone book as a fairly determinate representation of the phone numbers and addresses of individuals who live in a particular city. For most small to modest sized towns names can often uniquely identify individuals, so it is not difficult to find the phone number of, say, Michael R. Walters in a town of 40,000 residents. Sometimes, though, a name may be common enough even in a small town to provide multiple listings for it. If there are four Michael Walters in one town, then your certainty, or probability, of dialing the number of the specific Michael Walters whom you want is, *ceteris paribus*, 25%. While such indeterminacy may be irritating, we would only have to call at most four numbers before reaching the Michael Walters whom we want. The situation for certain names in large metropolitan areas—New York, Chicago, or Pittsburgh—may be a different matter, though. A common name like Robert Smith, appears 114 times in the Pittsburgh phone book. While we may be willing to dial four numbers to get the right Michael Walters in a small town, we would probably not be willing to dial anywhere near 114 numbers to find the right Robert Smith in Pittsburgh (especially if we are using a pay phone!). But the problem of even the most common name in an American phone directory is dwarfed by the repetition of names in China. Although the Chinese culture is several millennia old, there are only a few hundred family names to distinguish billions of individual Chinese. In Shanghai alone, there are several thousand individuals with the same name. If all were listed in a hypothetical Shanghai phone book, it would take many pages to list them. Such a high level of indeterminacy would militate against the accurate retrieval of a specific individual in Shanghai with that name.

Looking at the other side of the determinacy problem, we said that, in general, retrieving documents or images can often be fairly indeterminate, in particular, when looking for a specific intellectual content, or "subject." But there are situations where even this is not the case. Take the documents that go together to make a loan application at a bank: these documents are stored under the applicant's name. But because the uniqueness of these documents is essential, banks usually include the applicant's Social Security Number (SSN) along with the other information. In such a case, the SSN would uniquely identify

---

[394] This distinction in information systems was originally called the "Data : Document Distinction." [D.C. Blair. "The Data-Document Distinction in Information Retrieval," **Communications of the ACM**, vol. 27:4, pp. 369–374, April 1984.]

any single set of application documents. The SSN can be used in the application process because only bank employees or the applicant will need to have access to these records and they both know which SSN corresponds with a particular name. But the manner in which indeterminacy is resolved here—by the use of customer SSN's—is not available for resolving all cases of the indeterminacy of identity. For example, when there are a large number of duplicate names in a telephone book, it would be possible to also list everyone's unique SSN along with his or her name, address, and phone number. But, given the nature of the retrieval task, it is unlikely that this would prove useful. The reason for this is that even close friends usually do not know each other's SSNs so it would be of little value for distinguishing individuals with the same names. Further, most individuals, as an ordinary practice, would be reluctant to have their names and corresponding SSNs published together in a public document, since that information could be used to get access to personal information or to "steal identities." In the case of the duplicate names in the phone book there is usually another highly determinate item of information that would be better than an SSN for distinguishing duplicate phone book entries: the address. While there may be many Robert Smiths in the phone book, there may only be one on "Green Court" or one on "Randolph Street," for example. It is far more likely that a friend will know the street you live on than your SSN, and that may be enough to resolve the indeterminacy of even large numbers of duplicate names in a phone book. The discrimination power of additional information is directly related to how determinate that information is. The fact that it is more likely that a friend would know your address rather than your Social Security Number is not arbitrary. It is a natural consequence of the ways that we normally interact in our day-to-day activities. Friends often visit each other or write to each other, so they often know each other's addresses, if only the name of the city and street. There are no *common* activities, though, in which two friends might need to know each other's Social Security Numbers. There are, in contrast, activities such as applying for a bank loan, where Social Security Numbers are used regularly. The discrimination power of language, like meaning, is ultimately contingent on the day-to-day activities (Wittgenstein's Forms of Life) and Language Games, in which it appears.

## "Escalating Uncertainty of Retrieval": The Problem With Large Systems and Indeterminately Represented Information

One way to demonstrate the effects of the indeterminacy of representation in information systems is to show how it could effect the conceptually simpler data model. Consider the situation in which we want to know the office phone of a co-worker we met briefly whose last name we believe to be "Smith." If we have access to a relational database with employee information in the "Employee_Table" we might submit an SQL query of the following type:

**SELECT** Phone Number
**FROM** Employee_Table
**WHERE** Last_Name = "Smith";

If this is a small company and there is only one "Smith" who is an employee, then this query will retrieve the correct information. But, if the company is larger, there would likely be more Smiths who work there and the above query would return a set of phone numbers for all the Smiths. If there are just two or three Smiths, you might be willing to call each of them to find the Smith whom you want. But let's assume that there are too many Smiths to call up.[395] In this case, you would need to use more information in the query to distinguish the Smith whom you want. Suppose that you know that Smith is a computer programmer and that job titles are included in the employee information on the database. Here, you might extend your query in the following way:

> **SELECT**   Phone Number
> **FROM**      Employee_Table
> **WHERE**    Last_Name = "Smith"
> **AND**        Job_Title = "Programmer";

In some cases this would retrieve the phone number of a unique individual, and in some cases it would not. In the latter case, it would be necessary to add more information, for example, if we knew he was in the marketing department we might submit the query:

> **SELECT**   Phone Number
> **FROM**      Employee_Table
> **WHERE**    Last_Name = "Smith"
> **AND**        Job_Title = "Programmer"
> **AND**        Department = "Marketing";

This is a common way to deal with retrieving specific information from a large information system. One can increase the specificity of the query, that is, reduce the number of retrieved items, by conjoining additional information with the original query. With each additional item of information—here, the "Job Title" and then the "Department"—the number of items satisfying each successive query usually decreases making the searcher's efforts easier.[396] But this strategy for the reduction of retrieved set size only works with *highly determinate representations* of the information on the database. If the representations are *less* determinate then an interesting thing happens when we add information to the query— with the addition of each item of information, even though the number of items retrieved usually goes down, the certainty of retrieving the correct record *also goes down*—that is, it is *less certain* that the retrieved records, no matter how few, will include the one the searcher wants. For example, suppose that we are uncertain of the individual's exact name. We think it was "Smith" but it could have been something else, "Smythe" or "Schmit,"

---

[395] When too many records are retrieved we say that the size of the retrieved set is greater than the searcher's "futility point"—the point in a search when he gives up. A more detailed discussion of "futility points" and the biases that it can introduce into the retrieval process can be found in Blair's "Searching Biases in Large-Scale Document Retrieval Systems." **Journal of the American Society for Information Science**, pp. 271–277, 31 July 1980, or in the first chapter of his **Language and Representation in Information Retrieval** [Elsevier Science, 1990]. The phenomenon of excessively large retrieved sets is also referred to as "output overload" (Blair and Maron, 1985) or "Infoglut." [Rozak. **The Cult of Information**. Pantheon Books, New York, 1986.]

[396] The size of the retrieved set might remain the same from query to query, but it cannot not go up. For the purposes of this discussion we will assume that the common result obtains and that additional information in the query will reduce the number of retrieved items. It is also important to note that this reduction only occurs when additional information is added conjunctively (using "AND" in the above SQL statements), and not when it is added disjunctively (using "OR" instead of "AND").

perhaps. We could represent this uncertainty probabilistically saying that we are 60% certain that his name is, in fact, "Smith" (i.e., we estimate that there is a 60% likelihood that the set of records corresponding to employees by the name of "Smith" will include the record of the employee whom we want).[397] Now, even if we only retrieve one or two records with our first query—ostensibly, a good result—it may be the case that *neither* of them represents the individual we want. But, as in the previous example, let's assume that the first query returns too many records. We could then add the additional information about the individual we want, as we did before, that he is a "programmer." Again, instead of knowing this with certainty, consider our certainty of his being a programmer is 70%. Even though our certainty of his being a "programmer" is higher than our certainty of his name being "Smith," the overall certainty of the individual we want being among those employees who are represented as having both the name "Smith" and the job title "programmer" is the product of the individual certainties, that is, .60 × .70, or 42%.[398] If we add the information that he is likely to be in the "Marketing" department, with a certainty of 80%, we wind up with a combined certainty of our third query ("Smith" and "programmer" and "Marketing") retrieving the individual we want as .60 × .70 × .80, or .34. So, even though we are increasingly certain that each additional item of information represents the individual we want, our combined certainty goes *down* with the addition of each item of information until we have, here, only a 34% certainty that the retrieved records, however few, include the individual whom we want.[399]

But notice what happens when we combine information that we are certain of, which is usually the case in database management systems. If we are absolutely certain that the individual whom we are looking for has the name "Smith," a job title of "programmer" and is employed by the "Marketing" department, then the combined certainty of these descriptions is, assuming independence, the simple product of successive probabilities

[397] In reality, it may be very difficult to estimate accurately a numerical value for our uncertainty about whether a particular index represents the information we want. The numerical values here are hypothetical and are meant to demonstrate the general nature of the retrieval difficulties rather than provide a precise estimation of the numeric values which might occur.

[398] To make the combination of probabilities the simple product of the individual probabilities requires an assumption of the independence of the two probabilities, namely, that the fact that someone's name is "Smith" is not related in any significant way to the fact that he is a programmer. Such independence is not always the case since we can imagine instances where there may be a significant dependence between two facts; for example, it may be the case that certain job titles, such as "salesman" are more likely to be found in one department, say, "Marketing," than another. Thus, "salesman" and "Marketing" are not independent. But the lack of independence in some cases does not change the point we are making here. If the probabilities of the individual events are not independent and are less than 1.0, which we assume they are here, then the resulting probability of the combination of events still yields probability values that decrease as more events (additions of information) are combined. It is this trend of decreasing certainty, or, as we first termed it, "escalating uncertainty," that is important for our discussion, not the actual probability values themselves.

[399] The perceptive reader can see that a reasonable search strategy is to search using the terms with the highest probabilities of success first. In our example, it would probably be better to search with the terms "Smith" and "Marketing" whose conjunctive probability is .48, before searching with "Smith" and "programmer" whose conjunctive probability is .42. Of course, a higher probability is not an absolute indicator of search term utility since there are words, like "the" or "a," that are in every document or record and, although they have probabilities of 1.0, they do not discriminate the useful documents from the useless ones at all. To select the retrieved set that has the higher probability of returning the desired record, both retrieved sets need to be smaller than the searcher's "futility point."

of 1.0. As long as we can add items of information to our query that are certain, the resultant probabilities will not be subject to the "escalating uncertainty" that typifies the combination of indeterminate information. This is why the data model has been so successful, even in large applications. It deals almost exclusively with *certain* information. This is the most important difference in the comparative effect of determinate/certain and indeterminate/uncertain information in large systems.[400]

## The Nature of Representational Indeterminacy in Information Systems

Representational indeterminacy is one of the most significant factors affecting the success of a search for information, so it is important that we look at it more closely. When we do, we see that there are different kinds of representational indeterminacy and a number of factors that can make it better or worse.

1. **Semantic ambiguity.** Ambiguity about the meaning of a word is the most obvious source of representational indeterminacy since we frequently deal with it conversationally. Consider the word "head." We might find it used in the following kinds of sentences:

   > "He put his hat on his **head**."
   > "He went to the **head** of the line."
   > "She's the **head** of the Executive Board."
   > "The crisis quickly came to a **head**."

   > "They began the canoe trip at the **head** of the river."
   > "He wuz **headin'** North after he robbed the bank, sheriff!"

   The word "head" can be used in any of the above examples, as well as others. If we just look at the literal word by itself it could take on any of a number of different meanings and be correspondingly indeterminate in what it represents. We could imagine submitting the single word "head" to an Internet search engine and retrieving web pages with the above sentences in them. An actual Internet search with the word "head" is given below.

2. **System size and category overload.** The number of times a word is used to represent, or index, information on an information system will affect the level of indeterminacy of that word. If the word "head" occurs in only one document or is used to represent a single item of information, then it is presumably being used in just *one* way, and semantic indeterminacy is less of a problem. Certainly, it may be unclear which of the many semantic meanings of "head" is being used to index the information, but with a single occurrence it would be no great effort for the

---

[400] This problem of escalating uncertainty and its effect on the retrieval of documents was first discussed in a paper by Blair and Maron: "An Evaluation of Retrieval Effectiveness for a Full-Text Document Retrieval System." **Communications of the ACM**, vol. 28:3, pp. 289–299, March 1985. The first publication to relate conditional probabilities to document indexes was M.E. Maron and J.L. Kuhn's "On Relevance, Probabilistic Indexing and Information Retrieval," **Journal of the Association for Computing Machinery**, vol. 7:3, pp. 216–244, July 1960.

searcher to retrieve the information and see whether it is the semantic usage that he wants. But as the number of times a word is used to represent information goes up, the uncertainty of its meaning increases, too. If "head" is used to index 1,000 items of information, then it is likely that its inherent semantic variability will cause it to represent a variety of semantic content. One might ask how the mere increase in the number of times a word is used causes an increase in the number of different semantic ways it is used, that is, why couldn't all 1,000 uses of "head" refer to a single semantic sense? While this is a reasonable hypothesis, the statistical properties of language militate against it. George Kingsley Zipf was the first to describe some of the basic statistical properties of natural language. Among these statistical regularities of language, he found that there was a relationship between the number of occurrences of a word in natural language text and the number of different semantic ways in which it is used: if the number of occurrences of a word in a sample of text is equal to $n$, then the number of different semantic ways in which it is used is equal to the square root of $n$. In our example, if "head" occurs 1,000 times as an index for information, then it is likely to be used around 30 different semantic ways. The "different meanings" of words are, admittedly, not always precisely identifiable, so it is unclear how exact Zipf's formulation of the relationship between word frequency and meaning actually is, though he did claim empirical evidence for the relationship.[401] But a more general formulation of this relationship which states that as a word increases in frequency of usage, the number of different semantic ways it is used goes up too, but at a rate proportional to the square root, is very likely to be the case.[402] This explains one of the most persistent frustrations of using search engines on the World Wide Web, namely, that when a searcher uses an ordinary word in a search query, she not only will usually retrieve a large number of websites having that word occurring in them, but she will also see a wide semantic variability in the way that the word is used in the retrieved websites. If we submit the word "head" to the Google Internet Search Engine, we can find the following variability in the first 30 retrieved websites (out of 21,300,000 selected websites![403]):

i. **HEAD**-Document Head. Syntax, **<HEAD>**... **<HEAD>**. Attribute Specifications.

ii. **HEAD** NEW MEDIA: ecommerce, interactive television, intranets. **Head** creates relationships which are true to marketing strategy.

---

[401] Zipf. **Human Behavior and the Principle of Least Effort**. Hafner Publishing, NY, 1965. (Facsimile of the 1949 edition)

[402] It may be the case that there is some upper bound to the number of semantic meanings that a word can possess, and it is certainly the case that some words have more semantic meanings than others. But even if the maximum number of meanings is no more than 50, for example, it still means that semantic indeterminacy can pose a significant problem with searching for intellectual content on a large information retrieval system.

[403] Of course, when the retrieved set of websites or documents rises beyond 20 or 30, it is unlikely that an inquirer who is dissatisfied with these first retrieved sites will continue to look beyond them. Thus the effective size of the set of retrieved websites must be less than the inquirer's "futility point"—which may be defined as the maximum number of items of information, here, websites, that he is willing to look through before he either gives up his search, or, submits a different or revised query to the search engine.

   iii. **Head** of the Herd. Click here! All software... Check out past **Head** of the Herd selections!

   iv. Mr. Edible Starch Tuber **Head**... Mr. Potato **Head** is a trademark of Hasbro, Inc.

   v. Welcome to **Head** Start: It is with great sadness that we inform the **Head** Start Community that...

   vi. The Plug-in **Head** site is devoted to Adobe Photoshop compatible plug-ins.

   vii. Archives of Otolaryngology-**Head** and Neck Surgery.

  viii. The World's Internet window to Hilton **Head** Island since 1995.

   ix. See how North Carolina gubernatorial candidates Mike Easley and Richard Vinroot weigh in....The **Head** to**Head** feature changes daily.

   x. Boar's **Head** Inn.

   xi. Janus **Head**, an Interdisciplinary Journal.

   xii. Welcome to the official site of the XXXVI **Head** of the Charles [boat race].

  xiii. Italian design company joins Pixel **Head**. >> Why should you outsource?

  xiv. **Head** lice help from the NPA, the only non-profit agency....

   xv. The **Head** Element contains information about the current document, such as title, keywords, that may be useful to search engines.

  xvi. Welcome to the **Head**-Space project...

  xvii. Ethnographic material related to **head** hunting, cannibalism, sideshows, oddities and curiosities.

 xviii. FCC **Head** takes his agency to task....

  xix. **Head**-Driven Phrase Structure Grammar (HPSG)

  xx. Edith**Head**-A Retrospectacular! will merge the glamour and excitement of film and fashion using a salute to Edith Head as its focal point.

     ⋮

We can see that there is a lot of semantic variability for the word "head" in the above 20 websites of the 21+ million identified for retrieval. Whether these represent the first 20 meanings of a possible 4,615 (the square root of 21,300,000) is difficult to tell, but it is clear that if we see this much variability in the first 30 websites retrieved, we will probably see a great deal *more* variability were we to examine subsequent retrieved websites. In any event, since the typical web user would be looking for a single usage of "head" the majority of the websites identified for retrieval would *not* be useful to the inquirer.

3. **The Productivity of Language.** One of the salient characteristics of natural language is its "productivity." Language is productive in the sense that a relatively small vocabulary and a few rules of syntax and semantics can combine to produce an uncountabley large number of valid sentences or descriptions (this is the notion of a "generative grammar").[404] The productivity of language has proved to be both a help and a hindrance for information retrieval systems, as it has for any other computerized system that has a large semantic component. Productivity is a help because it is relatively simple to find a reasonable way to represent the intellectual

---

[404] D.T. Langendoen and P. Postal. **The Vastness of Natural Languages**. Basil Blackwell, Oxford, UK, 1984.

content of any document; but this productivity can also be a hindrance because language is so creative that the number of "reasonable" representations for a document's intellectual content is virtually unlimited. As a consequence, anticipating how a searcher might ask for a particular document content can be very difficult.[405]

Consider our example of the semantic variability of the word "head." There are two kinds of semantic variability here. First, as we have already shown, the word "head" can have a variety of meanings. But there is another kind of semantic variability, namely, that there is a wide variety of ways we can express the same semantic content of the word "head" *without using the word "head."* Consider our examples:

| **Original Sentences** | **Alternative Sentences** |
| --- | --- |
| "He put his hat on his **head**." | "He put his hat on." |
| "He went to the **head** of the line." | "He went to the front of the line." |
| "She's the **head** of the Executive Board." | "She's the chair of the Executive Board." |
| "The crisis quickly came to a **head**." | "The crisis quickly became critical." |
| "They began the canoe trip at the **head** of the river." | "They began the canoe trip at the source of the river." |
| "He wuz **headin'** North after he robbed the bank, sheriff!" | "He wuz ridin' North after he robbed the bank, sheriff!" |

4. **The two sides of indeterminacy: The indexer and the inquirer.** The examples that we have given of semantic indeterminacy are on the *index* or *document* side of the retrieval process. But semantic indeterminacy also affects the *inquirer* or *searching* side of this process, too, thus multiplying the effect of indeterminacy and lowering the likelihood of retrieving a useful item of information content.[406] That is, the word "head" as we have shown, has a large number of different semantic uses, or meanings, which the authors of different websites may use. But, that same variability can affect the inquirer, too: he has a lot of choices of words and phrases that he can use *instead of* "head"—these are like the "Alternative Sentences" shown above. So the person who must represent the intellectual content of a website must not only make decisions about the specific words that he or she uses to express what

---

[405] Swanson demonstrated this effect empirically in his "Studies of Indexing Depth and Retrieval Effectiveness" [Unpublished report, National Science Foundation Grant GN 380, February 1966]. The results of his unpublished test are discussed in Blair **Language and Representation in Information Retrieval**, pp. 170–171. Elsevier Science, 1990.

[406] D.C. Blair. "Indeterminacy in the Subject Access to Documents," **Information Processing and Management**, vol. 22:2, pp. 229–241, 1986. The pioneering work in modeling the indeterminacy of index and search terms is M.E. Maron and J.L. Kuhns' "On Relevance, Probabilistic Indexing and Information Retrieval" [**Journal of the Association for Computing Machinery**, vol. 7:3, pp. 216–244, July 1960]. Maron later extended this work in his writings on what he called the "Operational Definition of 'About'." ["On Indexing, Retrieval and the Meaning of About," **Journal of the American Society for Information Science**, vol. 28:1, pp. 38–43, January 1977.

they want to express, they must give some thought to what words a typical searcher who would be happy with the "content" of that website might use as search terms.

5. **What do search terms do?—Description and discrimination.** If we look more closely at the way that words are used in the search for intellectual content—what Wittgenstein might call the Language Game of searching—we can see that they have two major functions. In the first place, they must *describe* the intellectual content of the material they serve as indexes for. In the data model this was fairly straightforward: we usually call addresses by the word "address" and phone numbers by the words "phone number." For documents or images this is, as we have shown, a more indeterminate process, except for the limited contextual information such as the author's name and the title of the work. But while there may not be a single, agreed-upon way to represent the intellectual content of text or images, the goal of the indexing process is to *describe* that content in a way that will facilitate retrieving it by interested inquirers.

If all information systems were small, that is, if all the possible retrieved sets they might generate would be smaller than the futility point of even the most demanding inquirer, then we would need only to be concerned with how index terms *describe* the intellectual content of available items of information. But one of the lessons of the Information Age is that as the costs of storage have *decreased* dramatically, the sizes of information systems have *gone up* just as dramatically. We have, quite literally, reached the point where no item of information, no matter how trivial, need be thrown away. In fact, in many instances it may *cost more* to examine items of information and *decide* whether to keep them than to simply keep them and pay for their storage indefinitely. As a consequence, the size of the typical information system continues to grow. Index terms, then, must not only *describe* the intellectual content of information, they must also *discriminate* the intellectual content of a given item of information from the intellectual content of other information on the same system that is similar to it. *Description*, then is a process which is only concerned with a single item of information, while *discrimination* is a process which must consider how a given item of information, such as a document or an image, must be distinguished from other items of information on the same system. In short, *description* deals with single items of information while *discrimination* looks at how individual information items relate to the entire information system. For example, in a small public library, if there are only ten books on the subject of "Database Management Systems," it might be fine to index them all with that phrase, since ten is most likely smaller than the futility point of the typical inquirer. But in a computer science library at a major university there might be hundreds of books that have an intellectual content concerned in some way with "Database Management Systems" and there would be few inquirers with a futility point that reaches into the hundreds. As a result, it may be important to subdivide the description "Database Management Systems." Instead of describing every intellectual content which has to do with database management systems as "Database Management Systems" we might be able to discriminate, for example, between different kinds of "Database Management Systems": Hierarchical, Network, CODASYL, Relational, Object-Oriented, or Distributed; or we might distinguish different kinds of Database applications: Data Warehousing, Data Marts, Data Mining, OLAP (OnLine Analytical Processing); or, we might distinguish different Database design issues: Normalization, Storage Structures, Physical Storage; Access Methods: Hashing Algorithms, Data Loading; or we might distinguish between specific brands of Database Management Systems: ORACLE, ACCESS, DB2, TOTAL, FILEMAKER PRO, INFORMIX, etc. Such subdivisions will better discriminate between the intellectual content of the large number of books on the general topic of "Database Management Systems."

*Description* and *discrimination* also characterize the two major kinds of search failures. A *failure of description* occurs when either an index term does not accurately describe the intellectual content of a given item of information, or when a search term does not accurately describe the intellectual content of the information the inquirer is looking for. The result of a failure of description is that the information retrieved does not have the content the inquirer wanted. A *failure of discrimination* can occur when a given index term correctly *describes* the intellectual content of an item, but does not *discriminate* it well from the intellectual content of other items of information on the same system. The result of a *failure of discrimination* is the retrieval of exceptionally large sets of information—"output overload." From this we can see that the most troublesome search failure for Internet search engines is a *failure of discrimination*—even the simplest search for intellectual content can return a retrieved set of millions of websites. The traditional measures of document retrieval effectiveness, recall, and precision, can be seen in terms of description and discrimination: *recall*, the percentage of relevant documents that are retrieved, can also be seen as a measure of the success of *description*, while *precision*, the percentage of retrieved documents that are relevant, can be seen as a measure of the success of *discrimination*.[407]

6. **The requirements of use.** Typically we search for information, not as an end in itself, but as something we can use in an activity or practice. Thus, it is the activity or practice that the search serves that sets the criteria for successful searching. Likewise, the degree of indeterminacy that a representation can have is not just a matter of the number of times that representation occurs, but is also a function of what the information that is indexed by that representation *will be used for*. For example, we described how there was a direct relation between the number of occurrences of a person's name in a phone book and the level of indeterminacy of that name as an indicator of a particular individual. This is true, not just because there are multiple occurrences of the name in the phonebook, but because the *primary use* of the phone book is to look up the phone number of a single individual. But we could imagine another, albeit unusual, use of a phone book. We could imagine that someone, a genealogist for example, might have a quite different use for a phone book. The genealogist might use it to determine how many individuals with a particular surname live in a given city. In such a case, a name that occurs 50 times in the phone book might not be indeterminate at all, since the genealogist's

[407] D.C. Blair. "Information Retrieval and the Philosophy of Language." **Annual Review of Information Science and Technology**, vol. 37, pp. 3–50. Information Today, Medford, NJ, 2003.

goal, unlike the typical phonebook user, might not be to find a single individual, but to tabulate all the occurrences of the name in question.

Looking at the requirements of use, we can say that there are, from a quantitative point of view, a number of different kinds of searches: specific, exhaustive, and sample.

Types of search:

> **Specific**. The searcher wants to see a single specific item of information (only one item of a category is desired, e.g., a telephone book lookup, or a patent search where an inventor is looking for the existence of a specific patent.).

> **Exhaustive**. The searcher wants to see all the items of information of a particular type or category (e.g., scientific research or litigation support).

> **Sample**. The searcher wants to see some, but not all, of the items of information in a particular category (e.g., a market researcher retrieving a few examples of what consumers are saying about a particular new product).

7. **Indirectness of Representation**. As we described in 2 (above), indeterminacy affects both the indexer and the inquirer, but there is one kind of indeterminacy that is unique to the inquirer. Unlike the indexer, the inquirer's search terms may not be a precise description of the "content" that he or she wants. If the indexer is free to use whatever terms he wants, then he can use whatever index terms best express the content of the information as he sees it. The inquirer, on the other hand, does not generally have this freedom of expression when using an information retrieval system. The inquirer must select his search terms from the index terms which have been used to represent the information content on the system. The inquirer's search terms are, in effect, not pure expressions of what he wants, but are *hypotheses* about how the information content he wants is represented. This means that there are *two distinct stages* of a content search: The *First Stage* is not so much a direct search for content as it is a search for the best search terms for the inquirer to work with. This is why Swanson has characterized content searching as inevitably a trial-and-error process.[408] In this kind of situation the inquirer may know what he wants, but can only guess at how it's represented on the information system he is using. But there are other situations where the inquirer doesn't even know exactly for what he is looking—for example, a lawyer, in the defense or prosecution of a lawsuit might, during the pre-trial "discovery" stage of the lawsuit, be looking for what could only be generally described as some kind of "incriminating evidence"—a "smoking gun"—which might be valuable in the conduct of the lawsuit. Here, the lawyer doesn't know specifically what she is looking for, but can only say that she will recognize such incriminating evidence if and when she sees it. A similar situation obtains with scholarly research, where the researcher may not know *exactly* what

---

[408] D.R. Swanson. "Information Retrieval as a Trial-and-Error Process," **Library Quarterly**, vol. 47:2, pp. 128–148, April 1977.

she is looking for, but, like the lawyer, will recognize what she is looking for when she sees it. Here we should remember Wittgenstein's admonition that "language is a vehicle of thought" rather than a representation of thought—we use language as a means by which we think. Likewise, the index terms available to the inquirer represent the tools with which he can not only search, but, even more basically, they represent the tools with which he can *think* about what information content he wants. In so far as the index terms are limited in their utility for expressing what the inquirer wants, they also pose constraints on how he can *think* about what he wants.

**Indeterminacy of Representation:** This depends on several factors:

i. *The number of tokens/occurrences of the representation in the category.* For example, the number of documents which are represented by a particular term, or the number of websites linked to a particular term as a result of an Internet search.

ii. *The uniqueness requirement.* This is a requirement based on the particular needs of the application the information is being used in. For example, in most cases someone looking up "Michael Smith" wants one person, but someone doing a demographic study may want to know how many "Smiths" are in New York city. The difference here is between "Smith" when it denotes a particular individual and "Smith" when it denotes a class of individuals: the first is a semantic use of "Smith" where it connotes a particular individual, but may not have enough information or the right information for the searcher to discriminate the individual he wants from the other "Smiths." The second use of "Smith" is a use of it as an item of data. Here, the name "Smith" gives us all the information we need... no supplementary information is needed since we don't need to distinguish individuals. The names by themselves, even without addresses or phone numbers, would be sufficient for the task. In the second case, individual reference or discrimination doesn't matter.

iii. *The discrimination power of additional information.* If we know "Michael Smith's" street address we might be able to pick him out from the other "Michael Smith's in a phone directory, even if there are a lot of them." The ability to distinguish the "Michael Smith" we want is dependent on the granularity of description, that is, just knowing the borough of New York city where "Michael Smith" lives may be all we need to identify the one we want, but in other situations we may need the street name, and in others you may need the street address, too. The nature of the representation may give you additional discrimination power, for example, since the information you are dealing with consists of the names, addresses, and phone numbers, we also have the option of calling and talking to several of the "Michael Smiths" if we cannot otherwise distinguish the individual we want. We might call this the "Cost of Discrimination," which dictates the cost of indeterminate searches. In some cases the "Cost of Discrimination" is low, but we can imagine examples for which the "Cost of Discrimination" is intolerably high, higher than the inquirer's "futility point," such as when an Internet content search yields *thousands*, or *millions* of websites [the name "Michael Smith" returns 766,000 websites when used as a search phrase on the Google Internet search engine].

## Indeterminacy in Information Systems: An Empirical Study

The discussion of indeterminacy of representation so far has been largely conceptual, with mostly hypothetical examples. It is only natural to ask whether there are any documented examples of information systems where the indeterminacy of representation seriously affected the effectiveness of retrieval? There is. In 1985 the results of a study were published[409] that showed dramatically how the indeterminacy of natural language militated against the precise retrieval of documents with a particular intellectual content. The study examined, in detail, the retrieval effectiveness of a full-text document retrieval system (IBM's STAIRS—STorage And Information Retrieval System) used to support a large corporate litigation, in which the defendant, an engineering construction company, was defending its conduct in a large construction project.[410] The system provided access to 40,000 documents, about 350,000 pages of online text. Simple full-text document retrieval systems operate by having the inquirer formulate queries using words he believes are contained in the documents he wants but are not contained in the documents he doesn't want—that is, the selected search terms must both *describe* the content the inquirer wants as well as *discriminate* the desired documents from nonrelevant ones. The lawyers and paralegals using the retrieval system were actively working on the lawsuit and were intimately familiar with the case, having worked on it for over a year prior to the test. They were also quite specific in their insistence that they needed to retrieve a *minimum* of 75% of the desired, or relevant, documents to conduct the defense of the lawsuit successfully. After the lawyers and paralegals used 51 individual queries to retrieve what they considered to be over 75% of the desired documents, the experimenters then tried to find whether they had missed any relevant documents. The results were striking: while the lawyers and paralegals were convinced that they were retrieving over 75% of the desired documents, they were, in actuality, retrieving only 20%![411] The principal reason for such low success rates in retrieval can be directly attributed to the indeterminacy of meaning in natural language. Stated succinctly, it is impossibly difficult for inquirers using a large full-text retrieval system to predict, by means of their search queries, the exact words, word combinations, and phrases that are used to express the content of the documents they desire but are *not used* to express the content of the documents they do not desire. (Note: it is not enough for the inquirer to simply predict the words that occur in the documents she wants—this

---

[409] D.C. Blair and M.E. Maron. "An Evaluation of Retrieval Effectiveness for a Full-Text Document Retrieval System," **Communications of the ACM**, vol. 28:3, pp. 289–299, March 1985. This experiment is discussed in much more detail in chapter 3 of Blair's **Language and Representation in Information Retrieval**, Elsevier Science (1990).

[410] The litigation which the retrieval system supported was the defense of a $257 million lawsuit brought by the city of San Francisco against the contractors who built the Bay Area Rapid Transit (BART) system, for their alleged failures to meet all the specifications of the contract and to manage the costs of the construction effectively.

[411] The value of 20% for recall is a *maximum* value. The reason for this is simple. In order to search such a large document collection effectively, the experimenters could not examine the relevance of every single document for every query. They actually searched only small portions of the document collection looking for relevant unretrieved documents. Consequently, the experimenters could not say with any assurance that they had found *all* of the unretrieved relevant documents, they merely retrieved enough to make the point that many were missed by the original searchers. If *more* unretrieved relevant documents were found, the average recall value would have been *less than* 20%, perhaps significantly less. (details of the experimental procedures were given in Blair's **Language and Representation in Information Retrieval** (1990))

is the "*description* requirement" of searching. The inquirer must also predict which of those words *do not* occur in the documents she doesn't want—this is the "*discrimination* requirement" of searching. If the inquirer *only* had to predict a word that occurred in all the documents she might want, she would use the word "the" as a search term. That would retrieve all the desired documents, but it would also retrieve all the undesired documents, too.)

It's instructive to look at some of the examples of how this indeterminacy affected retrieval in this case:[412]

> In the legal case in question, one concern of the lawyers was an accident that had occurred and was an object of litigation. The lawyers wanted all the reports, correspondence, memoranda, and minutes of meetings that discussed this accident. Formal queries were constructed that contained the word "accident" along with the name of the [city] where it occurred. In the search for *unretrieved* relevant documents, the experimenters later found that the accident was not always referred to as an "accident," but as an "event," "incident," "situation," "problem," or "difficulty," often without mentioning the relevant proper name—the name of the city in which it occurred. The manner in which an individual referred to the accident was frequently dependent on his or her point of view. Those who discussed the event in a critical or accusatory way referred to it quite directly–as an "accident." Those who were personally involved in the event, and perhaps culpable, tended to refer to it euphemistically as, *inter alia*, an "unfortunate situation," or a "difficulty." Sometimes the accident was referred to obliquely as "the subject of your last letter," "what happened last week was . . . ," or, as in the opening lines of the minutes of a meeting discussing the issue, "Mr. A: We all know why we're here. . . ." [the words "accident" and the name of the city were not used at any time in the meeting either]. Sometimes relevant documents dealt with the problem by mentioning only the technical aspects of why the accident occurred, but neither the accident itself nor the people or place involved. Finally, much relevant information discussed [contributing factors in] the situation *prior* to the accident and, naturally, contained no reference to the accident itself.

> Another information request resulted in the identification of 3 key terms or phrases that were used to retrieve relevant information. Later, the experimenters were able to find 26 other words and phrases that retrieved additional relevant documents. The 3 original key terms could not have been used individually as they would have retrieved 420 documents, or approximately 4000 pages of hard copy, an unreasonably large set, most of which contained irrelevant information. Another request identified 4 key terms/phrases that retrieved relevant documents, but it was possible to find 44 additional terms and combinations of terms to retrieve relevant documents that had been missed.

> Sometimes the experimenters followed a trail of linguistic creativity through the database. In searching for documents discussing "trap correction" (one of the key engineering phrases), it was discovered that relevant, un-retrieved documents had discussed the same issue but referred to it as the "wire warp." Continuing our

[412] These quotations are from Chapter 3 of Blair's **Language and Representation in Information Retrieval** (1990).

search, we found that in still other documents "trap correction" was referred to in a third and novel way: the "shunt correction system." Finally, it was discovered that the inventor of this system was a man named "Coxwell" which directed the experimenters to some documents he had authored, only he referred to the system as the "Roman circle method." Using the "Roman circle method" in a query directed them to still more relevant but un-retrieved documents, but this was not the end either. Further searching revealed that the system had been tested in another city, and all documents germane to those tests referred to the system as the "air truck." At this point the search ended, having consumed over an entire 40-hour week of on-line searching, but there is no reason to believe that the experimenters had found all of the un-retrieved relevant documents; they simply ran out of time.

As the data base included many items of personal correspondence as well as the verbatim minutes of meetings, the use of slang frequently changed the way in which one would "normally" talk about a subject. Disabled or malfunctioning mechanisms with which the lawsuit was concerned were sometimes referred to as "sick" or "dead," and a burned-out circuit was referred to as being "fried." A critical issue under discussion was sometimes referred to as a "smoking gun."

Even misspellings proved an obstacle [to retrieval]. Key search terms like "flattening," "gauge," "memos," and "correspondence," which were essential parts of search phrases, were used effectively to retrieve relevant documents. However, the misspellings "flatening," "guage," "gage," "memoes," and "correspondance," using the same phrases, also retrieved relevant documents. Misspellings like these, which are tolerable in normal everyday correspondence, when included in a computerized database become literal traps for users who are asked not only to anticipate the key words and phrases that may be used to discuss an issue but also to foresee the whole range of possible misspellings, letter transpositions, and typographical errors that are likely to be committed. [While spelling correction sub routines in word-processing programs have improved such problems, they have not eliminated them since they generally cannot correct proper names which have been misspelled.]

Some information requests placed almost impossible demands on the ingenuity of the individual constructing the query. In one situation, the lawyer wanted "Company A's comments concerning [a specific subject]. . . ." Looking at the documents authored by Company A was not enough, as many relevant comments were embedded in the minutes of meetings or recorded secondhand in the documents authored by others. Retrieving all the documents in which Company A was mentioned was too broad a search; it retrieved over 5,000 documents (about 40,000+ pages of hard copy). However, predicting the exact phraseology of the text in which Company A commented on the issue was almost impossible; sometimes Company A was not even mentioned, only that so-and-so (who represented Company A):

"said/considered/remarked/pointedout/commented/noted/explained/    discussed," etc. [the fact that this individual represented Company A was not included in the document text and had to be known by the searcher.]

In some requests, the most important terms and phrases *were not used at all* in relevant documents. For example, "steel quantity" was a key phrase used to retrieve important relevant documents germane to an actionable issue in the lawsuit, but unretrieved relevant documents were also found that did not report *steel quantity* at all, but merely the *number* of such things as "girders," "beams," "frames," "bracings," etc. In another request, it was important to find documents that discussed "non-expendable components." In this case, relevant unretrieved documents merely listed the names of the components (of which there were hundreds) and made no mention of the broader generic description of these items as "nonexpendable."

It might be countered that such linguistic variability as this is uncommon—it is not. This linguistic variability is a consequence of the "productivity" of language which we discussed briefly above. Another question which arises is, why didn't the lawyers realize they were not getting all of the information relevant to a particular issue? Certainly they knew the lawsuit. They had been involved with it from the beginning—over a year—and were the principal attorneys representing the defense. In addition, one of the paralegals had been instrumental not only in setting up the information retrieval system, but also in supervising the selection of relevant information to be put on-line. Might it not be reasonable to expect them to be suspicious that they were not retrieving everything they wanted? Not really. Because the database was so large (providing access to over 350,000 pages of hard copy, all of which was in some way pertinent to the lawsuit), it would be unreasonable to expect four individuals (two lawyers and two paralegals) to have total, literal recall of all the important supporting facts, testimony, and related data that was germane to the case. If they had such recall they would have no need for a computerized, interactive retrieval system. It is well known among cognitive psychologists that man's power of literal recall is much less effective than his power of recognition. The lawyers could remember the exact text of some of the important information, but this was a very small subset of the total information relevant to a particular issue.

The system, above, as mentioned, contained 40,000 documents. Yet this was just a small part of the entire system which was projected to have over 1,000,000 documents, approximately 10,000,000 pages of online text, by the time the trial began. As we have pointed out, some of the indeterminacy of natural language is due to the size of the text in which it occurs. If the above linguistic variability was found in the comparatively small preliminary system, the linguistic variability and difficulty retrieving the desired documents in sets smaller than the inquirer's futility point would likely be significantly higher—again, the analogy of doing content searches on the Internet using an Internet search engine is apropos, especially since Internet search engines are basically full-text retrieval systems like STAIRS was. The difference is, of course, that most Internet searches are not in defense of a multi-million dollar lawsuit, as the above example was, so when relevant documents/websites are missed it is not nearly as crucial. Although this study was published over 20 years ago, the problems it identifies are still critical in information retrieval. The fact that an Internet search using the names of the authors "Blair and Maron" links to several hundred websites in 2004 shows that the issues it discussed are still relevant to today's information systems.

## The "Determinacy of Sense": An Old Logical Problem

Talking about the indeterminacy of language is a broad and conceptually deep endeavor, one in which we can easily lose our intellectual footing. But here, as elsewhere in this manuscript, Wittgenstein has left us some guideposts.

Computers are fundamentally logical systems, and the evolution of computer models has some parallels with the evolution of models of formal logic (the logic of relations existed for almost a century before the first relational database was proposed and built by a philosopher at the Rand Corporation[413]). The high determinacy of representation in the data model recalls the concern over the "determinacy of sense" in language that occupied several prominent philosophers in the early 20th century. Germany's Gottlob Frege and England's Bertrand Russell were the most prominent logicians of this period. For them, the primary purpose of language was to assert facts. Facts themselves are either true or false—there are no other choices. If language asserts facts, and facts are either true or false, then it is necessary that language should be able to represent these facts precisely. The words or assertions which correspond to the facts must have a "definite sense," that is, their meaning or application must be *only* one of two choices: true or false (what logicians call the "excluded middle" or "bivalence": If A is an assertion about a fact, then the expression (A v ¬A) is true for all values of A. That is, if A = "It is raining" then it is necessarily true that "It is raining" (A) or (v) "It is not raining" (¬A)). Frege and Russell believed that ordinary language was logically flawed and did not measure up to the criterion of *definite sense*. Consequently, they believed that the analytic precision that philosophical analysis required could only be attained by a specially constructed logical language which could maintain the requisite *definite sense* of its assertions. Wittgenstein was a student of Russell's and a protégé of Frege's. In his early work, the **Tractatus Logico-Philosophicus**, Wittgenstein agreed with Frege and Russell that language asserted facts and that its assertions about facts, what philosophers call "propositions," must be "bivalent." As he stated in the **Tractatus**:

A proposition must restrict reality to two alternatives: yes or no. [**TLP** 4.023]

But Wittgenstein went farther than his predecessors by saying that the logical structure of factual assertions was the factual structure of the world—a grand statement that assured that language would have the same *determinacy of sense* as the "facts" of the world.[414] But Wittgenstein broke with Frege and Russell's assertion that ordinary language was logically defective and needed to be replaced by a more precise logical language:

---

[413] The philosopher who designed the first working Relational Data Base was M.E. Maron [M.E. Maron. "Relational Data File I: Design Philosophy," **Information Retrieval: A Critical View**. Thompson Book, Washington, DC, 1966. Edited by G. Schector.] After designing it, Maron worked with R.E. Levien to build an actual working model. This was reported in: R.E. Levien. "Relational Data File II: Implementation" [**Information Retrieval: A Critical View**, Thompson Book, Washington, D C, 1966. Edited by G. Schector] and R. E. Levien and M. E. Maron. "A Computer System for Inference Execution and Data Retrieval," **Communications of the ACM**, vol. 10:11, pp. 715–721, November 1967.

[414] Wittgenstein presented this view in the **Tractatus**:

| 2.1 | We picture facts to ourselves. |
|---|---|
| 2.12 | A picture is a model of reality. |
| 2.141 | A picture is a fact. |
| 2.15 | The fact that the elements of a picture are related to one another in a determinate way represents that things are related to one another in the same way. |
| 2.1511 | *That* is how a picture is attached to reality; it reaches right out to it. |
| 2.1512 | It is laid against reality like a measure. |

> All the propositions of our everyday language, just as they stand, are in good logical order. [**TLP** 5.5563]

With this statement Wittgenstein is making a subtle, but important distinction with Frege and Russell. He is saying that language is *not* logically defective, that assertions about facts can, and do, make sense. He is *not* saying that language cannot be misunderstood, and that sometimes our assertions about facts are not vague or ambiguous. They can be. What ordinary language does is it *obscures* or *disguises* the underlying logical form of its assertions:

> Everyday language is part of the human organism and is no less complicated than it. It is not humanly possible to gather immediately from it what the logic of language is. [**TLP** 4.002]

> Most of the propositions and questions of philosophers arise from our failure to understand the logic of our language. [**TLP** 4.003]

We don't need to construct a separate logically precise language, we just need to analyse our assertions in ordinary language according to strict logical principles, as his mentor Bertrand Russell had done:

> It was Russell who performed the service of showing that the apparent logical form of a proposition need not be its real one. [**TLP** 4.0031]

The logical structure of language just needs to be brought out. Logic doesn't give us an ideal language, it simply gives us a form of notation and a method that we can use to bring out the logical order of ordinary language.

Over the next 3 decades, Wittgenstein gradually reassessed this position. In the first place, he saw that language did not have an underlying logical order which needed to be brought out to resolve ambiguities or determine the meaning of a statement. No logical order could do this because for it to work it must be able to not only tell us the meaning of a word, but the meaning of that word in *all possible circumstances and uses*. Issues of meaning, he began to see, are not resolved by uncovering something inherent in language, they are resolved by looking at how the statement in question is *used*. He also came to reject the notion that the meaning of a word had to have a *definite sense*, believing that such a notion was ultimately incoherent because it could be applied variously in different contexts of language use. That is, the notion of a *definite sense* is not one thing, since it varied in different contexts and circumstances. For example, suppose I am with a friend who is sitting at a desk and typing on his Macintosh computer. If he says that "the computer" works very well, I know exactly what "the computer" means. But if my friend says that "the computer" used by the IRS has proved unreliable, I have only the vaguest idea what "the computer" actually means here—it could be any one of hundreds of brands and models of computers. Even when such a thing as a *definite sense* does exist in language, it is not something that is a property of words. Words, by themselves, do not have precise meanings, but their *uses* could have. Wittgenstein's reassessment of his earlier position lead him to reject the single comprehensive notion of a *definite sense* and to adopt a more complex notion of meaning in language which recognized that the sense of language was precise in some contexts and uses but could have varying levels of *indeterminacy* in other contexts and uses. This break with what Wittgenstein called his "old way of thinking" comes out in his criticism of Frege in **Philosophical Investigations**:

> One might say that the concept "game" is a concept with blurred edges.—"But is a blurred concept a concept at all?"—Is an indistinct photograph a picture of a person at all? Is it even always an advantage to replace an indistinct picture by a sharp one? Isn't the indistinct one often exactly what we need?

> Frege compares a concept to an area and says that an area with vague boundaries cannot be called an area at all. This presumably means that we cannot do anything with it.—But is it senseless to say: "Stand roughly there?" Suppose that I were standing with someone in a city square and said that. As I say it I do not draw any kind of boundary, but perhaps point with my hand—as if I were indicating a particular spot. And this is just how one might explain to someone what a game is. One gives examples and intends them to be taken in a particular way.—I do not, however, mean by this that he is supposed to see in those examples that common thing which I—for some reason—was unable to express; but that he is now to employ those examples in a particular way. Here giving examples is not an indirect means of explaining—in default of a better. For any general definition can be misunderstood too. The point is that this is how we play the game. (I mean the language-game with the word "game.") [**PI** §71]

It is important to avoid an obvious misinterpretation of Wittgenstein here. He is *not* saying that vagueness is an essential feature of language, in a sense *promoting* vagueness in language as necessary and useful. What he is doing is simply resisting the requirement for the "strict determinacy of sense" in language that Frege and Russell insisted was necessary for language to express meanings clearly. For Frege and Russell, each individual word had to have a meaning that was clear and precisely determinate. If it didn't, Frege insisted, the indeterminacy of meaning would multiply as words were combined into sentences. But here again Wittgenstein debunks this view in his later writing:

> When I give the description: "The ground was quite covered with plants"—do you want to say I don't know what I am talking about until I can give a definition of a plant? [**PI** §70]

The meaning of this statement, as well as his other example, "stand roughly there," are, in the proper circumstances, perfectly clear even though they both use words—"plants" and "roughly"—that, by themselves, are somewhat vague. As Wittgenstein has shown us, we should "Let the use teach you the meaning" [**PI** p. 212]. Of course, this does not mean that these statements are always clear. We can imagine circumstances, that is, *uses*, in which they are not. For example, if I go to a store and ask the clerk for some weed killer saying that "*The ground was quite covered with plants* that I want to get rid of" the clerk might say that he needed to know exactly what kind of plants they were in order to give me the proper weed killer. Or, if I say "*Stand roughly here*" but point to the edge of a precipice, the person I am addressing might reasonably ask, "Where do you mean exactly?"

What is the relationship between the quest for a logical model of language with a *definite sense*, and the difference between data retrieval and content, or document, retrieval? In the first place, data are usually considered to be "facts," so an instance of a Data Model is, in some sense, an implicit assertion about the truth or falsity of the specific facts that are organized by it (e.g., the record that shows that Roy Blakney lives at 10 Green St Court, is an implicit assertion that an individual by that name currently lives at that address). The various editing and integrity constraints that can be applied to the data or facts on a database are aimed at preserving the recorded values of these facts. Further, the data manipulation and data definition languages of the Data Model have some of the characteristics of the ideal logical language which Frege and Russell sought—take **SQL** as an example: **SQL** is separate from natural language; its operators are precisely defined in a way that much of the grammar of natural language cannot be; and for most of the data it is used to specify it's application has a *definite sense*—it is either true or false.[415]

If we can take any lesson from Wittgenstein's evolving view of representation in language it is that the simple logical model with a *definite sense* and an *excluded middle*, while rigorous, has only a narrow range of application, namely, to only those items of data or information whose representations have a *definite sense*—a high level of representational *determinacy* (or low level of *indeterminacy*). As Wittgenstein saw the limitations of the model of language with a definite sense, in particular, that the logical model of language was not something that underlay language use and needed to be uncovered, and that even the idea of a strict determinacy of sense was a false ideal because a general universally applicable conception of such determinacy was incoherent. His own views evolved to a more complex assessment of language in which meaning was not a context-free property of individual words, but was often dependent on context and could be *determinate* in some contexts and uses and *indeterminate* in varying degrees in others (And "indeterminacy" is not a pejorative term. It merely expresses a particular state of the sense or meaning of an expression.). In the same manner we can view the transition from the Data Model to the Document Model of information systems as, not a break with the past and the creation of a new form of representation, but the natural evolution of a precise, but limited, data model to a more complex and comprehensive document model—a model that includes the precision of the data model in some circumstances, but also incorporates the capacity for the less *determinate* representations of intellectual content often found in the document model. In his later writings, Wittgenstein himself summarized the transition from the precise logical model of language to the more complex context-dependent model of his later writings:

> The more narrowly we examine language, the sharper becomes the conflict between it and our requirement (For the crystalline purity of logic was, of course, not a *result of investigation*; it was a requirement.). The conflict becomes intolerable; the requirement is now in danger of becoming empty.—We have got onto slippery ice where there is no friction and so in a certain sense the conditions are ideal, but also, just because of that, we are unable to walk. We want to walk; so we need *friction*. Back to the rough ground! [**PI** §107]

---

[415] In the Database literature, there is some discussion of the need for 3-valued logics rather than two, primarily because of the ambiguity of the "null" value—for example, when an employee record has a null value where an employee's spouse is to be listed, does it mean that he/she has no spouse, or does it mean that the spouse's name was simply not recorded? But, to date, data base management system manufacturers have not agreed on a uniform way to handle such ambiguities.

The Data Model has, as I have already stated, been enormously successful in its application to data management. But its implicit unstated requirement for determinacy of representation made for a neat, but bounded domain of application. This was fine as long as the principal applications dealt with precisely specifiable data whose correctness was evident, or decidable, in every case (e.g., that "Roger Picquet's address" is correct and the same in each of its occurrences on the multiple databases or files in which it appears). But as database applications have evolved, database management systems began to be used to manage information such as documents and images whose representations of intellectual content often didn't fall into the precisely defined categories or value ranges of the data model. If this indeterminate information is "forced" into the more precise data model, then the data model becomes a Procrustean bed in which everything "fits" but access may still not be adequate, because the apparent precision only hides an underlying indeterminacy of representation. The evolution from the Data to the Document Model is, in a metaphorical sense, a movement from the "crystalline purity of logic" back to Wittgenstein's "rough ground." What is the "rough ground?" The "rough ground" consists, in part, of the circumstances and context which help to give language meaning, and which can mitigate the ambiguity of document representations. If the evolution of the precise Data Model to the more complex—but more broadly applicable—Document Model is analogous to the development of Wittgenstein's idea of logic, representation, and *definite sense*, then the development of the Document Model is contingent on being able to build more of the context of information creation and use into the representation scheme of the Document Model—it is "information in context."

## Description and Discrimination (Either can be Indeterminate)

Representations of information, what we call indexes, have two fundamental objectives: *description* and *discrimination*: they must *describe* the "intellectual content" of a particular corpus of information, and they must *discriminate* that information from information that has a similar intellectual content. The judgment of the quality of indexes lies primarily (though not solely) with the searchers: the indexes must *describe* the information the way that searchers who are looking for that information would describe it.[416] But the indexes must also, through these descriptions, *discriminate* the information the searchers would find useful from similar information which they would not find useful. The goal of indexes is to identify *all* and *only* the information that the searcher would find useful— *description* identifies *all* the useful information, while *discrimination* identifies *only* the useful information.

The quality of *description* and *discrimination* vary quite widely in information systems. Databases which provide access to highly determinate data, such as bank accounts which are indexed by unique names or social security numbers, both *describe* and *discriminate* well. Descriptions such as, "name," "address," "account balance," or "social security number" have clear senses, or meanings, that are easily understood within the context and

---

[416]This is the "operational theory of about" put forward by M.E. Maron in his "On Indexing, Retrieval and the Meaning of About" [**Journal of the American Society for Information Science**, vol. 28:1, pp. 38–43, January 1977]. This definition, while insightful, only models description, not discrimination.

practice of banking. The description "social security number" *discriminates* well since it links account information to uniquely identifiable individuals, a requirement for the practice of banking.

But, as we pointed out before, there are kinds of data retrieval systems, like the hypothetical Shanghai phonebook, that, although they *describe* their data correctly, they do not *discriminate* it well enough to distinguish items of information (names) which have many occurrences.[417] Here we might say that some data retrieval systems while successful at *describing* the data or information that they provide access to, suffer from a failure to *discriminate* useful data for the searchers who use them. But other kinds of information systems may suffer from *failures of description* as well as *failures of discrimination.* This is the case, as we mentioned briefly before, for those information systems that provide access to the "intellectual content" of texts or images. A failure of *description* occurs when the intellectual content of a document or image is *described* in a way that the typical searcher, who wants that document or image, would not be able to anticipate. For example, a book that discusses what the searchers would call "continental drift" is indexed under the description "plate tectonics." This usually occurs when the index scheme—the vocabulary that has been selected to represent the intellectual content of texts or images— does not match very well the way that searchers might describe the intellectual content of those texts or images. But *descriptions* of intellectual content can fail to *discriminate* as well. This occurs when the index terms the searchers use to describe what they want identify categories that have very high numbers of members. This sort of problem occurs in the subject catalogues of large libraries, but is often seen as a consequence of using World Wide Web search engines to search for intellectual content. On the Web, searches using fairly general terms like "computers" or "travel" or "investing" return thousands, sometimes millions of websites that match them. This is a failure of discrimination.

## The Consequences of Indeterminacy in Information Retrieval

Since indeterminacy in language is the principal factor that determines the successful retrieval of information content, we should take a moment to look at the actual consequences of indeterminate searches on information systems. First of all, we should note that indeterminacy is not a property of individual index terms, or a property of information retrieval systems. As Wittgenstein showed us, indeterminacy is a function of how the searcher wants to use the information she is looking for: if she just wants to look at a few samples of information on a particular topic, then the determinacy of her search terms does not need to be high. But if she needs to find the "best" information on a very precisely defined topic, and is not at all interested in information with similar intellectual

---

[417] While most phone books rely only on the uniqueness of names to discriminate individual listings, instances like the hypothetical Shanghai phone book could still provide unique listings if the searcher knew both the name and the address of the person whose phone number he is looking up. This, of course, puts an additional burden on the searcher and makes his search more difficult. In fact, it is almost a truism that an information system that does not describe or discriminate well is often trading off indexing effort for searching effort: that is, less effort in indexing results in information systems that do not describe or discriminate well, and a system with such flaws makes effective searching much more difficult than a system that does a better job of description and/or discrimination.

content that is not the "best," the determinacy of her search terms needs to be very high. Previously, we drew the major distinction in information systems as being between Data Retrieval and Document Retrieval. While it is the case that Data Retrieval tends to be fairly determinate, and Document, or Content, Retrieval relatively indeterminate, there are instances as we have shown where Data Retrieval can be somewhat indeterminate and Document Retrieval can be relatively determinate. It all depends on the manner in which the information is represented and the use to which the searcher wants to put the information. The real distinction between Data Retrieval and Document retrieval is the distinction between "Determinate Searching" and "Indeterminate Searching." Since Data Retrieval is the exemplar of Determinate Searching, and Document Content Retrieval is the exemplar of Indeterminate Searching, we will refer to distinctions between Data Retrieval and Document Retrieval in the following discussion of the distinctions between Determinate and Indeterminate Searching. It will be easier for the reader to see the important distinctions if the examples are given of searching for Data and searching for Document Content.

## DISTINCTION 1: THE TYPE OF QUERY

The typical queries for document and data retrieval differ noticeably. For determinate data retrieval, the question names the desired information fairly precisely. An inquiry for Roy Blakney's phone number is described as a request for "Roy Blakney's phone number." There is very little ambiguity about how to describe it. Document content queries are often much more indirect and ambiguous. They tend to look like: "Give me information that discusses the economic tradeoffs between distributed database management systems and centralized systems for databases with high transaction rates." From this question it is impossible to determine what the exact formal query might be to retrieve the desired information. For example, should the inquirer look under specific subject terms like "distributed databases," "economics," "budgeting," "cost analysis," etc., or, under the names of computer vendors who might provide distributed databases or manage them such as IBM or Oracle—or, some Boolean combination of these terms. Further, does the inquirer want actual budgeting information for individual systems, or averaged over several systems; or does the inquirer want explanations of a more general or theoretical nature? Does the inquirer want comparative analysis of systems of different size, in different industries, or managing different kinds of data, etc? Such questions can go on indefinitely. It is also the case, that a determinate search for data on one system will be very much like a determinate search for the same data on another system, but an indeterminate search for document content, even though it is looking for the same information, might require vastly different search strategies on different systems.

## DISTINCTION 2: THE RELATIONSHIP BETWEEN THE FORMAL QUERY AND THE REPRESENTATION OF THE SATISFACTORY ANSWER

In retrieval we can identify three principal linguistic relationships:

> Between the **request for information** and the **formal query**;
> Between the **formal query** and the **representation of the information** desired;

Between the **representation of the information** desired and the **intellectual content** of that information.

The relationship between a **formal** *data* **retrieval query** and the **representation of a satisfactory answer** is typically deterministic. A request for Brian O'Connor's social security number will be satisfied only with *Brian O'Connor's social security number.* Hence, there is usually a clear mapping between the description in a **formal query** of what is desired—"O'Connor's social security number"—and the **representation of that information** in a data management system. In SQL, the de facto standard data access language, it might look like this:

```
SELECT   SSN
FROM     EMPLOYEE TABLE
WHERE    NAME = "O'Connor";
```

There is also a deterministic relationship between the **request for data** and the **formal query** which retrieves the right information. From a logical point of view, the relationship between a **data retrieval request** and the **formal query** that retrieves what you want is similar to the notion of "analytic" statements in language. Analytic statements are like "All bachelors are unmarried." This statement is analytic—that is, it is necessarily true— because the idea of being "unmarried" is part of the definition of what a bachelor is. No amount of empirical investigation can prove or disprove an analytic statement, it is true by definition. In a similar sense, the correct **formal data query** is often embedded in the description of the original **request for information**. If you ask, "What is Brian O'Connor's employee number?" the formal terms "SSN" and "O'Connor" used in the **formal SQL query** are part of the definition of "employee number" and "Brian O'Connor" in the original request. So, more formally, we might say that for most **data retrieval requests** the relation between the **data request** and the **correct formal query** is analytic.

In **document retrieval**, the **request for information** and the **query** that retrieves the desired document(s) may be entirely, and unpredictably, dissimilar. Consider again the example from the STAIRS study (see the quotation at footnote 412) where the request was for documents that discussed "steel quantity." Most of the relevant documents did not use the phrase "steel quantity" at all, but merely referred to the number of such things as "girders," "beams," "frames," "bracings," etc. While the relationship between a **determinate data query** and the **representation of the correct answer** is generally deterministic, the relationship between an **indeterminate document query** and the **representation of the most useful documents** is generally probabilistic.

DISTINCTION 3: CRITERION OF SUCCESSFUL RETRIEVAL

The evaluation of retrieval effectiveness for determinate data retrieval is fairly straight-forward: Did the system retrieve the *correct* answer to the query? If you asked for "Arpad Kerekes' address" then only Arpad Kerekes' *correct* address would be a successful answer. No other address will do, and there are no "partially correct" answers. Further, there are usually ways of verifying correctness independently of the information system itself. The decision whether data retrieval is successful or not is, thus, binary—either it got the right data, or it did not—this is what logicians call the "excluded middle." Since document retrieval has a less straightforward relation between the query and the representation of desired documents, the standard of success cannot be as rigid as *correctness*. Retrieved documents are judged to be *useful* or *not useful*, and some documents can be more, or less, useful than others. Hence, document retrieval success is often judged in terms of *degrees* of effectiveness, and only under special circumstances can a document be thought of as correct or not. The standard of effectiveness for document retrieval is one of *utility* rather than *correctness*. Utility is a much more complex and problematic performance criterion to measure than correctness, and, typically, there are no objective, user-independent standards of utility.[418]

Although documents may be judged useful or not useful, their utility is not just a property of the information itself, it is contingent on the background and abilities of those who would use the information, and on the use to which it will be put: one document may be useful for one individual, but not for another, even though both individuals are searching for information to solve the same problem (e.g., the retrieved document may be very "technical" and while one searcher has the necessary background to understand it, the other searcher does not). Since the effectiveness of data retrieval is, as we have observed, usually contingent on the *correctness* of the data, the background and abilities of those who use the information do not usually affect this judgment—that is, an item of data is *correct* whether or not it is thought to be correct by the searcher, but a document cannot usually be judged *useful* if the searcher does not think it is so. Thus, while *correctness* is an independent property of data itself, *utility* is a broader notion that extends beyond the information itself and includes the background, abilities, and intentions of the searcher.

## DISTINCTION 4: THE SPEED OF SUCCESSFUL RETRIEVAL

Since the process of determinate data retrieval generally consists of the simple matching of formal queries to descriptions of the data, the speed of successful data retrieval is primarily dependent on the physical searching speeds of the computer. Faster computers and more efficient methods of searching and storage translate into a "better" data retrieval system, all other things being equal. But, because of the indeterminacy of document content representation—that is, that there is usually no single, direct link between a formal query and the intellectual content of useful documents, document searches are typically characterized by trial-and-error: The inquirer submits a formal query, retrieves a number of documents, evaluates their utility, and, if not enough useful documents are retrieved, modifies the original query and retrieves a new set of documents. This process may repeat itself many times during a search, especially on large document collections. To understand this iterative process, one needs only to think of conducting a subject search on the World Wide Web. Here, individual websites are equivalent to the individual documents in our model. Because of the trial-and-error nature of document retrieval, the speed of successful retrieval is not primarily dependent on the physical searching speeds of the computer, but on the number of websites or documents the inquirer must evaluate, and the number of

---

[418] William Cooper was the first to show that utility was the principal criterion of success for document content retrieval: W.S. Cooper. "On Selecting a Measure of Retrieval Effectiveness, Part I: The 'Subjective' Philosophy of Evaluation," **Journal of the American Society for Information Science**, vol. 24, pp. 87–100, 1973.

revisions of his query he must make in the course of finding what he needs. In short, the speed of document retrieval is primarily contingent on the number of logical decisions the inquirer must make during the course of her search. No matter how fast the physical searching speeds of the retrieval systems are, the searcher is still faced with the task of evaluating the retrieved documents, and deciding on subsequent query revisions. Unlike data retrieval, simply using a faster computer does not guarantee better access to document content. A faster computer may only get you the useless documents faster, and there may be too many useless documents to look at in a reasonably large system.

The difference between the speeds of determinate data retrieval and document content retrieval is like the difference in speeds between a racecar and a delivery truck. Since a racecar merely goes from the start to the finish, its physical speed is a reasonably good indicator of how fast it will run the race. But for the delivery truck, its physical speed matters less than the number of stops (deliveries) it must make along the way—a Ferrari won't help a newspaper boy deliver his papers any faster than a bicycle if he has to stop and park it at every house and the houses are close together. But a delivery truck may also deliver things to the *wrong* addresses and must then take additional time to straighten this out. In such a case the delivery process is extended and may reach a point where it is never completed, that is, some customers never get their packages. Analogously, just as the delivery truck may deliver the wrong things to a customer, a document retrieval system can deliver *useless* documents to an inquirer. In some situations, the inquirer, like the hapless customer, may never get what he wants, and, likewise, the document search or "delivery" process may extend to the point where it is never finished. Because of these differences in how search speed may be assessed, data retrieval is improved by increasing the speed of physical access, while document retrieval can only be improved by reducing the number of logical decisions the inquirer must make. Automated document retrieval procedures may reduce the number of decisions an inquirer must make, but it does not eliminate them. The reduction of the number of logical decisions can be effected by improving the representation of the documents, by improving the inferences that a system needs to make to match formal requests to useful documents, or, by providing expert searchers to help the users of the system. Because of the dominance of the determinate Data Retrieval Model, some system designers have made the erroneous assumption that the increase in physical searching speed of a document content retrieval system will improve its effectiveness the way that such an increase in physical searching speed improves a determinate data retrieval system. Wittgenstein would call this a "disease of thinking."

## DISTINCTION 5: REPRESENTING INFORMATION: THE EFFECT OF SEMANTIC INDETERMINACY

Data items are typified by the relatively few ways in which they can be represented. An "address" is simply an "address," there are no obvious other simple ways to represent or refer to that kind of information. An "employee number" might be variously termed an "employee ID" or an "Social Security Number" or an "ID number" or an "SSN." But even here there is still a relatively limited number of ways to represent it. Documents with a particular subject content, on the other hand, can be represented in an almost unlimited number of ways. Suppose an inquirer wanted a document dealing with the "techniques of records management." How might such information be represented? Well, it might be under "techniques of records management," of course, but it might also be represented as:

> records management systems
> records organization
> records organizing systems
> file management
> techniques of file management
> file management systems
> systems of file management
> filing systems
> filing methods
> methods of filing
> methods of file management
> techniques of file organization
> file organization methods
> information systems
> techniques of information system design
> office systems
> office information systems[419]
>
> ⋮

With the aid of a thesaurus, such a list could be extended considerably. But even this does not exhaust the ways in which this kind of information could be represented. Useful documents might be listed under the names of the numerous specific commercial records management systems such as "FileNet," "PCDocs," or "Documentum" and might not have any generic descriptions like the ones above. The consequence of this phenomenon is that it becomes increasingly problematic for the inquirer to guess the description(s) that represent the documents he wants. An experiment conducted by Swanson[420] showed that when indexers were encouraged to assign as many subject terms as possible to short physics papers they were able to find pertinent subject descriptions with virtually no upper limit. Such unlimited semantic flexibility in language was first proposed by the mathematician/philosopher C.S. Peirce in the 19th century. He called this aspect of language "unlimited semiosis."[421] Peirce believed that most semantic "meaning" could be represented by an unlimited number of different words, word combinations, and phrases. In the 1960's the logician Yehoshua Bar-Hillel also recognized this combinatorial aspect of language drawing an *a propos* analogy between the representation of meaning for a linguistic

---

[419] This list was the result of some information systems work I was doing at a company. The managers I was talking to did not believe that it was problematic to represent document content, so I gave each of them a copy of the same document entitled "Techniques of Records Management" and asked them to each write down what he/she thought was the main subject description for it, and to not talk to each other in the process. This is the list that resulted.

[420] D. Swanson. "Studies of Indexing Depth and Retrieval Effectiveness." Unpublished report, National Science Foundation Grant GN 380, p. 9, February 1966. Although the report was not published, it is described in detail on pp. 170–171 of Blair's **Language and Representation in Information Retrieval**, Elsevier Science, 1990.

[421] C.S. Peirce. "Logic as Semiotic: The Theory of Signs," **Philosophical Writings of Peirce**. Dover Publications, New York, 1955. Edited by Justus Buchler.

expression and the endless—and undecidable—ways that the same number could be represented [e.g., $4 = (3 + 1) = (7 - 3) = (1765 - 1761) = (positive$ square root of 16), etc.].[422] More recently, Langendoen and Postal[423] have asserted that the collection of sentences which comprise a natural language is so vast that its magnitude cannot be represented by any number, finite or transfinite. As a consequence, no algorithm, Turing Machine or generative grammar can construct or produce all of the possible well-formed sentences in a language. *Prima facie*, this is a different problem than the one we have described by the phrase "unlimited semiosis." But it is still part of the same linguistic phenomenon. The fact that the set of all possible well-formed sentences in a language is uncountably infinite is certainly related to the phenomenon that Peirce observed that a given linguistic "meaning" has an unlimited number of representations. The practical consequences of this phenomenon have been a persistent irritant to work on "semantic networks." Here, unless the network is unusually small the number of words and phrases that can be linked to a set of semantic "meanings" can quickly grow to unmanageable proportions. This indeterminacy in language has been a significant problem for Artificial Intelligence which terms it the "exponential explosion"[424] and has undermined many attempts to provide realistic natural language processing or semantic networking.

## DISTINCTION 6: THE END-POINT OF SEARCHING

Because determinate data retrieval depends on a fairly straightforward matching of queries to representations, if the query does not retrieve what you want you can be fairly certain that the desired data does not exist on the information system. For example, if you submit a well-formed request for Mary Sinico's address and the system replies that no records match the query, it is very likely that that information does not exist on the database. This is a direct result of the low indeterminacy of representation for data.

On the other hand, for document retrieval, if you submit a query and retrieve no useful documents, it does *not* mean that there are no useful documents in the system. Because so many formal queries can be derived from a single topical request (see the "records management" example in Distinction 5, *supra*), the negative results may only mean that you have not guessed, in your formal query, the words that represent the documents you would find useful.

## DISTINCTION 7: TYPES OF SEARCHES

Determinate data retrieval is characterized by one kind of search: an exact match of the formal query with specific data representations. This may retrieve a single data item or it may retrieve an aggregate of data based on a number of exact matches, such as when the search looks for data in a specific range. Document retrieval, on the other hand, is typified

---

[422] Y. Bar-Hillel. "Theoretical Aspects of the Mechanization of Literature Searching," **Language and Information: Selected Essays on Their Theory and Application**, chapter 19. Addison-Wesley, London, 1964.
[423] D.T. Langendoen and P. Postal. **The Vastness of Natural Languages**. Basil Blackwell, Oxford, UK, 1984.
[424] P. Winston. **Artificial Intelligence**, 3rd ed. Addison-Wesley, Reading, MA, 1992.

by at least three different kinds of searches: *sample, exhaustive,* and *specific.*[425] *Sample* searches are those where the inquirer needs only a few of the documents on a given topic, so any reasonably good documents on the subject will suffice (one can imagine a marketing executive for a manufacturing firm wanting to see examples of what customers are saying about his company's products. He doesn't want *everything* written by or about customers who bought his products, but only a selection of such writings). *Exhaustive* searches are at the other extreme and require *all* the documents that might satisfy a particular information need. Legal searching and searching to support research often require exhaustive searches. *Specific* searches are those where one must either find a *specific* document that satisfies the information need, or find evidence that the desired document does not exist. Specific searches are typical of patent searching. Here, the inventor or patent attorney must either find a document that describes the existence of a previous patent that matches the one being applied for, or search enough to develop evidence that no such single prior patent exists.

One of the characteristic difficulties of document retrieval design is that often systems are designed to support one kind of searching, say, *sample,* but over time the needs of the inquirers change and the system is used more for *exhaustive* or *specific* searches. A system designed for sample searching is not well-suited for exhaustive or specific searching. Further, document representation schemes are especially difficult to change in a reasonably large system, so it may be difficult to convert a sample-oriented search system into an exhaustive or specific-oriented searching system. This is part of a more general problem of the structure of searching, that a lack of foresight in the selection of the searchable categories of a set of documents may leave a searcher without good access points for her searches. For example, in the STAIRS evaluation (*q.v.*) searching was based on the precise word content of the documents and a few categories such as "author" and "date." After the system was built it was discovered that the lawyers frequently wanted to find documents of a particular type (internal memos, outside letters, minutes of meetings, different types of reports, budget statements, etc). Since "document-type" was not a searchable field on the system, this kind of search could not be made. This is a common problem for document content retrieval systems that start as small systems but develop into much larger systems. Categories of documents that were relatively small and could be searched in their entirety on a small system, may grow larger than a typical inquirer would be willing to look through.[426] When the STAIRS system was smaller, the searchers could retrieve the documents with the words they wanted in them, then look through the retrieved set to find the document types that they wanted. But as the

[425] D.C. Blair. "The Challenge of Document Retrieval, Part I: Major Issues and a Framework Based on Search Exhaustivity, Determinacy of Representation and Document Collection Size," **Information Processing and Management,** vol. 38, pp. 273–291, 2002. D.C. Blair. "The Challenge of Document Retrieval, Part II: A Strategy for Document Searching Based on Identifiable Document Partitions," **Information Processing and Management,** vol. 38, pp. 293–304, 2002. W.S. Cooper. "On Selecting a Measure of Retrieval Effectiveness, Part I: The 'Subjective' Philosophy of Evaluation," **Journal of the American Society for Information Science,** vol. 24, pp. 87–100, 1973

[426] For a more detailed discussion of this phenomenon, see D.C. Blair. "Searching Biases in Large, Interactive Document Retrieval Systems," **Journal of the American Society for Information Science,** vol. 31:4, pp. 271–277, July 1980; or chapter 1 of D.C.Blair. **Language and Representation in Information Retrieval,** Elsevier Science, 1990.

system got larger and the retrieved sets got correspondingly larger, it became very time-consuming to look through entire retrieved sets for the document types that the searcher desired.

## DISTINCTION 8: SCALING UP THE SYSTEM

Increasing the size of an existing determinate data retrieval system generally does not cause any major difficulties with retrieval. The process of normalization, the principal method of database design, does not take the size of the database into consideration when normalizing record structures. Again, less determinate document content retrieval systems are more problematic. Size *does* influence document content retrieval effectiveness, all other things being equal. In fact, the fastest way to turn a *good* document content retrieval system into a *bad* one is simply to make it larger. Consider the following example. Suppose a document retrieval query consists of the following terms: "Databases" AND "Distributed" (This will retrieve documents that contain both words "Databases" and "Distributed" in their text, or as assigned index terms.). Let's suppose, further, that it retrieves 50 documents that match the query, and 1 of those documents is judged to be useful. Now, let's suppose that the document collection grows significantly. This generally means that the number of documents retrieved by our query will increase, too. Now let's say that the number of documents retrieved by our query is 500 instead of 50. While 50 documents might be tedious to browse through to find our one useful document, 500 documents would probably be too many to look through. This is what is known as "output overload." The easiest way to reduce the number of documents retrieved by a query is to simply add another term, conjunctively, to the original query. For example: "Databases" **AND** "Distributed" **AND** "Relational." We have now specified that the term "Relational" must appear in the text or indexing record of the retrieved documents, in addition to the two original terms. Suppose that this query now retrieves 50 documents. Since we now have only 50 documents in our retrieved set, are we in the same position as we were after submitting the original query to the smaller document collection? Not necessarily. While we have only 50 documents again, these are not likely to be the *same* 50 documents that we had originally. It is also possible that the one useful document that we found in the original 50 may not be included in the second 50. What has happened here is that a *quantitative* change in the system has caused a *qualitative* (i.e., *semantic*) change in the search strategy (i.e., the search query "Databases" **AND** "Distributed" **AND** "Relational" is semantically different from the search query "Databases" **AND** "Distributed"). This qualitative change means that it will require an increased searching effort to achieve the same level of effectiveness in the larger system as was achieved in the smaller system.

For some numerical information, data retrieval has other ways of dealing with large numbers of records that are not available to document retrieval systems—aggregation, graphical representation and data modeling. Many large sets of values can be represented meaningfully by totals, rates, averages or mathematical models: for example, the total sales for each salesperson, the average salary of COBOL programmers with 10 years experience, the backorder rate for new products, etc. The technique of Data Warehousing deals almost entirely with extremely large data sets of aggregated data—data that would be incomprehensible without being summarized in some way.[427] Other numerical information can be presented graphically in ways that make it easy to see the general characteristics, like trends, of un-aggregated information. Some relations might even be difficult—perhaps impossible—to see without being represented graphically.[428] For data values that occur in some complex but predictable pattern, a mathematical model may reduce a large data set into a single formula. None of these efficient ways of dealing with large amounts of information is available for document retrieval. Although documents can be summarized, there is no simple uniformly accepted way of doing this, and any such summarizing process inevitably reduces the amount of useful information available for retrieval (imagine how much less information there is in the abstract of a scientific paper than there is in the paper itself).

## DISTINCTION 9: MANAGEMENT AND THE DELEGATION PROBLEM

Because the typical data search is relatively straightforward, and the procedure of one search is often very similar to the procedures of other searches, these kinds of searches can usually be easily delegated to assistants. Without too much fear of misunderstanding, one person can ask another to get "Eveline Hill's pay rate," "The number of widgets in stock in the Centralia warehouse," or "The names of customers with backorders of more than two weeks." For document retrieval, on the other hand, a request for information may be interpreted in such a wide variety of ways that delegation is difficult. For example, when a manager asks her assistant to "Get me any reports that analyze Central European investment prospects," there are a lot of different ways that request could be interpreted, and a variety of information that might satisfy it. For example, is it a request for the investment records of specific investors, or is it a request for general investment trends? Is it a request for historical information combined with present results, or is it a request for an informed analysis of future prospects? Should the information be broken down by company, or industry, or by country? Should the information include just economic information/projections, or should it include an analysis of the political situations and economic stability of the concerned countries? Should the request only be directed toward internally done analysis, or should it be targeted towards gathering analysis done by those outside the organization? Are there free government sources of this kind of information— in which case, how would you find out where they are—or is this information maintained by commercial information brokers—in which case, how much do you want to pay to get it? Does the person who wants the information have a strong background in economics and finance? If so, the information can be very technical. If not, a more general level of analysis is needed, etc. This list of variations can be extended indefinitely. The managerial consequences of this difference are clear: managers can delegate most data searches to subordinates, but they cannot do so as easily with document searches (unless they have a high tolerance for misunderstanding or have assistants who understand their information needs in great detail). If the manager cannot easily delegate a task, what does she do? She has to do it herself. Consequently, document retrieval can quickly become a "black hole" for

---

[427] J. Bischoff and T. Alexander. **Data Warehouse: Practical Advice from the Experts**. Prentice Hall, Upper Saddle River, NJ, 1997

[428] Tufte's popular book gives many excellent examples of how much the graphical display of data can add to the data itself. E.R. Tufte. **The Visual Display of Quantitative Information**. Graphics Press, Cheshire, Conneticut, USA, 1992.

| Determinate Data Searching | Indeterminate Content Searching |
|---|---|
| 1. Direct ("I want to know X") | 1. Indirect ("I want to know about X") |
| 2. Necessary relation between a formal query and the representation of a satisfactory answer. | 2. Probabilistic relation between a formal query and the representation of a satisfactory answer. |
| 3. Criterion of success = CORRECTNESS | 3. Criterion of success = UTILITY |
| 4. Speed dependent on the time of physical access. | 4. Speed dependent on the number of logical decisions the searcher must make in the course of her search. |
| 5. Finite representation of information. | 5. Unlimited ways to represent information. |
| 6. A negative search result usually means the desired data is not in the database. | 6. A negative search result does not necessarily mean that there are no useful documents in the system. |
| 7. One type of search. (exact match or data aggregation based on a set of exact matches) | 7. Three types of searches: sample, exhaustive and specific. |
| 8. Scaling-up does not affect retrieval performance much. | 8. Scaling-up can seriously degrade the performance of a system. |
| 9. Searches can be delegated. | 9. Harder to delegate searches. |
| 10. Representations have low context dependency. | 10. Representations have high context dependency. |

**Summary of the Consequences of Indeterminacy in Information Retrieval**

time, drawing the manager away from his/her primary duties for significant periods. While data retrieval draws on the duties of lower level employees who carry out the requests of management, document retrieval tends to draw on the duties of management itself—those who are most responsible for decision-making in the organization. Document retrieval, then, can be a two-edged sword. It can assist the manager in getting what she needs for decision-making, but it may do this by increasing the amount of time she spends *away* from her primary duties. This is one of the reasons that document retrieval systems are perceived with such ambivalence. A good document retrieval system that gets you useful information quickly is certainly an asset, but one that contains crucial information but is difficult to use can be a source of frustration and a drain on managerial time.

One of the consequences of the construction of a poorly designed document retrieval system is that the users quickly learn how difficult it is to get what they want. If the system contains important information that they need to have access to, they meet this difficulty by forming their own personal document retrieval systems—usually paper-based ones— thereby duplicating much of the retrieval function and cost. If this happens frequently, a substantial amount of an organization's document retrieval cost may be duplicated. Further, these "personal" information systems are often designed idiosyncratically (since they have to satisfy only one user) and can be used effectively only by the designer. As a result, when the person who designed her own document retrieval system leaves her job or the organization, the knowledge needed to use the system leaves, too (for others it's like trying to make sense of another individual's personal filing system). Further, this need to create redundant systems is not a one-time effort. The next person to occupy the vacated position may have to create an entirely new system. This may result in two costs: the cost of creating a duplicate, personal retrieval system, and the cost of poor information retrieval while the personal system is being put together.

Since our only means of retrieving information from an information system is by using index terms in our search queries, it is easy to see how critical indexes are to the performance of an information system. If you can't anticipate the way that the information you want is indexed, be it data, text, images or audio, then it is very unlikely that you will be able to retrieve it, short of sequentially looking at every information item in the collection, an unworkable strategy for most information systems.

If we are to have any chance of reducing the indeterminacy of content indexing it is essential for us to understand the indexing process. On the most basic level, content indexing is a process by which we create brief descriptions of the information in question and link those descriptions logically or physically to that information. What is necessary for search terms and indexes to work? What do they do? On the face of it, an index term is simply a word that has a "meaning," and the "meaning" can, among other things, describe the intellectual content of the text in question:

Index Term $\longleftrightarrow$ ["Intellectual Content"][429]

The exemplars of this relationship are the drawers of $3 \times 5$ cards that used to comprise the subject catalogue of many libraries. Here an index phrase saying "20th Century Imagist Poetry" might be affixed to the top of the cards for specific books in the library. Each book with this phrase on it would presumably be concerned in whole or in part with "20th Century Imagist Poetry." This ostensibly simple basic relationship between index terms and the intellectual content of text is the kind of linguistic model of language that Wittgenstein discusses in the opening paragraph of **Philosophical Investigations**:

> When they (my elders) named some object, and accordingly moved towards something, I saw this and I grasped that the thing was called by the sound they uttered when they meant to point it out. Their intention was shewn by their bodily movements, as it were the natural language of all peoples: the expression of the face, the play of the eyes, the movement of other parts of the body, and the tone of voice which expresses our state of mind in seeking, having, rejecting, or avoiding something. Thus, as I heard words repeatedly used in their proper places in various sentences, I gradually learnt to understand what objects they signified; and after I had trained my mouth to form these signs, I used them to express my own desires.
> [**PI** §1]

These are the words of the medieval philosopher Augustine. They encapsulate an easy and intuitively attractive theory of language. Wittgenstein describes a more sophisticated version of this theory which seems to fit the relationship between indexes and intellectual content particularly well:

> These words, it seems to me, give us a particular picture of the essence of human language. It is this: the individual words in language name objects—sentences are

---

[429] An index term can, of course, describe other aspects of information in addition to its "intellectual content." An index term may be an author's name, date of publication, type of information, type of document, type of image (JPEG, TIFF, GIF), etc. But it is in the representation and retrieval of "intellectual content" that the more difficult and interesting issues arise. How intellectual content should be represented for retrieval will be the subject of much of the remainder of this discussion.

combinations of such names.—In this picture of language we find the roots of the following idea: Every word has a meaning. This meaning is correlated with the word. It is the object for which the word stands.

Augustine does not speak of there being any difference between kinds of word. If you describe the learning of language in this way you are, I believe, thinking primarily of nouns like "table," "chair," "bread," and of people's names, and only secondarily of the names of certain actions and properties; and of the remaining kind of words as something that will take care of itself. [**PI** §1]

This model of language matches very closely to the way that language often appears to be used in information systems. Specifically, index terms "stand for" information objects ("intellectual contents") in much the way that Augustine describes words as standing for objects, or, as Wittgenstein reformulated it, words have ("stand for") meanings. We discussed Augustine's model of language briefly in Part I in our exegesis of Wittgenstein's **Philosophical Investigations**. But because of its relevance to how language is used in information systems it is important to look at the model in more detail, and to bring out whatever implications or shortcomings it may have. To see the difficulties with Augustine's model of language and its more subtle descendents, lets enumerate its basic features:

1. Words name objects.

2. The meaning of a word is the object for which it stands,

3. Every word has a meaning.

4. The meaning of a word is independent of context.

5. The meaning of a sentence is composed of the meanings of its words.

6. Teaching consists of pointing to objects and saying their names.

7. Language is primarily used to assert facts.

1. and 2. *Words name objects—the meaning of a word is the object for which it stands.* If we consider examples of words such as "chair," "apple," and "pencil," language does seem to work this way. But if we look at examples such as "rectitude," "charisma," and "the day after tomorrow" it is harder to make the case that words name "objects." Wittgenstein gives us a hint of the complexity he sees in these kinds of statements when he asks rhetorically:

A dog believes his master is at the door. But can he also believe his master will come the day after to-morrow?—And what can he not do here?—How do I do it?—How am I supposed to answer this? [**PI** p. 174]

If "the day after to-morrow" were simply a phrase correlated with an object, or "meaning," of some kind, it would be plausible that even a dog could understand it and could come to expect his master then. A dog, after all, can recognize other kinds of objects: balls, bones, food, leashes, cats, and other dogs, as well as more abstract objects such as friends and enemies, and characteristic situations like his master coming home soon, playing, or being frightened. Further, as Pavlov showed, a dog can "expect" things to happen some short time in the future, such as getting fed. But can a dog expect his master "the day after to-morrow?" Wittgenstein does not answer his question explicitly, but it is clear from his previous writings that he does not believe that a dog can do this. For Wittgenstein, the "day after to-morrow" isn't so much a phrase that has a meaning, although we may speak of it this way, that is, there are Language Games in which we use the word "meaning" in this way (we can imagine someone who is learning English asking "What does the 'day-after-tomorrow' mean?"). But for Wittgenstein, as we showed in Part I, if we really want to understand the "meaning" of the "day after to-morrow" we need to look at its use. Consequently, to understand the "meaning" of the "day after to-morrow" we need to be able to use it in the right circumstances, and to use it we need the experiences of distinguishing one day from another—"today," "tomorrow," "the day-after-tomorrow"—of observing the succession of one day following another, and of using days as units of time in a variety of activities. And these are not independent activities that can be separated from our daily lives and practices like we can sometimes separate the "meaning" from a word, as we do with dictionary entries. To use the "day after to-morrow" correctly is not just to know a dictionary definition, it is to be able to discern the *appropriate circumstances and activities* in which it can be used, and this ability is further contingent on our ability to participate in a broad range of human activities in which understanding the "day after to-morrow" is important. Someone who is learning English and asks me "What does the 'day-after-tomorrow' mean?" can get along with this simple question because he is already familiar with the kinds of activities in which such a phrase is used. A dog, though, doesn't share with us the activities in which the "day-after-tomorrow" is important. Wittgenstein brings this out more strikingly with one of his more provocative statements:

> If a lion could talk we could not understand him. [**PI** p. 223]

The reason why we could not understand the speaking lion is because we have no personal experience with the activities in which he is generally engaged. If we can come to under-stand the meaning of a word by looking at its use, then meaning is intimately linked to the activities that we have in common with others. If we don't have any activities in common, then there is little that we can talk about. In Wittgenstein's words, we have too few "forms of life" in common with the lion on which we could base a common language. Someone might object that there *are* activities which we have in common with the lion—activities like eating, resting, being afraid, or raising children. But, in spite of the superficial sim-ilarity of these activities, the lion goes about them in such a different manner that they really are not the same for us both. For example, though the lion must eat regularly, the way that we do, eating for him is a basic, instinctive, opportunistic activity, while eating for us is intimately caught up in a complex system of social activities that involve issues of etiquette, socializing and the culinary arts, none of which has any role in the life of the lion. Our talking lion might use the word "eat" to refer to the same act as we do, but the real meaning of the word "eat" with all its connotations and implications would be vastly different for the lion than it would be for us. If our talking lion were to say that he was "stepping out for lunch" we could not be certain exactly what he was going to do, and if he said that he had a "lot of fun yesterday" we would not know at all what he meant. This is what Wittgenstein means when he says that even if a lion could talk, that is, use the same words we do, we would not really be able to understand him.

After consideration of these examples, which belie the Augustinian Model of Language, we may try to draw some comfort from the fact that language appears to work according to Augustine's Model at least in the cases where objects are referred to. But even here the relationship between language and "objects" is not simple. "Words" and "objects" recall the much debated topic of "reference." Frege, Wittgenstein's early mentor, was one of the first philosophers to discuss some of the complexities of reference, but these issues reach back at least to antiquity and Eubulides' "paradox of the Hooded Man."[430] Frege highlighted one of the important issues of reference with his example of the "Morning Star" and the "Evening Star." Both the Morning Star and the Evening Star refer to the same celestial object, the planet Venus. Yet the descriptions "Morning Star" and "Evening Star" do not have precisely the same meaning or "sense" for the simple reason that we cannot use them interchangeably in everyday discourse. That is, in ordinary usage we cannot say, in the morning, that we see the "Evening Star" and, in the evening, that we are looking at the "Morning Star."

In Frege's example we could at least tell what the speaker who refers to the "Morning Star" in the evening, or the "Evening Star" in the morning probably *means*. But Bertrand Russell gave us an example of a problem of reference where it is much less clear what the speaker means. Consider the following two statements:

> George the IV wanted to know if Scott was the author of **Waverly.**

> Scott is the author of **Waverly**.

Now if "Scott" and "the author of **Waverly**" refer to the same person, *and* the meaning of a word is completely explained by its reference, as Augustine claims, then we should be able to use "Scott" and "the author of **Waverly**" interchangeably. If we substitute "Scott" for "the author of **Waverly**" in Russell's first sentence, then we get: "George the IV wanted to know if Scott was Scott." Here, in contrast to Frege's example, the substitution of "Scott" for "the author of **Waverly**" leaves us with a sentence whose intended meaning would be impossible to figure out.

It is clear that even when a word or phrase has an obvious reference such as "Scott" and "the author of **Waverly**" do, the "meaning," or what Frege called the "sense," of that word or phrase is not limited to the object to which it refers. It is also the case that when we refer to a particular person we may not mean the person at all, but some salient aspect of the person. For example, Wittgenstein's father, Karl, was once referred to as "the Andrew Carnegie of Austria." By this, it was *not* meant that Karl looked like Carnegie, or had Scottish ancestry, but that he, like Carnegie, was a wealthy industrialist who patronized the arts. Finally, it is evident that many words, such as "rectitude" and "unicorn" do not refer to objects at all, yet we still use them regularly and are understood when we do so.

According to Putnam, reference is not established solely by some mental event which links words to objects, but is "socially fixed."[431] That is, I can refer to, or point out a "chair"

---

[430] See foonote 99 in Part II.***

[431] "...reference is socially fixed and not determined by conditions or objects in individual brains/minds." **Representation and Reality**, p. 25. MIT Press, Cambridge, MA, 1988.

only under particular circumstances and only to certain kinds of people. For example, for me to refer to a chair—"This is a chair"—what I refer to must be present and visible. It can't be hidden in some way, and there must be enough light for us to see it. Further, the people I am talking to must speak enough English to understand me, and be old enough to understand my point in referring to a chair. Pointing out a chair to infants in a dark nursery, just won't work. Finally, "chairs" need to be one of those things that people ordinarily refer to ostensively, they must "fit" into the practice or activity of "pointing things out"—for example, pointing out a chair as part of a request to move it. Augustine's model of language is a simple model and easy to comprehend. But there are some subtle aspects to it which are not obvious at first. In particular, Augustine's description of how he learned to speak is important. In his words, he "... heard words repeatedly used... [and] gradually learnt to understand what objects they signified... " [**PI** §1] This passage makes the point that we can hear and distinguish words *before* we understand them. That is, words can exist for us *without* meaning—as words we don't understand. Further, since we can have words without meaning, it follows that "meaning" can exist independently of words—it appears to be something that can be *added to* words by a specific act such as looking it up in a dictionary.[432] In some instances we can even have a "sense" or "meaning" without a word. We can see this sometimes when we compare words in two languages. For example, the Japanese have a word that means the point when a sound, such as the single stroke of a large bell, has diminished to a level where the listener cannot tell whether he can still hear it or not. In English, we don't have a word or simple phrase for this "meaning." Augustine's view of language dichotomizes words and meaning, and sets up a framework in which they can be considered separately, a framework that exists in various forms to this day: most prominently, in the belief in the independence of syntax and meaning that was the cornerstone of Chomsky's generative grammar.[433]

This dichotomy between words and meaning forces us to deal with questions of meaning in a predictable, almost unavoidable, way. Specifically, when we can no longer maintain the claim that meaning equals some entity such as a physical "object," we give up the physical "object" but we inevitably try to keep the framework in which the "meaning" of a word is an entity of *some* kind. We think of a word having a "meaning" in the same way that we think of people having biological parents. The orphaned child may not know who his parents are, but their existence at some time is beyond doubt. Wittgenstein, too, believed in the dichotomization of meaning and words or grammar early in his career.[434] But it was one of his major contributions to the philosophy of language to question this

---

[432] The separation of "meaning" from words has another unfortunate consequence, namely, when we believe that "meanings" can be separated from words it is easy to follow this belief into a kind of Platonism where the "meanings" of words have a kind of separate existence. This is a view that Frege held, and, in a more subtle version, Russell too.

[433] As discussed in Part I, this is a view that Wittgenstein held himself in his **TLP**, but later repudiated particularly in his rejection of the "calculus model of language" (see the section "Language as a Kind of Calculus" in Part I). George Lakoff's early work in linguistics directly challenged this notion of the independence of grammar, or syntax, and meaning. See his **Irregularity in Syntax**. The independence of words and meaning lead Frege to assert that the "meaning"—what he called the "sense"—of a word had actual existence in his own right (***see Muculloch's **The Mind and its World**).

[434] This was Wittgenstein's view of meaning in his **TLP**.

fundamental dichotomy, in short, to resist the "compulsion" that the Augustinian model of language seems to force on us.[435]

Augustine's model of language reinforced the basic dichotomy between words and meaning, leaving subsequent philosophers the task of trying to get them back together again. The fact that many words and phrases obviously do *not* refer to objects, yet are nonetheless meaningful, compels us to look for another entity that "meaning" could be. John Locke was able to articulate an alternative theory of meaning that preserved Augustine's separation of words and meaning but did not fall prey to its failures. For Locke:

> Words in their primary or immediate signification, stand for nothing but the ideas in the mind of him that uses them.[436]

Locke's linking of a word's signification, or "meaning," with an "idea" resolves the problem of words that do not refer to an object or type of object, yet are still meaningful. We may not be able to link all words to objects, but it seems evident to some theorists that when we know the meaning of the words "rectitude" or "unicorn" we do have something "in mind."

Locke's mentalistic theory of meaning has had a long history of support, and various forms of it survive today.[437] But, as appealing as mentalistic theories of meaning are, they suffer

---

[435] Much of Wittgenstein's later philosophy was directed at questioning this and other dichotomies that have been of concern to philosophy: dichotomies between "word" and "meaning," between "inner (mental) states" and "outer processes," between "mind" and "body," and between "mind" and "brain." He dealt with these dichotomies in a characteristic way. First, he showed how untenable such dichotomies were. We need both parts of the dichotomy to work together—the "mind" and the "brain" must work, somehow, in concert, "inner processes" obviously influence "outer processes"—but we are confronted with an infinite regress whenever we try to explain how they work together. Second, he tried to show where the source of these dichotomies comes from: these dichotomies arose not from empirical observation so much as they arose from distinctions we make in language. In short, most of the dichotomies which trouble us are chimera, they are grammatical distinctions which we have mistaken for empirical ones. As Wittgenstein stated, in another context, but no less relevant here: "We have only rejected the grammar which tries to force itself on us. . . " [**PI** §304]

[436] J. Locke. "An Essay Concerning Human Understanding." See Book III "Of Words." Quotation from section 3.2.2 in **British Empirical Philosophers**. Routledge and Kegan Paul, London, 1985. Edited by A.J. Ayer and R. Winch. Hilary Putnam places the origin of a mentalistic theory of meaning in the work of Aristotle:

> As he was the first to theorize in a systematic way about so many other things, so Aristotle was the first thinker to theorize in a systematic way about meaning and reference. In *De Interpretatione* he laid out a scheme which has proved remarkably robust. According to this scheme, when we understand a word or any other "sign," we associate that word with a "concept." This concept determines what the word refers to. Two millennia later, one can find the same theory in John Stuart Mill's Logic, and in the present century one finds variants of this picture in the writings of Bertrand Russell, Gottlob Frege, Rudolph Carnap, and many other important philosophers. Something like this picture also appears to be built into the English language. Etymologically, meaning is related to mind. To mean something was probably, in the oldest usage, just to have it in mind. [H. Putnam. **Representation and Reality**, p. 19. MIT Press, Cambridge, MA, 1991.]

[437] In particular, semiotic theory is often mentalistic, see Umberto Eco's **A Theory of Semiotics**, Indiana University Press, Bloomington, Indiana, 1976. This version of semiotics was described and critiqued in Chapter 4 of Blair's **Language and Representation in Information Retrieval**, Elsevier Science, Amsterdam, 1990. Hilary

from a number of fatal problems. In the first place, if the meaning or sense of a word that I understand is an idea, then that idea is something private to me. But if meaning is private, how do I teach you *my* idea of the meaning of a word, or learn the meaning of a word which you understand but I do not? We do explain the meaning of words and phrases to each other, but is this explanation really a presentation of our ideas? If the explanation we give turns out to be wrong, what is the source of our error? Did we have the right idea, but explained it incorrectly, or was our original idea incorrect in the first place? There is no way to tell. Yet to teach or learn the meaning of a word or phrase requires clear criteria of correctness, something a purely mentalistic theory of meaning does not, and cannot, have. The criterion for whether you understand the meaning of a word is not whether you have the "right idea," but whether you use it correctly in your day-to-day speech and writing. The question of whether you have the "right idea" doesn't come up in ordinary usage. Thus, if the criterion for correct understanding is correct usage, then ideas are not the foundation of our understanding—usage is. This is not to deny that there are some "mental phenomena" that accompany our language use, it only means that whatever those "mental phenomena" are they are not relevant to teaching or learning a language. But a replacement of "ideas" with "usage" has to be done carefully, too. If meaning is *only* resolved through a consideration of usage, then we must be careful not to be forced into the most obvious alternative to mentalism—behaviorism. This too, is a dead end as an unrestricted source for meaning, as we discussed in the final section of Part II. The problem is not what the definition of "meaning" is, the problem is the seeming dichotomy between words and meanings which forces us to see "meaning" as something separate from the words themselves.

The dichotomy between a word and its meaning is more harmful than helpful in our quest for understanding how language works. Equating "meaning" with some kind of object puts us in a position where "meanings" can have some kind of separate existence from the words that are somehow connected to them. But "meanings" are not separate things that can be looked at like a geologist looks at rock samples. Meanings are not "things" but are emergent from our day–to-day activities and practices. They are not simply mental entities, conscious or unconscious, because they are contingent on the circumstances and context of their usage; neither are they just behavior because they do have some mental component (otherwise we would not be able to distinguish between someone who lies but has the same statements and behavior as someone telling the truth).[438]

---

Putnam presents a criticism of current mentalistic theories of meaning in his **Representation and Reality**, MIT Press, Cambridge, MA, 1991.

[438] Wittgenstein's critique of mentalism comes in two forms. The first is his criticism of the "Picture Theory of Meaning"—a view that he held early in his career. Briefly, pictures, especially mental ones, cannot be the unequivocal foundation for meaning in language because pictures can be interpreted in any number of ways (see the examples in the previous section **"Wittgenstein at Work: Philosophical Investigations"**).

Wittgenstein's second criticism of mentalism is his well-known argument against a private language. Briefly, the issue of a private language concerns whether or not we can have meanings in language that only we can know. For example, private language advocates claim that although we all have a sense of what the word "pain" means, and can use it appropriately in ordinary discourse, in reality our notion of "pain" is based on our own experiences of "pain" and these personal experiences are unique and private. Wittgenstein's rejoinder to this is two-fold: in the first place, private meanings cannot be uniquely private since in order to discuss, describe, or compare them we must use our ordinary, public language. If we can only describe the private language using language that is public, then our private language is just a particular kind of public, that is, ordinary, language. As Wittgenstein

3. *Every word has a meaning.* If the "meaning" of a word is the object, actual or mental, for which it stands, this implies that the "meaning" is a clearly defined entity—a single thing. Again, if we think of tangible objects—chairs, cars, hammers, etc.—this view has a certain appeal. But on closer examination we can see that even the definitions of common objects can have cases where their application is indeterminate. Those who think that a chair is simply a chair, should go to a museum of contemporary art. Here, what an artist may call a chair can vary widely from our accepted notion of what it is. But even in ordinary usage, what we might call a chair can deviate from our normal expectations. A chair has a function, it is something to sit on. Such a function can give the status of "chair" to a lot of objects. For example, if we need to sit down, but there are no ordinary chairs available, we might use a low table or a box to sit on. In a functional sense, the low table or box *becomes* a chair for the period of time we use it for this purpose. Some may quibble that using something *as a chair* does not change the general definition of what a chair is, but arguments can be made on both sides of the issue. What is important is that the definition of what an ordinary object like a chair is can vary a lot and, like the "heap" in sorites, the boundary between what is a chair and what is not a chair may be unclear and may vary according to circumstances. In like manner, we can view a hammer as a specific kind of tool with a characteristic shape and heft, but we can also view a hammer as something that can be used in certain ways. In the functional sense, a lot of things can be used as hammers: rocks, iron bars, hatchets, even fists.

The words "hammer" and "chair" can also be used metaphorically, such as when the weatherman says that a storm "hammered Cape Cod" or when a reporter states that Senator X "chaired the Armed Services Committee." In other uses, some professional athletes and at least one popular singer have the nickname "hammer." These metaphorical uses of these words stretch our notion of what these words mean and where it is appropriate to use them.

Some names of objects find a wide variety of applications. We discussed before the many disparate uses or meanings of the word "head," but it is easy to come up with other examples of words with many acceptable uses. Consider the word "line":

> "He took a pencil and drew a **line**."
> "The soldiers stood in **line**."

put it, "What goes on within also has meaning only in the stream of life." [**RPP II** §687]

Wittgenstein's second criticism of private language has to do with how we determine correct usage. If we want to know how to use a word then we need to have some exemplary cases of the word's usage—what Wittgenstein called "übersichtliche Darstellungen"—which we can look to as examples of how to use it. But since, in a private language, any such exemplary uses of a word are also private, how would we know whether the exemplary cases we have are actually correct or whether we have used the exemplary cases appropriately to establish correct usage? What is private to us cannot be compared to other private entities in the way that we compare things in our daily activities—for example, comparing samples of shades of a color to see which are alike. This notion of the incomparability of private phenomena is one of the cornerstones of Wittgenstein's philosophy of mind.

Through all of this Wittgenstein is not saying that we have no mental process, conscious or unconscious, that is part of our correct use of language. He just says that any such mental process is neither necessary nor definitional. In his words, "It is not a something, but not a nothing either!" (see Part II section " Wittgenstein vs. Behaviorism: The Existence of Mental Phenomena")

"He put his reputation on the **line**."
"Give me the bottom **line** on the investment."
"The batter **lined** out to third."
"I can't follow his **line** of thought."
"The coat was **lined** with down."
"Don't give me that old **line**!"
"The actor forgot his **lines**."
"The ocean **liner** weighed anchor and put out to sea."
"The fishing **line** was hopelessly tangled."
"The store carried a **line** of small tools."
"His actions were completely out of **line**."
"Drop me a **line** when you get there."
"Make him toe the **line**!"

Such examples do not exhaust the different uses of the word "line" and this variability is typical of many other common words. Examples like these should disabuse us of any notion that word meaning is a precise or single thing. Hilary Putnam goes even farther. He shows that even when we agree on the meaning, or usage, of a particular word we still may not all have the same criteria for its use. Meaning, he proposes, is subject to a kind of "Division of Linguistic Labor." By Putnam's account, even when we agree on the "meaning of a word" we may not be using identical criteria for its application. Take the word "elm," I may recognize an elm tree by the general size and shape of its serrated leaf, while my friend may recognize elms just as reliably as I do by looking at the shape of the mature tree, the appearance of the bark and the size of the leaf buds. An expert botanist might be able to identify an elm by the particular cell structure of the wood which she can see under a microscope.[439] Putnam's point is that the ability to use a word, here, "elm," in the same way does not guarantee that the users possess the same criteria for the word's usage. Language, according to Putnam, is a co-operative activity. We may have useful heuristics that help us to identify things like elms, but no one, not even the expert, can identify things like elms in every possible circumstance (e.g., a botanist would probably not be able to identify an elm in complete darkness, but a blind person may have sensitive enough touch to do so by handling the bark and leaves). To distinguish an elm from trees that it looks very much like, or in the winter when it has no leaves, we would probably rely on expert botanists or on a tree-identification guide. But if we know very little about elms, we may just rely on our neighbor to help us identify them. This is what Putnam means by the "Division of Linguistic Labor." The expert, though, does not know a "more complete" definition of "elm" than we do, he simply knows more *about* elms than we do, and this additional information about elms may be useful for identifying elms in different circumstances—that is, the expert can use the word "elm" in a wider variety of circumstances than the average person can. But this additional information is not part of the meaning of the word "elm." Wittgenstein would say that what accounts for the different criteria that we have, even when we can each identify elms reliably, is that we use the word "elm" in different *language games*. We only need the criteria to identify elms in the *language games*, that is, the particular *uses*, that concern us. If we

---

[439] I have no idea whether cell-structure can be used to identify trees. My point is that the expert may have different criteria for identifying elms than non-experts, like myself, have.

are not botanists we may only want to identify the elms which we see in our own yard or neighborhood. The ability to distinguish species of elms, for example those that grow in the southern latitudes from those that grow in northern latitudes, may not be important to us. For some botanists, distinguishing various species of elm may be important, but understanding the cell structure of elm wood may not be important. For a botanist at a tree farm, understanding the different cell structures of elm species may be important, but understanding how to identify elms in the wild may be unimportant. And for a botany student studying for an exam, he may need only to be able to write down the scientific definition of an "elm" which might include its Latin name and its correct genus. Some of these *language games* may pick out the same trees as elms, and some may not. There is no sense of a "complete" definition of an "elm" that would enable us to pick out elms in *all* conceivable circumstances. It also should be clear that there is no *language game* that would require such an all-inclusive understanding of what an elm is. The criterion for whether an individual knows the meaning of a word like "elm" is not whether he has some arbitrarily "complete" definition of an elm, but whether he can use the word "elm" correctly in the *language games* in which he wishes to participate. A *language game*, as we pointed out in Part II, is not just a particular set of regularities in language but also includes the activities or practices in which it is normally used—as Wittgenstein put it:

> I shall also call the whole, consisting of language and the actions into which it is woven, the "language-game." [**PI** §7]

4. *The meaning of a word is independent of context.* Much of Part II of this manuscript was a discussion of the importance of context for meaning, so these discussions will not be repeated here (in particular, see the sections "Wittgenstein at Work" and "Language Games" in Part I). A couple of clear examples can serve to remind us of the importance of context.

Indexicals are good examples of strongly context-dependent words: words like "here," "now," "this," "that," "him," "her," and "it." The references these words make change from context to context and speaker to speaker. These examples are fairly obvious, but there are other examples that are more subtle and deal with aspects of context beyond the notion of physical presence or absence. Consider the example, "I am here." This sentence has the indexicals "I" and "here" and these would be clarified by ascertaining who spoke the sentence and on what occasion. But if you are sitting before me and are perfectly visible, and you utter "I am here" you probably mean something else entirely than the simple statement of where you are. That is, it is obvious to me that you are here, so you must be trying to tell me something else. One can imagine a situation in which one person is distraught over something and the other, a close friend or relative, goes to him and, patting him on the shoulder, says, "Don't worry, I am here," meaning, of course, not just that the speaker is physically present, but that the speaker is emotionally supportive. In this utterance the context needed to interpret the meaning of the sentence extends beyond the simple notion of physical presence and includes the relationship between the two individuals and the particular circumstances in which they find themselves. Context can often indicate which of the many meanings of a word is currently being used. For example, the word "pitch" can mean a lot of things: the slope of a roof, the tone of voice, a specific action in a baseball game, a tar-based substance, the description of a product that a salesman gives his customer, etc. But if two individuals are talking while they attend a baseball game and use the word "pitch" it is highly unlikely that it means anything other than a specific action in the game.

5. *The meaning of a sentence is composed of the meanings of its words.* If "meanings" are entities that are attached somehow to words, then it is no great intellectual leap to conclude that sentence meaning is somehow put together from the meanings of the words. If this is the case, then, most fundamentally, to understand the meaning of a sentence means that we must *be aware* of all the words in a sentence. Yet there is ample empirical evidence that, at least with speech, we often do not hear every word in a sentence. For example, suppose that you walk into a fast food restaurant and go up to the counter to order what you want. As you come up to the counter, a clerk approaches you and quickly says, "Kelp ya?" In spite of the fact that the clerk, strictly speaking, has not said any English words, we generally understand him to say, "Can I help you?"—a phrase we *do* understand. President Franklin Roosevelt would often dispel the boredom of a long receiving line before a White House dinner by saying completely inappropriate things to the guests as he greeted them, his favorite greeting being "I murdered my grandmother this morning." The guests, of course, would assume that the President had greeted them in a cordial and expected manner, and that even if they heard exactly what he said they would assume that they had misunderstood him.[440] In cases like these, it is clear that we understand the situation or circumstances *before* we understand what is said to us, and our expectations about what is likely to be said may override and supersede what is actually said. Thus, sentence meaning, in these examples, is not built up out of word meanings for the simple reason that we often do not hear the words in the sentence, or we hear them but the circumstances are so strong that we assume something else was said.

But what about cases where we *do* hear all the words in a sentence. Are there ever cases that the meaning of a sentence seems to have little to do with the individual meanings of the words? Yes there are. Consider the following example. I come into my office in the morning, and after greeting a colleague I ask her, "Is Bill back from vacation yet?" She answers, in a perfectly forthright manner, "I saw a yellow Volkswagon in the parking lot this morning." What did she mean? It is not difficult to see that she is saying that she believes Bill is back from vacation—that is, that Bill owns a yellow VW, that a yellow VW is an unusual appearing car so Bill probably has the only one, and if Bill is back from vacation he will have likely driven his car in to the office and parked it where it can be seen by others, etc. But no matter how extended and detailed a description of the meanings of "saw," "yellow," "Volkswagen," "parking lot," etc., are, there is no way that we can derive the meaning my colleague intended soley from the meanings of her words.

6. *Teaching consists of pointing to objects and saying their names.* If meaning is not an object then we cannot "point" to it, either literally or figuratively. This is not to say that we cannot convey the meaning of some words by pointing to an object, for we can certainly do this (Wittgenstein: ". . . the *meaning* of a name is sometimes explained by pointing to its *bearer*" [**PI** §43] ). But this is just a special case in language learning and is not the only way, nor even the most common way, that we learn what words mean. Further, even

---

[440] **Bartlett's Book of Anecdotes**, p. 465. Little Brown, New York, 2000. Edited by C. Fadiman and A. Bernard.

the simple act of pointing to an object to explain the meaning of a word is not the simple act that Augustine makes it out to be. If someone points to an automobile in response to a question about what a particular word means, what is it exactly that is being pointed to? One cannot state unequivocably that it was *the car* that was being pointed out. It could be that the car was pointed to as an example of a particular*color*; or, as an example of a particular*brand of car* (e.g. a Ford); or, as an example of a particular*kind of car* (e.g. a sedan); or, as a particular *person's car*. (Wittgenstein: "an ostensive definition can be variously interpreted in *every* case" [**PI** §28] ) It is interesting to note that even when we point to something to demonstrate what a word means, such as pointing to a chair when someone who is learning English asks us what "chair" means, the chair *itself* is not the meaning of the word "chair." The chair that we point to is a single entity, yet when we define the word "chair" by pointing to a chair we are indicating not a single thing but a *type* of object. As a consequence, even when we point at an object to explain the meaning of a word, we are not really pointing just to that single object, but indicating a type of object, so it is the *type of object* that is the meaning of the word, not the *object itself*. While we can point to an object in explaining the meaning of a word, we cannot point to a *type of object*. The person learning English who asks us what "chair" means must understand this; he must understand the Language Game of pointing things out to explain the meaning of a word. In other words, he must understand a lot about how language works before even the simple act of ostensive definition will make sense. Consequently, ostensive definition cannot be the foundation of language understanding as Augustine implies it is because one must have a clear grasp of how language works *before* ostensive definition can be understood. As Wittgenstein put it, succinctly:

> . . . the ostensive definition explains the use—the meaning—of the word when the overall role of the word in language is clear. [**PI** §30]

Wittgenstein scholar P.M.S. Hacker summarizes Wittgenstein's position on this issue:

> The meaning of a word is not an object in reality. It is not an abstract object (a Fregean "sense") which, by means of an ethereal mechanism, determines an entity in reality as its reference. Nor is it a psychological object (an idea in the mind) which resembles an entity or possible entity in reality. Rather it is, or is determined by, the use of the word, and it is given by an explanation of meaning, which is a rule for the use of that word. Ostensive definition, which appears to connect the network of language to reality, actually connects a word with a sample, which itself belongs to the method of representation and is an instrument of the language, not something represented by the ostensive definition. So language remains self-contained and autonomous. Of course, this does not mean that we do not refer to objects in the world by our uses of language, that we are not really talking about a language-independent reality. However, the intentionality of language is attributable not to connections between words and world, but to intra-grammatical connections, to explanations of meaning and of what we mean by the words we utter.[441]

7. *Language is primarily used to assert facts.* Early in his philosophical career, Wittgenstein also believed that the primary purpose of language was to make assertions about facts.

---

[441]**Wittgenstein's Place in 20th Century Analytic Philosophy**, p. 101. P.M.S. Hacker, Blackwell Publishers, Oxford, UK, 1996.

But this is one idea about language that he quite clearly revised (note Wittgenstein's reference to "the author of the **Tractatus Logico-Philosophicus**" at the end of the following quotation):

> But how many kinds of sentence are there? Say assertion, question, and command?—There are *countless* kinds: countless different kinds of use of what we call "symbols," "words," "sentences." And this multiplicity is not something fixed, given once for all; but new types of language, new language-games, as we may say, come into existence, and others become obsolete and get forgotten. (We can get a *rough picture* of this from the changes in mathematics.)

> Here the term "language-*game*" is meant to bring into prominence the fact that the *speaking* of language is part of an activity, or of a form of life.

> Review the multiplicity of language-games in the following examples, and in others:

> Giving orders, and obeying them—
> Describing the appearance of an object, or giving its measurements—
> Constructing an object from a description (a drawing)—
> Reporting an event—
> Speculating about an event—
> Forming and testing a hypothesis—
> Presenting the results of an experiment in tables and diagrams—
> Making up a story; and reading it—
> Play-acting—
> Singing catches—
> Guessing riddles—
> Making a joke; telling it—
> Solving a problem in practical arithmetic—
> Translating from one language into another—
> Asking, thanking, cursing, greeting, praying.

> —It is interesting to compare the multiplicity of the tools in language and of the ways they are used, the multiplicity of kinds of word and sentence, with what logicians have said about the structure of language. (Including the author of the **Tractatus Logico-Philosophicus**.) [PI §23]

## What Do Inquirers Want?

Traditionally, searchers have been thought to be retrieving information on specific topics or subjects; libraries and many Internet "portals" are arranged this way. Yahoo (www.yahoo.com) and the Library of Congress are the exemplars of this class of information system, developing and maintaining thousands of hierarchically arranged categories and linking them to existing information. Classifying information sources by subject has become such a compelling design for Internet searching that many of the search engines that began as just search engines have added subject access to websites, too, making them more like Yahoo. But as compelling as subject access is as a paradigm for searching, it is usually not what searchers are really looking for. More often than not, what prompts a search for information is not so much a lack of information on a particular subject, but the obstruction of an activity that the searcher wants to begin or continue. It may be that information on a particular topic *will* help a searcher continue an activity that has been impeded in some way, but it is rare that *any* information on that topic will do this. Consequently, the primary goal of most searching is to find something that will enable the searcher to continue the impeded activity.[442] Let's consider a few examples:

1. *An investor searching for stock information.* In this situation, the searcher is looking for information that will tell him how good his existing investments are, or whether there are present investment opportunities that he could take advantage of. Naturally, he could probably find pertinent information under the general topic of "investing," so it is tempting to say that he is looking for information on that subject. But if we look at the activity of investing, we can see a number of interesting aspects of it. In the first place, the searcher will probably not make an investment or change an existing investment without good reason to do so. In this sense, his activity of investing has been impeded or at least slowed, pending some information that would justify his doing something.

   It is also the case that not *every* item of information under the topic "investing" will be useful to the searcher. He may have very specific needs as far as what types of investments he is interested in and the level of detail or technicality in which the information is written. The principal criterion, then, is not *just* what topic the information is on but whether the information is *useful* to him, that is, does it help him further his investing activity? Topicality is a good starting point, but may not be precise enough to lead him to exactly what will be useful for him. Interestingly, it may be the case that information that is *not on the topic of* "*investing*" will be the most useful information that he finds. Useful information could take the form of economic forcasts which predict slowdowns in the industries in which our searcher is invested, dictating that he should move his investments to a more promising economic sector. He might also find a statement from the Federal Reserve announcing interest rate increases, thus making investments in bonds or money markets more attractive than his stocks. Neither of these items of information is, strictly speaking, on the topic of "investing."

2. *An inventor searching to see if his invention has already been patented.* Here, of course, the searcher is primarily looking for information that concerns the type of invention he has made, probably a very narrowly defined topic. A successful, though disappointing, conclusion to the search would occur if he finds that an invention like his has already been patented. But there is another kind of conclusion to his search, namely, his *not* being able to find patents for inventions like his. Here, the success of the search comes not with the acquisition of information about patents for inventions similar to his, but with the convincing *absence* of such information. In other words, the successful conclusion of the search has occurred because *no* information on that topic could be found. The inventor is now free to

---

[442] D.C. Blair. **Pragmatic Aspects of Inquiry**, Doctoral dissertation, University of California, Berkeley, 1981.

continue his application for a patent for his invention, something he could not do until he *could not* find the information he was searching for.[443]

3. *An academic researcher searching for information to support a research project (a grant, dissertation, or scholarly publication).* While academic research is often considered the exemplar of subject searching—"knowing more and more about less and less" as the saying goes—the researchers who are at the forefront of their respective fields are often engaged not so much in searching a topic as they are engaged in *creating* a topic, or at least re-defining it. Research is, by definition, working on something that has not been done before. Since the researcher is, in some sense, creating or modifying a topic, the information that she finds relevant to this endeavor can be unpredictably varied and may change from search to search.

One aspect of research is that it tends to be frequently associated with specific individuals, institutions or journals. Often a searcher will use a topic search to get her into the general intellectual area with which she is concerned. Once she gains access to her field of interest she then combs through the field's literature for the names of individuals, institutions and journals that deal with what she is interested in. These names can become the focus of her subsequent searches. Citations and bibliographic references can also become important access points to research literature, for example, when the searcher finds a paper that she considers useful, some of the papers that are cited by that paper are likely to be useful, too. It is also the case that papers that subsequently cite the useful paper may be of use, too (these can be found in the **Science** or **Social Science Citation Indexes**). The strategy of using citations to find related information comes from an understanding of how the activities of research and writing about research are done. Here we can see how closely dependent search strategy can be on understanding how the activity (research and publication) *uses* that kind of information. This is why the citation indexes are so popular among researchers.

4. *A biologist looking for information on a specific species of plant or animal.* Biological nomenclature is certainly one of the most precise classifications of information, and searching its categories is probably the closest searching comes to a pure subject search. It is usually the case, though, that a searcher in a biological field would not find *everything* in a particular classification useful for his purposes. But it is also the case that whatever he does find useful is often within a single established category.[444] Biological classifications have one characteristic, though,

---

[443] It is tempting to think that if the goal of the search is topic "A" then the conclusion of the search can be arrived at by finding "¬A." But finding that a topic does not exist is a very different sort of search than finding that it does exist. In order for the inventor to convince the patent office that "A" (the specific category for his invention) does not exist, he must either search all existing invention categories and not find it, or marshal evidence to support this assertion that "A" does not exist. Since it is unlikely that he can search all existing invention categories, there being too many even in narrowly-defined fields, he must then gather evidence for the category's nonexistence. This is, in part, a semantic notion (what kind of invention is it, that is, what does the category mean?), in part a logical notion (what categories are logically equivalent to the negation of topic "A"?), and in part a legal notion (what counts as evidence that topic "A" does not exist?).

[444] The field of biological classification is not without its differences of opinion, and competing methodologies. New methods like "cladistics" can produce classifications that compete with more traditional classifications,

that most other classification schemes do not: the classification scheme and how it is applied to flora and fauna is part of an established *practice*. The establishment, maintenance and understanding of the relevant classification scheme itself is part of the practice of being a biologist. It is also the case that the classification scheme marks the boundaries of what the biologist does: *she* is an expert on furbish louseworts, *he* works on the life-cycle of snail darters, *they* study the migration patterns of whooping cranes. Having the classification scheme so closely allied with the practice of being a biologist links it closely to what biologists do, making it more likely that biological classifications would distinguish *useful* information from the *less useful* or *useless* information. The classification system is also, in a sense, *normative*: an entity that has all the characteristics of one particular species *must* be classified as that species, and information about that entity must be classified in that species' category. We might hypothesize that the best candidates for pure subject searches are those that operate within a *normative* classification scheme, though even normative classification schemes can suffer from *category overload*, and normative schemes themselves are probably the most labor-intensive categorization mechanisms to use since they require their construction, support and maintenance to be carried out by many of the individuals who would use them, and, in the final analysis, the taxonomy must be agreed upon by the majority of practitioners (as Putnam pointed out, reference is "socially fixed.").

From these brief examples we can draw a number of conclusions: because the searcher often wants information that will enable him to begin an activity, or restart an activity that has been blocked in some way, we can say that what he is searching for is not so much information on a topic as it is information that he can apply to some purpose—information he can *use*. This can be true even when a searcher is looking explicitly for information on a particular topic. Topics, then, are usually not the primary goal of a search, but are more like heuristics that might get the searcher into the general area where there might be useful information. From this point, the searcher can use a variety of criteria to identify other, possibly useful information—authors' names, publication titles, time periods, publishing institutions, types of publication, citation references, recommendations of colleagues, literal occurrences of specific words, such as names, in the text of candidate documents, etc. In short, the early part of most content searches is not so much looking for the *right information* as it is looking for the *right questions* to base the search on (i.e., which subject terms, author names, journal names, or names of research institutions, are the best ones to base the search on?).

To represent the content of information, we must understand what it *means*, and to understand what it means we need to know how it is *used*. Since words in a sentence can be seen to have meaning, we think that they have meanings that they carry with them. In the same sense, we think that information has a meaning apart from its use. But neither words nor information really has determinate meaning apart from their usage.

---

and established classifications rarely survive indefinitely without some alteration. (See the website "What is Cladistics?" by L. M. Clos—www.fossilnews.com/1996/cladistics.html)

If it is true that a searcher is primarily interested in the *use* to which the information he finds can be put, then why don't we have classification schemes that emphasize the *utility of information* rather than its subject? There are some instances of classifications of information based on utility, many government publications have this kind of orientation, technical manuals and publications are categorized this way, and military publications are often specifically classified according to what kind of activity or skill they support. But the vast majority of publications are not classified according to their *use* but according to their perceived *subject.*

There are a number of reasons why information classifications are oriented more towards subjects and less towards utility. In the first place, while a unit of information might have a few subjects with which it may be reasonably associated, there are often a number of uses to which that information can be put. Identifying the possible uses for specific information, outside of a particular practice, can be difficult. But there is a more compelling reason for the dominance of subject description over utility in classification. Specifically, the classification process, whether automatic or human-based begins, and usually ends, with an examination of the information that is to be classified. From this information it is usually possible to get some idea of its subject, but it may be very difficult to get a sense of how that information might be used. The *subject* of information is a characteristic of individual information items, but its *utility* is more of a system-concept, a broader and more contextual notion of information. It must include not just a sense of what the information is about, but must also include some sense of how it may serve the skills and practices of those who use the information system. Such meta-information cannot usually be inferred from just the text of a document.

You can make a guess at a subject by reading a document text, but you cannot understand how it may be used without understanding the pragmatic context—the scaffolding and practices it's used in—of the publication. The primary reason subject searches are not precise descriptions of what the search is about is that it is almost never the case that *everything* on a subject will satisfy the searcher.

If we assume Andy Clark's perspective (*vide supra*) and look at information systems from a "scaffolding" point of view, we can see their relation to utility more clearly. That is, as part of our intellectual scaffolding, an information system is really an extension of our memories, storing information that would be difficult, if not impossible, to remember. But if we look at our own memories, we see that what we typically remember is not usually random bits of information, but things that are *useful* for us. If our memory is utility-oriented, then it makes sense for our information systems, as intellectual scaffolding, to be utility-oriented too.

## Information Systems—A Wittgensteinean View

> I am sitting with a philosopher in the garden; he says again and again "I know that that's a tree," pointing to a tree that is near us. Someone else arrives and hears this, and I tell him: "This fellow isn't insane. We are only doing philosophy." [**OC** §467]

What's the point of bringing philosophy into this discussion? If we have identified the determinacy of representation as a major factor in the retrieval of intellectual content, and that this is a property of language, then philosophy gives us some idea of the depth of this issue. What it shows us is that the indeterminacy of representation is not a superficial issue in language that can be easily eliminated with "clearer" or "more precise" descriptions. As Wittgenstein showed us, the meaning of language is not a property of individual words, but is intimately bound up in its use. Likewise, the meaning and determinacy of the descriptions of information are not properties of the descriptions themselves, but are contingent on how they are used. It shows that the determinacy of representation is a deep and complex aspect of language that cannot be clarified without reference to the context and circumstances of its usage. In information systems, other than the more determinate data retrieval systems, indeterminacy will be an essential characteristic of many content retrieval efforts, and will not lend itself to solution by Artificial Intelligence, Natural Language Processing, or any other techniques that do not/cannot understand language meaning as an emergent phenomenon arising from the day-to-day interactions of individuals engaged in their fundamental activities and practices. Indeterminacy cannot be "squeezed out" of language—there is no underlying logical clarity of meaning that we just need to uncover, as Frege and Russell thought. If indeterminacy is something that we are going to have to live with in content retrieval, then we need to understand what the consequences of it are for information system design and use. If we cannot eliminate indeterminacy in a lot of retrieval situations, then we need to investigate ways of mitigating it when it interferes with effective retrieval. We have discussed the consequences of indeterminacy in content retrieval, and we will look at some of the ways to mitigate this indeterminacy shortly. First, though, let's look at the problem of indeterminate retrieval from a Wittgensteinean point of view.

### The "Meaning" of a Document

Information systems are fundamentally linguistic processes. At the very least a searcher must describe the intellectual content he would like to find, and these descriptions must be matched against the descriptions of the content of available information (these descriptions of available information can come from a variety of sources: manual indexing, computer-assisted indexing, automatic indexing, or full-text retrieval). Looking at the linguistic nature of information, it is natural to see items of information, documents, databases, images, etc. as *meaning* something. This is implicit in the idea of information having "intellectual content." But just as Wittgenstein admonished us not to look for the meaning of a word, but to let the use teach us the meaning, we can also say that documents or other items of information don't having meanings so much as they have *uses*—that is, we should let the *use* of information "teach us the meaning."

### What are the "Diseases of Thinking" in Information Retrieval?

Wittgenstein believed, as we have shown, that many of the problems that philosophers had solving traditional philosophical problems were not a result of the intractability of the problems but resulted from a flawed way of thinking about them—his most salient example is, of course, that asking for the "meaning" of a word can lead our analysis of language in an unproductive direction. If we take a Wittgensteinean view of Information Retrieval, then we need to ask first whether there are any "Diseases of Thinking" in analyzing the less determinate activity of content retrieval, that is, are there ways of looking at the problems of indeterminate content retrieval that militate against the solution or mitigation of these problems. There are.

a. **The Data Model is an effective model for all Information Systems, regardless of what kind of information is managed by the system.** This assumption is the one that causes the most trouble in information retrieval design. It is not a "stupid" assumption, it merely overlooks the fact that the enormous success of the Data Model when managing determinate information is a kind of success that is strictly limited by the kind of information it provides access to. The attempt to apply the Data Model to all kinds of information systems is a lot like the attempt by some philosophers to apply the formal logical model of language, which is similarly bounded, to all questions of language meaning. This, of course, is precisely the "disease of thinking" that Wittgenstein spent his later life arguing against. The success of the Data Model of determinate retrieval has made this view very attractive and has lead to a number of other "Diseases of Thinking" in Information Retrieval:

b. **Information Content representation can be exact and unambiguous.** It's easy to assume that the determinacy of representation in the Data Model is a realistic goal for representing less determinate content for retrieval. But for a goal to be productive, it must be a realistic one, and as Wittgenstein showed us in detail, indeterminacy is not something that can be squeezed out of language by more rational or logical efforts. The belief that the representation of information content is *potentially* determinate leads to the erroneous assumption that content retrieval failures are the results of poor searching techniques. This, in fact, is exactly the rationale that IBM responded with when it was first confronted with the results of the STAIRS evaluation. The unacceptably low recall values, they claimed, were a product of lousy searching techniques (this explanation was not published, but was communicated to the company that sponsored the STAIRS study). This explanation overlooks a number of aspects of language that we have discussed here, in particular, that language is "productive" and that there are an unlimited number of ways that a particular intellectual content can be represented linguistically. By advocating that full-text retrieval was perfectly suited to the retrieval of precise content from a large system of related information, STAIRS forced the searchers into a position where it was impossible *not* to have poor searching techniques. To blame the searchers for the failures of the system was like, as M.E. Maron pointed out, a company selling someone a combination lock without giving them the combination, and when the customer asks for the combination the company replies that finding the combination is the customer's responsibility, not theirs. Now, although we have showed how pervasive indeterminacy in language is, and how severely it can affect content retrieval, it is important that we should not simply give up, believing there is no way to retrieve precise information from any content retrieval system. Just as Wittgenstein showed that there were definite nonlogical ways to resolve ambiguities in meaning, we will discuss shortly a number of non-Data Model strategies for mitigating the affects of indeterminacy in content retrieval.

c. **Improvements in Physical Access speed will improve Intellectual Access to information content.** This is another consequence of the belief that the Data Model works well for all kinds of retrieval. For very deterministic data retrieval, as we discussed, if you speed up the physical access speed of the system, it will speed up intellectual access too, that is, it will get you faster to the information you want. Again, this only works for highly determinate retrieval where given a typical query it is clear exactly what information will satisfy it. To recall our analogy for this issue, a physically faster race car will enable the racer to get to the finish faster, but a physically faster delivery truck doesn't necessarily speed up delivery over a slower truck.

d. **Size doesn't matter. Large retrieval systems work just as well as smaller systems.** For the determinate data retrieval model, as we pointed out, making a system larger does not typically reduce retrieval effectiveness. But with the less determinate content retrieval model, as the system gets larger the indeterminacy multiplies making it increasingly difficult to conduct successful specific or exhaustive searches. The indeterminacy of content representation has two principal effects: First, and most obviously, it may be very difficult for a searcher to anticipate how a particular information content is represented in a large system containing similar information. This can lead to the situation where the searcher cannot retrieve the information content that she wants. But there is another less obvious aspect of the indeterminacy of content representation, namely, that even when the searcher correctly anticipates how the information content she wants is represented, because of the indeterminacy of representation, there may be many other information contents that she doesn't want that are represented the same way. On large content retrieval systems this leads to the situation where the searcher retrieves a great deal of unwanted information, and this unwanted information may hide the retrieval of the desired information if the number of desired documents is small and the total number of retrieved documents is above the searcher's futility point. This belief that large less determinate retrieval systems work as well as small systems leads to a related "Disease of Thinking":

  i. **Information systems should be as comprehensive as possible: A bigger information system is always a better information system.** As the cost of the storage of information has dropped dramatically in recent years, organizations have gotten to the point where they need not throw away any of the documents they have gathered or written. In fact, for many organizations, it may cost them *more* to look at the information they have collected and decide which of it to keep, than it costs to simply keep it. By keeping everything, it appears that the organization is saving money and building a better more comprehensive information system, but if they are keeping increasing amounts of indeterminately represented information content, the "cost" of successful retrieval will go up significantly since it will be increasingly difficult for searchers to search through the growing body of existing information for what they want or need.

e. **Everything that we need to know in order to determine how to represent the intellectual content of a document is contained within the document itself.** Wittgenstein's predecessor Gottlob Frege claimed that the meaning of a sentence is composed of the meanings of its words. In his view, the meaning of a sentence cannot be something other than a composite of the meanings of its words. Wittgenstein disagreed strongly with this view, especially since it implied a kind of semantic "reduction" of sentence meaning to a combination of individual word meanings. It is easy to come up with an example where the meaning of a sentence is something other than an aggregate of the meanings of its words. Consider again the example of when I come into my office and ask a colleague whether Bill has returned from vacation yet. My colleague replies "I saw a yellow Volkswagen in the parking lot." Clearly, my colleague is telling me that she thinks Bill *has* returned from his vacation, since he has a comparatively uncommon yellow Volkswagen, and she saw it in the parking lot today. Thus the actual "meaning" of the sentence "I saw a yellow Volkswagen in the parking lot" is clearly "Yes, Bill has returned from vacation." But there is no way that you could derive the actual meaning of the sentence my colleague utters by looking only at the words in that sentence. As Wittgenstein showed us, to understand the meaning of the sentence we have to understand the circumstances in which it was uttered, and the background of the person who uttered it. Just as a sentence can be something more than the combination of the meanings of its words, the determination of how to represent the intellectual content of a document may require an understanding of more than the words in the text of the document.

This particular bias in the way that content searching for documents is seen is implicit in the belief that full-text searching will work for precise searches on large-scale information retrieval systems. That is, if everything you need to know about how a document is to be represented or understood is in the text of the document, what else could you possibly need to represent the document but the text itself? But it was clear from the STAIRS evaluation that what was in the documents was clearly not enough to support precise retrieval on a large system.

f.  **The only thing that a searcher is actively looking for is the information that he desires.** Again, the distinction between determinate and indeterminate searching is important here. With determinate data retrieval systems, since the desired information can be defined so precisely, it is clear that the searcher is primarily involved in finding that information. But for a large less determinate content retrieval system, since it is usually unclear what the exact search query is that will retrieve what is wanted, the initial part of the search is not so much looking for the *right information* as it is looking for the *right search queries*. Since, as Swanson showed, content retrieval is a trial-and-error process, the searcher must first be focused on identifying and correcting or mitigating the errors of retrieval that typify the first attempts to find what he wants. This two-stage approach to searching is often overlooked in the design of content retrieval systems. That is, if the searcher must begin his search for content by actively looking for the "right search terms/queries" with which to initiate his search, then a good content retrieval system must be designed to help the searcher in this process—most content retrieval systems do not do this. Thus, content retrieval systems must support both kinds of searches—the search for the best queries and then the search for the desired information. The only major document content retrieval system that actively helps searchers find the best queries with which to begin their searches is Swanson's Arrowsmith Project which provides this kind of support for active searches on Medline, the national medical research document retrieval system maintained by the National Library of Medicine. Swanson built Arrowsmith because he saw that the inherent indeterminacy in content representation, in even such a closely controlled and manually indexed retrieval system as Medline, was so great that it was possible to uncover "undiscovered medical knowledge" among the published writings of medical researchers by linking together medical research documents that had not previously been linked together by Medline's carefully constructed and applied content descriptions. Swanson brilliantly proved his point by proposing, for the first time, several treatments for illnesses that had not been proposed before (e.g., treating Raynaud's syndrome with Omega-3 fish-oil, and treating Migraine headaches with Magnesium). This inspired subsequent medical research which proved that Swanson's proposed treatments *were* effective.[445] Thus Swanson showed that indeterminacy in language is unavoidable even in such carefully constructed normative taxonomies as medical content descriptions.

## How Do Computers Influence Information Systems?

So far we have described how the determinate Data Model of information retrieval has influenced the less determinate Document Content Retrieval Model. But there is another major factor of influence on the Content Retrieval Model and that is the use of computers to build such retrieval systems. Computers have had a number of significant influences on the less determinate Document Content Retrieval Systems:

i. **Computers often force an unnatural precision on categories.** The majority of computerized information systems operate by performing exact matches between category descriptions and the items in that category. But there are situations where the membership in a particular category may not be that precisely determined. This is commonly the case in representing information content since it is rarely the case that one could say that a particular document is about only one thing. For example, if we had a biography of Aristotle, what category would you put it in? It could realistically be linked to the category of "Biography," of course, but it could also be linked to the category of "Ancient Greek History," or the category of "Ancient Greek Philosophy." Yet these obvious categories only scratch the surface of the possible categories that Aristotle's biography could be linked to. For example, the biography could be classified as an example of "good biographical writing" or "bad biographical writing," or "pioneering work in formal logic" or an example of the "life of an influential thinker." Of course the response to this categorical indeterminacy is to simply recommend that all possible categories be added to Aristotle's biography. But this overlooks the fact that some of these categories are more appropriate than

[445] D.R. Swanson. "Undiscovered Public Knowledge," **Library Quarterly**, vol. 5:2, pp. 103–118, 1986.

"Fish-oil, Raynaud's Syndrome, and Undiscovered Public Knowledge," **Perspectives in Biology and Medicine**, vol. 30:1, pp. 7–18, 1986.

"Migraine and Magnesium: Eleven Neglected Connections," **Perspectives in Biology and Medicine**, vol. 31:4, pp. 526–557.

Arrowsmith has active websites at kiwi.uchicago.edu/ and arrowsmith.psych.uic.edu/.

others, and some of them, while reasonable, may actually be misleading for a majority of the searchers. It is also the case that while adding all the possible category descriptions to a document is faithful to the demands of *content description*, it ignores the importance of *content discrimination*, that is, while each of the content descriptions will make it more likely that a searcher who would want the document will be able to anticipate the correct search query, it is also the case that it is more likely that the document will be retrieved by those who don't want that particular content. This is, as we have discussed, particularly true on large content retrieval systems. The recommendation to add as many content descriptions as possible to documents has been called "unlimited aliasing." We have discussed how there may be no upper limit to the number of possible content descriptions that can be added to a document, so while the addition of content descriptions may expand the description of document content, it ignores the fact that some content descriptions are more useful than others. The key to document representation is not unlimited aliasing— just adding as many content descriptions as possible—the key is to add *just the right* content descriptions, ones that simultaneously describe the documents well and discriminate them from other documents in the collection. In an empirical study, Brooks could not find evidence to support the unlimited aliasing recommended by Furnas, *et al.* "This experiment found no evidence to support the Strategy of Unlimited Aliasing... some index terms are simply better than others."[446]

ii. **Computerizing an information system often removes information from its active context.** As we discussed before, most categories of data—names, addresses, phone numbers, etc.—are fairly determinate, and because of this their precise meaning is not affected by changes in context. An address is still obviously an address whether you read it in a document or see it written on the side of a truck. Such is not the case, as we have said, for content descriptions. When considered by themselves, these descriptions can be quite indeterminate. For example, suppose that you saw the content description "Systems" assigned to a particular document that was not available to look at. So, on the basis of the content description "Systems," what do you think the document would be about? There is no clear answer to such a question. But if we refer back to Wittgenstein, he was quite clear about how you resolve ambiguities or indeterminacies in language—you look at how the words are actually *used*. The *use* of words is just another way of saying that you need to look at their active context. In our example, you may not be able to understand what the single word "Systems" actually means when it is used to represent the intellectual content of a document, but if you can look at the actual context of the document, for example, that it was a document that came from the filing cabinet of a computer technician who specialized in building and maintaining accounting systems, you would then have a much better idea of what kind of content

[446]T.A. Brooks. "All the Right Descriptors: A Test of the Strategy of Unlimited Aliasing," **Journal of the American Society for Information Science**, vol. 44:3, pp. 137–147, April 1993. Quotation is from p. 146. The advocate of "unlimited aliasing" that Brooks responded to was G.W. Furnas, T.K. Landauer, L.M. Gomez, and S.T. Dumais. "The Vocabulary Problem in Human-System Communication," **Communications of the ACM**, vol. 30:11, pp. 964–971, November 1987.

"Systems" actually refers to in this case. Prior to the widespread use of computerized information, documents often had a kind of social context—that is, if you worked in an organization when all documents were made of paper, and wanted a document on a particular subject, your best search strategy was to simply ask others in the organization if they had such a document or, if not, if they could recommend someone else in the organization who might have it or know where it might be. Since paper-based information was cumbersome to manage, people would generally only keep information that they found particularly useful. As a result, knowing who had what information, and what activities they participated in, could tell you a great deal about the information itself. By understanding what the social context of information was, it was also much easier to see what the "value" of the information was. Such a social organization of information was quickly bypassed when documents became machine-readable. As more and more information came to reside on computers, it tended to lose its social context. It was no longer as significant when someone kept a particular document on his computer, because, given the low cost of computer storage and the easy and rapid ability to copy documents, people could keep machine-readable copies of documents that were not necessarily that useful to them. In fact, it's not uncommon for people to have copies of documents on their computers that they have not even read. One of the major consequences of losing the social context of documents and not being able to see their value, is that it becomes increasingly hard to distinguish important information from less important or unimportant information. As a result, there is no incentive to throw any of that information away. This contributes to the continual growth of document collections on computers, and the resulting degradation of effective retrieval of needed information. In the early 1970's I worked for a company that had its headquarters in San Francisco. In this period, virtually all documents were kept and stored as paper copies. The company, in order to keep the comparatively expensive office space as small as possible, had a rigid company-wide rule that no one could have more than one filing cabinet in his or her office. This rigidly enforced rule meant that employees could not usually keep every document they received or used, but it had the beneficial effect of forcing employees to regularly "weed" their document collections and keep only that information that was really important to them and necessary for their jobs. As a consequence, the value of virtually all of the paper documents in the organization was well understood, and the organization was not littered with useless documents. Soon all of this changed when the company installed equipment that could convert paper documents into 16mm microfilm. Because a single microfilm roll could hold 6000 pages of documents, it became possible for employees to put all the documents on microfilm that they would have thrown away before. Now that nothing needed to be thrown away, they became very casual about deciding what to keep as paper and what to put on microfilm. Also, since what they kept on microfilm was often a jumble of documents with dissimilar content, there was no easy way to describe in detail what was contained in the 6000 pages of a film roll. As a result, in less than a year there were over 35 microfilm rolls—210,000 pages of documents—labeled "Miscellaneous," some of which actually contained documents that were important for the activities of the organization.

iii. **Computers can force searchers, indexers and content system designers into unnatural Language Games.** Since we have discussed how many organizations now have an economic disincentive for weeding out less useful and useless information—that it costs more to periodically examine the information on a computer and decide what to keep, than to simply keep everything—many organizations have gotten to the point that virtually nothing is thrown away. The obvious consequence of this is that computerized information systems will continue to grow larger at a rapid rate with no clear upper limit. The dramatic increase in the size of less determinate content retrieval systems has forced the designers and users into unnatural Language Games. Specifically, when there are thousands of documents that all have similar content, it becomes extremely difficult to use natural language to distinguish some of the content from the many other different, but similar contents of documents on the same system. In short, our natural language was never intended to make the kind of subtle distinctions that would be required to describe the slight differences of content of thousands or millions of documents with similar content. If our natural language cannot make the distinctions necessary to discriminate the different kinds of content in a large information retrieval system, then we have to find other means to make these distinctions manifest.

## Managing the Retrieval of Indeterminate Information Content—Some Practical Consequences

Since one of the themes of this discussion has been to look at how indeterminacy in language affects the retrieval of information content, it is appropriate that we end this discussion with a brief look at the practical consequences that such indeterminacy has for the actual management of information content.

First of all, as we stated before, indeterminacy in language is not something that can be squeezed out by a more rational approach such as defining words more precisely. In so far as indeterminacy in meaning is pervasive in ordinary language, it will be correspondingly pervasive in information systems, especially content-retrieval ones. But while indeterminacy cannot be eliminated, its effects *can* be mitigated. Let's look at how this might be done.

**Representing Intellectual Content.** The most fundamental question in the design of content retrieval systems is, of course, how do you represent the content of information? When an index term is assigned to represent some specific content, it is, in linguistic terms, a "reference" to that content. If we recall what Putnam stated about the character of "reference," we are reminded that referring words do not refer to some mental concept, their reference must be, as Putnam put it, "socially fixed"—that is, what enables a reference to work are not the concepts that people have "in their heads," but the active way that they use the words to refer to something. Although Putnam is a contemporary philosopher, he has acknowledged his affinity with Wittgenstein's philosophy, and it is clear that the notion of reference being "socially fixed" is a description that Wittgenstein would be sympathetic to since it fits with his idea of linguistic meaning being based on use. The importance of this view of reference for content-retrieval is that if a system designer wanted to represent a certain information document content with "term A," it cannot be justified by saying that "term A" appears within the title or the text of the document, or that people "think" that "term A" represents that content. The best justification for "term A" being used to represent the content of this document is whether the individuals who would use that document would actually refer to that content themselves by using "term A." In this way, "term A" would be "socially fixed" to the content of that document. Thus, the first step in representing information content is to examine how the potential users of the information system actually talk about this kind of information content—"Let the use teach you the meaning." [**PI** p. 212]

While the examination of how users talk about the information content on an information retrieval system is a good way to see how the information should be represented, it is not a solution without limitations. Specifically, although users might refer to a particular document content using "term B," this might be a useful way to represent this content if there are only a limited number of documents on the system with this content and the rest of the documents on the system are concerned with clearly different content that would not be represented by "term B." Using "term B" to represent the content of a document runs into a problem when the number of documents so represented is large. How many is a "large number of documents?" This is not an easy figure to estimate, but a good touchstone is the average "futility point" of the users of the system—the maximum number of documents that the searchers, on average, are willing to look through to find what they want. When the number of documents using "term B" to represent their content gets above the threshold of the average futility point, then there is the possibility that the users will not find "term B" by itself a very useful search term. The reason why this happens is that in ordinary usage, a particular reference to information content, for example "philosophy," is typically only used to make fairly obvious distinctions. For example, if a friend of mine tells me his son just declared his college major, and I ask him what major he declared, it's perfectly understandable for him to just say "philosophy." But if I am looking for some information on "philosophy," and there are thousands of documents on the information system with that content description, the chances are that I don't want just anything with that content, but some specific subset of it. This example is even more striking when we consider content searching on the World Wide Web. Using the Google search engine, the search term "philosophy" returns 18,200,000 websites. When this occurs, system designers must find ways for searchers to reduce the size of the retrieved sets without raising the probability of excluding the desired documents.

## Reducing Indeterminacy in Content Retrieval

As we pointed out before, indeterminacy in content retrieval is not one thing. There are several major kinds of indeterminacy, and each can have different mitigating strategies.

*Semantic Ambiguity.* This kind of indeterminacy is a consequence of the fact that the same word can be used in multiple contexts and have a different meaning in each context. Consider our examples of the words "head" or "line" which each have a number of distinct "meanings." How can these meanings be distinguished if they are used to represent the content of documents? The easiest way is to not represent the content of information with

a single word such as "head" but to represent it with the word "head" in its appropriate semantic context—for example, "*head* of the intelligence committee" or "medical treatment
of *head* injuries." One of the recent changes in some Internet search engines like Teoma and
Google is that they now include the sentence in which the search term appears at each selected website. This helps the searcher to see which retrieved websites are using the search
term the way she intended it. This would be a good model for full-text retrieval systems
to follow, although it certainly doesn't solve all the problems of full-text content retrieval.

*Category Overload.* One of the contributors to indeterminacy that is most characteristic of
content retrieval systems is the retrieval of large numbers of documents that are represented
by the same search term. As we pointed out before, Zipf showed that when a word is used
many times in ordinary usage, the number of different meanings it has will increase as its
usage increases. Consequently, as content-retrieval systems get larger, as they are inevitably
doing, the levels of indeterminacy will go up too. How can the effects of category overload
be mitigated? The most obvious way is to try to keep the retrieved sets as small as possible.
One way to do this is to keep the entire system as small as possible by regularly examining
the information in the system and removing any documents that are no longer useful. As
we pointed out, this is often not done because the cost of weeding out useless documents
is usually more than the cost of simply keeping everything. But there is another cost that
is important here, namely, the cost of less effective retrieval. As more useless documents
are kept on the retrieval system, the cost of retrieval will continue to increase. This cost of
retrieval is really two costs: first, as more useless documents fill the system, retrieved sets
will become larger, and the searcher will have to work harder to find what she wants if it's
buried in a large retrieved set. Secondly, as the retrieved sets get larger, it becomes more
likely that the searcher won't see the desired document even when it is in the retrieved set.
This can add the additional cost of not being able to retrieve the information that is wanted.

*Language Productivity.* Because there are so many different ways that the same content
can be represented by the system designer or indexer, and the searcher, there must be a
way to direct the searcher towards the right descriptions. One obvious way is to use a
normative classification scheme which states quite clearly that certain specific content
can only be represented in one way. This is what Medline, the medical research retrieval
system does when it classifies medical documents by using the same words that physicians
and medical researchers use to refer to medical subjects such as afflictions and treatments.
Of course, the use of a normative representation scheme generally requires that such a
scheme already exists and be supported by the active users of the information system. A
normative representation scheme is not something that can be declared by fiat, it must be a
reference scheme that is part of the practice that it supports. If it is not part of the practice
it supports, it will be hard for searchers to understand just what the terms of representation
actually "mean" because they will have no clear *usage*.

*Content Representation and "übersichtliche Darstellungen."* Since content representations
use ordinary language to describe content, then, like ordinary language these uses of
language should be "learnable." Since Wittgenstein showed how essential "perspicuous
representations" ("übersichtliche Darstellungen") were to learning what the meanings of
particular words are, it follows that if the language used to represent information content
is to be learnable it should have "perspicuous representations" too. This can be done in

a content retrieval system by explicitly linking each content representation term to an information content that best represents what the content term "means," and identifying these "perspicuous representations" for searchers so that they can more quickly get an idea of what particular content representations actually mean.

## Large Content Retrieval Systems vs. Small Content Retrieval Systems

While the results of the STAIRS evaluation (*q.v.*) are striking, when it was published there was a lot of resistance to its results. In particular, a number of previous studies of full-text retrieval systems were cited which had much better retrieval results. But when these evaluations were examined it was discovered that they were conducted on comparatively small retrieval systems of fewer than 200 documents (as compared with the 40,000 documents of the STAIRS study). Of course the problem was the assumption that if retrieval worked well on a small system, it would work well on a large system of the same design. We have already discussed the problem with such an assumption or "disease of thinking" (*q.v.*), and have shown why large content-retrieval systems have rates of retrieval effectiveness that decrease as the system gets larger. But if it is the case that even full-text retrieval can be adequate on small systems, this actually has a consequence for the design of large content-retrieval systems. In short, the best way to insure good retrieval on a large content-retrieval system is to turn it into a small system. This doesn't mean to get rid of most of the documents, but to develop partitions in the document collection so that searchers, instead of applying their search requests to the *entire* document collection will actually only apply them to a much smaller *partition* of the collection. If content retrieval is much more likely to be successful on systems of 200 documents or less, then it stands to reason that even a document collection of thousands of documents could be searched effectively if the searcher was assured that the documents she wanted were all in a particular partition of less than 200 documents. Without such partitions, the searchers are likely to apply their own form of active retrieved set reduction by conjunctively adding search terms to the original query. This is not a good strategy in indeterminate searching because, in the first place, it changes the searcher's original query to something that is semantically different, and with the addition of each indeterminate search term, while the number of documents retrieved goes down, the probability of retrieving the desired content goes down too [the details of this combinatoric problem were discussed in the previous section "'Escalating Uncertainty of Retrieval': The Problem with Large Systems and Indeterminately Represented Information."] How can such partitions be designed? There are a number of ways partitions can be constructed, for example:

1. **Partitions based on temporal values**. Most documents or other texts have a time when they were published or created or even a time when they become obsolete. Sometimes the time of creation can be an effective partition for content searching such as when a searcher desires information content that was created within a specific time period.

2. **Partitions based on authors.** Most documents have authors, and frequently this can be the basis of a useful partition. This is especially true in research-oriented information systems since authors' names can often be a good way of partitioning documents that pertain to a particular activity or subject.

3. **Partitions based on publishers.** Publishers, of course, often exercise critical judgment when deciding what documents or books to publish, and such judgment can be an effective way of partitioning texts that concern a particular topic, or are of a particular quality. Even the works of a single publisher can be partitioned by, for example, the names of the journals it publishes.

4. **Partitions based on the principal activities of the users.** Of course, it has been the theme of this discussion that the activities of the users of an information system can be an effective way to classify the information that they use in these activities. It stands to reason, then, that if the information on a system is being used in a number of specific activities, then these activities may be an effective basis for partitions.

5. **Partitions based on document type.** (internal memo, external letter, book, government publication, published document, financial analysis, etc.)

6. **Partitions based on normative taxonomies.** We have already discussed how the normative taxonomies of the sciences are, in some sense, "ideal" subject classifications. It seems logical, then, that such normative taxonomy partitions would be the goal of any large content-retrieval design. But it is important to understand that what makes a normative taxonomy such as Botany or Obstetric Medicine so effective as a way of partitioning information content is that such taxonomies are part of the *practice* of being a Botanist or an Obstetrician. Thus, effective normative taxonomies cannot be easily created by simply ordering system users to think this way. They are typically only effective if they already exist and are understood and supported by the potential users of the information retrieval system.

7. **Partitions based on physical separation.** It is often the case nowadays that existing information systems are combined with other information systems to produce larger and more comprehensive information systems. Sometimes, the previous information systems can be effective partitions for information that is used for a particular activity, or is concerned with a particular subject area. Consequently, when information systems are combined to produce larger systems, the system designers should consider whether to keep the different system contents as searchable partitions of the larger system. This decision should be made, of course, by interviewing the potential users of the larger system and determining whether they would find the previous systems useful searchable partitions of the new system. Even the information collected by individuals within an organization can sometimes be useful partitions for an information system. That is, if individuals frequently went to "Mary Ann..." or "Fred..." to find information on a particular topic or information useful in a particular activity, it stands to reason that the information that Mary Ann and Fred had in their possession may still be effective partitions in this regard. This is particularly true for individuals who leave an organization, and is a way of maintaining the usefulness of their information selection after they have gone.

8. **Partitions based on information usage.** We have already said that it is generally a good idea to regularly "weed out" useless documents/information. This keeps the retrieval system from growing larger with information that is of no use to the

searchers. One of the reasons some information system designers are reluctant to do this is that they feel that they can't absolutely say which documents are so useless that they can be discarded. If this is the case, then when you "weed" an information system, the documents that are not considered useful do not have to be thrown away, they merely have to be moved to a partition containing "less useful" documents that is separate from the active retrieval system. Such a partition can be the basis for an "archive" of information. Searchers who cannot find what they want on the active system, then would still be able to search the partition of "less useful" documents in case what they want is there.

9. **Partitions based on previous searches.** If the information system can maintain a record of successful searches, these could be used as heuristics for subsequent searches. For each successful search, a record should be kept of the natural language statement of the search query, the actual formal query which retrieved the desired documents, and the documents which satisfied the request.

It is essential that partitions satisfy two requirements:

1. The reference that defines a partition, such as a *time period, author's name, document type*, etc. must be completely determinate; that is, there can be no ambiguity about which partition a document belongs in. If a partition is not completely determinate then it cannot be an effective searchable subset of the entire collection.

2. The partition itself must divide the documents into searchable subsets of the entire collection, that is, the types of searches which the users engage in should, most of the time, fall within a single partition, or within a very few partitions. Once again, it is essential to examine the kinds of searching that the users engage in primarily to determine what kinds of partitions would satisfy these two criteria.

### Using Documents Themselves as Instruments of Organization and Indeterminacy Reduction—"Exemplary Documents" and "Seed Searching"

Since we have shown how "meaning" in language is best understood by looking at how words are *used*, it stands to reason that usage is an important criterion for determining how document content might be arranged and how it should be referred to or indexed. As we said, it is best to talk to the users of the system to find out how they discuss the information content held on the information system. But there is sometimes another source of this referential information—certain specific documents. The documents that can provide this segmentation and description of the content in an information system, are what have been called "exemplary documents."[447] Exemplary documents are those documents that describe or exhibit the intellectual structure of a particular area of intellectual content. In so doing, they provide both a referential/indexing vocabulary for that content area and, more importantly, a natural language context in which the terms which refer to this content have a clearer meaning, thus making it easier for searchers to understand how the

---

[447] D.C. Blair and S. Kimbrough. "Exemplary Documents: A Foundation for Information Retrieval Design," **Information Processing and Management**, vol. 38, pp. 363–379, 2002.

document/information content is arranged and referred to. The most obvious example of an exemplary document is the "survey article" that appears in the literature of a particular research area. This kind of article explicitly discusses the major issues or topics in a field of study, and often provides specific references from these issues to significant publications, authors and institutions that are important in this area. But survey articles don't just provide a "topography" of the intellectual landscape of the field, they also discuss the issues of the field using the professional vernacular of that field; that is, they are demonstrations of how the field refers to, and talks about, these issues and topics, and what the "socially fixed" references of that content area are. In this way, the survey article can act as a kind of conservative linguistic process that demonstrates how, out of the many ways a topic *could be discussed*, it usually is discussed in that field of inquiry. Survey articles, therefore, provide two essential elements for representing the intellectual content of documents in a particular field:

- A description of the major issues or topics in the field, or part of the field.

- A demonstration of the language used to refer to the issues and topics with which the field is concerned.

Another example of an exemplary document would be in litigation. Corporate and government litigation are just two areas where there is a dramatically increasing number of large-scale lawsuits—lawsuits in which attorneys may need to have access to thousands, or sometimes millions of documents. Further, the successful conduct of the lawsuit is critically dependent on effective document access. The intellectual structure of the information germane to a particular lawsuit is best exemplified in an exemplary document called the "complaint." The complaint identifies, very precisely, the issues or events being litigated, the individuals involved in the case, and, if relevant, the institutions involved also. In addition, the complaint will often identify the chronological sequence of events that ties all the individuals, issues and institutions together, and will often assert causal links between certain key events which can be useful in retrieval. Looking at the above examples of exemplary documents, we can start to see some of the characteristics that many of them have:

i. They provide a synoptic view or survey of at least some of the major topics and issues of an area of intellectual content.

ii. They often discuss these topics and issues with a vocabulary that is a restricted subset of all the possible ways these issues could be discussed. An exemplary document is a demonstration of the "dialect" of natural language that is used to talk about issues in that content area. In this way, an exemplary document can limit the "productivity" of language.

iii. They often indicate the structure or framework of the content by showing, explicitly or implicitly, the relationship between some or all of the issues or topics they identify (e.g., that certain issues are related causally; or chronologically).

Exemplary Documents enable inquirers to better understand the intellectual structure of the content of a document collection. One of the trade-offs of content-retrieval is that the more complex the intellectual structure of an indexing or representation scheme is, the harder it may be for the searchers to understand. Yet, if we want to provide high levels of retrieval effectiveness for some content retrieval systems, then we will need fairly complex and detailed intellectual structures for representing the various contents of the documents. But such complex representation schemes will require that inquirers must be able to learn them. Unfortunately, most indexed collections of documents are not constructed to facilitate the "learning" of the intellectual structure.[448] Often the only way an inquirer can learn how documents are represented on a system is by trial and error—by submitting queries and retrieving documents.[449] Such a piecemeal process is a very unsystematic and difficult way to learn, in any general way, how the documents in the collection have been represented. In the first place, the inquirer may never be able to see enough documents to form any general opinion about how the documents are represented[450]; and, in the second place, if the inquirer can only see individual documents it may be hard to infer what the broad intellectual relationships are that may exist among the different contents of groups of documents. Exemplary documents can help to defeat, or at least mitigate, this problem by providing access to not only the intellectual concepts of a content area, but also to the structure of those concepts and the specific vocabulary used to discuss them.

Given the capabilities of current information systems, there is a very useful way to present an exemplary document that structures the content of a particular information system. Specifically, the full text of the exemplary document can be placed on the information system with hypertext links from the statements in the text which refer to the information content of the system, to the actual documents on the system which have these referred to intellectual contents. This means that the searchers can begin their searches by reading the exemplary document that refers to their area of interest, and then directly follow the links from the exemplary document to the subset(s) of the content that they want. This is a much better way to provide access to the intellectual content of the retrieval system than by simply listing the different descriptions by themselves, like a subject catalogue in a library, and providing links to the appropriate documents. Such a list would not give searchers any indication of what the descriptions actually mean, whereas the exemplary document not only contains the appropriate descriptions which refer to various contents, it *uses* these words in a natural language discussion of the content, so it gives the searchers a better understanding of what the references actually "mean." An exemplary document would be a better introduction to the "meaning" of the references than any *definitions* of the references would be.

**Seed-Searching and "Pitching Horseshoes in the Dark":** One of the difficulties searchers have with content retrieval is learning how the content they want is actually represented on the retrieval system. As we said, the searcher often must try to find out how content is represented by trial and error. This is made more difficult because there are two kinds of indeterminacy which occur in content retrieval: the indeterminacy of search term

---

[448] D.C. Blair. **Language and Representation in Information Retrieval**. Elsevier Science, Amsterdam, 1990.

[449] D.R. Swanson. "Information Retrieval as a Trial-and-Error process," **Library Quarterly**, vol. 47:2, pp. 128–148, April 1977.

[450] D.C. Blair. "Searching Biases in Large Interactive Document Retrieval Systems," **Journal of the American Society for Information Science**, vol. 31:4, pp. 271–277, July 1980.

selection, and the indeterminacy of document representation. Together, they act to increase the overall indeterminacy of the retrieval system. Yet there is, in some retrieval situations, a way to reduce one of these indeterminacies. The method is called "Seed Searching."[451] When a searcher begins to use a content retrieval system for the first time to search for some specific content, it is very difficult for him to know with any certainty what the best candidates for search terms are. This is where the "trial and error" part of content retrieval begins. But unless the retrieval system uses a well-understood normative representation scheme, the searcher's initial queries may be no more than "wild guesses," and, if so, may lead to a lot of effort and frustration before he begins to retrieve the information content that he wants. Basically, when the searcher starts, he doesn't have a good idea how the information content he wants is represented on the system, because, as we have shown, given the "productivity" of language, there may be an uncountable number of ways that a particular content can be represented or referred to. It's like "pitching horseshoes in the dark"—if you can't see the post you're trying to hit with your horseshoe, then not only is it difficult to hit it, but you can't even tell how far and in what direction you're pitch of the horseshoe is off the mark, so it's hard to make an informed adjustment to the missing toss. Selecting the right search terms to look for specific content on a new information retrieval system has a similar character—not only is it hard to find the right search terms, but it may even be difficult to determine how "far off the mark" the initial search terms are if they did not retrieve what was wanted—basically, such search failures are relatively uninformative, if you don't get the content you want with a particular search query, it is hard to see how to change it to make a better query. Seed searching is a way to reduce the effect of this uncertainty. It works in the following way: instead of beginning a content search by guessing which search terms will work, the searcher should, if possible, begin by identifying a document he has already read that he knows has the content he wants and see if it already exists on the system (I'm assuming that such a document can be retrieved by specifying something other than the content representations, such as the title, the author's name, or the publisher and date of publication, etc.). If a searcher can find such a document on the retrieval system, then he can look at how the content of the document is represented by the system. This representation can then become the basis for a search query that will very likely retrieve the content that the searcher wants. Of course, it won't always be the case that a searcher can identify a document with the desired content that already exists on the retrieval system, but it is a strategy that is worth considering since it gives a far better starting search query than what the searcher would have if he just has to guess at how the content he wants is represented.[452]

---

[451] D.C. Blair. "Indeterminacy in the Subject Access to Documents," **Information Processing and Management**, vol. 22:2, pp. 229–241, 1986.

[452] The "Seed Searching" strategy for content retrieval was developed as a result of a request by one of the editors of **Mathematical Reviews** in the early 1980s. The editor told me that **Mathematical Reviews**, which publishes English language reviews of all the mathematical research articles published throughout the world, was in a difficult position because many of the subscribers said that they had a hard time determining how the articles that concerned the branch of mathematical research they were interested in were represented in the reviews. The editor told me that they were ready to spend up to $400,000 to redesign their classification scheme, so that their clients could find the content they wanted more easily. He then said that he had contacted me so that I could help in the redesign of the classification scheme. I pointed out, that instead of changing the representations of thousands of mathematical reviews stretching back to 1940, it would be far better for them to suggest that their clients first retrieve an article from **Mathematical Reviews** that they already knew had the content they wanted, then look at how the content of that article was represented. These representations could then be used to find

## Measuring the Effectiveness of Content Retrieval

Naturally, a well-run content retrieval system should have a sense of how well it is operating, that is, how successful the searches are that are conducted on the system. Of course, the system could keep track of the searchers' evaluations of the success of their searches. While this is revealing information, it is relatively hard to gather this kind of data because searchers rarely like to take the time to record their evaluations of their searches. In addition, it is hard to add evaluations from different searchers together because their evaluations may not actually be comparable. For example, if two searchers each say that their respective searches were "unsuccessful" they could still mean very different things by these descriptions. For one searcher, although the search was "unsuccessful" she immediately saw how to change her search query to retrieve the content that she wanted. But for the other searcher, the "unsuccessful" search left him completely in the dark, and became the first of many in a sequence of "unsuccessful" searches. This raises the question of whether there is a way to test the overall effectiveness of a content retrieval system without having to compensate for the probable differences in meaning of the searchers' evaluations. There is. Once again, we must look at how language is being used in the searching process.

> George Kingsley Zipf demonstrated that there were empirical ways to measure the effectiveness of language use.[453] He showed how one could tabulate the frequencies in which individual words occur in ordinary language usage and construct a rank-frequency distribution of these words and their frequencies. This distribution could then be examined to determine how effective the language usage which produced the data was. Zipf's rank-frequency distribution in language was used as a basis for estimating the effectiveness of content-retrieval by Blair(1990).[454] But there actually is a similar, but easier way to estimate the effectiveness of a content-retrieval system. Instead of using the Zipfian distribution as the measure of retrieval effectiveness, one needs only examine the similarity of the searchers' use of language and the language of representation for the retrieval system. That is, the system could keep track of the number of times individual search terms were used in queries by all searchers, and construct a rank-frequency distribution of the terms used. Another rank-frequency distribution could be constructed of the terms used to represent the content of the documents on the retrieval system. These two rank-frequency distributions could then be compared to see how similar they were. If they were similar, then it would mean that the searchers were using the language of content representation in a similar way to the way it was used to represent the intellectual content of the information. This homogeneity of usage between searching and content representation would most likely mean that content-retrieval on the system was relatively successful. By the same token, if there is a dissimilarity of

---

other reviews with similar content. The only requirement would be that the indexing representation process be consistent, so that even if the articles in a particular area were represented in a way that a client thought was unusual, once he determined what this representation was all other reviews of documents with similar content would be represented the same way.

[453] G.K. Zipf. **Human Behavior and the Principle of Least Effort.** Hafner, NY, 1965. (Facsimile of the 1949 edition)

[454] D.C. Blair. **Language and Representation in Information Retrieval**. Elsevier Science, Amsterdam, 1990. The importance of Zipf's examination of language for evaluating the effectiveness of content-retrieval is discussed in detail in Chapter 4 of this book: "Language and Representation: the Central Problem in Information Retrieval."

language usage between searching and content representation then it is clear that the searchers are using the language of content representation differently than it is being used by the retrieval system to represent the content of the documents. This would be a general indicator of probable poor searching results. The advantage of this method, of course, is that it is very easy to calculate since a retrieval system could be programmed to gather this data as searches are carried out on the system. It is also a feasible way to calculate the effectiveness of a content-retrieval system without forcing the searchers to record their judgments of retrieval effectiveness every time they search. The basic assumption of this method is that if searchers are to be successful at retrieving the intellectual content they desire, they must use language in searching in the same way that the language is used to represent the content of the information on the retrieval system. This assumption is clearly consistent with the Wittgensteinean view of language that we have discussed here.

## The STAIRS Evaluation: A Final Look

Given this discussion of the practical methods for mitigating the effects of indeterminate content retrieval, it may be instructive to discuss how these recommendations could have been used to make a better retrieval system out of the full-text content retrieval system investigated in the STAIRS evaluation. First of all, as the searchers used the STAIRS system it was clear that many of the searches required documents of a specific type. Consequently, document type would have been an effective partition for the collection. Each document on the system should have been classified according to its type so it could be retrieved with other documents of the same type. Since the document type was not something that could be inferred by the computer from the text of the document alone, these representations of the documents would have had to be applied to the documents manually. The type of document is a fairly determinate representation, so it would not have been a difficult description to add to the documents. The STAIRS study was conducted on a document collection used to defend a large corporate lawsuit, so the official "complaint" of the lawsuit which described the legal issues being contested was a complete description of the content of the document collection. In other words, only documents relevant to issues identified in the lawsuit were included in the information retrieval system. The complaint specified 13 issues that were being contested. Since every document had to be relevant to one of these issues, it is clear that these 13 issues could also serve as partitions for the document collection, and the complaint itself was a good candidate for an "exemplary document" to be included with the collection. Since each document included in the collection had to be personally examined and determined to be relevant, it would not have been much extra effort to also determine which partitions (document type and issue in the complaint) each relevant document fell into, and manually add these representations to the documents. Of course, the essence of full-text retrieval then was that such manual indexing procedures were not necessary, but the results of the STAIRS evaluation showed that full-text retrieval was not sufficient by itself to enable effective retrieval of specific content on a large retrieval system. How much these partitions would have improved the results of the STAIRS evaluation is, of course, not clear, but there is little doubt that they would have improved the performance of the system. This is because, instead of applying the search queries to all the 40,000 documents in the collection, the queries would have been applied to the much smaller partitions of the collection.

Finally, some content retrieval system designers remain expectant of a technical solution to the problems of retrieving specific content on a large retrieval system. This could, they think, take the form of either a particularly fast search engine or the development of a computer system that "understands" language use. To expect that there will be such a simple technical solution to the problem of indeterminacy in content retrieval is to ignore the complexity of language that the field of the philosophy of language is a testament to. If meaning in language is not something that is "in the head" but attains its meaning through the context and circumstances of usage, then no computer can ever have the understanding of language that an ordinary individual has, because a computer cannot participate in the activities and circumstances that an ordinary individual does. As Hilary Putnam put it, "Cut the pie any way you like, 'meanings' just ain't in the head!"[455] We could modify his statement to assert, just as convincingly:

> Cut the pie any way you like, "meanings" just ain't in the *computer*!

## Summary of the Design Criteria for Large Content-Retrieval Systems

While every content retrieval system is in some sense unique, there are some general guidelines which we can extract from the previous discussion that can help to improve the retrieval of information with specific content.

1. Regularly weed out useless documents, otherwise searchers may wind up "drinking from the firehose"—that is, having retrieved sets of documents that are too large to examine completely.

2. Talk to the potential searchers to determine:

   i. What kind of search will be most common: sample, exhaustive or specific. This will determine how important it will be to mitigate the inherent indeterminacy of content retrieval (i.e., if most searches are just sample searches, then indeterminacy will not be too much of a problem, but if specific or exhaustive searches are the norm, then mitigating strategies should be adopted).
   ii. How they actually talk about and refer to the intellectual content managed by the information system.
   iii. What possible partitions can be placed in the system that can reduce the number of documents being searched for individual queries, and can focus the searches on groups that likely contain the desired documents.

3. Try to find "exemplary documents" which discuss the intellectual content of information on the retrieval system. If they can be found, set them up as "entrances" and organizers of the content of the system.

---

[455] H. Putnam. "The Meaning of 'Meaning'," **Language, Mind and Knowledge, Minnesota Studies in the Philosophy of Science**, v. VII, pp. 131–193, 1975. Quotation is from p. 144.

4. If strategies are needed to mitigate indeterminacy look at the possibility of providing relatively determinate "partitions" of the collection that can focus searches on smaller parts of the document collection.

5. Consider keeping a record of the rank-frequency distributions of search terms and content representation terms.

6. Create a taxonomy of activities and practices that use the documents in the collection and link the documents to the activities and practices that use them.

7. For each of the terms in the indexing/searching vocabulary that has multiple meanings in everyday usage, link it explicitly to a "perspicuous representation" in the document collection which can provide the searchers with good examples of what the term actually "means," that is, how it is used, in the retrieval system.

8. Finally, educate the searchers to give them an understanding of the unavoidable indeterminacy of content representation, and of the various mitigating strategies for effective retrieval: Partitions, Exemplary documents, Seed Searching, and the relation of content to the activities that use it.

# The End

# Information Knowledge and Science Management